Hockey Scouting Report 2000

SHERRY ROSS

GREYSTONE
BOOKS

Douglas & McIntyre Publishing Group
Vancouver / Toronto / New York

To my niece and goddaughter, Chelsea Lorraine Ross.

Copyright © 1999 by Michael A. Berger

All rights reserved. No part of this book may be reproduced, stored in a retrieval system or transmitted in any form or by any means, without the prior permission of the publisher or, in the case of photocopying or other reprographic copying, a licence from CANCOPY (Canadian Reprography Collective), Toronto, Ontario.

Greystone Books
A division of Douglas & McIntyre Ltd.
2323 Quebec Street, Suite 201
Vancouver, British Columbia V5T 4S7

Editing by Anne Rose and Kerry Banks
Cover design by Peter Cocking
Cover photograph of John LeClair by Jim McIsaac/Bruce Bennett Studios
Typesetting by MicroMega Designs
Printed and bound in Canada   Canada

The publisher gratefully acknowledges the assistance of the Canada Council for the Arts and of the British Columbia Ministry of Tourism, Small Business and Culture. The publisher also acknowledges the financial support of the Government of Canada through the Book Publishing Industry Development Program for its publishing activities.

SHERRY ROSS

Yrs. of NHL service: 21
Born: Randolph, NJ
Position: press box
Height: no way
Weight: you gotta be kidding
Uniform no.: DKNJ
Shoots: straight

LAST SEASON
First season as hockey columnist for the *New York Daily News*.

THE FINESSE GAME
The versatile Ross began her career in 1978-79, covering the New York Rangers for the *Morristown (N.J.) Daily Record*. In addition to working as a sportswriter for the *Bergen (N.J.) Record*, *Newsday*, and the *National*, she became the NHL's first female team broadcaster in 1992, when she was hired as a colour commentator by the New Jersey Devils. In 1994, she became the first woman to call a major professional men's sports championship as the colour analyst for the NHL radio network in the Stanley Cup Finals.

As a freelance writer, Ross has also contributed to *Sports Illustrated*, the *Hockey News*, and *Beckett Hockey Monthly*. She is the secretary-treasurer for the Professional Hockey Writers' Association.

THE PHYSICAL GAME
Thanks to personal trainer Jason Montagna and a new fitness regime, Ross is still able to maintain an 82-game schedule and finds the time to ride her horse, Cody. Frequent trips to Walt Disney World replenish the mental aspect of her game.

THE INTANGIBLES
Although her hand-eye coordination may have diminished over the years, her enthusiasm for the game keeps Ross from unplugging her laptop.

ACKNOWLEDGEMENTS
There is only one name that appears on this book, but it is hardly a one-woman project. There are a number of men, who must remain anonymous, who contribute their expertise and insights year after year to the gathering of information for the book. It would not exist without them, and there is no way to express my gratitude for their generosity.

It has been a pleasure to watch this book grow from something of a trade manual for insiders to a book that can be appreciated by fans and pool players, and by NHL teams that use it as a resource. And as this is another expansion year, we hope to be able to introduce new fans to this great game and the athletes who play it.

This book would also not make it to print without the assistance of Frank Brown. My friend, former co-author and current vice-president of media relations for the National Hockey League never hesitated when I called requesting assistance. Andy McGowan, of the NHL office, and team public relations directors around the league were also quick to respond to my cries for help during the summer.

For their complete professionalism and patience, computer genius Kelly Dresser, and my editors Anne Rose and Kerry Banks, deserve Stanley Cup rings this year.

My family and friends also deserve my thanks for putting up with my long absences and short temper until this project is completed every year.

Thanks also to my *Daily News* hockey team — John Dellapina, Anthony McCarron and Ralph Vacchiano — for helping make my real job fun. And special thanks to my *News* sports editor, Barry Werner, for giving me a shot as the hockey columnist and for encouraging my more creative writing. You're a great boss.

And speaking of the Boss, thanks from this Jersey girl to Bruce, Max, Steve, Nils, Clarence, Patti, Gary, Roy and Danny for making the summer shimmer. There is magic in the night.

CONTENTS

Point Leaders 1
Anaheim Mighty Ducks 5
Atlanta Thrashers 22
Boston Bruins 38
Buffalo Sabres 55
Calgary Flames 73
Carolina Hurricanes 91
Chicago Blackhawks 107
Colorado Avalanche 125
Dallas Stars 141
Detroit Red Wings 158
Edmonton Oilers 176
Florida Panthers 194
Los Angeles Kings 211
Montreal Canadiens 228
Nashville Predators 245
New Jersey Devils 262
New York Islanders 278
New York Rangers 295
Ottawa Senators 311
Philadelphia Flyers 327
Phoenix Coyotes 342
Pittsburgh Penguins 359
San Jose Sharks 373
St. Louis Blues 389
Tampa Bay Lightning 406
Toronto Maple Leafs 422
Vancouver Canucks 438
Washington Capitals 455
Player Index 474

POINT LEADERS

NHL Scoring Statistics 1998-99

RANK	POS.	PLAYER	GP	G	A	PTS	+/-	PP	S	PCT
1.	R	JAROMIR JAGR	81	44	83	127	17	10	343	12.8
2.	R	TEEMU SELANNE	75	47	60	107	18	25	281	16.7
3.	L	PAUL KARIYA	82	39	62	101	17	11	429	9.1
4.	C	PETER FORSBERG	78	30	67	97	27	9	217	13.8
5.	C	JOE SAKIC	73	41	55	96	23	12	255	16.1
6.	C	ALEXEI YASHIN	82	44	50	94	16	19	337	13.1
7.	R	THEOREN FLEURY	75	40	53	93	26	8	301	13.3
8.	C	ERIC LINDROS	71	40	53	93	35	10	242	16.5
9.	L	JOHN LECLAIR	76	43	47	90	36	16	246	17.5
10.	R	PAVOL DEMITRA	82	37	52	89	13	14	259	14.3
11.	C	MARTIN STRAKA	80	35	48	83	12	5	177	19.8
12.	C	MATS SUNDIN	82	31	52	83	22	4	209	14.8
13.	C	MIKE MODANO	77	34	47	81	29	6	224	15.2
14.	C	JASON ALLISON	82	23	53	76	5	5	158	14.6
15.	R	TONY AMONTE	82	44	31	75	0	14	256	17.2
16.	L	LUC ROBITAILLE	82	39	35	74	-1	11	292	13.4
17.	C	STEVE YZERMAN	80	29	45	74	8	13	231	12.6
18.	C	ROD BRIND'AMOUR	82	24	50	74	3	10	191	12.6
19.	L	STEVE THOMAS	78	28	45	73	26	11	209	13.4
20.	C	PETR SYKORA	80	29	43	72	16	15	222	13.1
21.	C	JEREMY ROENICK	78	24	48	72	7	4	203	11.8
22.	R	DMITRI KHRISTICH	79	29	42	71	11	13	144	20.1
23.	C	ROBERT REICHEL	83	26	43	69	-13	8	236	11.0
24.	L	KEITH TKACHUK	68	36	32	68	22	11	258	14.0
25.	R	MIROSLAV SATAN	81	40	26	66	24	13	208	19.2
26.	L	MARKUS NASLUND	80	36	30	66	-13	15	205	17.6
27.	C	PIERRE TURGEON	67	31	34	65	4	10	193	16.1
28.	R	BILL GUERIN	80	30	34	64	7	13	261	11.5
29.	C	BOBBY HOLIK	78	27	37	64	16	5	253	10.7
30.	C	RAY WHITNEY	81	26	38	64	-3	7	193	13.5
31.	C	SERGEI FEDOROV	77	26	37	63	9	6	224	11.6
32.	C	IGOR LARIONOV	75	14	49	63	13	4	83	16.9
33.	C	KEITH PRIMEAU	78	30	32	62	8	9	178	16.9
34.	C	STEVE RUCCHIN	69	23	39	62	11	5	145	15.9
35.	D	AL MACINNIS	82	20	42	62	33	11	314	6.4
36.	C	WAYNE GRETZKY	70	9	53	62	-23	3	132	6.8
37.	C	ALEXEI ZHAMNOV	76	20	41	61	-10	8	200	10.0
38.	C	CLIFF RONNING	79	20	40	60	-3	10	257	7.8
39.	L	SERGEI BEREZIN	76	37	22	59	16	9	263	14.1
40.	R	SAMI KAPANEN	81	24	35	59	-1	5	254	9.4
41.	L	BRETT HULL	60	32	26	58	19	15	192	16.7
42.	L	BRENDAN SHANAHAN	81	31	27	58	2	5	288	10.8
43.	L	VYACHESLAV KOZLOV	79	29	29	58	10	6	209	13.9
44.	R	RAY SHEPPARD	74	25	33	58	4	5	188	13.3
45.	L	CORY STILLMAN	76	27	30	57	7	9	175	15.4

GP = games played; G = goals; A = assists; PTS = points; +/- = goals-for minus goals-against while player is on ice; PP = power-play goals; S = no. of shots; PCT = percentage of goals to shots; * = rookie

RANK	POS.	PLAYER	GP	G	A	PTS	+/-	PP	S	PCT
46.	L	BRIAN ROLSTON	82	24	33	57	11	5	210	11.4
47.	L	JEFF FRIESEN	78	22	35	57	3	10	215	10.2
48.	D	NICKLAS LIDSTROM	81	14	43	57	14	6	205	6.8
49.	D	RAY BOURQUE	81	10	47	57	-7	8	262	3.8
50.	L	SHAWN MCEACHERN	77	31	25	56	8	7	223	13.9
51.	C	MICHAEL PECA	82	27	29	56	7	10	199	13.6
52.	R	RICK TOCCHET	81	26	30	56	5	6	178	14.6
53.	D	FREDRIK OLAUSSON	74	16	40	56	17	10	121	13.2
54.	C	DOUG GILMOUR	72	16	40	56	-16	7	110	14.5
55.	L	GERMAN TITOV	72	11	45	56	18	3	113	9.7
56.	R	PETER BONDRA	66	31	24	55	-1	6	284	10.9
57.	C	JOE NIEUWENDYK	67	28	27	55	11	8	157	17.8
58.	R	JOHN MACLEAN	82	28	27	55	5	11	231	12.1
59.	D	BRIAN LEETCH	82	13	42	55	-7	4	184	7.1
60.	R	JASON ARNOTT	74	27	27	54	10	8	200	13.5
61.	L	MARTY MCINNIS	81	19	35	54	-15	11	146	13.0
62.	C	ADAM OATES	59	12	42	54	-1	3	79	15.2
63.	D	PHIL HOUSLEY	79	11	43	54	14	4	193	5.7
64.	L	ADAM GRAVES	82	38	15	53	-12	14	239	15.9
65.	R	VALERI BURE	80	26	27	53	0	7	260	10.0
66.	R	ALEXEI KOVALEV	77	23	30	53	2	6	191	12.0
67.	R	KEITH JONES	78	20	33	53	23	3	135	14.8
68.	R	MARK RECCHI	71	16	37	53	-7	3	171	9.4
69.	R	SCOTT YOUNG	75	24	28	52	8	8	205	11.7
70.	L	DEREK KING	81	24	28	52	15	8	150	16.0
71.	C	RON FRANCIS	82	21	31	52	-2	8	133	15.8
72.	R	JERE LEHTINEN	74	20	32	52	29	7	173	11.6
73.	D	LARRY MURPHY	80	10	42	52	21	5	168	6.0
74.	C	JAROME IGINLA	82	28	23	51	1	7	211	13.3
75.	R	CLAUDE LEMIEUX	82	27	24	51	0	11	292	9.2
76.	L	SERGEI SAMSONOV	79	25	26	51	-6	6	160	15.6
77.	C	ROB NIEDERMAYER	82	18	33	51	-13	6	142	12.7
78.	C	VIKTOR KOZLOV	65	16	35	51	13	5	209	7.7
79.	D	ERIC DESJARDINS	68	15	36	51	18	6	190	7.9
80.	D	SERGEI ZUBOV	81	10	41	51	9	5	155	6.5
81.	R	ZIGMUND PALFFY	50	22	28	50	-6	5	168	13.1
82.	L	MICHAL GROSEK	76	20	30	50	21	4	140	14.3
83.	L	PATRIK ELIAS	74	17	33	50	19	3	157	10.8
84.	C	GREG JOHNSON	68	16	34	50	-8	2	120	13.3
85.	R	ANDREAS DACKELL	77	15	35	50	9	6	107	14.0
86.	R	ADAM DEADMARSH	66	22	27	49	-2	10	152	14.5
87.	L	JOSEF BERANEK	66	19	30	49	6	7	160	11.9
88.	C	VINCENT DAMPHOUSSE	77	19	30	49	-4	6	190	10.0
89.	D	BORIS MIRONOV	75	11	38	49	13	5	173	6.4
90.	L	WENDEL CLARK	77	32	16	48	-24	11	215	14.9
91.	R	SERGEI KRIVOKRASOV	70	25	23	48	-5	10	208	12.0
92.	R	JOE MURPHY	76	25	23	48	10	7	176	14.2
93.	R	*MILAN HEJDUK	82	14	34	48	8	4	178	7.9
94.	D	DARRYL SYDOR	74	14	34	48	-1	9	163	8.6
95.	C	MARK MESSIER	59	13	35	48	-12	4	97	13.4
96.	L	MAGNUS ARVEDSON	80	21	26	47	33		136	15.4
97.	C	PETR NEDVED	56	20	27	47	-6	9	153	13.1
98.	C	TREVOR LINDEN	82	18	29	47	-14	8	167	10.8
99.	C	CURTIS BROWN	78	16	31	47	23	5	128	12.5
100.	C	IGOR KOROLEV	66	13	34	47	11	1	99	13.1

GP = games played; G = goals; A = assists; PTS = points; +/- = goals-for minus goals-against while player is on ice; PP = power-play goals; S = no. of shots; PCT = percentage of goals to shots; * = rookie

GOAL LEADERS

RANK	PLAYER	G
1.	TEEMU SELANNE	47
2.	JAROMIR JAGR	44
3.	ALEXEI YASHIN	44
4.	TONY AMONTE	44
5.	JOHN LECLAIR	43
6.	JOE SAKIC	41
7.	THEOREN FLEURY	40
8.	ERIC LINDROS	40
9.	MIROSLAV SATAN	40
10.	PAUL KARIYA	39
11.	LUC ROBITAILLE	39
12.	ADAM GRAVES	38
13.	PAVOL DEMITRA	37
14.	SERGEI BEREZIN	37
15.	KEITH TKACHUK	36
16.	MARKUS NASLUND	36
17.	MARTIN STRAKA	35
18.	MIKE MODANO	34
19.	BRETT HULL	32
20.	WENDEL CLARK	32
21.	MATS SUNDIN	31
22.	PIERRE TURGEON	31
23.	BRENDAN SHANAHAN	31
24.	SHAWN MCEACHERN	31
25.	PETER BONDRA	31
26.	PETER FORSBERG	30
27.	BILL GUERIN	30
28.	KEITH PRIMEAU	30
29.	STEVE YZERMAN	29
30.	PETR SYKORA	29
31.	DMITRI KHRISTICH	29
32.	VYACHESLAV KOZLOV	29
33.	STEVE THOMAS	28
34.	JOE NIEUWENDYK	28
35.	JOHN MACLEAN	28
36.	JAROME IGINLA	28
37.	BOBBY HOLIK	27
38.	CORY STILLMAN	27
39.	MICHAEL PECA	27
40.	JASON ARNOTT	27
41.	CLAUDE LEMIEUX	27
42.	ROBERT REICHEL	26
43.	RAY WHITNEY	26
44.	SERGEI FEDOROV	26
45.	RICK TOCCHET	26
46.	VALERI BURE	26
47.	RAY SHEPPARD	25
48.	SERGEI SAMSONOV	25
49.	SERGEI KRIVOKRASOV	25
50.	JOE MURPHY	25

ASSIST LEADERS

PLAYER	A
JAROMIR JAGR	83
PETER FORSBERG	67
PAUL KARIYA	62
TEEMU SELANNE	60
JOE SAKIC	55
THEOREN FLEURY	53
ERIC LINDROS	53
JASON ALLISON	53
WAYNE GRETZKY	53
PAVOL DEMITRA	52
MATS SUNDIN	52
ALEXEI YASHIN	50
ROD BRIND'AMOUR	50
IGOR LARIONOV	49
MARTIN STRAKA	48
JEREMY ROENICK	48
JOHN LECLAIR	47
MIKE MODANO	47
RAY BOURQUE	47
STEVE YZERMAN	45
STEVE THOMAS	45
GERMAN TITOV	45
PETR SYKORA	43
ROBERT REICHEL	43
NICKLAS LIDSTROM	43
PHIL HOUSLEY	43
DMITRI KHRISTICH	42
AL MACINNIS	42
BRIAN LEETCH	42
ADAM OATES	42
LARRY MURPHY	42
ALEXEI ZHAMNOV	41
SERGEI ZUBOV	41
CLIFF RONNING	40
FREDRIK OLAUSSON	40
DOUG GILMOUR	40
STEVE RUCCHIN	39
RAY WHITNEY	38
BORIS MIRONOV	38
BOBBY HOLIK	37
SERGEI FEDOROV	37
MARK RECCHI	37
DANIEL MCGILLIS	37
ERIC DESJARDINS	36
MARC SAVARD	36
LUC ROBITAILLE	35
SAMI KAPANEN	35
JEFF FRIESEN	35
MARTY MCINNIS	35
VIKTOR KOZLOV	35

P.I.M. LEADERS

RANK	PLAYER	PIM
1.	ROB RAY	261
2.	JEFF ODGERS	259
3.	*PETER WORRELL	258
4.	*PATRICK COTE	242
5.	KRZYSZTOF OLIWA	240
6.	PAUL LAUS	218
7.	DENNY LAMBERT	218
8.	DONALD BRASHEAR	209
9.	BOB PROBERT	206
10.	*BRAD BROWN	205
11.	TIE DOMI	198
12.	CRAIG BERUBE	194
13.	JIM CUMMINS	190
14.	*SEAN BROWN	188
15.	SEAN O'DONNELL	186
16.	KEN BELANGER	182
17.	GARY ROBERTS	178
18.	JASON WIEMER	177
19.	MATTHEW BARNABY	177
20.	DARCY TUCKER	176
21.	SANDY MCCARTHY	160
22.	STU GRIMSON	158
23.	RONNIE STERN	158
24.	DAVE MANSON	155
25.	TODD SIMPSON	151

P-PLAY LEADERS

PLAYER	PP
TEEMU SELANNE	25
ALEXEI YASHIN	19
ADRIAN AUCOIN	18
JOHN LECLAIR	16
BRETT HULL	15
PETR SYKORA	15
MARKUS NASLUND	15
TONY AMONTE	14
ADAM GRAVES	14
PAVOL DEMITRA	14
DMITRI KHRISTICH	13
MIROSLAV SATAN	13
STU BARNES	13
STEVE YZERMAN	13
BILL GUERIN	13
SERGEI GONCHAR	13
JOE SAKIC	12
PAUL KARIYA	11
MARTY MCINNIS	11
CLAUDE LEMIEUX	11
WENDEL CLARK	11
LUC ROBITAILLE	11
JOHN MACLEAN	11
KEITH TKACHUK	11
AL MACINNIS	11

GOALIE WIN LEADERS

RANK	PLAYER	W
1.	MARTIN BRODEUR	39
2.	CURTIS JOSEPH	35
3.	ED BELFOUR	35
4.	CHRIS OSGOOD	34
5.	BYRON DAFOE	32
6.	NIKOLAI KHABIBULIN	32
7.	PATRICK ROY	32
8.	GUY HEBERT	31
9.	DOMINIK HASEK	30
10.	ARTURS IRBE	27
11.	JOHN VANBIESBROUC	27
12.	MIKE RICHTER	27
13.	JEFF HACKETT	26
14.	*OLAF KOLZIG	26
15.	TOMMY SALO	25
16.	JOCELYN THIBAULT	24
17.	DAMIAN RHODES	22
18.	RON TUGNUTT	22
19.	SEAN BURKE	21
20.	GARTH SNOW	20
21.	TOM BARRASSO	19
22.	STEPHANE FISET	18
23.	GRANT FUHR	16
24.	MIKE DUNHAM	16
25.	MIKE VERNON	16

GOALIE G.A.A. LEADERS

PLAYER	GAA
RON TUGNUTT	1.79
DOMINIK HASEK	1.87
BYRON DAFOE	1.99
ED BELFOUR	1.99
ROMAN TUREK	2.08
NIKOLAI KHABIBULI	2.13
JOHN VANBIESBROUC	2.18
ARTURS IRBE	2.22
STEVE SHIELDS	2.22
MIKE VERNON	2.27
MARTIN BRODEUR	2.29
PATRICK ROY	2.29
JAMIE MCLENNAN	2.38
JAMIE STORR	2.40
CHRIS OSGOOD	2.42
GUY HEBERT	2.42
DAMIAN RHODES	2.44
GRANT FUHR	2.44
FRED BRATHWAITE	2.45
JEFF HACKETT	2.49
KEN WREGGET	2.53
TOM BARRASSO	2.55
CURTIS JOSEPH	2.56
OLAF KOLZIG	2.58
STEPHANE FISET	2.60

ANAHEIM MIGHTY DUCKS

Players' Statistics 1998-99

POS	NO.	PLAYER	GP	G	A	PTS	+/-	PIM	PP	SH	GW	GT	S	PCT
R	8	TEEMU SELANNE	75	47	60	107	18	30	25		7	1	281	16.7
L	9	PAUL KARIYA	82	39	62	101	17	40	11	2	4		429	9.1
C	20	STEVE RUCCHIN	69	23	39	62	11	22	5	1	5	1	145	15.9
D	2	FREDRIK OLAUSSON	74	16	40	56	17	30	10		2		121	13.2
L	16	MARTY MCINNIS	81	19	35	54	-15	42	11	1	5		146	13.0
R	17	TOMAS SANDSTROM	58	15	17	32	-5	42	7		2		107	14.0
C	39	TRAVIS GREEN	79	13	17	30	-7	81	3	1	2		165	7.9
C	11	MATT CULLEN	75	11	14	25	-12	47	5	1	1	1	112	9.8
D	24	RUSLAN SALEI	74	2	14	16	1	65	1				123	1.6
C	18	TED DRURY	75	5	6	11	2	83					79	6.3
L	33	JIM MCKENZIE	73	5	4	9	-18	99	1		1		59	8.5
R	19	JEFF NIELSEN	80	5	4	9	-12	34			2		94	5.3
C	22	*JOHAN DAVIDSSON	64	3	5	8	-9	14	1		1		48	6.3
C	14	*ANTTI AALTO	73	3	5	8	-12	24	2				61	4.9
D	23	JASON MARSHALL	72	1	7	8	-5	142					63	1.6
D	5	KEVIN HALLER	82	1	6	7	-1	122					64	1.6
D	27	*PASCAL TREPANIER	45	2	4	6	0	48			1		49	4.1
D	25	*MIKE CROWLEY	20	2	3	5	-10	16	1		1		41	4.9
D	7	PAVEL TRNKA	63		4	4	-6	60					50	
L	32	STU GRIMSON	73	3		3	0	158			1		10	30.0
D	4	JAMIE PUSHOR	70	1	2	3	-20	112					75	1.3
D	21	*SCOTT FERGUSON	2		1	1	0						1	
G	31	GUY HEBERT	69		1	1	0							
D	34	DANIEL TREBIL	6				-2						1	
L	12	*MIKE LECLERC	7				-2	4					1	
G	30	DOMINIC ROUSSEL	18				0							

GP = games played; G = goals; A = assists; PTS = points; +/- = goals-for minus goals-against while player is on ice; PIM = penalties in minutes; PP = power-play goals; SH = shorthanded goals; GW = game-winning goals; GT = game-tying goals; S = no. of shots; PCT = percentage of goals to shots; * = rookie

MATT CULLEN

Yrs. of NHL service: 2
Born: Virginia, Minn; Nov. 2, 1976
Position: centre
Height: 6-1
Weight: 195
Uniform no.: 11
Shoots: left

Career statistics:

GP	G	A	TP	PIM
136	17	35	52	70

1997-98 statistics:

GP	G	A	TP	+/-	PIM	PP	SH	GW	GT	S	PCT
61	6	21	27	4	23	2	0	0	0	75	8.0

1998-99 statistics:

GP	G	A	TP	+/-	PIM	PP	SH	GW	GT	S	PCT
75	11	14	25	-12	47	5	1	1	1	112	9.8

LAST SEASON
Second NHL season. Missed one game with ankle injury. Missed three games due to coach's decision. Appeared in three games with Cincinnati (AHL), scoring 1-2 — 3.

THE FINESSE GAME
Cullen received a tryout as the number one centre for Paul Kariya and Teemu Selanne, and it was definitely a learning experience. Cullen has first-line potential and above-average dedication, which means he can get even better.

Cullen has good speed and a good slap shot. He handles the puck well in traffic and is willing to take it there. He is strong on his skates with a quick first step. He has soft hands for passing and a nice scoring touch, but he needs to shoot more. He is more of a playmaker, which will be an advantage if he gets to play with finishers like Kariya and Selanne. But when his wingers are covered, Cullen shouldn't force the pass but take the shot.

An intelligent player, Cullen has improved his defensive awareness, but it is the one area where he needs to show more improvement. Think of how Steve Rucchin handles his safety-valve role when he is on the top line. He's the kind of two-way centre Cullen has to emulate.

THE PHYSICAL GAME
Cullen is strong and fast, and he has an aggressive streak to go along with his work ethic. He plays hard every shift.

THE INTANGIBLES
Cullen is valued for his character as well as his skills. He is going to get another shot at the top job in training camp.

PROJECTION
Cullen struggled at times in his new role, but he could be ready this year to make the transition and score 60 points.

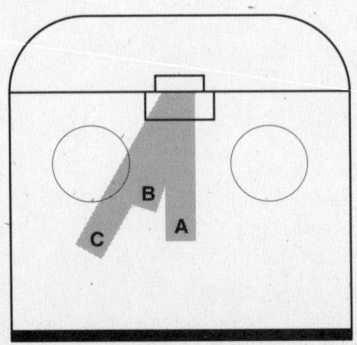

TED DONATO

Yrs. of NHL service: 7
Born: Dedham, Mass.; Apr. 28, 1969
Position: centre
Height: 5-10
Weight: 181
Uniform no.: 21
Shoots: left

Career statistics:

GP	G	A	TP	PIM
533	123	155	278	316

1995-96 statistics:

GP	G	A	TP	+/-	PIM	PP	SH	GW	GT	S	PCT
82	23	26	49	+6	46	7	0	1	0	152	15.1

1996-97 statistics:

GP	G	A	TP	+/-	PIM	PP	SH	GW	GT	S	PCT
67	25	26	51	-9	37	6	2	2	0	172	14.5

1997-98 statistics:

GP	G	A	TP	+/-	PIM	PP	SH	GW	GT	S	PCT
79	16	23	39	+6	54	3	0	5	1	129	12.4

1998-99 statistics:

GP	G	A	TP	+/-	PIM	PP	SH	GW	GT	S	PCT
82	11	16	27	-8	41	3	0	0	0	106	10.4

LAST SEASON

Acquired by N.Y. Islanders from Boston for Ken Belanger, Nov. 7, 1998. Acquired by Ottawa from N.Y. Islanders for fourth-round draft pick, Mar. 20, 1999. Acquired by Anaheim from Ottawa with Antti-Jussi Niemi for Patrick Lalime, June 18, 1999.

THE FINESSE GAME

Donato is a small man who is able to survive in a big man's game because of his hockey sense. He is a good power-play man on the second unit. When Donato gets the chance, he can work down low or use a shot from the point.

He is also a strong penalty killer. He can thrive as a forward on the shorthanded unit because opponents are more concerned about getting the puck than hitting, and Donato is usually in the middle part of the ice. He gets a lot of defensive assignments but creates offense with his anticipation.

Donato is, like a quarterback, very aware of what is going on around him and always communicating with his teammates so that they know what is going on, too. He has good hands and makes hard or soft passes as the occasion warrants.

THE PHYSICAL GAME

Donato is cunning and doesn't allow himself to get into situations where he's close to the boards and could get taken out. He is an elusive skater. He can be outmuscled, but he hustles for the puck and often manages to keep it alive along the boards.

THE INTANGIBLES

Donato had to change uniforms four times in eight months after spending the first six years of his career with the Boston organization that originally drafted him. The rapid shifts had to be unsettling, but Anaheim has made it clear they want him here as a veteran character guy.

PROJECTION

Donato's game is best suited to his being a third-line checker — in that position he could chip in 20 goals.

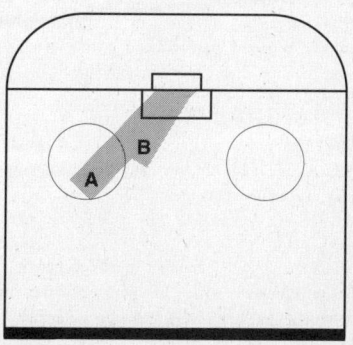

TED DRURY

Yrs. of NHL service: 6
Born: Boston, Mass.; Sept. 13, 1971
Position: centre
Height: 6-0
Weight: 185
Uniform no.: 18
Shoots: left

Career statistics:

GP	G	A	TP	PIM
347	38	50	88	330

1995-96 statistics:

GP	G	A	TP	+/-	PIM	PP	SH	GW	GT	S	PCT
42	9	7	16	-19	54	1	0	1	1	80	11.3

1996-97 statistics:

GP	G	A	TP	+/-	PIM	PP	SH	GW	GT	S	PCT
73	9	9	18	-9	54	1	0	2	1	114	7.9

1997-98 statistics:

GP	G	A	TP	+/-	PIM	PP	SH	GW	GT	S	PCT
73	6	10	16	-10	82	0	1	0	0	110	5.5

1998-99 statistics:

GP	G	A	TP	+/-	PIM	PP	SH	GW	GT	S	PCT
75	5	6	11	+2	83	0	0	0	0	79	6.3

LAST SEASON
Missed seven games due to coach's decision.

THE FINESSE GAME
Drury is a cerebral player who is appreciated by coaches for his adaptability on the penalty kill. He sticks to the game plan. If a strong forecheck is needed, he provides it. If the team has to key on a special opponent, a Brett Hull or a Jaromir Jagr, Drury plays it the way it's drawn on the chalkboard. He can play centre or left wing as needed.

Drury is a shifty skater with decent speed. His forte is his passing ability. He isn't much of a finisher. He is an asset on the power play because of his effort and timing in moving the puck, and he can stickhandle through traffic. He's a poor man's Craig Janney, but with better defensive instincts. He has superb hockey sense, which makes him an asset on the checking line.

THE PHYSICAL GAME
Drury is underrated by opponents, who see a rather average-sized forward and underestimate his wiry strength. He plays a determined game to stay at the NHL level.

THE INTANGIBLES
Drury still has great wheels and a good head, which will keep him in the lineup despite challenges from younger players.

PROJECTION
Drury is in the Mighty Ducks' plans again as a third-liner, but because his offensive production is minimal, he'll be on the bubble if the team gets deeper.

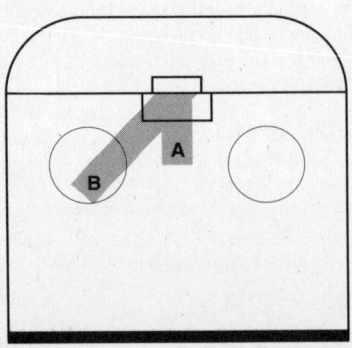

KEVIN HALLER

Yrs. of NHL service: 9
Born: Trochu, Alberta; Dec. 5, 1970
Position: left defense
Height: 6-2
Weight: 192
Uniform no.: 5
Shoots: left

Career statistics:

GP	G	A	TP	PIM
544	37	87	124	788

1995-96 statistics:

GP	G	A	TP	+/-	PIM	PP	SH	GW	GT	S	PCT
69	5	9	14	+18	92	0	2	2	0	89	5.6

1996-97 statistics:

GP	G	A	TP	+/-	PIM	PP	SH	GW	GT	S	PCT
62	2	11	13	-12	85	0	0	0	0	77	2.6

1997-98 statistics:

GP	G	A	TP	+/-	PIM	PP	SH	GW	GT	S	PCT
65	3	5	8	-5	94	0	0	0	0	67	4.5

1998-99 statistics:

GP	G	A	TP	+/-	PIM	PP	SH	GW	GT	S	PCT
82	1	6	7	-1	122	0	0	0	0	64	1.6

LAST SEASON

Third on team in penalty minutes. One of two Mighty Ducks to appear in all 82 games.

THE FINESSE GAME

Haller is a gazelle on skates, with an amazingly light and quick first few strides. He makes skating look effortless and he likes to carry the puck — though he doesn't get involved much offensively once he is inside the offensive zone. In fact, he usually gets rid of the puck once he hits the redline.

Haller has a decent shot from the point. He keeps it low and it tends to get through traffic. He is also a fair passer. He can lead a rush by skating the puck out of his own zone or he will make a heads-up breakout pass.

Haller has worked hard at improving his defensive reads. He has concentrated so much on defense that he thinks little about getting involved in the attack. He doesn't have great hockey smarts, however, which probably is the most limiting factor in his development.

THE PHYSICAL GAME

Haller is tough and, frequently, mean. He'll stick the top players, like Wayne Gretzky (no one could be sorrier than Haller that 99 retired), and he won't back down from anyone. He isn't huge but he plays a pretty big game. He has an edge that a lot of defensemen don't have. Haller plays a lot like Darius Kasparaitis, but Haller is bigger and stronger. He gets in people's faces, but does it without taking a lot of dumb penalties.

THE INTANGIBLES

Haller doesn't provide much offense, but he's a handy number four or five defenseman who complements younger finesse players.

PROJECTION

Haller may be shoved down the depth chart if Anaheim brings in some younger defensemen.

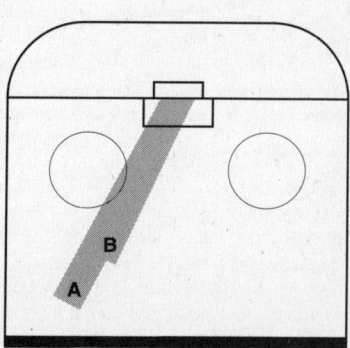

GUY HEBERT

Yrs. of NHL service: 7
Born: Troy, N.Y.; Jan. 7, 1967
Position: goaltender
Height: 5-11
Weight: 185
Uniform no.: 31
Catches: left

Career statistics:

GP	MIN	GA	SO	GAA	A	PIM
369	20963	984	22	2.82	4	20

1995-96 statistics:

GP	MIN	GAA	W	L	T	SO	GA	S	SAPCT	PIM
59	3326	2.83	28	23	5	4	157	1820	.914	6

1996-97 statistics:

GP	MIN	GAA	W	L	T	SO	GA	S	SAPCT	PIM
67	3863	2.67	29	25	12	4	172	2133	.919	4

1997-98 statistics:

GP	MIN	GAA	W	L	T	SO	GA	S	SAPCT	PIM
46	2660	2.93	13	24	6	3	130	1339	.903	4

1998-99 statistics:

GP	MIN	GAA	W	L	T	SO	GA	S	SAPCT	PIM
69	4083	2.42	31	29	9	6	165	2114	.922	0

LAST SEASON

Second among NHL goalies in minutes played. Tied for fourth among NHL goalies in shutouts. Career high in wins.

THE PHYSICAL GAME

Hebert is technically solid. He squares himself to the shooter and combines good angle play with quick reflexes. He stands up well and doesn't get flustered when he sees a lot of shots (which he frequently does), and he deadens pucks with his pads and doesn't leave big rebounds. He also challenges shooters but falls into lapses of staying too deep in his net. When he does, he struggles.

Hebert uses his stick effectively around the net to control rebounds and deflect passes, but he doesn't handle the puck aggressively outside his net. He doesn't have to whip the puck up-ice like Martin Brodeur, but he should be secure enough to make little passes to avoid pressure and help his defensemen.

Hebert's lateral movement has gotten better. He takes away a lot of the net low and forces shooters to go high. Since he is a small goalie, shooters expect him to go down and scramble, but he stands his ground effectively. He allows very few soft goals.

THE MENTAL GAME

Hebert still sees a lot of shots (2,114, the most faced by any goalie), but last season the Mighty Ducks did a good job of taking away the high-quality scoring chances and he was allowed to relax as a result. Hebert is coachable and willing to work to correct his flaws. He's become a much more reliable goalie.

THE INTANGIBLES

Hebert returned successfully from shoulder surgery and the Mighty Ducks thought enough of him to sign him to a three-year, $12-million contract extension before he could test free agency.

PROJECTION

The Mighty Ducks are ready to take the next step. Is Hebert ready? His 31 wins last season say yes. He should improve to 35 wins.

PAUL KARIYA

Yrs. of NHL service: 5
Born: North Vancouver, B.C.; Oct. 16, 1974
Position: left wing
Height: 5-11
Weight: 175
Uniform no.: 9
Shoots: left

Career statistics:

GP	G	A	TP	PIM
302	168	210	378	93

1995-96 statistics:

GP	G	A	TP	+/-	PIM	PP	SH	GW	GT	S	PCT
82	50	58	108	+9	20	20	3	9	0	349	14.3

1996-97 statistics:

GP	G	A	TP	+/-	PIM	PP	SH	GW	GT	S	PCT
69	44	55	99	+36	6	15	3	10	0	340	12.9

1997-98 statistics:

GP	G	A	TP	+/-	PIM	PP	SH	GW	GT	S	PCT
22	17	14	31	+12	23	3	0	2	1	103	16.5

1998-99 statistics:

GP	G	A	TP	+/-	PIM	PP	SH	GW	GT	S	PCT
82	39	62	101	+17	40	11	2	4	0	429	9.1

LAST SEASON

Led NHL in shots with the second-highest total in league history. Third in NHL and led team in assists. Led team in shorthanded goals. Second on team and third in NHL in points. Tied for second on team in power-play goals and plus-minus. Third in NHL in power-play assists (32). Fourth in NHL in power-play points (43). One of two Mighty Ducks to appear in all 82 games.

THE FINESSE GAME

One of the best skaters in the NHL, Kariya is so smooth and fluid his movements appear effortless. He's also explosive, with a good change of direction; he can turn a defender inside out on a one-on-one rush. His speed is a weapon, since he forces defenders to play off him for fear of being burnt, and that opens the ice for his playmaking options. He combines his skating with no-look passes that are uncanny.

Teemu Selanne is the perfect linemate for him, because the Finnish Flash breaks as soon as he sees Kariya with control of the puck. Kariya puts on a burst of speed and can lift his alley-oop pass over the sticks of defenders just ahead of Selanne, for him to skate into. Kariya uses his speed defensively, too, and is quick on the backcheck to break up passes. Kariya kills penalties by hounding the point men and pressuring them into bad passes, which he turns into scoring chances.

A magician with the puck, Kariya can make a play when it looks as if there are no possible options. He likes to use the net for protection, like his idol Wayne Gretzky, and make passes from behind the goal line.

His release on his shot is excellent. Playing with the defensively alert Steve Rucchin gives Kariya and Selanne the freedom to make their breakout dashes.

Kariya is a low-maintenance superstar. He has worked on his weaknesses, becoming stronger on the puck, less fancy in his passing and more willing to shoot. He is able to carry a team on his back.

THE PHYSICAL GAME

Kariya has powerful thighs and legs and has improved his upper body. He was able to make a successful comeback from a career-threatening concussion, and vowed to start carrying his stick a little higher to protect himself. With 40 penalty minutes, he was hardly a goon.

THE INTANGIBLES

Kariya and Selanne scored 40 per cent of Anaheim's goals last season. Teams know they have to shut these two down to stop the Mighty Ducks, but it's not always that easy to do. Kariya is expected to make a full recovery from a broken foot suffered in the playoffs.

Kariya signed a three-year $32-million contract extension. We don't expect it to go to his head.

PROJECTION

For Kariya, 100 points is a given.

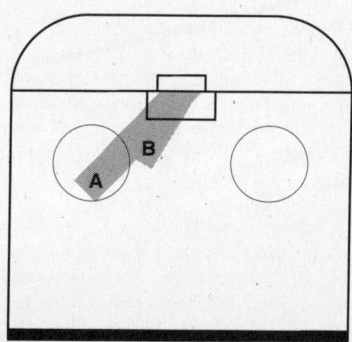

JASON MARSHALL

Yrs. of NHL service: 4
Born: Cranbrook, B.C.; Feb. 22, 1971
Position: right defense
Height: 6-2
Weight: 205
Uniform no.: 23
Shoots: right

Career statistics:

GP	G	A	TP	PIM
244	6	23	29	518

1995-96 statistics:

GP	G	A	TP	+/-	PIM	PP	SH	GW	GT	S	PCT
24	0	1	1	+3	42	0	0	0	0	9	0.0

1996-97 statistics:

GP	G	A	TP	+/-	PIM	PP	SH	GW	GT	S	PCT
73	1	9	10	+6	140	0	0	0	0	34	2.9

1997-98 statistics:

GP	G	A	TP	+/-	PIM	PP	SH	GW	GT	S	PCT
72	3	6	9	-8	189	1	0	0	0	68	4.4

1998-99 statistics:

GP	G	A	TP	+/-	PIM	PP	SH	GW	GT	S	PCT
72	1	7	8	-5	142	0	0	0	0	63	1.6

LAST SEASON

Second on team in penalty minutes. Missed six games with hamstring injury. Missed three games due to coach's decision.

THE FINESSE GAME

Marshall is big and mobile with good puck skills. He has been slow to come to hand, mostly from having to learn the mental discipline of playing his position.

He will never be involved much offensively. He lacks the instincts to be much of a factor from the point and his shot is only average. He is a good skater for his size.

Marshall can be his own worst enemy. If he makes a mistake he is very hard on himself. This held him back in his early development. He has started to feel more comfortable now that the Mighty Ducks have made him a regular, but coach Craig Hartsburg still sat him out for the final three games before the playoffs.

THE PHYSICAL GAME

Marshall is big and likes to play a physical game. He sticks up for his teammates and will take the initiative to set a physical tone. He is a hard worker and shows up most nights. He can have games where he gets a little headstrong and starts running around out of position, committing sins of commission rather than omission.

THE INTANGIBLES

Marshall is an unspectacular but steady member of the Mighty Ducks' top four. He blocks shots and has a high pain threshold that keeps him coming back shift after shift. He has evolved into a gamer. He is one tough Duck.

PROJECTION

Marshall will be hard-pressed to get points in double-digits, but his PIM should again be triple-digits.

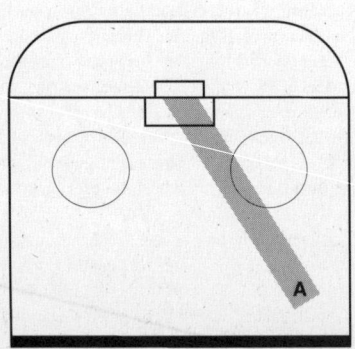

MARTY MCINNIS

Yrs. of NHL service: 7
Born: Hingham, Mass.; June 2, 1970
Position: left wing
Height: 5-11
Weight: 183
Uniform no.: 16
Shoots: right

Career statistics:

GP	G	A	TP	PIM
503	120	183	303	193

1995-96 statistics:

GP	G	A	TP	+/-	PIM	PP	SH	GW	GT	S	PCT
74	12	34	46	-11	39	2	0	1	0	167	7.2

1996-97 statistics:

GP	G	A	TP	+/-	PIM	PP	SH	GW	GT	S	PCT
80	23	26	49	-8	22	5	1	4	1	182	12.6

1997-98 statistics:

GP	G	A	TP	+/-	PIM	PP	SH	GW	GT	S	PCT
75	19	25	44	+1	34	5	4	0	0	128	14.8

1998-99 statistics:

GP	G	A	TP	+/-	PIM	PP	SH	GW	GT	S	PCT
81	19	35	54	-15	42	11	1	5	0	146	13.0

PROJECTION
McInnis came close to the 20 goals that should be expected from him annually.

LAST SEASON
Acquired from Chicago for a fourth-round draft pick Oct. 25, 1998. Tied for second on team in power-play and shorthanded goals. Third on team in shooting percentage. Missed one game due to coach's decision.

THE FINESSE GAME
McInnis does a lot of the little things well. He plays positionally, is smart and reliable defensively, and turns his checking work into scoring opportunities with quick passes and his work down low. He is a very patient shooter.

McInnis isn't fast but he is deceptive, with a quick first few strides to the puck. He seems to be more aware of where the puck is than his opponents are, so while they're looking for the puck, he's already heading towards it.

McInnis is a good penalty killer because of his tenacity and anticipation. He reads plays well on offense and defense. Playing the off-wing opens up his shot for a quick release. He's always a shorthanded threat.

THE PHYSICAL GAME
McInnis is not very big or tough, but he is sturdy and will use his body to bump and scrap for the puck. He always tries to get in the way, but he loses a lot of battles in tight to larger forwards because he is not that strong.

THE INTANGIBLES
McInnis should be a third-liner but plays the second line in Anaheim, where he makes pretty good use of the opportunities presented to him.

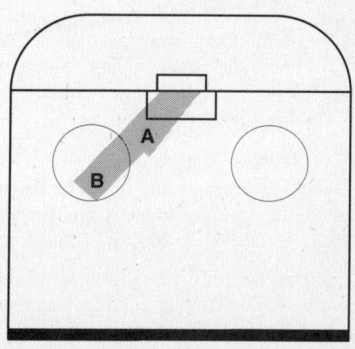

JEFF NIELSEN

Yrs. of NHL service: 2
Born: Grand Rapids, MN; Sept. 20, 1971
Position: right wing
Height: 6-0
Weight: 200
Uniform no.: 19
Shoots: left

Career statistics:

GP	G	A	TP	PIM
114	9	9	18	52

1996-97 statistics:

GP	G	A	TP	+/-	PIM	PP	SH	GW	GT	S	PCT
2	0	0	0	-1	2	0	0	0	0	1	0.0

1997-98 statistics:

GP	G	A	TP	+/-	PIM	PP	SH	GW	GT	S	PCT
32	4	5	9	-1	16	0	0	0	0	36	11.1

1998-99 statistics:

GP	G	A	TP	+/-	PIM	PP	SH	GW	GT	S	PCT
80	5	4	9	-12	34	0	0	2	0	94	5.3

LAST SEASON

Second NHL season. Missed two games due to coach's decision.

THE FINESSE GAME

Nielsen *can* skate, *can* use his great shot and *can* be physical. The question remains, on how many nights will he make use of his best assets? Considering how muce ice time Nielsen saw last season he should have produced more than five goals, even by accident. Although he skates well enough to earn shifts as a third-line checker, which reduces the pressure on him to score goals, even checking forwards these days are expected to chip in 10 goals.

The missing ingredients in Nielsen's game are hockey sense and the consistency to stay physically involved.

THE PHYSICAL GAME

Nielsen has to reach down and play to his size every night. The nights when he hits and gets involved are his best nights. If only they came along more often.

THE INTANGIBLES

Nielsen has all the tools to be a better player than he is. Anaheim is a bit thin at forward and as the team improves he'll be on the bubble unless he steps up his game, too. Nielsen needs to mature in his approach to this job, which is what it is.

PROJECTION

Nielsen should be a much better scorer for the number of games and the ice time he plays. Nielsen waited a long time for his shot at an NHL job, but he needs to show more.

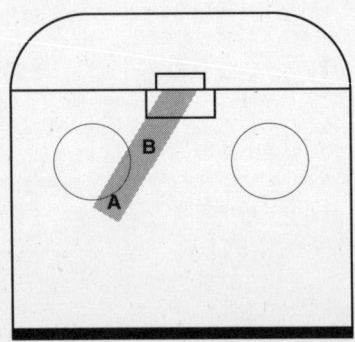

FREDRIK OLAUSSON

Yrs. of NHL service: 13
Born: Dadsejo, Sweden; Oct. 5, 1966
Position: right defense
Height: 6-2
Weight: 195
Uniform no.: 2
Shoots: right

Career statistics:

GP	G	A	TP	PIM
861	128	396	524	368

1995-96 statistics:

GP	G	A	TP	+/-	PIM	PP	SH	GW	GT	S	PCT
56	2	22	24	-7	38	1	0	0	0	83	2.4

1996-97 statistics:

GP	G	A	TP	+/-	PIM	PP	SH	GW	GT	S	PCT
71	9	29	38	+16	32	3	0	3	0	110	8.2

1997-98 statistics:

GP	G	A	TP	+/-	PIM	PP	SH	GW	GT	S	PCT
76	6	27	33	+13	42	2	0	1	0	89	6.7

1998-99 statistics:

GP	G	A	TP	+/-	PIM	PP	SH	GW	GT	S	PCT
74	16	40	56	+17	30	10	0	2	0	121	13.2

LAST SEASON

Signed as free agent Aug. 28, 1998. Led team defensemen and fourth among NHL defensemen in scoring. Tied for second on team and led team defensemen in plus-minus. Third on team in assists. Second in NHL in power-play assists (33). Tied for third in NHL in power-play points (43). Missed two games due to rib injuries. Missed six games due to coach's decision.

THE FINESSE GAME

One of the smarter free-agent signings last season, Olausson fit right into the Anaheim power play thanks to his ability to read off left point Paul Kariya. When penalty killers overload on Kariya, Olausson slips into the back door in the right circle, and is always ready for a Kariya feed. Olausson is a power-play specialist, and has the hand skills to cradle the puck when he is heading up-ice, plus decent hockey vision.

He gambles low on rare occasions, and usually stays at the point to prevent breakouts. He is adept at keeping the puck in at the point.

Olausson's skating helps him to recover from some of his mistakes, which have become less glaring in recent years. He is fundamentally sound, and does a lot of the little things well. His defensive reads are adequate, and he plays odd-man rushes with intelligence and poise.

THE PHYSICAL GAME

Olausson's work ethic is more evident in the attacking zone than in the defensive zone. His physical involvement is minimal, but he tries to compensate by playing an alert positional game. He uses his stick in the passing lanes.

THE INTANGIBLES

Olausson was well-spotted in Anaheim, but how will the arrival of Oleg Tverdovsky affect his ice time, especially on the power play?

PROJECTION

Another 50 points is about right for Olausson if he continues to see significant power-play time.

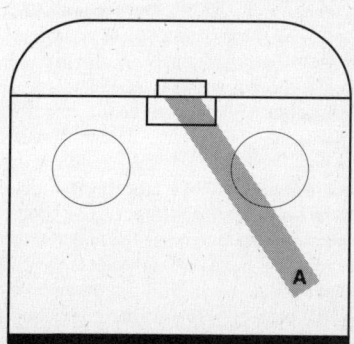

STEVE RUCCHIN

Yrs. of NHL service: 5
Born: London, Ont.; July 4, 1971
Position: centre
Height: 6-3
Weight: 210
Uniform no.: 20
Shoots: left

Career statistics:
GP	G	A	TP	PIM
327	84	159	243	94

1995-96 statistics:
GP	G	A	TP	+/-	PIM	PP	SH	GW	GT	S	PCT
64	19	25	44	+3	12	8	1	4	0	113	16.8

1996-97 statistics:
GP	G	A	TP	+/-	PIM	PP	SH	GW	GT	S	PCT
79	19	48	67	+26	24	6	1	2	1	153	12.4

1997-98 statistics:
GP	G	A	TP	+/-	PIM	PP	SH	GW	GT	S	PCT
72	17	36	53	+8	13	8	1	3	0	131	13.0

1998-99 statistics:
GP	G	A	TP	+/-	PIM	PP	SH	GW	GT	S	PCT
69	23	39	62	+11	22	5	1	5	1	145	15.9

LAST SEASON

Second on team in shooting percentage. Tied for second on team in game-winning goals. Third on team in goals with career high. Third on team in points. Missed 10 games with groin injury. Missed three games due to illness.

THE FINESSE GAME

Rucchin was two players in one last season. When in his usual role as centre for Paul Kariya and Teemu Selanne, he was the disher and the line's defensive conscience. When moved to the second line, Rucchin helped spread the wealth by shooting more and continuing to push the envelope of his talent.

Playing on a second line is more suited to Rucchin's level, but he is such a stabilizing force with the gunners that coach Craig Hartsburg went back to the combination for the playoffs. The role isn't easy for Rucchin, but he makes it look simple. First he has to concentrate on being back defensively. Then he has to rush to get into the play to get the puck to his linemates or give them some room to work. Since Rucchin was strictly a defensive centre in college, this has taken some adjusting over the years. He still doesn't think like a number one centre, and frankly, he doesn't have the ability, but Anaheim forces him to play like one.

Rucchin thinks offense more in his second-line role. He has good size and range, and good hockey sense that enables him to make the most of his above-average skating, passing and shooting skills. He grinds and digs the puck off the wall, and has the vision and the passing skills to find a breaking Kariya and Selanne. He is patient and protects the puck well.

THE PHYSICAL GAME

Rucchin can be a real force. He's strong and balanced, willing to forecheck hard and fight for the puck along the boards and in the corners. When he wins the puck, he's able to create a smart play with it. He has long arms and a long reach for holding off defenders and working the puck one-handed, or reaching in defensively to knock the puck away from an attacker.

Rucchin often matches up against other teams' big centres.

THE INTANGIBLES

Rucchin is more than just the water boy for Kariya and Selanne. He's one of the important leaders on the team.

PROJECTION

Rucchin had a nice bounce-back year and if he continues in a second-line role could score 60 to 65 points.

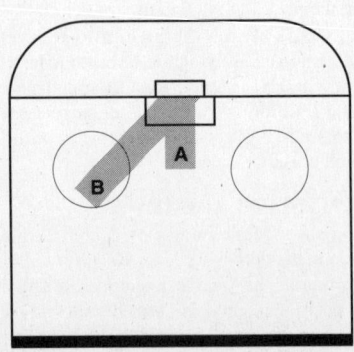

RUSLAN SALEI

Yrs. of NHL service: 3
Born: Minsk, Belarus; Nov. 2, 1974
Position: left defense
Height: 6-1
Weight: 200
Uniform no.: 24
Shoots: left

Career statistics:

GP	G	A	TP	PIM
170	7	25	32	172

1996-97 statistics:

GP	G	A	TP	+/-	PIM	PP	SH	GW	GT	S	PCT
30	0	1	1	-8	37	0	0	0	0	14	0.0

1997-98 statistics:

GP	G	A	TP	+/-	PIM	PP	SH	GW	GT	S	PCT
66	5	10	15	+7	70	1	0	0	1	104	4.8

1998-99 statistics:

GP	G	A	TP	+/-	PIM	PP	SH	GW	GT	S	PCT
74	2	14	16	+1	65	1	0	0	0	123	1.6

LAST SEASON

Missed five games due to suspension for dangerous hit. Missed two games with shoulder injury. Missed one game due to coach's decision.

THE FINESSE GAME

Salei is a fairly agile skater but doesn't have great breakaway speed. He skates well backwards, is mobile and is not easy to beat one-on-one.

His defensive reads are very good, and he can kill penalties. There is a possibility he could see time on a second power-play unit, because he moves the puck well and appears to have an NHL-calibre point shot. He shoots well off the pass — and it's high velocity.

Salei's skill level is high enough that the Mighty Ducks are able to use him up front in an emergency. On defense, he needs to develop more consistency.

THE PHYSICAL GAME

Salei is mature and solidly built and he initiates a lot of contact. He is not afraid to hit anyone. He has a little nasty streak that results in some cheap hits (and two suspensions in the last two seasons), but he can play it hard and clean, too. He will sometimes start running around and lose track of his man.

THE INTANGIBLES

Salei is still consistently inconsistent. This could be his last chance to prove himself before he loses a top four spot to a kid like Vitali Vishnevsky.

PROJECTION

Salei risks being dropped to the third defense pairing, though he will probably continue to see second-unit power-play time.

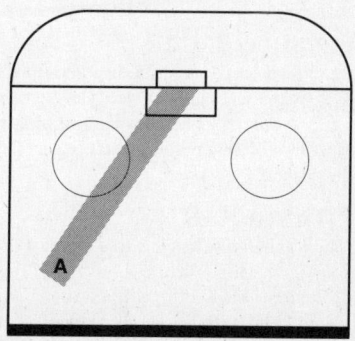

TOMAS SANDSTROM

Yrs. of NHL service: 15
Born: Jakobstad, Finland; Sept. 4, 1964
Position: right wing
Height: 6-2
Weight: 200
Uniform no.: 17
Shoots: left

Career statistics:

GP	G	A	TP	PIM
983	394	462	856	1193

1995-96 statistics:

GP	G	A	TP	+/-	PIM	PP	SH	GW	GT	S	PCT
58	35	35	70	+4	69	17	1	2	0	187	18.7

1996-97 statistics:

GP	G	A	TP	+/-	PIM	PP	SH	GW	GT	S	PCT
74	18	24	42	+6	69	1	2	2	1	139	12.9

1997-98 statistics:

GP	G	A	TP	+/-	PIM	PP	SH	GW	GT	S	PCT
77	9	8	17	-25	64	2	1	0	1	136	6.6

1998-99 statistics:

GP	G	A	TP	+/-	PIM	PP	SH	GW	GT	S	PCT
58	15	17	32	-5	42	7	0	2	0	107	14.0

PROJECTION

Sandstrom is a question mark and is no longer a big point producer. He can possibly score in the 30-point range, but we would look elsewhere for help in our pool or on the ice.

LAST SEASON

Third on team in shooting percentage. Missed 24 games with fractured wrist.

THE FINESSE GAME

Sandstrom is one of the few players in the league who can release a shot when the puck is in his feet. He uses a short backswing and surprises goalies with the shot's velocity and accuracy. He can beat a netminder in a number of ways, but this shot is unique. Sandstrom is also smart enough and skilled enough to work to get open and be ready for the puck.

Sandstrom combines size, speed, strength and skill. He needs to play to keep his legs going. His skating is impressive for someone of his dimensions. Quick and agile, he intimidates with his speed. He has a nice passing touch and shoots well on the fly or off the one-timer. He just isn't the same hungry player he was earlier in his career: he is less willing to pay the price that made him such an effective and annoying player to face.

THE PHYSICAL GAME

There are times when Sandstrom hits and runs, but he generally gets the last laugh as vengeance-crazed opponents take retaliatory penalties against him. He has lost his appetite for the one-on-one battles on the walls and in the corners.

THE INTANGIBLES

Sandstrom was an unrestricted free agent during the off-season. Increasingly brittle, he was mulling a return to Sweden and leaving the NHL, though the Ducks wanted him back for another year.

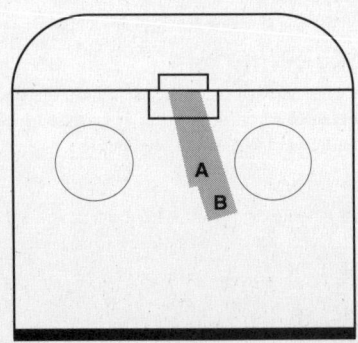

TEEMU SELANNE

Yrs. of NHL service: 7
Born: Helsinki, Finland; July 3, 1970
Position: right wing
Height: 6-0
Weight: 200
Uniform no.: 8
Shoots: right

Career statistics:

GP	G	A	TP	PIM
485	317	331	644	185

1995-96 statistics:

GP	G	A	TP	+/-	PIM	PP	SH	GW	GT	S	PCT
79	40	68	108	+5	22	9	1	5	0	267	15.0

1996-97 statistics:

GP	G	A	TP	+/-	PIM	PP	SH	GW	GT	S	PCT
78	51	58	109	+28	34	11	1	8	2	273	18.7

1997-98 statistics:

GP	G	A	TP	+/-	PIM	PP	SH	GW	GT	S	PCT
73	52	34	86	+12	30	10	1	10	3	268	19.4

1998-99 statistics:

GP	G	A	TP	+/-	PIM	PP	SH	GW	GT	S	PCT
75	47	60	107	+18	30	25	0	7	1	281	16.7

LAST SEASON

Winner of inaugural Rocket Richard Trophy for leading NHL in goals. Led team and second in NHL in scoring. Led NHL in power-play goals. Second on team and fourth in NHL in assists. Led team in plus-minus and shooting percentage. Second on team in shots. Missed seven games with strained right thigh.

THE FINESSE GAME

Selanne has Porsche turbo speed. He gets down low and then simply explodes past defensemen, even when he starts from a standstill. He gets tremendous thrust from his legs and has quick feet. Acceleration, balance, change of gears, it's all there.

Everything you could ask for in a shot is there as well. Selanne employs all varieties of attacks and is equally comfortable on either wing. He plays off Paul Kariya's puck control and exquisite lead passes. So often these two players will simply "alley oop" to the other with perfect timing, so that they receive the puck in full stride.

Selanne is constantly in motion. If his first attempt is stopped, he'll pursue the puck behind the net, make a pass and circle out again for a shot. He is almost impossible to catch and is tough to knock down because of his balance. He will set up on the off-wing on the power play and can score on the backhand. His shot is not especially hard, but it is quick and accurate.

Selanne doesn't just try to overpower with his skating, he also outwits opponents. He has tremendous hockey instincts and vision, and is as good a playmaker as a finisher. He has a reputation for being selfish with the puck, but he is more generous with Kariya and feeds him for one-timers.

THE PHYSICAL GAME

Anaheim is pretty much a one-line team, so Kariya, Selanne and Steve Rucchin (or whoever might inherit the role) have to deal with checking pressure every night. Teams set out to bump and grind Selanne from the first shift, and he has to fight his way through the junk. When the referees are slow on the whistle, he takes matters into his own hands, usually with his stick. He is one of the toughest players in the league, European or otherwise. He is big and uses his strength along the wall, but he takes a beating.

THE INTANGIBLES

Coach Craig Hartsburg tried several times during the season to break up the Kariya-Selanne combo to get them away from checking pressure, but they are much better together than apart. Selanne can have 55 quiet minutes and kill you when you let up for the other two shifts.

Those power-play totals could soar even higher next year with the addition of Oleg Tverdovsky to the point.

PROJECTION

Selanne is a consistent 50-goal, 100-point scorer.

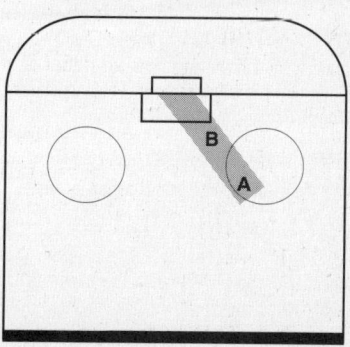

PAVEL TRNKA

Yrs. of NHL service: 2
Born: Plzen, Czech Republic; July 27, 1976
Position: left defense
Height: 6-3
Weight: 200
Uniform no.: 7
Shoots: left

Career statistics:

GP	G	A	TP	PIM
111	3	8	11	100

1997-98 statistics:

GP	G	A	TP	+/-	PIM	PP	SH	GW	GT	S	PCT
48	3	4	7	-4	40	1	0	0	1	46	6.5

1998-99 statistics:

GP	G	A	TP	+/-	PIM	PP	SH	GW	GT	S	PCT
63	0	4	4	-6	60	0	0	0	0	50	.0

LAST SEASON

Second NHL season. Missed 19 games due to coach's decision.

THE FINESSE GAME

Trnka watched an awful lot of games from the press box last season as part of his continuing NHL education. He is a fine puck-carrying defenseman, though he lost the first-unit power-play time to the reborn Fredrik Olausson, which may have weighed on his confidence.

Trnka is a highly skilled player, though he will not put a lot of points on the board. He hasn't been a scorer at the minor-league level. He uses his finesse skills in a defensive role by making the smart first pass or skating the puck out of the zone. He lacks a shot or the puck movement from the point that would make him a more productive player.

Trnka is continuing to learn the defensive part of the game. He tends to back in, back in, back in until he is almost on top of the goalie. He will also lose his checking assignment.

THE PHYSICAL GAME

Trnka can handle a lot of ice time, when he gets it. He is a willing hitter but not a big banger. He is more of a bumper.

THE INTANGIBLES

After making a fairly impressive debut at age 21, Trnka took a step back last year. He is still very young and still a project.

PROJECTION

If Trnka gets 20 points, it would be a bonus.

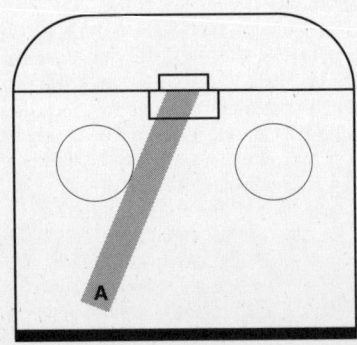

OLEG TVERDOVSKY

Yrs. of NHL service: 5
Born: Donetsk, Ukraine; May 18, 1976
Position: left defense
Height: 6-0
Weight: 185
Uniform no.: 10
Shoots: left

Career statistics:

GP	G	A	TP	PIM
328	34	107	141	129

1995-96 statistics:

GP	G	A	TP	+/-	PIM	PP	SH	GW	GT	S	PCT
82	7	23	30	-7	41	2	0	0	0	119	5.9

1996-97 statistics:

GP	G	A	TP	+/-	PIM	PP	SH	GW	GT	S	PCT
82	10	45	55	-5	30	3	1	2	0	144	6.9

1997-98 statistics:

GP	G	A	TP	+/-	PIM	PP	SH	GW	GT	S	PCT
46	7	12	19	+1	12	4	0	1	1	83	8.4

1998-99 statistics:

GP	G	A	TP	+/-	PIM	PP	SH	GW	GT	S	PCT
82	7	18	25	+11	32	2	0	2	0	117	6.0

LAST SEASON

Acquired from Phoenix for a first-round draft pick in 1999 and Travis Green, June 26, 1999. One of four Coyotes to appear in all 82 games.

THE FINESSE GAME

Tverdovsky is an impressive talent. A weakness in the offensive zone is tough to find because this defenseman passes the puck well and shoots bullets. He is clearly an "offenseman." He has not learned how to pick his spots well, though, and wants to go at every opportunity. He can make some world-class errors or produce world-class goals. There are nights when he is simply brilliant, but he hasn't achieved consistency yet.

Defensively, Tverdovsky can be a nightmare. He is often very casual moving the puck around the wall or banging it off the glass.

Tverdovsky has Brian Leetch potential. He's an explosive skater and can carry the puck at high tempo. He works the point on the power play, utilizing a nice lateral slide along the blueline, and he kills penalties. He also sees his options and makes his decisions at lightning speed. He needs to develop Leetch's commitment to team defense.

THE PHYSICAL GAME

Some of Tverdovsky's defensive weaknesses can be attributed to the fact that he sometimes plays the puck instead of the man, or tries to poke-check without backing it up with his body. Physically, when he makes the right decision he can eliminate the man, and he looks to be improving in this area by at least tying up his man.

This youngster is a devoted practice player who almost has to be wrestled off the ice. He loves to play and is enthusiastic and extremely competitive.

THE INTANGIBLES

Tverdovsky returns to the Mighty Ducks, where he started his career. He can expect to be booed by fans who remember his anti-Anaheim remarks of two seasons ago, and cheered once fans get a gander of him on the Ducks' power play with Paul Kariya and Teemu Selanne.

PROJECTION

Tverdovsky needs to score in the 55- to 60-point range to overcome his defensive shortcomings.

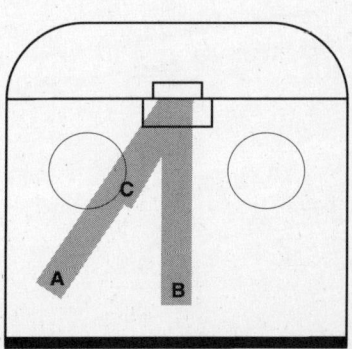

ATLANTA THRASHERS

Expansion team — no statistics available for the 1998-99 season.

KELLY BUCHBERGER

Yrs. of NHL service: 10
Born: Langenburg, Sask.; Dec. 2, 1966
Position: left wing
Height: 6-2
Weight: 200
Uniform no.: 16
Shoots: left

Career statistics:

GP	G	A	TP	PIM
795	82	158	230	1747

1995-96 statistics:

GP	G	A	TP	+/-	PIM	PP	SH	GW	GT	S	PCT
82	11	14	25	-20	184	0	2	3	0	119	9.2

1996-97 statistics:

GP	G	A	TP	+/-	PIM	PP	SH	GW	GT	S	PCT
81	8	30	38	+4	159	0	0	3	0	78	10.3

1997-98 statistics:

GP	G	A	TP	+/-	PIM	PP	SH	GW	GT	S	PCT
82	6	17	23	-10	122	1	1	1	0	86	7.0

1998-99 statistics:

GP	G	A	TP	+/-	PIM	PP	SH	GW	GT	S	PCT
52	4	4	8	-6	68	0	2	1	0	29	13.8

LAST SEASON

Selected from Edmonton in Expansion Draft, June 25, 1999. Missed 30 games with fractured forearm.

THE FINESSE GAME

What's not to like? Buchberger is an ideal third-line player. Night in and night out, he faces other teams' top forwards and does a terrific shadow job, harassing without taking bad penalties.

Buchberger works hard and provides a consistent effort. He will grind, go to the net, kill penalties — all of the grunt work. He can finish off some plays now and then, but that is not his objective. The biggest change in Buchberger is that he has developed a degree of confidence in his finesse moves and is now willing to try something that looks too difficult for a "defensive" player. Sometimes it works, sometimes it doesn't, but he can surprise opponents.

Buchberger has some straight-ahead speed and will go to the net and muck, but this kind of player needs some luck to get goals. He has earned a great deal of respect for his work ethic. He doesn't quit. He has five career playoff-overtime goals simply because he's a gamer.

THE PHYSICAL GAME

Buchberger's injury (which required a plate and screws to repair) was his first serious setback in the past eight seasons (he had missed only three games in the prior seven seasons). When he returned, he was obviously not as strong usual. But he is a legitimately tough customer. Honest and gritty, he won't get knocked around and is a solid hitter who likes the physical part of the game. He is a very disciplined player. He's also very determined. He keeps his legs moving constantly, and a player who lets up on this winger will be sorry, because Buchberger will keep plugging with the puck or go to the net.

THE INTANGIBLES

Buchberger will be a great player to have on hand for the expansion Thrashers to start off their team. Hopefully at the trade deadline, they'll do the right thing and trade him to a playoff contender, so he can get another shot at a Cup. Buchberger is one of the most unsung leaders in the NHL. Even at 32, he is one of the best crunch-time players in the league.

PROJECTION

Point totals in this case are minimal and meaningless. Buchberger could score 10 points and be a candidate for team MVP.

SYLVAIN CLOUTIER

Yrs. of NHL service: 0
Born: Mont-Laurier, Que.; Feb. 13, 1974
Position: C
Height: 6-0
Weight: 195
Uniform no.: 14
Shoots: left

Career statistics:

GP	G	A	TP	PIM
7	0	0	0	0

1998-99 statistics:

GP	G	A	TP	+/-	PIM	PP	SH	GW	GT	S	PCT
7	0	0	0	-1	0	0	0	0	0	3	.0

LAST SEASON
Acquired from Chicago in Expansion Draft, June 25, 1999. Appeared in 73 games with Indianapolis (IHL), scoring 21-33 — 54. Will be entering first NHL season.

THE FINESSE GAME
Cloutier is a solid enough young player, but one without too many offensive skills. He was a scorer at the junior and minor-league levels, but isn't able to translate that into any kind of NHL numbers.

He has decent hands and a shot that is best from close range (he has a quick release on his shot). He is very good on face-offs.

Cloutier understands the game well and is coachable. He's like a sponge when it comes to soaking up hockey information. He won't make the same mistake twice once a coach has pointed something out to him.

THE PHYSICAL GAME
Cloutier has an edge to his game and can be chippy. He is hardworking and pushes himself every night. His effort is consistently intense. He has decent size that he puts to good use.

THE INTANGIBLES
Even an expansion team like the Thrashers may have trouble figuring out how to use Cloutier. He may not skate well enough to be a checking-line player, and won't score enough to be a top six forward.

PROJECTION
Cloutier isn't likely to break double digits in goals.

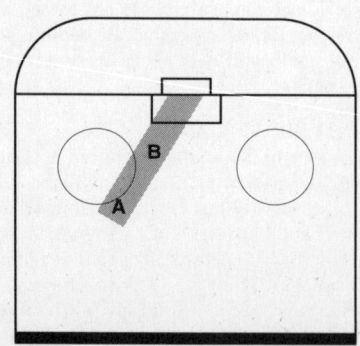

KEVIN DEAN

Yrs. of NHL service: 4
Born: Madison, WI; Apr. 1, 1969
Position: left defense
Height: 6-3
Weight: 205
Uniform no.: 28
Shoots: left

Career statistics:

GP	G	A	TP	PIM
181	4	28	26	68

1995-96 statistics:

GP	G	A	TP	+/-	PIM	PP	SH	GW	GT	S	PCT
41	0	6	0	+4	28	0	0	0	0	29	0.0

1996-97 statistics:

GP	G	A	TP	+/-	PIM	PP	SH	GW	GT	S	PCT
28	2	4	6	+2	6	0	0	0	0	21	9.5

1997-98 statistics:

GP	G	A	TP	+/-	PIM	PP	SH	GW	GT	S	PCT
50	1	8	9	+12	12	1	0	0	0	28	3.6

1998-99 statistics:

GP	G	A	TP	+/-	PIM	PP	SH	GW	GT	S	PCT
62	1	10	11	+4	22	1	0	0	0	51	2.0

LAST SEASON

Acquired from New Jersey in Expansion Draft, June 25, 1999. Missed five games with strained right knee. Missed three games with irregular heartbeat. Missed one game with flu. Missed nine games with groin injury. Missed two games due to coach's decision.

THE FINESSE GAME

Dean doesn't do anything special, which was what kept him hovering around as the sixth or seventh defenseman through much of his Devils tenure. He is a good, solid skater, but not overly fast or agile. He has good size but he isn't physical.

Dean has some hand skills, especially passing, but doesn't do much offensively because he doesn't have terrific vision. A smart player, he understands game situations well. And he can be used on special teams, at least in a secondary role.

THE PHYSICAL GAME

Dean is tall but lean, and he leans on people as opposed to hitting them. He plays hard and competes but has no tough edge to him at all.

THE INTANGIBLES

Dean is a quiet leader and was a captain in the AHL, but has never developed confidence in himself at the NHL level. He is another of the well-schooled Devils defensemen who will be a top four blueliner with the expansion Thrashers.

PROJECTION

Dean could score 15 to 20 points with the ice time he will get in Atlanta.

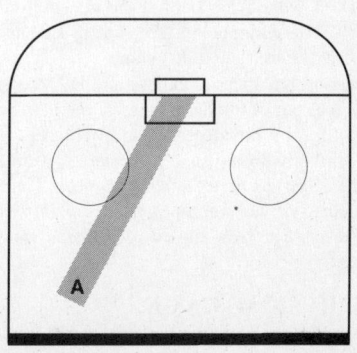

NELSON EMERSON

Yrs. of NHL service: 8
Born: Hamilton, Ont.; Aug. 17, 1967
Position: centre/left wing
Height: 5-11
Weight: 175
Uniform no.: 7
Shoots: right

Career statistics:

GP	G	A	TP	PIM
589	164	260	424	449

1995-96 statistics:

GP	G	A	TP	+/-	PIM	PP	SH	GW	GT	S	PCT
81	29	29	58	-7	78	12	2	5	0	247	11.7

1996-97 statistics:

GP	G	A	TP	+/-	PIM	PP	SH	GW	GT	S	PCT
66	9	29	38	-21	34	2	1	2	0	194	4.6

1997-98 statistics:

GP	G	A	TP	+/-	PIM	PP	SH	GW	GT	S	PCT
81	21	24	45	-17	50	6	0	4	1	203	10.3

1998-99 statistics:

GP	G	A	TP	+/-	PIM	PP	SH	GW	GT	S	PCT
65	13	24	37	+8	51	3	0	1	2	188	6.9

LAST SEASON

Signed as free agent, July 20, 1999. Acquired from Chicago for Chris Murray, Mar. 23, 1999. Acquired by Chicago from Carolina for Paul Coffey, Dec. 28, 1998. Third on team in shots. Missed 18 games with shoulder injury.

THE FINESSE GAME

On the power play, which has become his specialty, Emerson can either play the point or work down low. He has an excellent point shot: keeping it low, on target and tippable. He is intelligent with the puck and doesn't always fire from the point, but works it to the middle of the blueline, and he uses screens well. When he carries in one-on-one against a defender, especially on a shorthanded rush, he always manages to use the defenseman to screen the goalie.

Emerson works well down low at even strength. He is mature and creative, with a terrific short game. He has quick hands for passing or snapping off a shot. He likes to work from behind the net, tempting the defense to chase him behind the cage. Speed and puck control are the essence of his game.

Emerson has nice quickness and balance, and he darts in and out of traffic in front of the net. He's too small to do any physical damage, which is why he needs to play with physical linemates. Unfortunately for him, Ottawa is pretty small and meek. He can use his speed to drive wide on a defenseman, who will think he has Emerson angled off only to watch him blast past.

THE PHYSICAL GAME

Emerson has good skating balance, and that will give him a little edge to knock a bigger player off-stride once in awhile. He works hard defensively but has to play a smart, small man's game to avoid getting pasted. He plays bigger than his size but isn't really feisty.

THE INTANGIBLES

As a power-play specialist, Emerson will continually find himself on the bubble, but thanks to expansion he should continue to find gainful employment.

PROJECTION

Emerson's career and his point totals are on the wane. His top end is 40 points.

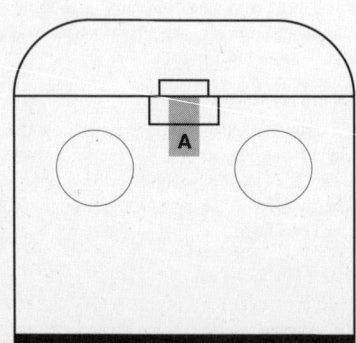

MAXIM GALANOV

Yrs. of NHL service: 1
Born: Krasnoyarsk, USSR; Mar. 13, 1974
Position: left defense
Height: 6-1
Weight: 195
Uniform no.: 47
Shoots: left

Career statistics:

GP	G	A	TP	PIM
57	4	4	8	16

1997-98 statistics:

GP	G	A	TP	+/-	PIM	PP	SH	GW	GT	S	PCT
6	0	1	1	+1	2	0	0	0	0	5	0.0

1998-99 statistics:

GP	G	A	TP	+/-	PIM	PP	SH	GW	GT	S	PCT
51	4	3	7	-8	14	2	0	0	1	44	9.1

LAST SEASON

Acquired from Pittsburgh in Expansion Draft, June 25, 1999. Acquired by Pittsburgh from N.Y. Rangers in waiver draft, Oct. 5, 1998. First NHL season. Missed 23 games with shoulder injuries. Missed eight games due to coach's decision.

THE FINESSE GAME

Galanov is one of those basic defensemen who don't do much out of the ordinary, but who, in a rapdily expanding NHL world, can hang onto a job for many years with a package of average skills.

Galanov gets the puck and gets it out of trouble. He can skate with the puck with good mobility, or he can make a smart first pass to move it out of the zone. He can see some second-unit power-play time. He has a decent shot from the point.

Galanov is a good fit for an expansion team because of his age.

THE PHYSICAL GAME

Galanov isn't a real imposing sort. He suffered a shoulder injury last year, which hampered his development and may affect his willingness to hit.

THE INTANGIBLES

Galanov is a fairly low-intensity, unemotional player, which doesn't endear him to coaches who like to see a bit more fire. He is unspectacular, but steady and reliable.

PROJECTION

Atlanta is building its inaugural season on the strength of its defense, and Galanov will be part of the core group for the first few seasons. He is capable of scoring 30 points if he gets the ice time. He is going to get a chance to flourish for the first time in his career.

JOHAN GARPENLOV

Yrs. of NHL service: 8
Born: Stockholm, Sweden; Mar. 21, 1968
Position: left wing
Height: 5-11
Weight: 185
Uniform no.: 29
Shoots: left

Career statistics:

GP	G	A	TP	PIM
536	112	183	295	245

1995-96 statistics:

GP	G	A	TP	+/-	PIM	PP	SH	GW	GT	S	PCT
82	23	28	51	-10	36	8	0	7	1	130	17.7

1996-97 statistics:

GP	G	A	TP	+/-	PIM	PP	SH	GW	GT	S	PCT
53	11	25	36	+10	47	1	0	1	2	83	13.3

1997-98 statistics:

GP	G	A	TP	+/-	PIM	PP	SH	GW	GT	S	PCT
39	2	3	5	-6	8	0	0	0	0	43	4.7

1998-99 statistics:

GP	G	A	TP	+/-	PIM	PP	SH	GW	GT	S	PCT
64	8	9	17	-9	42	0	1	0	1	71	11.3

LAST SEASON

Acquired from Florida in Expansion Draft, June 25, 1999.

THE FINESSE GAME

Garpenlov's best asset is his skating, which has kept him around in the NHL even as his offensive contributions wane.

A strong skater with good balance, he carries the puck through checks. He has a hard wrist shot from the off-wing and shoots well in stride, but he has been shy of shooting throughout his career and that isn't expected to change at this late stage.

Garpenlov's quickness gets him into high-quality scoring areas, but then he looks to make a pass. He's a better playmaker than finisher. A solid forechecker, he creates turnovers and then looks to do something intelligent with the puck. He is a good penalty killer and will handle power-play time with Atlanta.

THE PHYSICAL GAME

Garpenlov is not physical. His forechecking pressure comes not from physical contact but from his skating, which gets him on top of a player to hurry a pass.

THE INTANGIBLES

Garpenlov is not an assertive player and doesn't have elite skills. There are many nights when you have to check the game sheet to make sure he played.

PROJECTION

Garpenlov will probably get significant ice time as a veteran forward on an expansion team, but 20 goals is his absolute top end.

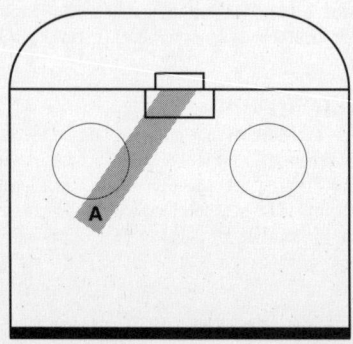

DAVID HARLOCK

Yrs. of NHL service: 1
Born: Toronto, Ont.; Mar. 16, 1971
Position: left defense
Height: 6-2
Weight: 205
Uniform no.: 6
Shoots: left

Career statistics:

GP	G	A	TP	PIM
84	2	6	8	72

1995-96 statistics:

GP	G	A	TP	+/-	PIM	PP	SH	GW	GT	S	PCT
1	0	0	0	0	0	0	0	0	0	0	0.0

1996-97 statistics:
Did not play in NHL

1997-98 statistics:

GP	G	A	TP	+/-	PIM	PP	SH	GW	GT	S	PCT
6	0	0	0	+2	4	0	0	0	0	2	0.0

1998-99 statistics:

GP	G	A	TP	+/-	PIM	PP	SH	GW	GT	S	PCT
70	2	6	8	-16	68	0	0	0	0	35	5.7

LAST SEASON

Acquired from N.Y. Islanders in Expansion Draft, June 25, 1999. Missed one game with bruised foot. Missed 11 games due to coach's decision.

THE FINESSE GAME

Harlock is an unspectacular sort, a defensive defenseman who does nothing special, just does his job. He plays a very sound positional game in his own end.

Harlock is an average skater. He is not flashy but he gets the puck and gets it out of danger. He can be used against other teams' top lines because he has a high panic point. He is a solid penalty killer. He uses his stick well to break up plays and take away passing lanes. He always seems to be in the right spot.

Harlock has bounced around the minors and through four other organizations before ending up in Atlanta.

THE PHYSICAL GAME

Harlock has good size. He has a very strong upper body and when he pins guys, they stay pinned. He's not very aggressive, but he keeps the front of the net cleared.

THE INTANGIBLES

Harlock is a perfect pickup for an expansion team. He is a steady, low-risk defenseman.

PROJECTION

Harlock's offensive contribution will be negligible.

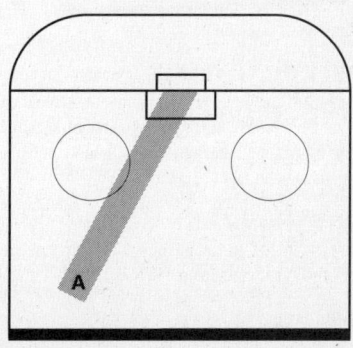

JODY HULL

Yrs. of NHL service: 11
Born: Cambridge, Ont; Feb. 2, 1969
Position: right wing
Height: 6-2
Weight: 195
Uniform no.: 8
Shoots: right

Career statistics:

GP	G	A	TP	PIM
598	102	116	218	122

1995-96 statistics:

GP	G	A	TP	+/-	PIM	PP	SH	GW	GT	S	PCT
78	20	17	37	+5	25	2	0	3	1	120	16.7

1996-97 statistics:

GP	G	A	TP	+/-	PIM	PP	SH	GW	GT	S	PCT
67	10	6	16	+1	4	0	1	2	1	92	10.9

1997-98 statistics:

GP	G	A	TP	+/-	PIM	PP	SH	GW	GT	S	PCT
49	4	4	8	+3	8	0	1	2	0	51	7.8

1998-99 statistics:

GP	G	A	TP	+/-	PIM	PP	SH	GW	GT	S	PCT
72	3	11	14	-2	12	0	0	1	1	73	4.1

PROJECTION

Hull was little used by Philadelphia coach Roger Neilson — probably his single biggest fan in the NHL — and isn't likely to leave much of an impression in Atlanta. Ten goals would be a huge contribution.

LAST SEASON

Acquired from Philadelphia in Expansion Draft, June 25, 1999. Missed five games with concussion and post-concussion syndrome. Missed two games with groin injury. Missed two games with sprained left knee. Missed one game due to coach's decision.

THE FINESSE GAME

Hull has some fine natural skills. His powerful skating style is almost syrupy smooth. He has some range and can skate with people, slowing them down and picking off passes.

His snap shot is heavy and effective, though his release isn't the fastest. There are times when you could swear you hear him thinking. He will cut into the middle at the blueline, then outguess himself on the proper play. Even if he has skating room and could take the puck closer to the net, he does not penetrate, drive the defense and pull the goalie to him.

Hull kills penalties well and will play positionally in a checking role. He can handle a lot of defensive responsibility.

THE PHYSICAL GAME

Hull is a polite player. He has no mean streak to speak of. He can be goaded into an occasional slash, but his lack of an aggressive game is what has kept him on the bubble throughout his career.

THE INTANGIBLES

Hull plays a lot of quiet games, but expansion teams need sensible veterans, and Hull is that.

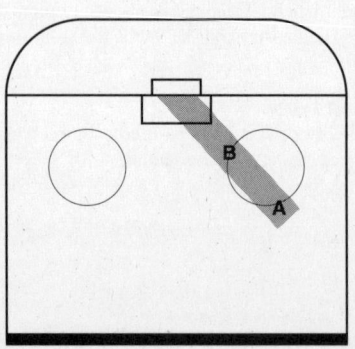

GORD MURPHY

Yrs. of NHL service: 11
Born: Willowdale, Ont.; Mar. 23, 1967
Position: right defense
Height: 6-2
Weight: 191
Uniform no.: 5
Shoots: right

Career statistics:

GP	G	A	TP	PIM
762	81	215	296	605

1995-96 statistics:

GP	G	A	TP	+/-	PIM	PP	SH	GW	GT	S	PCT
70	8	22	30	+5	30	4	0	0	0	125	6.4

1996-97 statistics:

GP	G	A	TP	+/-	PIM	PP	SH	GW	GT	S	PCT
80	8	15	23	+3	51	2	0	0	0	137	5.8

1997-98 statistics:

GP	G	A	TP	+/-	PIM	PP	SH	GW	GT	S	PCT
79	6	11	17	-3	46	3	0	0	0	123	4.9

1998-99 statistics:

GP	G	A	TP	+/-	PIM	PP	SH	GW	GT	S	PCT
51	0	7	7	+4	16	0	0	0	0	56	.0

LAST SEASON

Acquired from Florida with Herbert Vasiljevs, Daniel Tarnqvist and a sixth-round draft pick for Trevor Kidd, June 25, 1999. Missed 23 games with neck injury.

THE FINESSE GAME

Murphy has concentrated on becoming a better defensive player. He uses his finesse skills in a two-way role. A strong and agile skater, he executes tight turns and accelerates in a stride or two. He moves the puck well and then joins the play eagerly.

Murphy also carries the puck well, though he gets into trouble when he overhandles in his own zone. He usually makes a safe pass, holding on until he is just about decked and then making a nice play. He plays the point on the power play and uses a pull-and-drag shot, rather than a big slapper, giving him a very quick release. He is patient with the puck along the blueline, sliding laterally until he spots the open lane.

Murphy plays a smart positional game and makes intelligent defensive reads. He doesn't get suckered into pulling out of his position. He makes a steady, reliable partner for a more offensive-minded or inexperienced player.

THE PHYSICAL GAME

Murphy uses his finesse skills to defend. His long reach makes him an effective poke-checker, and he would rather wrap his arms around an attacker than move him out of the crease with a solid hit. He's more of a pusher than a hitter. He is responsible defensively and is used to killing penalties. He logs a lot of ice time and holds up well under the grind.

THE INTANGIBLES

Murphy is not, and will never be, a tough customer, but he has improved his positional play and can step up and provide some offensive spark. He is often asked to work as part of a top defensive pairing, which is beyond his ability, though he is likely to play that role with the expansion Thrashers.

PROJECTION

Murphy will be one of Atlanta's top four defensemen and is likely to get some power-play point time, so his totals should improve to around 20 points.

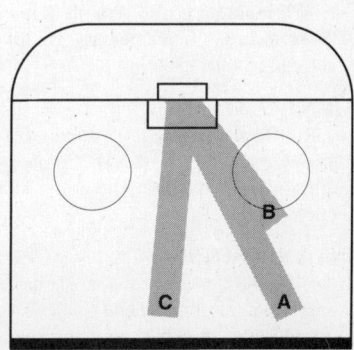

DAMIAN RHODES

Yrs. of NHL service: 5
Born: St. Paul, MN; May 28, 1969
Position: goaltender
Height: 6-0
Weight: 190
Uniform no.: 1
Catches: left

Career statistics:

GP	MIN	GA	SO	GAA	A	PIM
228	12937	556	11	2.58	6	16

1995-96 statistics:

GP	MIN	GAA	W	L	T	SO	GA	S	SAPCT	PIM
47	2747	2.77	14	27	5	2	127	1342	.905	4

1996-97 statistics:

GP	MIN	GAA	W	L	T	SO	GA	S	SAPCT	PIM
50	2934	2.72	14	20	14	1	133	1213	.890	2

1997-98 statistics:

GP	MIN	GAA	W	L	T	SO	GA	S	SAPCT	PIM
50	2743	2.34	19	19	7	5	107	1148	.907	0

1998-99 statistics:

GP	MIN	GAA	W	L	T	SO	GA	S	SAPCT	PIM
45	2480	2.44	22	13	7	3	101	1060	.905	4

LAST SEASON

Acquired from Ottawa for future considerations, June 18, 1999. Career high in wins. Credited with scoring a goal.

THE PHYSICAL GAME

Rhodes makes good first saves and doesn't give up bad rebounds. He either guides the pucks to the corners or deadens the puck in front of him. He is better off the less he plays the puck. Don't be fooled by the goal he "scored" last season. It was put into an empty net by Devils defenseman Lyle Odelein, and Rhodes got credit because he was the last opposition player to touch the puck. He's not Martin Brodeur, though sometimes he thinks he is, which is when he gets into real trouble.

Rhodes is technically sound. Uncontrolled rebounds allow the shooter to drive in for the second chance, but he doesn't give away many. You have to beat him; he won't beat himself.

Rhodes is a stand-up goalie who plays his angles well and is solid in his fundamentals. He gives his team a chance to win the game.

THE MENTAL GAME

In Ottawa, Ron Tugnutt gradually usurped Rhodes as the number one goalie, but Rhodes will be able to take over the role with the expansion Thrashers. At 30, it's now or never.

THE INTANGIBLES

Rhodes is still a bit of a loose cannon. He has not yet proven himself as a true number one goalie. He will be good enough to give an expansion team some solid goaltending, but he is not the guy to take his club to the next level.

PROJECTION

Rhodes will be able to play behind a pretty nice defense — for an expansion team — but he will be forced to win a lot of low-scoring games. He would do well to get 15 wins.

ULF SAMUELSSON

Yrs. of NHL service: 15
Born: Fagersta, Sweden; Mar. 26, 1964
Position: left defense
Height: 6-1
Weight: 195
Uniform no.: 2
Shoots: left

Career statistics:

GP	G	A	TP	PIM
1031	56	273	329	2395

1995-96 statistics:

GP	G	A	TP	+/-	PIM	PP	SH	GW	GT	S	PCT
74	1	18	19	+9	122	0	0	0	0	66	1.5

1996-97 statistics:

GP	G	A	TP	+/-	PIM	PP	SH	GW	GT	S	PCT
73	6	11	17	+3	138	1	0	1	0	77	7.8

1997-98 statistics:

GP	G	A	TP	+/-	PIM	PP	SH	GW	GT	S	PCT
73	3	9	12	+1	122	0	0	2	0	59	5.1

1998-99 statistics:

GP	G	A	TP	+/-	PIM	PP	SH	GW	GT	S	PCT
71	4	8	12	+5	99	0	0	0	0	39	10.3

LAST SEASON

Acquired from N.Y. Rangers for a second-round draft pick in 1999 and a third-round draft pick in 2000, Mar. 23, 1999. Missed nine games with broken foot.

THE FINESSE GAME

Samuelsson always picks his spots in the neutral zone, setting up cartilage-jarring hits on unsuspecting opponents. His willingness to launch himself into the play as the late man in the attacking zone catches more than a few teams by surprise, as well.

Samuelsson can't carry the puck at a high tempo and is better off making the escape pass than trying to rush it up-ice himself. Although he likes trying to handle the puck, this is a mistake. He has a nice shot but lacks poise and confidence in the attacking zone.

Samuelsson has wonderful skills that are often overshadowed by the more irritating aspects of his nature. He is a very good skater for his size, with flat-out speed and one-step quickness, agility, mobility and balance. He skates backwards very well, and generally makes good defensive reads and is always well-positioned. He is difficult to beat one-on-one and sometimes even two-on-one because of his anticipation.

THE PHYSICAL GAME

Samuelsson plays with so much extra padding that you wonder how he can even move. He looks like a kid whose overprotective parent has stuffed him into a snowsuit, with his arms sticking out at right angles. But the protection does permit him to be absolutely fearless in shot-blocking, at which he is among the best in the league, and in throwing those roadblock body blasts.

Samuelsson is a big hitter. He will try to put someone through the wall, though sometimes a simple take-out would do. He could hit cleaner, but bringing his stick up on a hit is his most natural move, and he takes many unnecessary penalties because of this tendency.

Samuelsson absorbs a lot of punishment in addition to dishing it out. His gloves are always in an opponent's face. Some of the physical wear and tear appears to be taking a toll on him.

THE INTANGIBLES

Samuelsson has just enough goon in him to distract opponents, and enough talent to take advantage when the other team is too busy being enraged. He probably has a season left as an effective defender.

PROJECTION

Samuelsson was an unrestricted free agent during the off-season. If he lands in a spot where he can partner a mobile, offensive defenseman, he can score 15 points and play the bad cop.

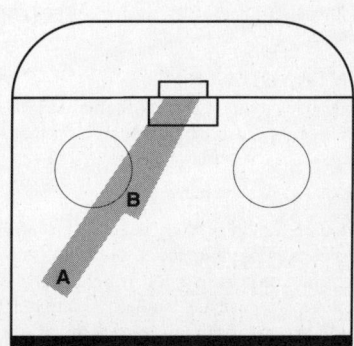

PATRIK STEFAN

Yrs. of NHL service: 0
Born: Pribham, Czech.; Sept. 16, 1980
Position: centre
Height: 6-1
Weight: 205
Uniform no.: n.a.
Shoots: left

Career IHL statistics:

GP	G	A	TP	PIM
68	17	40	57	36

LAST SEASON
Selected first overall in 1999 Entry Draft. Appeared in 33 games with Long Beach (IHL), scoring 11-24 — 35. Missed games with concussion.

THE FINESSE GAME
Playing two seasons in the minor leagues has given Stefan the kind of seasoning his other contemporaries lacked, which marked him as the player most ready to step right into the NHL this season.

There is little doubt Stefan is a special talent. He is a tall skater whose stance is upright, allowing him to keep his head up to see all of the ice and all of his options. He uses a long stick for a long reach to beat defenders one-on-one in open ice. He loves to carry the puck and has drawn comparisons to Jaromir Jagr for his end-to-end ability.

An excellent passer who can thread a puck through a crowd, he shoots well forehand and backhand and isn't shy about using his shot. He is good on draws and can run a power play.

Stefan has a polished two-way game. He has hockey smarts.

THE PHYSICAL GAME
Stefan is a bit lean but very strong; he should be able to handle NHL checking attention. He isn't just making the move from junior. He has already played against men.

THE INTANGIBLES
The single question mark about Stefan was his medical clearance, because of the concussion that forced him to miss half a season.

PROJECTION
If he's sound, Stefan is ready to make an impression with the expansion Thrashers. He is the complete package. He won't have a lot of help, but he is the kind of player who can make others around him better, and he will be among the top rookies of the year.

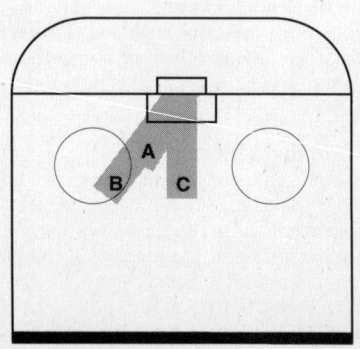

CHRIS TAMER

Yrs. of NHL service: 5
Born: Dearborn, Mich.; Nov. 17, 1970
Position: left defense
Height: 6-2
Weight: 212
Uniform no.: 2
Shoots: left

Career statistics:

GP	G	A	TP	PIM
305	9	26	35	680

1995-96 statistics:

GP	G	A	TP	+/-	PIM	PP	SH	GW	GT	S	PCT
70	4	10	14	+20	153	0	0	1	0	75	5.3

1996-97 statistics:

GP	G	A	TP	+/-	PIM	PP	SH	GW	GT	S	PCT
45	2	4	6	-25	131	0	1	0	0	56	3.6

1997-98 statistics:

GP	G	A	TP	+/-	PIM	PP	SH	GW	GT	S	PCT
79	0	7	7	+4	181	0	0	0	0	55	.0

1998-99 statistics:

GP	G	A	TP	+/-	PIM	PP	SH	GW	GT	S	PCT
63	1	5	6	-14	124	0	0	1	0	48	2.1

LAST SEASON

Drafted from N.Y. Rangers in Expansion Draft, June 25, 1999. Acquired by N.Y. Rangers with Petr Nedved and Sean Pronger for Alexei Kovalev and Harry York, Nov. 25, 1998. Led Rangers in penalty minutes. Missed 11 games due to coach's decision.

THE FINESSE GAME

Tamer is a conservative, stay-at-home defenseman. He has limited skating and stick skills but is smart enough to stay within his limitations and play a positional game.

He plays a poised game and learns from his mistakes. He does the little things well, chipping a puck off the boards or angling an attacker to the wall.

Tamer is smart enough when he is shooting from the point to make sure his shot doesn't get blocked. He will take something off his shot, or put it wide so the forwards could attack the puck off the end boards.

THE PHYSICAL GAME

Tamer doesn't nail people, but he has some strength and will use it to push people out of the crease, and he'll battle in the corners. He doesn't have a good skating base to be a punishing open-ice hitter, but he defends himself or sticks up for a teammate. He doesn't have a serious nasty side, though he is often guilty of late hits.

Tamer is a well-conditioned athlete and he can handle a lot of ice time. He kills penalties well and blocks shots. Tamer plays despite having asthma.

THE INTANGIBLES

Tamer will become a fixture among the Thrashers' top four defensemen. He will never be a star, but he gives solid support and can complement a more offensive player. His point production will be low, but he is an intelligent defenseman who will only get better.

PROJECTION

Tamer won't get many points, but his PIM total will always be in triple digits.

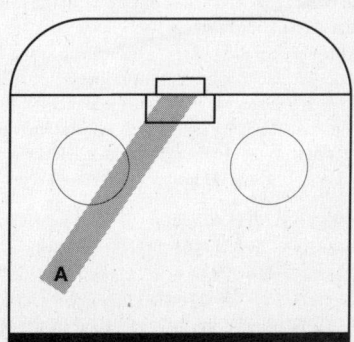

MARK TINORDI

Yrs. of NHL service: 11
Born: Deer River, Alta.; May 9, 1966
Position: left defense
Height: 6-4
Weight: 213
Uniform no.: 24
Shoots: left

Career statistics:

GP	G	A	TP	PIM
663	52	148	200	1514

1995-96 statistics:

GP	G	A	TP	+/-	PIM	PP	SH	GW	GT	S	PCT
71	3	10	13	+26	113	2	0	0	0	82	3.7

1996-97 statistics:

GP	G	A	TP	+/-	PIM	PP	SH	GW	GT	S	PCT
56	2	6	8	+3	118	0	0	1	0	53	3.8

1997-98 statistics:

GP	G	A	TP	+/-	PIM	PP	SH	GW	GT	S	PCT
47	8	9	17	+9	39	0	1	0	0	57	14.0

1998-99 statistics:

GP	G	A	TP	+/-	PIM	PP	SH	GW	GT	S	PCT
48	0	6	6	-6	108	0	0	0	0	32	.0

LAST SEASON

Acquired from Washington in Expansion Draft, June 25, 1999. Second on Capitals in penalty minutes. Missed 25 games with ankle injury. Missed eight games with groin injury. Missed one game with knee injury. Missed one game due to coach's decision.

THE FINESSE GAME

Tinordi can play both sides and with any partner. He can be the point man on the power play and he can kill penalties. You can use him in the first minute and in the last minute, when you're trying to protect a lead.

Tinordi doesn't have much in the way of finesse skills, but, oh, how he loves to go to the net. He starts out at the point on the power play yet doesn't hesitate to crash down low. He is an impact player and a major force on the ice.

Tinordi has an effective point shot: low, hard and accurate. He also sees the play well and moves his passes crisply. He intimidates when he moves low and bulls his way to the net. He is poised with the puck and will use a wrist shot in deep.

An above-average skater, Tinordi is mobile for his large size. He lacks one-step quickness, but once in gear he has a long stride with good balance and mobility. He can use his long reach well around the net or to take the puck away from a defender. He is a strong penalty killer with good hockey sense.

THE PHYSICAL GAME

It's impossible to discuss Tinordi's game without making reference to the injuries that hit him every season. He plays with the throttle wide open and doesn't recognize any other playing style. One of the reasons why he is so susceptible to getting hurt is that he is more concerned with making the play than with protecting himself, and he ends up in vulnerable situations. A little less reckless abandon would help keep him in one piece, but we're not sure if Tinordi knows how to play that way. He usually ends up missing a big chunk of playing time each year with some serious ailment.

As honest and tough as they come, Tinordi commands respect on the ice. He has too short a fuse, though in recent years he has done a better job of curbing his temper, realizing he is more important to his team on the ice than in the penalty box. He is competitive and fearless and stands up for his teammates for any slight.

THE INTANGIBLES

Tinordi is so fragile that it will be hard for his team to rely upon him heavily. A great leader when he is healthy, he will make a fine addition to the expansion Thrashers.

PROJECTION

Tinordi could score 25 goals and have a great season, or five goals and still have a great season. He's that important in that many ways. Take him for your pool or your team with the usual caveat: some major part of him will be broken.

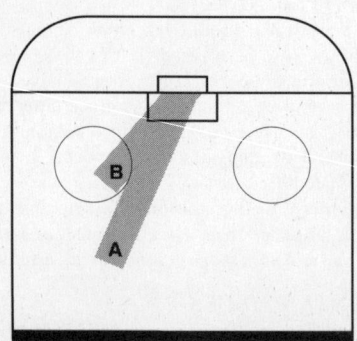

TERRY YAKE

Yrs. of NHL service: 6
Born: New Westminster, B.C.; Oct. 22, 1968
Position: centre
Height: 5-11
Weight: 185
Uniform no.: 27
Shoots: right

Career statistics:

GP	G	A	TP	PIM
330	67	103	170	178

1995-96 statistics:
Did not play in NHL

1996-97 statistics:
Did not play in NHL

1997-98 statistics:

GP	G	A	TP	+/-	PIM	PP	SH	GW	GT	S	PCT
65	10	15	25	+1	38	3	1	4	0	60	16.7

1998-99 statistics:

GP	G	A	TP	+/-	PIM	PP	SH	GW	GT	S	PCT
60	9	18	27	-9	34	3	0	4	0	59	15.3

LAST SEASON
Acquired from St. Louis in Expansion Draft, June 25, 1999. Tied for third on team in game-winning goals. Appeared in 24 games with Worcester (AHL), scoring 8-11 — 19.

THE FINESSE GAME
Yake makes life easy on a coach because he is so versatile. Although he is not exceptional in any area, he is capable in most. He can play right wing or centre, work on the power play, kill penalties, play four-on-four, step up to fill in on a number one line or check.

Moving around from line to line and position to position hurts some players, but Yake gets too comfortable if he is in one spot for very long, so the new challenges seem to wake his game up.

He moves with good speed and acceleration. He stickhandles and controls the puck well while on the move. He can pass equally well off his forehand or backhand. He has a knack around the net. He doesn't have a great NHL shot, but he is clever, creative and poised.

THE PHYSICAL GAME
Yake can play a feisty game when the mood strikes. He's not a very aggressive player, but he will forecheck tenaciously.

THE INTANGIBLES
The biggest knock on Yake was always his lack of intensity. He is a useful player when motivated, and he is someone the Blues are going to miss. Yake started the season in the minors, as the Blues gave some jobs to younger players, but was then called up and didn't miss a game.

PROJECTION
Yake is well-liked by his coaches and he can produce 30 points or so in his chameleon role.

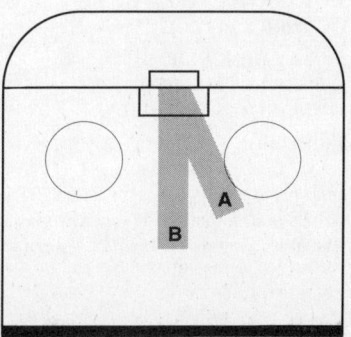

BOSTON BRUINS

Players' Statistics 1998-99

POS	NO.	PLAYER	GP	G	A	PTS	+/-	PIM	PP	SH	GW	GT	S	PCT
C	41	JASON ALLISON	82	23	53	76	5	68	5	1	3		158	14.6
R	12	DMITRI KHRISTICH	79	29	42	71	11	48	13	1	6	1	144	20.1
D	77	RAY BOURQUE	81	10	47	57	-7	34	8		3		262	3.8
L	14	SERGEI SAMSONOV	79	25	26	51	-6	18	6		8	1	160	15.6
C	6	JOE THORNTON	81	16	25	41	3	69	7		1		128	12.5
L	33	ANSON CARTER	55	24	16	40	7	22	6		6		123	19.5
R	23	STEVE HEINZE	73	22	18	40	7	30	9		3		146	15.1
D	18	KYLE MCLAREN	52	6	18	24	1	48	3				97	6.2
L	19	ROB DIMAIO	71	7	14	21	-14	95	1				121	5.8
D	20	DARREN VAN IMPE	60	5	15	20	-5	66	4				92	5.4
R	11	P.J. AXELSSON	77	7	10	17	-14	18			2		146	4.8
R	42	PETER FERRARO	46	6	8	14	10	44	1		1		61	9.8
D	36	GRANT LEDYARD	47	4	8	12	-8	33	1		2		47	8.5
D	32	DON SWEENEY	81	2	10	12	14	64					79	2.5
C	26	TIM TAYLOR	49	4	7	11	-10	55			1		76	5.3
D	25	HAL GILL	80	3	7	10	-10	63			2		102	2.9
C	17	*SHAWN BATES	33	5	4	9	3	2					30	16.7
C	38	CHRIS TAYLOR	37	3	5	8	-3	12		1			60	5.0
R	10	*CAMERON MANN	33	5	2	7	0	17	1		1	1	42	11.9
L	16	KEN BELANGER	54	2	5	7	-1	182					19	10.5
R	27	LANDON WILSON	22	3	3	6	0	17					32	9.4
D	37	MATTIAS TIMANDER	22		6	6	4	10					22	
D	44	DAVE ELLETT	54		6	6	11	25					45	
L	22	KEN BAUMGARTNER	69	1	3	4	-6	119				1	15	6.7
L	57	*ANTTI LAAKSONEN	11	1	2	3	-1	2					8	12.5
C	21	*RANDY ROBITAILLE	4		2	2	-1						5	
G	34	BYRON DAFOE	68		2	2	0	25						
C	28	*ANDRE SAVAGE	6	1		1	2						8	12.5
C	72	*ERIC NICKULAS	2				0							
R	56	*PETER NORDSTROM	2				-1							
D	29	DENNIS VASKE	3				-3	6						
D	55	*JONATHAN GIRARD	3				1						3	
D	71	TERRY VIRTUE	4				2						2	
L	51	*JAY HENDERSON	4				-1	2					4	
D	53	*BRANDON SMITH	5				2						2	
C	61	*MARQUIS MATHIEU	9				-1	8					4	
G	35	ROBBIE TALLAS	17				0							

GP = games played; G = goals; A = assists; PTS = points; +/- = goals-for minus goals-against while player is on ice; PIM = penalties in minutes; PP = power-play goals; SH = shorthanded goals; GW = game-winning goals; GT = game-tying goals; S = no. of shots; PCT = percentage of goals to shots; * = rookie

JASON ALLISON

Yrs. of NHL service: 3
Born: North York, Ontario; May 29, 1975
Position: centre
Height: 6-3
Weight: 205
Uniform no.: 41
Shoots: right

Career statistics:

GP	G	A	TP	PIM
268	66	134	200	170

1995-96 statistics:

GP	G	A	TP	+/-	PIM	PP	SH	GW	GT	S	PCT
19	0	3	3	-3	2	0	0	0	0	18	0.0

1996-97 statistics:

GP	G	A	TP	+/-	PIM	PP	SH	GW	GT	S	PCT
72	8	26	34	-6	34	2	0	1	0	99	8.1

1997-98 statistics:

GP	G	A	TP	+/-	PIM	PP	SH	GW	GT	S	PCT
81	33	50	83	+33	60	5	0	8	2	158	20.9

1998-99 statistics:

GP	G	A	TP	+/-	PIM	PP	SH	GW	GT	S	PCT
82	23	53	76	+5	68	5	1	3	0	158	14.6

LAST SEASON

Led team in assists and points for second consecutive season. Tied for sixth in the NHL in assists. Third on team in shots. Only Bruin to appear in all 82 games.

THE FINESSE GAME

Allison is capable of completely dominating games. He is strong on the puck, skates well, has excellent vision and sure, soft hands to put the passes where they need to go. He is the complete package offensively.

Allison faced top checkers every shift and still excelled. He makes players on his line better, and has established good chemistry with Anson Carter in particular. Allison is night in and night out one of the best forwards on the ice whenever the Bruins win.

The puck follows Allison around the rink. He has great patience, uncanny hockey sense and was one of the top 10 centres in the league. While his game is predominantly offense, he was often put on the ice to protect leads late in games, so his defense is hardly suspect.

Allison wants to get even better, and worked with a speed skater in the off-season to step up his foot speed.

THE PHYSICAL GAME

Allison is not quite as strong or tough as some of the league's best power forwards, but he goes through traffic and makes plays despite the checking attention focussed on him. He is hungry to score and will pay the price to do so. He showed an edge in a tiff with Keith Tkachuk last season.

Allison plays through pain. He didn't miss a game despite a sore wrist in the second half that frequently prevented him from taking draws.

THE INTANGIBLES

Scouts say Allison tends to be a bit on the lazy side, and Pat Burns benched him during one midseason game. After the playoffs, GM Harry Sinden publicly criticized Allison's postseason, in which he scored only two goals in 12 games.

PROJECTION

Allison is Boston's number one centre. How he responds to Sinden's blast will show early on in his attitude. He can still improve, and a 30-goal, 85-point season is not beyond his ability.

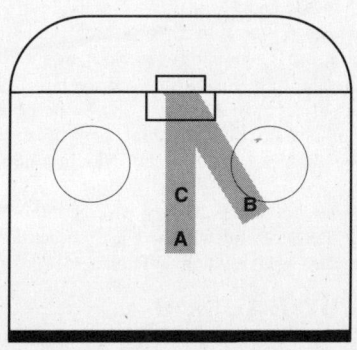

DAVE ANDREYCHUK

Yrs. of NHL service: 17
Born: Hamilton, Ont.; Sept. 29, 1963
Position: left wing
Height: 6-3
Weight: 220
Uniform no.: 23
Shoots: right

Career statistics:

GP	G	A	TP	PIM
1226	532	604	1139	862

1995-96 statistics:

GP	G	A	TP	+/-	PIM	PP	SH	GW	GT	S	PCT
76	28	29	57	-9	64	14	2	3	1	241	11.6

1996-97 statistics:

GP	G	A	TP	+/-	PIM	PP	SH	GW	GT	S	PCT
82	27	34	61	+38	48	4	1	2	1	233	11.6

1997-98 statistics:

GP	G	A	TP	+/-	PIM	PP	SH	GW	GT	S	PCT
75	14	34	48	+19	26	4	0	2	0	180	7.8

1998-99 statistics:

GP	G	A	TP	+/-	PIM	PP	SH	GW	GT	S	PCT
52	15	13	28	+1	20	4	0	3	1	110	13.6

LAST SEASON

Signed as free agent, July 22, 1999. Third on Devils in shooting percentage. Missed 21 games with fractured right ankle. Missed six games with bruised sternum. Missed three games due to coach's decision.

THE FINESSE GAME

Andreychuk just can't get enough of the game, but defenders have certainly had their fill of him. The big winger uses a very stiff shaft on his long stick, enabling him to lean on it hard in front of the net. He tries to keep his blade on the ice for deflections, and by pushing his 220 pounds on the stick, he makes it almost impossible for a defender to lift it off the ice. His touch just isn't as deadly as it once was.

Andreychuk has slow feet but a cherry-picker reach, which he uses with strength and intelligence. He is a lumbering skater. He works in tight areas, though, so he only needs a big stride or two to plant himself where he wants to be. He has marvellous hand skills in traffic and is one of the Devils' best passers. He can use his stick to artfully pick pucks out of midair, to slap at rebounds or for wraparounds.

From the hash marks in, Andreychuk has long been one of the most dangerous snipers in the league. On the other four-fifths of the ice, he is a liability because of his lack of foot speed, which is now even slower.

Andreychuk needs to play with people who can get him the puck and with people who can skate, to compensate for his skating deficiencies.

THE PHYSICAL GAME

If you're looking for someone to protect his smaller teammates, or to inspire a team with his hitting, Andreychuk is not your man. Andreychuk is a giant shock absorber, soaking up hits without retaliating. He has a long fuse and seldom takes a bad penalty, especially when his team is on the power play.

He's tough in his own way — in front of the opponent's net — at least. He is nearly impossible to budge, and with his long arms can control pucks. He isn't dominating, but he is physically prominent within five feet of the crease. He pays the price to score goals, but the goals aren't coming.

THE INTANGIBLES

The Bruins have been searching for a pair of power-play hands around the net, ever since Cam Neely retired in 1996. Andreychuk is well past his prime, but he can put his touch and his reach to good use in a limited role. He also possesses one of the best hockey brains in the league.

PROJECTION

Andreychuk's days as a big-timer scorer are over. He could score 20 goals again, though, if he stays healthy.

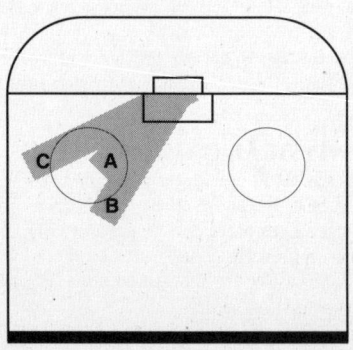

P. J. AXELSSON

Yrs. of NHL service: 2
Born: Kungalv, Sweden; Feb. 26, 1975
Position: right wing
Height: 6-1
Weight: 174
Uniform no.: 11
Shoots: left

Career statistics:

GP	G	A	TP	PIM
159	15	29	44	56

1997-98 statistics:

GP	G	A	TP	+/-	PIM	PP	SH	GW	GT	S	PCT
82	8	19	27	-14	38	2	0	1	0	144	5.6

1998-99 statistics:

GP	G	A	TP	+/-	PIM	PP	SH	GW	GT	S	PCT
77	7	10	17	-14	18	0	0	2	0	146	4.8

LAST SEASON
Second NHL season. Missed four games with concussion. Missed one game with flu.

THE FINESSE GAME
Axelsson is a smart player with a real head for the game. He has the skills, especially skating, that stamp him as a bona fide NHLer.

Axelsson is a role player but happily accepts that job. He is a very fast skater, yet unlike a lot of Swedish players he is not strong on the puck. His hand skills are just about average, though he was a fairly decent scorer in the Swedish Elite League, and he doesn't fumble with the puck. His future in this league will be based less on his scoring than on his defensive ability. Killing penalties is where he excells.

Axelsson's primary asset, however, is his work ethic. He never stops skating, never stops fighting for the puck and he loves big checking assignments against other teams' top lines.

THE PHYSICAL GAME
Axelsson is very competitive. He is a solid checker who will finish all of his hits. He will stand up to players like Eric Lindros and won't be intimidated, despite the fact that Axelsson is the kind of tall but scrawny player that Lindros could use as a toothpick. Axelsson is not fun to play against.

THE INTANGIBLES
Axelsson is a catalyst. He and his checking linemates (last season, Tim Taylor and Rob DiMaio) had trouble with nagging injuries and suspensions and the like, which made it hard for the third line to maintain its pace and consistency through the season.

PROJECTION
Axelsson may be able to score 10 to 15 goals, but not much more than that. However, he could earn Selke Trophy recognition somewhere down the road.

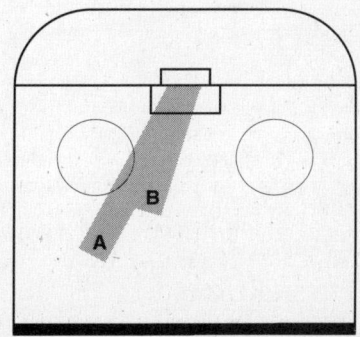

SHAWN BATES

Yrs. of NHL service: 1
Born: Melrose, MA; Apr. 3, 1975
Position: centre
Height: 5-11
Weight: 205
Uniform no.: 17
Shoots: right

Career statistics:

GP	G	A	TP	PIM
46	7	4	11	4

1997-98 statistics:

GP	G	A	TP	+/-	PIM	PP	SH	GW	GT	S	PCT
13	2	0	2	-3	2	0	0	0	0	12	16.7

1998-99 statistics:

GP	G	A	TP	+/-	PIM	PP	SH	GW	GT	S	PCT
33	5	4	9	+3	2	0	0	0	0	30	16.7

LAST SEASON
First NHL season. Appeared in 37 games with Providence (AHL), scoring 25-21 — 46.

THE FINESSE GAME
Bates's calling card is his speed. He has NHL quickness and skating ability. He will develop into an excellent penalty killer, and his skills are close enough to possibly earn him some time on the second power-play unit. He has been able to score at a pretty good clip in the minors.

Bates has very quick hands and is an accurate shot. He is also a good passer, who sees his options and holds onto the puck to create time and space for his wingers.

He protects the puck well with his body, and does everything with the puck at a high tempo and in heavy traffic. He is an intelligent player who understands all aspects of the game.

THE PHYSICAL GAME
Size is a problem for Bates. He is an average-sized player with average strength, but his skating will keep him out of trouble. He will hit when he forechecks, but with minimal impact.

THE INTANGIBLES
Bates's biggest enemy is himself. He didn't have a great attitude when he was promoted to the big team, and he had a worse attitude when he was sent back down to the minors. While teammate Landon Wilson hustled to Providence to play for the Calder Cup after the Bruins were eliminated from the Stanley Cup playoffs, Bates declined. Perhaps he was injured, but it's not a great way to make an impression on any coach, especially one like Pat Burns. If Bates thinks he is going to inherit the third-line role vacated by Tim Taylor, he could be mistaken. He'll have to earn it.

PROJECTION
Bates will have to fight for the third-line job in training camp and could score 10 to 15 goals if he snags it.

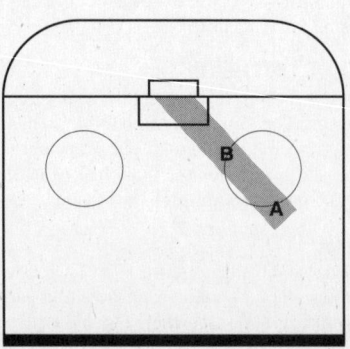

RAY BOURQUE

Yrs. of NHL service: 20
Born: Montreal, Que.; Dec. 28, 1960
Position: right defense
Height: 5-11
Weight: 210
Uniform no.: 77
Shoots: left

Career statistics:

GP	G	A	TP	PIM
1453	385	1083	1468	1067

1995-96 statistics:

GP	G	A	TP	+/-	PIM	PP	SH	GW	GT	S	PCT
82	20	62	82	+31	58	9	2	2	1	390	5.1

1996-97 statistics:

GP	G	A	TP	+/-	PIM	PP	SH	GW	GT	S	PCT
62	19	31	50	-11	18	8	1	3	1	230	8.3

1997-98 statistics:

GP	G	A	TP	+/-	PIM	PP	SH	GW	GT	S	PCT
82	13	35	48	+2	80	9	0	3	1	264	4.9

1998-99 statistics:

GP	G	A	TP	+/-	PIM	PP	SH	GW	GT	S	PCT
81	10	47	57	-7	34	8	0	3	0	262	3.8

LAST SEASON

Tied for second in NHL and led team defensemen in points. Led team in shots. Second on team in assists. Third on team in points and power-play goals. Missed one game with hip flexor.

THE FINESSE GAME

Bourque has tremendous defensive instincts, though his offensive skills usually get the headlines. He suffered through some scoring slumps last season but was never less than invaluable to the Bruins. His defensive reads are almost unmatched in the NHL, and he is an excellent transition player. He is not too proud to make the simple play, if it is the right one, instead of making a flashy play. If he is under pressure and his team is getting scrambly, Bourque will simply flip the puck over the glass for a face-off.

As a passer, Bourque can go tape-to-tape as well as anybody in the NHL. He has the touch and the vision of a forward, and eagerly makes what for anyone else would be a low-percentage play, because his passes and skating are so sure.

Bourque is adept at keeping the puck in the zone at the point. He is a key performer on special-team units. On the point, he has a low, heavy shot with a crisp release. He is an excellent skater who will also shoot from midrange with a handy snap shot, or in close with a wrist shot. He does not squander his scoring chances and is a precise shooter down low. He is able to go top shelf to either corner, which few other defensemen, let alone forwards, can match.

Willing to lead a rush or jump up into the play, Bourque is a balanced skater, with speed, agility and awesome balance. It takes a bulldozer to knock him off the puck.

THE PHYSICAL GAME

Bourque is single-minded in his approach to fitness. Only twice in his 19 seasons has he failed to play more than 60 games a season (and one of those was the 1994-95 lockout year). He is no perimeter player, either. The minutes he routinely logs (25 to 28 per game) are quality, crunch-time minutes.

Bourque plays a physical game when he has to. It's amazing what kind of punishment he has been able to absorb over the years. He is not very big by today's standards for defensemen (or forwards, for that matter). Other teams try to eliminate him physically, and the Bruins superstar has paid a big price because of it.

THE INTANGIBLES

As high as Bourque's level of play is, the fact remains he will turn 40 at midseason and the end of his career is not far off. If he doesn't get a ring, Bourque's legacy will be the quality defensemen, such as Kyle McLaren and Hal Gill, whose careers have been boosted immeasurably by playing alongside him.

PROJECTION

The amazing Bourque may have yet another 50-point season in him.

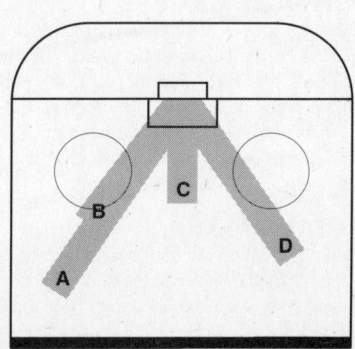

ANSON CARTER

Yrs. of NHL service: 3
Born: Toronto, Ont.; June 6, 1974
Position: centre/right wing
Height: 6-1
Weight: 175
Uniform no.: 33
Shoots: right

Career statistics:

GP	G	A	TP	PIM
171	51	50	101	62

1996-97 statistics:

GP	G	A	TP	+/-	PIM	PP	SH	GW	GT	S	PCT
38	11	7	18	-7	9	2	1	2	0	79	13.9

1997-98 statistics:

GP	G	A	TP	+/-	PIM	PP	SH	GW	GT	S	PCT
78	16	27	43	+7	31	6	0	4	0	179	8.9

1998-99 statistics:

GP	G	A	TP	+/-	PIM	PP	SH	GW	GT	S	PCT
55	24	16	40	+7	22	6	0	6	0	123	19.5

PROJECTION
Carter's ice time and prominent role in the attack means he should hit the 30-goal mark this season.

LAST SEASON
Fourth in NHL and second on team in shooting percentage. Third on team in goals and game-winning goals. Missed 15 games with sprained ankle. Missed 12 games in contract dispute. Appeared in five games with Utah (IHL), scoring 1-1 — 2.

THE FINESSE GAME
Carter is a deceptive skater with a long, rangy, loping stride, but he isn't a bit awkward in turns. What really sets him apart, though, is his hockey intelligence. He thinks the game well in all zones. He has very good hands and a good shot.

Carter has pushed himself hard to improve his skating and shooting, and both skills are now polished. He has graduated to playing on the top line with Jason Allison.

Carter drives to the net well. He has good balance and is hard to knock off his skates. He isn't a power forward, but he goes into the high-traffic areas and has soft hands for receiving passes and releasing a quick shot.

THE PHYSICAL GAME
A late bloomer physically, Carter still needs to add some muscle but he is not afraid to hit, not afraid to take a hit and, like Eric Lindros and Peter Forsberg, will make a preemptive hit while carrying the puck. He's not dirty or mean, just honestly tough. As one of the few blacks to make it to the NHL, you know he's mentally tough.

THE INTANGIBLES
Carter is a positive, driven and likable athlete, but the Bruins believe there is more in the tank. He had a slow start last season (six goals in 24 games) due to his contract dispute.

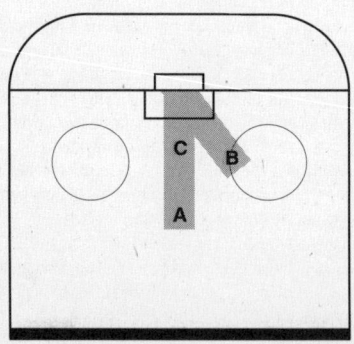

BYRON DAFOE

Yrs. of NHL service: 4
Born: Sussex, England; Feb. 25, 1971
Position: goaltender
Height: 5-11
Weight: 175
Uniform no.: 34
Catches: left

Career statistics:

GP	MIN	GA	SO	GAA	A	PIM
230	12940	579	17	2.68	5	33

1995-96 statistics:

GP	MIN	GAA	W	L	T	SO	GA	S	SAPCT	PIM
47	2666	3.87	14	24	8	1	172	1539	.888	6

1996-97 statistics:

GP	MIN	GAA	W	L	T	SO	GA	S	SAPCT	PIM
40	2162	3.11	13	17	5	0	112	1178	.905	0

1997-98 statistics:

GP	MIN	GAA	W	L	T	SO	GA	S	SAPCT	PIM
65	3693	2.24	30	25	9	6	138	1602	.914	2

1998-99 statistics:

GP	MIN	GAA	W	L	T	SO	GA	S	SAPCT	PIM
68	4001	1.99	32	23	11	10	133	1800	.926	25

LAST SEASON

Led NHL in shutouts with career best. Second in NHL in save percentage. Tied for third in NHL in minutes played. Tied for third in NHL in goals-against average with career best. Tied for fifth in NHL in wins with career best.

THE PHYSICAL GAME

Dafoe's game is technically sound and quite aggressive, sometimes overly slow. He usually controls his rebounds well, but on nights when he doesn't his challenging style leaves him vulnerable on second shots.

He can get a bit scrambly, probably a vestige of playing for a worse defensive team in Los Angeles. Goalies for weaker teams tend to do too much. He plays a better game the less he tries to accomplish.

Dafoe is slightly smaller than many of today's larger goalies, but when he stands up and plays his angles he is able to maximize his size.

He is quite average in a lot of areas — especially stickhandling. He thinks the game well, though, and he stays alert and doesn't beat himself. Those 10 shutouts weren't a fluke.

THE MENTAL GAME

Dafoe has battled to get his playing chance and he handles adversity well. Now that he knows coach Pat Burns will come back with him after good games or bad, Dafoe is more relaxed and confident. He gives the Bruins the goaltending stability they have lacked for a number of seasons.

THE INTANGIBLES

Dafoe was a number one goalie at every level he played until he first reached the NHL (his first full season was with Los Angeles in 1995-96). He can't be considered among the league's elite yet, but he is building some solid credentials at the top of the second echelon of goaltenders.

PROJECTION

Dafoe should be able to surpass 30 wins, and maybe he'll even get on the NHL All-Star ballot this time.

HAL GILL

Yrs. of NHL service: 2
Born: Concord, Mass.; Apr. 6, 1975
Position: right defense
Height: 6-7
Weight: 240
Uniform no.: 25
Shoots: left

Career statistics:

GP	G	A	TP	PIM
148	5	11	15	110

1997-98 statistics:

GP	G	A	TP	+/-	PIM	PP	SH	GW	GT	S	PCT
68	2	4	6	+4	47	0	0	0	0	56	3.6

1998-99 statistics:

GP	G	A	TP	+/-	PIM	PP	SH	GW	GT	S	PCT
80	3	7	10	-10	63	0	0	2	0	102	2.9

LAST SEASON
Second NHL season. Missed two games with hip injury.

THE FINESSE GAME
Gill's only drawback is his skating. He has slow feet, which may keep him from becoming an elite defenseman, but every other facet of his game is Grade A.

He can be used in any game situation and when the heat is on, Gill excells. He has a huge shot from the point, though his lack of mobility along the blueline makes it a less effective scoring weapon. His puck movement is advanced. He was not much of a scorer at the college level and he won't be in the NHL, either, but his finesse skills serve him well in a defensive role. He makes the first pass on the breakout or gets the puck and moves it out of the zone.

Gill is one of the tallest players in the NHL and he uses his reach well. Playing with Ray Bourque a lot obviously helped his development, as it did Kyle McLaren's. Gill is calm with the puck and has a high panic threshold.

THE PHYSICAL GAME
Gill competes hard every night. He is not intimidated by some of the league's tough customers and is one of the few defensemen in the East who can stay on his feet after a hit by someone like New Jersey's Bobby Holik. Gill is solid and imposing, and can intimidate with his size. He is strong on the boards, strong in the corners and he clears out the front of his net. He doesn't fight. He doesn't have to. He has a pretty long fuse, but don't confuse that with a lack of bravery. Gill is a gamer.

THE INTANGIBLES
How's this for a compliment? Jaromir Jagr called Gill the toughest player he competes against. And Gill is only in his second NHL season.

PROJECTION
Gill will be a top four defenseman again this year with Boston, and will become a mainstay. He is one of the best young rearguards in the league, but he doesn't get the attention he deserves because his point totals are so tiny.

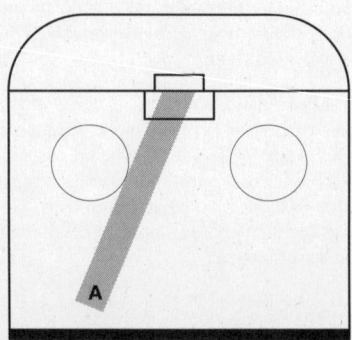

STEVE HEINZE

Yrs. of NHL service: 7
Born: Lawrence, Mass.; Jan. 30, 1970
Position: right wing
Height: 5-11
Weight: 193
Uniform no.: 23
Shoots: right

Career statistics:

GP	G	A	TP	PIM
440	119	95	214	239

1995-96 statistics:

GP	G	A	TP	+/-	PIM	PP	SH	GW	GT	S	PCT
76	16	12	28	-3	43	0	1	3	0	129	12.4

1996-97 statistics:

GP	G	A	TP	+/-	PIM	PP	SH	GW	GT	S	PCT
30	17	8	25	-8	27	4	2	2	0	96	17.7

1997-98 statistics:

GP	G	A	TP	+/-	PIM	PP	SH	GW	GT	S	PCT
61	26	20	46	+8	54	9	0	6	0	160	16.3

1998-99 statistics:

GP	G	A	TP	+/-	PIM	PP	SH	GW	GT	S	PCT
73	22	18	40	+7	30	9	0	3	0	146	15.1

PROJECTION

Until the Bruins get a little deeper, Heinze will continue to get his ice time on the first or second line and produce another 20 to 25 goals.

LAST SEASON

Second on team in power-play goals. Missed five games with hip flexor. Missed three games with flu. Missed one game with finger laceration.

THE FINESSE GAME

Heinze is a traditional, grinding Bruins forward who skates up and down his wing. He has surprisingly good hands for a grinder, with a quick snap shot. He gets goals that go in off his legs, arms and elbows from his work in front of the net.

He's smart at trailing plays along the way and digging out loose pucks, which he either takes to the net himself or, more often, passes off.

Heinze has a good first step to the puck, which helps in his penalty killing, as he forces the puck carrier. He was a big scorer at Boston College with David Emma and Marty McInnis (the HEM Line), but he succeeded at that level mainly because he was able to overpower people; he doesn't have that same edge in the pros. He plays an intelligent game and is a good playmaker with passing skills on his forehand and backhand.

THE PHYSICAL GAME

Heinze is hampered by his lack of size and strength. His probable future is as a third-line checking winger, but he doesn't have the power to line up against other teams' top forwards. He is willing to get in the way and force people to go through him. The trouble is, they usually do.

THE INTANGIBLES

Heinze is a grinder playing in a prettier role.

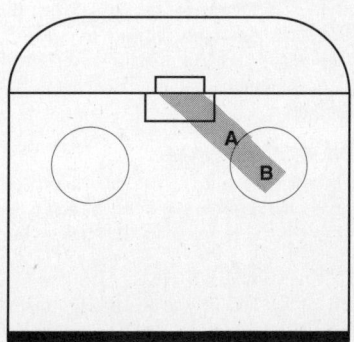

DMITRI KHRISTICH

Yrs. of NHL service: 9
Born: Kiev, Ukraine; July 23, 1969
Position: left wing
Height: 6-2
Weight: 195
Uniform no.: 12
Shoots: right

Career statistics:

GP	G	A	TP	PIM
627	226	282	507	290

1995-96 statistics:

GP	G	A	TP	+/-	PIM	PP	SH	GW	GT	S	PCT
76	27	37	64	0	44	12	0	3	0	204	13.2

1996-97 statistics:

GP	G	A	TP	+/-	PIM	PP	SH	GW	GT	S	PCT
75	19	37	56	+8	38	3	0	2	0	135	14.1

1997-98 statistics:

GP	G	A	TP	+/-	PIM	PP	SH	GW	GT	S	PCT
82	29	37	66	+25	42	13	2	1	0	144	20.1

1998-99 statistics:

GP	G	A	TP	+/-	PIM	PP	SH	GW	GT	S	PCT
79	29	42	71	+11	48	13	1	6	1	144	20.1

LAST SEASON

Led NHL in shooting percentage. Led team in goals and power-play goals. Second on team in points and plus-minus. Tied for second on team in game-winning goals. Missed three games with shoulder injuries.

THE FINESSE GAME

Khristich has good hand-eye coordination for deflections and can even take draws. He is not an especially fast skater, but he has a long, strong stride and very good balance. His hockey sense is excellent, and he is responsible defensively as well.

One weakness is his tendency to put himself in a position where he gets hit, and hurt. Part of that stems from holding onto the puck to make a perfect play.

Khristich played on the second line in Boston, usually with Joe Thornton and rookie Sergei Samsonov. Playing with an effective point man, Ray Bourque, boosted Khristich's power-play production. He likes to lurk just off to the goalie's right, with his forehand open and ready for the pass. When the puck reaches his blade, he slams the shot in one quick motion. If the penalty killers are drawn to him, it then opens ice for another forward. Either way, Khristich gets the job done.

THE PHYSICAL GAME

Khristich is a very sturdy skater but lacks physical presence. He will go into the trenches and is tough to knock off the puck. He protects the puck well.

THE INTANGIBLES

The Bruins have had it with Khristich's inconsistent effort and were looking to deal their second-leading scorer during the off-season.

PROJECTION

Even with the ability to score 30 goals and 70 points, Khristich's inability to show up every night drives coaches crazy.

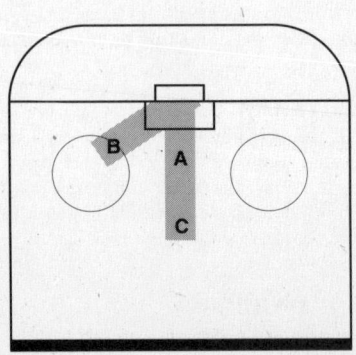

CAMERON MANN

Yrs. of NHL service: 1
Born: Thompson, Man.; Apr. 20, 1977
Position: right wing
Height: 6-0
Weight: 194
Uniform no.: 10
Shoots: right

Career statistics:

GP	G	A	TP	PIM
42	5	3	8	21

1997-98 statistics:

GP	G	A	TP	+/-	PIM	PP	SH	GW	GT	S	PCT
9	0	1	1	+1	4	0	0	0	0	6	0.0

1998-99 statistics:

GP	G	A	TP	+/-	PIM	PP	SH	GW	GT	S	PCT
33	5	2	7	0	17	1	0	1	1	42	11.9

LAST SEASON

First NHL season. Appeared in 43 games with Providence (AHL), scoring 21-25 — 46. Missed one game with flu.

THE FINESSE GAME

Mann is a good skater: he has good speed, a quick start from standstill and his skating is effortless. Capable of beating a player one-on-one, he plays well at both ends of the ice.

Mann has a good scoring touch around the net with a hard shot. His stickhandling is above average. He can certainly develop into a better player than Steve Heinze, who has given the Bruins a lot of mileage over the years.

Mann would be a good fit among the team's young forwards. There won't be a lot of pressure on him behind Anson Carter. Mann can't carry a team but he can add to its depth. He has enough skill.

THE PHYSICAL GAME

Mann has fair size and strength but he is not a physical force. He seldom instigates, but he does not back down when challenged and he possesses a good work ethic. He has picked up his work in the corners a notch.

THE INTANGIBLES

Mann had a strong playoffs with Providence. The only knock on him is that some scouts believe he is soft and won't pay the price, but he had a preseason toe-to-toe with Trent McCleary and beat him in a fight. He was a different player after that.

PROJECTION

Mann has the potential to earn a spot on the top two lines with Boston. He's been able to score in the minors and could be a 20-goal scorer if he gets a fairly major role this season.

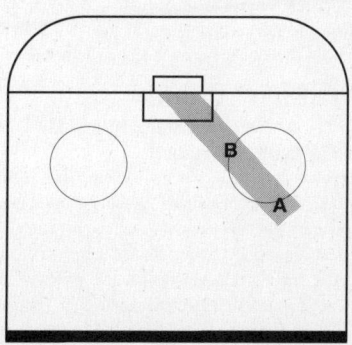

KYLE MCLAREN

Yrs. of NHL service: 4
Born: Humbolt, Sask.; June 18, 1977
Position: left defense
Height: 6-4
Weight: 210
Uniform no.: 18
Shoots: left

Career statistics:

GP	G	A	TP	PIM
250	21	59	80	231

1995-96 statistics:

GP	G	A	TP	+/-	PIM	PP	SH	GW	GT	S	PCT
74	5	12	17	+16	73	0	0	0	0	74	6.8

1996-97 statistics:

GP	G	A	TP	+/-	PIM	PP	SH	GW	GT	S	PCT
58	5	9	14	-9	54	0	0	1	0	68	7.4

1997-98 statistics:

GP	G	A	TP	+/-	PIM	PP	SH	GW	GT	S	PCT
66	5	20	25	+13	56	2	0	0	0	101	5.0

1998-99 statistics:

GP	G	A	TP	+/-	PIM	PP	SH	GW	GT	S	PCT
52	6	18	24	+1	48	3	0	0	0	97	6.2

LAST SEASON

Missed 15 games due to contract dispute. Missed 14 games with shoulder injury. Missed one game with foot injury.

THE FINESSE GAME

McLaren is big and mobile. His puckhandling ability is well above average, and he moves the puck out of the zone quickly and without panicking. He can rush with the puck or make the cautious bank off the boards to clear the zone if that is his best option.

He can play either right or left defense, and his advanced defensive reads allow him to adapt, which is very hard to do for a young player.

McLaren is an effective penalty killer because he is fearless. He blocks shots and takes away passing lanes. He can also play on the power play, and probably will improve in this area because he plays heads-up and has a hard and accurate slap shot with a quick release. As he gains more confidence he will become more of an offensive factor, but frequently he puts the cart before the horse and goes on the attack — before he has taken care of his own end of the ice.

THE PHYSICAL GAME

McLaren is a mean, punishing hitter. He is almost scary in his fierce checking ability. He is tough and aggressive, but he doesn't go looking for fights and doesn't take foolish penalties. When he does get into a scrap, he can go toe-to-toe and has already earned some respect around the league as a player you don't want to tick off. He is strong on the puck, strong on the wall and doesn't allow loitering in front of his crease.

McLaren has a tendency to lose his edge and get more freewheeling and offensive. Every time he lapses into this bad habit, the coaching staff have to rein him in a bit and bring him back to a simple game.

THE INTANGIBLES

The next Ray Bourque? How unfair to saddle this kid with that cumbersome label, but McLaren has learned well from playing with Bourque and he is Boston's top defenseman of the future.

PROJECTION

The less McLaren thinks about getting points the more easily he will score. He should get close to 40 points this season.

SERGEI SAMSONOV

Yrs. of NHL service: 2
Born: Moscow, Russia; Oct. 27, 1978
Position: left wing
Height: 5-8
Weight: 184
Uniform no.: 14
Shoots: left

Career statistics:

GP	G	A	TP	PIM
160	47	51	98	26

1997-98 statistics:

GP	G	A	TP	+/-	PIM	PP	SH	GW	GT	S	PCT
81	22	25	47	+9	8	7	0	3	0	159	13.8

1998-99 statistics:

GP	G	A	TP	+/-	PIM	PP	SH	GW	GT	S	PCT
79	25	26	51	-6	18	6	0	8	1	160	15.6

LAST SEASON

Second NHL season. Led team and tied for third in the NHL in game-winning goals. Second on team in goals and shots. Third on team in shooting percentage. Missed two games with sinus infection. Missed one game with thigh contusion.

THE FINESSE GAME

Following his Calder Trophy-winning season, a little setback could have been predicted, and Samsonov was less consistent last season.

When he's on, he is an absolute treat to watch. He is an outstanding skater and the puck doesn't slow him down a hair. He performs the hockey equivalent of a between the legs dribble, putting pucks between the legs (his or the defenders') and executing cutbacks.

Samsonov has outstanding quickness and breakaway speed. He plays on his off-wing but uses all of the ice. He is a better scorer than playmaker. He has a quick release on his shot. He tends to be streaky/slumpy, but that's to be expected in a young player.

Samsonov is reliable enough defensively.

THE PHYSICAL GAME

Sturdily built, Samsonov is a little tank. He can't be scared off the play and he handles himself well in traffic and in tight spaces along the boards and corners.

THE INTANGIBLES

Samsonov should get his skates back under him. He is a top six forward who is still learning the day-in, day-out dedication the job requires.

PROJECTION

Samsonov came through with the 25-goal season we predicted for him. He should move up to the 30-goal level this season.

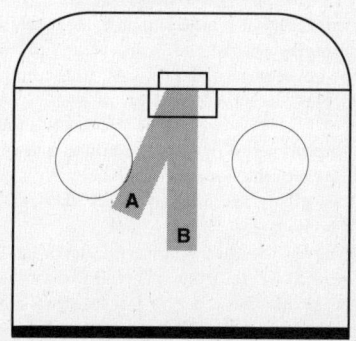

DON SWEENEY

Yrs. of NHL service: 11
Born: St. Stephen, N.B.; Aug. 17, 1966
Position: left defense
Height: 5-10
Weight: 188
Uniform no.: 32
Shoots: left

Career statistics:

GP	G	A	TP	PIM
751	43	167	210	530

1995-96 statistics:

GP	G	A	TP	+/-	PIM	PP	SH	GW	GT	S	PCT
77	4	24	28	-4	42	2	0	3	0	142	2.8

1996-97 statistics:

GP	G	A	TP	+/-	PIM	PP	SH	GW	GT	S	PCT
82	3	23	26	-5	39	0	0	0	0	113	2.7

1997-98 statistics:

GP	G	A	TP	+/-	PIM	PP	SH	GW	GT	S	PCT
59	1	15	16	+12	24	0	0	0	0	55	1.8

1998-99 statistics:

GP	G	A	TP	+/-	PIM	PP	SH	GW	GT	S	PCT
81	2	10	12	+14	64	0	0	0	0	79	2.5

LAST SEASON

Led team in plus-minus. Missed one game due to coach's decision.

THE FINESSE GAME

Sweeney has found a niche for himself in the NHL. He's mobile, physical and greatly improved in the area of defensive reads. He has good hockey sense for recognizing offensive situations as well.

He mostly stays at home and out of trouble, but Sweeney is a good enough skater to get involved in the attack and to take advantage of open ice. He is a good passer and has an adequate shot, and he has developed more confidence in his skills. He skates his way out of trouble and moves the puck well.

Sweeney is also a clever player who knows his strengths and weaknesses. Despite being a low draft pick (166th overall), he doesn't let anyone overlook him because of his effort and intelligence.

THE PHYSICAL GAME

Sweeney is built like a little human Coke machine. He is tough to play against and, while wear and tear is a factor, he never hides. He is always in the middle of physical play. He utilizes his lower-body drive and has tremendous leg power. He is also shifty enough to avoid a big hit when he sees it coming, and many a large forechecking forward has sheepishly picked himself up off the ice after Sweeney has scampered away from the boards with the puck.

Sweeney is the ultimate gym rat, devoting a great deal of time to weightlifting and overall conditioning. Pound for pound, he is one of the strongest defensemen in the NHL.

THE INTANGIBLES

Sweeney is highly competitive. Despite his small size, a lot of teams would welcome him on their blueline. Boston has gotten a little deeper on the blueline, but Sweeney remains a top four staple.

PROJECTION

Sweeney's point totals won't go much higher than 20.

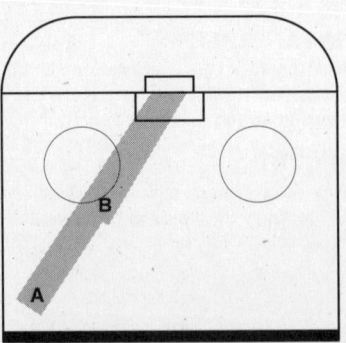

JOE THORNTON

Yrs. of NHL service: 2
Born: London, Ont.; July 2, 1979
Position: centre
Height: 6-4
Weight: 198
Uniform no.: 6
Shoots: left

Career statistics:

GP	G	A	TP	PIM
136	19	29	48	88

1997-98 statistics:

GP	G	A	TP	+/-	PIM	PP	SH	GW	GT	S	PCT
55	3	4	7	-6	19	0	0	1	0	33	9.1

1998-99 statistics:

GP	G	A	TP	+/-	PIM	PP	SH	GW	GT	S	PCT
81	16	25	41	+3	69	7	0	1	0	128	12.5

LAST SEASON

Second NHL season. Missed one game with chest injury.

THE FINESSE GAME

The first thing you notice about Thornton is his size, but his key assets are his exceptional vision of the ice and the hand skills to make things happen. All the tools, and the toolbox, too.

Thornton is so good at finding holes and passing lanes that teammates will have to be exceptionally alert when playing with him, because he will create something out of nothing. He also loves to shoot and work the boards, corners and front of the net. He needs to be prodded to keep his feet moving, as he often drifts into a bad habit of standing and waiting for things to happen. He needs to make things happen.

Thornton's skating could use some improvement, but it's NHL calibre. He handled the promotion to second-line duty last season as a centre and showed every sign of being able to handle the full-time role.

THE PHYSICAL GAME

Thornton has a short fuse and can be goaded off his game. He digs and bangs and plays with an edge, but he needs to keep his natural aggression under control.

THE INTANGIBLES

The Bruins brought Thornton along slowly and carefully his rookie season, so much so that Thornton was almost stuck with a "bust" label before he was 20. Their patience paid off as Thornton made the logical next step in his development. He is going to progress.

PROJECTION

Thornton fell shy of the 20 goals predicted for him last season but should move past that mark this year.

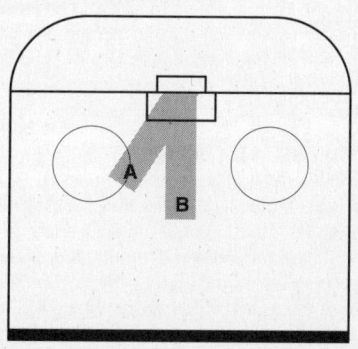

LANDON WILSON

Yrs. of NHL service: 3
Born: St. Louis, Mo.; Mar. 13, 1975
Position: right wing
Height: 6-2
Weight: 202
Uniform no.: 27
Shoots: right

Career statistics:

GP	G	A	TP	PIM
106	13	20	33	102

1995-96 statistics:

GP	G	A	TP	+/-	PIM	PP	SH	GW	GT	S	PCT
7	1	0	1	+3	6	0	0	0	0	6	16.7

1996-97 statistics:

GP	G	A	TP	+/-	PIM	PP	SH	GW	GT	S	PCT
49	8	12	20	-5	72	0	0	0	0	83	9.6

1997-98 statistics:

GP	G	A	TP	+/-	PIM	PP	SH	GW	GT	S	PCT
28	1	5	6	+3	7	0	0	0	0	26	3.8

1998-99 statistics:

GP	G	A	TP	+/-	PIM	PP	SH	GW	GT	S	PCT
22	3	3	6	0	17	0	0	0	0	32	9.4

LAST SEASON

Appeared in 48 games with Providence, scoring 31-22-53. Missed two games with concussion. Missed one game with shoulder injury.

THE FINESSE GAME

The Bruins have been searching for a power winger ever since Cam Neely was forced to retire; they're hoping Wilson will be the man. They traded a first-round draft pick to get him, but so far continue to be discouraged by his development.

The question is not Wilson's skills. A fine all-around athlete with good stamina, Wilson has developed a variety of shots. He can stickhandle around a defender and release a quick snap shot, or he can unload a powerful slap shot from the top of the circles. He has keen offensive instincts and he's a finisher.

Wilson doesn't have blazing speed, but he has good anticipation that buys him a step in a race. He powers his way to the net with the puck or in pursuit of a rebound. He has decent hands, and on Boston he doesn't have to beat out a lot of people to play with some of the better players on the Bruins. The issue is how hard Wilson will play to earn a spot on the top two lines.

THE PHYSICAL GAME

The only way Wilson is going to be an NHL player is if he uses his body and finishes his checks. There are some troubling question marks about his intensity. He is big, solidly built and strong on his skates. He competes for the puck in the high-traffic areas. On nights when he is on he can physically dominate a game.

THE INTANGIBLES

Wilson has to make the decision to be an NHL player. Pat Burns made a player out of Jason Allison. Wilson is his next project, and the 24-year-old is the type of player who does take awhile to develop. The Bruins need some size on the wing desperately, but Wilson has to play some desperate hockey. Burns is not about to hand him a job just because he's so darned big. If the Bruins are successful in moving Dmitri Khristich during the off-season, that could mean a job is wide open for Wilson to take.

PROJECTION

A job on one of the top two lines is his if Wilson shows enough fire. He needs to score 20 to 25 goals if he sticks. He is at the right age now to make his mark.

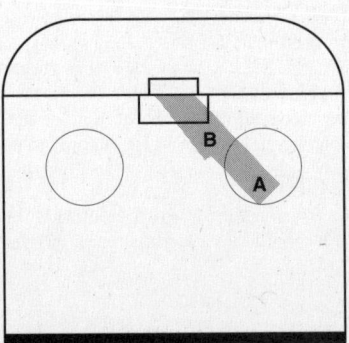

BUFFALO SABRES

Players' Statistics 1998-99

POS	NO.	PLAYER	GP	G	A	PTS	+/-	PIM	PP	SH	GW	GT	S	PCT
R	81	MIROSLAV SATAN	81	40	26	66	24	44	13	3	6	1	208	19.2
C	27	MICHAEL PECA	82	27	29	56	7	81	10		8	1	199	13.6
L	18	MICHAL GROSEK	76	20	30	50	21	102	4		3	1	140	14.3
C	37	CURTIS BROWN	78	16	31	47	23	56	5	1	3	3	128	12.5
R	15	DIXON WARD	78	20	24	44	10	44	2	1	4	1	101	19.8
C	90	JOE JUNEAU	72	15	28	43	-4	22	2	1	3		150	10.0
D	5	JASON WOOLLEY	80	10	33	43	16	62	4		2	1	154	6.5
C	41	STU BARNES	81	20	16	36	-11	30	13		3		180	11.1
C	19	BRIAN HOLZINGER	81	17	17	34	2	45	5		2		143	11.9
D	44	ALEXEI ZHITNIK	81	7	26	33	-6	96	3	1	2		185	3.8
R	25	VACLAV VARADA	72	7	24	31	11	61	1		1		123	5.7
L	80	GEOFF SANDERSON	75	12	18	30	8	22	1		1		155	7.7
D	8	DARRYL SHANNON	71	3	12	15	28	52	1			1	80	3.8
D	42	RICHARD SMEHLIK	72	3	11	14	-9	44					61	4.9
C	22	WAYNE PRIMEAU	67	5	8	13	-6	38				1	55	9.1
C	9	*ERIK RASMUSSEN	42	3	7	10	6	37					40	7.5
D	3	JAMES PATRICK	45	1	7	8	12	16					31	3.2
D	4	RHETT WARRENER	61	1	7	8	2	84					44	2.3
D	74	JAY MCKEE	72		6	6	20	75					57	
L	17	RANDY CUNNEYWORTH	14	2	2	4	1				1		12	16.7
R	32	ROB RAY	76		4	4	-2	261					23	
L	24	PAUL KRUSE	43	3		3	0	114					33	9.1
D	34	*J-LUC GRAND-PIERRE	16		1	1	0	17					11	
D	21	MIKE HURLBUT	1				2						2	
R	46	*DEAN SYLVESTER	1				-1						1	
C	83	*DOMENIC PITTIS	3				0	2					1	
D	29	*JASON HOLLAND	3				-1	8					2	
D	6	*CORY SARICH	4				3						2	
G	43	*MARTIN BIRON	6				0							
G	30	DWAYNE ROLOSON	18				0	4						
G	39	DOMINIK HASEK	64				0	14						

GP = games played; G = goals; A = assists; PTS = points; +/- = goals-for minus goals-against while player is on ice; PIM = penalties in minutes; PP = power-play goals; SH = shorthanded goals; GW = game-winning goals; GT = game-tying goals; S = no. of shots; PCT = percentage of goals to shots; * = rookie

STU BARNES

Yrs. of NHL service: 8
Born: Edmonton, Alta.; Dec. 25, 1970
Position: centre
Height: 5-11
Weight: 175
Uniform no.: 41
Shoots: right

Career statistics:

GP	G	A	TP	PIM
514	141	168	309	214

1995-96 statistics:

GP	G	A	TP	+/-	PIM	PP	SH	GW	GT	S	PCT
72	19	25	44	-12	46	8	0	5	2	158	12.0

1996-97 statistics:

GP	G	A	TP	+/-	PIM	PP	SH	GW	GT	S	PCT
81	19	30	49	-23	26	5	0	3	3	176	10.8

1997-98 statistics:

GP	G	A	TP	+/-	PIM	PP	SH	GW	GT	S	PCT
78	30	35	65	+15	30	15	1	5	0	196	15.3

1998-99 statistics:

GP	G	A	TP	+/-	PIM	PP	SH	GW	GT	S	PCT
81	20	16	36	-11	30	13	0	3	0	180	11.1

LAST SEASON
Acquired from Pittsburgh for Matthew Barnaby, Mar. 11, 1999. Tied for team lead in power-play goals. Tied for third on team in goals.

THE FINESSE GAME
It's hard to begrudge Barnes any of the success he enjoys. He pursues the puck intelligently and finishes his checks. He employs these traits at even strength, whether killing penalties or on the power play. He reads the play coming out of the zone and uses his anticipation to pick off passes. He plays with great enthusiasm. He has sharply honed puck skills and offensive instincts, which he puts to especially effective use on the power play. He has good quickness and can control the puck in traffic. He uses a slap shot or a wrist shot in tight.

Barnes wastes few of the quality chances that come his way. He has a quick release and is accurate with his shot. One of his favourite plays is using his right-handed shot for a one-timer on the power play.

He has a good work ethic; his effort overcomes his deficiency in size. He's clever and plays a smart small man's game.

THE PHYSICAL GAME
Barnes is not big but he gets in the way. He brings a little bit of grit to the lineup, but what really stands out is his intensity and spirit. He can energize his team with one gutsy shift. Barnes always keeps his feet moving and draws penalties.

THE INTANGIBLES
The epitome of hard work, Barnes was fortunate to be transferred to a team that thrives on it. He went through an astounding goal slump after his arrival in Buffalo, but never got down on himself, and helped the Sabres reach the Final round.

PROJECTION
Realistically, 20 goals is the right target for Barnes, and that's where we expect him to be again this year.

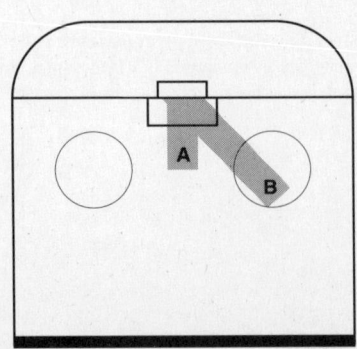

CURTIS BROWN

Yrs. of NHL service: 3
Born: Unity, Sask.; Feb. 12, 1976
Position: centre
Height: 6-0
Weight: 190
Uniform no.: 37
Shoots: left

Career statistics:

GP	G	A	TP	PIM
174	33	47	80	110

1995-96 statistics:

GP	G	A	TP	+/-	PIM	PP	SH	GW	GT	S	PCT
4	0	0	0	0	0	0	0	0	0	1	0.0

1996-97 statistics:

GP	G	A	TP	+/-	PIM	PP	SH	GW	GT	S	PCT
28	4	3	7	+4	18	0	0	1	0	31	12.9

1997-98 statistics:

GP	G	A	TP	+/-	PIM	PP	SH	GW	GT	S	PCT
63	12	12	24	+11	34	1	1	2	1	91	13.2

1998-99 statistics:

GP	G	A	TP	+/-	PIM	PP	SH	GW	GT	S	PCT
78	16	31	47	+23	56	5	1	3	3	128	12.5

LAST SEASON

Led team in assists. Third on team in plus-minus. Missed three games with bruised knee.

THE FINESSE GAME

Brown is a little cannonball, strong and quick on his skates and unafraid to get involved around the net. He is an excellent penalty killer, with terrific reads and anticipation, and the jump to pick off passes and turn them into shorthanded chances.

Brown was a left wing who was converted to the number two centre (behind Michael Peca), and while he is really a number three, he has enough offensive skills to try to make his wingers go. He is a playmaker first. Brown will create things with his speed on the forecheck and then has the hands to make the tape-to-tape pass.

Brown's hockey sense and defensive awareness are exceptional. If Peca weren't around, he would probably get some Selke Trophy recognition.

THE PHYSICAL GAME

Brown is little but plays with a bit of swagger. He isn't really tough. He just gives the impression that he won't back off. He is abrasive and annoying.

THE INTANGIBLES

Last year was a big breakthrough for Brown. He wore down a bit in the playoffs, but will probably come back with renewed energy.

PROJECTION

Brown will get a lot of ice time again and should produce 50 points.

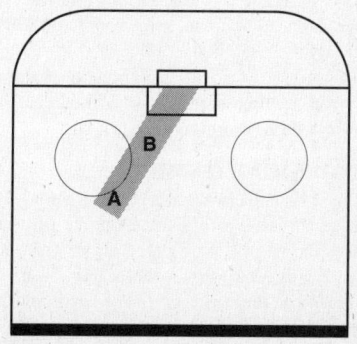

MICHAL GROSEK

Yrs. of NHL service: 5
Born: Vszkov, Czech Republic; June 1, 1975
Position: left wing
Height: 6-2
Weight: 296
Uniform no.: 18
Shoots: right

Career statistics:

GP	G	A	TP	PIM
275	54	77	131	285

1995-96 statistics:

GP	G	A	TP	+/-	PIM	PP	SH	GW	GT	S	PCT
23	6	4	10	-1	31	2	0	1	1	34	17.6

1996-97 statistics:

GP	G	A	TP	+/-	PIM	PP	SH	GW	GT	S	PCT
82	15	21	36	+25	71	1	0	2	1	117	12.8

1997-98 statistics:

GP	G	A	TP	+/-	PIM	PP	SH	GW	GT	S	PCT
67	10	20	30	+9	60	2	0	1	0	114	8.8

1998-99 statistics:

GP	G	A	TP	+/-	PIM	PP	SH	GW	GT	S	PCT
76	20	30	50	+21	102	4	0	3	1	140	14.3

LAST SEASON

Second on team in assists with career high. Third on team in points with career high. Tied for third on team in goals with career high. Third on team in shooting percentage and penalty minutes. Missed five games with back spasms. Missed one game due to suspension for elbowing incident.

THE FINESSE GAME

Maddeningly inconsistent, Grosek has an array of NHL-calibre skills at his disposal but doesn't always have the inclination to use them. He is still very young and has an eagerness to succeed at the NHL level. He is an excellent stickhandler, and he can be absolutely magical with the puck. He is good enough to play his off-wing (left) as well as the right. He doesn't have a great shot, but he intimidates with his speed and drives to the net. With more confidence, his release may improve.

Grosek is a bundle of talent whose first shot at an NHL job was derailed by two serious injuries. He uses his speed and size to create some room and he is genuinely tough.

Defensively, Grosek's game has improved, largely from getting to play with Mike Peca. If only Peca's work ethic would rub off as well.

THE PHYSICAL GAME

On his best nights, Grosek plays like a young Claude Lemieux, abrasive and a little undisciplined. But Lemieux played that way every night. Grosek only plays that way every few weeks. He is an impact player when he takes the bit in his teeth and goes a little wild. If he could do it over the majority of the 82-game schedule, he would be a star.

THE INTANGIBLES

Grosek was sidelined with injuries for much of the playoffs. When he returned, he was not as effective as he had been during what was a pretty good regular season for him. Buffalo's patience may run out soon, though Grosek has a patron saint in his good friend Dominik Hasek.

PROJECTION

Grosek fell shy of the 25 goals we predicted for him last season, though he was more consistent than he has been in the past and showed some positive signs. He needs to continue with his commitment to get to the 25- to 30-goal level, which his skills indicate he should reach.

DOMINIK HASEK

Yrs. of NHL service: 8
Born: Pardubice, Czech Republic; Jan. 29, 1965
Position: goaltender
Height: 5-11
Weight: 168
Uniform no.: 39
Catches: left

Career statistics:

GP	MIN	GA	SO	GAA	A	PIM
414	23903	901	42	2.26	9	78

1995-96 statistics:

GP	MIN	GAA	W	L	T	SO	GA	S	SAPCT	PIM
59	3417	2.83	22	30	6	2	161	2011	.920	6

1996-97 statistics:

GP	MIN	GAA	W	L	T	SO	GA	S	SAPCT	PIM
67	4037	2.27	37	20	10	5	153	2177	.930	30

1997-98 statistics:

GP	MIN	GAA	W	L	T	SO	GA	S	SAPCT	PIM
72	4220	2.09	33	23	13	13	147	2149	.932	12

1998-99 statistics:

GP	MIN	GAA	W	L	T	SO	GA	S	SAPCT	PIM
64	3817	1.87	30	18	14	9	119	1877	.937	14

LAST SEASON

Won 1999 Vezina Trophy. Named to First NHL All-Star Team. Led NHL in save percentage for sixth consecutive season with career best. Second in NHL in GAA with career best. Second in NHL in shutouts. Missed 12 games with groin injury. Missed one game with back injury.

THE PHYSICAL GAME

Nobody has worse technique nor better leg reflexes than Hasek; his foot speed is simply tremendous. He wanders and flops and sprawls. But he stops the puck. Usually, what Hasek sees he stops, and to him the puck seems to be moving more slowly than it does for other goalies. He watches it come off the shooter's stick into his glove or body, and he always seems in control, even while he looks to be flopping like a trout.

Hasek is adept at directing his rebounds away from onrushing attackers. He prefers to hold pucks for face-offs — in fact, he chases into the face-off circles for them — and the Sabres have a decent corps of centres so that tactic works fine for his team. Hasek instructs his defensemen to get out of the way so he can see the puck, and they follow orders.

Hasek learned to come out of his net a little bit more but he still doesn't cut down his angles well. He also has to work on his puckhandling. He has the single most bizarre habit of any NHL goalie we've seen in recent years. In scrambles around the net he abandons his stick entirely and grabs the puck with his blocker hand. His work with the stick is brutal, which may be why he lets go of it so often. Opponents have been complaining that he just happens to drop the stick in the way of the shooter trying to get to the loose puck.

THE MENTAL GAME

On the ice, Hasek is competitive and unflappable. He is always prepared for tough saves early in a game, and has very few lapses of concentration. His excitable style doesn't bother his teammates, who have developed faith in his ability. When he dives, when he blows up at an opponent's nudge, it's all with a purpose.

THE INTANGIBLES

The Stanley Cup still eludes Hasek, but he is probably one of the few goalies who doesn't have to win it to prove his greatness.

PROJECTION

Buffalo takes pride in being more than a one-man team, but Hasek is still the man who should rack up 30 wins for the Sabres.

BRIAN HOLZINGER

Yrs. of NHL service: 4
Born: Parma, Ohio; Oct. 10, 1972
Position: centre
Height: 5-11
Weight: 180
Uniform no.: 19
Shoots: right

Career statistics:

GP	G	A	TP	PIM
293	63	80	143	172

1995-96 statistics:

GP	G	A	TP	+/-	PIM	PP	SH	GW	GT	S	PCT
58	10	10	20	-21	37	5	0	1	0	71	14.1

1996-97 statistics:

GP	G	A	TP	+/-	PIM	PP	SH	GW	GT	S	PCT
81	22	29	51	+9	54	2	2	6	0	142	15.5

1997-98 statistics:

GP	G	A	TP	+/-	PIM	PP	SH	GW	GT	S	PCT
69	14	21	35	-2	36	4	2	1	1	116	12.1

1998-99 statistics:

GP	G	A	TP	+/-	PIM	PP	SH	GW	GT	S	PCT
81	17	17	34	+2	45	5	0	2	0	143	11.9

LAST SEASON
Missed one game with flu.

THE FINESSE GAME
Holzinger has a fine touch down low and patience with the puck to find the open passing lane. He needs to work with a big grinder on one wing, because he is too small to do much work effectively in the corners. He is not as gritty as a number of smaller forwards and plays too much on the perimeter.

Holzinger is not a natural scorer but he has some speed, which he could learn to use to his advantage. He is crafty and deceptively quick.

The key to Holzinger's development will be adding the little things to his game that make a complete player. He has to ask himself how he can contribute if he's not scoring. He can play, but can he win? He has a lot of raw talent, but at the moment he's an open-ice break player. He has a lot of hockey sense and may be adaptable. His defense has improved.

THE PHYSICAL GAME
Holzinger will have to work for his open ice in the NHL. He is not very big, nor very strong. Strength and conditioning work must figure in his summer vacation plans again, and every season for as long as he wants to stay in the NHL. He did seem to tick off a number of stars in the playoffs, which is a positive sign that he is adding some sandpaper to his game.

THE INTANGIBLES
Lack of depth among the Sabres' corps of forwards made Holzinger the number one centre (he played on a line with 40-goal scorer Miroslav Satan), but he is not really up to that role. He needs to work on a number of his weak points to keep that job — if and when the team upgrades the position.

PROJECTION
Holzinger will probably get enough ice time for 40 to 45 points, but he is not an impact player.

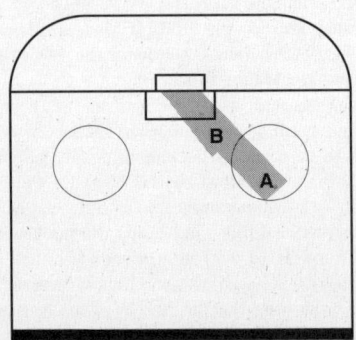

JOE JUNEAU

Yrs. of NHL service: 7
Born: Pont-Rouge, Que.; Jan. 5, 1968
Position: centre/left wing
Height: 6-0
Weight: 195
Uniform no.: 90
Shoots: right

Career statistics:

GP	G	A	TP	PIM
482	114	263	429	172

1995-96 statistics:

GP	G	A	TP	+/-	PIM	PP	SH	GW	GT	S	PCT
80	14	50	64	-3	30	7	2	2	2	0	8.0

1996-97 statistics:

GP	G	A	TP	+/-	PIM	PP	SH	GW	GT	S	PCT
58	15	27	42	-11	8	9	1	3	0	124	12.1

1997-98 statistics:

GP	G	A	TP	+/-	PIM	PP	SH	GW	GT	S	PCT
56	9	22	31	-8	26	4	1	1	0	87	10.3

1998-99 statistics:

GP	G	A	TP	+/-	PIM	PP	SH	GW	GT	S	PCT
72	15	28	43	-4	22	2	1	3	0	150	10.0

LAST SEASON

Acquired from Washington with third-round draft pick in 1999 for Alexei Tesikov, Mar. 23, 1999. Missed eight games with concussions. Missed three games with flu. Missed one game to due coach's decision.

THE FINESSE GAME

A natural centre, even when playing in the middle, Juneau gravitates to the left wing and generates most of his scoring chances from there. He varies his play selection. He will take the puck to the net on one rush, then pull up at the top of the circle and hit the trailer late on the next rush.

While the circles are his office, Juneau is not exclusively a perimeter player. He will go into traffic, and is bigger than he looks on the ice. His quick feet and light hands make him seem smaller, because he is so crafty with the puck.

Laterally, Juneau is among the best skaters in the NHL. He has an extra gear that allows him to pull away from people. He does not have breakaway speed, but he has great anticipation and gets the jump on a defender with his first few steps.

Juneau doesn't shoot the puck enough and gets a little intimidated when there is a scramble for a loose puck in front of the net. He is not always willing to sacrifice his body that way. He shoots a tad prematurely. When he could wait and have the goalie down and out, he unloads quickly, because he hears footsteps. His best shot is a one-timer from the left circle.

Juneau is fine on draws and kills penalties.

THE PHYSICAL GAME

Juneau has improved his toughness and willingness to take a hit to make a play — probably dressing room osmosis — but he is still something of a featherweight. You can almost see him psych himself up to make or take a hit. It doesn't come naturally to him.

THE INTANGIBLES

Juneau didn't have a big playoffs. For the second consecutive season he was nearly invisible in the Final series (with Washington in 1998 and Buffalo last season).

PROJECTION

Juneau would be a nice free agent pickup for a team needing some complementary offensive help, but his playoffs won't exactly drive his price tag up.

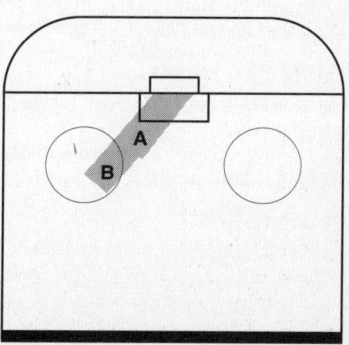

JAY MCKEE

Yrs. of NHL service: 3
Born: Kingston, Ont.; Sept. 8, 1977
Position: left defense
Height: 6-3
Weight: 195
Uniform no.: 74
Shoots: left

Career statistics:
GP	G	A	TP	PIM
172	2	29	31	154

1995-96 statistics:
GP	G	A	TP	+/-	PIM	PP	SH	GW	GT	S	PCT
1	0	1	1	+1	2	0	0	0	0	2	0.0

1996-97 statistics:
GP	G	A	TP	+/-	PIM	PP	SH	GW	GT	S	PCT
43	1	9	10	+3	35	0	0	0	0	29	3.4

1997-98 statistics:
GP	G	A	TP	+/-	PIM	PP	SH	GW	GT	S	PCT
56	1	13	14	-1	42	0	0	0	0	55	1.8

1998-99 statistics:
GP	G	A	TP	+/-	PIM	PP	SH	GW	GT	S	PCT
72	0	6	6	+20	75	0	0	0	0	57	.0

LAST SEASON
Missed six games with bruised foot. Missed two games with flu. Missed one game with bruised hand. Missed one game due to coach's decision.

THE FINESSE GAME
McKee has been studiously applying his skills to the defensive aspects of his game, to the point where his offensive game has been totally neglected. He has a future as more of a two-way defenseman if he builds off the confidence his defensive game should have provided him.

McKee is a strong skater, which powers his open-ice hits. He has good acceleration and quickness to carry the puck out of the zone. He gets involved in the attack because of his skating, but he doesn't have elite hands or playmaking skills.

He has sharp hockey sense and plays an advanced positional game for a young player. With Rhett Warrener's acquisition, McKee found a sympatico defense partner and his game picked up over the latter part of the season and into the playoffs.

THE PHYSICAL GAME
McKee has good size and is wiry and tough, if a little on the lean side. He exhibited a mean streak in junior but has been a little quieter at the pro level; he could get a little more involved.

THE INTANGIBLES
Given his mature game, it's easy to forget that McKee was only 22 when last season started, and top-four defensemen usually take longer than that to develop. He has recovered from some of the damage done by rushing him at age 19.

PROJECTION
McKee has a lot of upside, but expect him to concentrate on defense first. The Sabres are a low-scoring team, so 20 points would be a fine output from McKee.

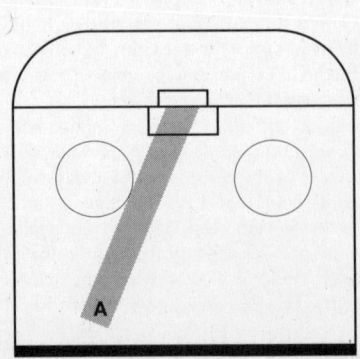

MICHAEL PECA

Yrs. of NHL service: 5
Born: Toronto, Ont.; March 26, 1974
Position: centre
Height: 5-11
Weight: 180
Uniform no.: 27
Shoots: right

Career statistics:

GP	G	A	TP	PIM
327	82	106	188	317

1995-96 statistics:

GP	G	A	TP	+/-	PIM	PP	SH	GW	GT	S	PCT
68	11	20	31	-1	67	4	3	1	0	109	10.1

1996-97 statistics:

GP	G	A	TP	+/-	PIM	PP	SH	GW	GT	S	PCT
79	20	29	49	+26	80	5	6	4	0	137	14.6

1997-98 statistics:

GP	G	A	TP	+/-	PIM	PP	SH	GW	GT	S	PCT
61	18	22	40	+12	57	6	5	1	1	132	13.6

1998-99 statistics:

GP	G	A	TP	+/-	PIM	PP	SH	GW	GT	S	PCT
82	27	29	56	+7	81	10	0	8	1	199	13.6

LAST SEASON

Led team in game-winning goals. Second on team in goals and points with career highs. Second on team in shots. Third on team in assists and power-play goals. Only Sabre to appear in all 82 games. Finalist for 1999 Selke Trophy.

THE FINESSE GAME

In street clothes and with his glasses on, Peca looks like a librarian. But don't judge this book by its demure cover. Peca is a strong, sure skater who plays every shift as if a pink slip will be waiting on the bench if he slacks off. He's good with the puck but not overly creative. He just reads offensive plays well and does a lot of the little things — especially when forechecking — that create turnovers and scoring chances. His goals come from his quickness and his effort. He challenges anyone for the puck.

Although Peca is known for his dogged defensive play, he is intelligent enough to be a useful offensive player. The Sabres skate him on their power-play unit. His hustle and attitude have earned him his NHL job, and league-wide respect. Peca thinks the game well and can be used in all situations.

Peca is at his worst offensively when he has too much time to think. He creates breakaway chances with his reads and anticipation but seldom converts. He is smart about disrupting plays and knows what to do once he gains control of the puck.

THE PHYSICAL GAME

Peca plays much bigger than his size. He's gritty and honest, and is always trying to add more weight. He has a tough time even keeping an extra five pounds on, and the Sabres have to be cautious about overplaying him, though they frequently have no choice.

He's among the best open-ice hitters in the league. Peca is able to launch successful strikes against bigger players because of his timing, balance and leg strength. He will also drop the gloves and go after even the biggest foe. He is prickly and in-your-face, though opponents are less impressed with his diving skills.

THE INTANGIBLES

Peca is an ideal third-line player who is forced to function as a centre on one of Buffalo's top two lines. Although he lacks the size to match up with some of the league's bigger forwards, he is tireless in his pursuit and effort. He adds energy to the lineup. That deal for Alexander Mogilny looked so lopsided in Vancouver's favour in 1995, but the Sabres got a player who cares and shows up every night. Can't say the same for the Canucks.

PROJECTION

Peca should produce 50 points and a fourth consecutive Selke nomination (he won in 1997).

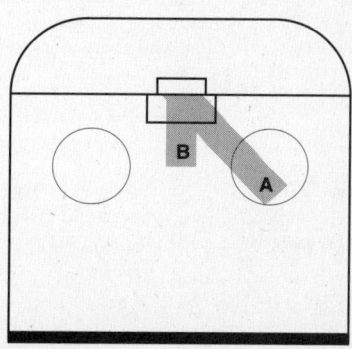

ERIK RASMUSSEN

Yrs. of NHL service: 1
Born: Minneapolis, Minn.; Mar. 28, 1977
Position: centre
Height: 6-2
Weight: 193
Uniform no.: 9
Shoots: left

Career statistics:

GP	G	A	TP	PIM
63	5	10	15	51

1997-98 statistics:

GP	G	A	TP	+/-	PIM	PP	SH	GW	GT	S	PCT
21	2	3	5	+2	14	0	0	0	0	28	7.1

1998-99 statistics:

GP	G	A	TP	+/-	PIM	PP	SH	GW	GT	S	PCT
42	3	7	10	+6	37	0	0	0	0	40	7.5

LAST SEASON

Second NHL season. Appeared in 37 games with Rochester (AHL), scoring 12-14 — 26. Missed one game with bruised foot.

THE FINESSE GAME

Big, tough and skilled, Rasmussen is the type of forward the Sabres have been waiting for. They're still waiting, because Rasmussen doesn't bring his "A" game to the ice every night. If both he and Vaclav Varada make the commitment to flex their muscles this season, the Sabres will become a much harder team to play through every night.

Rasmussen doesn't have great hands, but he has good ones to complement a scoring instinct and a desire to drive to the net. He usually looks to make a play first; the Sabres will try to encourage him to make better use of his wrist shot. He also has a hard slap shot.

Rasmussen is a strong skater with a long stride. He has good balance and agility and is tough to knock off his feet. He needs to learn to play a full 60 minutes and not take any shifts off.

THE PHYSICAL GAME

Rasmussen is abrasive and annoying to play against. He isn't huge, but he is strong and willing to throw his weight around and get in people's faces. He competes hard and will lead by example. He is still young and learning that he has to play hard every night to stick.

THE INTANGIBLES

Rasmussen is not a finished player, but he's an interesting project.

PROJECTION

A blue-chip prospect, Rasmussen could have a solid 30-point season coming up in the next season or two.

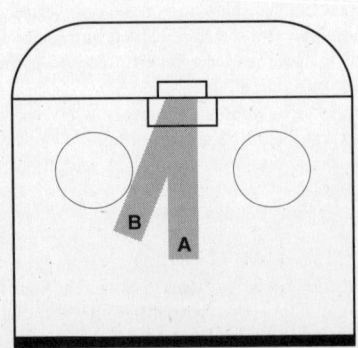

GEOFF SANDERSON

Yrs. of NHL service: 8
Born: Hay River, N.W.T.; Feb. 1, 1972
Position: left wing
Height: 6-0
Weight: 185
Uniform no.: 80
Shoots: left

Career statistics:

GP	G	A	TP	PIM
589	212	199	411	241

1995-96 statistics:

GP	G	A	TP	+/-	PIM	PP	SH	GW	GT	S	PCT
81	34	31	65	0	40	6	0	7	0	314	10.8

1996-97 statistics:

GP	G	A	TP	+/-	PIM	PP	SH	GW	GT	S	PCT
82	36	31	67	-9	29	12	1	4	1	297	12.1

1997-98 statistics:

GP	G	A	TP	+/-	PIM	PP	SH	GW	GT	S	PCT
75	11	18	29	+1	38	2	0	2	1	197	5.6

1998-99 statistics:

GP	G	A	TP	+/-	PIM	PP	SH	GW	GT	S	PCT
75	12	18	30	+8	22	1	0	1	0	155	7.7

LAST SEASON

Missed one game with back spasms. Missed one game with sore hip. Missed five games due to coach's decision.

THE FINESSE GAME

Sanderson doesn't make the best use of his speed, which prevents him from becoming the southpaw version of Mike Gartner in that player's prime. Still, his skating speed gives him a tremendous edge over the majority of NHL players, though it's not as big a weapon as it should be.

Sanderson has to go, go, go, and take lots of shots. When he plays that way he is far more dangerous. He can drive wide on a defenseman or open up space by forcing the defense to play back off him. He doesn't score often off the rush because he doesn't have a heavy shot. He can create chaos off the rush, though, and finish up by getting open in the slot for a pass.

He has a superb one-timer on the power play, where he likes to score on his off-wing in the deep right slot. Sanderson has become a better all-around player: he is more intelligent in his own end and his checking is more consistent. He can also kill penalties. His speed makes him a shorthanded threat.

THE PHYSICAL GAME

Sanderson has to learn and desire to fight his way through checkers. He is wiry but gets outmuscled, and although his speed keeps him clear of a lot of traffic, he has to battle when the room isn't there. He would benefit if the team added a little muscle up front.

THE INTANGIBLES

Sanderson has to decide how badly he wants a full-time job. He didn't appear too interested last season. On a team that desperately needed scoring, Sanderson did not step up.

PROJECTION

Sanderson's 30 points are an indication that he is on the bubble.

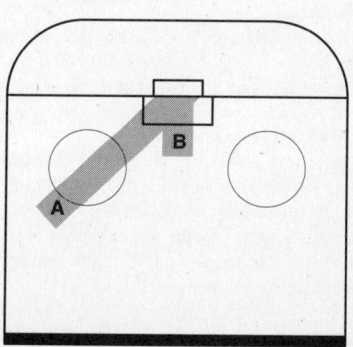

Buffalo Sabres

MIROSLAV SATAN

Yrs. of NHL service: 4
Born: Topolcany, Slovakia; Oct. 22, 1974
Position: left wing
Height: 6-1
Weight: 185
Uniform no.: 81
Shoots: left

Career statistics:

GP	G	A	TP	PIM
298	105	80	185	126

1995-96 statistics:

GP	G	A	TP	+/-	PIM	PP	SH	GW	GT	S	PCT
62	18	17	35	0	22	6	0	4	0	113	15.9

1996-97 statistics:

GP	G	A	TP	+/-	PIM	PP	SH	GW	GT	S	PCT
76	25	13	38	-3	26	7	0	3	0	119	21.0

1997-98 statistics:

GP	G	A	TP	+/-	PIM	PP	SH	GW	GT	S	PCT
79	22	24	46	+2	34	9	0	4	0	139	15.8

1998-99 statistics:

GP	G	A	TP	+/-	PIM	PP	SH	GW	GT	S	PCT
81	40	26	66	+24	44	13	3	6	1	208	19.2

LAST SEASON

Led team in points for second consecutive season. Led team in goals, shorthanded goals and shots. Tied for team lead in power-play goals. Second on team in plus-minus, game-winning goals and shooting percentage. Fifth in NHL in shooting percentage. Tied for seventh in NHL in goals. Missed one game with flu.

THE FINESSE GAME

Satan has terrific breakaway speed, which allows him to pull away from many defenders. He uses his skills in a strictly offensive sense. He developed as a fairly conscientious two-way player but in recent years has become more of a high-risk player.

Satan isn't shy about shooting. He keeps his head up and looks for his shooting holes, and is accurate with a wrist and snap shot. He sees his passing options and will sometimes make the play, but he is the sniper on whatever line he is playing and prefers to take the shot himself. One fault is his tendency to hold onto the puck too long.

Satan's biggest drawback is his lack of intensity, and with it, a lack of consistency. When he isn't scoring, he isn't doing much else to help his team win.

THE PHYSICAL GAME

Satan isn't huge, and being the prime checking objective on a team that isn't exactly loaded with offensive options takes its toll at crunch time. This was proven in the playoffs, when Satan was invisible in the Final against Dallas. He has a wiry strength, and shouldn't be as intimidated as he appears to be.

THE INTANGIBLES

There are a lot of questions about Satan's desire, though he did come back (from a broken foot) to help the Sabres reach the Finals. There can be few doubts about his raw ability. To be able to score 40 goals on this team was no small feat.

PROJECTION

Goals, goals, goals. Forget playmaking. Look at that goals-to-assists ratio. Satan wants to score. Forty goals will be hard to duplicate without a true number one centre, which Buffalo does not have.

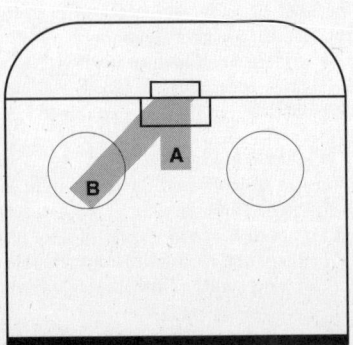

RICHARD SMEHLIK

Yrs. of NHL service: 6
Born: Ostrava, Czech Republic; Jan. 23, 1970
Position: right defense
Height: 6-3
Weight: 208
Uniform no.: 42
Shoots: left

Career statistics:

GP	G	A	TP	PIM
409	39	108	147	323

1995-96 statistics:
Did not play -- Injured

1996-97 statistics:

GP	G	A	TP	+/-	PIM	PP	SH	GW	GT	S	PCT
62	11	19	30	+19	43	2	0	1	0	100	11.0

1997-98 statistics:

GP	G	A	TP	+/-	PIM	PP	SH	GW	GT	S	PCT
72	3	17	20	+11	62	0	1	0	0	90	3.3

1998-99 statistics:

GP	G	A	TP	+/-	PIM	PP	SH	GW	GT	S	PCT
72	3	11	14	-9	44	0	0	0	0	61	4.9

LAST SEASON
Missed seven games with bruised quadricep.

THE FINESSE GAME
Smehlik's skating is his strong suit. He is agile with good lateral movement and very solid on his skates. Because his balance is so good, he is tough to knock down.

He thinks defense, and his impressive finesse skills are dedicated to the defensive aspect of the game. If Smehlik takes more responsibility offensively, he can respond. He has good passing skills and fair hockey vision, and he can spot and hit the breaking forward. Most of his assists will be traced back to a headman feed out of the defensive zone. He plays well at the point and has a rocket shot, but isn't clever enough with the puck to be a really effective member of the power play.

Smehlik is vulnerable to a strong forecheck. Teams are aware of this deficiency and try to work his corner.

THE PHYSICAL GAME
Smehlik can use his body well but has to be more consistent and authoritative. He has to clean up his crease better, something he doesn't do well since he's not a mean hitter. He prefers to use his stick to break up plays, and he does that effectively. He has a long reach and is able to intercept passes, or reach in around a defender to pry the puck loose. He gets a lot of minutes playing with Alexei Zhitnik against top lines and needs to keep up his conditioning.

THE INTANGIBLES
Smehlik would have a hard time being a top four defenseman on a stronger team, but he has developed a comfortable partnership with Zhitnik, and if it ain't broke . . . .

PROJECTION
Smehlik has some decent skills, but his probable level is the 25- to 30-point range. He will continue to get a lot of ice time.

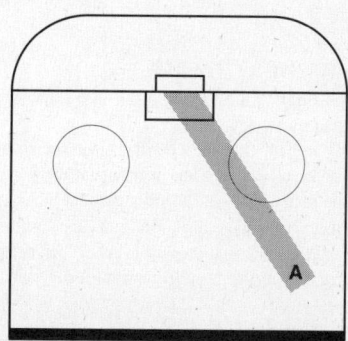

VACLAV VARADA

Yrs. of NHL service: 2
Born: Vsetin, Czech Republic; Apr. 26, 1976
Position: right wing
Height: 6-0
Weight: 200
Uniform no.: 25
Shoots: left

Career statistics:

GP	G	A	TP	PIM
105	12	30	42	78

1995-96 statistics:

GP	G	A	TP	+/-	PIM	PP	SH	GW	GT	S	PCT
1	0	0	0	0	0	0	0	0	0	2	0.0

1996-97 statistics:

GP	G	A	TP	+/-	PIM	PP	SH	GW	GT	S	PCT
5	0	0	0	0	2	0	0	0	0	2	0.0

1997-98 statistics:

GP	G	A	TP	+/-	PIM	PP	SH	GW	GT	S	PCT
27	5	6	11	0	15	0	0	1	1	27	18.5

1998-99 statistics:

GP	G	A	TP	+/-	PIM	PP	SH	GW	GT	S	PCT
72	7	24	31	+11	61	1	0	1	0	123	5.7

PROJECTION
Varada has a 30-goal season in his future, but that future could be another three seasons away yet. Power forwards take awhile to develop, and in the meantime, an increase to 10 to 15 goals should be expected next season.

LAST SEASON
Second NHL season. Missed 10 games with sprained ankle.

THE FINESSE GAME
Varada is the closest thing the Sabres have to a power forward, but he has yet to demonstrate the kind of scoring touch that the role demands. He has been learning the game as a defensive winger on Michael Peca's line. When he is on, he plays with such intensity and reckless abandon that by the end of the game his face is cut and scraped, as if he had been attacked by crazed weasels.

Varada has excellent size and great hands. He is wonderful with the puck, an excellent stickhandler. He can also make plays, though his future is as a scorer. He has a good wrist and slap shot. He needs to be an involved player and not stay on the perimeter. He has a passion for scoring and drives to the net for his best chances. He handles himself well in traffic. He is a solidly balanced skater and an effective forechecker.

THE PHYSICAL GAME
Varada is thick: thick arms, thick legs, thick thighs. He is much more powerful than he looks. He gives the Sabres some desperately needed size on the right side, but he needs to play like a power forward every night. He can be gritty and hard to play against.

The biggest knock on Varada, as it is with many young players, is his intensity level. If he brings his game up every night, he will be a budding star. There is plenty of room on this team for anyone who can put the puck in the net.

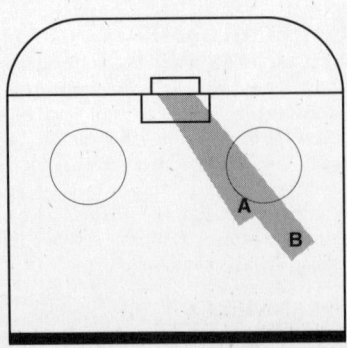

DIXON WARD

Yrs. of NHL service: 7
Born: Leduc, Alta.; Sept. 23, 1968
Position: left wing
Height: 6-0
Weight: 200
Uniform no.: 15
Shoots: right

Career statistics:

GP	G	A	TP	PIM
395	79	107	186	323

1995-96 statistics:

GP	G	A	TP	+/-	PIM	PP	SH	GW	GT	S	PCT
8	2	2	4	+4	6	0	0	1	0	12	16.7

1996-97 statistics:

GP	G	A	TP	+/-	PIM	PP	SH	GW	GT	S	PCT
79	13	32	45	+17	36	1	2	4	0	93	14.0

1997-98 statistics:

GP	G	A	TP	+/-	PIM	PP	SH	GW	GT	S	PCT
71	10	13	23	+23	42	0	2	3	1	99	10.1

1998-99 statistics:

GP	G	A	TP	+/-	PIM	PP	SH	GW	GT	S	PCT
78	20	24	44	+10	44	2	1	4	1	101	19.8

LAST SEASON

Led team in shooting percentage. Tied for third on team in goals. Third on team in game-winning goals. Missed two games with bruised sternum.

THE FINESSE GAME

Ward is a powerful skater with good anticipation and he can put on a quick burst of speed. His work along the boards and in front of the net is consistent and effective. He has good hands to take advantage of whatever opportunities are created from his efforts. He has a good shot from the top of the slot and also drives to the net to follow up his shot.

Ward is alert defensively and is a good penalty killer. He isn't overly creative, but he can handle second-unit power-play shifts. He has good enough hockey sense to play in almost any situation.

Ward scored a lot of big goals at key times last season for the Sabres.

THE PHYSICAL GAME

Ward has average size but he uses his body willingly. He plays the game with enthusiasm and finishes his checks.

THE INTANGIBLES

Ward is a nifty two-way forward who nearly disappeared off the NHL radar screen a few years ago, but he has made the most of his second chance with the Sabres.

PROJECTION

Ward is a feisty, intelligent player who could chip in another 20 goals for the Sabres.

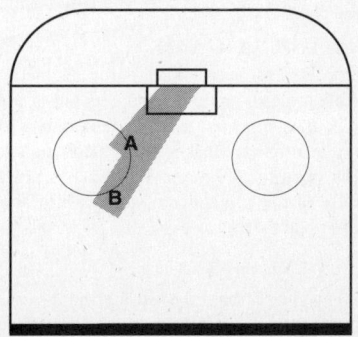

RHETT WARRENER

Yrs. of NHL service: 4
Born: Shaunavon, Sask.; Jan. 27, 1976
Position: left defense
Height: 6-1
Weight: 209
Uniform no.: 4
Shoots: left

Career statistics:

GP	G	A	TP	PIM
230	5	23	28	317

1995-96 statistics:

GP	G	A	TP	+/-	PIM	PP	SH	GW	GT	S	PCT
28	0	3	3	+4	46	0	0	0	0	19	0.0

1996-97 statistics:

GP	G	A	TP	+/-	PIM	PP	SH	GW	GT	S	PCT
62	4	9	13	+20	88	1	0	1	0	58	6.9

1997-98 statistics:

GP	G	A	TP	+/-	PIM	PP	SH	GW	GT	S	PCT
79	0	4	4	-16	99	0	0	0	0	66	.0

1998-99 statistics:

GP	G	A	TP	+/-	PIM	PP	SH	GW	GT	S	PCT
61	1	7	8	+2	84	0	0	0	0	44	2.3

LAST SEASON

Acquired from Florida with fifth-round draft pick in 1999 for Mike Wilson, Mar. 23, 1999. Missed 12 games with strained groin.

THE FINESSE GAME

Warrener's game is heavily slanted to defense, which made his shift from Florida to Buffalo an extremely comfortable fit.

He has a foundation of good hockey sense, completed by his size and firm passing touch. Warrener plays a simple game, wins a lot of the one-on-one battles and sticks within his limitations. His defensive reads are quite good for a young player. He plays his position well and moves people out from in front of the net. He blocks shots, and he can start a quick transition with a breakout pass.

Warrener might struggle a bit with his foot speed. His turns and lateral movement are okay but he lacks quickness and acceleration, which hampers him from becoming a more effective two-way defenseman.

THE PHYSICAL GAME

Warrener likes the aggressive game. Sometimes he gets a little too rambunctious and gets out of position, but that is to be expected from a young player looking to make an impact. He's a solid hitter but doesn't make the open-ice splatters. Warrener is not a self-starter. He needs someone to stay on him about his conditioning and his effort.

THE INTANGIBLES

When Warrener is paired with a stay-at-home type like Jay McKee, he gets more involved in the attack. He can be the defensive partner, too, if he is teamed with a more offensive defenseman.

PROJECTION

Warrener instantly became one of the Sabres' top four defensemen, and while he has some growing up to do, he is on the right track. He won't win any Norris Trophies, but he can be a foundation defenseman who produces 20 points a year.

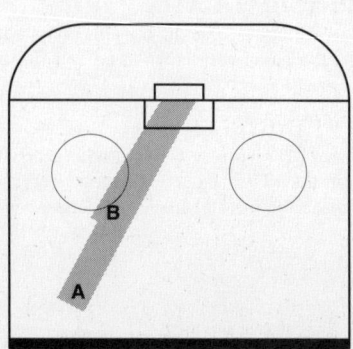

JASON WOOLLEY

Yrs. of NHL service: 7
Born: Toronto, Ont.; July 27, 1969
Position: right defense
Height: 6-1
Weight: 188
Uniform no.: 5
Shoots: left

Career statistics:

GP	G	A	TP	PIM
334	36	130	166	191

1995-96 statistics:

GP	G	A	TP	+/-	PIM	PP	SH	GW	GT	S	PCT
52	6	28	34	-9	32	3	0	0	0	98	6.1

1996-97 statistics:

GP	G	A	TP	+/-	PIM	PP	SH	GW	GT	S	PCT
60	6	30	36	+4	30	2	0	1	0	86	7.0

1997-98 statistics:

GP	G	A	TP	+/-	PIM	PP	SH	GW	GT	S	PCT
71	9	26	35	+8	35	3	0	2	1	129	7.0

1998-99 statistics:

GP	G	A	TP	+/-	PIM	PP	SH	GW	GT	S	PCT
80	10	33	43	+16	62	4	0	2	1	154	6.5

LAST SEASON

Led team defensemen in scoring. Career highs in goals, assists and points. Missed one game with flu. Missed one game with groin injury.

THE FINESSE GAME

Woolley is pretty much a one-way defenseman, but since that one way has never been at the elite level of a Paul Coffey, he was always considered something of a journeyman.

That changed last season when Woolley stepped up to make an impact on the Sabres' power play. He rushes the puck well and sets up from the point. He does not have a bullet shot but he gets it away quickly and keeps it low and on net. He has the vision to spot a man low for a pass.

Woolley is mobile but doesn't possess blazing speed. He can lug the puck or make an outlet pass.

THE PHYSICAL GAME

Woolley uses his finesse skills in his defense. He has good size but isn't an intimidating physical presence.

THE INTANGIBLES

Woolley had a career year and astoundingly tied for the team lead in playoff scoring.

PROJECTION

Woolley has elevated his game and will score in the 40-point range.

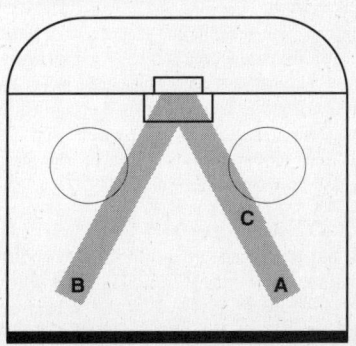

ALEXEI ZHITNIK

Yrs. of NHL service: 7
Born: Kiev, Ukraine; Oct. 10, 1972
Position: left defense
Height: 5-11
Weight: 204
Uniform no.: 44
Shoots: left

Career statistics:

GP	G	A	TP	PIM
500	63	200	263	593

1995-96 statistics:

GP	G	A	TP	+/-	PIM	PP	SH	GW	GT	S	PCT
80	6	30	36	-25	58	5	0	0	0	193	3.1

1996-97 statistics:

GP	G	A	TP	+/-	PIM	PP	SH	GW	GT	S	PCT
80	7	28	35	+10	95	3	1	0	1	170	4.1

1997-98 statistics:

GP	G	A	TP	+/-	PIM	PP	SH	GW	GT	S	PCT
78	15	30	45	+19	102	2	3	3	2	191	7.9

1998-99 statistics:

GP	G	A	TP	+/-	PIM	PP	SH	GW	GT	S	PCT
81	7	26	33	-6	96	3	1	2	0	185	3.8

LAST SEASON

Third on team in shots. Missed one game with bruised chest.

THE FINESSE GAME

Zhitnik has shored up some of the weaker points of his game, developing into a solid all-around defenseman who could be a top four on almost any team in the league. Being able to work with Buffalo assistant coach Mike Ramsey has helped him progress.

Zhitnik has a bowlegged skating style that ex-coach Barry Melrose once compared to Bobby Orr's. Zhitnik is no Orr, but he was born with skates on. He has speed, acceleration and lateral mobility.

Zhitnik plays the right point on the power play to open up his forehand for the one-timer. And he likes to rush the puck and shoots well off the fly. He needs to develop his lateral movement better, to use all of the blueline and stop his shots from getting blocked. He has a good, hard shot, and he keeps it low for deflections in front.

A player who sees the ice well and is a good playmaker, Zhitnik can snap a long, strong headman pass or feather a short pass on a give-and-go. He can also grab the puck and skate it out of danger. He plays a smarter game now and is less of a defensive liability. He still likes to think about going on the attack and will occasionally make the risky play.

THE PHYSICAL GAME

Zhitnik has paid close attention to his conditioning. Now that he is in better shape he is more willing and able to play a more physical style. Where he once made rather wild checks, he now knows when to step up for the hit. He plays sensibly and doesn't take bad penalties. His lower-body strength is impressive. He can really unload on some checks, as he did on Brett Hull in the playoffs. Zhitnik takes pride in his game and competes hard most nights.

THE INTANGIBLES

Dominik Hasek is still the best defenseman on the Sabres, but Zhitnik is an underrated member of the club's defense corps. We haven't see his best yet.

PROJECTION

Zhitnik gets prime ice time and should produce in the 45- to 50- point range.

CALGARY FLAMES

Players' Statistics 1998-99

POS.	NO.	PLAYER	GP	G	A	PTS	+/-	PIM	PP	SH	GW	GT	S	PCT
L	16	CORY STILLMAN	76	27	30	57	7	38	9	3	5	1	175	15.4
D	6	PHIL HOUSLEY	79	11	43	54	14	52	4		1		193	5.7
R	8	VALERI BURE	80	26	27	53	0	22	7		4		260	10.0
C	12	JAROME IGINLA	82	28	23	51	1	58	7		4	1	211	13.3
C	21	ANDREW CASSELS	70	12	25	37	-12	18	4	1	3		97	12.4
D	53	DEREK MORRIS	71	7	27	34	4	73	3		2	2	150	4.7
L	20	RENE CORBET	73	13	18	31	1	68	3		1		127	10.2
C	11	JEFF SHANTZ	76	13	17	30	14	44	1	1	3		82	15.9
C	24	JASON WIEMER	78	8	13	21	-12	177	1		1		128	6.3
C	23	*CLARKE WILM	78	10	8	18	11	53	2	2			94	10.6
R	62	ANDREI NAZAROV	62	7	9	16	-4	73			2	1	71	9.9
D	55	STEVE SMITH	69	1	14	15	3	80					42	2.4
C	18	STEVE DUBINSKY	62	4	10	14	-7	14		2			70	5.7
D	32	CALE HULSE	73	3	9	12	-8	117					83	3.6
C	17	HNAT DOMENICHELLI	23	5	5	10	-4	11	3				45	11.1
D	27	TODD SIMPSON	73	2	8	10	18	151					52	3.8
R	42	ED WARD	68	3	5	8	-4	67					56	5.4
D	3	*DENIS GAUTHIER	55	3	4	7	3	68					40	7.5
L	25	DAVE ROCHE	36	3	3	6	-1	44	1		2		30	10.0
D	5	TOMMY ALBELIN	60	1	5	6	-11	8					54	1.9
L	28	BOB BASSEN	41	1	2	3	-13	35					47	2.1
R	33	GREG PANKEWICZ	18		3	3	0	20					10	
R	26	TOM CHORSKE	26		3	3	-8	8					44	
C	15	*MARTIN ST. LOUIS	13	1	1	2	-2	10					14	7.1
G	40	FRED BRATHWAITE	28		2	2	0	2						
C	26	*ERIC LANDRY	3		1	1	1						1	
D	19	CHRIS O'SULLIVAN	10		1	1	-1	2					10	
G	30	*TYLER MOSS	11		1	1	0							
D	38	ERIC CHARRON	12		1	1	-6	14					9	
G	47	*J GIGUERE	15		1	1	0	4						
R	44	*RICO FATA	20		1	1	0	4					13	
G	31	KEN WREGGET	27		1	1	0	8						
D	29	*WADE BELAK	31		1	1	1	94					7	
D	33	*LEE SOROCHAN	2				-3						5	
D	22	*ROCKY THOMPSON	3				0	25						
G	1	*TYRONE GARNER	3				0							
G	35	ANDREI TREFILOV	5				0							

GP = games played; G = goals; A = assists; PTS = points; +/- = goals-for minus goals-against while player is on ice; PIM = penalties in minutes; PP = power-play goals; SH = shorthanded goals; GW = game-winning goals; GT = game-tying goals; S = no. of shots; PCT = percentage of goals to shots; * = rookie

TOMMY ALBELIN

Yrs. of NHL service: 12
Born: Stockholm, Sweden; May 21, 1964
Position: defense
Height: 6-1
Weight: 190
Uniform no.: 5
Shoots: left

Career statistics:

GP	G	A	TP	PIM
674	36	168	204	367

1995-96 statistics:

GP	G	A	TP	+/-	PIM	PP	SH	GW	GT	S	PCT
73	1	13	14	+1	18	0	0	0	0	121	0.8

1996-97 statistics:

GP	G	A	TP	+/-	PIM	PP	SH	GW	GT	S	PCT
72	4	11	15	8-	14	2	0	0	0	103	3.9

1997-98 statistics:

GP	G	A	TP	+/-	PIM	PP	SH	GW	GT	S	PCT
69	2	17	19	+9	32	1	0	2	0	88	2.3

1998-99 statistics:

GP	G	A	TP	+/-	PIM	PP	SH	GW	GT	S	PCT
60	1	5	6	-11	8	0	0	0	0	54	1.9

LAST SEASON
Missed six games with groin injury. Missed 16 games due to coach's decision.

THE FINESSE GAME
Albelin is a strong but not quick skater, though he is agile enough to be used as a checking forward in a pinch. He is fluid, with a big, loping stride that covers a lot of ground with little wasted motion. He skates backwards well and keeps his body positioned to break up passes. He can quickly turn an interception into a breakout pass, as he sees his options well and doesn't panic with the puck.

Albelin doesn't like to carry the puck; he prefers to use his teammates, but he can lug it if necessary. He has good hand skills for handling the puck if he goes in deep, though he usually stays at the tops of the circle (unless, of course, he is playing forward).

Albelin isn't a great power-play quarterback because his shot is not overpowering, nor does it always get through to the net. He is a smart penalty killer and in recent years has settled more and more into a defensive role.

THE PHYSICAL GAME
Albelin gets good drive from his powerful legs to take his man out along the boards, but he's not a big open-ice hitter. He won't be intimidated and he's slow to rile, which is unpopular with coaches who would prefer more emotion.

THE INTANGIBLES
As one of the few veterans on a very young Flames defense, Albelin is invaluable because of his patience and steady play. Nothing Albelin does leaves you thinking, "Fabulous!" But he is versatile enough to play forward or defense, or play the right or left side on D. He can complement nearly any kind of player. He is like a utility infielder in baseball. He may not have his own niche, but he can fill a lot of cracks in a team.

PROJECTION
Albelin will get 15 to 20 points playing an increasingly modest offensive role.

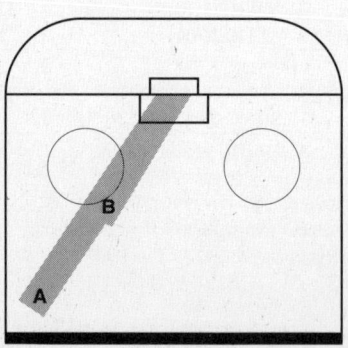

VALERI BURE

Yrs. of NHL service: 4
Born: Moscow, Russia; June 13, 1974
Position: right wing
Height: 5-10
Weight: 168
Uniform no.: 8
Shoots: right

Career statistics:

GP	G	A	TP	PIM
311	77	95	172	97

1995-96 statistics:

GP	G	A	TP	+/-	PIM	PP	SH	GW	GT	S	PCT
77	22	20	42	+10	28	5	0	1	2	143	15.4

1996-97 statistics:

GP	G	A	TP	+/-	PIM	PP	SH	GW	GT	S	PCT
64	14	21	35	+4	6	4	0	2	1	131	10.7

1997-98 statistics:

GP	G	A	TP	+/-	PIM	PP	SH	GW	GT	S	PCT
66	12	26	38	-5	35	2	0	2	0	179	6.7

1998-99 statistics:

GP	G	A	TP	+/-	PIM	PP	SH	GW	GT	S	PCT
80	26	27	53	0	22	7	0	4	0	260	10.0

LAST SEASON

Led team in shots. Tied for second on team in power-play goals and game-winning goals. Third on team in goals, points and shooting percentage. Tied for third on team in assists. Career highs in goals, assists and points. Missed two games with concussion.

THE FINESSE GAME

Although he is not as lightning-fast as big brother Pavel, Valeri does have his own distinct qualities, which might be appreciated more if he had a different last name. He has a great sense of anticipation and wants the puck every time he's on the ice. And he can make things happen, though he sometimes tries to force the action rather than let the game flow naturally. He gets carried away in his pursuit of the puck and gets caught out of position, whereas if he just showed patience the puck would come to him.

Bure works well down low on the power play, but will also switch off and drop back to the point. He is gaining confidence in his shot and scoring ability, and is very tough to defend against one-on-one.

He has good hands to go along with his speed and seems to get a shot on goal or a scoring chance on every shift. He is smart and creative, and can make plays as well as finish.

THE PHYSICAL GAME

Bure is strong for his size and last season was more willing to pay the price. He has to keep a little grit in his game to succeed.

THE INTANGIBLES

Bure was a third-line player in Montreal who needed to be a top six forward. He earned that job and the respect of coach Brian Sutter, who is not that easy to impress. Bure's always had the knack. He either found the right guy to push him or decided it was time to push himself.

PROJECTION

Bure should be ready to take the next step to be a consistent 25- to 30-goal scorer.

RENE CORBET

Yrs. of NHL service: 4
Born: Victoriaville, Que.; June 25, 1973
Position: left wing
Height: 6-0
Weight: 187
Uniform no.: 20
Shoots: left

Career statistics:

GP	G	A	TP	PIM
267	45	55	100	303

1995-96 statistics:

GP	G	A	TP	+/-	PIM	PP	SH	GW	GT	S	PCT
33	3	6	9	+10	33	0	0	0	0	35	8.6

1996-97 statistics:

GP	G	A	TP	+/-	PIM	PP	SH	GW	GT	S	PCT
76	12	15	27	+14	67	1	0	3	1	128	9.4

1997-98 statistics:

GP	G	A	TP	+/-	PIM	PP	SH	GW	GT	S	PCT
68	16	12	28	+8	133	4	0	4	2	117	13.7

1998-99 statistics:

GP	G	A	TP	+/-	PIM	PP	SH	GW	GT	S	PCT
73	13	18	31	+1	68	3	0	1	0	127	10.2

PROJECTION

Corbet scored five goals in 20 games since the move to Calgary. He can score 15 to 20 goals as a role player with the Flames.

LAST SEASON

Acquired from Colorado with Wade Belak, Robyn Regehr and a conditional draft pick for Theo Fleury and Chris Dingman, Feb. 28, 1999. Missed two games with groin injury.

THE FINESSE GAME

Corbet had a tough go getting ice time because he wasn't in the same elite class as teammates Joe Sakic and Peter Forsberg, but he is getting more use in Calgary. He has solid NHL credentials as a defensively responsible forward, who also has some offensive upside.

He has a terrific shot with a great release. He was a scoring champion in junior (QMJHL) and tore it up pretty good in the AHL, so he has confidence in his ability to find the net.

Corbet's defensive work has improved, as has his skating. As a young player, he hired Olympic speed skater Gaetan Boucher as a coach. Corbet has quick acceleration, and carrying the puck doesn't slow him down.

THE PHYSICAL GAME

Corbet is of average height but a little on the light side. He actually looks somewhat fragile, since he tends to work in the high-traffic areas and gets bounced around. He has added a little grit to his game.

THE INTANGIBLES

Corbet can play on the third line in Calgary as a winger and handle some second-unit power-play shifts.

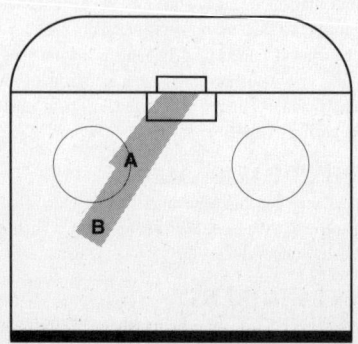

HNAT DOMENICHELLI

Yrs. of NHL service: 2
Born: Edmonton, Alberta; Feb. 17, 1976
Position: centre/left wing
Height: 6-0
Weight: 175
Uniform no.: 17
Shoots: left

Career statistics:

GP	G	A	TP	PIM
77	17	15	32	26

1996-97 statistics:

GP	G	A	TP	+/-	PIM	PP	SH	GW	GT	S	PCT
23	3	3	6	-3	9	1	0	0	0	30	10.0

1997-98 statistics:

GP	G	A	TP	+/-	PIM	PP	SH	GW	GT	S	PCT
31	9	7	16	+4	6	1	0	1	2	70	12.9

1998-99 statistics:

GP	G	A	TP	+/-	PIM	PP	SH	GW	GT	S	PCT
23	5	5	10	-4	11	3	0	0	0	45	11.1

LAST SEASON

Second NHL season. Appeared in 51 games with Saint John (AHL), scoring 25-21 — 46.

THE FINESSE GAME

Domenichelli's size is a big drawback. He's of average height but very, very slender and easy to knock off the puck. But he is quick enough to jump in and out of holes and he has great hands and a good shot.

His best asset is his hockey sense, and he can play centre or wing hands. He is a creative playmaker with good vision, but won't pass up a good shot if he has it. Domenichelli saw a lot of power-play time towards the end of last season and needs to earn his way onto the top unit this year, where he can make an impact.

He is a good skater with quickness and agility, but doesn't possess real breakaway speed.

THE PHYSICAL GAME

Domenichelli tries, but he's just not going to win one-on-one battles. He has strength more than size, but doesn't yet seem to have the appetite for battling in the high-traffic areas. Another smallish guy who is no longer in Calgary, Theo Fleury, excelled because he did pay the price, and Domenichelli must learn to do the same.

THE INTANGIBLES

The Flames acquired Domenichelli largely because he was Jarome Iginla's linemate in junior; they would like to recapture some of that old Kamloops magic. Although this thinking doesn't always result in great results at the NHL level (see Pat Falloon-Ray Whitney), the offense-starved Flames can't be blamed for trying. Domenichelli is done with the minor league/major league shuffle. He has to be ready to stick.

PROJECTION

Domenichelli could be a 25/25 man (that's goals and points) — if he plays on one of the Flames' top two forward lines.

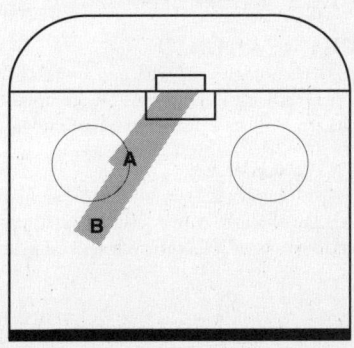

STEVE DUBINSKY

Yrs. of NHL service: 6
Born: Montreal, Quebec; July 9, 1970
Position: centre
Height: 6-0
Weight: 190
Uniform no.: 18
Shoots: left

Career statistics:

GP	G	A	TP	PIM
235	13	32	45	109

1995-96 statistics:

GP	G	A	TP	+/-	PIM	PP	SH	GW	GT	S	PCT
43	2	3	5	+3	14	0	0	0	0	33	6.1

1996-97 statistics:

GP	G	A	TP	+/-	PIM	PP	SH	GW	GT	S	PCT
5	0	0	0	+2	0	0	0	0	0	4	0.0

1997-98 statistics:

GP	G	A	TP	+/-	PIM	PP	SH	GW	GT	S	PCT
82	5	13	18	-6	57	0	1	0	0	112	4.5

1998-99 statistics:

GP	G	A	TP	+/-	PIM	PP	SH	GW	GT	S	PCT
62	4	10	14	-7	14	0	2	0	0	70	5.7

PROJECTION

Dubinsky will never have great offensive numbers, but given increased playing time should produce 10 to 15 goals.

LAST SEASON

Acquired from Chicago with Jeff Shantz for Marty McInnis, Jamie Allison and Erik Andersson, Oct. 27, 1998. Missed nine games with knee injury. Missed two games with hand injury.

THE FINESSE GAME

Whatever Dubinsky can bring to a team is the output from his skating and forechecking. He doesn't get many points, but he brings a lot of energy to every shift. He creates turnovers, yet doesn't have the great hands or instincts to make much happen offensively when he does. He needs to play with opportunistic linemates who can feed off the mistakes he churns up when he harries opposing defensemen.

Dubinsky is also a top face-off man. His future probably lies in a checking-line role. He's smart and dedicated enough to play that style if it means keeping an NHL job, and his skating allows him to go up against other teams' fleet forwards. He is versatile and can play centre or left wing.

THE PHYSICAL GAME

Dubinsky isn't big but he is wiry and enthusiastic, and he gets a crash-bang shift going to wake up his team. He has become rather valuable in a modest way.

THE INTANGIBLES

Coaches like his positive attitude, and Dubinsky will be given a fair shake to earn continued ice time on the third and fourth lines. His problem will be getting his shifts.

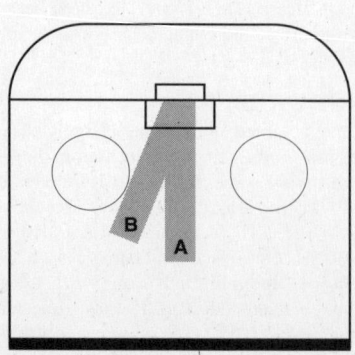

DENIS GAUTHIER

Yrs. of NHL service: 1
Born: Montreal, Que.; Oct. 1, 1976
Position: left defense
Height: 6-2
Weight: 195
Uniform no.: 3
Shoots: left

Career statistics:

GP	G	A	TP	PIM
65	3	4	7	84

1997-98 statistics:

GP	G	A	TP	+/-	PIM	PP	SH	GW	GT	S	PCT
10	0	0	0	-5	16	0	0	0	0	3	0.0

1998-99 statistics:

GP	G	A	TP	+/-	PIM	PP	SH	GW	GT	S	PCT
55	3	4	7	+3	68	0	0	0	0	40	7.5

LAST SEASON

First NHL season. Appeared in 16 games with Saint John (AHL), scoring 0-2 — 2.

THE FINESSE GAME

Gauthier is going to be one of those defensemen you have to watch every night in order to appreciate him, because he is a stay-at-home type whose numbers will never be gaudy.

A good skater, he is strong and balanced on his skates. His lower-body strength and speed power his hitting. He is capable of hitting in open ice because of his mobility.

Gauthier won't take off on many rushes. He prefers to skate the puck out of his zone or make the outlet pass or the bank off the boards.

THE PHYSICAL GAME

Gauthier is a powerful, fierce hitter. Anyone on the receiving end of a Gauthier check knows he has been rocked. One of his role models is Dave Manson. Another is Scott Stevens. Ouch.

Gauthier is in excellent physical condition. He can handle a lot of ice time.

THE INTANGIBLES

Gauthier has a good chance to stick as a fifth defenseman for now and will quickly move up the depth chart as he gains more experience.

PROJECTION

Gauthier will have minor point totals and major penalties.

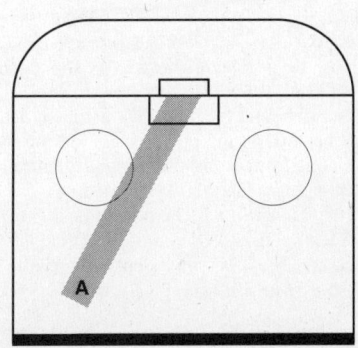

PHIL HOUSLEY

Yrs. of NHL service: 17
Born: St. Paul, Minn.; Mar. 9, 1964
Position: right defense
Height: 5-10
Weight: 185
Uniform no.: 6
Shoots: left

Career statistics:
GP	G	A	TP	PIM
1210	302	773	1075	714

1995-96 statistics:
GP	G	A	TP	+/-	PIM	PP	SH	GW	GT	S	PCT
81	17	51	68	-6	30	6	0	1	0	205	8.3

1996-97 statistics:
GP	G	A	TP	+/-	PIM	PP	SH	GW	GT	S	PCT
77	11	29	40	-10	24	3	1	2	0	167	6.6

1997-98 statistics:
GP	G	A	TP	+/-	PIM	PP	SH	GW	GT	S	PCT
64	6	25	31	-10	24	4	1	0	0	116	5.2

1998-99 statistics:
GP	G	A	TP	+/-	PIM	PP	SH	GW	GT	S	PCT
79	11	43	54	+14	52	4	0	1	0	193	5.7

LAST SEASON
Led team in assists. Led team defensemen and second on team in points. Sixth among NHL defensemen in points. Tied for second on team in plus-minus. Third on team in shots. Missed three games with abdominal injury.

THE FINESSE GAME
Among the best-skating defensemen in the NHL, Housley, like Paul Coffey, takes a lot of heat for his defensive shortcomings. A better team could afford to use Housley as a pure power-play specialist, but in Calgary he shoulders the full workload.

Housley's skating fuels his game. He can accelerate in a heartbeat and his edges are deep and secure, giving him the ability to avoid checks with gravity-defying moves. Everything he does is at high tempo. He intimidates with his speed and skills, forcing defenders back and opening up more ice for himself and his teammates. He can continue to be an effective offensive weapon because he has barely lost a step over the years.

Housley has an excellent grasp of the ice. On the power play he is a huge threat. His shots are low, quick and heavy, either beating the goalie outright or setting up a rebound for the forwards down deep. He also sets up low on the power play, and he doesn't mind shooting from an impossible angle that can catch a goalie napping on the short side.

Housley has great anticipation and can break up a rush by picking off a pass and turning the play into a counterattack. He is equally adept with a long headman or short cup-and-saucer pass over a defender's stick.

THE PHYSICAL GAME
Housley is not the least bit physical. He is not strong enough to shove anyone out of the zone, so his defensive play is based on his pursuit of the puck. He is likely to avoid traffic areas unless he feels he can get in and out with the puck quickly enough.

Success on a rush, even a two-on-one, against Housley is not guaranteed, since he is a good enough skater to position himself properly and break up the play with his stick.

THE INTANGIBLES
Housley has found a comfortable niche with the Flames and their core of young defensemen.

PROJECTION
Housley nearly doubled the output we expected for him last season. He should score 50 points again given his apparent comfort level with the team and the West.

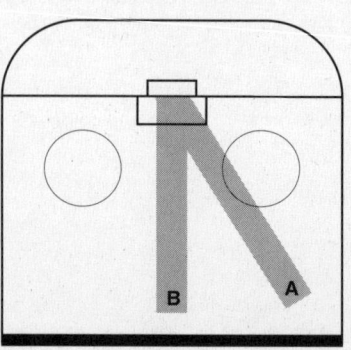

CALE HULSE

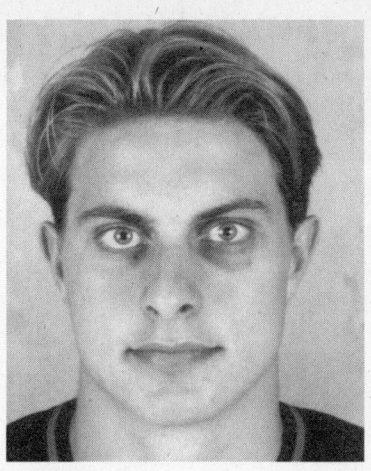

Yrs. of NHL service: 3
Born: Edmonton, Alberta; Nov. 10, 1973
Position: right defense
Height: 6-3
Weight: 210
Uniform no.: 32
Shoots: right

Career statistics:

GP	G	A	TP	PIM
226	9	37	46	397

1995-96 statistics:

GP	G	A	TP	+/-	PIM	PP	SH	GW	GT	S	PCT
11	0	0	0	+1	20	0	0	0	0	9	0.0

1996-97 statistics:

GP	G	A	TP	+/-	PIM	PP	SH	GW	GT	S	PCT
63	1	6	7	-2	91	0	1	0	0	58	1.7

1997-98 statistics:

GP	G	A	TP	+/-	PIM	PP	SH	GW	GT	S	PCT
79	5	22	27	+1	169	1	1	0	0	117	4.3

1998-99 statistics:

GP	G	A	TP	+/-	PIM	PP	SH	GW	GT	S	PCT
73	3	9	12	-8	117	0	0	0	0	83	3.6

LAST SEASON

Third on team in penalty minutes. Missed six games with abdominal injury.

THE FINESSE GAME

Hulse has worked hard over the past few seasons to improve what was one of his most glaring weaknesses, his slow skating. He works diligently during the off-season on speed drills, and the result is that Hulse is probably one of the fastest straight-ahead skaters on the Flames. This has helped him improve his puck movement; he can now lug the puck out of the zone if needed.

Hulse is a better-than-average skater. He has a long, strong stride with good balance. Like many defensemen schooled in the Devils system, he is sound in the defensive aspects of the game but is reluctant to get involved even modestly in the attack.

Hulse has a decent shot from the point. Once he comprehends he can actually cross the far blueline once in awhile, he could work on a second power-play unit with more experience, though his future is as a defensive mainstay. Intelligent and steady, he may also develop into a key penalty killer.

THE PHYSICAL GAME

Hulse is tough, an outstanding fighter who doesn't go looking for trouble but won't back down from a challenge, either. He isn't mean by nature. He understands, however, that he has a job in the NHL because of his physical ability. You have to pay the price against him in front of the net or in the corners. His limited skating prevents him from being a strong open-ice hitter, but he plays well positionally.

THE INTANGIBLES

Hulse's chief flaw continues to be a lack of intensity. He will play well for three games and then take a night off. This is one of those players who needs a kick in the butt now and then. He usually responds.

PROJECTION

Hulse graduated to becoming one of Calgary's top four defensemen in his second season. He will never have gaudy numbers, but he can score 20 points and be a physical complement to a more offensive partner.

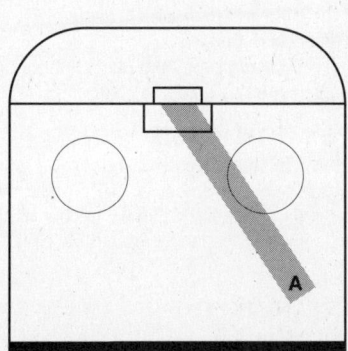

JAROME IGINLA

Yrs. of NHL service: 3
Born: Edmonton, Alberta; July 1, 1977
Position: right wing
Height: 6-1
Weight: 193
Uniform no.: 12
Shoots: right

Career statistics:

GP	G	A	TP	PIM
234	62	71	133	124

1996-97 statistics:

GP	G	A	TP	+/-	PIM	PP	SH	GW	GT	S	PCT
82	21	29	50	-4	37	8	1	3	0	169	12.4

1997-98 statistics:

GP	G	A	TP	+/-	PIM	PP	SH	GW	GT	S	PCT
70	13	19	32	-10	29	0	2	1	0	154	8.4

1998-99 statistics:

GP	G	A	TP	+/-	PIM	PP	SH	GW	GT	S	PCT
82	28	23	51	+1	58	7	0	4	1	211	13.3

LAST SEASON

Led team in goals with career high. Second on team in shots. Tied for second on team in power-play goals and game-winning goals. Only Flame to appear in all 82 games.

THE FINESSE GAME

Iginla doesn't have great speed but he's smart and energetic. What puts him ahead of other 22-year-olds is his defensive play, which he developed first in junior. The scoring touch came later (the reverse of how most young players develop), and it's one of the reasons why Iginla was able to step into the NHL with such success. He has a veteran's understanding of the game, though he may never be a great scorer and will have to work hard for his goals. Throw out Adam Graves's one 50-goal season and you are looking at Iginla's future, if he can bring up his level of consistency.

Iginla does his best work in the corners and in front of the net. He is strong and doesn't mind the trench warfare. In fact, he thrives on it. He plays well in all three zones — a power forward who plays both ends of the rink, and there aren't many NHL players who fit that description.

Iginla is versatile enough to play all three forward positions, but is best suited as a centre.

THE PHYSICAL GAME

Gritty, powerful and aggressive, Iginla will take a hit to make a play but, even better, will initiate the hits. He has a mean streak and will have to control himself while he is proving his mettle around the NHL; a fine line to walk.

THE INTANGIBLES

Iginla still has trouble with his consistency, but it's quite a natural learning phase for a young player, and Iginla was better at it last season than in his sophomore year. A coach has to find the right buttons on Iginla and know when to push them and when to lay off without damaging his confidence.

PROJECTION

Iginla will score 25 to 30 goals again this season.

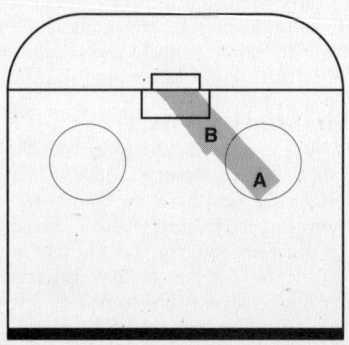

DEREK MORRIS

Yrs. of NHL service: 2
Born: Edmonton, Alberta; Aug. 24, 1978
Position: right defense
Height: 6-0
Weight: 200
Uniform no.: 53
Shoots: right

Career statistics:

GP	G	A	TP	PIM
153	16	47	63	161

1997-98 statistics:

GP	G	A	TP	+/-	PIM	PP	SH	GW	GT	S	PCT
82	9	20	29	+1	88	5	1	1	1	120	7.5

1998-99 statistics:

GP	G	A	TP	+/-	PIM	PP	SH	GW	GT	S	PCT
71	7	27	34	+4	73	3	0	2	2	150	4.7

LAST SEASON

Second NHL season. Led team defensemen in points for second consecutive season. Tied for third on team in assists. Missed 10 games with shoulder injury.

THE FINESSE GAME

Morris possesses all high-level skills, but what truly sets him apart from the other defensemen of his generation is his brain. For a young player, he has a real grasp for the technical part of the game. He is a thinker and understands hockey thoroughly. He is already a steady performer and the Flames' top defenseman — at age 21.

Morris plays in all game situations, on the first penalty-killing unit and on the first power-play unit. He is a fan of Paul Coffey, and he possesses the kind of skating that brings to mind his role model. Morris is better defensively, however, and will become a better all-around player. He handles the puck well in an up-tempo game and may develop into the kind of defenseman who can take over a game.

Morris needs only to improve his one-on-one play and get a little stronger to continue on the path to becoming an elite defenseman.

THE PHYSICAL GAME

Morris has improved his stamina but will always need to maintain a serious strength and conditioning program. He is not overly big, but he is very strong. You can't run him over and he gets a lot of power from his legs for hitting and moving people out of the front of the net.

THE INTANGIBLES

Morris is very well-liked by his teammates and coaches for his desire to learn and willingness to listen. He is a blue chipper who is going to start earning the attention he deserves. Playing with Housley will help him develop his offensive skills even more.

PROJECTION

As Morris continues to mature he will gain confidence in his offensive game without losing anything from his defense. There is a 60-point season in his not-too-distant future.

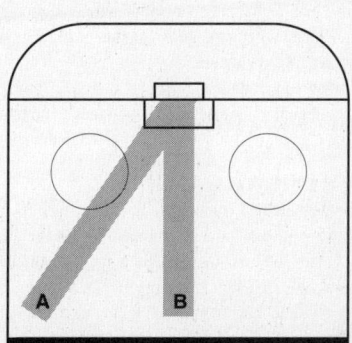

ANDREI NAZAROV

Yrs. of NHL service: 5
Born: Chelyabinsk, Russia; May 22, 1974
Position: right wing
Height: 6-5
Weight: 230
Uniform no.: 62
Shoots: right

Career statistics:

GP	G	A	TP	PIM
245	31	38	69	621

1995-96 statistics:

GP	G	A	TP	+/-	PIM	PP	SH	GW	GT	S	PCT
42	7	7	14	-15	62	2	0	1	0	55	12.7

1996-97 statistics:

GP	G	A	TP	+/-	PIM	PP	SH	GW	GT	S	PCT
60	12	15	27	-4	222	1	0	1	0	116	10.3

1997-98 statistics:

GP	G	A	TP	+/-	PIM	PP	SH	GW	GT	S	PCT
54	2	2	4	-13	170	0	0	0	0	50	4.0

1998-99 statistics:

GP	G	A	TP	+/-	PIM	PP	SH	GW	GT	S	PCT
62	7	9	16	-4	73	0	0	2	1	71	9.9

LAST SEASON

Acquired from Tampa Bay for Michael Nylander, Jan. 19, 1999. Missed seven games due to suspension for high-sticking incident.

THE FINESSE GAME

Nazarov isn't overly creative with the puck, but with his size does he have to be? This giant has decent hand skills around the net, though he does have some trouble fishing out loose pucks from his feet in goalmouth scrambles, presumably because his head is so far from the ice it's tough to see.

The biggest improvement in Nazarov's game is in his skating. He can handle second-line and second-unit power-play time with assurance. He is not at his best handling the puck for long and is insecure if forced to rush with it; defenders have a relatively easy time stripping it from him because the puck is so far from his feet. He plops himself in front of the net on power plays and creates a wall that is nearly impossible for the goalie to see around. Nazarov needs to play with linemates who will get him the puck. He has decent hands and can shoot.

Nazarov is smart and understands the game well. He is aware of his limitations and won't try to do too much. He has an obvious love for the game.

THE PHYSICAL GAME

Nazarov was asked by coach Brian Sutter to cut out the stupid penalties and be more of a hockey player. Nazarov already has enough of a reputation to scare off all but the most fearless opponents. It was the lazy penalties that he had to cut back on, and for the most part, he has.

Nazarov is rattlesnake-mean and he has a short fuse. One scout says of him, "He's sick." He will fight anyone, and his long reach makes him tough for even some of the league's best fighters to cope with. He will protect his teammates. Anyone checked by Nazarov does not get back into the play quickly. He could star in a lot of very ugly highlight tapes.

THE INTANGIBLES

Nazarov is still raw and rough. Calgary used him as a third-line winger and he was able to get some ice time.

PROJECTION

If he can earn enough minutes, Nazarov could produce 30 points and 150 penalty minutes. By all means, take him if your pool includes PIM.

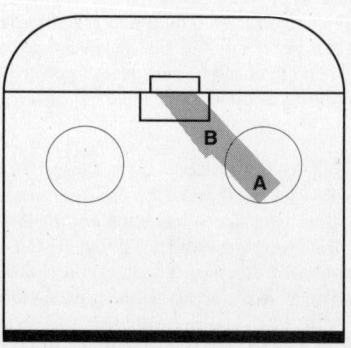

MARC SAVARD

Yrs. of NHL service: 2
Born: Ottawa, Ont.; July 17, 1977
Position: centre
Height: 5-11
Weight: 185
Uniform no.: 10
Shoots: left

Career statistics:

GP	G	A	TP	PIM
98	10	41	51	42

1997-98 statistics:

GP	G	A	TP	+/-	PIM	PP	SH	GW	GT	S	PCT
28	1	5	6	-4	4	0	0	0	0	32	3.1

1998-99 statistics:

GP	G	A	TP	+/-	PIM	PP	SH	GW	GT	S	PCT
70	9	36	45	-7	38	4	0	1	0	116	7.8

LAST SEASON

Acquired from N.Y. Rangers with a 1999 first-round draft pick for Jan Hlavac, a 1999 first-round draft pick, and a 1999 third-round draft, June 26, 1999. Second NHL season. Third on Rangers in assists. Appeared in nine games for Hartford (AHL), scoring 3-10 — 13.

THE FINESSE GAME

Savard grew up as a Wayne Gretzky fan, and was awed by playing on the same team with the Great One. Savard's size and skating will prevent him from ever playing a game like Gretzky's, however, though he is an intelligent playmaker whose points will always be heavier in assists than goals. He doesn't have a very quick or accurate shot.

Savard really has a knack for delivering the puck to a guy who can do something dangerous with it, instead of passing just because he's tired of carrying it. He possesses good vision and instincts for the power play. A left-handed shot, he favours the attacking right-wing corner/half-boards for his "office." He will not even try one-on-one moves. He's a distributor.

Savard is not very quick off the mark and his speed is about average. He is pretty sturdy though, which makes his dives all the more comical. He is one of the most blatant actors in the game. It's a wonder NHL referees have not cottoned onto his act, because he's really terrible at it and still draws a huge share of penalties.

THE PHYSICAL GAME

Savard won't touch a soul with an intentional, clean hit. He is sneaky mean, however, and if he can, he'll pay you back. He is small and is targeted by a lot of bigger guys, so that's how he has learned to defend himself. He absorbs some pretty stiff hits without being the least bit intimidated. He is actually quite strong for his size. His defensive play will be limited to stick-checking.

THE INTANGIBLES

Savard is not a blue-chip prospect. He will probably be a number two centre in Calgary by default.

PROJECTION

Depending on his ice time, Savard could score from 30 to 40 points, with an emphasis on assists.

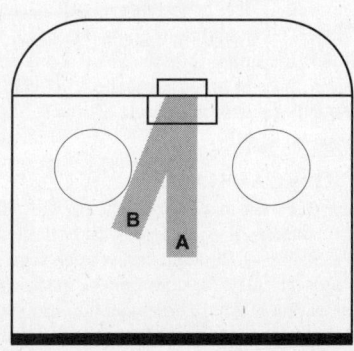

JEFF SHANTZ

Yrs. of NHL service: 6
Born: Duchess, Alta; Oct. 10, 1973
Position: centre
Height: 6-1
Weight: 185
Uniform no.: 11
Shoots: right

Career statistics:

GP	G	A	TP	PIM
381	48	97	145	195

1995-96 statistics:

GP	G	A	TP	+/-	PIM	PP	SH	GW	GT	S	PCT
78	6	14	20	+12	24	1	2	0	0	72	8.3

1996-97 statistics:

GP	G	A	TP	+/-	PIM	PP	SH	GW	GT	S	PCT
69	9	21	30	+11	28	0	1	1	0	86	10.5

1997-98 statistics:

GP	G	A	TP	+/-	PIM	PP	SH	GW	GT	S	PCT
61	11	20	31	0	36	1	2	2	0	69	15.9

1998-99 statistics:

GP	G	A	TP	+/-	PIM	PP	SH	GW	GT	S	PCT
76	13	17	30	+14	44	1	1	3	0	82	15.9

LAST SEASON

Acquired from Chicago with Steve Dubinsky for Marty McInnis, Jamie Allison and Erik Andersson, Oct. 27, 1999. Led team in shooting percentage for second consecutive season. Tied for second on team in plus-minus. Missed four games with shoulder injury. Missed two games with concussion.

THE FINESSE GAME

Shantz doesn't excel in many technical areas, but he possesses good hockey sense and good skills, though his game is heavily defense-oriented. Ideally, he is a number three forward (he can play centre or right wing). If injuries arise, however, he can fill in on a more offensive-minded line.

A good skater, Shantz is smooth in his turns with average quickness. He handles the puck well and sees his passing options. He won't be forced into many bad passes — he prefers to eat the puck rather than toss it away.

Shantz has a decent touch around the net but doesn't score many highlight goals. He has a heavy shot without the quick release. Most of his scoring comes from in tight off his forechecking efforts — perfect for a dump-and-chase style of attack. Shantz is very good on face-offs.

THE PHYSICAL GAME

The major question mark about Shantz was whether he was big and strong enough to prosper in the NHL, but he checks pretty hard and seems to be acquiring a taste for physical play. He doesn't have much size and will need to keep up his conditioning and strength work. He's gritty, doesn't take bad penalties and plays hard but clean.

THE INTANGIBLES

Shantz is developing into a solid two-way forward.

PROJECTION

A healthy Shantz could reach 40 points this season.

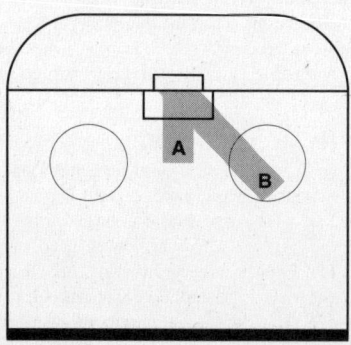

TODD SIMPSON

Yrs. of NHL service: 3
Born: Edmonton, Alta.; May 28, 1973
Position: left defense
Height: 6-3
Weight: 215
Uniform no.: 27
Shoots: left

Career statistics:

GP	G	A	TP	PIM
214	4	26	29	500

1995-96 statistics:

GP	G	A	TP	+/-	PIM	PP	SH	GW	GT	S	PCT
6	0	0	0	0	32	0	0	0	0	3	0.0

1996-97 statistics:

GP	G	A	TP	+/-	PIM	PP	SH	GW	GT	S	PCT
82	1	13	14	-14	208	0	0	1	0	85	1.2

1997-98 statistics:

GP	G	A	TP	+/-	PIM	PP	SH	GW	GT	S	PCT
53	1	5	6	-10	109	0	0	1	0	51	2.0

1998-99 statistics:

GP	G	A	TP	+/-	PIM	PP	SH	GW	GT	S	PCT
73	2	8	10	+18	151	0	0	0	0	52	3.8

LAST SEASON

Led team in plus-minus. Second on team in penalty minutes. Missed nine games with concussion.

THE FINESSE GAME

Simpson is a poor man's Mark Tinordi. He is a defensive defenseman, one who made his initial reputation by fighting, just as Tinordi did. But Simpson has also worked his tail off to become a solid defenseman.

Although he still has a lot to learn, Simpson is coachable and will play intelligent position defense, making attackers pay the price for coming into his area of the ice. His stickhandling and shooting skills are average. His skating is just about NHL level and could stand some improvement.

What sets Simpson apart (besides his size), though, is his determination. He won't give up on a play in any zone. He kills penalties on the first unit and blocks shots. He's smart enough to make some plays offensively, though he doesn't have much confidence in that part of the game. Put it this way: when he decides to go to the net, there aren't too many people who can stop him.

Simpson is highly competitive and will go out against other teams' top lines night after night, despite a gap in skills.

THE PHYSICAL GAME

Simpson is unafraid of big guys and big names. If he has to hit Pavel Bure and Peter Forsberg, he'll hit them. If he has to drop his gloves against a goon, he'll do that, too. He loves a good tilt, but he has learned to take a quality player with him on most nights.

THE INTANGIBLES

Simpson is captain material, a leader and a player who fights for his teammates on the ice and goes out of his way to make them feel a part of the Flames off the ice. He's a tremendous heart-and-soul player, a team guy and a tough guy.

PROJECTION

Simpson's value can't be measured in points. It's unlikely he'll score more than 20 points.

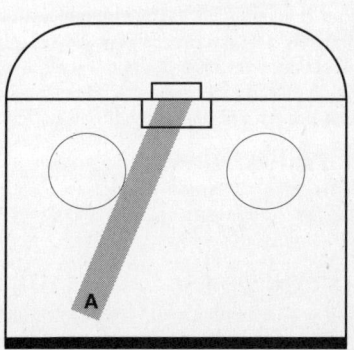

CORY STILLMAN

Yrs. of NHL service: 4
Born: Peterborough, Ont.; Dec. 20, 1970
Position: centre
Height: 6-0
Weight: 180
Uniform no.: 16
Shoots: left

Career statistics:

GP	G	A	TP	PIM
290	76	93	169	135

1995-96 statistics:

GP	G	A	TP	+/-	PIM	PP	SH	GW	GT	S	PCT
74	16	19	35	-5	41	4	1	3	0	132	12.1

1996-97 statistics:

GP	G	A	TP	+/-	PIM	PP	SH	GW	GT	S	PCT
58	6	20	26	-6	14	2	0	0	0	112	5.4

1997-98 statistics:

GP	G	A	TP	+/-	PIM	PP	SH	GW	GT	S	PCT
72	27	22	49	-9	40	9	4	1	1	178	15.2

1998-99 statistics:

GP	G	A	TP	+/-	PIM	PP	SH	GW	GT	S	PCT
76	27	30	57	+7	38	9	3	5	1	175	15.4

LAST SEASON

Led team in points with career high. Led team in power-play goals, game-winning goals and short-handed goals. Second on team in goals, matching career high. Second on team in assists with career high. Missed five games with knee injury.

THE FINESSE GAME

A natural centre, Stillman brings a centre's playmaking ability to the wing. He's intelligent and has sound hockey instincts, but doesn't have that extra notch of speed an elite player at the NHL level needs. Since he's not very big (which hampers his odds of playing centre), he needs every advantage he can get.

Stillman has a good enough point shot to be used on the power play. He can beat a goalie with his shot from just inside the blueline. He has good hands and a keen understanding of the game. He possesses great patience and puckhandling skills, and is efficient in small areas. He has the potential to become an effective player if he is supported by gifted forwards.

Stillman is a goal scorer, and possesses a kind of selfishness that is intrinsic to good scorers. He wants the puck, and he wants to shoot it. He creates off the forecheck, not with his size but with his anticipation.

THE PHYSICAL GAME

Stillman is thick and sturdy enough to absorb some hard hits. He is not overly aggressive but will protect the puck.

THE INTANGIBLES

Stillman came to training camp two seasons ago without a contract and has worked hard to get and keep a job. It took a long time for the Flames to have as much faith in Stillman as he has in himself.

PROJECTION

Stillman can be a consistent 30-goal scorer.

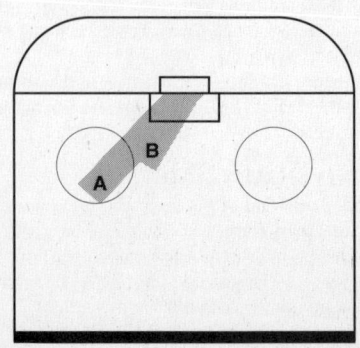

JASON WIEMER

Yrs. of NHL service: 5
Born: Kimberley, B.C.; Apr. 14, 1976
Position: left wing
Height: 6-1
Weight: 215
Uniform no.: 24
Shoots: left

Career statistics:

GP	G	A	TP	PIM
322	39	41	90	596

1995-96 statistics:

GP	G	A	TP	+/-	PIM	PP	SH	GW	GT	S	PCT
66	9	9	18	-9	81	4	0	1	0	89	10.1

1996-97 statistics:

GP	G	A	TP	+/-	PIM	PP	SH	GW	GT	S	PCT
63	9	5	14	-13	134	2	0	0	0	103	8.7

1997-98 statistics:

GP	G	A	TP	+/-	PIM	PP	SH	GW	GT	S	PCT
79	12	10	22	-10	160	3	0	2	0	122	9.8

1998-99 statistics:

GP	G	A	TP	+/-	PIM	PP	SH	GW	GT	S	PCT
78	8	13	21	-12	177	1	0	1	0	128	6.3

LAST SEASON

Led team in penalty minutes. Missed three games with hand injury.

THE FINESSE GAME

Wiemer has the build and the touch for standing in the traffic areas and picking pucks out of scrambles. He also has a touch of mean that merits him some room and time to execute. His release has improved, but he does not have an NHL-calibre shot that will make him a power forward who can post big numbers. Wiemer has to grind out his goals.

Wiemer does the dirty work in the corners, but needs to play with some skilled linemates because he doesn't have the finesse or creativity to make any pretty plays. He can finish off what someone with more vision opens up for him, however.

Wiemer's major shortcoming is his skating (though his foot speed is improving), but it is not enough of a problem to prevent him from becoming an impact player. He is very strong and well balanced for work around the net. He relies on his strength and his reach.

THE PHYSICAL GAME

Wiemer relishes body contact and will usually initiate checks to intimidate. He is very strong and can hit to hurt. He drives to the net and pushes defenders back, and he isn't shy about dropping his gloves or raising his elbows. He functions as the grinder on a line, since he will scrap along the boards and in the corners for the puck. He can complement almost any linemate.

The next step is for Wiemer to do this on a consistent basis. Power forwards are useless when they take a night off. Wiemer is exactly the kind of player the Flames need.

THE INTANGIBLES

Life got a lot easier for Wiemer once coaches accepted the idea that he was not going to be the next Cam Neely. Wiemer had to learn his job and he had to be pushed, and playing him as a checking-line centre accomplished both. He was rushed into the NHL before he was ready. Some of the damage has been undone by the confidence he rebuilt in his game last season.

PROJECTION

Wiemer will probably score in the 15-goal range as he continues in his third-line role and picks up some second-unit power-play time.

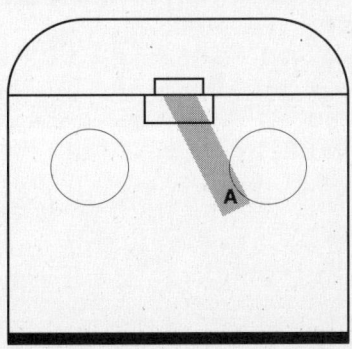

CLARKE WILM

Yrs. of NHL service: 1
Born: Central Butte, Sask.; Oct. 24, 1976
Position: centre
Height: 6-0
Weight: 202
Uniform no.: 23
Shoots: left

Career statistics:

GP	G	A	TP	PIM
78	10	8	18	53

1998-99 statistics:

GP	G	A	TP	+/-	PIM	PP	SH	GW	GT	S	PCT
78	10	8	18	+11	53	2	2	0	0	94	10.6

LAST SEASON
First NHL season. Missed two games with concussion. Missed two games due to coach's decision.

THE FINESSE GAME
Wilm has great hands — but he has to be right on the doorstep for his shot to be effective, because he doesn't have much velocity on it.

He can check adequately and can kill penalties on a second or third unit. His major weakness is his skating, which will have to improve in order for him to get more ice time, as he does not have many skills.

The few assets that Wilm has are accentuated by his effort.

THE PHYSICAL GAME
Wilm is tough but not a fighter. He stands in the traffic areas and takes his licks. He's basically a Saskatchewan farm kid who likes playing hockey a lot more than farming and will pay the price to hold an NHL job.

THE INTANGIBLES
Like his usual linemate, Steve Dubinsky, Wilm is an energy guy who is learning his trade on the fourth line. He doesn't have the skill to have much of a future elsewhere. But the Flames will use him in front of the net on a second power-play unit because of his uncanny short-range accuracy.

PROJECTION
Wilm will have trouble getting many shifts; 10 to 15 goals would be the best numbers to expect from him.

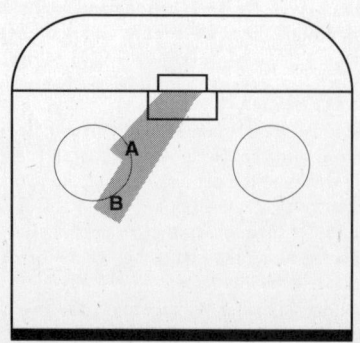

CAROLINA HURRICANES

Players' Statistics 1998-99

POS.	NO.	PLAYER	GP	G	A	PTS	+/-	PIM	PP	SH	GW	GT	S	PCT
C	55	KEITH PRIMEAU	78	30	32	62	8	75	9	1	5	1	178	16.9
R	24	SAMI KAPANEN	81	24	35	59	-1	10	5		7		254	9.4
R	26	RAY SHEPPARD	74	25	33	58	4	16	5		4	1	188	13.3
C	21	RON FRANCIS	82	21	31	52	-2	34	8		2	1	133	15.8
L	10	GARY ROBERTS	77	14	28	42	2	178	1	1	4		138	10.1
L	51	ANDREI KOVALENKO	74	19	21	40	-6	32	3		4	1	104	18.3
C	92	JEFF O'NEILL	75	16	15	31	3	66	4		2		121	13.2
L	23	MARTIN GELINAS	76	13	15	28	3	67			2	2	111	11.7
R	18	ROBERT KRON	75	9	16	25	-13	10	3	1	2		134	6.7
D	2	GLEN WESLEY	74	7	17	24	14	44			2	1	112	6.3
L	28	PAUL RANHEIM	78	9	10	19	4	39		2	1		67	13.4
R	11	KEVIN DINEEN	67	8	10	18	5	97			1		86	9.3
L	13	JON BATTAGLIA	60	7	11	18	7	22				2	52	13.5
C	44	KENT MANDERVILLE	81	5	11	16	9	38					71	7.0
D	4	NOLAN PRATT	61	1	14	15	15	95			1		46	2.2
D	77	PAUL COFFEY	54	2	12	14	-7	28	1				87	2.3
D	5	MAREK MALIK	52	2	9	11	-6	36	1				36	5.6
D	22	SEAN HILL	54		10	10	9	48					44	
D	7	CURTIS LESCHYSHYN	65	2	7	9	-1	50					35	5.7
D	3	STEVE CHIASSON	28	1	8	9	7	16	1				74	1.4
D	14	*STEVEN HALKO	20		3	3	5	24					6	
D	33	DAVE KARPA	33		2	2	1	55					21	
D	46	*MIKE RUCINSKI	15		1	1	1	8					8	
C	15	*BYRON RITCHIE	3					0						
R	45	*SHANE WILLIS	7				-2						1	
C	31	*CRAIG MACDONALD	11				0						5	
G	37	TREVOR KIDD	25					0						
G	1	ARTURS IRBE	62					0	10					

GP = games played; G = goals; A = assists; PTS = points; +/- = goals-for minus goals-against while player is on ice; PIM = penalties in minutes; PP = power-play goals; SH = shorthanded goals; GW = game-winning goals; GT = game-tying goals; S = no. of shots; PCT = percentage of goals to shots; * = rookie

BATES BATTAGLIA

Yrs. of NHL service: 2
Born: Chicago, Illinois; Dec. 5, 1975
Position: left wing
Height: 6-2
Weight: 185
Uniform no.: 33
Shoots: left

Career statistics:

GP	G	A	TP	PIM
93	9	15	24	32

1997-98 statistics:

GP	G	A	TP	+/-	PIM	PP	SH	GW	GT	S	PCT
33	2	4	6	-1	10	0	0	1	0	21	9.5

1998-99 statistics:

GP	G	A	TP	+/-	PIM	PP	SH	GW	GT	S	PCT
60	7	11	18	+7	22	0	0	0	2	52	13.5

LAST SEASON

Second NHL season. Missed 22 games due to coach's decision.

THE FINESSE GAME

Battaglia had a hard time getting into the lineup last season after making such a splash in the second half of his rookie season. He is a very entertaining young forward who should recover from his sophomore setback.

Battaglia is a good skater and is strong on the puck. He has had to drill hard to perfect most of his skills, because he is not a natural — now he is making it look easy. His first strides are a bit sluggish, but he is a powerful skater once he gets moving.

He goes hard to the net to create his scoring chances. He moves the puck alertly and plays smart positional hockey. He won't gamble or try to do anything fancy with the puck, which makes it easy for other grinders to play with him. He has a good head for the game, and the heart, too.

Battaglia is versatile and can play all three forward positions. He is a natural centre but will probably be used on the wing. He is skilled enough to take an occasional spin on the first line with players like Keith Primeau and Sami Kapanen.

THE PHYSICAL GAME

Battaglia has good size and is willing to use it. He works hard and his enthusiasm alone will bug other players. A Chicago native, he grew up emulating Jeremy Roenick. He'll never have Roenick's scoring touch, but he'll bring the nonstop work ethic of a young Roenick every night.

THE INTANGIBLES

Battaglia has a solid, 10-year NHL future in store as a third-line forward. He'll bring energy to every shift. He made a big jump going from college to the NHL and he is still finding his niche.

PROJECTION

Battaglia was a fair scorer at the college level (Lake Superior State), but if he scores 10 to 15 goals a year in his checking role he'll be fulfilling his destiny. He needs a chance to play.

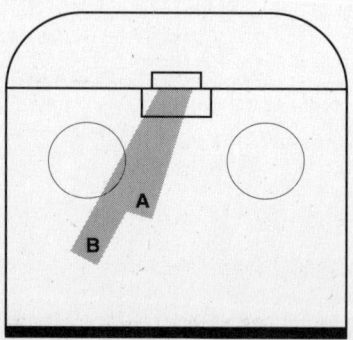

RON FRANCIS

Yrs. of NHL service: 18
Born: Sault Ste. Marie, Ont.; Mar. 1, 1963
Position: centre
Height: 6-2
Weight: 200
Uniform no.: 21
Shoots: left

Career statistics:

GP	G	A	TP	PIM
1329	449	1037	1486	867

1995-96 statistics:

GP	G	A	TP	+/-	PIM	PP	SH	GW	GT	S	PCT
77	27	92	119	+25	56	12	1	4	0	158	17.1

1996-97 statistics:

GP	G	A	TP	+/-	PIM	PP	SH	GW	GT	S	PCT
81	27	63	90	+7	20	10	1	2	0	183	14.8

1997-98 statistics:

GP	G	A	TP	+/-	PIM	PP	SH	GW	GT	S	PCT
81	25	62	87	+12	20	7	0	5	2	189	13.2

1998-99 statistics:

GP	G	A	TP	+/-	PIM	PP	SH	GW	GT	S	PCT
82	21	31	52	-2	34	8	0	2	1	133	15.8

LAST SEASON
Second on team in power-play goals. Led team in power-play points (18). Only Hurricane to appear in all 82 games.

THE FINESSE GAME
Francis could still put points on the board, but his value now is as a two-way centre with an emphasis on defense. Technically, he is a choppy skater who gets where he has to be with a minimum amount of style. His understanding of the game is key because he has great awareness of his positioning. He gets loads of ice time, so he has learned to pace himself to conserve energy. There are few useless bursts of speed.

Francis is Dr. Draw. On rare nights when he is struggling with an opposing centre, he'll tinker with his changes in the neutral zone, then save what he has learned for a key draw deep in either zone. Just as a great scorer never shows a goalie the same move twice in a row, Francis never uses the same technique twice in succession. He has good hand-eye coordination and uses his body well at the dot. Few players win their draws as outright as Francis does on a consistent basis.

When he focusses on a defensive role, Francis has the vision to come out of a scramble into an attacking rush. He anticipates passes, blocks shots, then springs an odd-man breakout with a smart play.

Francis doesn't have a screamingly hard shot, nor is he a flashy player. He works from the centre of the ice, between the circles, and has a quick release on a one-timer. He can kill penalties or work the point on the power play with equal effectiveness. He complements any kind of player.

THE PHYSICAL GAME
Not a big, imposing hitter, Francis will still use his body to get the job done. He will bump and grind and go into the trenches. Back on defense, he can function as a third defenseman; on offense, you will find him going into the corners or heading for the front of the net for tips and rebounds. He keeps himself in great shape. Francis was healthy all year, but suffered a sprained ankle in the playoffs, when the 'Canes needed him most.

THE INTANGIBLES
People look at a four-year, $20.8-million free agent and expect points to match, but Francis isn't playing with Mario Lemieux and Jaromir Jagr anymore. Francis is no longer a number one centre, and he doesn't have to be in Carolina, since he has the powerful Keith Primeau in front of him. Primeau will learn more about the all-around game by playing with Francis, and Francis will give the 'Canes a nifty one-two punch up the middle.

PROJECTION
Expect Francis's production to continue to decline slowly, to around 50 points.

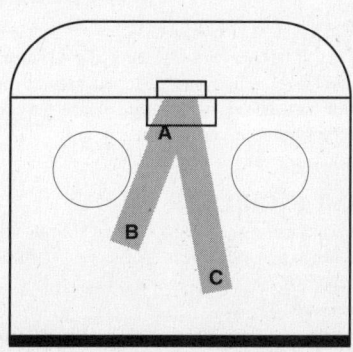

MARTIN GELINAS

Yrs. of NHL service: 10
Born: Shawinigan, Que.; June 5, 1970
Position: left wing
Height: 5-11
Weight: 195
Uniform no.: 23
Shoots: left

Career statistics:
GP	G	A	TP	PIM
663	181	176	357	434

1995-96 statistics:
GP	G	A	TP	+/-	PIM	PP	SH	GW	GT	S	PCT
81	30	26	56	+8	59	3	4	5	1	181	16.6

1996-97 statistics:
GP	G	A	TP	+/-	PIM	PP	SH	GW	GT	S	PCT
74	35	33	68	+6	42	6	1	3	1	177	19.8

1997-98 statistics:
GP	G	A	TP	+/-	PIM	PP	SH	GW	GT	S	PCT
64	16	18	34	-5	40	3	2	5	0	147	10.9

1998-99 statistics:
GP	G	A	TP	+/-	PIM	PP	SH	GW	GT	S	PCT
76	13	15	28	+3	67	0	0	2	2	111	11.7

PROJECTION
Gelinas lacks the talent to score more than 20 goals, but that kind of production from a third-liner, combined with his energy and work ethic, make him a valuable role player.

LAST SEASON
Missed four games with quadriceps strain. Missed two games with bruised thigh.

THE FINESSE GAME
Gelinas plays a grinding game on the dump-and-chase. Much of his scoring is generated by his forechecking, with the majority of his goals tap-ins from about five feet out. He is strong along the boards and in front of the net. He is not a natural scorer, but he has good instincts and works hard for his chances. He is a good penalty killer.

Gelinas is ideally a third-line winger, but he can play fill-in stints on better lines in case of injuries. His hockey sense and puckhandling prevent him from blossoming in a bigger role.

Gelinas is an energetic player who provides momentum-changing shifts. He's not a goal scorer, though, and gets into trouble when he starts thinking and playing like one.

THE PHYSICAL GAME
Gelinas is a small player and seems to get himself into situations where he just gets flattened. He isn't intimidated, but he does get wiped out of the play and he needs to be smarter about jumping in and out of holes, paying the price only when necessary.

THE INTANGIBLES
Gelinas went through several scoring slumps with the 'Canes, but when he scores, he scores at important times: 12 of his 13 goals last season either tied a game or put his team ahead.

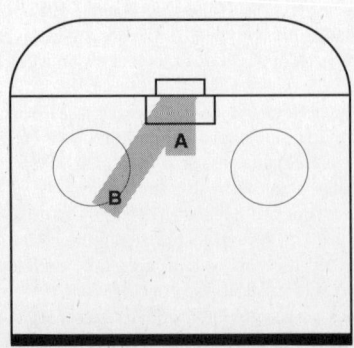

Carolina Hurricanes

SEAN HILL

Yrs. of NHL service: 7
Born: Duluth, Minn.; Feb. 14, 1970
Position: right defense
Height: 6-0
Weight: 195
Uniform no.: 22
Shoots: right

Career statistics:

GP	G	A	TP	PIM
338	18	70	88	362

1995-96 statistics:

GP	G	A	TP	+/-	PIM	PP	SH	GW	GT	S	PCT
80	7	14	21	-26	94	2	0	2	0	157	4.5

1996-97 statistics:

GP	G	A	TP	+/-	PIM	PP	SH	GW	GT	S	PCT
5	0	0	0	+1	4	0	0	0	0	9	0.0

1997-98 statistics:

GP	G	A	TP	+/-	PIM	PP	SH	GW	GT	S	PCT
55	1	6	7	-5	54	0	0	0	0	53	1.9

1998-99 statistics:

GP	G	A	TP	+/-	PIM	PP	SH	GW	GT	S	PCT
54	0	10	10	+9	48	0	0	0	0	44	.0

LAST SEASON

Tied for third on team in plus-minus. Missed 16 games with broken ankle. Missed six games with abdominal strain. Missed four games with sprained ankle. Missed two games with fractured cheekbone.

THE FINESSE GAME

A good skater, Hill is agile, strong and balanced, if not overly fast. He can skate the puck out of danger or make a smart first pass. He learned defense in the Montreal system but has since evolved into more of a specialty-team player.

Hill has a good point shot and good offensive sense. He likes to carry the puck and start things off a rush or he will jump into the play. He can handle power-play time but is not exceptional. He is more suited to a second-unit role, though that ice time will fall off on an improved team. He has not played for many quality teams in the past few seasons (Anaheim, Ottawa, Carolina). It would be interesting to see how he could perform with a better defensive team if he got the chance.

Hill's best quality is his competitiveness. He will hack and whack at puck carriers like an annoying terrier ripping and nipping your socks and ankles.

THE PHYSICAL GAME

For a smallish player, Hill gets his share of points, and he gets them by playing bigger than his size. He has a bit of a mean streak, and though he certainly can't overpower people, he is a solidly built player who doesn't get pushed around easily.

THE INTANGIBLES

Hill has had four serious injuries in the last three seasons: major reconstructive knee surgery in October, 1996; a broken leg in 1997-98; and last year a fractured ankle and a fractured face (from a puck) that required reconstructive surgery. That is the only red flag for an otherwise capable defenseman who could remain as a number five to six on most teams.

PROJECTION

A poor man's Al MacInnis, Hill brings a veteran's composure. He doesn't have elite skills, but he can kick in 25 points a season if he remains healthy. It's a big "if" the way things have been going for Hill.

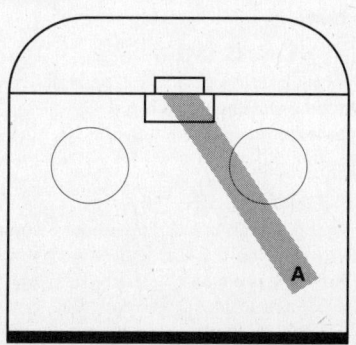

ARTURS IRBE

Yrs. of NHL service: 7
Born: Riga, Latvia; Feb. 2, 1967
Position: goaltender
Height: 5-8
Weight: 175
Uniform no.: 1
Catches: left

Career statistics:

GP	MIN	GA	SO	GAA	A	PIM
321	17893	909	19	3.05	5	54

1995-96 statistics:

GP	MIN	GAA	W	L	T	SO	GA	S	SAPCT	PIM
22	1112	4.49	4	12	4	0	85	607	.860	4

1996-97 statistics:

GP	MIN	GAA	W	L	T	SO	GA	S	SAPCT	PIM
35	1965	2.69	17	12	3	3	88	825	.825	8

1997-98 statistics:

GP	MIN	GAA	W	L	T	SO	GA	S	SAPCT	PIM
41	1999	2.73	14	11	6	2	91	982	.982	2

1998-99 statistics:

GP	MIN	GAA	W	L	T	SO	GA	S	SAPCT	PIM
62	3643	2.22	27	20	12	6	135	1753	.923	10

LAST SEASON

Tied for fourth in NHL in save percentage. Tied for fourth in NHL in shutouts with career best. Career best goals-against.

THE PHYSICAL GAME

If you didn't know Irbe was a goalie, you might guess he was a gymnast — he has that kind of slender, muscular build. And if Mary Lou Retton played goal, she would probably play it as Irbe does: diving, rolling, scrambling and sticking the landing. Irbe is so flexible that when he does a split, he doesn't have to use his stick to cover what little five-hole is left. His, er, cup, is right on the ice. Teams have to try to beat him high.

Irbe is unbelievably quick. He has great confidence in his abilities and will challenge shooters by coming out well beyond his crease.

Irbe needs to improve on his work outside the net. He doesn't move the puck well and gets caught while he's making decisions. He can get mixed up with his defensemen.

THE MENTAL GAME

Irbe's unusual style matches his personality. He is quite outgoing and unpredictable. It was a long stretch between number one goaltending jobs for Irbe, who is a mature competitor.

THE INTANGIBLES

Irbe arrived in Carolina's camp without a contract in 1998 and by spring the Hurricanes were unloading Trevor Kidd. He is not an elite goalie or one who will take the 'Canes to the next level, but apparently Carolina is content to make do with him for now.

Because of his age, size, and especially because of his active style, Irbe needs to be held to 60 starts a year.

PROJECTION

Irbe will be the number one goalie in Carolina and should record 25 wins.

SAMI KAPANEN

Yrs. of NHL service: 4
Born: Vantaa, Finland; June 14, 1973
Position: left wing
Height: 5-10
Weight: 170
Uniform no.: 24
Shoots: left

Career statistics:

GP	G	A	TP	PIM
242	68	88	156	34

1995-96 statistics:

GP	G	A	TP	+/-	PIM	PP	SH	GW	GT	S	PCT
35	5	4	9	0	6	0	0	0	0	46	10.9

1996-97 statistics:

GP	G	A	TP	+/-	PIM	PP	SH	GW	GT	S	PCT
45	13	12	25	+6	2	3	0	2	0	82	15.9

1997-98 statistics:

GP	G	A	TP	+/-	PIM	PP	SH	GW	GT	S	PCT
81	26	37	63	+9	16	4	0	5	0	190	13.7

1998-99 statistics:

GP	G	A	TP	+/-	PIM	PP	SH	GW	GT	S	PCT
81	24	35	59	-1	10	5	0	7	0	254	9.4

LAST SEASON

Led team in assists, game-winning goals and shots. Second on team in points. Third on team in goals. Tied for third on team in power-play goals. Missed one game with bruised knee.

THE FINESSE GAME

Kapanen is a small, skilled forward who is always moving. He handles the puck well while in motion, though like a lot of European forwards he tends to hold onto the puck a tad too long. He will shoot on the fly, however, and has an NHL shot when he does release it. He has a fine wrist shot and he can score off the rush.

Kapanen has quickness, good balance, good strength, and he's smart. He makes few mistakes. He knows where to be on the ice and how to use big players as picks and screens. He sticks to the perimeter until he darts into holes. He takes care of his defensive assignments, and even though he's too small to body check, he is able to harrass opponents by lifting up a stick and swiping the puck. Kapanen is strong on the puck.

Kapanen uses a very short stick to keep the puck in close to his body. He might lose a little off his shot because of it, but he is able to create some terrific scoring chances with his passing because of his control. It also means defenders are forced to reach in for the puck.

THE PHYSICAL GAME

Kapanen plays without fear and draws a lot of penalties with his speed. He is lean without much muscle mass. He plays a spunky game and picks up the team on its quieter nights, because he sprints to the pucks and tries on every shift.

THE INTANGIBLES

Kapanen is a clone of Montreal's Saku Koivu, who gets much better press. Kapanen is Carolina's most consistent player, most dangerous player and most exciting player.

PROJECTION

With a little more depth to take some of the checking pressure off Kapanen, he could score 35 goals. Without it, 25 to 30 is his range.

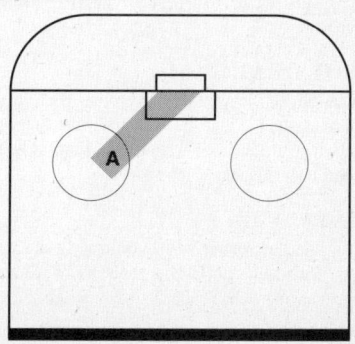

DAVE KARPA

Yrs. of NHL service: 6
Born: Regina, Sask.; May 7, 1971
Position: right defense
Height: 6-1
Weight: 202
Uniform no.: 33
Shoots: right

Career statistics:

GP	G	A	TP	PIM
356	12	58	70	1018

1995-96 statistics:

GP	G	A	TP	+/-	PIM	PP	SH	GW	GT	S	PCT
72	3	16	19	-3	270	0	1	1	0	62	4.8

1996-97 statistics:

GP	G	A	TP	+/-	PIM	PP	SH	GW	GT	S	PCT
69	2	11	13	+11	210	0	0	1	0	90	2.2

1997-98 statistics:

GP	G	A	TP	+/-	PIM	PP	SH	GW	GT	S	PCT
78	1	11	12	-3	217	0	0	0	0	64	1.6

1998-99 statistics:

GP	G	A	TP	+/-	PIM	PP	SH	GW	GT	S	PCT
33	0	2	2	+1	55	0	0	0	0	21	.0

PROJECTION

Over a full season, Karpa is a sure bet for 200 PIM.

LAST SEASON

Acquired from Anaheim with a fourth-round pick in 2000 for Stu Grimson and Kevin Haller, Aug. 11, 1998. Missed 41 games with torn knee ligaments. Missed eight games with bruised shoulder.

THE FINESSE GAME

Karpa is a grate defenseman. He plays an irritating, aggravating game. He usually gets a lot of minutes but injuries cut him down to half a season, and opponents were probably, well, grateful.

Karpa's skating is adequate for strength and balance, but he's on the slow side. He masks it well with proper positioning. His reputation helps him defensively, too. He plays hard, and anyone skating in on him will play it safe, go outside and just shoot or dump the puck. They know if they try to drive to the net on him he will make them pay the price with a check or a two-hander. It helps to have him paired with a more mobile partner.

Karpa has little interest in getting involved offensively.

THE PHYSICAL GAME

Karpa is a physical veteran who plays with a natural sneer on his face. He is highly competitive and aggressive. He will fight anyone and although he doesn't always win his fights, he is game.

THE INTANGIBLES

There are a lot of teams who would love a Karpa on their side. He stands up for his teammates, plays hard every night and makes people who wander into his area of the ice pay.

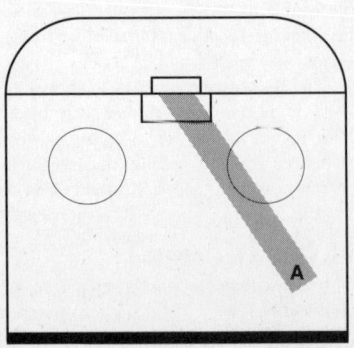

ANDREI KOVALENKO

Yrs. of NHL service: 7
Born: Balakovo, Russia; June 7, 1970
Position: right wing
Height: 5-10
Weight: 215
Uniform no.: 51
Shoots: left

Career statistics:

GP	G	A	TP	PIM
468	142	161	303	324

1995-96 statistics:

GP	G	A	TP	+/-	PIM	PP	SH	GW	GT	S	PCT
77	28	28	56	+20	49	6	0	6	1	131	21.4

1996-97 statistics:

GP	G	A	TP	+/-	PIM	PP	SH	GW	GT	S	PCT
74	32	27	59	-5	81	14	0	2	0	163	19.6

1997-98 statistics:

GP	G	A	TP	+/-	PIM	PP	SH	GW	GT	S	PCT
59	6	17	23	-14	28	1	0	2	1	89	6.7

1998-99 statistics:

GP	G	A	TP	+/-	PIM	PP	SH	GW	GT	S	PCT
74	19	21	40	-6	32	3	0	4	1	104	18.3

LAST SEASON

Acquired from Philadelphia for Adam Burt, Mar. 7, 1999. Acquired by Philadelphia from Edmonton for Alexandre Daigle, Jan. 29, 1999. Led team in shooting percentage.

THE FINESSE GAME

Kovalenko has the skills associated with many Russian forwards, but he also has a brisk, sometimes abrasive, style. When he is on his best game, he can play on a top line and make things happen. He is woefully inconsistent, however.

Kovalenko bustles right into traffic. He is an intelligent player who doesn't panic with the puck and is a natural on the power play. He doesn't hang onto the puck long but likes to make short give-and-go plays in the offensive zone. He always keeps his wheels in motion. He is an accurate shooter with a quick release on his wrist shot. He should shoot more, but like many Russian players he hates to take a low-percentage shot and would rather work to get into position for a better one.

Defensive work is his downfall, but he has become more conscientious and makes fewer high-risk plays.

THE PHYSICAL GAME

Kovalenko's nickname is the "Little Tank," because of his chunky build. Checks often bounce right off him because he is so solid. He can be tough around the net and in the offensive corners. He will take some punishment in front of the net on the power play, and gets a lot of goals off the rebounds.

THE INTANGIBLES

Three teams in a year isn't the best way to build confidence. Kovalenko scored 6-6 — 12 in 18 games with Carolina, and then went into the, uh, tank, with no goals in four playoff games.

PROJECTION

Kovalenko will get a fresh start in Carolina. He has the skills to score 30 goals, but he hasn't done it since 1996-97.

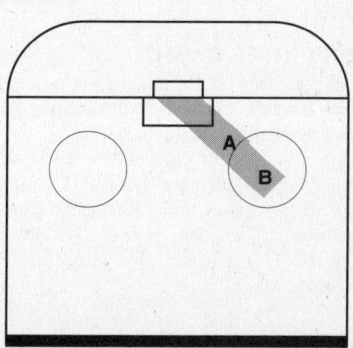

CURTIS LESCHYSHYN

Yrs. of NHL service: 11
Born: Thompson, Man.; Sept. 21, 1969
Position: left defense
Height: 6-1
Weight: 205
Uniform no.: 7
Shoots: left

Career statistics:

GP	G	A	TP	PIM
731	41	135	176	636

1995-96 statistics:

GP	G	A	TP	+/-	PIM	PP	SH	GW	GT	S	PCT
77	4	15	19	+32	73	0	0	1	0	76	5.3

1996-97 statistics:

GP	G	A	TP	+/-	PIM	PP	SH	GW	GT	S	PCT
77	4	18	22	-18	38	1	1	1	0	102	3.9

1997-98 statistics:

GP	G	A	TP	+/-	PIM	PP	SH	GW	GT	S	PCT
73	2	10	12	-2	45	1	0	1	0	53	3.8

1998-99 statistics:

GP	G	A	TP	+/-	PIM	PP	SH	GW	GT	S	PCT
65	2	7	9	-1	50	0	0	0	0	35	5.7

LAST SEASON

Missed 12 games with groin injuries. Missed three games with back spasms. Missed one game with bruised sternum.

THE FINESSE GAME

Leschyshyn has average skills for a defensive defenseman. He has very slow feet, though he is balanced and strong in a containment game. His passes are soft, but he has a rather low panic point and will try to lug it out himself — not the best option given his limited skills.

Leschyshyn has a nice point shot. It's low and accurate and he gets it away quickly, but it's not elite enough to warrant any significant power-play time. He knows the importance of getting the shot on target, though. He'd rather take a little velocity off the puck to make sure his aim is true.

Leschyshyn is not overly creative and has become more defense-oriented in the past season. His reads are excellent.

THE PHYSICAL GAME

Leschyshyn is very fit. He made a successful comeback from a potentially career-threatening knee injury, a challenge that is more mental than physical. He provides consistency and strong defensive-zone coverage, though he's rather passive and doesn't use his size well. But he does make efficient take-outs to eliminate his man, and doesn't run around the ice trying to pound people. He competes harder in some games than others.

THE INTANGIBLES

Leschshyn is a number five or six defenseman on a thin Carolina team. With the loss of Steve Chiasson, his experience will be an asset.

PROJECTION

Leschyshyn will only score in the 15- to 20-point range.

MAREK MALIK

Yrs. of NHL service: 2
Born: Ostrava, Czech.; June 24, 1975
Position: left defense
Height: 6-5
Weight: 190
Uniform no.: 5
Shoots: left

Career statistics:
GP	G	A	TP	PIM
107	3	15	18	90

1995-96 statistics:
GP	G	A	TP	+/-	PIM	PP	SH	GW	GT	S	PCT
7	0	0	0	-3	4	0	0	0	0	2	0.0

1996-97 statistics:
GP	G	A	TP	+/-	PIM	PP	SH	GW	GT	S	PCT
47	1	5	6	+5	50	0	0	1	0	33	3.0

1997-98 statistics:
Did not play in NHL

1998-99 statistics:
GP	G	A	TP	+/-	PIM	PP	SH	GW	GT	S	PCT
52	2	9	11	-6	36	1	0	0	0	36	5.6

PROJECTION
Malik needs to win a steady job first. If he does, he could chip in 20 points.

LAST SEASON
Appeared in 21 games with New Haven (AHL), scoring 2-8 — 10.

THE FINESSE GAME
Malik has very good potential because of his high skill level in all areas. He is a good skater for his towering size, though he is a straight-legged skater and not quick. He uses his range mostly as a defensive tool and is not much involved in the attack.

Malik is poised with the puck. He is a good passer and playmaker, and moves the puck out of his own end quickly. He won't try to do too much himself but will utilize his teammates well. He's big, but does a lot of little things well, which makes him a solid defensive player. He limits his offensive contributions to a shot from the point. However, he may yet develop better skills as a playmaker.

THE PHYSICAL GAME
Tall but weedy, Malik needs to fill out more to be able to handle some of the NHL's big boys one-on-one. Like Kjell Samuelsson, he takes up a lot of space with his arms and stick, and is more of an octopus-type defenseman than a solid hitter. He is strong in front of his net. He has some aggressiveness in him but needs to compete every night on a more consistent level.

THE INTANGIBLES
Malik has had a lot of chances but lingers on the bubble. He has split three of the last four seasons between the NHL and the minors and spent the entire 1997-98 season in Sweden. He's 24 now, and it's time to step up, if he's going to.

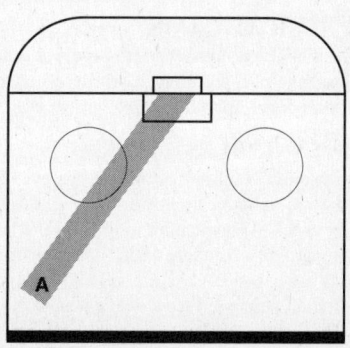

JEFF O'NEILL

Yrs. of NHL service: 4
Born: Richmond Hill, Ont.; Feb. 23, 1976
Position: centre
Height: 6-0
Weight: 190
Uniform no.: 92
Shoots: right

Career statistics:

GP	G	A	TP	PIM
286	57	70	127	213

1995-96 statistics:

GP	G	A	TP	+/-	PIM	PP	SH	GW	GT	S	PCT
65	8	19	27	-3	40	1	0	1	0	65	12.3

1996-97 statistics:

GP	G	A	TP	+/-	PIM	PP	SH	GW	GT	S	PCT
72	14	16	30	-24	40	2	1	2	0	101	13.9

1997-98 statistics:

GP	G	A	TP	+/-	PIM	PP	SH	GW	GT	S	PCT
74	19	20	39	-8	67	7	1	4	1	114	16.7

1998-99 statistics:

GP	G	A	TP	+/-	PIM	PP	SH	GW	GT	S	PCT
75	16	15	31	+3	66	4	0	2	0	121	13.2

LAST SEASON
Missed seven games with neck injury.

THE FINESSE GAME
To be a Pat LaFontaine — to whom O'Neill was often compared early in his career — a player needs all the tools. And except for his skating, O'Neill's intensity isn't good enough to place him among the top centres, though his skills are.

An excellent skater, with balance, speed, acceleration and quickness, he has a good sense of timing and is patient with his passes. He doesn't have a big-time release but he has a decent one-timer.

O'Neill likes to carry the puck down the left-wing boards to protect the puck, and with his speed he is able to blow by defensemen. He does not follow this move up by driving to the net. Defensively, he has to remind himself not to leave the zone before the puck does. He is often too anxious to counterattack before his team has control.

THE PHYSICAL GAME
O'Neill could always be in better shape. He is considered something of a soft player, whose effort and intensity don't come up to his skill level.

THE INTANGIBLES
The knock on O'Neill is that no one has ever looked better in a rookie game or in warmups — when he is not being checked or when nothing is on the line. He is showing progress, though, which keeps us from giving up on him. And if Carolina gets a big winger to play with him, you could see a whole new O'Neill this season. He seems satisfied to have an NHL job — not that tough to do in a league that just keeps expanding — but he has never shown the desire to take his game to the next level.

PROJECTION
O'Neill could provide 45 to 50 points in a second-line role. He has the untapped resources to do much more.

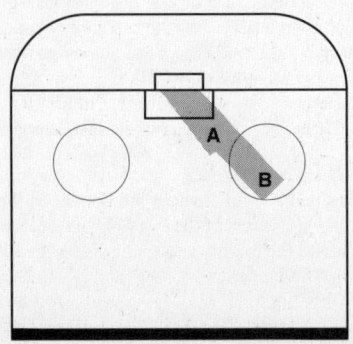

KEITH PRIMEAU

Yrs. of NHL service: 9
Born: Toronto, Ont.; Nov. 24, 1971
Position: centre
Height: 6-4
Weight: 210
Uniform no.: 55
Shoots: left

Career statistics:

GP	G	A	TP	PIM
597	179	229	406	1127

1995-96 statistics:

GP	G	A	TP	+/-	PIM	PP	SH	GW	GT	S	PCT
74	27	25	52	+19	168	6	2	7	0	150	18.0

1996-97 statistics:

GP	G	A	TP	+/-	PIM	PP	SH	GW	GT	S	PCT
75	26	25	51	-3	161	6	3	2	2	169	15.4

1997-98 statistics:

GP	G	A	TP	+/-	PIM	PP	SH	GW	GT	S	PCT
81	26	37	63	+19	110	7	3	2	0	180	14.4

1998-99 statistics:

GP	G	A	TP	+/-	PIM	PP	SH	GW	GT	S	PCT
78	30	32	62	+8	75	9	1	5	1	178	16.9

LAST SEASON

Led team in goals, points and power-play goals. Second on team in game-winning goals and shooting percentage. Third on team in assists and shots. Missed three games with back injury. Missed one game with wrist injury.

THE FINESSE GAME

Although Primeau would probably make a better left wing, he has persevered at centre. He is effective there, because of his size and skating, but he doesn't have the good playmaking skills, vision or sense to make the most of the centre ice position. He doesn't have the puck on his stick much, nor does he use his wingers well or establish much chemistry. He showed some gradual improvement learning from Ron Francis, and Francis could continue to help Primeau evolve.

Primeau's assets — his strength, his speed, his work along the boards — would serve him much better as a winger. The middle sometimes stops him from hitting as much as he should, though last season he was more consistent at it. There is less contact in the middle, and he limits himself by thinking more like a scorer than a power forward.

Primeau has a huge stride with a long reach. A left-hand shot, he will steam down the right side, slide the puck to his backhand, get his feet wide apart for balance, then shield the puck with his body and use his left arm to fend off the defenseman before shovelling the puck to the front of the net. He's clever enough to accept the puck at top speed and, instead of wondering what to do with it, make a move.

Primeau has worked hard at all aspects of his game and can be used in almost any role, including penalty killing and four-on-four play. His face-off work has improved dramatically. He wants to be the go-to guy and has earned that right.

THE PHYSICAL GAME

It's not that Primeau doesn't like to hit, because he does. When he plays with a little bit of an edge he can dominate for a period or an entire game. He has a fiery temper and can lose control. Emotion is a desirable quality, but he has become too valuable a player to spend too much time in the penalty box. He can't be overly tame, though. He needs to wig out once in awhile to scare people.

It used to be that if Primeau had contact with someone, he would be the one to fall. Now, he has improved his posture and balance, and can knock some pretty big men on their cans.

THE INTANGIBLES

Because he is a left-handed shot and not adept with his backhand pass, Primeau needs to play with a suitable right-winger, and he is a good fit with Sami Kapanen. Primeau was a Group 2 free agent during the off-season, and may not start the year if the contract dispute is as prolonged as expected.

PROJECTION

Primeau came close to the 70-point milepost last season and should go past it. He keeps getting better.

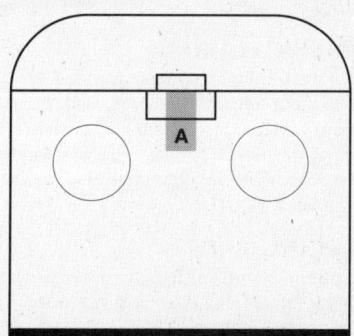

GARY ROBERTS

Yrs. of NHL service: 12
Born: North York, Ont.; May 23, 1966
Position: left wing
Height: 6-1
Weight: 200
Uniform no.: 10
Shoots: left

Career statistics:

GP	G	A	TP	PIM
723	291	305	596	2017

1995-96 statistics:

GP	G	A	TP	+/-	PIM	PP	SH	GW	GT	S	PCT
35	22	20	42	+15	78	9	0	5	1	84	26.2

1996-97 statistics:
Did not play in NHL

1997-98 statistics:

GP	G	A	TP	+/-	PIM	PP	SH	GW	GT	S	PCT
61	20	29	49	+3	103	4	0	2	1	106	18.9

1998-99 statistics:

GP	G	A	TP	+/-	PIM	PP	SH	GW	GT	S	PCT
77	14	28	42	+2	178	1	1	4	0	138	10.1

PROJECTION
Roberts plays on Carolina's top line and can provide another 20 goals, but at 33 he is beginning the downhill slide.

LAST SEASON
Led team in penalty minutes. Tied for third on team in game-winning goals. Missed four games with strained wrist. Missed one game with neck injury.

THE FINESSE GAME
Roberts has excellent hands and terrific instincts around the net. He works hard for loose pucks and, when he gets control, doesn't waste time trying anything fancy. As soon as the puck is on his blade, it's launched towards the net. He shoots by instinct and is not very creative. His rule is: throw the puck at the front of the net and see what happens.

Roberts is not an agile skater. He can beat the defender one-on-one on the occasional rush, powered by his strong stride and his ability to handle the puck at a fair clip.

He sees the ice well and will spot an open teammate for a smart pass. He forechecks intelligently and creates turnovers with his persistent work. An excellent penalty killer, he anticipates well and turns mistakes into shorthanded scoring chances.

THE PHYSICAL GAME
Despite a neck injury that nearly ended his career, Roberts is still a tough customer around the net. Can there be any better evidence that the Hurricanes are in dire need of an enforcer? A guy who was almost crippled by a neck injury should not be leading a team in penalty minutes.

THE INTANGIBLES
Roberts suffered through a lengthy slump last year (no goals in 18 games); his days as a big-time, 40-goal scorer are in his healthy past.

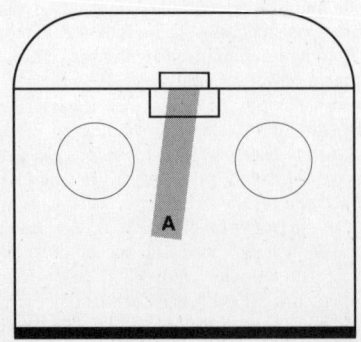

RAY SHEPPARD

Yrs. of NHL service: 12
Born: Pembroke, Ont.; May 27, 1966
Position: right wing
Height: 6-1
Weight: 195
Uniform no.: 26
Shoots: right

Career statistics:

GP	G	A	TP	PIM
770	347	290	637	208

1995-96 statistics:

GP	G	A	TP	+/-	PIM	PP	SH	GW	GT	S	PCT
70	37	23	60	-19	16	14	0	7	0	231	16.0

1996-97 statistics:

GP	G	A	TP	+/-	PIM	PP	SH	GW	GT	S	PCT
68	29	31	60	+4	4	13	0	7	0	226	12.8

1997-98 statistics:

GP	G	A	TP	+/-	PIM	PP	SH	GW	GT	S	PCT
71	18	19	37	-11	23	7	0	2	0	169	10.7

1998-99 statistics:

GP	G	A	TP	+/-	PIM	PP	SH	GW	GT	S	PCT
74	25	33	58	+4	16	5	0	4	1	188	13.3

LAST SEASON

Second on Hurricanes in goals, assists and shots. Third on Hurricanes in points. Tied for third on Hurricanes in power-play goals and game-winning goals. Missed three games with bruised foot. Missed two games with neck injury. Missed two games with groin strain. Missed one game with back spasms.

THE FINESSE GAME

There are times when Sheppard looks like a puck magnet. He is always eager to move to the puck and has good hockey sense and vision. Although he is a winger, he has a centre's view of the ice. He is also unselfish; he loves to shoot but will dish off if he spies a teammate with a better percentage shot. He has good hands with a quick release and doesn't waste time with a big backswing. He prefers efficiency and accuracy.

Sheppard has great hands but is a liability everywhere on the ice except for a 10-foot radius around the net. He is not a great skater. He looks excruciatingly slow, but this is deceptive because he is almost always in a good scoring position. He doesn't turn quickly and doesn't have great balance, but he can curl out of the right circle on his backhand and get off a wrist or snap shot. He is also strong enough to ward off a defender with one hand and shovel a pass or push a shot towards the net with his other. He must play with a centre who will get him the puck.

Sheppard is at his best on the power play, where he moves into the open ice and converts passes. However, he is usually the last player back when play breaks back out of the offensive zone.

THE PHYSICAL GAME

Sheppard does not play a big game. He's an average-sized forward who plays below his size. He won't work along the boards but will go to the front of the net, so he has to play with one grinder to get him the puck and one quick forward to serve as the safety valve. Sheppard has improved his lower-body strength.

THE INTANGIBLES

Sheppard became the first player to score at least 20 goals with six different NHL teams. He could be trying to do it with a seventh team this season, as the 'Canes showed no interest in re-signing the unrestricted free agent during the off-season.

PROJECTION

We don't envision more than 25 goals in his future, no matter where Sheppard ends up.

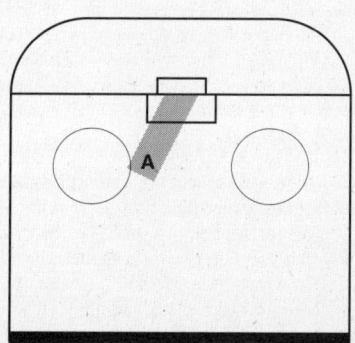

GLEN WESLEY

Yrs. of NHL service: 12
Born: Red Deer, Alta.; Oct. 2, 1968
Position: left defense
Height: 6-1
Weight: 197
Uniform no.: 20
Shoots: left

Career statistics:

GP	G	A	TP	PIM
877	106	322	428	679

1995-96 statistics:

GP	G	A	TP	+/-	PIM	PP	SH	GW	GT	S	PCT
68	8	16	24	-9	88	6	0	1	0	129	6.2

1996-97 statistics:

GP	G	A	TP	+/-	PIM	PP	SH	GW	GT	S	PCT
68	6	26	32	0	40	3	1	0	0	126	4.8

1997-98 statistics:

GP	G	A	TP	+/-	PIM	PP	SH	GW	GT	S	PCT
82	6	19	25	+7	36	1	0	1	0	121	5.0

1998-99 statistics:

GP	G	A	TP	+/-	PIM	PP	SH	GW	GT	S	PCT
74	7	17	24	+14	44	0	0	2	1	112	6.3

LAST SEASON

Second on team in plus-minus. Led team defensemen in points. Missed eight games with sprained ankle.

THE FINESSE GAME

Wesley simply isn't an offensive force, though he keeps being shoehorned into that role. He is at best a number two defenseman, and is ideally suited as a three or four. He toils in the one to two slot for Carolina because the team is so thin defensively.

Wesley is solid, but not elite. He is very good with the puck. He clicks on the power play because he knows when to jump into the holes. He has good but not great offensive instincts, gauging when to pinch, when to rush, when to pass the puck and when to back off. He is a decent skater who is not afraid to veer into the play deep; he seldom gets trapped there. He has a good slap shot from the point and snap shot from the circle.

You could count on two hands the number of times Wesley has been beaten one-on-one during his career, and there are very few defensemen you can say that about. He makes defensive plays with confidence and is poised even when outnumbered in the rush. He has to keep his feet moving.

THE PHYSICAL GAME

Wesley is not a bone-crunching defenseman, but neither was Jacques Laperriere, and he's in the Hall of Fame. We're not suggesting that Wesley is in that class, only that you don't have to shatter glass to be a solid checker, which he is. He's not a mean hitter, but he will execute a takeout check and not let his man get back into the play.

He is also sly about running interference for his defense partner, allowing him time to move the puck and giving him confidence that he won't get hammered by a forechecker. He is also quite durable. His ankle injury ended a 185 consecutive games-played streak.

THE INTANGIBLES

Wesley is a more relaxed player in Carolina, and is helping to break in some of the younger defensemen. He is happy not having to be the star.

PROJECTION

Wesley is, at best, a 30-point scorer. He doesn't get nearly the amount of points he should for the ice time he receives.

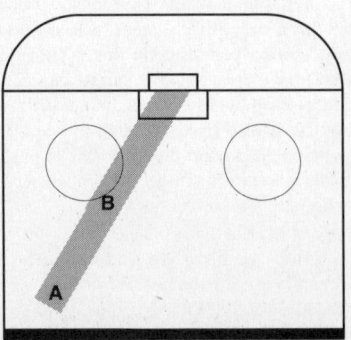

CHICAGO BLACKHAWKS

Players' Statistics 1998-99

POS.	NO.	PLAYER	GP	G	A	PTS	+/-	PIM	PP	SH	GW	GT	S	PCT
R	10	TONY AMONTE	82	44	31	75	0	60	14	3	8		256	17.2
C	36	ALEXEI ZHAMNOV	76	20	41	61	-10	50	8	1	2	1	200	10.0
C	93	DOUG GILMOUR	72	16	40	56	-16	56	7	1	4		110	14.5
D	3	BORIS MIRONOV	75	11	38	49	13	131	5		4	1	173	6.4
L	55	ERIC DAZE	72	22	20	42	-13	22	8		2	3	189	11.6
L	34	DEAN MCAMMOND	77	10	20	30	8	38	1		1		138	7.2
R	16	ED OLCZYK	61	10	15	25	-3	29	2	1	2		88	11.4
D	22	DAVE MANSON	75	6	17	23	1	155	2				145	4.1
L	24	BOB PROBERT	78	7	14	21	-11	206			3		87	8.0
D	8	ANDERS ERIKSSON	72	2	18	20	11	34			1		79	2.5
R	17	*JEAN-PIERRE DUMONT	25	9	6	15	7	10			2		42	21.4
D	4	DOUG ZMOLEK	62		14	14	1	102					33	
C	26	*TODD WHITE	35	5	8	13	-1	20	2				43	11.6
L	33	REID SIMPSON	53	5	4	9	2	145	1				23	21.7
L	25	*DANIEL CLEARY	35	4	5	9	-1	24					49	8.2
L	23	JEAN-YVES LEROUX	40	3	5	8	-7	21					47	6.4
C	44	JOSEF MARHA	32	2	6	8	1	4	1		1		45	4.4
D	2	*BRAD BROWN	66	1	7	8	-4	205				1	26	3.8
R	15	CHRIS MURRAY	42	1	6	7	-2	79					37	2.7
D	37	*BRYAN MUIR	54	1	4	5	1	50					82	1.2
D	38	JAMIE ALLISON	39	2	2	4	0	62					24	8.3
C	20	MARK JANSSENS	60	1		1	-11	65					27	3.7
G	30	MARK FITZPATRICK	27		1	1	0	8						
G	41	JOCELYN THIBAULT	62		1	1	0	2						
R	19	RYAN VANDENBUSSCHE	6				0	17					3	
C	14	*SYLVAIN CLOUTIER	7				-1							3	
R	39	*CRAIG MILLS	7				-2	2					1	
R	27	*TY JONES	8				-1	12					3	
R	44	*DENNIS BONVIE	11				-4	44					1	
D	32	RADIM BICANEK	14				-4	10					13	
D	6	*REMI ROYER	18				-10	67					24	
D	5	TRENT YAWNEY	20				-6	32					11	

GP = games played; G = goals; A = assists; PTS = points; +/- = goals-for minus goals-against while player is on ice; PIM = penalties in minutes; PP = power-play goals; SH = shorthanded goals; GW = game-winning goals; GT = game-tying goals; S = no. of shots; PCT = percentage of goals to shots; * = rookie

JAMIE ALLISON

Yrs. of NHL service: 2
Born: Lindsay, Ontario; May 13, 1975
Position: left defense
Height: 6-1
Weight: 195
Uniform no.: 38
Shoots: left

Career statistics:

GP	G	A	TP	PIM
103	5	10	15	201

1995-96 statistics:
Did not play in NHL

1996-97 statistics:

GP	G	A	TP	+/-	PIM	PP	SH	GW	GT	S	PCT
20	0	0	0	-4	35	0	0	0	0	8	0.0

1997-98 statistics:

GP	G	A	TP	+/-	PIM	PP	SH	GW	GT	S	PCT
43	3	8	11	+3	104	0	0	1	0	27	11.1

1998-99 statistics:

GP	G	A	TP	+/-	PIM	PP	SH	GW	GT	S	PCT
39	2	2	4	0	62	0	0	0	0	24	8.3

PROJECTION
Allison is on the cusp of becoming a top four defenseman. Once he does, he could score in the 20- to 25-point range.

LAST SEASON
Acquired from Calgary with Marty McInnis and Erik Andersson for Jeff Shantz and Steve Dubinsky, Oct. 27, 1998. Missed 23 games with fractured wrist. Missed three games with groin injury. Missed 10 games due to coach's decision.

THE FINESSE GAME
Allison concentrates on defense, and could develop into a Ken Daneyko type rock-solid blueliner, but with better talent. He uses his skills and his skating in a defensive role; with more experience he could get involved in the attack. He has good lateral movement and plays well positionally. He makes the good first pass out of the zone. He is a good puckhandler with a decent point shot, and could earn time on the second power-play unit.

Allison has good hockey sense. He reads plays well and contributes an intense game. No one aspect of his technique is overwhelming. It's the complete package that will make him an NHL regular.

THE PHYSICAL GAME
Allison is as tough as they come. He is very strong and highly competitive. He checks with authority and his skating powers his hits. He blocks shots and will do whatever it takes to help his team win games.

THE INTANGIBLES
Allison hasn't yet put all the pieces of his game together to earn a spot in the top four. He's close, though. He has a good head for the game and needs the confidence that will come from a full-time role. He may be on the move again since things didn't go well for him in Chicago.

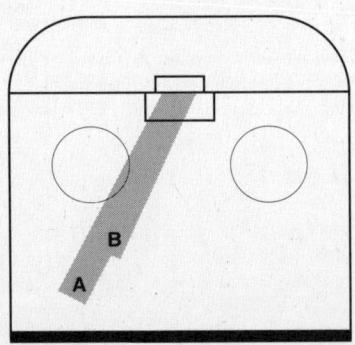

TONY AMONTE

Yrs. of NHL service: 8
Born: Hingham, Mass.; Aug. 2, 1970
Position: right wing
Height: 6-0
Weight: 190
Uniform no.: 10
Shoots: left

Career statistics:

GP	G	A	TP	PIM
615	247	263	510	434

1995-96 statistics:

GP	G	A	TP	+/-	PIM	PP	SH	GW	GT	S	PCT
81	31	32	63	+10	62	5	4	5	0	216	14.4

1996-97 statistics:

GP	G	A	TP	+/-	PIM	PP	SH	GW	GT	S	PCT
81	41	36	77	+35	64	9	2	4	2	266	15.4

1997-98 statistics:

GP	G	A	TP	+/-	PIM	PP	SH	GW	GT	S	PCT
82	31	42	73	+21	66	7	3	5	0	296	10.5

1998-99 statistics:

GP	G	A	TP	+/-	PIM	PP	SH	GW	GT	S	PCT
82	44	31	75	0	60	14	3	8	0	256	17.2

LAST SEASON

Tied for second in NHL in goals. Led team in goals and points for third consecutive season. Led team in power-play goals, game-winning goals, shorthanded goals, shots and shooting percentage. Only Blackhawk to appear in all 82 games.

THE FINESSE GAME

Amonte is blessed with exceptional speed and acceleration. His timing is accurate and his anticipation keen. He has good balance and he can carry the puck at a pretty good clip, though he is more effective when streaking down the wing and getting the puck late. Playing on the left side leaves his forehand open for one-timers, but Amonte is equally secure on the right wing, where he played most of last season. He's been called a young Yvan Cournoyer for the way he uses his speed to drive wide around the defense to the net.

Amonte has a quick release on his wrist shot. He likes to go top shelf, just under the crossbar, and can also go to the backhand shot or a wrist shot off his back foot, like a fadeaway jumper. He is a top power-play man, since he is always working himself into open ice. Amonte's power-play numbers will improve with the addition of Boris Mironov and Anders Eriksson to the points. An accurate shooter, Amonte is also creative in his playmaking. He passes very well and is conscious of where his teammates are; he usually makes the best percentage play. He has confidence in his shot and wants the puck when the game is on the line.

Offensively, Amonte is a smart player away from the puck. He sets picks and creates openings for his teammates. He is an aggressive penalty killer and a shorthanded threat.

THE PHYSICAL GAME

Amonte's speed and movement keep him out of a lot of trouble zones, but he will also drive to the front of the net and take punishment there if that's the correct play. He loves to score, he loves to help his linemates score, and although he is outweighed by a lot of NHL defensemen he is seldom outworked. He's intense and is not above getting chippy and rubbing his glove in someone's face.

Amonte takes a lot of abuse and plays through the checks. He seldom takes bad retaliatory penalties. He just keeps his legs driving and draws calls with his nonstop skating.

THE INTANGIBLES

Amonte's numbers are staggering when you take into account the stifling attack preached by ex-coach Dirk Graham and a tendinitis injury that required off-season arthoscopic surgery.

PROJECTION

Amonte is primed for a career year: 50 goals and 100 points.

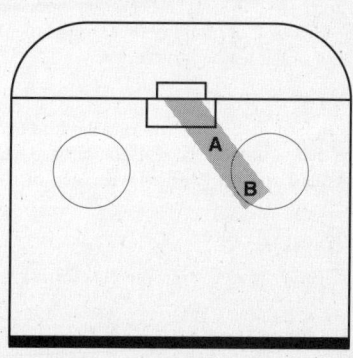

BRAD BROWN

Yrs. of NHL service: 1
Born: Baie Verte, Nfld.; Dec. 27, 1975
Position: right defense
Height: 6-4
Weight: 218
Uniform no.: 2
Shoots: right

Career statistics:

GP	G	A	TP	PIM
74	1	7	8	227

1996-97 statistics:

GP	G	A	TP	+/-	PIM	PP	SH	GW	GT	S	PCT
8	0	0	0	-1	22	0	0	0	0	1	0.0

1997-98 statistics:
Did not play in NHL

1998-99 statistics:

GP	G	A	TP	+/-	PIM	PP	SH	GW	GT	S	PCT
66	1	7	8	-4	205	0	0	0	1	26	3.8

LAST SEASON
First NHL season. Second on team in penalty minutes. Missed two games with bruised foot. Missed six games with back injury. Missed one game due to suspension. Missed four games due to coach's decision.

THE FINESSE GAME
Brown's desire elevates a pretty modest package of skills to a degree that allows him to perform at the NHL level. He is a strong skater, though not a fast one; he will need to work on his skating for the rest of his career.

Because he doesn't move well, Brown is limited in the game situations in which he can be used. He cannot be employed on the penalty-killing unit, for example, and he has limited offensive ability, so his ice time comes only at full strength.

Brown needs to be paired with a mobile partner.

THE PHYSICAL GAME
Brown is mean and tough and plays with a lot of heart. One of his childhood idols was Marty McSorley, which gives you a pretty good idea of what Brown is about. He is a punishing hitter when someone comes into his turf. He can't make the killer open-ice hits because of his lack of mobility, but around the boards and in front of the net he is effective.

THE INTANGIBLES
Brown's lack of foot speed will prevent him from being more than a number five or six defenseman. His toughness and competitiveness will keep him in the lineup.

PROJECTION
Little offensive upside. Big potential for major PIM totals.

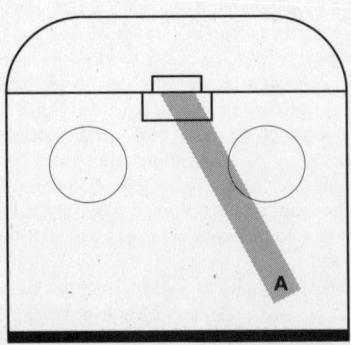

ERIC DAZE

Yrs. of NHL service: 4
Born: Montreal, Que.; July 2, 1975
Position: left wing
Height: 6-4
Weight: 215
Uniform no.: 55
Shoots: left

Career statistics:

GP	G	A	TP	PIM
307	106	74	180	80

1995-96 statistics:

GP	G	A	TP	+/-	PIM	PP	SH	GW	GT	S	PCT
80	30	23	53	+16	18	2	0	2	0	167	18.0

1996-97 statistics:

GP	G	A	TP	+/-	PIM	PP	SH	GW	GT	S	PCT
71	22	19	41	-4	16	11	0	4	0	176	12.5

1997-98 statistics:

GP	G	A	TP	+/-	PIM	PP	SH	GW	GT	S	PCT
80	31	11	42	+4	22	10	0	7	1	216	14.4

1998-99 statistics:

GP	G	A	TP	+/-	PIM	PP	SH	GW	GT	S	PCT
72	22	20	42	-13	22	8	0	2	3	189	11.6

LAST SEASON

Second on team in goals. Tied for second on team in power-play goals. Missed six games with groin injury. Missed three games with bruised left ankle. Missed one game due to coach's decision.

THE FINESSE GAME

Although the most impressive thing about Daze is his size, it is his skating ability that sets him apart from other lumbering big men. He isn't a speed demon, but he skates well enough to not look out of place with faster linemates.

Daze keeps his hands close together on his stick and is able to get a lot on his shot with very little backswing. He has excellent hands for shooting or scoring, and is an adept stickhandler who can draw defenders to him and then slip a pass through to a teammate. He sets screens on the power play. He has good hockey vision and an innate understanding of the game. He has also advanced defensively.

Daze excells when he drives wide, protects the puck and takes it to the net. Very few defensemen can handle him when he does, but he frequently stops working and stops moving his feet. When he stands around rooted to one spot on the power play, he is useless. Although the right wing is his off-side, Daze has played it through most of his NHL career and is more comfortable there than on the left.

Daze's best weapon is his one-timer, which may be one of the most unstoppable in the NHL.

THE PHYSICAL GAME

Daze doesn't back down, but he doesn't show much initiative, either. He is not a prototypical power forward. There will be the occasional night when he tries to run guys over, but those games are infrequent. He doesn't have the strength or the taste for it.

Daze has a long reach — he can pass or shoot the puck even when a defenseman thinks he has him all wrapped up and under control. He must compete harder on a more consistent basis. This is the hardest lesson to hammer home with a young player, but one Daze must learn.

THE INTANGIBLES

Daze was ridden hard by former coach Dirk Graham and may have been one of the more relieved 'Hawks when Lorne Molleken took over. Daze's laid-back personality may be his ticket out of Chicago.

He suffered a sprained knee in the World Championships, but was expected to be okay for the start of training camp.

PROJECTION

Daze needs to play with forwards who will get him the puck. As long as Chicago can provide the passers, Daze will provide the finish. Thirty goals is probably his top end, though.

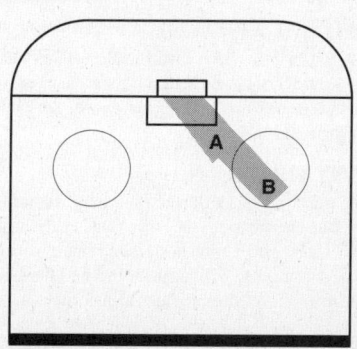

J. P. DUMONT

Yrs. of NHL service: 0
Born: Montreal, Que,; Apr. 1, 1978
Position: right wing
Height: 6-1
Weight: 187
Uniform no.: 17
Shoots: left

Career statistics:

GP	G	A	TP	PIM
25	9	6	15	10

1998-99 statistics:

GP	G	A	TP	+/-	PIM	PP	SH	GW	GT	S	PCT
25	9	6	15	+7	10	0	0	2	0	42	21.4

LAST SEASON
Will be entering first full NHL season. Appeared in 50 games with Portland (AHL), scoring 32-14 — 46. Missed two games with back injury. Missed two games due to coach's decision.

THE FINESSE GAME
Few young players combine the ability to score with Dumont's willingness to pay the price. He has all of the weapons needed to become a scorer in the NHL. He is an instinctive shooter and playmaker, seeing his options a step ahead of everyone else. He disguises his intentions well. Because he is unselfish with the puck, defenders may expect the pass. But Dumont has an excellent wrist and slap shot so you can't allow him to cruise to the net. He is pure hands.

Dumont takes it to the net, too. He goes through and around players like the breeze, with excellent puck control. His skating is NHL calibre. He has good acceleration for short bursts or rink-long sprints. He has had to work on his conditioning and has taken power-skating lessons, so he is willing to work to improve his game. His hand-eye coordination for tip-ins and rebounds is outstanding.

As is typical with many young players, the knock on Dumont is his lack of intensity at times, but he is maturing. He is one of those rare players who finds the back of the net by any means possible.

THE PHYSICAL GAME
Dumont is tall but whippet-thin. He will need to fill out with some muscle now that he's no longer playing with boys. He has an edge to his game, which shows he may thrive in the pros.

THE INTANGIBLES
Dumont may have his detractors, who disparage his skating, but even though it is average or below he is going to score and score and score some more. The trade that sent him to Chicago should be Islanders GM Mike Milbury's career killer. Dumont is a special talent.

PROJECTION
Dumont is a future 50-goal scorer, and the likely Calder Trophy winner as rookie of the year. It would be no surprise to see Dumont net 20 goals in his first full season.

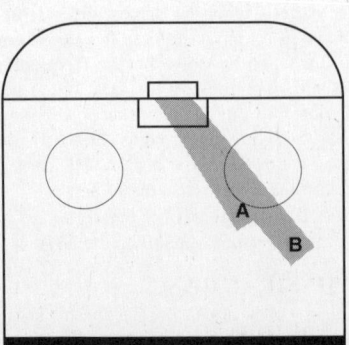

ANDERS ERIKSSON

Yrs. of NHL service: 2
Born: Bolinas, Sweden; Jan. 9, 1975
Position: defense
Height: 6-3
Weight: 218
Uniform no.: 8
Shoots: left

Career statistics:

GP	G	A	TP	PIM
161	9	38	47	76

1996-97 statistics:

GP	G	A	TP	+/-	PIM	PP	SH	GW	GT	S	PCT
23	0	6	6	+5	10	0	0	0	0	27	0.0

1997-98 statistics:

GP	G	A	TP	+/-	PIM	PP	SH	GW	GT	S	PCT
66	7	14	21	+21	32	1	0	2	0	91	7.7

1998-99 statistics:

GP	G	A	TP	+/-	PIM	PP	SH	GW	GT	S	PCT
72	2	18	20	+11	34	0	0	1	0	79	2.5

LAST SEASON

Second NHL season. Acquired from Detroit with first-round draft picks in 1999 and 2001 for Chris Chelios, Mar. 23, 1999. Second NHL season. Third on team in plus-minus. Missed nine games due to coach's decision.

THE FINESSE GAME

Eriksson is big for an NHL defenseman, even by today's standards, but his strength lies in his mobility and puckhandling skills. He sees the ice well; his biggest asset is his ability to get the puck out of his own end fast. He is a heads-up passer who is poised with the puck.

Eriksson is improving his defensive reads and reactions. He doesn't jump into the play unless it's safe, and he won't pinch unless that is the correct play. He may err on the side of caution until he develops a little more confidence, but he has the skill level to provide some offense as a playmaker. He will probably limit his shots to the point.

Eriksson is a very good skater with balance and agility. He doesn't have a big turning radius and he accelerates well.

THE PHYSICAL GAME

Eriksson is not a big hitter, but he is strong and he'll tie up his man along the boards and in front of the net. His conditioning is very good, and he has adjusted to the longer North American schedule well. He should be able to handle the league's big power forwards because of his body positioning. He will force people to try to go through him.

THE INTANGIBLES

Eriksson moved into a top four position with the Blackhawks and will be given much more ice time, power-play time and responsibilities than he had in Detroit.

PROJECTION

Eriksson will continue to focus on his defense, but may provide 35 to 40 points while he's doing it.

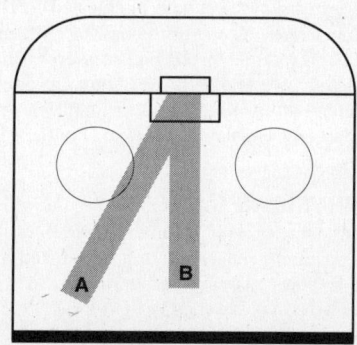

DOUG GILMOUR

Yrs. of NHL service: 16
Born: Kingston, Ont.; June 25, 1963
Position: centre
Height: 5-11
Weight: 172
Uniform no.: 93
Shoots: left

Career statistics:

GP	G	A	TP	PIM
1197	397	835	1232	1082

1995-96 statistics:

GP	G	A	TP	+/-	PIM	PP	SH	GW	GT	S	PCT
81	32	40	72	-5	77	10	2	3	0	180	17.8

1996-97 statistics:

GP	G	A	TP	+/-	PIM	PP	SH	GW	GT	S	PCT
81	22	60	82	+2	68	4	1	1	1	143	15.4

1997-98 statistics:

GP	G	A	TP	+/-	PIM	PP	SH	GW	GT	S	PCT
63	13	40	53	+10	68	3	0	5	0	94	13.8

1998-99 statistics:

GP	G	A	TP	+/-	PIM	PP	SH	GW	GT	S	PCT
72	16	40	56	-16	56	7	1	4	0	110	14.5

LAST SEASON

Second on team in assists and shooting percentage. Tied for second on team in game-winning goals. Third on team in points. Missed 10 games with back injury and season-ending back surgery.

THE FINESSE GAME

A creative playmaker, Gilmour has eschewed the banana blade for a nearly straight model, so he can handle the puck equally well on his forehand or backhand. He will bring people right in on top of him before he slides a little pass to a teammate, creating time and space. He is very intelligent and has great anticipation. He loves to set up from behind the net, and intimidates because he plays with such supreme confidence.

Gilmour doesn't shoot much; he's a set-up man who needs finishers around him. When he does shoot he won't use a big slapper, but instead scores from close range either as the trailer or after losing a defender with his subtle dekes and moves. He's not a smooth, gifted skater, but he is nimble and quick.

Gilmour ranks as one of the best face-off men in the NHL and routinely beats big, stronger centres on draws. In his own end he is very sound positionally. He is defensively solid player. His awful plus-minus reflects just how bad the 'Hawks and Gilmour's injury must have been.

THE PHYSICAL GAME

Gilmour competes with passion and savvy, challenging bigger opponents. Although he's listed at 185 pounds, he plays at around 165 during the season. He is more effective at the slightly lighter weight.

THE INTANGIBLES

Gilmour is a man with a $6-million annual salary, which means nothing he does will look like enough. He provides never-say-die leadership. He often responds with a big shift after his team has been scored upon and will ignite his teammates with an inspirational bump or goal. He will do everything he can to win a game, but the reservoir is only so deep at his age.

PROJECTION

Gilmour will be 36 when the season starts, and it's going to be a challenge to score 70 points, though an improved 'Hawks power play could boost him to that total.

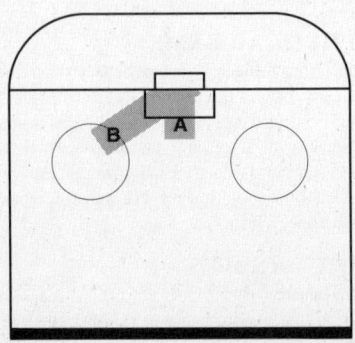

DAVE MANSON

Yrs. of NHL service: 13
Born: Prince Albert, Sask.; Jan. 27, 1967
Position: left defense
Height: 6-2
Weight: 202
Uniform no.: 22
Shoots: left

Career statistics:

GP	G	A	TP	PIM
919	97	270	367	2606

1995-96 statistics:

GP	G	A	TP	+/-	PIM	PP	SH	GW	GT	S	PCT
82	7	23	30	+8	205	3	0	0	0	189	3.7

1996-97 statistics:

GP	G	A	TP	+/-	PIM	PP	SH	GW	GT	S	PCT
75	4	18	22	-26	187	2	0	0	0	175	2.3

1997-98 statistics:

GP	G	A	TP	+/-	PIM	PP	SH	GW	GT	S	PCT
81	4	30	34	+22	122	2	0	0	0	148	2.7

1998-99 statistics:

GP	G	A	TP	+/-	PIM	PP	SH	GW	GT	S	PCT
75	6	17	23	+1	155	2	0	0	0	145	4.1

LAST SEASON

Acquired from Montreal with Jocelyn Thibault and Brad Brown for Jeff Hackett, Eric Weinrich, Alain Nasreddine and future considerations, Nov. 16, 1998. Third on team in penalty minutes. Missed two games with hip pointer. Missed three games due to suspension. Missed one game due to coach's decision.

THE FINESSE GAME

Manson is his own worst enemy. He makes mental errors that keep him from stepping up into the ranks of the NHL's best defensemen. He makes low-percentage plays, such as skating through his own crease under a heavy forecheck. Maybe skilled Russian defensemen can get away with that. Manson can't. He can be scary in his own end when he overhandles the puck. He is conscious of helping out his goalie, communicates well and clears rebounds when he keeps the game simple.

Manson will often take himself out of position with his poor defensive reads, then has to resort to using his stick to pull attackers down. Not all of his hefty PIM total are penalties of aggression.

He is smart and effective on the power play because he will mix up his shot with a big fake and freeze. But there isn't much that's subtle about Manson. His game is power. He doesn't have much lateral mobility so the shot isn't as effective as it would be in the hands of an Al MacInnis. He is not a bad skater for a big guy, though, and he gambles down deep and is canny enough to use an accurate wrist shot when in close.

THE PHYSICAL GAME

Manson has become more disciplined, but still has a knack for taking bad penalties at the worst times. He can throw himself off his game. He will lose control and run after people. He patrols the front of his net well, can hit to hurt and intimidates players into getting rid of the puck faster than they want to. They flinch from even the threat of a Manson body check.

THE INTANGIBLES

For all of his flaws, no one can fault Manson's effort. He's a trier if not a doer. He knows his shortcomings and wants to be a better player. He plays hurt and stands up for his teammates.

PROJECTION

Manson will be a fourth or fifth defenseman in Chicago and will probably score 25 points. His PIM totals will be impressive, as usual.

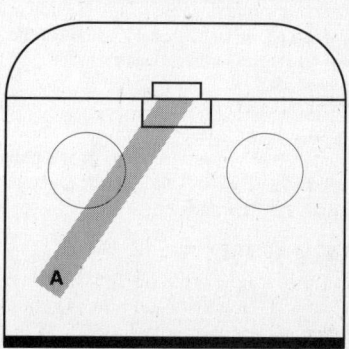

JOSEF MARHA

Yrs. of NHL service: 2
Born: Havlickuv Brod, Czech Republic; June 2, 1976
Position: centre
Height: 6-0
Weight: 176
Uniform no.: 44
Shoots: left

Career statistics:

GP	G	A	TP	PIM
63	11	17	28	8

1995-96 statistics:

GP	G	A	TP	+/-	PIM	PP	SH	GW	GT	S	PCT
2	0	1	1	+1	0	0	0	0	0	2	0.0

1996-97 statistics:

GP	G	A	TP	+/-	PIM	PP	SH	GW	GT	S	PCT
6	0	1	1	0	0	0	0	0	0	6	0.0

1997-98 statistics:

GP	G	A	TP	+/-	PIM	PP	SH	GW	GT	S	PCT
23	9	9	18	+4	4	3	0	0	0	31	29.0

1998-99 statistics:

GP	G	A	TP	+/-	PIM	PP	SH	GW	GT	S	PCT
32	2	6	8	+1	4	1	0	1	0	45	4.4

PROJECTION

Marha is a bit of a wild card, but even thinking conservatively, he could score 20 goals if he sticks and gets a job on the top two lines.

LAST SEASON

Second NHL season. Acquired from Anaheim for future considerations, Jan. 28, 1999. Appeared in three games with Cincinnati (AHL), scoring 1-0 — 1. Appeared in seven games with Portland (AHL), scoring 0-6 — 6. Missed nine games with ankle injury. Missed 22 games due to coach's decision.

THE FINESSE GAME

A strictly offensive player, Marha is a sensational power-play man. He is always in motion, finding holes, bursting past defenders with an outside move on the rush, looking for an open man or looking for the shot. He has great hands and protects the puck well. He is smart in all zones and can kill penalties because of his speed and anticipation.

Marha can finish or make a play, but he has to score one way or the other because he doesn't bring much else to the ice.

He has to earn his way into a spot among the top six Chicago forwards because of his playing style. He failed to score a goal in his last 17 games of the season — no way to impress a new coach.

THE PHYSICAL GAME

Marha hasn't shown a taste for physical play and will be made a target if he gets a reputation as a player who can be intimidated. He is solidly built and could handle tough play if he wanted to.

THE INTANGIBLES

Motivation is a key problem for Marha. He has bounced around the minors and now is with his third organization in three years.

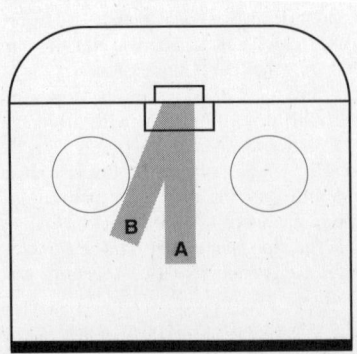

DEAN MCAMMOND

Yrs. of NHL service: 6
Born: Grand Cache, Alberta; June 15, 1973
Position: left wing
Height: 5-11
Weight: 200
Uniform no.: 37
Shoots: left

Career statistics:

GP	G	A	TP	PIM
320	62	106	168	153

1995-96 statistics:

GP	G	A	TP	+/-	PIM	PP	SH	GW	GT	S	PCT
53	15	15	30	+6	23	4	0	0	0	79	19.0

1996-97 statistics:

GP	G	A	TP	+/-	PIM	PP	SH	GW	GT	S	PCT
57	12	17	29	-15	28	4	0	6	0	106	11.3

1997-98 statistics:

GP	G	A	TP	+/-	PIM	PP	SH	GW	GT	S	PCT
77	19	31	50	+9	46	8	0	3	0	28	14.8

1998-99 statistics:

GP	G	A	TP	+/-	PIM	PP	SH	GW	GT	S	PCT
77	10	20	30	+8	38	1	0	1	0	138	7.2

PROJECTION

McAmmond isn't likely to become the scorer in the NHL that he was at the minor and junior levels, so 20 goals out of him would make for a positive season.

LAST SEASON

Acquired from Edmonton with Boris Mironov and Jonas Elofsson for Chad Kilger, Ethan Moreau, Christian Laflamme and Daniel Cleary, Mar. 19, 1999. Third on team in plus-minus.

THE FINESSE GAME

McAmmond's chief asset is his speed. He has excellent acceleration and quickness, and uses his speed to forecheck and force the play. He works the boards and the corners; he is effective in open ice as well because of his skating.

McAmmond developed as a centre, so he uses all of the ice even when he is in his regular slot on left wing. He handles the puck well in traffic and has good vision to see developing plays. He is unselfish and passes well on the forehand and backhand. He also has a nice shot in tight. He has needed some time to adjust to NHL tempo and now moves the puck more crisply.

He can handle second-unit power-play time.

THE PHYSICAL GAME

McAmmond is feisty and aggressive. He isn't very big but he creates a ruckus in the offensive zone with his tenacity. He will stick his nose in just about anywhere and he can be very irritating to play against. He drives to the net with authority, often right past bigger defenders.

THE INTANGIBLES

McAmmond isn't likely to earn top six ice time among the 'Hawks forwards, though he can step up in case of injuries.

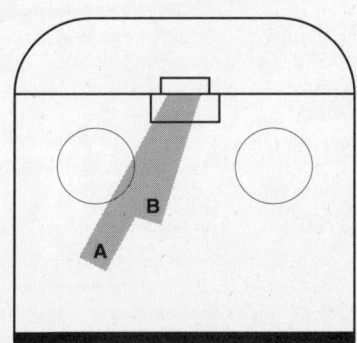

BRYAN MCCABE

Yrs. of NHL service: 4
Born: St. Catharines, Ont.; June 8, 1975
Position: left defense
Height: 6-2
Weight: 215
Uniform no.: 23
Shoots: left

Career statistics:

GP	G	A	TP	PIM
315	26	70	96	650

1995-96 statistics:

GP	G	A	TP	+/-	PIM	PP	SH	GW	GT	S	PCT
82	7	16	23	-24	156	3	0	1	0	130	5.4

1996-97 statistics:

GP	G	A	TP	+/-	PIM	PP	SH	GW	GT	S	PCT
82	8	20	28	-2	165	2	1	2	0	117	6.8

1997-98 statistics:

GP	G	A	TP	+/-	PIM	PP	SH	GW	GT	S	PCT
82	4	20	24	+19	209	1	1	0	0	123	3.3

1998-99 statistics:

GP	G	A	TP	+/-	PIM	PP	SH	GW	GT	S	PCT
69	7	14	21	-11	120	1	2	0	0	98	7.1

LAST SEASON

Acquired from Vancouver with a first-round draft pick in 2000 for a 1999 first-round draft pick, June 26, 1999. Missed 13 games due to contract dispute. Has never missed a game due to injury in four NHL seasons.

THE FINESSE GAME

McCabe's offensive game was supposed to be ahead of his defensive aspects, but he concentrated so much on learning the defensive side of the game that his offensive upside is high.

McCabe is an unorthodox skater with a bit of a hitch. He doesn't have a fluid, classic stride, but he moves his feet quickly and he can get to where he's going. When he has the puck or is jumping into the play he has decent speed, but his lack of mobility defensively is one of his flaws. He is hesitant in his own zone when reading the rush and will get caught, but he is willing to work to improve.

McCabe needs to develop more confidence in his offensive instincts. He knows when to jump up into the attacking zone. He has a heavy, major-league slap shot. He moves the puck well and can run an NHL power play.

Defensively, McCabe plays well positionally and doesn't get mesmerized by the puck. He kills penalties well and blocks shots.

THE PHYSICAL GAME

McCabe is willing to drop his gloves and can handle himself in a bout, though it's not a strong part of his game. Asking him to be a top cop is a waste of his ability. He's not tough but he is very competitive. He is also a sturdy body checker, and if his skating improves he will become a more efficient hitter. He is big and strong and shows leadership. He handled a lot of tough checking assignments against other teams' top physical lines.

THE INTANGIBLES

McCabe has strong leadership qualities and will be a top two defenseman with Chicago. He pushes himself and competes hard. He is maturing into a reliable, all-around defender and is progressing every season.

PROJECTION

McCabe can bump up his production to 35 to 40 points without detracting from his defense.

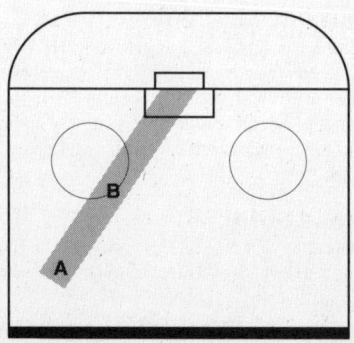

BORIS MIRONOV

Yrs. of NHL service: 7
Born: Moscow, Russia; March 21, 1972
Position: right defense
Height: 6-3
Weight: 220
Uniform no.: 3
Shoots: right

Career statistics:

GP	G	A	TP	PIM
397	49	149	198	567

1995-96 statistics:

GP	G	A	TP	+/-	PIM	PP	SH	GW	GT	S	PCT
78	8	24	32	-23	101	7	0	1	0	158	5.1

1996-97 statistics:

GP	G	A	TP	+/-	PIM	PP	SH	GW	GT	S	PCT
55	6	26	32	+2	85	2	0	1	0	147	4.1

1997-98 statistics:

GP	G	A	TP	+/-	PIM	PP	SH	GW	GT	S	PCT
81	16	30	46	-8	100	10	1	1	1	203	7.9

1998-99 statistics:

GP	G	A	TP	+/-	PIM	PP	SH	GW	GT	S	PCT
75	11	38	49	+13	131	5	0	4	1	173	6.4

LAST SEASON

Acquired from Edmonton with Dean McAmmond and Jonas Elofsson for Chad Kilger, Ethan Moreau, Christian Laflamme and Daniel Cleary, Mar. 19, 1999. Led team defensemen and 10th among NHL defensemen in points. Led team in plus-minus. Tied for second on team in game-winning goals. Third on team in assists. Career highs in assists and points. Missed one game with charley horse. Missed five games due to coach's decision.

THE FINESSE GAME

Mironov has a huge slap shot and is a good puckhandler as well, so he can start a rush out of his own zone and finish things up at the other end. He has improved the release on his shot and sets things up well from the point with his passing.

Mironov has improved his defensive play to the stage where he belongs as part of a team's top defense against other teams' top lines. He uses his size well to protect the puck. He has made the game easier by allowing the play to come to him instead of trying to make too many things happen by himself.

Mironov helps his team most with his ability to carry or pass the puck out of his own zone. Attacking teams have to back off their forecheck, because Mironov will start his team on a breakout and jump into the play to create an odd-man rush.

THE PHYSICAL GAME

Mironov is big and mobile. He isn't a thumper, but he's strong and he eliminates people. He can and does handle a lot of minutes (around 28 per night).

THE INTANGIBLES

Mironov is a good fit with Chicago, a team that has upgraded its defense and played a more relaxed style since last season's coaching change to Lorne Molleken. Mironov was a restricted free agent and could miss the start of training camp as a protracted negotiation is anticipated.

PROJECTION

Last season we predicted Mironov would be among the top 15 defenseman scorers (he was number 10). He has more in him. A 60-point season is not out of the question.

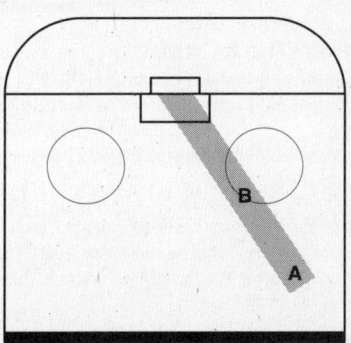

CHRIS MURRAY

Yrs. of NHL service: 4
Born: Port Hardy, B.C.; Oct. 25, 1974
Position: right wing
Height: 6-2
Weight: 209
Uniform no.: 15
Shoots: right

Career statistics:

GP	G	A	TP	PIM
210	14	17	31	488

1995-96 statistics:

GP	G	A	TP	+/-	PIM	PP	SH	GW	GT	S	PCT
48	4	3	7	+5	163	0	0	1	0	32	9.4

1996-97 statistics:

GP	G	A	TP	+/-	PIM	PP	SH	GW	GT	S	PCT
64	5	3	8	-7	124	0	0	0	0	41	12.2

1997-98 statistics:

GP	G	A	TP	+/-	PIM	PP	SH	GW	GT	S	PCT
53	5	4	9	+3	118	0	0	2	0	51	9.8

1998-99 statistics:

GP	G	A	TP	+/-	PIM	PP	SH	GW	GT	S	PCT
42	1	6	7	-2	79	0	0	0	0	37	2.7

PROJECTION
Murray is a few seasons away from a full-time role. He could score five to 10 goals and rack up some serious PIM.

LAST SEASON
Acquired from Ottawa for Nelson Emerson, Mar. 23, 1999. Missed four games with dislocated shoulder. Missed three games due to personal reasons. Missed 31 games due to coach's decision.

THE FINESSE GAME
Murray did not play much early in his NHL career, and when he did, all he did was fight. At 25, he is starting to focus on his other skills, in an effort to be much more than a goon winger.

For starters, Murray is a pretty good skater, and he has decent hands. He will bust a move occasionally that leaves people wondering just where it came from, as he dangles a puck through a defenseman's legs and drives to the net, going top shelf with his shot.

Murray will never be a 40-goal power forward, but he can contribute more offensively than he has done in the past. He played on Memorial Cup winners in junior, so he knows how to win. He is highly competitive.

THE PHYSICAL GAME
Murray isn't a super heavyweight but he will go with anybody, and he likes it. He has to learn to pick his spots better, to maintain his tough reputation without spending too much time in the penalty box.

THE INTANGIBLES
Murray could be just a fourth-line banger and crasher, or he could develop into the successor to Bob Probert, though he is unlikely to ever post Probert-like numbers (in goals or PIMs).

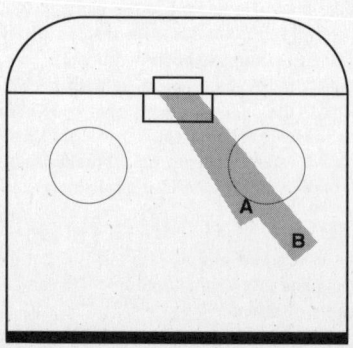

ED OLCZYK

Yrs. of NHL service: 15
Born: Chicago, Ill.; Aug. 16, 1966
Position: centre
Height: 6-1
Weight: 205
Uniform no.: 16
Shoots: left

Career statistics:

GP	G	A	TP	PIM
998	340	450	790	862

1995-96 statistics:

GP	G	A	TP	+/-	PIM	PP	SH	GW	GT	S	PCT
51	27	22	49	0	65	16	0	1	0	147	18.4

1996-97 statistics:

GP	G	A	TP	+/-	PIM	PP	SH	GW	GT	S	PCT
79	25	30	55	-14	51	5	1	6	0	195	12.8

1997-98 statistics:

GP	G	A	TP	+/-	PIM	PP	SH	GW	GT	S	PCT
56	11	11	22	-9	35	5	1	1	0	123	8.9

1998-99 statistics:

GP	G	A	TP	+/-	PIM	PP	SH	GW	GT	S	PCT
61	10	15	25	-3	29	2	1	2	0	88	11.4

It was Graham who banished Olczyk to the minors for the first time in the veteran's career. He played well in Chicago after the coaching change, scoring 17 points in his last 23 games.

PROJECTION

The versatile Olczyk can produce 20 to 25 goals and an equal number of assists.

LAST SEASON

Appeared in seven games with Chicago (IHL), scoring 2-2 — 4. Missed 11 games due to coach's decision.

THE FINESSE GAME

It's been hard for Olczyk to get playing time in recent seasons as he is not a first-line player anymore, but he can fill in nicely as a versatile second-line and specialty teams player.

He doesn't have great speed but he is deceptive, and Olczyk works hard to get open. He loves to shoot, without being selfish. He can play all three forward positions and he brings a centre's playmaking sense to the wing. He is most effective from the left side, from the top of the circle in. He has a long reach with a fair backhand shot.

Olczyk is at his best on the power play. He likes the extra open ice and is creative. He also kills penalties well, and is smart enough to function as a safety valve on a line with a one-way forward.

THE PHYSICAL GAME

The reason Olczyk falls out of favour with so many coaches is that he is a big guy who doesn't play big. He fights for the puck but isn't as determined in his play away from the puck. He will take a hit to make a play, yet he doesn't initiate and isn't strong along the wall.

THE INTANGIBLES

An unrestricted free agent, Olczyk's ice time and production will depend on where he signs; he was another 'Hawk who suffered under the Dirk Graham system.

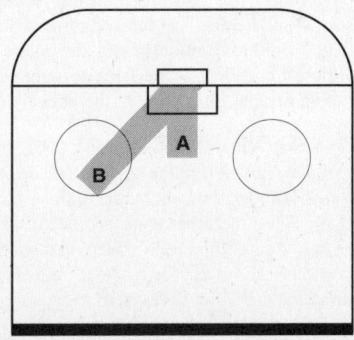

BOB PROBERT

Yrs. of NHL service: 13
Born: Windsor, Ont.; June 5, 1965
Position: right wing
Height: 6-3
Weight: 225
Uniform no.: 24
Shoots: left

Career statistics:

GP	G	A	TP	PIM
726	151	195	346	2907

1995-96 statistics:

GP	G	A	TP	+/-	PIM	PP	SH	GW	GT	S	PCT
78	19	21	40	+15	237	1	0	3	0	97	19.6

1996-97 statistics:

GP	G	A	TP	+/-	PIM	PP	SH	GW	GT	S	PCT
82	9	14	23	-3	326	1	0	3	0	111	8.1

1997-98 statistics:

GP	G	A	TP	+/-	PIM	PP	SH	GW	GT	S	PCT
14	2	1	3	-7	48	2	0	0	0	18	11.1

1998-99 statistics:

GP	G	A	TP	+/-	PIM	PP	SH	GW	GT	S	PCT
78	7	14	21	-11	206	0	0	3	0	87	8.0

LAST SEASON

Led team in penalty minutes. Missed one game due to suspension. Missed four games due to coach's decision. Scored final goal at Maple Leaf Gardens.

THE FINESSE GAME

Probert is a slugger with a nice touch. He needs a little time to get away his shot, but, let's face it, not too many brave souls play him that tight. In traffic, he can stickhandle and even slide a backhand pass down low. His shots aren't heavy, but he is accurate and shoots mostly from close range. He is smart with the puck and doesn't give it away.

Probert has diminished to where he is a borderline third-line player. He doesn't have open-ice speed, but in tight he has one-step quickness and can even pivot surprisingly well with the puck. He has to play with linemates who get him the puck since he can't help out in pursuing it. He plays a low-risk game and doesn't make mistakes that hurt his team.

Chicago didn't use him much on the power play last season. When he does get the assignment, Probert parks himself right in front of the net; the goalie looks like a bobble-head doll as he tries to peer around Probert's giant frame for a view of the puck.

THE PHYSICAL GAME

Still one of the scariest fighters in the NHL, Probert is strong, quick-fisted and mean, but he is slow to rile on some nights, when the other team decides it's best to let a sleeping dog lie. If he falls asleep on the ice, he's a nonfactor. He steps up for his teammates and is strong along the wall. He works hard every night.

THE INTANGIBLES

Probert has become a fairly skilled tough guy with a terrific attitude and dedication to the game and his teammates. He was urged to fight when Dirk Graham was coaching the team last season, then urged to be a hockey player when Lorne Molleken stepped in. His ice time will no doubt be reduced, but he is still a valuable team guy.

PROJECTION

Probert is a solid contributor who works hard and knows his role. He will score 25 points and make everyone around him braver.

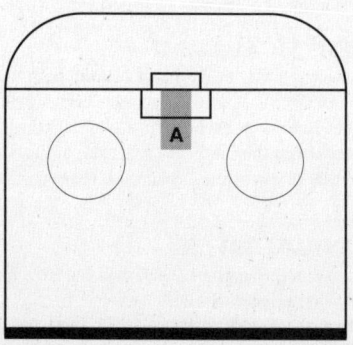

JOCELYN THIBAULT

Yrs. of NHL service: 6
Born: Montreal, Que.; Jan. 12, 1975
Position: goaltender
Height: 5-11
Weight: 170
Uniform no.: 41
Catches: left

Career statistics:

GP	MIN	GA	SO	GAA	A	PIM
267	14886	688	16	2.77	3	6

1995-96 statistics:

GP	MIN	GAA	W	L	T	SO	GA	S	SAPCT	PIM
50	2892	2.86	26	17	5	3	138	1480	.907	2

1996-97 statistics:

GP	MIN	GAA	W	L	T	SO	GA	S	SAPCT	PIM
61	3397	2.90	22	24	11	1	164	1815	.910	0

1997-98 statistics:

GP	MIN	GAA	W	L	T	SO	GA	S	SAPCT	PIM
47	2652	2.47	19	15	8	2	109	1109	.902	0

1998-99 statistics:

GP	MIN	GAA	W	L	T	SO	GA	S	SAPCT	PIM
52	3014	2.71	21	26	5	4	136	1435	.905	2

LAST SEASON

Acquired from Montreal with Dave Manson and Brad Brown for Jeff Hackett, Eric Weinrich, Alain Nasreddine and future considerations, Nov. 16, 1998. Career best goals-against average. Career high in games played.

THE PHYSICAL GAME

Thibault is a small goalie whose technique makes him look even smaller. He is a butterfly-style goalie, but when he goes to his knees he doesn't keep his torso upright (as Patrick Roy does so splendidly), and that costs Thibault a big chunk of net.

Thibault plays deep in his net and does not challenge shooters. He relies on his reflexes — which, happily for him, happen to be excellent. He is a battler and doesn't give up on a puck, but he creates problems for himself by making the easy saves more difficult than they would be if his fundamentals were better. Thibault has a good glove hand and quick feet, and he is a good skater with lateral mobility.

Thibault has improved his stickhandling, and how he directs his rebounds. He is not very strong on his stick, which means he fails to make key poke-checks or knock away cross-crease passes.

Thibault weighs about 160 pounds, sopping wet, so he needs a light workload (55 starts) to be effective down the stretch without wearing down.

THE MENTAL GAME

Although being traded to Montreal (in 1995) was a dream come true for the French-speaking goalie, getting out was the end to a nightmare. Thibault is a far more relaxed athlete in Chicago. The pressure to be a number one goalie is sufficient without having to do it for the Canadiens.

THE INTANGIBLES

Thibault has yet to prove he belongs among the NHL's top-level goalies. The notoriously chintzy Blackhawks should hire an experienced backup, one who could not only handle 20 to 25 starts but would tutor and bolster Thibault. The likelihood of that happening equals the chances of the 'Hawks winning the Cup this year.

PROJECTION

Thibault managed 24 wins last season with two non-playoff teams. He will need a better team in front of him to flirt with 30.

ALEXEI ZHAMNOV

Yrs. of NHL service: 7
Born: Moscow, Russia; Oct. 1, 1970
Position: centre
Height: 6-1
Weight: 195
Uniform no.: 26
Shoots: left

Career statistics:

GP	G	A	TP	PIM
455	164	275	439	372

1995-96 statistics:

GP	G	A	TP	+/-	PIM	PP	SH	GW	GT	S	PCT
58	22	37	59	-4	65	5	0	2	0	199	11.1

1996-97 statistics:

GP	G	A	TP	+/-	PIM	PP	SH	GW	GT	S	PCT
74	20	42	62	+18	56	6	1	2	0	208	9.6

1997-98 statistics:

GP	G	A	TP	+/-	PIM	PP	SH	GW	GT	S	PCT
70	21	28	49	+16	61	6	2	3	1	193	10.9

1998-99 statistics:

GP	G	A	TP	+/-	PIM	PP	SH	GW	GT	S	PCT
76	20	41	61	-10	50	8	1	2	1	200	10.0

LAST SEASON

Led team in assists. Second on team in points and shots. Tied for second on team in power-play goals. Third on team in goals. Missed four games with back injury. Missed one game with bruised ankle. Missed one game with flu.

THE FINESSE GAME

Zhamnov chafed under Dirk Graham's dump-and-chase system, and was one of the most relieved Blackhawks when Lorne Molleken took over and opened up the attack.

Zhamnov's game is puck control: he can carry it at top speed or work the give-and-go. The Russian is a crafty playmaker and is not too unselfish. He has an accurate if not overpowering shot. As well, he can blast off the pass, or manoeuvre until he has a screen and then wrist it. On the power play, he works the left point or, if used low, can dart in and out in front of the goalie, using his soft hands for a tip.

Defensively, Zhamnov is sound and was frequently used against other teams' top forward lines. He is a dedicated backchecker and never leaves the zone too quickly.

THE PHYSICAL GAME

Zhamnov will bump to prevent a scoring chance or go for a loose puck, but body work is not his forte. The knock on Zhamnov is his lack of physical play, but he works hard and competes. He is strong and fights his way through traffic in front of the net to get to a puck, when he wants to. He needs to do a better job of tying up the opposing centre on face-offs, since he wins few draws cleanly.

THE INTANGIBLES

Zhamnov alone lacks the consistency and personality needed to lift his game to an elite level, which is why the continued presence of Doug Gilmour would be a help to him. He's not an initiator or a team leader, as Gilmour is. Zhamnov could even play on a line with Gilmour as a winger.

PROJECTION

Zhamnov has 100-point potential, but 80 is more likely.

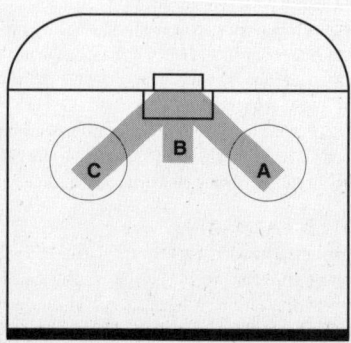

COLORADO AVALANCHE

Players' Statistics 1998-99

POS.	NO.	PLAYER	GP	G	A	PTS	+/-	PIM	PP	SH	GW	GT	S	PCT
C	21	PETER FORSBERG	78	30	67	97	27	108	9	2	7		217	13.8
C	19	JOE SAKIC	73	41	55	96	23	29	12	5	6	1	255	16.1
R	14	THEOREN FLEURY	75	40	53	93	26	86	8	3	5	2	301	13.3
R	22	CLAUDE LEMIEUX	82	27	24	51	0	102	11		8	1	292	9.2
R	18	ADAM DEADMARSH	66	22	27	49	-2	99	10		3	1	152	14.5
R	23	*MILAN HEJDUK	82	14	34	48	8	26	4		5		178	7.9
C	37	*CHRIS DRURY	79	20	24	44	9	62	6		3	1	138	14.5
L	13	VALERI KAMENSKY	65	14	30	44	1	28	2		2		123	11.4
D	8	SANDIS OZOLINSH	39	7	25	32	10	22	4		3		81	8.6
D	52	ADAM FOOTE	64	5	16	21	20	92	3				83	6.0
D	2	SYLVAIN LEFEBVRE	76	2	18	20	18	48					64	3.1
R	12	SHEAN DONOVAN	68	7	12	19	4	37	1		1		81	8.6
D	3	AARON MILLER	76	5	13	18	3	42	1		2		87	5.7
C	26	STEPHANE YELLE	72	8	7	15	-8	40	1				99	8.1
D	5	ALEXEI GUSAROV	54	3	10	13	12	24	1				28	10.7
C	32	DALE HUNTER	62	2	9	11	-7	119					24	8.3
L	25	SHJON PODEIN	55	3	6	9	-5	24					75	4.0
D	29	ERIC MESSIER	31	4	2	6	0	14	1		1		30	13.3
R	36	JEFF ODGERS	75	2	3	5	-3	259	1				39	5.1
D	7	GREG DE VRIES	73	1	3	4	-7	64					57	1.8
D	24	JON KLEMM	39	1	2	3	4	31					28	3.6
D	4	CAM RUSSELL	42	1	2	3	-4	94					15	6.7
R	17	*CHRISTIAN MATTE	7	1	1	2	-2						9	11.1
L	16	WARREN RYCHEL	28		2	2	3	63					15	
G	33	PATRICK ROY	61		2	2	0	28						
D	15	*MICHAEL GAUL	1				0						1	
C	44	*SERGE AUBIN	1				0						1	
D	59	*BRIAN WHITE	2				0							
L	6	CHRIS DINGMAN	3				-2	24					1	
G	30	*MARC DENIS	4				0							
D	32	JEFF BUCHANAN	6				1	6					1	
D	43	*DAN SMITH	12				5	9					6	
G	1	CRAIG BILLINGTON	21				0	2						
D	27	*SCOTT PARKER	27				-3	71					3	

GP = games played; G = goals; A = assists; PTS = points; +/- = goals-for minus goals-against while player is on ice; PIM = penalties in minutes; PP = power-play goals; SH = shorthanded goals; GW = game-winning goals; GT = game-tying goals; S = no. of shots; PCT = percentage of goals to shots; * = rookie

ADAM DEADMARSH

Yrs. of NHL service: 5
Born: Trail, B.C.; May 10, 1975
Position: right wing
Height: 6-0
Weight: 195
Uniform no.: 18
Shoots: right

Career statistics:

GP	G	A	TP	PIM
343	107	110	217	558

1995-96 statistics:

GP	G	A	TP	+/-	PIM	PP	SH	GW	GT	S	PCT
78	21	27	48	+20	142	3	0	2	0	151	13.9

1996-97 statistics:

GP	G	A	TP	+/-	PIM	PP	SH	GW	GT	S	PCT
78	33	27	60	+8	136	10	3	4	0	198	16.7

1997-98 statistics:

GP	G	A	TP	+/-	PIM	PP	SH	GW	GT	S	PCT
73	22	21	43	0	125	10	0	6	3	187	11.8

1998-99 statistics:

GP	G	A	TP	+/-	PIM	PP	SH	GW	GT	S	PCT
66	22	27	49	-2	99	10	0	3	1	152	14.5

LAST SEASON

Tied for second on team in shooting percentage. Matched career high in assists. Missed five games with eye injury. Missed two games with rib injury. Missed three games with elbow injury. Missed six games with back injury.

THE FINESSE GAME

Deadmarsh is capable of playing in every situation. He's not as accomplished as some of the other forwards on the team, but he has a meanness and a toughness about him. He's relentless in finishing his checks. He's very strong on the puck, very strong on the boards, and he's one of the faster players in the NHL in a power package. He doesn't have the same touch around the net as Keith Tkachuk or John LeClair, but he's a bona fide 30-goal scorer. Although better at centre than wing, he is versatile enough to handle either role.

Deadmarsh is a bigger version of Kevin Dineen. He's feisty and tough and can work in a checking role, but he can also score off the chances he creates with his defense and can be moved onto the top two scoring lines and not look out of place. His game is incredibly mature. He is reliable enough to be put out on the ice to protect a lead in the late minutes of a game, because he'll do what it takes to win.

Deadmarsh doesn't have to be the glamour guy (Colorado is loaded with those types, anyway), but that doesn't mean he provides unskilled labour. He has dangerous speed and quickness, and a nice scoring touch to convert the chances he creates off his forechecking. He can play centre as well as both wings, so he's versatile. He doesn't play a complex game. He's a basic up-and-down winger, a nice complement to all of the flash and dash on the Avalanche. He excells as a dedicated penalty killer.

THE PHYSICAL GAME

Deadmarsh always finishes his checks. He has a strong work ethic with honest toughness. He never backs down from a challenge and issues some of his own. He isn't a dirty player, but he will fight when challenged or stand up for his teammates.

THE INTANGIBLES

Deadmarsh has a smirk on his face all the time. Either you want to kiss it or punch it. No one knows whether that's just the way his face is, or if he's laughing at you, and that can be a real irritant when he's playing. He runs over you with that little smile and you think, "Are you serious? Are you pulling my leg?" You just don't know with him, which really makes him a tough guy to play against, and he plays like this every night. Yet, he doesn't say boo off the ice. He's not a comedian by any means. He's actually a pretty quiet guy.

Deadmarsh has a huge upside. There just aren't enough good things scouts can find to say about him. He is the kind of player who will seldom be one of the three stars of the game, but he'll be one of the guys who found five ways to help win a game.

PROJECTION

Deadmarsh lacks the fine touch to be an elite scorer, but he should consistently score in the 30-goal, 60-point range. He is still a pretty well-kept secret thanks to his more flamboyant teammates.

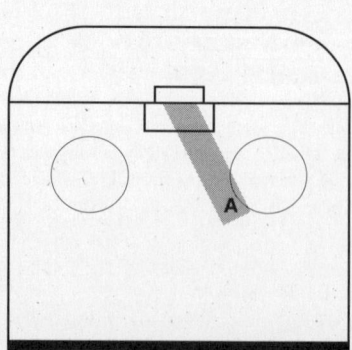

SHEAN DONOVAN

Yrs. of NHL service: 4
Born: Timmins, Ont.; Jan. 22, 1975
Position: right wing
Height: 6-2
Weight: 190
Uniform no.: 12
Shoots: right

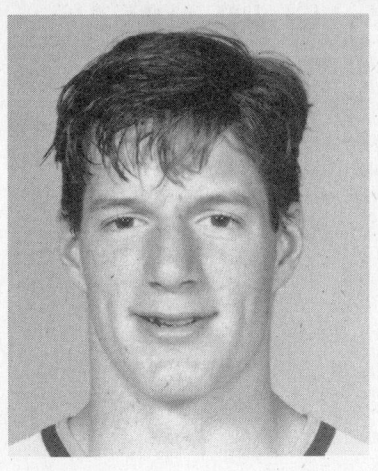

Career statistics:

GP	G	A	TP	PIM
296	37	36	73	194

1995-96 statistics:

GP	G	A	TP	+/-	PIM	PP	SH	GW	GT	S	PCT
74	13	8	21	-17	39	0	1	2	0	73	17.8

1996-97 statistics:

GP	G	A	TP	+/-	PIM	PP	SH	GW	GT	S	PCT
73	9	6	15	-18	42	0	1	0	0	115	7.8

1997-98 statistics:

GP	G	A	TP	+/-	PIM	PP	SH	GW	GT	S	PCT
67	8	10	18	+6	70	0	0	0	0	81	9.9

1998-99 statistics:

GP	G	A	TP	+/-	PIM	PP	SH	GW	GT	S	PCT
68	7	12	19	+4	37	1	0	1	0	81	8.6

LAST SEASON

Missed two games with hip injury. Missed one game with concussion. Missed one game with shoulder injury. Missed 10 games due to coach's decision.

THE FINESSE GAME

Donovan has big-league speed, but lacks the hand skills to make the best use of it. His quickness and powerful stride allow him to shift directions with agility. And he doesn't waste energy. He knows where he is supposed to be positioned and reads plays well. He has good anticipation, which stamps him as a strong penalty killer, though he is not a shorthanded scoring threat yet because of his lack of moves on a breakaway.

Donovan may never be a great point getter because of his lack of scoring or playmaking touch. For the second straight season he showed fatal lapses in effort and, as a result, was a healthy scratch down the stretch and into the playoffs. He has a future as a third-line checking winger, but has to become more consistent. He isn't fazed by facing some of the league's better wingers, and has the skating ability to shadow almost anyone.

THE PHYSICAL GAME

Donovan is always busy making hits, and he brings a lot of energy to a game when he is in the mood. He doesn't have much of a mean streak but showed an occasional willingness to agitate last season; he needs to get under his opponents' skin a little more. He takes the body but doesn't punish people. He is well-conditioned and has good stamina. He doesn't get pushed off the puck easily.

THE INTANGIBLES

A player with Donovan's kind of speed can have a comfortable, 10-year NHL career, but he'll only be successful if he can add more scoring and intensity. He is likely on his way out of Colorado, which didn't use him at all in the playoffs.

PROJECTION

All speed, no finish. He is a longshot to score much more than 20 points.

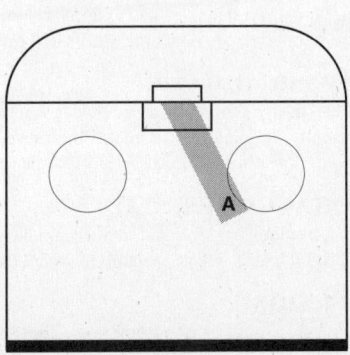

CHRIS DRURY

Yrs. of NHL service: 1
Born: Trumbull, CT; Aug. 20, 1976
Position: centre
Height: 5-10
Weight: 180
Uniform no.: 37
Shoots: right

Career statistics:

GP	G	A	TP	PIM
79	20	24	44	62

1998-99 statistics:

GP	G	A	TP	+/-	PIM	PP	SH	GW	GT	S	PCT
79	20	24	44	+9	62	6	0	3	1	138	14.5

LAST SEASON
Won 1999 Calder Trophy. Named to NHL All-Rookie Team. Led NHL rookies in power-play goals. Second among NHL rookies and tied for second on team in shooting percentage. Third among NHL rookies in points and shots. Second among NHL rookies in goals. Fourth among NHL rookies in assists. Missed two games with hip pointer.

THE FINESSE GAME
Few rookies can step into a veteran roster like Colorado's and make the kind of impact Drury did last season. He has a wealth of assets, starting with his quick skating. He gets in on top of a goalie very quickly — and we mean right on top, because he isn't afraid of crease-crashing — and is able to control the puck while charging in. He knows where the net is and isn't afraid to get there by the shortest route possible, even though he isn't the biggest guy in the world.

Drury has quick and soft hands, and is a steady scorer. His effort is so consistent, and that's what produces his points. He already has an advanced defensive side to his game, so even on nights when he isn't putting points on the board, he is doing something to help his team win.

He is capable of playing wing or centre and was used extensively at both positions, although centre is his natural position. He is a smart player who quickly grasps any concepts the coaching staff pitch him.

THE PHYSICAL GAME
Small but sturdy, Drury doesn't back down an inch and is usually the player who makes the pre-emptive hit. He sure doesn't play little.

THE INTANGIBLES
Drury is remarkably poised and mature and has excellent leadership skills. He is probably a future captain.

PROJECTION
Drury will score a lot of important goals for this franchise in the future. He is likely to at least match his rookie goal total and probably exceed it by five to 10 goals.

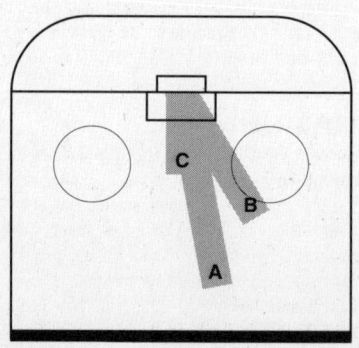

ADAM FOOTE

Yrs. of NHL service: 8
Born: Toronto, Ont.; July 10, 1971
Position: right defense
Height: 6-1
Weight: 202
Uniform no.: 52
Shoots: right

Career statistics:

GP	G	A	TP	PIM
499	23	89	112	770

1995-96 statistics:

GP	G	A	TP	+/-	PIM	PP	SH	GW	GT	S	PCT
73	5	11	16	+27	88	1	0	1	0	49	10.2

1996-97 statistics:

GP	G	A	TP	+/-	PIM	PP	SH	GW	GT	S	PCT
78	2	19	21	+16	135	0	0	0	0	60	3.3

1997-98 statistics:

GP	G	A	TP	+/-	PIM	PP	SH	GW	GT	S	PCT
77	3	14	17	-3	124	0	0	1	0	64	4.7

1998-99 statistics:

GP	G	A	TP	+/-	PIM	PP	SH	GW	GT	S	PCT
64	5	16	21	+20	92	3	0	0	0	83	6.0

LAST SEASON
Missed 15 games with elbow injury. Missed three games with concussion.

THE FINESSE GAME
Foote is frequently overlooked because of flashier teammates like Peter Forsberg and Sandis Ozolinsh, but he is one of the most important foot soldiers (aw, we couldn't resist) on the Avalanche.

He has great foot speed and quickness. Defensively, he's strong in his coverage as a stay-at-home type, but he's not creative with the puck, probably his major deficiency. Still, all of the Avalanche defensemen are encouraged to jump into the attack and Foote eagerly does so when given the chance. He is wise in his pinches and knows when to drive to the slot, and he has a useful shot. He won't take wild chances. The Avalanche would like to wring more offensive production out of him, but at this stage of his career it is not likely to happen. Foote believes his job is to concentrate on defense, though he handled some power-play time before Sandis Ozolinsh returned to the fold after his contract hassle.

Foote usually skates the puck out of his zone and is less likely to find the man for an outlet pass. There are few defensemen in the league who can match him in getting the first few strides in and jumping out of the zone. He is an excellent penalty killer.

THE PHYSICAL GAME
Foote is big and solid and uses his body well. He plays the man and not the puck. He is highly aggressive in his defensive zone; anyone trying to get through Foote to the net will pay a price. He plays it smart and takes few bad penalties. In recent seasons, he has really stepped up his physical play and he dishes out some powerful checks. He has good lower-body strength and drives his body upwards, resulting in a heavy impact with his unfortunate target. Foote can fight when provoked and stands up for his teammates.

THE INTANGIBLES
Colorado's defense gets far less credit than its forwards and goalie, but Foote is an excellent two-way defenseman whose skills are just a notch below elite class. He is one of the more underrated defensemen around. What sets him apart is his competitiveness. He thrives on the challenge of playing against other teams' top forwards.

PROJECTION
Foote plays a defense-heavy game but can still score 25 to 30 points.

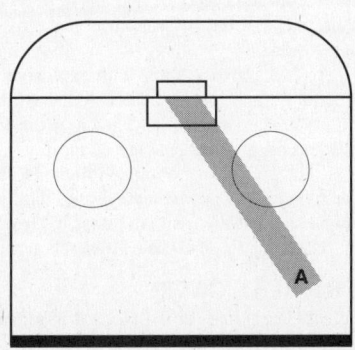

PETER FORSBERG

Yrs. of NHL service: 5
Born: Ornskoldsvik, Sweden; July 20, 1973
Position: centre
Height: 6-0
Weight: 190
Uniform no.: 21
Shoots: left

Career statistics:

GP	G	A	TP	PIM
344	128	312	440	338

1995-96 statistics:

GP	G	A	TP	+/-	PIM	PP	SH	GW	GT	S	PCT
82	30	86	116	+26	47	7	3	3	0	217	13.8

1996-97 statistics:

GP	G	A	TP	+/-	PIM	PP	SH	GW	GT	S	PCT
65	28	58	86	+31	73	5	4	4	0	188	14.9

1997-98 statistics:

GP	G	A	TP	+/-	PIM	PP	SH	GW	GT	S	PCT
72	25	66	91	+6	94	7	3	7	1	202	12.4

1998-99 statistics:

GP	G	A	TP	+/-	PIM	PP	SH	GW	GT	S	PCT
78	30	67	97	+27	108	9	2	7	0	217	13.8

LAST SEASON

Led team in assists and points for third consecutive season. Fourth in NHL in points. Second in NHL in assists. Led team in plus-minus. Second on team in game-winning goals. Third on team in goals, penalty minutes and power-play goals. Missed two games with elbow injury. Missed one game with groin injury. Missed one game with thigh injury.

THE FINESSE GAME

Forsberg is used in all game situations: power play, penalty killing and four-on-four. His skill level is world class in every department.

Forsberg protects the puck as well as anybody in the league. He is so strong that he can control the puck with one arm while fending off a checker, and still make an effective pass. His passing is nearly as good as teammate Joe Sakic's. He can be off-balance with his head down, digging the puck out of his skates, and he can still put a pass on a teammate's stick. Forsberg seems to be thinking a play or two ahead of everyone else on the ice and has an amazing sense of every player's position.

Forsberg is a smooth skater with explosive speed (think Teemu Selanne) and can accelerate while carrying the puck. He has excellent vision of the ice and is an outstanding playmaker. One of the few knocks on him is that he doesn't shoot enough. He works most effectively down between the circles with a wrist or backhand shot off the rush, and does his best work in traffic. There's a lot of Gordie Howe about him.

THE PHYSICAL GAME

Forsberg is better suited for the North American style than most Europeans — or many North Americans, for that matter. He is tough to knock down. He loves the game and dishes out more than he receives. He relishes contact; just try to knock him off the puck. He has a wide skating base and great balance. He can be cross-checked while he's on his backhand and still not lose control of the puck. Jaromir Jagr may be the only other player in the league who can do that.

Forsberg has a cockiness that many great athletes carry about them like an aura; he dares people to try to intimidate him. His drive to succeed helps him handle the cheap stuff and keep going. He's got a mean streak, too: bringing his stick up into people's faces. He also takes abuse, as he did from Edmonton's Bill Guerin in the playoffs. Forsberg plays equally hard on any given inch of the ice. His physical game sometimes goes over the top and robs him of his offensive game, which is why rivals are so eager to engage him.

THE INTANGIBLES

Forsberg suffered a shoulder injury during the playoffs that required surgery. It will cost him at least the first month of the season. Colorado gave him a three-year, $30-million contract extension in April.

PROJECTION

Forsberg could be the best all-around forward in the NHL. The only question mark about him this season is his recovery from his operation.

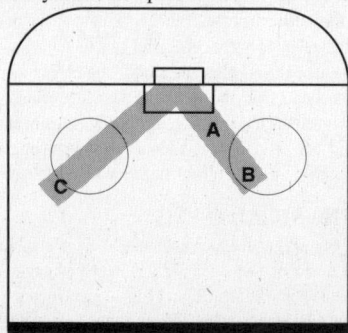

ALEXEI GUSAROV

Yrs. of NHL service: 9
Born: Leningrad, Russia; July 18, 1964
Position: left defense
Height: 6-3
Weight: 185
Uniform no.: 5
Shoots: left

Career statistics:

GP	G	A	TP	PIM
522	36	118	154	285

1995-96 statistics:

GP	G	A	TP	+/-	PIM	PP	SH	GW	GT	S	PCT
65	5	15	20	+29	56	0	0	0	0	42	11.9

1996-97 statistics:

GP	G	A	TP	+/-	PIM	PP	SH	GW	GT	S	PCT
58	2	12	14	+4	28	0	0	0	0	33	6.1

1997-98 statistics:

GP	G	A	TP	+/-	PIM	PP	SH	GW	GT	S	PCT
72	4	10	14	+9	42	0	1	1	0	47	8.5

1998-99 statistics:

GP	G	A	TP	+/-	PIM	PP	SH	GW	GT	S	PCT
54	3	10	13	+12	24	1	0	0	0	28	10.7

LAST SEASON

Missed 25 games with broken finger. Missed one game with stiff neck.

THE FINESSE GAME

Gusarov's game was once offense-heavy, but in recent years he has used his finesse skills to defensive purpose. A shifty skater with a long reach and great range, he can handle the puck on the rush or move it out of his zone. He doesn't mind gambling on offense if the ice opens up for him. Sometimes he will get overly involved in the attack and has to be reined in by coaches.

Gusarov is aggressive and confident in his skills, but he can get careless in the neutral zone and get his partner into trouble by overcommitting. He has improved his positional play but will sometimes get caught puck-watching.

He is a good penalty killer and sees spot duty on the second power-play unit.

THE PHYSICAL GAME

Gusarov does not like the physical game. He would rather use his long reach and stick to fish around for the puck than bump people. He's tall and lean and doesn't have the best build or base for contact.

THE INTANGIBLES

With Sylvain Lefebvre lost to free agency, Gusarov — who got a new contract during the off-season — will have to step up as a veteran.

PROJECTION

Gusarov is a likely 25-point scorer.

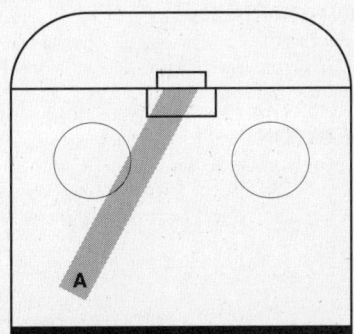

MILAN HEJDUK

Yrs. of NHL service: 1
Born: Usti-nad-Labem, Czech.; Feb. 14, 1976
Position: right wing
Height: 5-11
Weight: 165
Uniform no.: 23
Shoots: right

Career statistics:

GP	G	A	TP	PIM
82	14	34	48	26

1998-99 statistics:

GP	G	A	TP	+/-	PIM	PP	SH	GW	GT	S	PCT
82	14	34	48	+8	26	4	0	5	0	178	7.9

LAST SEASON

Finalist for 1999 Calder Trophy. Named to NHL All-Rookie Team. Led NHL rookies in points and shots. Led NHL rookies in assists. Tied for first among NHL rookies in game-winning goals. Fifth among NHL rookies in goals. Tied for fourth among NHL rookies in power-play goals. One of two Avalanche players to appear in all 82 games.

THE FINESSE GAME

Hejduk was part of a powerful one-two rookie punch with teammate and occasional linemate Chris Drury, who won the Calder Trophy. Hejduk has quick hands and is a finisher. He is willing to pay the price around the net to score.

An absolute late bloomer (he was a 1994 draft pick), Hejduk was well down the Colorado depth chart until he performed well for the gold medal-winning Czech team in 1998, not looking out of place among his veteran teammates.

Hejduk has excellent speed, hockey sense and vision. He was durable (not getting hurt until the playoffs) and has great stamina.

THE PHYSICAL GAME

Hejduk is small but has a solid build. He doesn't stay out of the high-traffic areas.

THE INTANGIBLES

Hejduk spoke little English and played on a team with no other Czech players. Imagine how he'll do when he starts feeling comfortable.

PROJECTION

Hejduk is only going to get better. He will get more ice time, as the Avalanche have lost some veteran forwards to free agency, and he could step up to 20 to 25 goals.

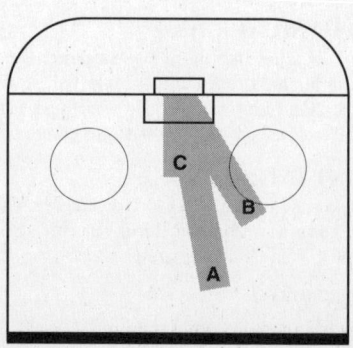

JON KLEMM

Yrs. of NHL service: 4
Born: Cranbrook, B.C.; Jan. 8, 1970
Position: right defense
Height: 6-3
Weight: 200
Uniform no.: 24
Shoots: right

Career statistics:

GP	G	A	TP	PIM
257	20	38	58	124

1995-96 statistics:

GP	G	A	TP	+/-	PIM	PP	SH	GW	GT	S	PCT
56	3	12	15	+12	20	0	1	1	0	61	4.9

1996-97 statistics:

GP	G	A	TP	+/-	PIM	PP	SH	GW	GT	S	PCT
80	9	15	24	+12	37	1	2	1	0	103	8.7

1997-98 statistics:

GP	G	A	TP	+/-	PIM	PP	SH	GW	GT	S	PCT
67	6	8	14	-3	30	0	0	0	1	60	10.0

1998-99 statistics:

GP	G	A	TP	+/-	PIM	PP	SH	GW	GT	S	PCT
39	1	2	3	+4	31	0	0	0	0	28	3.6

LAST SEASON

Missed 29 games with torn knee ligaments. Missed six games with appendectomy.

THE FINESSE GAME

Klemm has enough finesse skills that the Avalanche can use him up front in a pinch. His defensive skills are good enough that he is frequently assigned the unenviable task of playing the stay-at-home partner to the wayward Sandis Ozolinsh. Let's just say he's had a lot of experience facing two-on-ones.

Klemm is an all-purpose defenseman who does everything the team asks of him. His skating is average, but he plays within his limitations. When he's moved up front he fills the role of a grinding winger.

THE PHYSICAL GAME

Klemm doesn't go looking for hits. He eliminates his man but doesn't have the explosive drive from his legs to make powerful highlight hits.

THE INTANGIBLES

Klemm is a sportswriter's nightmare, because he's so quiet, yet he's appreciated by his coaches and teammates for his willingness to do anything for the team. He is an underrated member of the Colorado defense corps. Injuries and surgery kept him from playing at peak form last season, but he'll be needed this year with Sylvain Lefebvre lost to free agency.

PROJECTION

Klemm keeps his game conservative, but probably has a little better offensive upside than he has shown. He is capable of 25 to 30 points a season.

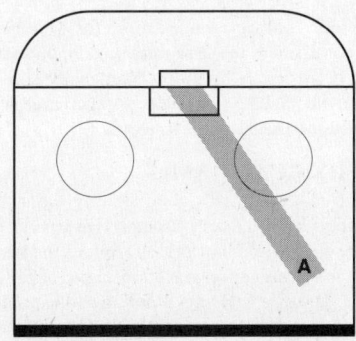

CLAUDE LEMIEUX

Yrs. of NHL service: 15
Born: Buckingham, Que.; July 16, 1965
Position: right wing
Height: 6-1
Weight: 215
Uniform no.: 22
Shoots: right

Career statistics:

GP	G	A	TP	PIM
920	325	326	651	1494

1995-96 statistics:

GP	G	A	TP	+/-	PIM	PP	SH	GW	GT	S	PCT
79	39	32	71	+14	117	9	2	10	0	315	12.4

1996-97 statistics:

GP	G	A	TP	+/-	PIM	PP	SH	GW	GT	S	PCT
45	11	17	28	-4	43	5	0	4	0	168	6.5

1997-98 statistics:

GP	G	A	TP	+/-	PIM	PP	SH	GW	GT	S	PCT
78	26	27	53	-7	115	11	1	1	1	261	10.0

1998-99 statistics:

GP	G	A	TP	+/-	PIM	PP	SH	GW	GT	S	PCT
82	27	24	51	0	102	11	0	8	1	292	9.2

LAST SEASON

Led team and tied for third in NHL in game-winning goals. Second on team in power-play goals and shots. One of two Avalanche players to appear in all 82 games.

THE FINESSE GAME

Lemieux is a shooter, a disturber, a force. He loves the puck, wants the puck, needs the puck and is sometimes obsessed with the puck. When he is struggling, that selfishness hurts the team. But when he gets into his groove everyone is happy to stand back and let him roll, and on the talented Avalanche team, he fits right in.

When Lemieux is on, he can rock the house. He has a hard slap shot and shoots well off the fly. He isn't afraid to jam the front of the net for tips and screens and will battle for loose pucks. He has great hands for close-in shots. Although he isn't asked to do much defensively for Colorado, he can kill penalties and check top forwards.

Lemieux is always valued more for what he does in the playoffs than in the regular season, but with the Avalanche losing both Valeri Kamensky and Theo Fleury to free agency, Lemieux's experience will be needed during the 82-game schedule.

THE PHYSICAL GAME

Lemieux is strong, with good skating balance and great upper-body and arm strength. He is very tough along the boards and in traffic in front of the net, out-duelling many bigger opponents because of his fierce desire. Because he is always whining and yapping, the abuse Lemieux takes is often ignored, but it's not unusual to find him with welts across his arms and cuts on his face. The satisfaction comes from knowing that his opponent usually looks even worse, but he still takes dumb penalties by jawing at the referees, who have little patience with him after all these years.

Of course, he also infuriates opponents by goading them into dropping their gloves and then turtling. Lemieux will gleefully inform you he's a lover, not a fighter.

THE INTANGIBLES

Lemieux is in his walk year, and will likely want to audition for a big new contract here or elsewhere. Since he thrives on pressure, it's unlikely to weigh on him.

PROJECTION

Lemieux will probably score 25 goals during the regular season. He is one of the great playoff performers of his generation; he's never played on a team that missed the playoffs.

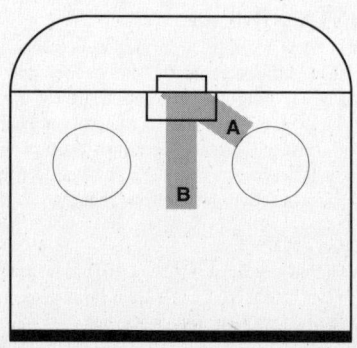

SANDIS OZOLINSH

Yrs. of NHL service: 7
Born: Riga, Latvia; Aug. 3, 1972
Position: left defense
Height: 6-1
Weight: 195
Uniform no.: 8
Shoots: left

Career statistics:

GP	G	A	TP	PIM
424	99	218	317	323

1995-96 statistics:

GP	G	A	TP	+/-	PIM	PP	SH	GW	GT	S	PCT
73	14	40	54	+2	54	8	1	1	1	166	8.4

1996-97 statistics:

GP	G	A	TP	+/-	PIM	PP	SH	GW	GT	S	PCT
80	23	45	68	+4	88	13	0	4	1	232	9.9

1997-98 statistics:

GP	G	A	TP	+/-	PIM	PP	SH	GW	GT	S	PCT
66	13	38	51	-12	65	9	0	2	1	135	9.6

1998-99 statistics:

GP	G	A	TP	+/-	PIM	PP	SH	GW	GT	S	PCT
39	7	25	32	+10	22	4	0	3	0	81	8.6

LAST SEASON

Led team defensemen in scoring for the second consecutive season. Missed 40 games with contract dispute. Missed two games with bruised sternum. Missed one game with sprained wrist.

THE FINESSE GAME

Ozolinsh is a pure "offensemen," but one who never knows when not to go. Unlike more intelligent rushing defensemen, such as Brian Leetch and Ray Bourque, Ozolinsh sees only one traffic light, and it's stuck on green.

He likes to start things by pressing in the neutral zone, where he will gamble and try to intercept cross-ice passes. His defense partner and the forwards will always have to be alert to guard against odd-man rushes back, because he doesn't recognize when it's a good time to be aggressive or when to back off.

He will start the breakout play with his smooth skating, then spring a teammate with a crisp pass. He can pass on his forehand or backhand, which is a good thing because he is all over the ice. He will follow up the play to create an odd-man rush, trail in for a drop pass or drive to the net for a rebound.

Ozolinsh has good straightaway speed, but he can't make a lot of agile, pretty moves. Because he can't weave his way through a number of defenders, he has to power his way into open ice with the puck and drive the defenders back through intimidation. His speed does help him recover to get back and help out on the odd-man rushes against that he helps create.

He sometimes hangs onto the puck too long. He has a variety of shots, with his best being a one-timer from the off-side on the power play. He is not as effective when he works down low. He does not stop and start well, especially when moving backwards.

THE PHYSICAL GAME

Ozolinsh goes into areas of the ice where he gets hit a lot, but he is stronger than he looks. He is all business on the ice and pays the price to get the puck, but he needs to develop more strength to clear out his crease.

THE INTANGIBLES

Ozolinsh led team defensemen in scoring despite missing half the season.

PROJECTION

If he had not been absent half the season, Ozolinsh would have finished with a pro-rated 64 points and would have led all NHL defensemen in scoring, which is precisely what we expect him to do this season.

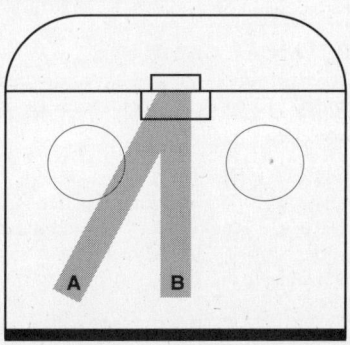

SHJON PODEIN

Yrs. of NHL service: 7
Born: Rochester, Minn.; Mar. 5, 1968
Position: left wing
Height: 6-2
Weight: 200
Uniform no.: 25
Shoots: left

Career statistics:

GP	G	A	TP	PIM
410	46	54	100	240

1995-96 statistics:

GP	G	A	TP	+/-	PIM	PP	SH	GW	GT	S	PCT
79	15	10	25	+25	89	0	4	4	0	115	13.0

1996-97 statistics:

GP	G	A	TP	+/-	PIM	PP	SH	GW	GT	S	PCT
82	14	18	32	+7	41	0	0	4	0	153	9.2

1997-98 statistics:

GP	G	A	TP	+/-	PIM	PP	SH	GW	GT	S	PCT
82	11	13	24	+8	53	1	1	2	0	126	8.7

1998-99 statistics:

GP	G	A	TP	+/-	PIM	PP	SH	GW	GT	S	PCT
55	3	6	9	-5	24	0	0	0	0	75	4.0

PROJECTION

In his defensive role, Podein can pop in 15 to 20 goals a season.

LAST SEASON

Acquired from Philadelphia with a conditional draft pick in 2000 for Keith Jones and a 2000 conditional draft pick, Nov. 12, 1998. Missed 25 games with fractured leg, ending consecutive games-played streak at 223. Missed one game with bruised foot.

THE FINESSE GAME

Podein is a labourer. He works hard, loves his job and uses his size well. He started out as a centre, but he is better suited as a winger because his hands aren't great. He is happiest in a dump-and-chase game, where he can use his straightaway speed to bore in on the puck carrier.

A mucker, Podein is not a fancy scorer. He gets most of his goals from digging around the net for rebounds and loose pucks. He doesn't have particularly good hockey sense.

Podein is not an agile skater but he is sturdy for work along the boards, and he can work up a pretty good head of steam. Just don't ask him to turn.

THE PHYSICAL GAME

Podein is antagonistic, with a bit of a mean streak, and he tends to be a bit careless with his stick. He can take bad penalties because of that tendency.

THE INTANGIBLES

Podein plays well on a checking line. He is a high-energy player and penalty killer who can lift the bench with a strong shift. He has taken a long route to the NHL and will have to work to stay here.

PATRICK ROY

Yrs. of NHL service: 14
Born: Quebec City, Que.; Oct. 5, 1965
Position: goaltender
Height: 6-0
Weight: 192
Uniform no.: 33
Catches: left

Career statistics:

GP	MIN	GA	SO	GAA	A	PIM
778	45404	2014	46	2.66	34	196

1995-96 statistics:

GP	MIN	GAA	W	L	T	SO	GA	S	SAPCT	PIM
61	3565	2.78	34	24	2	2	165	1797	.908	10

1996-97 statistics:

GP	MIN	GAA	W	L	T	SO	GA	S	SAPCT	PIM
62	3698	2.32	38	15	7	7	143	1861	.923	15

1997-98 statistics:

GP	MIN	GAA	W	L	T	SO	GA	S	SAPCT	PIM
65	3835	2.39	31	19	13	4	153	1825	.916	39

1998-99 statistics:

GP	MIN	GAA	W	L	T	SO	GA	S	SAPCT	PIM
61	3648	2.29	32	19	8	5	139	1673	.917	28

LAST SEASON

Tied for fourth in NHL in wins. Second among NHL goalies in penalty minutes (27). Missed four games with knee injury. Missed four games with back spasms. Missed two games with groin injury.

THE PHYSICAL GAME

Roy is the butterfly goalie by whom all others are judged. He tempts shooters with a gaping hole between his pads, then, when he has the guy suckered, snaps the pads closed at the last second to deny the goal. There is no one in the NHL better at this tantalizing technique.

Although he is tall but not broad, Roy uses his body well. He plays his angles, stays at the top of his crease and squares his body to the shooter. He is able to absorb the shot and deaden it, so there are few juicy rebounds left on his doorstep.

He goes down much sooner than he did earlier in his career. The book on Roy is to try to beat him high. Usually there isn't much net there and it's a small spot for a shooter to hit. He gets into slumps when he allows wide-angle shots taken from the blueline to the top of the circle, but those lapses are seldom prolonged.

Roy comes back to the rest of the pack in his puckhandling, where he is merely average. As for his skating, he seldom moves out of his net. When he gets in trouble he moves back and forth on his knees rather than trying to regain his feet. His glove hand isn't great, either. It's good, but he prefers to use his body. If he is under a strong forecheck, he isn't shy about freezing the puck for a draw, especially since he plays with excellent face-off men in Colorado.

THE MENTAL GAME

Roy is still considered one of the best money goalies in the game. He believes it, too, which is the most important thing. Few goalies play with as much visible attitude as Roy, which can intimidate shooters.

THE INTANGIBLES

Given the supporting cast of young studs in front of him, Roy might be able to play effectively until he's 40. Thanks to Roy, up-and-comer Marc Denis will not have to worry about getting rushed into the lineup, though his time may be coming sooner than expected.

PROJECTION

Another 30-win season is in store.

Colorado Avalanche

JOE SAKIC

Yrs. of NHL service: 11
Born: Burnaby, B.C.; July 7, 1969
Position: centre
Height: 5-11
Weight: 185
Uniform no.: 19
Shoots: left

Career statistics:

GP	G	A	TP	PIM
792	375	604	979	340

1995-96 statistics:

GP	G	A	TP	+/-	PIM	PP	SH	GW	GT	S	PCT
82	51	69	120	+14	44	17	6	7	1	339	15.0

1996-97 statistics:

GP	G	A	TP	+/-	PIM	PP	SH	GW	GT	S	PCT
65	22	52	74	-10	34	10	2	5	0	261	8.4

1997-98 statistics:

GP	G	A	TP	+/-	PIM	PP	SH	GW	GT	S	PCT
64	27	36	63	0	50	12	1	2	1	254	10.6

1998-99 statistics:

GP	G	A	TP	+/-	PIM	PP	SH	GW	GT	S	PCT
73	41	55	96	+23	29	12	5	6	1	255	16.1

LAST SEASON

Led team and sixth in NHL in goals. Led team and tied for NHL lead in shorthanded goals. Second on team and fifth in NHL in assists and points. Led team in power-play goals and shooting percentage. Third on team in plus-minus and game-winning goals. Missed seven games with bruised right shoulder.

THE FINESSE GAME

Sakic is one of the game's best playmakers. It's not a secret that he has also become one of the game's best shooters, and he isn't shy about it. But how do you defend against him? Try to keep the puck far, far away.

Sakic has one of the most explosive first steps in the league. He finds and hits the holes in a hurry — even with the puck — to create his chances. He uses a stick shaft with a little "whip" in it that makes his shots more dangerous. He has one of the best wrist shots and snap shots in the NHL and one of the quickest releases in the game.

Sakic's most impressive gift, however, is his great patience with the puck. He will hold it until the last minute, when he has drawn the defenders to him and opened up ice, creating time and space for his linemates. This makes him a gem on the power play, where he works down low and just off the half-boards on the right wing. He can also play the point, as he did during Sandis Ozolinsh's absence.

Sakic is a scoring threat every time he is on the ice because he can craft a dangerous scoring chance out of a situation that looks innocent. He is lethal trailing the rush. He takes a pass in full stride without slowing, then dekes and shoots before the goalie can even flinch. He is a good face-off man, and if he's tied up he uses his skates to kick the puck free.

THE PHYSICAL GAME

Sakic is not a physical player. He's stronger than he looks and, like Wayne Gretzky in his prime, spins off his checks when opponents take runs at him. He uses his body to protect the puck when he is carrying deep; you have to go through him to get it away. He will try to keep going through traffic or along the boards with the puck, and often squirts free with it because he is able to maintain control and his balance. He creates turnovers with his quickness and hands, but not by initiating contact. He has been quite durable through his career.

THE INTANGIBLES

Sakic will face more intense checking pressure until Peter Forsberg is able to return from his shoulder injury. Sakic is a quiet leader, a soft-spoken guy who doesn't draw much attention to himself. His game does that. He may be one of the most respected NHLers for his talent, competitive nature and class.

PROJECTION

Sakic should flirt with 100 points again this season.

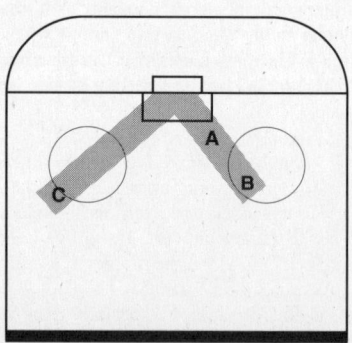

ALEX TANGUAY

Yrs. of NHL service: 0
Born: Ste-Justine, Que.; Nov. 21, 1979
Position: centre
Height: 6-0
Weight: 180
Uniform no.: n.a.
Shoots: left

Career junior statistics:
GP	G	A	TP	PIM
152	101	114	214	122

LAST SEASON
Will be entering first NHL season. Appeared in five games with Hershey (AHL), scoring 1-2 — 3. Appeared in 31 games with Halifax (QMJHL), scoring 27-34 — 61. Missed games with concussion.

THE FINESSE GAME
You will notice Tanguay when he gets to the NHL because he is known for scoring highlight-reel goals. A strong skater with breakaway speed, he goes from zero to 60 in a flash. And he does it with the puck, too. He is absolutely dynamic. He loves to have the puck but he isn't selfish and is a good playmaker.

Like any young player, Tanguay needs to develop the defensive aspect of his game, but this was an asset for him in junior.

He likes his team to rely on him and will develop into a player who can be used in all game situations.

THE PHYSICAL GAME
Tanguay isn't big but he has an aggressive side. He is highly competitive and will do what it takes to win. He is in good shape and handles a lot of minutes.

THE INTANGIBLES
Tanguay finished the season in the minors and may start there, but the Avalanche will be looking for a few good young men and he might just crack the roster. He missed two months early in the season with a concussion in juniors, but he came back strong.

PROJECTION
Tanguay scored eight goals in the 1998 preseason and was close to making the Avs, but he couldn't reach a contract agreement. He is ready for the pros. He could score 15 goals in his initial year.

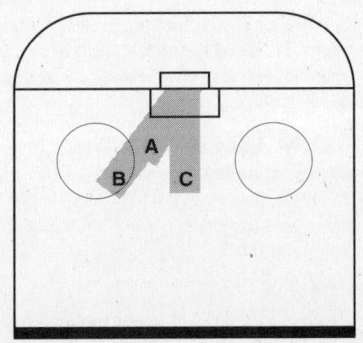

STEPHANE YELLE

Yrs. of NHL service: 4
Born: Ottawa, Ont.; May 9, 1974
Position: centre
Height: 6-1
Weight: 162
Uniform no.: 26
Shoots: left

Career statistics:

GP	G	A	TP	PIM
303	37	53	90	156

1995-96 statistics:

GP	G	A	TP	+/-	PIM	PP	SH	GW	GT	S	PCT
71	13	14	27	+15	30	0	2	1	0	93	14.0

1996-97 statistics:

GP	G	A	TP	+/-	PIM	PP	SH	GW	GT	S	PCT
79	9	17	26	+1	38	0	1	1	0	89	10.1

1997-98 statistics:

GP	G	A	TP	+/-	PIM	PP	SH	GW	GT	S	PCT
81	7	15	22	-10	48	0	1	0	0	93	7.5

1998-99 statistics:

GP	G	A	TP	+/-	PIM	PP	SH	GW	GT	S	PCT
72	8	7	15	-8	40	1	0	0	0	99	8.1

LAST SEASON

Missed nine games with sprained wrist. Missed one game with hip injury.

THE FINESSE GAME

Yelle is a smart player who reads the play extremely well, and it's his knowledge of the game that has made him an NHL player. His other skills are average: he's a good skater, but he sees the ice in terms of his defensive role. He's a player you want on the ice to kill penalties or to protect a lead.

Yelle doesn't take many face-offs. He doesn't have the hands to get involved in the offense. He isn't even a real shorthanded threat because he doesn't have breakaway speed and will make the safe play instead of the prettier high-risk one. He kills penalties but has to be paired with a better-skating partner.

On a team of glamorous forwards, Yelle is blue-collar.

THE PHYSICAL GAME

Yelle is a tall and stringy-looking athlete with toothpicks for legs. He handles himself well, because even though he doesn't look strong he finds a way to get the puck out.

THE INTANGIBLES

Yelle was injured during the playoffs and was sorely missed by the Avalanche at crunch time. He is a smart player and works diligently, which compensates for some of his other flaws.

PROJECTION

Yelle's absolute top end is 15 goals, though he is more likely to score goals in single digits. His value is as a defensive forward.

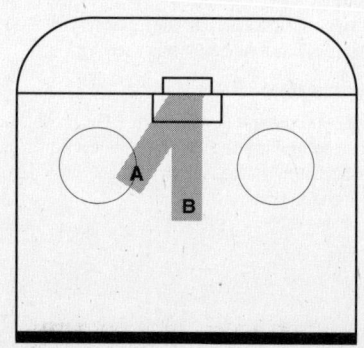

DALLAS STARS

Players' Statistics 1998-99

POS.	NO.	PLAYER	GP	G	A	PTS	+/-	PIM	PP	SH	GW	GT	S	PCT
C	9	MIKE MODANO	77	34	47	81	29	44	6	4	7	1	224	15.2
L	22	BRETT HULL	60	32	26	58	19	30	15		11		192	16.7
C	25	JOE NIEUWENDYK	67	28	27	55	11	34	8		8	1	157	17.8
R	26	JERE LEHTINEN	74	20	32	52	29	18	7	1	2		173	11.6
D	56	SERGEI ZUBOV	81	10	41	51	9	20	5		3		155	6.5
D	5	DARRYL SYDOR	74	14	34	48	-1	50	9		2	1	163	8.6
L	15	JAMIE LANGENBRUNNER	75	12	33	45	10	62	4		1		145	8.3
R	16	PAT VERBEEK	78	17	17	34	11	133	8		2	1	134	12.7
R	29	GRANT MARSHALL	82	13	18	31	1	85	2		4		112	11.6
D	2	DERIAN HATCHER	80	9	21	30	21	102	3		2		125	7.2
C	33	BENOIT HOGUE	74	12	17	29	-10	54	2		3		121	9.9
R	12	MIKE KEANE	81	6	23	29	-2	62	1	1	1		106	5.7
C	41	TONY HRKAC	69	13	14	27	2	26	2		2	2	67	19.4
C	18	DEREK PLANTE	51	6	14	20	4	16	1				90	6.7
L	14	DAVE REID	73	6	11	17	0	16	1		1		81	7.4
C	21	GUY CARBONNEAU	74	4	12	16	-3	31			2		60	6.7
D	24	RICHARD MATVICHUK	64	3	9	12	23	51	1				54	5.6
D	27	SHAWN CHAMBERS	61	2	9	11	6	18	1		1		82	2.4
D	3	CRAIG LUDWIG	80	2	6	8	5	87					39	5.1
C	10	BRIAN SKRUDLAND	40	4	1	5	2	33			1		33	12.1
D	37	*BRAD LUKOWICH	14	1	2	3	3	19					8	12.5
L	17	BRENT SEVERYN	30	1	2	3	-2	50					22	4.5
C	49	*JONATHAN SIM	7	1		1	1	12					8	12.5
C	39	*KELLY FAIRCHILD	1				0						4	
G	30	*EMMANUEL FERNANDEZ	1				0							
D	34	*PETR BUZEK	2				0	2						
C	23	AARON GAVEY	7				-1	10					4	
L	46	*JAMIE WRIGHT	11				-3						10	
R	11	*BLAKE SLOAN	14				-1	10					7	
D	6	DOUG LIDSTER	17				0	10					7	
L	28	*JASON BOTTERILL	17				-2	23					8	
G	1	ROMAN TUREK	26				0							
G	20	ED BELFOUR	61				0	26						

GP = games played; G = goals; A = assists; PTS = points; +/- = goals-for minus goals-against while player is on ice; PIM = penalties in minutes; PP = power-play goals; SH = shorthanded goals; GW = game-winning goals; GT = game-tying goals; S = no. of shots; PCT = percentage of goals to shots; * = rookie

ED BELFOUR

Yrs. of NHL service: 9
Born: Carman, Man.; Apr. 21, 1965
Position: goaltender
Height: 5-11
Weight: 182
Uniform no.: 20
Catches: left

Career statistics:

GP	MIN	GA	SO	GAA	A	PIM
550	31553	1319	45	2.51	15	294

1995-96 statistics:

GP	MIN	GAA	W	L	T	SO	GA	S	SAPCT	PIM
50	2956	2.74	22	17	10	1	2.74	1373	.902	36

1996-97 statistics:

GP	MIN	GAA	W	L	T	SO	GA	S	SAPCT	PIM
46	2723	2.89	14	24	6	2	131	1317	.900	34

1997-98 statistics:

GP	MIN	GAA	W	L	T	SO	GA	S	SAPCT	PIM
61	3581	1.88	37	12	10	9	112	1335	.916	18

1998-99 statistics:

GP	MIN	GAA	W	L	T	SO	GA	S	SAPCT	PIM
61	3536	1.99	35	15	9	5	117	1373	.915	26

LAST SEASON

Won 1999 Jennings Trophy. Became first goalie in NHL history to record 35 or more wins in five seasons. Tied for second among NHL goalies in wins. Tied for third among NHL goalies in goals-against average with career best.

THE PHYSICAL GAME

Belfour's style relies more on athleticism than technique. He is always on his belly, his side, his back. He's a runner-up only to Dominik Hasek as the best goalie with the worst style in the NHL.

Belfour has great instincts and reads the play well in front of him. He plays with an inverted-V, giving the five-hole but usually taking it away from the shooter with his quick reflexes. He is very aggressive and frequently comes so far out of his crease that he gets tangled with his own defenders — as well as running interference on the opponents. He knows he is well-padded and is not afraid to use his body, though injuries have made him less aggressive than in the past.

In fact, Belfour uses his body more than his stick or glove, and that is part of his problem. He tries to make the majority of saves with his torso, making the routine saves more difficult. Fortunately, playing behind a strong team keeps his quality shots to a minimum.

Belfour tends to keep his glove low. The book on him is to shoot high, but that's the case with most NHL goalies — and a lot of NHL shooters have trouble picking that spot. He sometimes gives up bad rebounds, but his defense is so good and so quick they will swoop in on the puck before the opposition gets a second or third whack.

Belfour has a lot of confidence and an impressive ability to handle the puck, though he sometimes overdoes it. He will usually go for short passes, but can go for the home-run play as well. He uses his body to screen when handling the puck for a 15-foot pass, and often sets picks for his forwards.

THE MENTAL GAME

Belfour kept his cool during the Stars' Cup run, and a number of the players attributed much of their success to his improved demeanour. He prevailed in a number of tight games, a testament to his strong mental game.

THE INTANGIBLES

A goalie isn't a winner until he wins the Cup. It had to be a huge source of personal satisfaction to Belfour to be the goalie of record on a championship squad. It will only make him a better goalie.

PROJECTION

Belfour was well-spotted with Roman Turek last season. Now that Turek has been dealt to St. Louis, the Stars need to find Belfour a compatible number two to repeat the 60-start, 35-win pattern that was so successful last season.

SHAWN CHAMBERS

Yrs. of NHL service: 11
Born: Royal Oaks, Mich.; Oct. 11, 1966
Position: left defense
Height: 6-2
Weight: 200
Uniform no.: 297
Shoots: left

Career statistics:

GP	G	A	TP	PIM
621	50	185	235	360

1995-96 statistics:

GP	G	A	TP	+/-	PIM	PP	SH	GW	GT	S	PCT
64	2	21	23	+1	18	2	0	1	0	112	1.8

1996-97 statistics:

GP	G	A	TP	+/-	PIM	PP	SH	GW	GT	S	PCT
73	4	17	21	+17	19	1	0	0	0	114	3.5

1997-98 statistics:

GP	G	A	TP	+/-	PIM	PP	SH	GW	GT	S	PCT
57	2	22	24	+11	26	1	1	0	0	73	2.7

1998-99 statistics:

GP	G	A	TP	+/-	PIM	PP	SH	GW	GT	S	PCT
61	2	9	11	+6	18	1	0	1	0	82	2.4

LAST SEASON

Missed 12 games with hip flexor. Missed seven games with fractured hand. Missed one game with sprained thumb.

THE FINESSE GAME

Much of Chambers's success is due to his ability to understand his limitations and play within them. The ill-advised gambles that plagued his early career are now a rarity. His career has been revived by moves in the past few seasons to two teams that play a strong defensive system, first in New Jersey, and now in Dallas.

Chambers can work on a second power-play unit. He has an awkward looking shot but he manages to get it away quickly, low and on net. He has the poise and the hand skills to be able to fake out a checker with a faux slapper, move to the top of the circle and drill it. He has a nice touch for keeping the puck in along the blueline.

Chambers's smarts put him a cut above the rest. Although his finesse skills may be average, he has great anticipation. He also understands the game well and knows where the puck is going before the play is made. He does the little things well — little wrist shots, little dump-ins, nothing that shouts out.

Chambers prefers to move the puck out of the zone with a quick pass rather than lug it. His skating isn't dazzling, but he's got some wheels and is more efficient than his style indicates.

THE PHYSICAL GAME

Although he won't put people into the third row of the stands, Chambers will hit often enough and hard enough so that, later in a game, the puck carrier will move the puck a little faster and maybe get hurried into a mistake. Dallas demands that its defensemen play a hard game. Although Chambers occasionally emerged a little worse for the wear, he deserves credit for not bailing out. Many do.

Chambers plays with a lot of enthusiasm and is a workhorse. He thrives on ice time and seems to have fun playing the game.

THE INTANGIBLES

Chambers has landed in a lot of right spots at the right time, and he now owns two Cups (plus an ankle tattoo to commemorate them). He is one of those players who isn't missed until he's out of the lineup.

PROJECTION

Chambers continues to be nibbled to death by injuries: he has averaged only 60 games a season over the past three years. Keep that in mind when assessing his potential input.

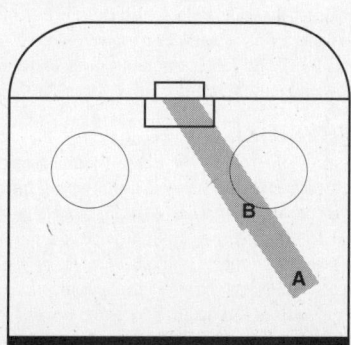

DERIAN HATCHER

Yrs. of NHL service: 8
Born: Sterling Heights, Mich.; June 4, 1972
Position: left defense
Height: 6-5
Weight: 225
Uniform no.: 2
Shoots: left

Career statistics:

GP	G	A	TP	PIM
528	54	138	192	1042

1995-96 statistics:

GP	G	A	TP	+/-	PIM	PP	SH	GW	GT	S	PCT
79	8	23	31	-12	129	2	0	1	0	125	6.4

1996-97 statistics:

GP	G	A	TP	+/-	PIM	PP	SH	GW	GT	S	PCT
63	3	19	22	+8	97	0	0	0	0	96	3.1

1997-98 statistics:

GP	G	A	TP	+/-	PIM	PP	SH	GW	GT	S	PCT
70	6	25	31	+9	132	3	0	2	0	74	8.1

1998-99 statistics:

GP	G	A	TP	+/-	PIM	PP	SH	GW	GT	S	PCT
80	9	21	30	+21	102	3	0	2	0	125	7.2

LAST SEASON

Second on team in penalty minutes. Missed two regular-season games plus five playoff games due to suspension for hit on Jeremy Roenick.

THE FINESSE GAME

Hatcher plays in all key situations and has developed confidence in his decision-making process. His skating is laboured, so he lets the play come to him. He is sturdy and well-balanced. The fewer strides he has to take, the better.

He has very good hands for a big man, and he has a good head for the game. Hatcher is fairly effective from the point on the power play — not because he has a big, booming slap shot, but because he has a good wrist shot and will get the puck on net quickly. He will join the rush eagerly once he gets into gear (his first few strides are sluggish), and he handles the puck nicely.

Hatcher plays hard in every zone, every night. His skills are just a shade below elite level, but he takes steps forward every season as a leader. He is a character player, and one his teammates look to for setting the tempo and seizing control of a game.

THE PHYSICAL GAME

Hatcher is a big force. He has a mean streak when provoked (ask Roenick) and is a punishing hitter. But he is smart enough to realize that opponents target him and want to take him off his game. It's a huge detriment to the Stars when Hatcher is in the box, and not just because he is one of their key penalty killers. He plays physically every night and demands respect and room. He's fearless. He's also a big horse and eats up all the ice time Dallas gives him, which can be 25 minutes a night. The more work he gets, the better.

THE INTANGIBLES

Hatcher will not provide big numbers, but he and Mike Modano are the cornerstones of the franchise. Hatcher is the kind of player the team looks to for consistent effort and intensity. He is a fine role model for the younger Stars and the veterans respect him as well. He is a quiet player who wants to make a big impact.

PROJECTION

Hatcher is poised to become one of the top six defensemen in the league, though he will never have the kind of numbers that inspire Norris Trophy voters. He will be a defenseman you want on your team when you have to win a clutch game. He can provide 30 points and invaluable leadership.

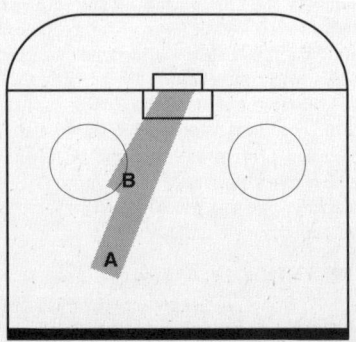

BENOIT HOGUE

Yrs. of NHL service: 11
Born: Repentigny, Que.; Oct. 28, 1966
Position: centre/right wing
Height: 5-10
Weight: 194
Uniform no.: 33
Shoots: left

Career statistics:

GP	G	A	TP	PIM
744	209	296	505	804

1995-96 statistics:

GP	G	A	TP	+/-	PIM	PP	SH	GW	GT	S	PCT
78	19	45	64	+10	104	5	0	5	0	155	12.3

1996-97 statistics:

GP	G	A	TP	+/-	PIM	PP	SH	GW	GT	S	PCT
73	19	24	43	+8	54	5	0	5	0	131	14.5

1997-98 statistics:

GP	G	A	TP	+/-	PIM	PP	SH	GW	GT	S	PCT
53	6	16	22	+7	35	3	0	1	0	55	10.9

1998-99 statistics:

GP	G	A	TP	+/-	PIM	PP	SH	GW	GT	S	PCT
74	12	17	29	-10	54	2	0	3	0	121	9.9

LAST SEASON

Acquired from Tampa Bay with a conditional draft pick in 2001 for Sergey Gusev, Mar. 21, 1999.

THE FINESSE GAME

Hogue's chief asset is his speed, which is explosive; he leaves defenders flat-footed with his acceleration. Add to that his anticipation and ability to handle the puck at a high tempo, and he's a breakaway threat. Still, Hogue is not a great puckhandler or shooter, though he capitalizes on each situation with his quickness and agility. He is a threat to score whenever he is on the ice.

Hogue has to be more accountable under the Stars system, something he finds restrictive since he loves to freewheel and freelance. He plays primarily on the left side, and even when playing centre will cut to the left-wing boards as he drives down the ice. He is not a great playmaker, but he creates scoring chances off his rushes.

Hogue is an excellent, aggressive penalty killer, a shorthanded threat who can also be used on the power play, though he lacks the patience to be as effective as he could be. He is very good on draws, though the Stars are so deep at centre he seldom has to fulfil this role.

THE PHYSICAL GAME

Hogue is a strong one-on-one player who uses his body to lean on an opponent. He is not a big checker, but he gets involved and uses his speed as a weapon to intimidate. He is a crunch-time player, whether a team needs to protect a lead or create one. He can get into ruts where he takes bad penalties.

THE INTANGIBLES

Hogue had a nightmare season personally, first playing in Tampa with a terrible team. Of course, that paled by comparison to the murder of his sister.

PROJECTION

Hogue may be little more than a rent-a-player with the Stars, and could be on the move again after helping them win a Cup. He could score 25 to 30 points on a team where he gets a little more ice time.

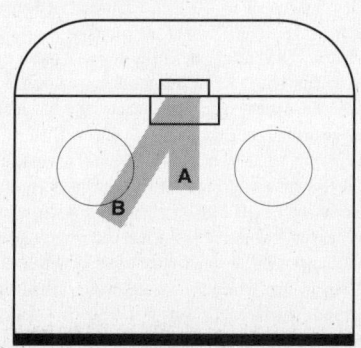

BRETT HULL

Yrs. of NHL service: 12
Born: Belleville, Ont.; Aug. 9, 1964
Position: right wing
Height: 5-10
Weight: 201
Uniform no.: 22
Shoots: right

Career statistics:

GP	G	A	TP	PIM
861	586	459	1045	328

1995-96 statistics:

GP	G	A	TP	+/-	PIM	PP	SH	GW	GT	S	PCT
70	43	40	83	+4	30	16	5	6	0	327	13.1

1996-97 statistics:

GP	G	A	TP	+/-	PIM	PP	SH	GW	GT	S	PCT
77	42	40	82	-9	10	12	2	6	2	302	13.9

1997-98 statistics:

GP	G	A	TP	+/-	PIM	PP	SH	GW	GT	S	PCT
66	27	45	72	-1	26	10	0	6	0	211	12.8

1998-99 statistics:

GP	G	A	TP	+/-	PIM	PP	SH	GW	GT	S	PCT
60	32	26	58	+19	30	15	0	11	0	192	16.7

LAST SEASON

Led team in power-play goals and game-winning goals. Second on team in goals, points, shots and shooting percentage. Missed 11 games with hamstring strain. Missed seven games with groin strain. Missed two games with bruised kidney.

THE FINESSE GAME

When Brett Hull lifted a puck over Dominik Hasek in triple overtime to win the Stanley Cup, everyone thought, "That's why the Stars got Brett Hull." When everyone found out after the game that he had played the final three shifts on one good knee and no groins, the thought was, "That's Brett Hull?"

Signing with the Stars was the best career move Hull ever made. His 80-goal days well behind him, Hull's overall game has improved enough over the past few seasons that he was not out of place on the disciplined Stars, and his dedication was evident from his first shift in Dallas.

Hull plays well in all three zones but remains a shooter first. His shot is seldom blocked — he gets it away so quickly that the defense doesn't have time to react. And his shots have tremendous velocity, especially his one-timers from the tops of the circles in.

Hull is always working to get himself in position for a pass, but he doesn't look like he's working. He sort of drifts into open ice and before a defender can react, he is firing off any kind of shot accurately. He usually moves to his off-wing on the power play. He can play the point but is a better asset down low.

Hull is an underrated playmaker who can thread a pass through traffic right onto the tape of a teammate. He will find the open man because he has soft hands and good vision. When the opponent overplays him, he makes smart decisions about whether to shoot or pass.

THE PHYSICAL GAME

Hull is compact and when he wants to hit, it's a solid check. His chronic groin injuries, though, make him high-risk. He is not as physically involved as he was when he was scoring goals at an absurd rate, but he will bump people.

THE INTANGIBLES

Hull might not be the prototypical team leader, but once he's on the ice he's as competitive as any of the elite players. His presence helped keep a once uptight Dallas room loose.

PROJECTION

Hull's big-point days are over, and 70 points this season is a reasonable target. He faces extensive rehab during the off-season for his injuries and might not be ready to start the year.

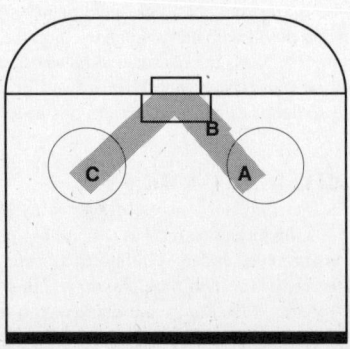

MIKE KEANE

Yrs. of NHL service: 11
Born: Winnipeg, Man.; May 28, 1967
Position: right wing
Height: 5-10
Weight: 185
Uniform no.: 12
Shoots: right

Career statistics:

GP	G	A	TP	PIM
806	116	242	368	713

1995-96 statistics:

GP	G	A	TP	+/-	PIM	PP	SH	GW	GT	S	PCT
73	10	17	27	-5	46	0	2	2	0	84	11.9

1996-97 statistics:

GP	G	A	TP	+/-	PIM	PP	SH	GW	GT	S	PCT
81	10	17	27	+2	63	0	1	1	0	91	11.0

1997-98 statistics:

GP	G	A	TP	+/-	PIM	PP	SH	GW	GT	S	PCT
83	10	13	23	-12	52	2	0	1	0	128	7.8

1998-99 statistics:

GP	G	A	TP	+/-	PIM	PP	SH	GW	GT	S	PCT
81	6	23	29	-2	62	1	1	1	0	106	5.7

LAST SEASON

Most assists and points since 1993-94. Missed one game with ankle contusion.

THE FINESSE GAME

Keane is one of the NHL's most underrated forwards. There are few better on the boards and in the corners, and he's the perfect linemate for a finisher. If you want the puck, he'll get it. Not only will he win the battle for it, he'll make a pass and then set a pick or screen. His game is skewed more to defense but he can still contribute with a big goal.

Keane's chief assets are his intelligence and desire. He doesn't waste much energy. He's a good skater and will use his speed to forecheck or create shorthanded threats when killing penalties. He can play all three forward positions, but is most effective on the right side. He is a smart player who can be thrust into almost any playing situation — a valuable role player.

THE PHYSICAL GAME

Keane is a physical catalyst. He is constantly getting in someone's way. He always finishes his checks in all three zones, and he's aggressive and will stand up for his teammates, though he is not a fighter. He has a ridiculously high pain threshold and has to be locked in a closet to keep him out of the lineup.

THE INTANGIBLES

Keane is valued as much for his character as for his hard-nosed and heads-up play. He is the kind of ideal role player who will elevate a team from good to better, but not take a mediocre (or worse) squad up a notch. Ideal for Dallas, that is.

PROJECTION

As a checking forward Keane probably won't score more than 15 goals a year, but since he prevents that many, it's not a bad trade-off. If injuries hit he can step in almost anywhere but in the net.

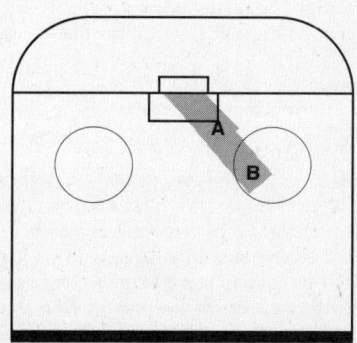

JAMIE LANGENBRUNNER

Yrs. of NHL service: 4
Born: Duluth, Minn.; July 24, 1975
Position: centre
Height: 5-11
Weight: 190
Uniform no.: 15
Shoots: right

Career statistics:

GP	G	A	TP	PIM
246	50	90	140	182

1995-96 statistics:

GP	G	A	TP	+/-	PIM	PP	SH	GW	GT	S	PCT
12	2	2	4	-2	6	1	0	0	0	15	13.3

1996-97 statistics:

GP	G	A	TP	+/-	PIM	PP	SH	GW	GT	S	PCT
76	13	26	39	-2	51	3	0	3	0	112	11.6

1997-98 statistics:

GP	G	A	TP	+/-	PIM	PP	SH	GW	GT	S	PCT
81	23	29	52	+9	61	8	0	6	1	159	14.5

1998-99 statistics:

GP	G	A	TP	+/-	PIM	PP	SH	GW	GT	S	PCT
75	12	33	45	+10	62	4	0	1	0	145	8.3

LAST SEASON

Career high in assists. Missed five games with shoulder injury. Missed one game with abdominal strain.

THE FINESSE GAME

Langenbrunner has terrific hand skills. He is intelligent and poised with the puck, and can play as a centre or a right wing, though his style of play makes him more suitable as a winger. He has good hockey vision and can pick his spots for shots. He is also a smart passer on either his forehand or backhand.

Langenbrunner is only an average skater, so he won't be coming in with speed and driving a shot off the wing. He's not dynamic at all. He has a strong short game, with his offense generated within 15 to 20 feet of the net. He has a quick release on his shot. Any deficiencies he may have are offset by his desire to compete and succeed.

Langenbrunner is a plumber, but one who is talented enough to play with the likes of Joe Nieuwendyk. Nieuwendyk's creativity has also helped Langenbrunner's awareness that a pass may come at any time, that a scoring chance may evolve at any moment. He is an aggressive forechecker who creates turnovers for his linemates.

THE PHYSICAL GAME

Langenbrunner plays a very intense game, bigger than his size allows him to. He will wear down physically. He competes hard in the hard areas of the ice, to either get a puck or get himself into a space to get the puck. He is showing signs of being a tough, competitive forward. He lacks the size to be a power forward, but he's one of the gritty types who are so annoying to play against. He won't just hang on the perimeter and won't back down — he'll even try to stir things up.

THE INTANGIBLES

Langenbrunner had to compete with Brett Hull and Pat Verbeek for ice time on the right side, and earned his spot with Nieuwendyk — a great education for a player in only his third NHL season. He has an excellent attitude to succeed.

PROJECTION

Langenbrunner is a smart, determined player, but with limited hand skills. Twenty goals appears to be his level.

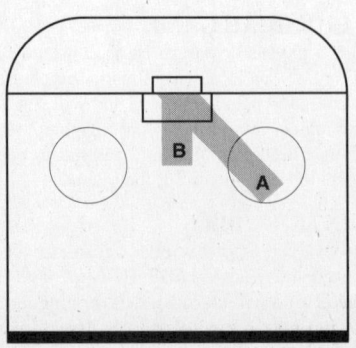

JERE LEHTINEN

Yrs. of NHL service: 4
Born: Espoo, Finland; June 24, 1973
Position: right wing
Height: 6-0
Weight: 185
Uniform no.: 26
Shoots: right

Career statistics:

GP	G	A	TP	PIM
266	65	100	165	56

1995-96 statistics:

GP	G	A	TP	+/-	PIM	PP	SH	GW	GT	S	PCT
57	6	22	28	+5	16	0	0	1	0	109	5.5

1996-97 statistics:

GP	G	A	TP	+/-	PIM	PP	SH	GW	GT	S	PCT
63	16	27	43	+26	2	3	1	2	0	134	11.9

1997-98 statistics:

GP	G	A	TP	+/-	PIM	PP	SH	GW	GT	S	PCT
72	23	19	42	+19	20	7	2	6	1	201	11.4

1998-99 statistics:

GP	G	A	TP	+/-	PIM	PP	SH	GW	GT	S	PCT
74	20	32	52	+29	18	7	1	2	0	173	11.6

LAST SEASON

Won 1999 Selke Trophy. Tied for team lead in plus-minus. Third on team in shots. Missed five games with fractured thumb. Missed two games with ankle sprain. Missed one game due to coach's decision.

THE FINESSE GAME

Lehtinen is the smartest positional player on the Stars; his second consecutive Selke win was well-deserved. He is remarkably hockey astute. He is so honest and so reliable that the other players, almost through osmosis, have to come on board.

As much as Mike Modano did on his own in the past three seasons, much of his progress can be traced to his teaming with Lehtinen. Modano returned the favour, because he is enhancing the latent offensive ability of Lehtinen, who was never noted for his scoring before. Both players have become more complete because of the other, and some of their best games have come as linemates. It was a natural move to keep Lehtinen on the line with Modano and Brett Hull to provide a defensive safeguard, but Lehtinen never hurts the line offensively, either.

Lehtinen's skating is well above adequate. He's not really top flight, but he has enough quickness and balance to play with highly skilled people. He controls the puck well and is an unselfish playmaker.

Lehtinen struggles only in his finishing. He appears to have a good shot with a quick release but at times is reluctant to shoot. He is gaining more confidence, thanks to Modano.

THE PHYSICAL GAME

Is there a loose puck that Lehtinen ever loses a battle for? Lehtinen is very strong on the puck: he protects it and won't be intimidated, and he competes along the boards. He completes his checks and never stops trying. He is very durable.

THE INTANGIBLES

Lehtinen never asks anything of the club, never complains, just asks what he can do to become better. He's a coach's dream.

PROJECTION

Selke Trophy play and 20 to 25 goals . . . it's hard to imagine asking much more out of player. Lehtinen will deliver.

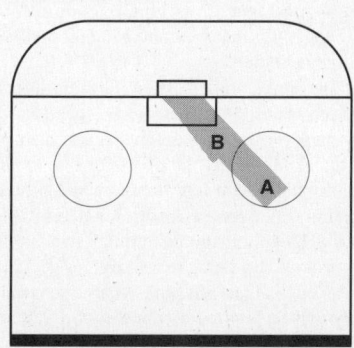

MIKE MODANO

Yrs. of NHL service: 10
Born: Livonia, Mich.; June 7, 1970
Position: centre
Height: 6-3
Weight: 200
Uniform no.: 9
Shoots: left

Career statistics:

GP	G	A	TP	PIM
710	311	424	705	518

1995-96 statistics:

GP	G	A	TP	+/-	PIM	PP	SH	GW	GT	S	PCT
78	36	45	81	-12	63	8	4	4	1	320	11.3

1996-97 statistics:

GP	G	A	TP	+/-	PIM	PP	SH	GW	GT	S	PCT
80	35	48	83	+43	42	9	5	9	2	291	12.0

1997-98 statistics:

GP	G	A	TP	+/-	PIM	PP	SH	GW	GT	S	PCT
52	21	38	59	+25	32	7	5	2	1	191	11.0

1998-99 statistics:

GP	G	A	TP	+/-	PIM	PP	SH	GW	GT	S	PCT
77	34	47	81	+29	44	6	4	7	1	224	15.2

LAST SEASON

Led team in goals, assists, points, shorthanded goals and shots. Tied for team lead in plus-minus. Third on team in game-winning goals and shooting percentage. Missed four games with groin injury.

THE FINESSE GAME

Like Steve Yzerman, Modano learned that flirting with 100-point seasons was fun, but to become a champion one has to sacrifice some of the offensive spark to play a better all-around game. Modano did so last season, and his stock is deservedly at an all-time high.

Modano has world-class skills that match up with those of just about any player in the NHL, and he's added a physical element. When there is a lot of open ice, he's a thrilling player to watch. He has outstanding offensive instincts and great hands, and he is a smooth passer and a remarkable skater in all facets. A solid, skating defensive team like Detroit can take the neutral zone away from him, but not many teams can challenge him that way and Modano makes good use of his speed there.

Modano makes other players around him better, which is the mark of a superstar. His speed and agility with the puck mesmerizes defenders and opens up ice for his linemates. He is the pivot for one of the best lines in the game, with Jere Lehtinen and Brett Hull.

Modano has become a top penalty killer (with Lehtinen). His anticipation and quick hands help him intercept passes. By going to a straighter stickblade he has improved his face-offs, and became so reliable defensively that he is thrown onto the ice in the closing minutes of a period or a game.

THE PHYSICAL GAME

Modano joined the list of Stanley Cup legends by taking the Stars to the Cup with a fractured wrist. Not only did he keep playing through the injury, but he was probably Dallas' best forward, and possibly their best player, in the final series. In his own way he is strong and tough — maybe not aggressive and feisty, but all questions about his hockey courage have been quelled forever.

THE INTANGIBLES

Modano is a true leader, molded by the example of teammate Joe Nieuwendyk. He has finally lived up to his potential and more great hockey can be expected.

PROJECTION

If scoring ever starts inching back upwards in the NHL, Modano could return to the 90-point ranks without losing one iota of his new, responsible game.

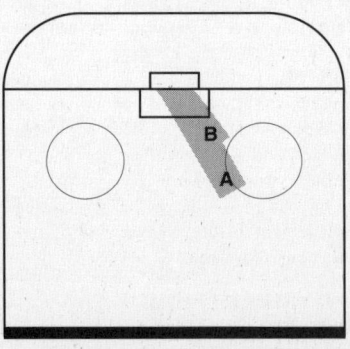

JOE NIEUWENDYK

Yrs. of NHL service: 12
Born: Oshawa, Ont.; Sept. 10, 1966
Position: centre
Height: 6-1
Weight: 195
Uniform no.: 25
Shoots: left

Career statistics:
GP	G	A	TP	PIM
835	425	398	823	453

1995-96 statistics:
GP	G	A	TP	+/-	PIM	PP	SH	GW	GT	S	PCT
52	14	18	32	-17	41	8	0	3	0	138	10.1

1996-97 statistics:
GP	G	A	TP	+/-	PIM	PP	SH	GW	GT	S	PCT
66	30	21	51	-5	32	8	0	2	2	173	17.3

1997-98 statistics:
GP	G	A	TP	+/-	PIM	PP	SH	GW	GT	S	PCT
73	39	30	69	+16	30	14	0	11	0	203	19.2

1998-99 statistics:
GP	G	A	TP	+/-	PIM	PP	SH	GW	GT	S	PCT
67	28	27	55	+11	34	8	0	8	1	157	17.8

LAST SEASON

Led team in shooting percentage. Second on team in game-winning goals. Third on team in goals and points. Tied for third on team in power-play goals. Won Conn Smythe Trophy as playoff MVP. Missed five games with inflammation in knee. Missed one game with sprained ankle. Missed one game with back spasms. Missed one game with sore knee. Missed three games due to coach's decision.

THE FINESSE GAME

Hands down, Nieuwendyk has the best hands in the NHL for tipping pucks in front of the net. This skill is priceless on power plays. He has fantastic hand-eye coordination and not only gets his blade on the puck, he acts as if he knows where he's directing it. He also has a long, powerful reach for snaring loose pucks around the crease.

Nieuwendyk is aggressive, tough and aware around the net. He can finish or make a play down low. He has the good vision, poise and hand skills to make neat little passes through traffic. He's a better playmaker than finisher, but he never doubts that he will convert his chances. He has good anticipation and uses his long stick to break up passes.

One of his best moves comes on the rush, when Nieuwendyk cuts wide to the right-wing boards then pulls the puck to his forehand for a dangerous shot.

Those same hand skills serve Nieuwendyk well on draws and he's defensively sound.

THE PHYSICAL GAME

Nieuwendyk does not initiate, but he will take the punishment around the front of the net and stand his ground. He won't be intimidated, but he won't scare anyone, either. He would like to carry more weight, but physical problems (two knee surgeries in 1998) require him to stay on the lean side.

THE INTANGIBLES

Nieuwendyk had to go through intense rehab to be ready for the 1998-99 season, and he saw the payoff in the playoffs. Dallas without Nieuwendyk couldn't get past Detroit in 1998; with him, they were carrying the Stanley Cup in 1999. It's no coincidence. The Conn Smythe went to the right Star.

PROJECTION

Recurring injuries indicate an increasing fragility for the 33-year-old centre. It's unlikely he will stay healthy through a full season and 70 points is probably his top range.

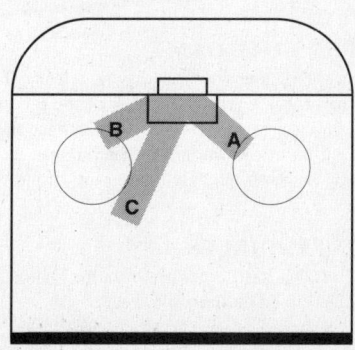

DEREK PLANTE

Yrs. of NHL service: 6
Born: Cloquet, Minn.; Jan. 17, 1971
Position: centre
Height: 5-11
Weight: 180
Uniform no.: 18
Shoots: left

Career statistics:

GP	G	A	TP	PIM
405	93	148	241	130

1995-96 statistics:

GP	G	A	TP	+/-	PIM	PP	SH	GW	GT	S	PCT
76	23	33	56	-4	28	4	0	5	0	203	11.3

1996-97 statistics:

GP	G	A	TP	+/-	PIM	PP	SH	GW	GT	S	PCT
82	27	26	53	+14	24	5	0	6	1	191	14.1

1997-98 statistics:

GP	G	A	TP	+/-	PIM	PP	SH	GW	GT	S	PCT
72	13	21	34	+8	26	5	0	1	0	150	8.7

1998-99 statistics:

GP	G	A	TP	+/-	PIM	PP	SH	GW	GT	S	PCT
51	6	14	20	+4	16	1	0	0	0	90	6.7

PROJECTION

In a full-time role and with the right wingers, 50 points is Plante's ceiling.

LAST SEASON

Acquired from Buffalo for a 1999 second-round draft pick, Mar. 23, 1999. Missed two games with back spasms. Missed one game with flu. Missed 18 games due to coach's decision.

THE FINESSE GAME

Plante has a frail-looking build, yet is remarkably durable. He compensates for his lack of stature with quickness and hand skills. He does not have blazing speed, but he can get the edge on a defender with a quick initial burst. He's very mobile, with a change of gears.

It would obviously help Plante to play with a big winger who could convert his setups. He is an excellent passer, with sharp instincts around the net, and he works very well with the open ice on the power play. He would rather pass than shoot.

Despite his good hand-eye coordination, Plante is average on draws and really loses an edge to bigger centres.

THE PHYSICAL GAME

Plante has a slender frame and is not strong. He has always had trouble with the length of the pro season, tending to wear down if he gets too much ice time. He pays attention to conditioning, which helps, but he is limited by his physique. He loses a lot of one-on-one battles.

THE INTANGIBLES

Plante found it hard cracking a tough Dallas lineup and is likely to be on the move again.

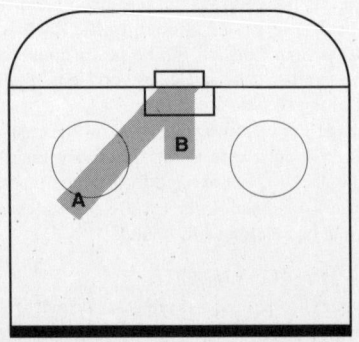

JAMIE PUSHOR

Yrs. of NHL service: 3
Born: Lethbridge, Alberta; Feb. 11, 1973
Position: right defense
Height: 6-3
Weight: 225
Uniform no.: 4
Shoots: right

Career statistics:

GP	G	A	TP	PIM
214	7	17	24	339

1995-96 statistics:

GP	G	A	TP	+/-	PIM	PP	SH	GW	GT	S	PCT
5	0	1	1	+2	17	0	0	0	0	6	0.0

1996-97 statistics:

GP	G	A	TP	+/-	PIM	PP	SH	GW	GT	S	PCT
75	4	7	11	+1	129	0	0	0	0	63	6.3

1997-98 statistics:

GP	G	A	TP	+/-	PIM	PP	SH	GW	GT	S	PCT
64	2	7	9	+3	81	0	0	0	0	51	3.9

1998-99 statistics:

GP	G	A	TP	+/-	PIM	PP	SH	GW	GT	S	PCT
70	1	2	3	-20	112	0	0	0	0	75	1.3

PROJECTION

Pushor won't compile points or penalty minutes, but will play a steady, stay-at-home style.

LAST SEASON

Acquired by Dallas from Atlanta for Jason Botterill, July 15, 1999. Acquired by Atlanta from Anaheim in Expansion Draft, June 25, 1999. Missed five games with shoulder injury. Missed two games with eye injury. Missed five games due to coach's decision.

THE FINESSE GAME

Pushor is a steady defenseman who has paid his dues. He is a good skater with average speed and accleration and above-average balance. He won't rush the puck up-ice, but he will make the smart first pass to get the puck out of the zone. He can get panicky and make the risky pass in front of his own goal.

Pushor reads plays well defensively. He uses his range to take away passing lanes and force attackers to the boards. He does the dirty work along the boards and in the corners. He knows his size is what got him to the NHL and it's his willingness to use his strength that will keep him there.

Pushor doesn't get involved much offensively because he lacks the hand skills and vision. He will not push his way in much beyond the blueline.

THE PHYSICAL GAME

Pushor is not overly aggressive, but he is strong on his skates and strong along the wall. He has good size and can be a solid hitter. Once in awhile he gets carried away with his checking and steps up to make risky open-ice hits in the neutral zone.

THE INTANGIBLES

Pushor was a number five or six defenseman with the Mighty Ducks. He'll get a chance to be in the top four in Dallas.

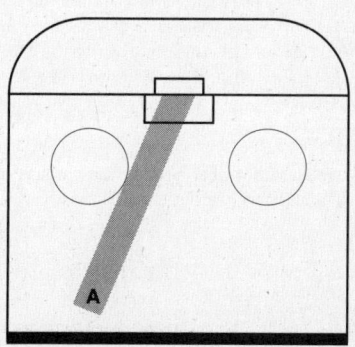

BLAKE SLOAN

Yrs. of NHL service: 0
Born: Park Ridge, IL; July 27, 1975
Position: right wing
Height: 5-10
Weight: 193
Uniform no.: 11
Shoots: right

Career statistics:

GP	G	A	TP	PIM
14	0	0	0	10

1998-99 statistics:

GP	G	A	TP	+/-	PIM	PP	SH	GW	GT	S	PCT
14	0	0	0	-1	10	0	0	0	0	7	.0

LAST SEASON

Will be entering first full NHL season. Appeared in 62 games with Houston (IHL), scoring 8-10 — 18. Missed five games due to coach's decision.

THE FINESSE GAME

Sloan played in the minors as a defenseman, but because of his size and his less-than-elite skills will make his way in the NHL as a winger.

The Stars were actually scouting another player in the farm system when Sloan caught their eye and earned a contract and a late-season promotion. He also appeared in 19 playoff games with the Stars, playing a fourth-line role.

Sloan has no hands to speak of, but he finishes his checks and on the forecheck can churn up loose pucks with his effort. He is disciplined and plays within Dallas' strict system, which earned him points with the coaching staff. Sloan skates well.

THE PHYSICAL GAME

Small but solid, Sloan uses every ounce of his muscle and hustle. He was an undrafted player and lived every minor leaguer's dream when the Stars sought him out. He ended up with a job and a ring.

THE INTANGIBLES

Honest effort should be rewarded and Sloan's was last season. He will probably keep a spot on the fourth line but could get more playing time, since the Stars are a little light on the left side. He will provide energy with every shift.

PROJECTION

Sloan's goals will probably be of the garbage variety, and if he breaks double digits it will be a surprise.

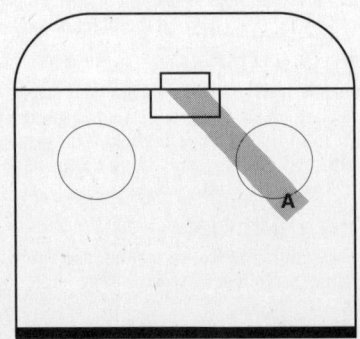

DARRYL SYDOR

Yrs. of NHL service: 7
Born: Edmonton, Alta.; May 13, 1972
Position: right defense
Height: 6-0
Weight: 195
Uniform no.: 5
Shoots: left

Career statistics:

GP	G	A	TP	PIM
549	55	200	255	439

1995-96 statistics:

GP	G	A	TP	+/-	PIM	PP	SH	GW	GT	S	PCT
84	3	17	20	-12	75	2	0	0	0	117	2.6

1996-97 statistics:

GP	G	A	TP	+/-	PIM	PP	SH	GW	GT	S	PCT
82	8	40	48	+37	51	2	0	2	0	142	5.6

1997-98 statistics:

GP	G	A	TP	+/-	PIM	PP	SH	GW	GT	S	PCT
79	11	35	46	+17	51	4	1	1	0	166	6.6

1998-99 statistics:

GP	G	A	TP	+/-	PIM	PP	SH	GW	GT	S	PCT
74	14	34	48	-1	50	9	0	2	1	163	8.6

LAST SEASON

Second on team in power-play goals. Third on team in assists. Career high in goals. Missed eight games with knee injuries.

THE FINESSE GAME

Sydor broke into the league in Los Angeles as an offensive defenseman, lost all confidence in that aspect of his game, came to Dallas, put his defensive play in order without even thinking offense, and now has a well-balanced game. Dallas asked him to be more accountable defensively, and he has emerged as a top four defenseman on one of the league's top defensive teams.

A forward in junior until he was converted to a defenseman (by Dallas coach Ken Hitchcock), Sydor is a very good skater with balance and agility and excellent lateral movement. He can accelerate well and he changes directions easily. He's not a dynamic defenseman, but he's better than average. He can be used up front with the Stars during injury emergencies.

Sydor's offensive game can kick in at anytime. He has a fine shot from the point and can handle power-play time. He has good sense for jumping into the attack and controls the puck ably when carrying it, though he doesn't always protect it well with his body. He makes nice outlet passes and has good vision of the ice. He can rush with the puck or play dump-and-chase. In his own zone, he has developed into a safe, reliable defender.

THE PHYSICAL GAME

Sydor wants and needs to establish more of a physical presence. He is intense and has to be reined in. He has learned that sometimes going nowhere is better than trying to go everywhere. He competes hard and could still get stronger.

THE INTANGIBLES

Sydor continues to gain confidence in his all-around game; a Cup ring has only added to his development.

PROJECTION

Last year we said Sydor was poised to move into elite scoring range with a 50- to 60-point season. Injuries prevented him from doing so, but he should move into that neighbourhood this season.

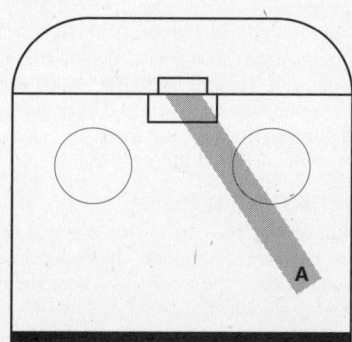

PAT VERBEEK

Yrs. of NHL service: 16
Born: Sarnia, Ont.; May 24, 1964
Position: right wing
Height: 5-9
Weight: 192
Uniform no.: 16
Shoots: right

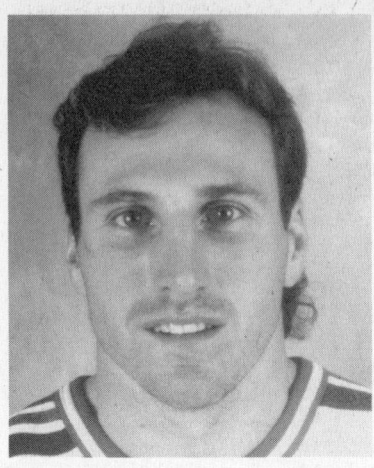

Career statistics:

GP	G	A	TP	PIM
1225	478	487	965	2665

1995-96 statistics:

GP	G	A	TP	+/-	PIM	PP	SH	GW	GT	S	PCT
69	41	41	82	+29	129	17	0	6	2	252	16.3

1996-97 statistics:

GP	G	A	TP	+/-	PIM	PP	SH	GW	GT	S	PCT
81	17	36	53	+3	128	5	0	4	0	172	9.9

1997-98 statistics:

GP	G	A	TP	+/-	PIM	PP	SH	GW	GT	S	PCT
82	31	26	57	+15	170	9	0	8	1	190	16.3

1998-99 statistics:

GP	G	A	TP	+/-	PIM	PP	SH	GW	GT	S	PCT
78	17	17	34	+11	133	8	0	2	1	134	12.7

LAST SEASON

Led team in penalty minutes for third consecutive season. Tied for third on team in power-play goals. Missed three games with sprained knee.

THE FINESSE GAME

Verbeek has a choppy stride, so much of his best work is done in small spaces rather than in open ice. He is very strong on his skates and he likes to go into traffic zones. Larger players think they can hit him, but he's so chunky, with a low centre of gravity, that he's nearly impossible to bowl over. He's very good at carrying the puck along the boards but is no stickhandler in open ice. He has no better than fair speed.

Verbeek plays low on the power play. He wastes few quality scoring chances, though. Most of his shots come from in tight. Nothing brings out his competitive edge more than some serious crashing around the crease, most of which he initiates. When Verbeek goes into scoring slumps, as he did last season, he becomes frustrated and starts cheating on his defensive responsibilities; his game proceeds to fall apart.

Verbeek's hands are quick enough to surprise with a backhand shot. He feels the puck on his stick and looks for openings in the net instead of scrapping with his head down and taking poor shots. He is also effective coming in late and drilling the shot.

THE PHYSICAL GAME

Verbeek is among the best in the league at drawing penalties. He can cleverly hold the opponent's stick and fling himself to the ice as if he were the injured party, and it's an effective tactic. He also draws calls honestly with his hard work by driving to the net and forcing the defender to slow him down by any means possible.

Verbeek is tough, rugged and strong, with a nasty disposition that he can tame without losing his ferocious edge, and he takes more than his share of bad penalties.

THE INTANGIBLES

Verbeek usually has strong seasons in contract years. Last season was an exception to that trend. He is still an underrated crunch-time player, and in the right spot could be a valuable free agent pickup for a team — if Dallas decides not to re-sign him.

PROJECTION

Verbeek's production is on the wane. He is no longer a first-line player, but he can still contribute 30 to 40 points in a reduced role.

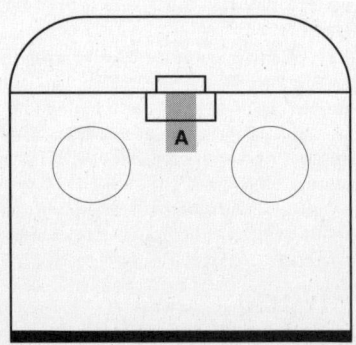

SERGEI ZUBOV

Yrs. of NHL service: 7
Born: Moscow, Russia; July 22, 1970
Position: right defense
Height: 6-1
Weight: 200
Uniform no.: 56
Shoots: right

Career statistics:

GP	G	A	TP	PIM
461	74	299	373	143

1995-96 statistics:

GP	G	A	TP	+/-	PIM	PP	SH	GW	GT	S	PCT
64	11	55	66	+28	22	3	2	1	0	141	7.8

1996-97 statistics:

GP	G	A	TP	+/-	PIM	PP	SH	GW	GT	S	PCT
78	13	30	43	+19	24	1	0	3	0	133	9.8

1997-98 statistics:

GP	G	A	TP	+/-	PIM	PP	SH	GW	GT	S	PCT
73	10	47	57	+16	16	5	1	2	1	148	6.8

1998-99 statistics:

GP	G	A	TP	+/-	PIM	PP	SH	GW	GT	S	PCT
81	10	41	51	+9	20	5	0	3	0	155	6.5

LAST SEASON

Tied for eighth among NHL defensemen in scoring. Led team defensemen in scoring for second consecutive season. Second on team in assists. Missed one game with bruised wrist.

THE FINESSE GAME

Zubov remains primarily an offenseman, though he is playing a more responsible game in the strict Dallas system. He has the ability to run a power play but is not in the elite class of NHL point men, like Brian Leetch. Zubov is still very effective, though, despite his occasional reluctance to shoot the puck when he has an obvious lane.

Zubov has some world-class skills. He skates with with good balance and generates power from his leg drive. He is agile in his stops and starts, even backwards. He also has a good slap shot and one-times the puck with accuracy — when he deigns to use it. He masks his intentions well, faking a shot and finding the open man with a slick pass. He's not afraid to come in deep, either. Zubov will occasionally frustrate his teammates when he slows things down with the puck on a rush or breakout while the rest of the team has already taken off like racehorses.

Zubov has very strong lateral acceleration, but he is also educated enough to keep skating stride for stride with the wing who is trying to beat him to the outside. So many other defensemen speed up a couple of strides then try to slow their men with stick checks.

Zubov will use his reach, superior body positioning or his agility to force the play and compel the puck carrier to make a decision. However, he doesn't always search out the right man or, when he does, he doesn't always eliminate the right man. A team has to live with that because Zubov's offensive upside is huge.

THE PHYSICAL GAME

Zubov is not physical, but he is solidly built and will take a hit to make a play. He can give a team a lot of minutes and not wear down physically.

His boyhood idol was Viacheslav Fetisov, and that role model should give you some idea of Zubov's style. He gets his body in the way with his great skating, then strips the puck when the attacker finds no path to the net. He doesn't initiate much but doesn't mind getting hit to make a play.

THE INTANGIBLES

Mentally, Zubov will still lose his focus and is capable of the most astounding giveaways. He can often atone with a terrific offensive play, but his lapses keep him from being rated among the league's best.

PROJECTION

As the Stars' top offensive defenseman, Zubov should score between 50 to 60 points again this season.

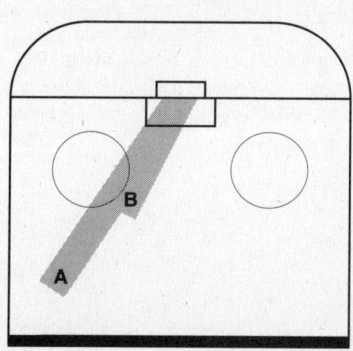

DETROIT RED WINGS

Players' Statistics 1998-99

POS	NO.	PLAYER	GP	G	A	PTS	+/-	PIM	PP	SH	GW	GT	S	PCT
C	19	STEVE YZERMAN	80	29	45	74	8	42	13	2	4		231	12.6
C	91	SERGEI FEDOROV	77	26	37	63	9	66	6	2	3		224	11.6
C	8	IGOR LARIONOV	75	14	49	63	13	48	4	2	2	1	83	16.9
L	14	BRENDAN SHANAHAN	81	31	27	58	2	123	5		5		288	10.8
L	13	VYACHESLAV KOZLOV	79	29	29	58	10	45	6	1	4	2	209	13.9
D	5	NICKLAS LIDSTROM	81	14	43	57	14	14	6	2	3		205	6.8
D	55	LARRY MURPHY	80	10	42	52	21	42	5	1	2		168	6.0
L	71	WENDEL CLARK	77	32	16	48	-24	37	11		3	1	215	14.9
R	25	DARREN MCCARTY	69	14	26	40	10	108	6		1	1	140	10.0
D	24	CHRIS CHELIOS	75	9	27	36	1	93	3	1	1	1	187	4.8
L	96	TOMAS HOLMSTROM	82	13	21	34	-11	69	5		4		100	13.0
R	20	MARTIN LAPOINTE	77	16	13	29	7	141	7	1	4		153	10.5
R	17	DOUG BROWN	80	9	19	28	5	42	3	1	1		180	5.0
C	33	KRIS DRAPER	80	4	14	18	2	79		1	1		78	5.1
L	18	KIRK MALTBY	53	8	6	14	-6	34		1	2		76	10.5
R	11	MATHIEU DANDENAULT	75	4	10	14	17	59					94	4.3
C	23	*STACY ROEST	59	4	8	12	-7	14			1		50	8.0
D	2	ULF SAMUELSSON	71	4	8	12	5	99					39	10.3
D	27	AARON WARD	60	3	8	11	-5	52					46	6.5
D	34	JAMIE MACOUN	69	1	10	11	-1	36					62	1.6
D	15	TODD GILL	51	4	5	9	-10	27	1		1	1	61	6.6
R	26	JOEY KOCUR	39	2	5	7	0	87					20	10.0
D	4	UWE KRUPP	22	3	2	5	0	6					32	9.4
G	30	CHRIS OSGOOD	63		3	3	0	8						
C	41	BRENT GILCHRIST	5	1		1	-1				1		4	25.0
R	85	PETR KLIMA	13	1		1	-3	4			1		12	8.3
D	3	DOUG HOUDA	3		1	1	-2						1	
D	28	*YAN GOLUBOVSKY	17		1	1	4	16					10	
C	21	*DARRYL LAPLANTE	3				0							
L	22	*PHILIPPE AUDET	4				-2						3	
G	38	*NORM MARACLE	16				0							
G	40	BILL RANFORD	36				0	2						

GP = games played; G = goals; A = assists; PTS = points; +/- = goals-for minus goals-against while player is on ice; PIM = penalties in minutes; PP = power-play goals; SH = shorthanded goals; GW = game-winning goals; GT = game-tying goals; S = no. of shots; PCT = percentage of goals to shots; * = rookie

DOUG BROWN

Yrs. of NHL service: 12
Born: Southborough, Mass.; June 12, 1964
Position: right wing
Height: 5-10
Weight: 185
Uniform no.: 17
Shoots: right

Career statistics:

GP	G	A	TP	PIM
743	141	193	334	184

1995-96 statistics:

GP	G	A	TP	+/-	PIM	PP	SH	GW	GT	S	PCT
62	12	15	27	+11	4	0	1	1	0	115	10.4

1996-97 statistics:

GP	G	A	TP	+/-	PIM	PP	SH	GW	GT	S	PCT
49	6	7	13	-3	8	1	0	0	0	69	8.7

1997-98 statistics:

GP	G	A	TP	+/-	PIM	PP	SH	GW	GT	S	PCT
80	19	23	42	+17	12	6	1	5	0	145	13.1

1998-99 statistics:

GP	G	A	TP	+/-	PIM	PP	SH	GW	GT	S	PCT
80	9	19	28	+5	42	3	1	1	0	180	5.0

LAST SEASON
Missed one game due to coach's decision.

THE FINESSE GAME
Brown approaches the game with intelligence and enthusiasm, blocks shots fearlessly and never stops working. He always attains his level of play but seldom surpasses it, which is why coaches often give younger players ice time ahead of him at the start of the season, then tend to go back to the old reliable redhead.

A determined penalty killer and a weapon when shorthanded, Brown never quits around the net. His goals come from deflections or wraparounds. Because his shot isn't much of a threat at all, he is so unsure of his ability to create a rebound with it that he falls back to a defensive posture rather than following the play to the net. He is always alert, and he fits in with the skilled Russians on the Red Wings, even though he plays a far less creative style.

Brown depends more on side-to-side quickness than on straight-ahead speed. Always hustling, he gets a lot of breakaways because of the quick jumps he gets on the opposition, however, he lacks the finishing touch to score as many goals as he should. He wipes out frequently after losing his edges. When carrying the puck, Brown does not always move it at the right time; sometimes he holds onto it too long, either because he doesn't see the proper play or because he can't make it in time.

THE PHYSICAL GAME
Brown is not big or strong, but he is one of the better grinders along the wall, since he will hang in there and not give up on a puck. He won't fight, but he won't be intimidated, either.

THE INTANGIBLES
Teams need star players and they need Doug Browns to do the support work, the glamourless, faceless stuff that trustworthy players provide. Difficult as it is to muster consistent play when dropped from the lineup for long stretches of games, Brown gets that job done. Any points he provides are a bonus, but they often come at important times. He is a very competitive player. Anyone who skates and hustles like Brown is guaranteed a long NHL career.

PROJECTION
Brown lacks world-class skills, but serves as the perfect complement to world-class players and is just as comfortable doing the grunt work on a checking line. He hustles and grinds and does all of the little things it takes to win a hockey game. He has spent most of his career on the bubble. He'll be there again this fall.

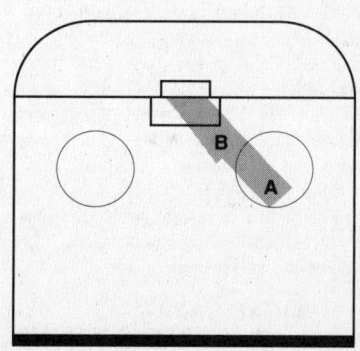

CHRIS CHELIOS

Yrs. of NHL service: 15
Born: Chicago, Ill.; Jan. 25, 1962
Position: right defense
Height: 6-1
Weight: 186
Uniform no.: 24
Shoots: right

Career statistics:

GP	G	A	TP	PIM
1076	165	633	798	2282

1995-96 statistics:

GP	G	A	TP	+/-	PIM	PP	SH	GW	GT	S	PCT
81	14	58	72	+25	140	7	0	3	0	219	6.4

1996-97 statistics:

GP	G	A	TP	+/-	PIM	PP	SH	GW	GT	S	PCT
72	10	38	48	+16	112	2	0	2	0	194	5.2

1997-98 statistics:

GP	G	A	TP	+/-	PIM	PP	SH	GW	GT	S	PCT
81	3	39	42	-7	151	1	0	0	0	205	1.5

1998-99 statistics:

GP	G	A	TP	+/-	PIM	PP	SH	GW	GT	S	PCT
75	9	27	36	+1	93	3	1	1	1	187	4.8

LAST SEASON

Acquired from Chicago for Anders Eriksson and first-round draft picks in 1999 and 2000, Mar. 23, 1999. Missed seven games with groin injuries.

THE FINESSE GAME

Whatever the team needs, Chelios will bleed to give. He can become a top offensive defenseman, pinching boldly at every opportunity. He can create offense off the rush, make a play through the neutral zone or quarterback the power play from the point. He has a good, low, hard slap shot. He is not afraid to skate in deep, where he can handle the puck well and use a snap shot or wrist shot with a quick release.

If defense is needed, Chelios will rule in his own zone. He is extremely confident and poised with the puck and doesn't overhandle it. He wants to get the puck away from his net by the most expedient means possible. He is aggressive in forcing the puck carrier to make a decision by stepping up. He also steps up in the neutral zone to break up plays with his stick.

Chelios is an instinctive player. When he is on his game, he reacts and makes plays few other defensemen can. When he struggles, which is seldom, he is back on his heels. He tries to do other people's jobs and becomes undisciplined.

Chelios has excellent anticipation and is a strong penalty killer. He's a mobile, smooth skater with good lateral movement. He is seldom beaten one-on-one, and he's even tough facing a two-on-one. In his mind, he can do anything. He usually does.

THE PHYSICAL GAME

Chelios has an absurdly high pain threshold, often playing despite injuries that would have a baseball player on the DL for a lifetime. He doesn't seem to tire, no matter how much ice time he gets, and he routinely plays 30 minutes or handles four-minute shifts. He is not that big but plays like an enormous defenseman. He is mean, tough and physical, strong and solid on his skates, and fearless.

THE INTANGIBLES

Chelios wants to go out a winner. The late-season trade to Detroit nearly guaranteed that he would, but he and the Red Wings failed in the second round. A full season playing in the Detroit system will help Chelios physically and mentally.

PROJECTION

Chelios was paired with Nicklas Lidstrom against other teams' top lines. If the gifted Swede returns, this could be one of the top defense pairs in the league. Chelios will be relied upon for less offense, but can still score 40 to 45 points.

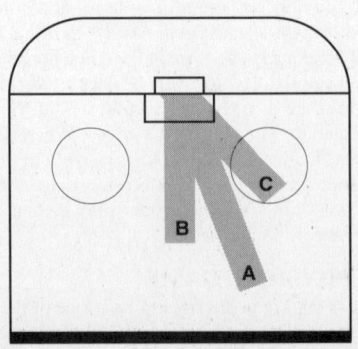

WENDEL CLARK

Yrs. of NHL service: 14
Born: Kelvington, Sask.; Oct. 25, 1966
Position: left wing
Height: 5-11
Weight: 194
Uniform no.: 71
Shoots: left

Career statistics:

GP	G	A	TP	PIM
760	356	232	712	1656

1995-96 statistics:

GP	G	A	TP	+/-	PIM	PP	SH	GW	GT	S	PCT
71	32	26	58	-5	76	8	0	3	1	237	13.5

1996-97 statistics:

GP	G	A	TP	+/-	PIM	PP	SH	GW	GT	S	PCT
65	30	19	49	-2	75	6	0	6	0	212	14.2

1997-98 statistics:

GP	G	A	TP	+/-	PIM	PP	SH	GW	GT	S	PCT
47	12	7	19	-21	80	4	0	3	0	140	8.6

1998-99 statistics:

GP	G	A	TP	+/-	PIM	PP	SH	GW	GT	S	PCT
77	32	16	48	-24	37	11	0	3	1	215	14.9

LAST SEASON

Acquired from Tampa Bay for Kevin Hodson and a second-round draft pick in 1999. Led team in goals with highest total since 1993-94. Second on team in power-play goals and shooting percentage.

THE FINESSE GAME

Let other players zig and zag. Clark's game is all straight lines. The shortest distance to the goal is the path he'll pursue, and he'll do so with all of the diligence his aging body allows.

Clark is an accurate shooter. He uses a slightly shorter stick than he did early in his career and keeps his hands higher on the stick than most, like Brett Hull. He is shooting from close to his feet, and his snap shots are quick and accurate. He can still overpower a goalie from the blueline, even with his wrist shot, which has tremendous power. His shooting percentage is usually quite high because he places himself in an optimum position to score.

Not a clever player, Clark rarely passes the puck. His effectiveness depends on him charging down the ice, wreaking havoc and letting his teammates trail in his wake, picking through the debris to make a play. He needs to play with a centre who can give him the puck late. When Clark gets the puck he has to shoot it in. He gets into trouble when he makes plays.

Clark is not a smart player positionally, either. Although a strong skater, he's not agile, fast or mobile. When he's playing well, he uses his leg drive like a linebacker in football to hit hard.

THE PHYSICAL GAME

Clark is just plain mean. He hits when it's least expected, often well away from the play. And he's a big, big hitter who hurts. He's a strong forechecker, but he gets frustrated when his scoring touch deserts him and will run around and take bad penalties. Last year there was less frustration, and, as a result, a much lower than average PIM total.

THE INTANGIBLES

Clark was able to stay relatively healthy last season, and the results showed in his production. But it was also his option year — when players have extra motivation to put up some numbers. It might have been Clark's last hurrah.

PROJECTION

Expect a decline in goals, but if Clark stays healthy and ends up with the right team, he could still chip in 25 goals.

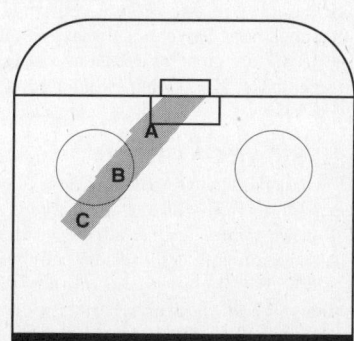

KRIS DRAPER

Yrs. of NHL service: 8
Born: Toronto, Ont.; May 24, 1971
Position: centre
Height: 5-11
Weight: 185
Uniform no.: 33
Shoots: left

Career statistics:

GP	G	A	TP	PIM
367	42	52	94	291

1995-96 statistics:

GP	G	A	TP	+/-	PIM	PP	SH	GW	GT	S	PCT
52	7	9	16	+2	32	0	1	0	0	51	13.7

1996-97 statistics:

GP	G	A	TP	+/-	PIM	PP	SH	GW	GT	S	PCT
76	8	5	13	-11	73	1	0	1	0	85	9.4

1997-98 statistics:

GP	G	A	TP	+/-	PIM	PP	SH	GW	GT	S	PCT
64	13	10	23	+5	45	1	0	4	0	96	13.5

1998-99 statistics:

GP	G	A	TP	+/-	PIM	PP	SH	GW	GT	S	PCT
80	4	14	18	+2	79	0	1	1	0	78	5.1

LAST SEASON
Missed two games due to suspension.

THE FINESSE GAME
Draper is unselfish and a good passer, especially in traffic. Also a good skater, he is strong on his feet and well-balanced, but not fast. Clever play makes him seem much quicker than he is and heightens his usefulness as a penalty killer.

Draper lacks a true finisher's touch. He plays his position well and is proud of his checking role; the strength of his game is his defense. His goals are hard-work goals that often come off his forecheck and his anticipation. When a linemate forces a defender into a giveaway, he's there to jump on the free puck and get a good shot away quickly.

Draper makes things happen on Detroit's Grind Line with usual left-wing partner Kirk Maltby. Although Draper is mostly a meat-and-potatoes forechecker, he has some hand quickness and cleverness with the puck in one-on-one confrontations. Rather than make the conventional play, he makes a fake, goes to a more creative option and buys some time for teammates. His skating is quite good on an up-tempo team.

THE PHYSICAL GAME
Scotty Bowman has always made his teams play hard, and Draper fits in well with that philosophy. A no-frills defensive centre with a strong work ethic, Draper has wiry strength and uses his body well. He works the boards and corners and relishes physical play. Although short on size, he's intense, ready to play every night and completes his checks.

THE INTANGIBLES
Draper has plenty of heart. He sees limited ice time but is ready for every shift, and Detroit looks to his Grind Line for an energy boost. He figures to be a role player for another season with the Red Wings thanks to his character.

PROJECTION
A hard worker, yes. The scorer you need for your pool? Hardly.

SERGEI FEDOROV

Yrs. of NHL service: 9
Born: Pskov, Russia; Dec. 13, 1969
Position: centre
Height: 6-1
Weight: 200
Uniform no.: 91
Shoots: left

Career statistics:

GP	G	A	TP	PIM
607	274	398	672	437

1995-96 statistics:

GP	G	A	TP	+/-	PIM	PP	SH	GW	GT	S	PCT
78	39	68	107	+49	48	11	2	11	1	306	12.7

1996-97 statistics:

GP	G	A	TP	+/-	PIM	PP	SH	GW	GT	S	PCT
74	30	33	63	+29	30	9	2	4	0	273	11.0

1997-98 statistics:

GP	G	A	TP	+/-	PIM	PP	SH	GW	GT	S	PCT
21	6	11	17	+10	25	2	0	2	0	68	8.8

1998-99 statistics:

GP	G	A	TP	+/-	PIM	PP	SH	GW	GT	S	PCT
77	26	37	63	+9	66	6	2	3	0	224	11.6

LAST SEASON

Tied for team lead in shorthanded goals. Tied for second on team in points. Third on team in shots. Missed five games due to suspension.

THE FINESSE GAME

Versatility is a Fedorov hallmark. He has played left wing and centre, and even defense, and he fuels a power play and kills penalties. Fedorov is a tremendous package of offensive and defensive skills. He can go from checking the opponent's top centre to powering the power play from shift to shift. His skating is nothing short of phenomenal, and he can handle the puck while dazzling everyone with his blades.

Fedorov likes to gear up from his own defensive zone, using his acceleration and balance to drive wide to his right, carrying the puck on his backhand and protecting it with his body. If the defenseman lets up at all, Fedorov is by him, pulling the puck quickly to his forehand. Nor is he by any means selfish. He has 360-degree vision of the ice and makes solid, confident passes right under opponents' sticks and smack onto the tape of his teammates'.

Fedorov will swing behind the opposing net from left to right, fooling the defense into thinking he is going to continue to curl around, but he can quickly reverse with the puck on his backhand, shake his shadow and wheel around for a shot or goalmouth pass. He does it all in a flash, and skating with the puck doesn't slow him down one whit.

THE PHYSICAL GAME

When you are as gifted as Fedorov, opponents will do all they can to hit you and hurt you; when your medical history includes a concussion and a separated shoulder from such contact, you may become gunshy. Nonetheless, although the wiry Fedorov seems reluctant to absorb big hits or deliver any, he will leave the relative safety of open ice and head to the trenches when he has to.

Much of his power is generated from his strong skating. For the most part, his defense is dominated by his reads, anticipation and quickness in knocking down passes and breaking up plays. He is not much of a body checker, and he gets most of his penalties from stick and restraining fouls.

THE INTANGIBLES

Fedorov was a non-factor in the playoffs, then complained it was because he didn't get enough ice time. The Red Wings, who need to get younger and deeper, might be willing to move him if the price is right.

PROJECTION

Fedorov has the skill to dominate any game, any night. He can be "on" one night, "off" the next. Again, we anticipate an unspectacular 70-point regular season.

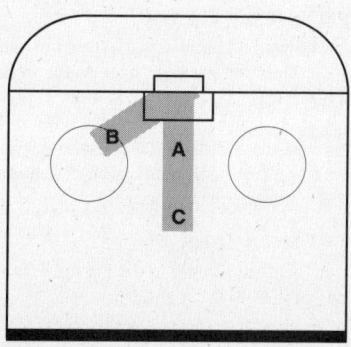

TOMAS HOLMSTROM

Yrs. of NHL service: 3
Born: Pitea, Sweden; Jan 23, 1973
Position: left wing
Height: 6-0
Weight: 210
Uniform no.: 96
Shoots: left

Career statistics:

GP	G	A	TP	PIM
186	24	41	65	134

1996-97 statistics:

GP	G	A	TP	+/-	PIM	PP	SH	GW	GT	S	PCT
47	6	3	9	-10	33	3	0	0	0	53	11.3

1997-98 statistics:

GP	G	A	TP	+/-	PIM	PP	SH	GW	GT	S	PCT
66	7	14	21	+21	32	1	0	2	0	91	7.7

1998-99 statistics:

GP	G	A	TP	+/-	PIM	PP	SH	GW	GT	S	PCT
82	13	21	34	-11	69	5	0	4	0	100	13.0

LAST SEASON

Only Red Wing to appear in all 82 games.

THE FINESSE GAME

He has a toothless grin and a gutsy game. He plays in the hard five feet outside the crease, sometimes inside it, and drives goalies wild. He is Sweden's answer to Dino Ciccarelli.

With the desire and work ethic of every low draft pick to ever make it to the NHL (257th in 1994), Holmstrom is a rough-cut stone among the polished gems that are the Stanley Cup champions' forwards. That makes him even more important, because Holmstrom provides an element of grit.

He has style, too, and can score in the clutch. He has an excellent close-range shot, and it was just a matter of time before he learned to use it. He is also a smart passer.

The change in the man-in-the-crease rule will be a boon to Holmstrom's game, since that is the high-toll area where he makes his living. He is a power-play mainstay because of his ability to screen and distract defensemen.

THE PHYSICAL GAME

Stocky and strong on his skates, Holmstrom can take a bloody pounding and get right back in the trenches to position himself for a pass. What is most impressive is how he is able to provoke the attacks without getting penalized himself. He rarely takes a bad penalty. The fact that he bounces back with a jack-o'-lantern smile is especially infuriating to opponents.

THE INTANGIBLES

Holmstrom is always better in the playoffs (four goals in 10 games) than in the regular season.

PROJECTION

Last season was Holmstrom's first true, full NHL year. The Red Wings expect more from him this year, like 20 to 25 goals.

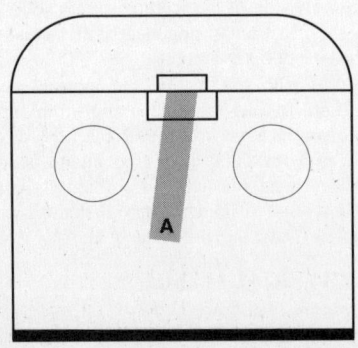

VYACHESLAV KOZLOV

Yrs. of NHL service: 6
Born: Voskresensk, Russia; May 3, 1972
Position: centre/left wing
Height: 5-10
Weight: 180
Uniform no.: 13
Shoots: left

Career statistics:
GP	G	A	TP	PIM
463	164	177	341	318

1995-96 statistics:
GP	G	A	TP	+/-	PIM	PP	SH	GW	GT	S	PCT
82	36	37	73	+33	70	9	0	7	0	237	15.2

1996-97 statistics:
GP	G	A	TP	+/-	PIM	PP	SH	GW	GT	S	PCT
75	23	22	45	+21	46	3	0	6	0	211	10.9

1997-98 statistics:
GP	G	A	TP	+/-	PIM	PP	SH	GW	GT	S	PCT
80	25	27	52	+14	46	6	0	1	0	221	11.3

1998-99 statistics:
GP	G	A	TP	+/-	PIM	PP	SH	GW	GT	S	PCT
79	29	29	58	+10	45	6	1	4	2	209	13.9

LAST SEASON
Tied for second on team in game-winning goals. Tied for third on team in goals. Third on team in shooting percentage. Missed three games due to suspension for elbowing incident.

THE FINESSE GAME
Kozlov has a very quick getaway step that allows him to jump into holes and openings. His darting style makes it impossible for defenders to chase him and easy for them to lose him.

Kozlov can play as freewheeling offensively as the team wants. He seems to materialize at the right place at the right time, much like Brett Hull in his prime. He can split the defense if it plays him too close, or drive the defense back with his speed and use the open ice to find a teammate. He has great control of the puck at high speed and plays an excellent transition game. Unlike many Russian players, he does not have to be coaxed into shooting, and he has a quick release — generally to the top corners of the net.

That said, there are also times when Kozlov can be frustrating to watch. He will hold the puck past the point when he either should make a play with it or make a pass. He then either loses control of it or takes himself to lesser ice. The reasonable speculation is that by holding the puck he is buying time for teammates to break into open ice; other times, he simply appears incapable of making a decision about what to do or he is trying to make the perfect play instead of a good enough play more quickly.

THE PHYSICAL GAME
Just as a defender comes to hit him, Kozlov gets rid of the puck. Usually it goes to a teammate, sometimes it simply goes up for grabs. It would be easy to infer Kozlov is like a quarterback who gets rid of the ball rather than getting sacked. More likely, he's taking the hit to create space for someone else by allowing the defender to take himself — and Kozlov — out of the play. Kozlov is not tall but he is solidly built. He's got a little mean streak, too, as that elbow to the head of Joe Nieuwendyk proved.

THE INTANGIBLES
Kozlov has star-level talent, and the Red Wings want him to produce more. He could be moved to centre this season to get him more ice time, and to get him more involved.

PROJECTION
Kozlov scored in the range (25 to 30 goals) we expected last season. He is ready to bump those numbers up into the 30- to 35- goal range.

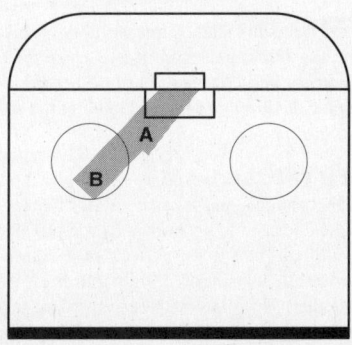

UWE KRUPP

Yrs. of NHL service: 13
Born: Cologne, West Germany; June 24, 1965
Position: right defense
Height: 6-6
Weight: 235
Uniform no.: 4
Shoots: right

Career statistics:

GP	G	A	TP	PIM
717	69	211	280	642

1995-96 statistics:

GP	G	A	TP	+/-	PIM	PP	SH	GW	GT	S	PCT
6	0	3	3	+4	4	0	0	0	0	9	0.0

1996-97 statistics:

GP	G	A	TP	+/-	PIM	PP	SH	GW	GT	S	PCT
60	4	17	21	+12	48	2	0	1	0	107	3.7

1997-98 statistics:

GP	G	A	TP	+/-	PIM	PP	SH	GW	GT	S	PCT
78	9	22	31	+21	38	5	0	2	0	149	6.0

1998-99 statistics:

GP	G	A	TP	+/-	PIM	PP	SH	GW	GT	S	PCT
22	3	2	5	0	6	0	0	0	0	32	9.4

LAST SEASON

Missed 52 games with back injury. Missed seven games with hamstring injury. Missed one game with bruised knee.

THE FINESSE GAME

The key to Krupp's game is his awareness of his limitations. Not a quick skater even before his knee surgery of four seasons ago, he is now more conservative, yet effective. He reads plays well both offensively and defensively and he positions himself well in his own zone, so he needs only one long stride to cut off the attacker.

Krupp has a hard shot, but it takes him far too long to get his big slapper underway and it's often blocked. Because he is so tall and uses such a long stick, Krupp doesn't one-time the puck well but, instead, must stop it and tee it up. He has a good wrist shot, which he could use to better purpose because he can get it away cleanly and with some velocity. He protects the puck well.

Krupp helps his team immeasurably by his ability to move the puck smartly out of the zone. He is a smooth passer and creates a lot of odd-man rushes by spotting the developing play and making the solid first pass.

THE PHYSICAL GAME

Krupp is enormous and takes up a lot of space on the ice, but he doesn't use his body as a weapon. It's more of a roadblock, and it's one heck of a detour to get around. He blocks shots willingly and is an excellent penalty killer. He plays with restraint and takes few bad penalties. Checkers seem to bounce off him. On the rare nights when he gets physical he can dominate, but he doesn't often play that way. It's just not his nature, and given his recent injuries, it's likely he'll avoid unnecessary contact now more than ever.

THE INTANGIBLES

Krupp could turn into one of the big-ticket free agent busts of 1998 because of the serious back injury that derailed his season. His future is very much in doubt.

PROJECTION

Given that Detroit invested heavily in defensemen such as Chris Chelios and Ulf Samuelsson for the playoff run, it's obvious the Red Wings aren't counting on Krupp to contribute much this season. Neither should you.

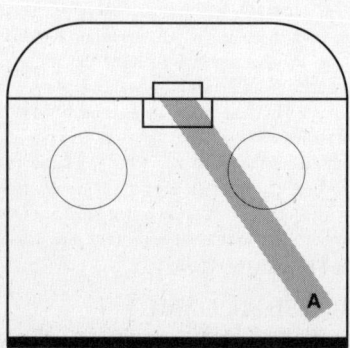

MARTIN LAPOINTE

Yrs. of NHL service: 6
Born: Ville Ste. Pierre, Que.; Sept. 12, 1973
Position: right wing
Height: 5-11
Weight: 200
Uniform no.: 20
Shoots: right

Career statistics:
GP	G	A	TP	PIM
388	65	67	132	640

1995-96 statistics:
GP	G	A	TP	+/-	PIM	PP	SH	GW	GT	S	PCT
58	6	3	9	0	93	1	0	0	0	76	7.9

1996-97 statistics:
GP	G	A	TP	+/-	PIM	PP	SH	GW	GT	S	PCT
78	16	17	33	-14	167	5	1	1	0	149	10.7

1997-98 statistics:
GP	G	A	TP	+/-	PIM	PP	SH	GW	GT	S	PCT
79	15	19	34	0	106	4	0	3	2	154	9.7

1998-99 statistics:
GP	G	A	TP	+/-	PIM	PP	SH	GW	GT	S	PCT
77	16	13	29	+7	141	7	1	4	0	153	10.5

LAST SEASON
Led team in penalty minutes. Third on team in power-play goals. Matched career high in goals. Missed one game with back spasms. Missed three games due to other injuries. Missed one game due to coach's decision.

THE FINESSE GAME
Everything about Lapointe's game stems more from what is between his ribs than what is between his ears. It all comes from the heart: the competitiveness, the drive that sends him to the net in the straightest line possible. If a defenseman or opposing forward — or goalie — happens to get knocked down in the process, that's their problem.

Lapointe's goals and assists result more from his acceleration than his speed. He doesn't have breakaway speed, but his eagerness, his intensity and his willingness to compete make him seem faster than he actually is. He doesn't have a great shot, though he has a nice, quick release and uses a wrist or snap shot as opposed to a big windup. Most of his goals are scored in the hard areas around the crease. He screens goalies, tips shots and works for loose pucks.

As important, Lapointe does not let a stick-check slow him down. He'll pull a checker along like a boat tugging a water-skier. He'll steam into the play to create an odd-man rush, and he creates lots of options with a nice passing touch that prevents goalies from overplaying him to shoot.

THE PHYSICAL GAME
Lapointe wants to play, wants to win and won't take an easy way out, which means a lot of opponents end up flat on the ice. He hits them all, big or small, and hits hard. He is low but wide, with a broad upper body and solid centre of gravity that powers his physical game. He can be a menace in the corners and a force in front of the net.

THE INTANGIBLES
Lapointe could be the heir apparent to Claude Lemieux as the Grate One. He drives opponents crazy, then backs up his activity with big goals. He has become a clutch playoff performer in many ways.

There is a snarl in Lapointe's game, however, a fire that always seems close to the fuse. Yet although he takes a good share of over-emotional penalties, Lapointe has better control than earlier in his career. He wakes things up, and never lets opponents take the easy way out. He never lets himself take the easy way, either. He came to the team as a big-time scorer in the Quebec League and dedicated himself to learning how to check. His approach is summarized in his statement, "I'd rather change my role and have the team win instead of being a one-man show."

PROJECTION
Lapointe scored only 16 goals in the regular season, and can produce more. He scores the big goals, however, and like Lemieux is turning into a player who is far more valuable in the playoffs than the regular season.

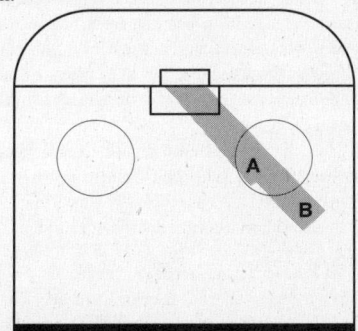

NICKLAS LIDSTROM

Yrs. of NHL service: 8
Born: Vasteras, Sweden; Apr. 28, 1970
Position: left defense
Height: 6-2
Weight: 185
Uniform no.: 5
Shoots: left

Career statistics:

GP	G	A	TP	PIM
612	101	322	423	164

1995-96 statistics:

GP	G	A	TP	+/-	PIM	PP	SH	GW	GT	S	PCT
81	17	50	67	+29	20	8	1	1	1	211	8.1

1996-97 statistics:

GP	G	A	TP	+/-	PIM	PP	SH	GW	GT	S	PCT
79	15	42	57	+11	30	8	0	1	0	214	7.0

1997-98 statistics:

GP	G	A	TP	+/-	PIM	PP	SH	GW	GT	S	PCT
80	17	42	59	+22	18	7	1	1	1	205	8.3

1998-99 statistics:

GP	G	A	TP	+/-	PIM	PP	SH	GW	GT	S	PCT
81	14	43	57	+14	14	6	2	3	0	205	6.8

LAST SEASON

Finalist for 1999 Norris and Lady Byng Trophies. Led team defensemen and tied for second among NHL defensemen in points. Tied for team lead in shorthanded goals. Third on team in assists and plus-minus. Led team in power-play points (29). Missed one game due to coach's decision.

THE FINESSE GAME

Lidstrom is an excellent skater and he has good vision of the ice. He prefers to look for the breakout pass, rather than carry the puck, and he has a superb point shot that stays low and accurate. His work at the point on the power play has improved significantly. His rink management is solid, his decision-making is better and his passing — especially to set up one-timers — is tape-to-tape. Lidstrom is also confident about moving down low to poach for goals.

Defensively, Lidstrom uses exceptional anticipation to position himself perfectly and has improved his reads. He is almost impossible to beat one-on-one, and sometimes even two-on-one, in open ice. He neatly breaks up passes with a quick stick. He kills penalties and willingly blocks shots. He also plays either side — an underrated asset — and is dependable in the last minute of a close period or game.

Lidstrom has added enough muscle to become a wiry, strong athlete who can handle an astounding amount of quality ice time. He wastes little energy, and his innate talent maximizes his stamina.

THE PHYSICAL GAME

Lidstrom truly perseveres. He does not take the body much and depends on his wits more than hard hits. But on the other side of the puck, he has little fear of contact and will accept a hit to make a play. It is a tribute to his style that he can play with quiet toughness and still be a Lady Byng candidate. This is how the game is meant to be played.

Although not a physical player, Lidstrom plays smart. With body positioning and stick positioning, he leaves opposing puck carriers no place to go and no alternative to giving up the puck — usually to him. He finds a way to tie up the opponent's stick. He has stepped up his physical play. He's not a punishing hitter, but puck carriers are wary of him because he makes them pay a price. He won't be intimidated; many teams have tried and failed with that tactic.

THE INTANGIBLES

Will he or won't he? Lidstrom was contemplating a return to Sweden to raise his family. If he decides to leave the NHL there will be a gaping hole on Detroit's roster. Lidstrom has matured into the best two-way defenseman in the NHL.

PROJECTION

Since he is used against the opposition's top offensive threat every night, Lidstrom's production may never rise above 60-some points, pretty nice numbers given his all-around game.

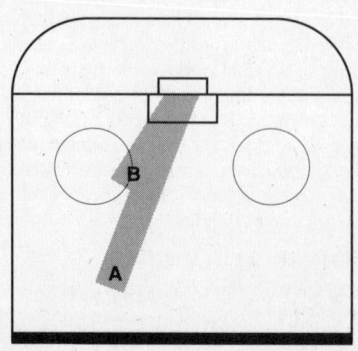

KIRK MALTBY

Yrs. of NHL service: 6
Born: Guelph, Ont.; Dec. 22, 1972
Position: right wing
Height: 6-0
Weight: 180
Uniform no.: 18
Shoots: right

Career statistics:

GP	G	A	TP	PIM
354	47	37	84	388

1995-96 statistics:

GP	G	A	TP	+/-	PIM	PP	SH	GW	GT	S	PCT
55	3	6	9	-16	67	0	0	1	0	55	5.5

1996-97 statistics:

GP	G	A	TP	+/-	PIM	PP	SH	GW	GT	S	PCT
66	3	5	8	+3	75	0	0	0	0	62	4.8

1997-98 statistics:

GP	G	A	TP	+/-	PIM	PP	SH	GW	GT	S	PCT
65	14	9	23	+11	89	2	1	3	0	106	13.2

1998-99 statistics:

GP	G	A	TP	+/-	PIM	PP	SH	GW	GT	S	PCT
53	8	6	14	-6	34	0	1	2	0	76	10.5

LAST SEASON

Missed 19 games with lower abdominal strain. Missed five games with knee injuries. Missed one game with ankle injury. Missed four games due to suspension.

THE FINESSE GAME

Maltby's skating helps keep him in position defensively; he seldom is caught up-ice. He plays well without the puck, understands the game well and is very coachable. He kills penalties well and blocks shots.

Maltby isn't overly creative, but he works tirelessly along the boards and in the corners to keep the puck alive. He has an average wrist and snap shot, yet has enough moves to be a threat when his team in shorthanded. Most of Maltby's goals are of the opportunistic type; he jumps on loose pucks and creates turnovers with his forechecking.

Astute hockey sense stamps Maltby as a two-way winger. He plays a key role for the Red Wings on the Grind Line (with Kris Draper and, frequently, Darren McCarty), and the line provided some tempo-changing shifts.

THE PHYSICAL GAME

There are few nights when you don't notice that Maltby is on the ice. He has good speed and he just loves to flatten people with clean, hard hits. He's fearless. He is not very big, but he is solid and won't back down from a challenge. He draws more than his fair share of penalties, either by forcing opponents to pull him down or by aggravating them enough that they take a whack at him.

Maltby's power emanates from his lower-body drive. He is strong and balanced and will punish with his hits. His work ethic and conditioning are strong. He wants to win the races to loose pucks.

THE INTANGIBLES

Maltby is valuable in his ability to stabilize a game. He wants to play, wants to learn, wants to do whatever he can to help the team. He will seldom make a mistake, with the puck or without it.

PROJECTION

A healthy Maltby will do the job defensively, add energy, and produce 15 goals.

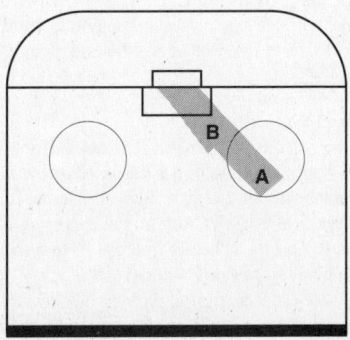

DARREN MCCARTY

Yrs. of NHL service: 6
Born: Burnaby, B.C.; April, 1972
Position: right wing
Height: 6-1
Weight: 210
Uniform no.: 25
Shoots: right

Career statistics:

GP	G	A	TP	PIM
369	77	117	194	818

1995-96 statistics:

GP	G	A	TP	+/-	PIM	PP	SH	GW	GT	S	PCT
63	15	14	29	+14	158	8	0	1	1	102	14.7

1996-97 statistics:

GP	G	A	TP	+/-	PIM	PP	SH	GW	GT	S	PCT
68	19	30	49	+14	126	5	0	6	1	171	11.1

1997-98 statistics:

GP	G	A	TP	+/-	PIM	PP	SH	GW	GT	S	PCT
71	15	22	37	0	157	5	1	2	0	166	9.0

1998-99 statistics:

GP	G	A	TP	+/-	PIM	PP	SH	GW	GT	S	PCT
69	14	26	40	+10	108	6	0	1	1	140	10.0

LAST SEASON

Third on team in penalty minutes. Missed 13 games with groin injuries.

THE FINESSE GAME

McCarty has an awkward stride and his first few steps are rather slow, but he is strong on his skates. When he reaches top speed his acceleration is serviceable, and he has decent finishing skills to go with a physical aspect. His balance is underrated. He absorbs (or delivers) big hits from some of the biggest skaters in the league, but hardly ever staggers.

McCarty has the ability to execute the consummate pro's perfecta: the poise to follow a great play with a good one. He can deke a defender with an inside-outside move, then go backhand-forehand to finish the play with a huge goal — providing a huge boost to his team while utterly deflating the opposition.

McCarty has decent hands and will score the majority of his goals in tight. He is not terribly creative but stays with a basic power game and is solid on the forecheck. Note that six of his 14 goals came on the power play.

THE PHYSICAL GAME

Mean, big, strong, tough and fearless. All the ingredients are there, along with the desire to throw his body at any player or puck he can reach. If a game is off to a quiet start, look for McCarty to wake everyone up. He forechecks and backchecks fiercely — and tries to go through players, not just to them.

McCarty is not a great fighter but he is willing. He's intelligent in picking his spots. His teammates know he is always there to back them up, which is why McCarty gets to play with some of Detroit's skilled players when he's not on the Grind Line with Kirk Maltby and Kris Draper.

THE INTANGIBLES

McCarty continues to work hard to polish the rougher aspects of his game. He made himself a huge leader on his team and backed up his big heart with big plays. The Red Wings are a smaller team in many ways when McCarty is out of the lineup.

PROJECTION

The Yzermans and the Fedorovs carry so much of the load and the scrutiny, but McCarty is a key role player. He can provide 20 goals and 50 points.

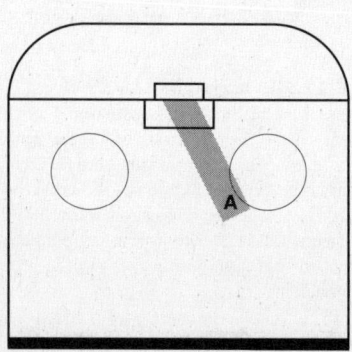

LARRY MURPHY

Yrs. of NHL service: 19
Born: Scarborough, Ont.; Mar. 8, 1961
Position: right defense
Height: 6-2
Weight: 210
Uniform no.: 55
Shoots: right

Career statistics:

GP	G	A	TP	PIM
1477	275	874	1155	1027

1995-96 statistics:

GP	G	A	TP	+/-	PIM	PP	SH	GW	GT	S	PCT
82	12	49	61	-2	34	8	0	1	2	182	6.6

1996-97 statistics:

GP	G	A	TP	+/-	PIM	PP	SH	GW	GT	S	PCT
81	9	36	45	+3	20	5	0	1	1	158	5.7

1997-98 statistics:

GP	G	A	TP	+/-	PIM	PP	SH	GW	GT	S	PCT
82	11	41	52	+35	37	2	1	2	0	129	8.5

1998-99 statistics:

GP	G	A	TP	+/-	PIM	PP	SH	GW	GT	S	PCT
80	10	42	52	+21	42	5	1	2	0	168	6.0

LAST SEASON

Led team in plus-minus. Missed one game due to injury. Missed one game due to coach's decision. Set NHL record for most regular-season games played by a defenseman (1,477).

THE FINESSE GAME

Murphy has never been a great skater. He actually has a rather choppy stride, but he has some agility and more quickness than speed. Partnering with Nicklas Lidstrom, as Murphy does frequently, helps him because Lidstrom's excellent skating keeps Murphy from getting mired in the defensive zone.

However, it's not all Lidstrom, though he and Murphy complement each other well. Murphy can read the ice, and will either rush the puck out of his zone under pressure or make the nice first pass that gives his team the jump on opponents. When he snares the puck, his first impulse is to make a quick pass, then sprint up-ice and join the breakout. He made a nice, intelligent partner with the developing Aaron Ward late in the season.

Murphy is smart and poised, the perfect guy to collect the puck behind his goal line and start the rush up-ice on the power play. He has a fairly high panic point with the puck, and often will hold it until the last moment before passing.

Although he has been known to give away the puck, Murphy generally will not force bad passes up the middle and almost always picks the safest passing option. His pinches are well-timed, and he has the reach to prevent a lot of pucks from getting by him at the point. He has the good sense, and balance, to drop to one knee and get his body in front of clearing attempts he is trying to block at the point, thus fewer pucks get past him.

Murphy's shot selection is intelligent. He loves to shoot but he won't fire blindly. He uses a low wrist shot rather than a big slap to keep the puck on net. His positional play is where he has shown the most improvement. He reads plays well and seldom seems to be floundering on the ice.

THE PHYSICAL GAME

Murphy does not like to play a physical game, but the Detroit system demands it, and he pays the price. He will bump his man in front but doesn't make strong takeouts. He prefers to position his body and force the shooter to make a play while he himself goes for the puck or stick. In his quiet way, Murphy is a tough customer.

THE INTANGIBLES

Murphy has a lot of hockey mileage on him. He doesn't miss many games or the playoffs (not since 1988). The Red Wings wrung a lot more out of Murphy than some other teams might have — this guy was booed out of Toronto two years ago — but he might be reaching a breaking point.

PROJECTION

Murphy might be the quietest 1,000-point scorer in NHL history. Rings make a big noise, however, and Murphy has earned four with two different organizations. He is big, but not physical. He is skilled, but not flashy. He plays a low-maintenance game, stays healthy, gets his minutes and he's going to score goals in double digits or set them up for another 50-point season.

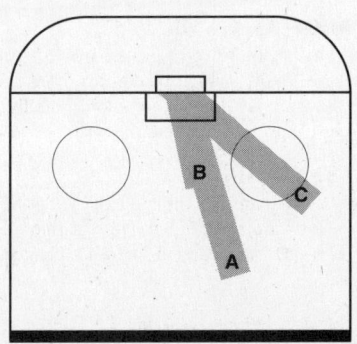

CHRIS OSGOOD

Yrs. of NHL service: 6
Born: Peace River, Alta.; Nov. 26, 1972
Position: goaltender
Height: 5-10
Weight: 175
Uniform no.: 30
Catches: left

Career statistics:

GP	MIN	GA	SO	GAA	A	PIM
284	16493	647	23	2.35	7	53

1995-96 statistics:

GP	MIN	GAA	W	L	T	SO	GA	S	SAPCT	PIM
50	2933	2.17	39	6	5	5	106	1190	.911	4

1996-97 statistics:

GP	MIN	GAA	W	L	T	SO	GA	S	SAPCT	PIM
47	2769	2.30	23	13	9	6	106	1175	.910	6

1997-98 statistics:

GP	MIN	GAA	W	L	T	SO	GA	S	SAPCT	PIM
64	3807	2.21	33	20	11	6	140	1605	.913	31

1998-99 statistics:

GP	MIN	GAA	W	L	T	SO	GA	S	SAPCT	PIM
63	3691	2.42	34	25	4	3	149	1654	.910	8

PROJECTION

By all means, make him a high pool pick, since he's good for another 30 to 35 wins on a team that will still be among the elite this season.

LAST SEASON

Fourth in NHL in wins. Missed six games with hip injury.

THE PHYSICAL GAME

Osgood is a small goalie, but by challenging shooters he makes himself look bigger in the net. He plays his angles well and has very quick feet. His reflexes are excellent for close shots and he stays on his skates and doesn't flop. He has a superb glove — he's tough to beat high. Osgood's problems arise when he loses his concentration and his angles, and fails to square himself to the shooter.

He controls his rebounds well and doesn't have to scramble for too many second or third shots. His lateral movement is very good.

Osgood can handle the puck; in fact, he has scored a goal. He also uses his stick effectively to poke pucks off attackers' sticks around the net. He is no Martin Brodeur, however, and he tends to get overambitious.

THE MENTAL GAME

Osgood has been allowed to settle into his role as a number one goalie, which made him more comfortable last season. He doesn't get a lot of credit, but he doesn't lose games for his team.

THE INTANGIBLES

Osgood has his name on the big trophy, but he won't win any hardware on his own. He was injured in the playoffs, which handicapped Detroit's chances for a three-peat.

BRENDAN SHANAHAN

Yrs. of NHL service: 12
Born: Mimico, Ont.; Jan. 23, 1969
Position: left wing
Height: 6-3
Weight: 218
Uniform no.: 14
Shoots: right

Career statistics:

GP	G	A	TP	PIM
869	394	407	801	1749

1995-96 statistics:

GP	G	A	TP	+/-	PIM	PP	SH	GW	GT	S	PCT
74	44	34	78	+2	125	17	2	6	0	280	15.7

1996-97 statistics:

GP	G	A	TP	+/-	PIM	PP	SH	GW	GT	S	PCT
81	47	41	88	+32	131	20	3	7	2	336	14.0

1997-98 statistics:

GP	G	A	TP	+/-	PIM	PP	SH	GW	GT	S	PCT
75	28	29	57	+6	154	15	1	9	1	266	10.5

1998-99 statistics:

GP	G	A	TP	+/-	PIM	PP	SH	GW	GT	S	PCT
81	31	27	58	+2	123	5	0	5	0	288	10.8

LAST SEASON
Led team in game-winning goals for third consecutive season. Led team in shots for second consecutive season. Second on team in goals and penalty minutes. Missed one game due to injury.

THE FINESSE GAME
Skating is one of Shanahan's few flaws. He isn't very quick, isn't very agile and he often looks awkward with the puck. Most of the time he's better off making the hit that frees the puck, then passing it to a teammate and breaking to a spot, because he can score from anywhere. He is far more polished as a starter and a finisher than as the middle man who beats a couple of checkers with the puck and feeds an open man.

A wonderful package of grit, skills and smarts, Shanahan will battle in front of the net for a puck, but he is also savvy enough to avoid an unnecessary thrashing. On the power play, he is one of the best at staying just off the crease, waiting for a shot to come from the point, then timing his arrival at the front of the net for the moving screen, the tip or the rebound. He can get a lot on his shot even when the puck is near his feet, because of a short backswing and strong wrists.

Shanahan has wonderfully soft hands for nifty goalmouth passes, and he has a hard, accurate snap and slap shot with a quick release, which he never tires of using. He also loves the one-time shot and is a good enough athlete to bury it — even if the pass he receives isn't perfect. Shanahan was even used to kill penalties late last season.

THE PHYSICAL GAME
The dilemma for rival teams: If you play Shanahan aggressively, it brings out the best in him. If you lay off and give him room, he will kill you with his skills. Shanahan spent his formative NHL years establishing his reputation by dropping his gloves with anybody who challenged him, but he has gotten smarter without losing his tough edge.

Shanahan takes or makes a hit to create a play. He's willing to eat glass to make a pass, but would rather strike the first blow. He does that by using his strength to overcome the hooking and holding, by fighting through checks to get himself in position to score. He sees the puck, goes and gets it and puts it towards the front of the net.

THE INTANGIBLES
Shanahan is a leader, a gamer who revels in pressure situations. Teammates thrive on his intensity. With all due respect to Steve Yzerman, Shanahan is the behind-the-scenes captain of the Red Wings. His ongoing discord with coach Scotty Bowman may wear on him eventually, even though GM Ken Holland and teammates like Yzerman have plunked themselves squarely in Shanahan's corner.

Detroit played him mostly on his off-wing last season, and while he can handle it, he will be more comfortable if the Red Wings move him back to the left side as planned this season.

Other than his willingness to hit or to scrap, no aspect of his game is elite. But he's there when you need him to make a play that will win for you, to say the right thing in the dressing room or to orchestrate the Stanley Cup handoff. And he's always there for the fans; Shanahan is one of the most popular players in the NHL.

PROJECTION
We expect him to score in the 50- to 60-point range, with most of his goals coming on the power play.

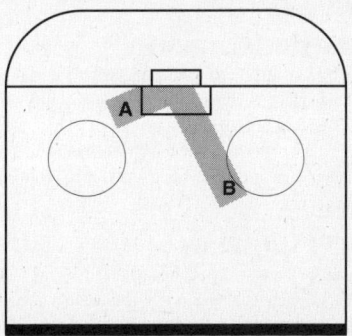

AARON WARD

Yrs. of NHL service: 3
Born: Windsor, Ont.; Jan. 17, 1973
Position: left defense
Height: 6-2
Weight: 200
Uniform no.: 27
Shoots: right

Career statistics:

GP	G	A	TP	PIM
167	11	19	30	157

1995-96 statistics:
Did not play in NHL

1996-97 statistics:

GP	G	A	TP	+/-	PIM	PP	SH	GW	GT	S	PCT
49	2	5	7	-9	52	0	0	0	0	40	5.0

1997-98 statistics:

GP	G	A	TP	+/-	PIM	PP	SH	GW	GT	S	PCT
52	5	5	10	-1	47	0	0	1	0	47	10.6

1998-99 statistics:

GP	G	A	TP	+/-	PIM	PP	SH	GW	GT	S	PCT
60	3	8	11	-5	52	0	0	0	0	46	6.5

LAST SEASON

Missed two games with rotator cuff injury. Missed 20 games due to coach's decision.

THE FINESSE GAME

Ward's game favours finesse over physicality, but he doesn't seem to have the skills for that style. Although his quickness has improved he could use a step in his skating. And even though his puck movement has improved he makes questionable decisions in both ends of the rink. He's still learning. The question becomes when, exactly, will he graduate to fill out a first-rounder's promise?

Ward is adequate from a positional standpoint and plays the percentages. He makes attackers try to beat his strength and reach to the outside, because he knows there aren't many forwards capable of taking the inside route.

Ward does an acceptable job in confined spaces, such as the corners, but like other big defensemen he has trouble winning a race back to the front of the net if the puck squirts loose.

THE PHYSICAL GAME

Ward's got all kinds of size but doesn't use it particularly well. He can be physical, big-hit physical, but does not play a consistently physical game, which the Detroit system demands of its defensemen. He's not an aggressive player. Scouts question his intensity and toughness.

THE INTANGIBLES

Ward can be a pepperpot, but doesn't seem to want to be one consistently. He has completed his sixth season with the organization, and must step up his play this year or he will be moved elsewhere. He will face another training camp challenge from Yan Golubovsky.

Ward makes impact with his hits but has not had significant impact on the coaching staff. Since the Red Wings have been desperate to find a physical defenseman to replace Vladimir Konstantinov, it seems telling that Ward, with such physical promise, hasn't leaped at the chance.

PROJECTION

It won't be too surprising if Ward ends up making a name for himself with another team. He has never been much of a scorer at any level. His top end would be 20 points over a full season of regular playing time, which he has yet to earn as he continues to perplex his coaches.

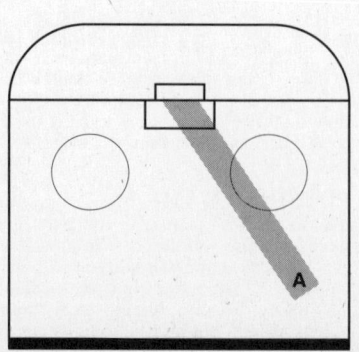

STEVE YZERMAN

Yrs. of NHL service: 16
Born: Cranbrook, B.C.; May 9, 1965
Position: centre
Height: 5-11
Weight: 185
Uniform no.: 19
Shoots: right

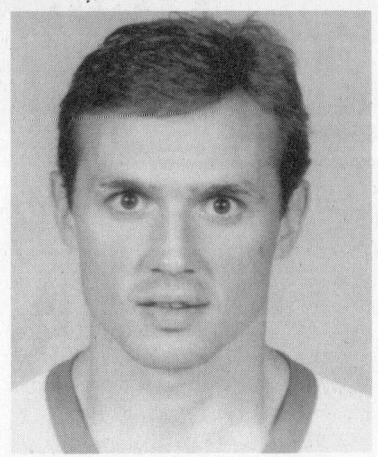

Career statistics:

GP	G	A	TP	PIM
1178	598	891	1483	782

1995-96 statistics:

GP	G	A	TP	+/-	PIM	PP	SH	GW	GT	S	PCT
80	36	59	95	+29	64	16	2	8	0	220	16.4

1996-97 statistics:

GP	G	A	TP	+/-	PIM	PP	SH	GW	GT	S	PCT
81	22	63	85	+22	78	8	0	3	0	232	9.5

1997-98 statistics:

GP	G	A	TP	+/-	PIM	PP	SH	GW	GT	S	PCT
75	24	45	69	+3	46	6	2	0	2	188	12.8

1998-99 statistics:

GP	G	A	TP	+/-	PIM	PP	SH	GW	GT	S	PCT
80	29	45	74	+8	42	13	2	4	0	231	12.6

LAST SEASON

Led team in points and power-play goals. Tied for team lead in shorthanded goals. Second on team in assists and shots. Tied for second on team in game-winning goals. Third on team in goals. Missed one game due to facial lacerations and broken nose. Missed one game due to coach's decision.

THE FINESSE GAME

Yzerman is no longer a 100-point scorer, but he's a better player than he was in those days. Now he will score 70 points and prevent the opponent from scoring 30.

Yzerman is a sensational skater. He zigs and zags all over the ice, spending very little time in the centre. He has great balance and quick feet, and is adroit at kicking the puck up onto his blade for a shot in one, seamless motion. He's also strong for an average-sized forward. He protects the puck well with his body and has the arm strength for wraparound shots and off-balance shots through traffic.

Yzerman prefers to stickhandle down the right side of the ice. In addition to using his body to shield the puck, he uses the boards to protect it. If a defender starts reaching in with his stick he usually ends up pulling Yzerman down for a penalty.

Yzerman has steadily improved his work on draws. He is a great penalty killer because of his speed and anticipation.

THE PHYSICAL GAME

Yzerman sacrifices his body willingly in the right circumstances and thinks nothing of diving to block a shot. He pays the price along the boards and around the net, and he's deceptively strong and durable.

Yzerman knows he isn't big enough to be an intimidating hitter, but he gets his body and stick in the way and at least makes the puck carrier change direction abruptly. He simply does not give up on a play, and he plays all 200 feet of the rink.

THE INTANGIBLES

Yzerman's lapses during the season are few, and he seldom experiences a prolonged scoring slump. Considering how much ice time he gets and how active a skater he is, this is a tribute to his devotion to conditioning and mental preparation. He has always seemed mature beyond his years, even when he broke into the NHL at age 18.

Yzerman is one of the game's great quiet captains, a leader by example who says and does all the right things.

PROJECTION

Yzerman will again score in the 70-point range. He is a model of consistency.

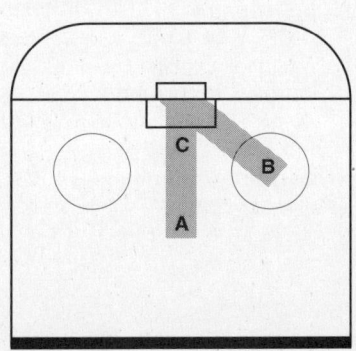

EDMONTON OILERS

Players' Statistics 1998-99

POS	NO.	PLAYER	GP	G	A	PTS	+/-	PIM	PP	SH	GW	GT	S	PCT
R	9	BILL GUERIN	80	30	34	64	7	133	13		2	1	261	11.5
L	20	JOSEF BERANEK	66	19	30	49	6	23	7		2		160	11.9
R	25	MIKE GRIER	82	20	24	44	5	54	3	2	1		143	14.0
R	10	PAT FALLOON	82	17	23	40	-4	20	8		2		152	11.2
L	17	REM MURRAY	78	21	18	39	4	20	4	1	4	1	116	18.1
C	39	DOUG WEIGHT	43	6	31	37	-8	12	1			1	79	7.6
L	26	TODD MARCHANT	82	14	22	36	3	65	3	1	2		183	7.7
R	28	ALEXANDER SELIVANOV	72	14	19	33	-8	42	2		1		177	7.9
D	22	ROMAN HAMRLIK	75	8	24	32	9	70	3				172	4.7
L	94	RYAN SMYTH	71	13	18	31	0	62	6		2	2	161	8.1
D	44	JANNE NIINIMAA	81	4	24	28	7	88	2		1		142	2.8
C	15	CHAD KILGER	77	15	12	27	-4	34	2	1	1	1	81	18.5
L	18	ETHAN MOREAU	80	10	11	21	-3	92			2		96	10.4
D	5	*TOM POTI	73	5	16	21	10	42			3		94	5.3
D	21	JASON SMITH	72	3	12	15	-9	51					68	4.4
C	19	BOYD DEVEREAUX	61	6	8	14	2	23		1	4	1	39	15.4
D	24	CHRISTIAN LAFLAMME	73	2	12	14	-3	70					68	2.9
R	16	KELLY BUCHBERGER	52	4	4	8	-6	68		2	1		29	13.8
D	23	*SEAN BROWN	51		7	7	1	188					27	
R	42	KEVIN BROWN	12	4	2	6	-2		2				13	30.8
R	27	*GEORGES LARAQUE	39	3	2	5	-1	57					17	17.6
D	46	TODD REIRDEN	17	2	3	5	-1	20					26	7.7
D	33	MARTY MCSORLEY	46	2	3	5	-5	101					29	6.9
D	8	FRANK MUSIL	39		3	3	0	34					9	
R	34	VLADIMIR VOROBIEV	2	2		2	1	2					5	40.0
D	32	*CRAIG MILLAR	24		2	2	-6	19					18	
R	38	CHRIS FERRARO	2	1		1	1						1	100.0
G	29	*STEVE PASSMORE	6		1	1	0	2						
G	30	BOB ESSENSA	39		1	1	0							
C	34	JIM DOWD	1			0							1	
L	12	JOE HULBIG	1		1	1		2					2	
L	28	BILL HUARD	3			0							2	
L	15	*DAN LACOUTURE	3		1									
C	21	DANIEL LACROIX	4			0		13					5	
R	7	*FREDRIK LINDQUIST	8				-2	2					6	
G	35	TOMMY SALO	64				0	12						

GP = games played; G = goals; A = assists; PTS = points; +/- = goals-for minus goals-against while player is on ice; PIM = penalties in minutes; PP = power-play goals; SH = shorthanded goals; GW = game-winning goals; GT = game-tying goals; S = no. of shots; PCT = percentage of goals to shots; * = rookie

JOSEF BERANEK

Yrs. of NHL service: 8
Born: Litvinov, Czech.; Oct, 25, 1969
Position: left wing
Height: 6-2
Weight: 195
Uniform no.: 20
Shoots: left

Career statistics:

GP	G	A	TP	PIM
390	96	118	214	298

1995-96 statistics:

GP	G	A	TP	+/-	PIM	PP	SH	GW	GT	S	PCT
61	6	14	20	-11	60	0	0	1	0	131	4.6

1996-97 statistics:
Did not play in NHL

1997-98 statistics:

GP	G	A	TP	+/-	PIM	PP	SH	GW	GT	S	PCT
8	3	1	4	-1	4	4	1	0	0	15	20.0

1998-99 statistics:

GP	G	A	TP	+/-	PIM	PP	SH	GW	GT	S	PCT
66	19	30	49	+6	23	7	0	2	0	160	11.9

LAST SEASON
Second on team in points. Third on team in assists, power-play goals and shooting percentage. Missed six games with knee surgery. Missed three games with sprained knee. Missed two games with thigh contusion.

THE FINESSE GAME
Defenders can usually guess "pass" when playing against Beranek. He thinks to make a play first before taking a shot, though he has an accurate shot, especially his wrister. He will often try to force a pass to a teammate instead of taking the shot himself, even when he is in a superior shooting position.

Beranek uses all of the ice, which makes him a natural for the European-style attack used by the Oilers. He can play centre or wing; when on the wing he brings a centre's playmaking ability and vision to the position.

Beranek needs to keep his feet moving. He is a good skater, but not a great one.

THE PHYSICAL GAME
Beranek played in Europe the previous season, and may have hit the wall around midyear in his return to the NHL schedule. His knee surgery is also a concern, though he did return to play two games in the playoffs. He doesn't play with much grit.

THE INTANGIBLES
The Oilers are relying heavily on Beranek to be a top line forward.

PROJECTION
Beranek has never been able to come close to the 28-goal season he had with Philadelphia in 1993-94. He is likely to stay around the 20-goal mark with 40 assists.

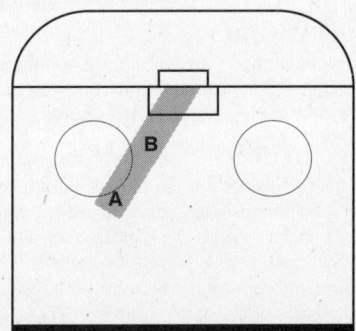

DANIEL CLEARY

Yrs. of NHL service: 1
Born: Carbonear, Nfld.; Dec. 19, 1978
Position: left wing
Height: 6-0
Weight: 203
Uniform no.: 25
Shoots: left

Career statistics:

GP	G	A	TP	PIM
41	4	5	9	24

1997-98 statistics:

GP	G	A	TP	+/-	PIM	PP	SH	GW	GT	S	PCT
6	0	0	0	-2	0	0	0	0	0	4	0.0

1998-99 statistics:

GP	G	A	TP	+/-	PIM	PP	SH	GW	GT	S	PCT
35	4	5	9	-1	24	0	0	0	0	49	8.2

LAST SEASON

Acquired from Chicago with Chad Kilger, Ethan Moreau and Christian Laflamme for Boris Mironov, Deam McAmmond and Jonas Elofsson, Mar. 19, 1999. First NHL season. Appeared in 30 games with Portland (AHL), scoring 9-17 — 26. Appeared in nine games with Hamilton (AHL), scoring 0-1 — 1.

THE FINESSE GAME

Cleary is a good skater and puckhandler, but he hasn't shown a desire to battle for his space and his scoring chances.

He has a smooth stride and acclerates quickly. He can handle the puck at a high pace and is very good one-on-one in open ice. He has a decent scoring touch but doesn't work himself into the optimum scoring areas, and he tends to rush his shots.

Cleary has to play in a second-line capacity, because he doesn't play third- or fourth-line style. He has the potential to do so. Some players look awfully shy in their first year of pro, and then suddenly the light gets switched on. Cleary has to make that jump.

THE PHYSICAL GAME

Cleary needs to pay the price. He doesn't get enough chances to score because he lacks a work ethic. He shies away from physical play too much.

THE INTANGIBLES

Cleary is something of an enigma. He seemed to sulk in the minors and his attitude needs an adjustment. He needs to show something extra this season.

PROJECTION

Cleary needs to take a page out of teammate J. P. Dumont's book and work harder to use his considerable skills, or he'll be on the bubble instead of in the top six forwards with Edmonton — which is where he's expected to play and where he would fit in very nicely with the team's speed.

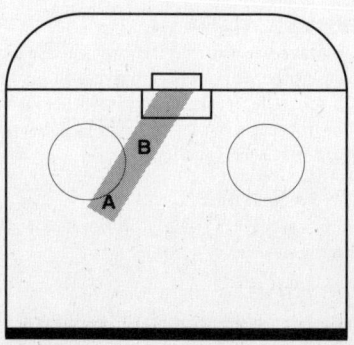

BOYD DEVEREAUX

Yrs. of NHL service: 2
Born: Seaforth, Ont.; Apr. 16, 1978
Position: centre
Height: 6-2
Weight: 195
Uniform no.: 19
Shoots: left

Career statistics:

GP	G	A	TP	PIM
99	7	12	19	29

1997-98 statistics:

GP	G	A	TP	+/-	PIM	PP	SH	GW	GT	S	PCT
38	1	4	5	-5	6	0	0	0	0	27	3.7

1998-99 statistics:

GP	G	A	TP	+/-	PIM	PP	SH	GW	GT	S	PCT
61	6	8	14	+2	23	0	1	4	1	39	15.4

LAST SEASON

Tied for team lead in game-winning goals. Appeared in seven games with Hamilton (AHL), scoring 4-6 — 10. Missed six games due to coach's decision.

THE FINESSE GAME

Devereaux has a lot of speed and gets the puck to the net, but he tends to try a lot of moves that work at the minor-league level; NHL defenders just eat those up. His hands are a question mark, which means he will probably never be a scorer at this level.

Devereaux can bring other things to the table, however. His skating makes him an above-average checking winger and penalty killer. He might not get to the second line, but he has the sense to be a valuable role player.

THE PHYSICAL GAME

Devereaux isn't much of a big hitter. He has decent size, but on the forecheck he intimidates more with his speed than the threat of a body check. He could stand to get a little stronger and more involved.

THE INTANGIBLES

Devereaux was bounced around a bit in the lineup, playing most of the year as a fourth-liner. He could graduate to the third line as a checker.

PROJECTION

Devereaux is an NHL player, with a chance at scoring 15 goals in a checking role if he wins a full-time job.

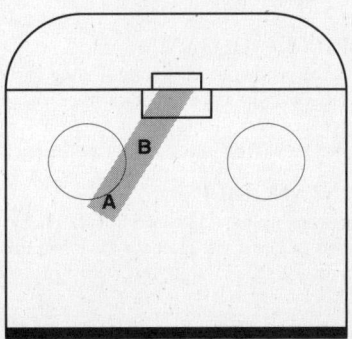

PAT FALLOON

Yrs. of NHL service: 10
Born: Foxwarren, Man.; Sept. 22, 1972
Position: right wing
Height: 5-11
Weight: 190
Uniform no.: 10
Shoots: right

Career statistics:

GP	G	A	TP	PIM
512	134	157	291	127

1995-96 statistics:

GP	G	A	TP	+/-	PIM	PP	SH	GW	GT	S	PCT
71	25	26	51	+14	10	9	0	2	1	170	14.7

1996-97 statistics:

GP	G	A	TP	+/-	PIM	PP	SH	GW	GT	S	PCT
52	11	12	23	-8	10	2	0	4	0	124	8.9

1997-98 statistics:

GP	G	A	TP	+/-	PIM	PP	SH	GW	GT	S	PCT
58	8	10	18	-8	16	3	0	0	0	136	5.9

1998-99 statistics:

GP	G	A	TP	+/-	PIM	PP	SH	GW	GT	S	PCT
82	17	23	40	-4	20	8	0	2	0	152	11.2

PROJECTION

Falloon should score 15 to 20 goals and around 45 points if he can keep his job on the second line.

LAST SEASON

Second on team in power-play goals. One of three Oilers to appear in all 82 games.

THE FINESSE GAME

Falloon needs to play with people who can get him the puck, which is why he's turned out to be a better winger for a player like Doug Weight or Todd Marchant in Edmonton than he was at centre earlier in his NHL career.

Not a natural goal scorer, Falloon scoops up his opportunities around the net, following up and pouncing on loose rebounds. He works to get open and always has his stick ready. He is not very big, so he has to dart in and out of holes and get his timing right. He has soft hands and good instincts.

Falloon uses an array of shots, and likes to cut against the grain from the right wing to the middle of the ice to pick up a screen for his wrist shot. He slows down considerably when he has to carry the puck. His defensive game is flawed. He is not a great skater.

THE PHYSICAL GAME

Falloon had problems with conditioning early in his career but has paid more attention in recent years, as his career was backsliding. He is far from a physical player, but he will go into traffic after the puck.

THE INTANGIBLES

Falloon probably wouldn't be a top six player on any other team, but he is adequate for the job in Edmonton and is a decent second-unit power-play guy.

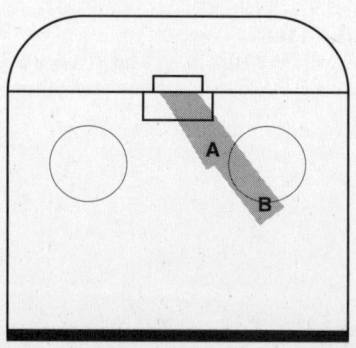

MIKE GRIER

Yrs. of NHL service: 3
Born: Detroit, Mich.; Jan. 5, 1975
Position: right wing
Height: 6-1
Weight: 232
Uniform no.: 25
Shoots: right

Career statistics:

GP	G	A	TP	PIM
227	44	47	91	172

1996-97 statistics:

GP	G	A	TP	+/-	PIM	PP	SH	GW	GT	S	PCT
79	15	17	32	+7	45	4	0	2	0	89	16.9

1997-98 statistics:

GP	G	A	TP	+/-	PIM	PP	SH	GW	GT	S	PCT
66	9	6	15	-3	73	1	0	1	0	90	10.0

1998-99 statistics:

GP	G	A	TP	+/-	PIM	PP	SH	GW	GT	S	PCT
82	20	24	44	+5	54	3	2	1	0	143	14.0

LAST SEASON

Led team in shorthanded goals. Second on team in shooting percentage. Third on team in goals and points with career highs. One of three Oilers to appear in all 82 games.

THE FINESSE GAME

Grier is a hockey player in a football player's body. He is an aggressive forechecker and bores in on the unfortunate puck carrier with all the intensity of a lineman blitzing a quarterback. But Grier doesn't waste energy. He is intelligent about when to come in full-tilt or when to back off a bit and pick off a hasty pass. He frightens a lot of people into mistakes, and the savvier he gets at reading their reactions the better he'll be.

Grier definitely believes that the most direct route to the net is the best path to choose. He won't hesitate to bull his way through two defensemen to get there.

The knock on Grier has always been his skating, which is getting much better. He has a slow first couple of strides, but he then gets into gear and is strong and balanced with fair agility. He scores his goals like Adam Deadmarsh does, by driving to the net after loose pucks. Grier was a scorer at the collegiate level and has decent hands. Since he always keeps his legs pumping, he draws a good share of penalties.

THE PHYSICAL GAME

Grier can't be too bulky or he won't be agile enough for his pursuit. He isn't a fighter. It takes a lot to provoke him. He's just an honest, tough, physical winger.

THE INTANGIBLES

Grier has dealt admirably with racism in his sport, and accepts the responsibility of being a role model for younger athletes. He made an amazing jump from college to the pros, and he keeps getting better. His attitude and work ethic are unassailable. He is the unsung hero of the Oilers.

PROJECTION

We told you last year that although Grier was not a natural goal scorer, he should get 15 to 20 goals with his effort. He did. Twenty seems to be his top end, but added to his other qualities, it's plenty.

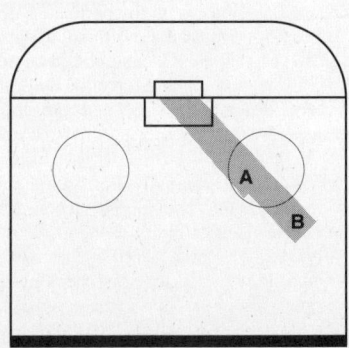

BILL GUERIN

Yrs. of NHL service: 7
Born: Wilbraham, Mass.; Nov. 9, 1970
Position: right wing
Height: 6-2
Weight: 200
Uniform no.: 9
Shoots: right

Career statistics:

GP	G	A	TP	PIM
500	151	156	307	682

1995-96 statistics:

GP	G	A	TP	+/-	PIM	PP	SH	GW	GT	S	PCT
80	23	30	53	+7	116	8	0	6	1	216	10.6

1996-97 statistics:

GP	G	A	TP	+/-	PIM	PP	SH	GW	GT	S	PCT
82	29	18	47	-2	95	7	0	9	0	177	16.4

1997-98 statistics:

GP	G	A	TP	+/-	PIM	PP	SH	GW	GT	S	PCT
59	18	21	39	+1	93	9	0	4	0	178	10.1

1998-99 statistics:

GP	G	A	TP	+/-	PIM	PP	SH	GW	GT	S	PCT
80	30	34	64	+7	133	13	0	2	1	261	11.5

LAST SEASON

Led team in goals, assists and points with career highs. Led team in power-play goals and shots. Second on team in penalty minutes. Tied for third on team in plus-minus. Missed two games with knee injury.

THE FINESSE GAME

Leaving New Jersey for Edmonton brought the change Guerin always thought it could. With newfound confidence, he has developed into a gamer, but one whose game could still use a little more polish. He has a terrifying slap shot, a wicked screamer that he unleashes off the wing in full flight. But like a young pitcher who lives off his fastball, he must master the change-up. There are times when a snap or wrist shot is the better choice, especially when he is set up for a one-timer.

What he must do is keep driving to the net instead of curling around and looking to make a pass. Guerin becomes ineffective when he stops playing like a power forward and dances on the perimeter; he starts playing an east-west instead of north-south game. His speed and power are potent weapons. But he needs to drive down the right wing and force the defense back with his speed. When he backs off and takes the easier route to the off-wing, his scoring chances decrease drastically in quality.

Hockey sense and creativity are lagging a tad behind his other attributes, but Guerin is a conscientious player and those qualities should develop. He is aware defensively and has worked hard at that part of the game, though he will still lose his checking assignments and start running around in the defensive zone.

THE PHYSICAL GAME

The more physical the game is, the more Guerin gets involved. He is big, strong and tough in every sense of the word, and, frankly, is useless when he plays otherwise.

The kind of game Guerin is going to have can usually be judged in the first few shifts. He can play it clean or mean, with big body checks or the drop of a glove. He will move to the puck carrier and battle for control until he gets it, and he's hard to knock off his skates.

In front of the net, Guerin digs hard. He works to establish position and has the hand skills to make something happen when the puck gets to his stick. Guerin is in great shape and can routinely handle 25 minutes a night.

THE INTANGIBLES

Guerin would have put up even better numbers if his linemate Doug Weight hadn't been injured nearly half the season. Guerin was expected to take the Oilers to salary arbitration in the off-season, but he has been down this contact road before and it's unlikely to bother him.

PROJECTION

Now that Guerin has cracked the mental barrier of being a 30-goal scorer, he has to get into the 35 to 40 range, which he could do if Weight remains healthy.

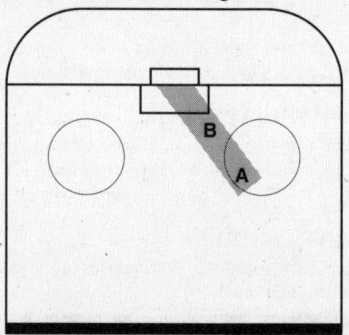

ROMAN HAMRLIK

Yrs. of NHL service: 7
Born: Gottwaldov, Czech Republic; Apr. 12, 1974
Position: left defense
Height: 6-2
Weight: 202
Uniform no.: 22
Shoots: left

Career statistics:

GP	G	A	TP	PIM
493	66	177	243	592

1995-96 statistics:

GP	G	A	TP	+/-	PIM	PP	SH	GW	GT	S	PCT
82	16	49	65	-24	103	12	0	2	3	281	5.7

1996-97 statistics:

GP	G	A	TP	+/-	PIM	PP	SH	GW	GT	S	PCT
79	12	28	40	-29	57	6	0	0	1	238	5.0

1997-98 statistics:

GP	G	A	TP	+/-	PIM	PP	SH	GW	GT	S	PCT
78	9	32	41	-15	70	5	1	3	0	198	4.5

1998-99 statistics:

GP	G	A	TP	+/-	PIM	PP	SH	GW	GT	S	PCT
75	8	24	32	+9	70	3	0	0	0	172	4.7

LAST SEASON
Led team defensemen in points. Second on team in plus-minus. Missed six games with fractured toe.

THE FINESSE GAME
Hamrlik is tantalizingly close to becoming the NHL's next star defenseman, a player who can handle marathon ice time and has the desire to dominate a game. He has all the tools. He is a fast, strong skater forwards and backwards. And although he still needs to improve his reads, he's getting better.

Hamrlik is a mobile defenseman with a solid shot and good passing skills, but he is not very creative. Right now, he thinks he can just overpower people, and he frequently can, but he could also learn to outsmart them and not make the game so difficult. He loves to get involved offensively. He plays nearly the full two minutes of a power play on the point, but he won't hesitate to jump into the play low. He has an excellent shot with a quick release. He could be smarter about taking some velocity off his shot in order to get a less blockable shot through.

Hamrlik has adjusted to the NHL pace because of his strong skating. He makes high-risk plays, however. Defensively, he runs into problems when he is trying to move the puck out of his zone and when he is forced to handle the puck on his backhand, but that is about the only way the opposition can cope with him.

THE PHYSICAL GAME
Hamrlik is aggressive and likes physical play, though he is not a huge, splashy hitter. He is in great shape and routinely plays 25 or more minutes a night, and wants to.

THE INTANGIBLES
Hamrlik is a high-maintenance defenseman. He has clashed with his coaches but is happier now with Edmonton, playing on a team that embraces an international style. Given the Oilers' financial woes, it's likely Hamrlik will be dealt during the season.

PROJECTION
Hamrlik should be a 20-goal, 50-point scorer and be among the top 10 defensemen in scoring, but his game and his head have to be straightened out first. He hasn't yet found the right mentor (coach or player) to bring out his best. Maybe Kevin Lowe can.

CHAD KILGER

Yrs. of NHL service: 4
Born: Cornwall, Ont.; Nov. 27, 1976
Position: centre
Height: 6-3
Weight: 204
Uniform no.: 15
Shoots: left

Career statistics:

GP	G	A	TP	PIM
207	29	34	63	91

1995-96 statistics:

GP	G	A	TP	+/-	PIM	PP	SH	GW	GT	S	PCT
74	7	10	17	-4	34	0	0	1	0	57	12.3

1996-97 statistics:

GP	G	A	TP	+/-	PIM	PP	SH	GW	GT	S	PCT
24	4	3	7	-5	13	1	0	0	0	30	13.3

1997-98 statistics:

GP	G	A	TP	+/-	PIM	PP	SH	GW	GT	S	PCT
32	3	9	12	0	10	2	0	1	0	32	9.4

1998-99 statistics:

GP	G	A	TP	+/-	PIM	PP	SH	GW	GT	S	PCT
77	15	12	27	-4	34	2	1	1	1	81	18.5

LAST SEASON

Acquired from Chicago with Daniel Cleary, Ethan Moreau and Christian Laflamme for Dean McAmmond, Boris Mironov and Jonas Elofsson, Mar. 20, 1999. Career highs in games played, goals, assists and points.

THE FINESSE GAME

Kilger joined his fourth organization when he was traded to the Oilers, and now has to deal with yet another new coach. That's a lot of upheaval for a young player who has yet to find his niche.

Kilger plays an intelligent game and is poised for a youngster. He sees the ice well and is a good passer. The release on his shot is too slow for the NHL level right now and needs to be improved. He has a long reach, which works to his advantage in dangling the puck away from defenders. Kilger is very strong on draws.

Kilger's size and skating ability are NHL calibre. Few big players skate as well as he does, and he's at his best when he accelerates through the neutral zone. When he gets the puck, if he wants it, he can get a lot of chances by busting through. He could become a go-to guy.

THE PHYSICAL GAME

Kilger is big, but needs to fill out and get stronger. The biggest knock on him at this stage is that he doesn't play well in traffic, and he will need to in order to establish himself as a top six forward.

THE INTANGIBLES

The Oilers tend to get a lot of mileage out of their young players, and this could be Kilger's big chance to establish himself as an NHL regular.

PROJECTION

Kilger is still raw and immature. He needs to have a regular role and not be a part-timer. He has a 20-goal season in him, and it better show up soon.

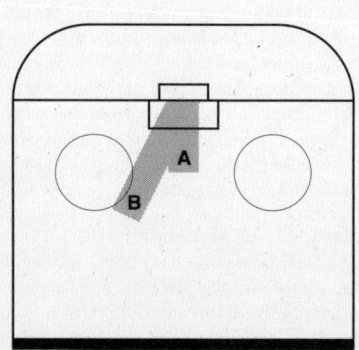

CHRISTIAN LAFLAMME

Yrs. of NHL service: 2
Born: St. Charles, Que.; Nov. 24, 1976
Position: defense
Height: 6-1
Weight: 195
Uniform no.: 19
Shoots: right

Career statistics:
GP	G	A	TP	PIM
149	2	24	26	131

1996-97 statistics:
GP	G	A	TP	+/-	PIM	PP	SH	GW	GT	S	PCT
4	0	1	1	+3	2	0	0	0	0	3	0.0

1997-98 statistics:
GP	G	A	TP	+/-	PIM	PP	SH	GW	GT	S	PCT
72	0	11	11	+14	59	0	0	0	0	75	.0

1998-99 statistics:
GP	G	A	TP	+/-	PIM	PP	SH	GW	GT	S	PCT
73	2	12	14	-3	70	0	0	0	0	68	2.9

PROJECTION
Laflamme can add more offensive upside to his game and move into the 20- to 25-point range.

LAST SEASON
Acquired from Chicago with Daniel Cleary, Ethan Moreau and Chad Kilger for Dean McAmmond, Boris Mironov and Jonas Elofsson, Mar. 20, 1999. Missed one game with concussion. Missed eight games due to coach's decision.

THE FINESSE GAME
Laflamme is a steady defenseman, advanced for his age because of his good hockey sense. Reliable, if not flashy, he will make a bonehead play every once in awhile, but he is still very early in the learning process.

Laflamme skates well forwards and backwards. He is a good penalty killer, holding his position well, and he seldom gets suckered into running around and missing his checking assignment. He usually worked on the second penalty-killing unit last season.

Laflamme hasn't been shortchanged in any skills department. Although he is primarily a defensive defenseman, he can jump up into the play. He will look to pass rather than shoot, though he has an accurate shot from the point. He can work on the second power-play unit. He handles the puck well and finds the open man. If he keeps the game simple, he's very effective.

THE PHYSICAL GAME
Laflamme takes pride in his play in his own end and patrols the front of his net with authority. He is a good body checker and finishes his checks. He enjoys hitting. He adds grit, without taking dumb penalties.

THE INTANGIBLES
Laflamme wants to make you pay to play against his team. He could be a top four defenseman with the Oilers.

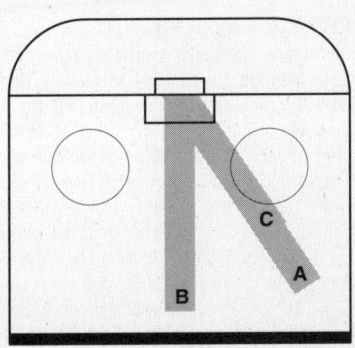

TODD MARCHANT

Yrs. of NHL service: 5
Born: Buffalo, N.Y.; Aug. 12, 1973
Position: centre
Height: 5-10
Weight: 175
Uniform no.: 26
Shoots: left

Career statistics:

GP	G	A	TP	PIM
367	74	96	170	280

1995-96 statistics:

GP	G	A	TP	+/-	PIM	PP	SH	GW	GT	S	PCT
81	19	19	38	-19	66	2	3	2	1	221	8.6

1996-97 statistics:

GP	G	A	TP	+/-	PIM	PP	SH	GW	GT	S	PCT
79	14	19	33	+11	44	0	4	3	0	202	6.9

1997-98 statistics:

GP	G	A	TP	+/-	PIM	PP	SH	GW	GT	S	PCT
76	14	21	35	+9	71	2	1	3	0	194	7.2

1998-99 statistics:

GP	G	A	TP	+/-	PIM	PP	SH	GW	GT	S	PCT
82	14	22	36	+3	65	3	1	2	0	183	7.7

LAST SEASON

Second on team in shots. One of three Oilers to appear in all 82 games.

THE FINESSE GAME

A speed merchant, Marchant is a strong one-on-one player with zippy outside speed. His quick hand skills keep pace with his feet, and he is particularly adept at tempting the defender with the puck then dragging it through the victim's legs. He then continues to the net for his scoring chances.

Marchant is opportunistic, and, with his pace, reminds scouts of a young Theo Fleury. However, he has a long way to go to match Fleury's scoring touch. He will never be a 50-goal, 100-point scorer like Fleury, because he doesn't have the hands.

Marchant is smart, sees the ice well and is a solid playmaker as well as shooter. He is no puck hog. He is an excellent penalty killer and a shorthanded threat because of his speed.

THE PHYSICAL GAME

His teammates have nicknamed him "Mighty Mouse," as Marchant is fearless in the face of bigger, supposedly tougher, opposition. He hurls his body at larger foes. He is really irritating to play against, because a big lug like Derian Hatcher looks foolish trying to chase down and swat a little bitty guy like Marchant.

Marchant is average size but his grit makes him look bigger. He sacrifices his body, but you wonder how long his body will last under the stress he puts it through. He is well-conditioned and can handle a lot of ice time. The mental toughness is there, too. He will take a hit to make a play but has to get smarter about picking his spots in order to survive. Edmonton is a very mobile team and Marchant's lack of size is not as much of a detriment as it could be on other teams.

THE INTANGIBLES

Marchant suffered from the absence of Doug Weight, since Weight's absence due to injury left the Oilers very thin up the middle and teams were able to key on Marchant.

PROJECTION

Marchant is a role player with a big heart. His top end is 20 goals, and that would be a career year.

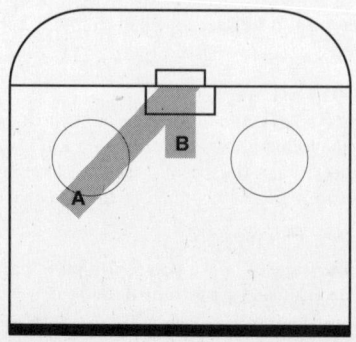

ETHAN MOREAU

Yrs. of NHL service: 3
Born: Huntsville, Ont.; Sept. 22, 1975
Position: left wing
Height: 6-2
Weight: 205
Uniform no.: 18
Shoots: left

Career statistics:

GP	G	A	TP	PIM
224	34	37	71	292

1995-96 statistics:

GP	G	A	TP	+/-	PIM	PP	SH	GW	GT	S	PCT
8	0	1	1	+1	4	0	0	0	0	1	0.0

1996-97 statistics:

GP	G	A	TP	+/-	PIM	PP	SH	GW	GT	S	PCT
82	15	16	31	+13	123	0	0	1	1	114	13.2

1997-98 statistics:

GP	G	A	TP	+/-	PIM	PP	SH	GW	GT	S	PCT
54	9	9	18	0	73	2	0	0	0	87	10.3

1998-99 statistics:

GP	G	A	TP	+/-	PIM	PP	SH	GW	GT	S	PCT
80	10	11	21	-3	92	0	0	2	0	96	10.4

LAST SEASON
Acquired from Chicago with Daniel Cleary, Chad Kilger and Christian Laflamme for Dean McAmmond, Boris Mironov and Jonas Elofsson, Mar. 20, 1999.

THE FINESSE GAME
For a young player, Moreau has been very consistent in the stretches he has played when healthy during the past three seasons. He is an intelligent player with good hockey sense. He can also play centre, though his future is clearly at left wing. He is not a natural scorer but has to work for his goals; his scoring touch improves with effort. Funny how that works.

Moreau has a long reach and uses a long stick, which allow him to get his strong wrist shots away around a defenseman who may think he has Moreau tied up. Defensively, he's on his way because he has an understanding of positional play. He's a budding power forward who goes to the net hard. When he plays on a line with Mike Grier, as he did when he arrived in Edmonton last season, he helped create a high-energy line.

THE PHYSICAL GAME
Moreau has good size and strength and is starting to develop more of a presence. He finishes his checks, especially around the net. There may be a latent aggressive streak that will emerge with more ice time and confidence. He works hard, is strong in the corners and will take a hit to make a play.

THE INTANGIBLES
Size is a desirable commodity in the NHL, and when it's combined with Moreau's drive around the net, that makes for an exciting young prospect. Former coach Craig Hartsburg compared Moreau to a young Bob Gainey, both for his playing style and budding leadership ability.

Moreau is very well-liked and he has some good leadership qualities. He made a good first impression on the Oilers with a solid playoffs.

PROJECTION
We think Moreau has some ability. Power forwards need time to develop, and Moreau will get that time this season. He has a 20-goal year in his immediate future.

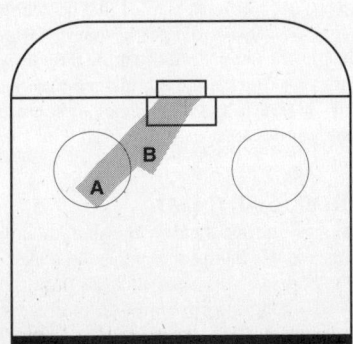

JANNE NIINIMAA

Yrs. of NHL service: 3
Born: Raahe, Finland; May 22, 1975
Position: right defense
Height: 6-1
Weight: 196
Uniform no.: 24
Shoots: left

Career statistics:

GP	G	A	TP	PIM
235	12	103	115	208

1996-97 statistics:

GP	G	A	TP	+/-	PIM	PP	SH	GW	GT	S	PCT
77	4	40	44	+12	58	1	0	2	0	141	2.8

1997-98 statistics:

GP	G	A	TP	+/-	PIM	PP	SH	GW	GT	S	PCT
77	4	39	43	+13	62	3	0	1	0	134	3.0

1998-99 statistics:

GP	G	A	TP	+/-	PIM	PP	SH	GW	GT	S	PCT
81	4	24	28	+7	88	2	0	1	0	142	2.8

LAST SEASON

Tied for third on team in plus-minus. Missed one game with back spasms.

THE FINESSE GAME

A left-handed shot who plays the right side, Niinimaa's excellent skating and puckhandling skills allow him to handle the amount of body shifting necessary to open his body to the rink and keep the forehand available as often as possible.

A nimble, agile player, he sets his feet wide apart for outstanding drive, power and balance, and uses a long stride and long reach to win races to the puck. He can turn the corners at near top speed and doesn't have to slow down when carrying the puck. When the opportunity to jump into the play presents itself he is gone in a vapour trail.

Like Paul Kariya, Niinimaa does a great job of "framing" his stick and giving his teammate a passing target. He keeps the blade on the ice and available, his body position saying, "Put it here, so I can do something with it."

Having stepped into the league at age 21, a middle-aged rookie, Niinimaa learned that he could create just as much offensive danger by merely flipping a puck towards the net instead of taking the full-windup slap shot every time. Although his one-timers can be blistering, he doesn't always shoot to score; sometimes, he shoots to create a rebound or possible deflection.

THE PHYSICAL GAME

Niinimaa plays a fairly physical game, though he is not aggressive. He bumps and jolts, and makes opponents pay a price for every inch of important ice gained. He seems to relish one-on-one battles. He wants the puck and does whatever is necessary to win control of it.

THE INTANGIBLES

Niinimaa is a dynamic player with elite skills. He is a gambler at heart, and will make high-risk plays that cost his team defensively.

PROJECTION

Niinimaa is going to play a lot, is going to get power-play time and is going to score 40 points.

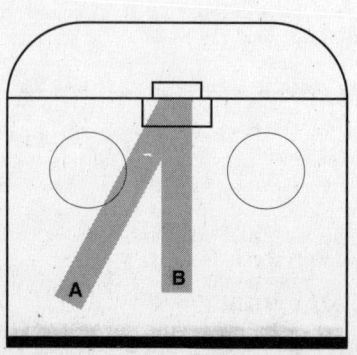

TOM POTI

Yrs. of NHL service: 1
Born: Worcester, Mass.; Mar. 22, 1977
Position: defense
Height: 6-2
Weight: 185
Uniform no.: 5
Shoots: left

Career statistics:

GP	G	A	TP	PIM
73	5	16	21	42

1998-99 statistics:

GP	G	A	TP	+/-	PIM	PP	SH	GW	GT	S	PCT
73	5	16	21	+10	42	2	0	3	0	94	5.3

LAST SEASON
First NHL season. Named to NHL All-Rookie Team. Led team in plus-minus. Ninth among NHL rookies in assists.

THE FINESSE GAME
Poti is a very good offensive defenseman who could be on his way to being an outstanding one. He is an excellent skater whose playing style fits in well with this fast Oilers team that embraces a European style of play.

Poti is a fine puckhandler and passer. He has been compared to Paul Coffey for his vision and his ability to spring teammates with headman passes. He has a long way to go to match Coffey's offensive reputation, but he didn't show many negative signs, either.

Poti uses a low shot from the point that isn't a rocket, so teammates can take advantage of it for tip-ins.

He needs to work on his defense to become a better all-around player. He is intelligent and should keep learning.

THE PHYSICAL GAME
Poti has good size but doesn't use it well. He is still adding some muscle and needs to throw his weight around a bit more and add some grit to his game. He can skate all night.

THE INTANGIBLES
Poti made a huge leap after playing only two seasons of college hockey.

PROJECTION
Poti is a blue chip defenseman who should score in the 30-point range as he gains more confidence and gets more ice time.

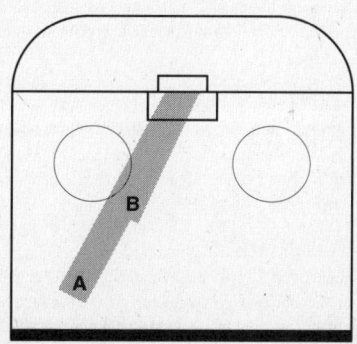

TOMMY SALO

Yrs. of NHL service: 4
Born: Surahammar, Sweden; Feb. 1, 1971
Position: goaltender
Height: 5-11
Weight: 173
Uniform no.: 35
Catches: left

Career statistics:

GP	MIN	GA	SO	GAA	A	PIM
200	11268	515	19	2.74	3	47

1995-96 statistics:

GP	MIN	GAA	W	L	T	SO	GA	S	SAPCT	PIM
10	523	4.02	1	7	1	0	35	250	.860	0

1996-97 statistics:

GP	MIN	GAA	W	L	T	SO	GA	S	SAPCT	PIM
58	3208	2.82	20	27	7	5	151	1576	.904	4

1997-98 statistics:

GP	MIN	GAA	W	L	T	SO	GA	S	SAPCT	PIM
62	3461	2.64	23	29	5	4	152	1617	.906	31

1998-99 statistics:

GP	MIN	GAA	W	L	T	SO	GA	S	SAPCT	PIM
51	3018	2.62	17	26	7	5	132	1368	.904	12

LAST SEASON

Acquired from N.Y. Islanders for Mats Lindgren and a 1999 eighth-round draft pick, Mar. 20, 1999. Career high in wins. Missed six games with broken finger.

THE PHYSICAL GAME

Salo's game is unconventional. He plays deep in his net and is excellent on low shots. He has adjusted to playing with traffic, which is one of the biggest adjustments for European goalies. He has quick feet but is not a great skater; he needs to improve his lateral movement.

Salo has a bad habit of not holding his stick at a proper angle. When he gets into this slump he might as well not bother playing with a stick at all. He has a quick glove and tends to try and catch everything instead of using other parts of his body. Since he doesn't use his stick well, he will try to cover up on every loose puck for face-offs. Better stickhandling work would elevate his game a notch.

Because of his style, Salo makes himself appear small in the net. He is an acrobatic goalie with crowd-pleasing moves.

THE MENTAL GAME

The big knock on Salo was always his lack of concentration. He seemed to let in a bad goal or two at the worst times, but he's gotten over that hump and his effort is far more consistent.

THE INTANGIBLES

Salo could be a Dominik Hasek type who needs to wait until he's 27 or 28 to hit his peak. Or he could be the guy who is just good enough to keep the Oilers competitive until their next budget goalie comes along. Salo had a very nice showing in the playoffs.

PROJECTION

Salo is among the middle of the pack of NHL netminders. If he gets 60 starts he should manage 25 to 28 wins.

JASON SMITH

Yrs. of NHL service: 6
Born: Calgary, Alta.; Nov. 2, 1973
Position: right defense
Height: 6-3
Weight: 205
Uniform no.: 21
Shoots: right

Career statistics:

GP	G	A	TP	PIM
338	9	33	42	334

1995-96 statistics:

GP	G	A	TP	+/-	PIM	PP	SH	GW	GT	S	PCT
64	2	1	3	+5	86	0	0	0	0	52	3.8

1996-97 statistics:

GP	G	A	TP	+/-	PIM	PP	SH	GW	GT	S	PCT
78	1	7	8	-12	54	0	0	0	0	74	1.4

1997-98 statistics:

GP	G	A	TP	+/-	PIM	PP	SH	GW	GT	S	PCT
81	3	13	16	-5	100	0	0	0	0	97	3.1

1998-99 statistics:

GP	G	A	TP	+/-	PIM	PP	SH	GW	GT	S	PCT
72	3	12	15	-9	51	0	0	0	0	68	4.4

LAST SEASON

Acquired from Toronto for 1999 fourth-round draft pick and 2000 second-round draft pick, Mar. 23, 1999.

THE FINESSE GAME

Smith has a low-key personality and will never be the kind of defenseman who can control a game. Knee surgery has affected his skating somewhat, but he has better than average speed and fair mobility. He can be erratic in his defensive reads, though he is showing constant improvement and making better decisions. He was one of the Leafs' most consistent defensemen last season.

As he gains confidence, Smith will start doing a little more and gain more presence. He doesn't give himself enough credit. He is the kind of player who needs to have the coaches give him a pat on the back.

Smith won't make anyone forget Brian Leetch. He has a fairly heavy shot but it has little movement on it. He's not very creative offensively and he doesn't gamble. However, he can kill penalties, though he'll get into trouble against a team that cycles well down low. He needs to work on his puckhandling skills.

THE PHYSICAL GAME

Smith is a solid hitter with a latent mean streak; his takeouts are effective along the boards and in front of the net. He's not as good in open ice because his mobility is not exceptional. He has a fairly long fuse but is a capable fighter.

Smith worked hard to make a speedy recovery from reconstructive knee surgery three seasons ago. He is very fit and can handle 22 to 25 minutes a game.

THE INTANGIBLES

Smith has to build on his strong foundation. He's a little insecure but wants to learn and will work hard to improve. He is very coachable, quietly confident and has good leadership ability. He will work best paired with an offensive defenseman.

PROJECTION

Smith is evolving into a reliable crunch-time player, but his numbers will never be gaudy.

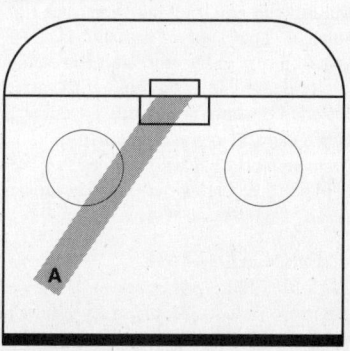

RYAN SMYTH

Yrs. of NHL service: 4
Born: Banff, Alta.; Feb. 21, 1976
Position: left wing
Height: 6-1
Weight: 195
Uniform no.: 94
Shoots: left

Career statistics:

GP	G	A	TP	PIM
269	74	62	136	210

1995-96 statistics:

GP	G	A	TP	+/-	PIM	PP	SH	GW	GT	S	PCT
48	2	9	11	-10	28	1	0	0	0	65	3.1

1996-97 statistics:

GP	G	A	TP	+/-	PIM	PP	SH	GW	GT	S	PCT
82	39	22	61	-7	76	20	0	4	0	265	14.7

1997-98 statistics:

GP	G	A	TP	+/-	PIM	PP	SH	GW	GT	S	PCT
65	20	13	33	-24	44	10	0	2	2	205	9.8

1998-99 statistics:

GP	G	A	TP	+/-	PIM	PP	SH	GW	GT	S	PCT
71	13	18	31	0	62	6	0	2	2	161	8.1

LAST SEASON

Missed seven games with fractured jaw. Missed one game with thigh contusion. Missed two games due to coach's decision.

THE FINESSE GAME

Smyth's knee injury in 1997-98 robbed him of the best part of his game: his willingness to play a reckless, headstrong style. When he broke the Oilers' power-play goals record (held by a fellow named Wayne Gretzky) in his sophomore year, Smyth was fearless. But the last two seasons he has looked nothing like that younger player.

Smyth is not a great, fluid skater, so he has to keep his feet moving. But he stopped doing that, stopped driving to the net and stopped scoring. Playing poorly in his own end didn't help his overall contribution to the team.

Smyth possesses little subtlety. Most of his goals come from the hash marks in, and probably half of them weren't the result of his shots, but tip-ins and body bounces. That's an art in itself, because Smyth has a knack for timing his moves to the net, along with a shooter's release. He has a long reach for getting to rebounds and is strong on his stick for deflections.

Smyth is at a disadvantage when he is forced to shoot or make a play because he doesn't have a quick release. When he carries the puck, he doesn't have much sense of what to do with it.

THE PHYSICAL GAME

Smyth isn't built like a power forward, but when he is playing with confidence he sure tries to play like one. He is a pesky net crasher and can be an irritating presence. He doesn't throw bombs, but he is a willing thrasher along the boards and gets good leg drive for solid hits. He's not a fighter, yet he won't back down.

THE INTANGIBLES

Smyth nearly redeemed his season with a strong playoffs, but three goals in three games is a very small sample by which to judge this enigma.

PROJECTION

Until he proves he has regained his confidence and his scoring touch, it is best to expect a modest 15 to 20 goals from Smyth.

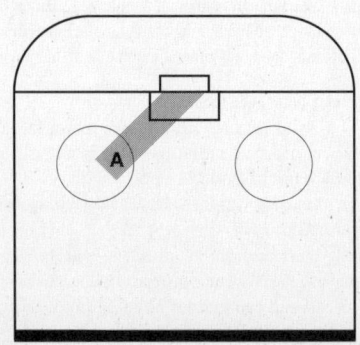

DOUG WEIGHT

Yrs. of NHL service: 8
Born: Warren, Mich.; Jan. 21, 1971
Position: centre
Height: 5-11
Weight: 191
Uniform no.: 39
Shoots: left

Career statistics:
GP	G	A	TP	PIM
547	134	342	485	460

1995-96 statistics:
GP	G	A	TP	+/-	PIM	PP	SH	GW	GT	S	PCT
82	25	70	104	-19	95	9	0	2	1	204	12.3

1996-97 statistics:
GP	G	A	TP	+/-	PIM	PP	SH	GW	GT	S	PCT
80	21	61	82	+1	80	4	0	2	0	235	8.9

1997-98 statistics:
GP	G	A	TP	+/-	PIM	PP	SH	GW	GT	S	PCT
79	26	44	70	+1	69	9	0	4	0	205	12.7

1998-99 statistics:
GP	G	A	TP	+/-	PIM	PP	SH	GW	GT	S	PCT
43	6	31	37	-8	12	1	0	0	1	79	7.6

LAST SEASON
Second on team in assists. Missed 34 games with knee surgery. Missed four games with contract dispute.

THE FINESSE GAME
Playmaking is Weight's strong suit. He has good vision and passes well to either side. His hands are soft and sure. When he utilizes his shot he has quick and accurate wrist and snap shots. He handles the puck well in traffic, is strong on the puck and creates a lot of scoring chances. Weight is an outstanding one-on-one player, but doesn't have to challenge all the time. He will trail the play down the right wing (his preferred side) and jump into the attack late.

Weight won't win many foot races, but he keeps his legs pumping and he often surprises people on the rush who think they had him contained, only to see him push his way past. He frequently draws penalties. He has decent quickness, good balance and a fair change of direction.

Weight has improved his defensive play slightly. He is an offensive Doug Risebrough. A late bloomer, he has succeeded on a weak team in the role of a number one centre, though a number two role would probably suit him better. Weight's point production is amazingly consistent. He seldom slumps.

THE PHYSICAL GAME
Weight is inconsistent in his physical play. He shows flashes of grittiness but doesn't bring it to the ice every night. Still, he is built like a fire hydrant, and on the nights he's on he hits with enthusiasm, finishing every check. He initiates and annoys.

He's also a bit of a trash talker, yapping and playing with a great deal of spirit. He has worked on his strength and conditioning and can handle a lot of ice time. He is very strong on his skates and hard to knock off the puck.

THE INTANGIBLES
Weight made a nice partner for the bigger, faster Bill Guerin. If both can stay healthy this season, their numbers will get healthier, too.

PROJECTION
Weight's production should move back up to the 80- to 85-point range.

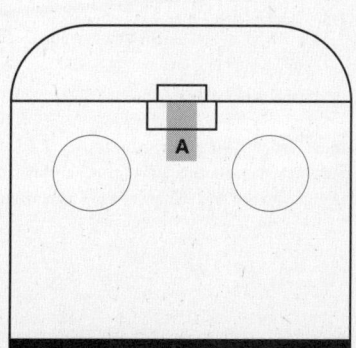

FLORIDA PANTHERS

Players' Statistics 1998-99

POS.	NO.	PLAYER	GP	G	A	PTS	+/-	PIM	PP	SH	GW	GT	S	PCT
C	14	RAY WHITNEY	81	26	38	64	-3	18	7		6	1	193	13.5
C	44	ROB NIEDERMAYER	82	18	33	51	-13	50	6	1	3	2	142	12.7
C	25	VIKTOR KOZLOV	65	16	35	51	13	24	5	1	1		209	7.7
R	27	SCOTT MELLANBY	67	18	27	45	5	85	4		3	3	136	13.2
R	19	RADEK DVORAK	82	19	24	43	7	29		4			182	10.4
R	21	*MARK PARRISH	73	24	13	37	-6	25	5		5	1	129	18.6
D	24	ROBERT SVEHLA	80	8	29	37	-13	83	4			1	157	5.1
L	11	BILL LINDSAY	75	12	15	27	-1	92		1	2		135	8.9
L	16	*OLEG KVASHA	68	12	13	25	5	45	4		2	1	138	8.7
D	4	BRET HEDICAN	67	5	18	23	5	51		2	1	1	90	5.6
L	29	JOHAN GARPENLOV	64	8	9	17	-9	42		1		1	71	11.3
R	10	PAVEL BURE	11	13	3	16	3	4	5	1		1	44	29.5
C	9	KIRK MULLER	82	4	11	15	-11	49			1		107	3.7
D	8	*JAROSLAV SPACEK	63	3	12	15	15	28	2	1			92	3.3
D	2	TERRY CARKNER	62	2	9	11	0	54					25	8.0
D	3	PAUL LAUS	75	1	9	10	-1	218					54	1.9
L	28	*PETER WORRELL	62	4	5	9	0	258			2		50	8.0
D	26	*DAN BOYLE	22	3	5	8	0	6	1		1		31	9.7
R	22	DINO CICCARELLI	14	6	1	7	-1	27	5		1		23	26.1
D	5	GORD MURPHY	51		7	7	4	16					56	
L	18	ALEX HICKS	55		7	7	-5	62					51	
G	31	SEAN BURKE	59		4	4	0	27						
D	7	MIKE WILSON	34	1	2	3	12	47			1		48	2.1
L	12	*MARCUS NILSON	8	1	1	2	2	5			1		7	14.3
D	6	*PETER RATCHUK	24	1	1	2	-1	10					34	2.9
C	23	CHRIS WELLS	20		2	2	-4	31					28	
C	17	*RYAN JOHNSON	1	1		1	0						1	100.0
R	26	DAVID NEMIROVSKY	2		1	1	1						2	
D	33	*FILIP KUBA	5		1	1	2						5	
D	15	*JEFF WARE	6		1	1	-6	6					1	
D	12	*CHRIS ALLEN	1				1							
D	15	*JOHN JAKOPIN	3				-1							
R	37	*HERBERT VASILJEVS	5				-1	2					6	
L	12	*DWAYNE HAY	9				-1						3	
G	1	KIRK MCLEAN	30				0	2						

GP = games played; G = goals; A = assists; PTS = points; +/- = goals-for minus goals-against while player is on ice; PIM = penalties in minutes; PP = power-play goals; SH = shorthanded goals; GW = game-winning goals; GT = game-tying goals; S = no. of shots; PCT = percentage of goals to shots; * = rookie

PAVEL BURE

Yrs. of NHL service: 8
Born: Moscow, Russia; Mar. 31, 1971
Position: right wing
Height: 5-10
Weight: 189
Uniform no.: 10
Shoots: left

Career statistics:

GP	G	A	TP	PIM
439	267	227	494	332

1995-96 statistics:

GP	G	A	TP	+/-	PIM	PP	SH	GW	GT	S	PCT
15	6	7	13	-2	8	1	1	0	0	78	7.7

1996-97 statistics:

GP	G	A	TP	+/-	PIM	PP	SH	GW	GT	S	PCT
63	23	32	55	-14	40	4	1	2	0	265	8.7

1997-98 statistics:

GP	G	A	TP	+/-	PIM	PP	SH	GW	GT	S	PCT
82	51	39	90	+5	48	13	6	4	1	329	15.5

1998-99 statistics:

GP	G	A	TP	+/-	PIM	PP	SH	GW	GT	S	PCT
11	13	3	16	+3	4	5	1	0	1	44	29.5

LAST SEASON

Acquired from Vancouver with Bret Hedican, Brad Ference and an optional draft pick for Ed Jovanovski, Dave Gagner, Mike Brown, Kevin Weekes and an optional draft pick, Jan. 17, 1999. Missed 29 games with right knee surgery. Missed 42 games due to contract dispute.

THE FINESSE GAME

Goalies never know when Bure's shot is going to come. He keeps his legs churning and the shot is on net before the goalie knows it. He does not telegraph his shot by breaking stride, and it's an awesome sight.

The Russian Rocket's quickness — and his control of the puck at supersonic speed — means anything is possible. He intimidates with his skating, driving back defenders who must play off him or risk being deked out of their skates at the blueline. He opens up tremendous ice for his teammates and will leave a drop pass or, more often, try to do it himself.

Bure's major weakness is his failure to use his teammates better. He will attempt to go through a team one-on-five rather than use his support. Of course, once in awhile he can actually do it — that's the scary part. He has great balance and agility, and he moves equally well with the puck or without it.

Bure doesn't do much defensively. He prefers to hang out at centre ice, and when he is going through a slump he doesn't do the other little things that can make a player useful until the scoring starts to click again. He is a shorthanded threat because of his breakaway speed and anticipation. His explosive skating comes from his thick, powerful thighs, which look like a speed skater's.

THE PHYSICAL GAME

Bure has a little nasty edge to him, and will make solid hits for the puck, though he doesn't apply himself as enthusiastically in a defensive role. He has to play a reckless game to drive to the net and score goals. He takes a lot of punishment getting there and that's what makes him vulnerable to injuries.

THE INTANGIBLES

Bure held out half a season to get traded from the Canucks, and appeared briefly but brilliantly for the Panthers before injuring his knee (one that had previously been surgically repaired). Bure's off-season rehab was going well, and with a heavy European influence on the Florida roster, he should be ready to turn on the afterburners in October.

PROJECTION

Fifty-goal scorers are rare these days, but Bure could be one of those gems.

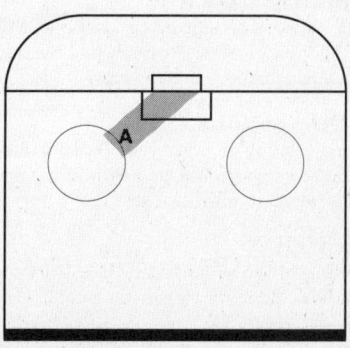

SEAN BURKE

Yrs. of NHL service: 10
Born: Windsor, Ont.; Jan. 29, 1967
Position: goaltender
Height: 6-4
Weight: 208
Uniform no.: 1
Catches: left

Career statistics:

GP	MIN	GA	SO	GAA	A	PIM
529	29828	1598	19	3.21	21	242

1995-96 statistics:

GP	MIN	GAA	W	L	T	SO	GA	S	SAPCT	PIM
66	3669	3.11	28	28	6	4	190	2034	.907	16

1996-97 statistics:

GP	MIN	GAA	W	L	T	SO	GA	S	SAPCT	PIM
51	2985	2.69	22	22	6	4	134	1560	.914	14

1997-98 statistics:

GP	MIN	GAA	W	L	T	SO	GA	S	SAPCT	PIM
52	2885	2.95	16	23	9	2	142	1362	.896	20

1998-99 statistics:

GP	MIN	GAA	W	L	T	SO	GA	S	SAPCT	PIM
59	3402	2.66	21	24	14	3	151	1624	.907	27

LAST SEASON

Fifth season with 20 or more wins. Career best goals-against average.

THE PHYSICAL GAME

Burke is a big goalie, and when he is on his game he challenges the shooter well and comes out to the top of his crease. Playing a lot of international hockey has given him an edge in East-West play.

He handles the puck well, and is confident and active on the dump-ins. He gives his defensemen a chance to handle the puck more easily and break out of the zone with less effort.

Burke fills up the net and is very quick for a netminder of his size. He has a quick glove hand, but he will often drop it and give the shooter the top corner over his left shoulder. He also holds his blocker hand too low on his stick, which makes him lean over too far and throws him off balance.

THE MENTAL GAME

Burke's status as a number one goalie will be challenged by the arrival of Trevor Kidd, but Burke has faced similar situations in his career.

THE INTANGIBLES

At 32 and entering his walk year, Burke will be looking to find enough gainful employment to land a new contract. He was healthy last year.

PROJECTION

Depending on how much ice time Burke nets in Florida, he could reach 20 wins again.

RADEK DVORAK

Yrs. of NHL service: 4
Born: Tabor, Czech Republic; Mar. 9, 1977
Position: left wing
Height: 6-2
Weight: 187
Uniform no.: 19
Shoots: left

Career statistics:

GP	G	A	TP	PIM
299	62	83	145	112

1995-96 statistics:

GP	G	A	TP	+/-	PIM	PP	SH	GW	GT	S	PCT
77	13	14	27	+5	20	0	0	4	0	126	10.3

1996-97 statistics:

GP	G	A	TP	+/-	PIM	PP	SH	GW	GT	S	PCT
76	18	21	39	-2	30	2	0	1	0	139	12.9

1997-98 statistics:

GP	G	A	TP	+/-	PIM	PP	SH	GW	GT	S	PCT
64	12	24	36	-1	33	2	3	0	1	112	10.7

1998-99 statistics:

GP	G	A	TP	+/-	PIM	PP	SH	GW	GT	S	PCT
82	19	24	43	+7	29	0	4	0	0	182	10.4

PROJECTION

Although teams will always want more out of Dvorak, his likely future is as a 20-goal scorer.

LAST SEASON

Led team and tied for fourth in NHL in shorthanded goals. Third on team in goals, plus-minus and shots. One of three Panthers to appear in all 82 games.

THE FINESSE GAME

Dvorak has exceptional speed. He might be one of the five fastest skaters in the Eastern Conference. He bursts down the left wing and will mix up the defense by sometimes driving wide and sometimes cutting through the middle. He takes the puck with him at a high tempo and creates off the rush.

Dvorak is a natural, gifted scorer who has to develop more confidence in his shot. Although he showed signs of improvement last season, with his speed he should be getting over 200 shots a season. He is a heads-up passer but needs to be more of a finisher.

Dvorak has become a more complete player by adding defensive awareness to his game. He is a fine penalty killer.

THE PHYSICAL GAME

Dvorak has very strong legs, which power his explosive skating, and he's not a bit intimidated by North American play.

THE INTANGIBLES

Dvorak was publicly singled out by coach Terry Murray, and under pressure to produce more Dvorak scored nine of his 19 goals in the last 20 games. He is developing into a third-line winger who will be an offensive threat, because of his ability to force mistakes and turn them into scoring chances.

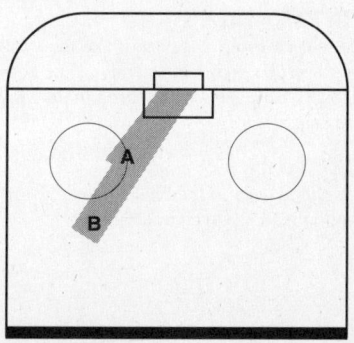

BRAD FERENCE

Yrs. of NHL service: 0
Born: Calgary, Alta.; Apr. 2, 1979
Position: right defense
Height: 6-3
Weight: 196
Uniform no.: n.a.
Shoots: right

Career junior statistics:

GP	G	A	TP	PIM
177	24	89	113	796

LAST SEASON
Will be entering first NHL season. Acquired from Vancouver with Pavel Bure, Bret Hedican and an optional draft pick for Ed Jovanovski, Dave Gagner, Mike Brown, Kevin Weekes and an optional draft pick, Jan. 19, 1999. Appeared in 31 games with Spokane (WHL), scoring 3-22 — 25 with 125 PIM. Appeared in 20 games with Tri-City (WHL), scoring 6-15 — 21 with 116 PIM.

THE FINESSE GAME
Ference is an average skater who will have to work on his foot speed to keep up with the NHL pace.

A two-way player in junior, he will likely develop into a more stay-at-home defenseman in the NHL. He moves the puck well out of his zone. He can play the point on the power play and has a pretty hard slap shot, but he doesn't have the lateral mobility to make his shot a more dangerous weapon.

Ference works the boards and the front of the net with enthusiasm. He will likely develop into a penalty killer who likes to block shots.

THE PHYSICAL GAME
Ference needs to add some weight to what is a tall but somewhat lean frame. He loves to compete and play a physical game. He just needs the strength to do it.

THE INTANGIBLES
Ference will be given a shot to make the Panthers in training camp as a sixth defenseman. If he doesn't, he will probably be given a half-season in the minors before a call-up.

PROJECTION
Until he gets a taste of the NHL, Ference's offensive contribution is likely to be minimal.

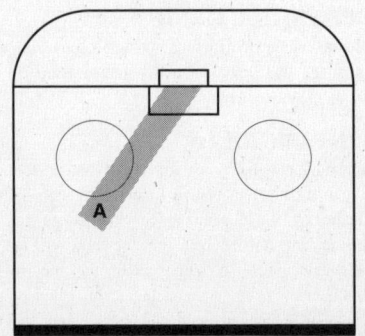

BRET HEDICAN

Yrs. of NHL service: 7
Born: St. Paul, Minn.; Aug. 10, 1970
Position: left defense
Height: 6-2
Weight: 195
Uniform no.: 4
Shoots: left

Career statistics:

GP	G	A	TP	PIM
442	21	111	132	371

1995-96 statistics:

GP	G	A	TP	+/-	PIM	PP	SH	GW	GT	S	PCT
77	6	23	29	+8	83	1	0	0	0	113	5.3

1996-97 statistics:

GP	G	A	TP	+/-	PIM	PP	SH	GW	GT	S	PCT
67	4	15	19	-3	51	2	0	1	0	93	4.3

1997-98 statistics:

GP	G	A	TP	+/-	PIM	PP	SH	GW	GT	S	PCT
71	3	24	27	+3	79	1	0	0	1	84	3.6

1998-99 statistics:

GP	G	A	TP	+/-	PIM	PP	SH	GW	GT	S	PCT
67	5	18	23	+5	51	0	2	1	1	90	5.6

LAST SEASON

Acquired from Vancouver with Pavel Bure, Brad Ference and an optional draft pick for Ed Jovanovski, Dave Gagner, Mike Brown, Kevin Weekes and an optional draft pick, Jan. 17, 1999. Tied for second on team in shorthanded goals. Missed eight games with eye injury.

THE FINESSE GAME

Hedican is among the best-skating defensemen in the NHL. He has a nice, deep knee bend and his fluid stride provides good acceleration; each stride eats up lots of ice. His steady balance allows him to go down to one knee and use his stick to challenge passes from the corners. He uses quickness, range and reach to make a confident stand at the defensive blueline.

Hedican happily uses his speed with the puck to drive down the wing and create trouble in the offensive zone. He also varies the attack. He seems to prefer the left-wing boards, but will also take the right-wing route to try to make plays off the backhand.

Hedican is a good enough stickhandler to try one-on-one moves. He is eager to jump into the play. He will never be a great point getter or playmaker because he doesn't think the game well enough, but he tries to help his team on the attack. He is a better player in the playoffs, when he doesn't think as much and lets his natural instincts rule.

Hedican knows that if an attacker beats him, he will be able to keep up with him and steer him to bad ice. He is the perfect guy to pick up the puck behind the net and get it to the redline and start the half-court game. He doesn't always just put his head down and go. He will move up the middle and look for a pass to a breaking wing.

THE PHYSICAL GAME

Hedican has decent size but not a great deal of strength or toughness. He won't bulldoze people in front of the net, but prefers to tie people up and go for the puck. He is more of a stick-checker than a body checker, though he will sometimes knock a player off the puck at the blueline, control it and make a smart first pass. His preference is to use body positioning to nullify an opponent rather than initiate hard body contact.

THE INTANGIBLES

Hedican has steady skills to complement a more offensive player like Robert Svehla, and he is a capable top two or three defenseman.

PROJECTION

Hedican is developing into a solid two-way defenseman and can be expected to improve sharply over the next few seasons as he gains confidence and experience. He should score around 40 points.

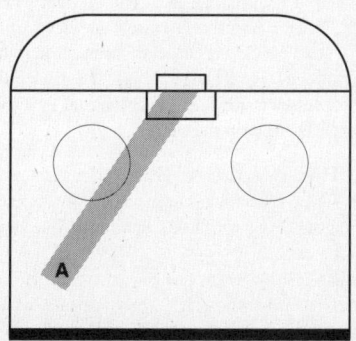

VIKTOR KOZLOV

Yrs. of NHL service: 4
Born: Togliatti, Russia; Feb. 14, 1975
Position: right wing
Height: 6-5
Weight: 225
Uniform no.: 25
Shoots: right

Career statistics:

GP	G	A	TP	PIM
285	57	86	143	88

1995-96 statistics:

GP	G	A	TP	+/-	PIM	PP	SH	GW	GT	S	PCT
62	6	13	19	-15	6	1	0	0	0	107	5.6

1996-97 statistics:

GP	G	A	TP	+/-	PIM	PP	SH	GW	GT	S	PCT
78	16	25	41	-16	40	4	0	4	0	184	8.7

1997-98 statistics:

GP	G	A	TP	+/-	PIM	PP	SH	GW	GT	S	PCT
64	17	13	30	-3	16	5	2	0	0	165	10.3

1998-99 statistics:

GP	G	A	TP	+/-	PIM	PP	SH	GW	GT	S	PCT
65	16	35	51	+13	24	5	1	1	0	209	7.7

LAST SEASON

Led team in shots. Second on team in assists and plus-minus. Tied for second on team in points. Tied for third on team in power-play goals. Missed eight games with shoulder injury. Missed seven games with fractured finger.

THE FINESSE GAME

Kozlov is a beautiful skater for his size. He has the moves of a 150-pounder, with quickness and agility. He has learned to come off the boards much quicker. As a huge right-handed shooter attacking the left side, he has a move that — dare we say it — makes him look like Mario Lemieux. He can undress a defender with his stickhandling and create a scoring chance down low. He has a keen sense of timing and pace.

Kozlov can play either centre or wing. He loves to shoot, and he shoots hard. He has an accurate wrist shot with a quick release.

He won't float and he has defensive principles. He won't hang at the redline, but he is an attentive backchecker. With deceptively quick acceleration for a player of his size he excells at the transition game.

Kozlov needs to learn to protect the puck better by keeping it closer to his feet. He often makes it too easy for a defender to strip the puck.

THE PHYSICAL GAME

Kozlov's physique makes him sturdy in contact, and when he goes down on a hook or a hold, nine times out of 10 it's a dive.

He has a long reach but doesn't care to play the body defensively, though offensively he will work with the puck to get in front of the net and into scoring position. He handles the puck well in traffic. He has added some muscle but it would help to add more, since he is likely going to be Florida's number one centre.

THE INTANGIBLES

Kozlov will probably get the centre's job alongside Pavel Bure.

PROJECTION

If he plays with Bure, Kozlov should post career numbers in the 70- to 80-point range.

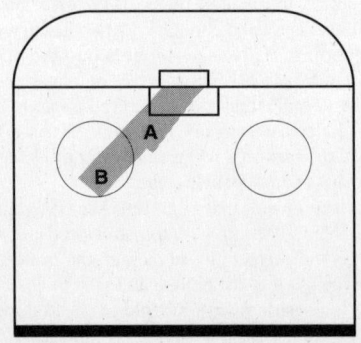

OLEG KVASHA

Yrs. of NHL service: 1
Born: Moscow, Russia; July 26, 1978
Position: left wing
Height: 6-5
Weight: 205
Uniform no.: 16
Shoots: left

Career statistics:

GP	G	A	TP	PIM
68	12	13	25	45

1998-99 statistics:

GP	G	A	TP	+/-	PIM	PP	SH	GW	GT	S	PCT
68	12	13	25	+5	45	4	0	2	1	138	8.7

LAST SEASON
First NHL season. Second among NHL rookies in shots. Tied for fourth among NHL rookies in power-play goals. Tied for 10th among NHL rookies in goals. Missed 14 games with shoulder separation and knee injury.

THE FINESSE GAME
Kvasha has tremendous speed and great hands. He can make a lot of things happen with the puck in full stride, which will make him the mirror image of right wing Pavel Bure should the two end up on the same line. They could become the East coast version of Paul Kariya and Teemu Selanne.

Kvasha can also play centre, and he brings a centre's vision to the left wing. He has terrific hockey sense and vision. He anticipates well and sees holes a split second before they open.

Kvasha can use his shot more. He has an excellent wrist shot that is his best weapon.

THE PHYSICAL GAME
Kvasha is strong, has good size and will drive to the net. He is not above crashing the goalie.

THE INTANGIBLES
Kvasha played in the minors a year ago instead of returning to junior, so his development has been accelerated.

PROJECTION
Another of the young Panthers with great potential, Kvasha should score in the 20- to 25-goal range. He has even bigger things ahead of him.

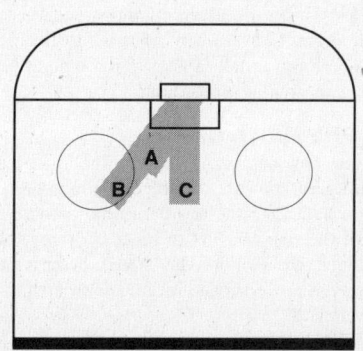

PAUL LAUS

Yrs. of NHL service: 6
Born: Beamsville, Ont.; Sept. 26, 1970
Position: right defense
Height: 6-1
Weight: 216
Uniform no.: 3
Shoots: right

Career statistics:

GP	G	A	TP	PIM
383	6	45	51	1307

1995-96 statistics:

GP	G	A	TP	+/-	PIM	PP	SH	GW	GT	S	PCT
78	3	6	9	-2	236	0	0	0	0	45	6.7

1996-97 statistics:

GP	G	A	TP	+/-	PIM	PP	SH	GW	GT	S	PCT
77	0	12	12	+13	313	0	0	0	0	63	0.0

1997-98 statistics:

GP	G	A	TP	+/-	PIM	PP	SH	GW	GT	S	PCT
77	0	11	11	-5	293	0	0	0	0	64	.0

1998-99 statistics:

GP	G	A	TP	+/-	PIM	PP	SH	GW	GT	S	PCT
75	1	9	10	-1	218	0	0	0	0	54	1.9

LAST SEASON

Second on team in penalty minutes. Missed seven games with torn hamstring.

THE FINESSE GAME

People don't like to play against a club that has Laus on its side. He is a legitimate tough guy, but one who has worked at the other aspects of his game to become a more useful player.

Laus has borderline NHL skating speed. He is powerful and well-balanced for battles along the boards and in the corners. He seems to know his limitations and doesn't try to overextend himself. Since he doesn't cover a lot of ice, he needs to be paired with a mobile partner. Of course, he also gets a lot of room since only the brave venture into his territory, and that buys him some time.

Laus uses his size and strength effectively at all times. He has to control both his temper and his playing style. His success in the NHL will come from playing his position and not running around headhunting. He doesn't have much offensive instinct, but he gets some room to take shots from the point because no one wants to come near him.

THE PHYSICAL GAME

Laus hits. Anyone. At any opportunity. Since his skating isn't great, he can't catch people in open ice, but he's murder along the boards, in the corners and in front of the net. He hits to hurt. He's big, but not scary-sized like a lot of today's NHL defensemen. He is, however, powerful and mean, and he stands up for his teammates.

THE INTANGIBLES

Laus has worked hard to become more than a mere goon, and the work has paid off. He is a perfectly serviceable fifth or sixth defenseman. He makes his teammates braver and, if his skills keep improving as they have been over the past three seasons, that will keep him on the ice. Peter Worrell's development has taken some of the heat off of Laus to fight every night. He may find it tough to get ice time depending on how some of Florida's young defensemen fare in training camp.

PROJECTION

If you're in a goon pool, Laus is a pretty sure bet for 200 PIM. However, he also scored his first goal in three seasons, so he could be on a tear.

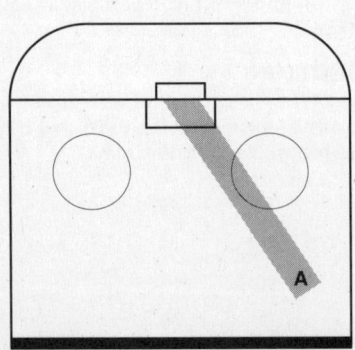

BILL LINDSAY

Yrs. of NHL service: 7
Born: Big Fork, Mont.; May 17, 1971
Position: left wing
Height: 5-11
Weight: 190
Uniform no.: 11
Shoots: left

Career statistics:

GP	G	A	TP	PIM
510	69	104	173	522

1995-96 statistics:

GP	G	A	TP	+/-	PIM	PP	SH	GW	GT	S	PCT
73	12	22	34	+13	57	0	3	2	0	118	10.2

1996-97 statistics:

GP	G	A	TP	+/-	PIM	PP	SH	GW	GT	S	PCT
81	11	23	34	+1	120	0	1	3	0	168	6.5

1997-98 statistics:

GP	G	A	TP	+/-	PIM	PP	SH	GW	GT	S	PCT
82	12	16	28	-2	80	0	2	5	0	150	8.0

1998-99 statistics:

GP	G	A	TP	+/-	PIM	PP	SH	GW	GT	S	PCT
75	12	15	27	-1	92	0	1	2	0	135	8.9

PROJECTION

Lindsay would be on the bubble if it weren't for his intensity. Scoring 20 goals would be a real stretch for him.

LAST SEASON

Missed seven games with knee injuries.

THE FINESSE GAME

Lindsay has a big shot but an average release. His first instinct is to try to beat the goalie between the pads. A long reach enables him to score many of his goals from his work in front of the net. He has decent hands, but it's his second and third effort that make the difference.

Lindsay is a support player who, teamed with more offensive linemates, acts as a safety valve. He is not particularly creative but he will follow the play to the net.

Although his skating speed and agility are average, Lindsay is balanced and strong on his skates. He has good size, which he uses in a checking role. He sometimes gets a bit lazy and doesn't keep his feet moving. When he doesn't take that extra step, he takes a bad hooking or tripping penalty. There is no subtlety to his forechecking. He skates in a straight line with limited agility.

THE PHYSICAL GAME

Lindsay uses his body effectively but doesn't thrash people. He is sturdy and sometimes gets it into his head to stir things up, to try and give his team a bit of a spark. He plays much bigger than his size. He takes a hit to make a play, but more often initiates the contact.

THE INTANGIBLES

Lindsay is a borderline third-winger because of his skill level, but he is a glue guy whose value to the team is immeasurable.

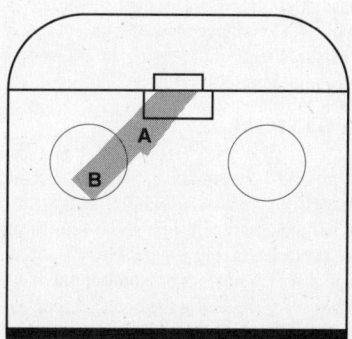

SCOTT MELLANBY

Yrs. of NHL service: 13
Born: Montreal, Que,; June 11, 1966
Position: right wing
Height: 6-1
Weight: 199
Uniform no.: 27
Shoots: right

Career statistics:

GP	G	A	TP	PIM
939	256	318	574	1819

1995-96 statistics:

GP	G	A	TP	+/-	PIM	PP	SH	GW	GT	S	PCT
79	32	38	70	+4	160	19	0	3	1	225	14.2

1996-97 statistics:

GP	G	A	TP	+/-	PIM	PP	SH	GW	GT	S	PCT
82	27	29	56	+7	170	9	1	4	0	221	12.2

1997-98 statistics:

GP	G	A	TP	+/-	PIM	PP	SH	GW	GT	S	PCT
79	15	24	39	-14	127	6	0	1	0	188	8.0

1998-99 statistics:

GP	G	A	TP	+/-	PIM	PP	SH	GW	GT	S	PCT
67	18	27	45	+5	85	4	0	3	3	136	13.2

LAST SEASON

Third on team in penalty minutes and shooting percentage. Tied for third on team in game-winning goals. Missed 15 games with groin injury.

THE FINESSE GAME

Not having a great deal of speed or agility, Mellanby generates most of his effectiveness in tight spaces, where he can use his size. On the power play, where he sees second-unit duty, Florida leans to the right when working the power play and looks to set Mellanby up below the hash marks. He works for screens and tips. He doesn't have many moves but he can capitalize on a loose puck. Goals don't come naturally to him, however, he's determined and he pays the price in front of the net.

Mellanby has developed a quicker release and more confidence in his shot, but still needs to shoot more, since he is quite accurate with his shot.

He has become more of a defensive player in recent seasons, though he no longer sees many penalty-killing shifts. He is not much of a shorthanded threat. He lacks the speed and scoring instincts to convert turnovers into dangerous chances.

THE PHYSICAL GAME

Mellanby forechecks aggressively, using his body well to hit and force mistakes in the attacking zone. He engages in one-on-one battles in tight areas and tries to win his share. He is also willing to mix it up and take penalties of aggression. He seldom misses an opportunity to rub his glove in an opponent's face.

He's very strong along the boards and uses his feet when battling for the puck.

THE INTANGIBLES

Mellanby is the Panthers' captain, but the team management considers him a little too laid-back for the job. He is going to lose ice time on the right side to Pavel Bure and Mark Parrish.

PROJECTION

Mellanby's production will continue to decline and he will find it tough getting ice time unless Florida moves him.

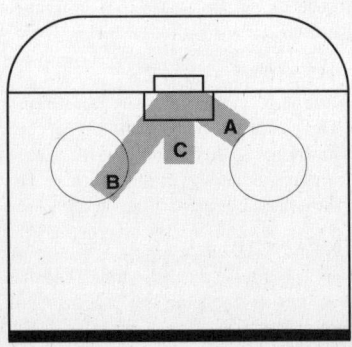

ROB NIEDERMAYER

Yrs. of NHL service: 6
Born: Cassiar, B.C.; Dec. 28, 1974
Position: centre
Height: 6-2
Weight: 201
Uniform no.: 44
Shoots: left

Career statistics:

GP	G	A	TP	PIM
525	79	122	201	339

1995-96 statistics:

GP	G	A	TP	+/-	PIM	PP	SH	GW	GT	S	PCT
82	26	35	61	+1	107	11	0	6	0	155	16.8

1996-97 statistics:

GP	G	A	TP	+/-	PIM	PP	SH	GW	GT	S	PCT
60	14	24	38	+4	54	3	0	2	0	136	10.3

1997-98 statistics:

GP	G	A	TP	+/-	PIM	PP	SH	GW	GT	S	PCT
33	8	7	15	-9	41	5	0	2	0	64	12.5

1998-99 statistics:

GP	G	A	TP	+/-	PIM	PP	SH	GW	GT	S	PCT
82	18	33	51	-13	50	6	1	3	2	142	12.7

LAST SEASON

Second on team in power-play goals. Tied for second on team in points. Third on team in assists. Tied for third on team in game-winning goals. One of three Panthers to appear in all 82 games.

THE FINESSE GAME

Niedermayer has to get a lot smarter about his position on the ice. He tends to go along the boards and leave himself in a vulnerable position. He needs to use the open ice more, though he appears much more comfortable along the wall.

He is an excellent skater. Big and strong, Niedermayer has the speed to stay with some of the league's best power centres. He drives to the net and is learning to play that way on a nightly basis.

Niedermayer is a strong passer and an unselfish player, probably too unselfish. He controls the puck well at tempo and can beat a defender one-on-one. He has started to finish better and play with much more authority.

Niedermayer is a mainstay on Florida's power play. One of his flaws is a slight hesitation in his shot release, but he is developing more confidence in his shot.

THE PHYSICAL GAME

Although not overly physical, Niedermayer has good size and is still growing. He is an intelligent player and doesn't hurt his team by taking bad penalties. The Panthers would actually prefer to see more attitude. He has lost a lot of confidence over the past few seasons, mostly due to injuries.

THE INTANGIBLES

Niedermayer rebounded strongly from a concussion a season ago. He had a strong start: 12 of his goals were scored in the first half; six in the second. The drop in production may have been due to his hitting a wall (his previous two seasons were interrupted by serious injuries).

PROJECTION

Niedermayer isn't a number one centre, which is how he has been used most of his career, but he is developing into a two-way number two centre who could score 20 to 25 goals.

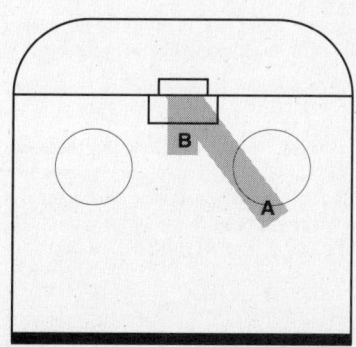

IVAN NOVOSELTSEV

Yrs. of NHL service: 0
Born: Golitsino, USSR; Jan. 23, 1979
Position: left wing
Height: 6-1
Weight: 183
Uniform no.: n.a.
Shoots: left

Career junior statistics:

GP	G	A	TP	PIM
121	83	61	144	86

LAST SEASON
Will be entering first NHL season. Appeared in 68 games with Sarnia (OHL), leading team in goals (57) and scoring 39 assists for 96 points.

THE FINESSE GAME
This kid is already being called the "Pocket Rocket," not for Henri Richard, but for being a smaller version of legendary Maurice "Rocket" Richard. There are some who think Novoseltsev might someday claim the goal-scoring trophy that is named for Richard.

Novoseltsev is a left-handed shot who plays the right wing. This opens up his forehand for one-timers.

He has blinding speed and the ability to pick up the puck behind his own net and go end-to-end. He intimidates with his speed, driving defensemen back on their heels before he cuts inside or outside. His wrist shot is his favourite weapon.

The usual red flag attached to Novoseltsev is his lack of defensive awareness. He can also be a bit selfish with the puck and doesn't always use his teammates well.

THE PHYSICAL GAME
Novoseltsev doesn't get overly involved in physical play. For one thing, you can't hit what you can't catch.

THE INTANGIBLES
If Novoseltsev makes the main squad this year, opposing teams will be clocking Panthers forwards with radar guns.

PROJECTION
Florida is trying to stay cautious, but there is a lot of buzz about this kid. He could use a season in the minors, but don't be surprised if he shows up as a Pavel Bure linemate midway through the season. He could score 20 goals in his first full NHL season.

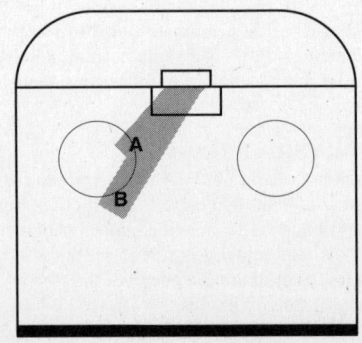

MARK PARRISH

Yrs. of NHL service: 1
Born: Edina, MN; Feb. 2, 1977
Position: left wing
Height: 6-0
Weight: 185
Uniform no.: 21
Shoots: right

Career statistics:

GP	G	A	TP	PIM
73	24	13	37	25

1998-99 statistics:

GP	G	A	TP	+/-	PIM	PP	SH	GW	GT	S	PCT
73	24	13	37	-6	25	5	0	5	1	129	18.6

LAST SEASON
First NHL season. Led NHL rookies and second on team in goals. Led NHL rookies and team in shooting percentage. Tied for lead among NHL rookies and second on team in game-winning goals. Second among NHL rookies and tied for third on team in power-play goals. Fourth among NHL rookies in shots. Fifth among NHL rookies in points. Appeared in two games with New Haven (AHL), scoring 1-0 — 1.

THE FINESSE GAME
Parrish made the jump from junior to the NHL, and has played only three career games in the minors. While he went through a few lulls during the season, he was pretty consistent for a rookie and a first-year pro.

Parrish has excellent outside speed and reads. He was able to beat a mobile defender like Brian Leetch for a goal last season. Parrish is a goal scorer by skill and by nature. He goes to the net hard because he knows he has to score to make his impact in the lineup.

Parrish has terrific hands and a great shot. He may lose some power-play time to Pavel Bure, unless Bure is used on the point. This would be great news for Parrish, who does some of his best work around the front of the net.

THE PHYSICAL GAME
Parrish doesn't have great size but he doesn't avoid the high-traffic areas. His speed is his best weapon. Florida coach Terry Murray used him wisely last year. His midseason benchings were as much to keep Parrish on his toes defensively as to prevent him from wearing down in the second half.

THE INTANGIBLES
Parrish is the real goods. He will be the number two right wing behind Bure and will be able to escape much of the checking pressure he faced last season.

PROJECTION
A sophomore slump is always a possibility, but Parrish should repeat with at least a 25-goal season.

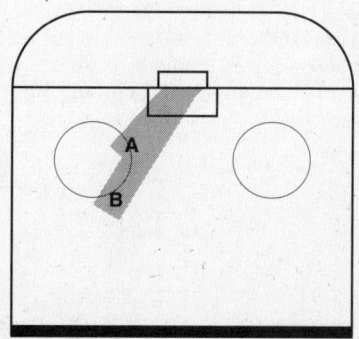

JAROSLAV SPACEK

Yrs. of NHL service: 1
Born: Rokycany, Czech.; Feb. 11, 1974
Position: left defense
Height: 5-11
Weight: 198
Uniform no.: 8
Shoots: left

Career statistics:

GP	G	A	TP	PIM
63	3	12	15	28

1998-99 statistics:

GP	G	A	TP	+/-	PIM	PP	SH	GW	GT	S	PCT
63	3	12	15	+15	28	2	1	0	0	92	3.3

LAST SEASON

First NHL season. Led team in plus-minus. Appeared in 14 games with New Haven (AHL), scoring 4-8 — 12 in 14 games. Missed three games with flu.

THE FINESSE GAME

An older rookie, Spacek started the season in the minors, but by the end of the season was among the Panthers' top four defensemen. He probably could have used a full season in the minors to acclimate himself to pro hockey.

Spacek is an agile skater. He is good one-on-one and even defending against a two-on-one. He moves the puck very well and has some offensive upside.

Spacek uses his finesse skills in a defensive manner, positioning himself intelligently and anticipating plays. He kills penalties, and last season played the point on the first power-play unit.

THE PHYSICAL GAME

Spacek is shy of the North American style of play. Strength-wise he loses a lot of battles along the boards and in front of the net.

THE INTANGIBLES

Spacek needs to get more battle-tough, but he was among the few good things that happened to the Panthers last season.

PROJECTION

Florida's power play should be more effective this season with a healthy Pavel Bure, and Spacek will benefit. He could score in the 35-point range.

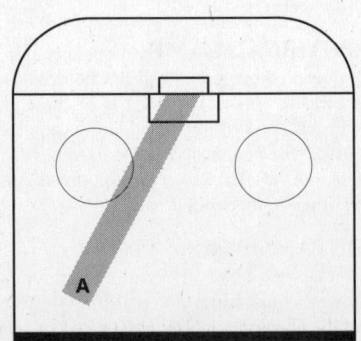

ROBERT SVEHLA

Yrs. of NHL service: 4
Born: Martin, Slovakia; Jan. 2, 1969
Position: right defense
Height: 6-1
Weight: 190
Uniform no.: 24
Shoots: right

Career statistics:

GP	G	A	TP	PIM
327	39	145	184	376

1995-96 statistics:

GP	G	A	TP	+/-	PIM	PP	SH	GW	GT	S	PCT
81	8	49	57	-3	94	7	0	0	0	146	5.5

1996-97 statistics:

GP	G	A	TP	+/-	PIM	PP	SH	GW	GT	S	PCT
82	13	32	45	+2	86	5	0	3	0	159	8.2

1997-98 statistics:

GP	G	A	TP	+/-	PIM	PP	SH	GW	GT	S	PCT
79	9	34	43	-3	113	3	0	0	0	144	6.3

1998-99 statistics:

GP	G	A	TP	+/-	PIM	PP	SH	GW	GT	S	PCT
80	8	29	37	-13	83	4	0	0	1	157	5.1

LAST SEASON
Led team defensemen in points for third consecutive season.

THE FINESSE GAME
Svehla is among the best in the league at the lost art of the sweep-check. If he does lose control of the puck, and an attacker has a step or two on him on a breakaway, Svehla has the poise to dive and use his stick to knock the puck away without touching the man's skates.

He is a terrific skater. No one, not even Jaromir Jagr, can beat Svehla wide, because he skates well backwards and laterally. He plays a quick transition. He is among the best NHL defensemen one-on-one in open ice. He pinches aggressively and intelligently and makes high-risk plays . . . unfortunately for the Panthers, he gambled too frequently in his own zone last season and was guilty of some horrendous giveaways.

Svehla works on the first power play, moving to the left point. He uses a long wrist shot from the point to make sure the puck will get through on net. When he kills penalties, he makes safe plays off the boards.

THE PHYSICAL GAME
Svehla is strong or naturally aggressive, but he competes. He gets into the thick of things by battling along the wall and in the corners for the puck. He is not a huge checker, but he pins his man and doesn't allow him back into the play. He is in peak condition and needs little recovery time between shifts, so he can handle a lot of ice time.

THE INTANGIBLES
Svehla took a huge step backwards last season, to the point where it must have been tough for coach Terry Murray to keep him in the lineup. He needs to redefine his intensity and pay more attention to the defensive part of his game.

PROJECTION
This is an important season for Svehla to recapture his form. He is capable of a 50-point season if he does.

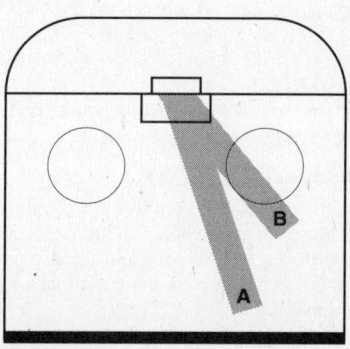

RAY WHITNEY

Yrs. of NHL service: 7
Born: Fort Saskatchewan, Alberta; May 8, 1972
Position: left wing/centre
Height: 5-10
Weight: 175
Uniform no.: 14
Shoots: right

Career statistics:

GP	G	A	TP	PIM
358	107	143	250	98

1995-96 statistics:

GP	G	A	TP	+/-	PIM	PP	SH	GW	GT	S	PCT
60	17	24	41	-23	16	4	2	2	0	106	16.0

1996-97 statistics:

GP	G	A	TP	+/-	PIM	PP	SH	GW	GT	S	PCT
12	0	2	2	-6	4	0	0	0	0	24	0.0

1997-98 statistics:

GP	G	A	TP	+/-	PIM	PP	SH	GW	GT	S	PCT
77	33	32	65	+9	28	12	0	2	0	175	18.9

1998-99 statistics:

GP	G	A	TP	+/-	PIM	PP	SH	GW	GT	S	PCT
81	26	38	64	-3	18	7	0	6	1	193	13.5

LAST SEASON

Led team in goals, points and power-play goals for second consecutive season. Led team in assists and game-winning goals. Second on team in shots and shooting percentage.

THE FINESSE GAME

Whitney is not a fast skater, but he is shifty in tight quarters and that makes him very tough to check. A defender will think he is about to nail him, but Whitney just wriggles out of the line of sight. He likes to cut to the middle of the ice and use his forehand. He is dangerous every shift.

Savvy and determined, Whitney compensates for his lack of speed with a keen sense of anticipation. He jumps into the right spot simply by knowing before his checker that it's the right place to be. That makes him appear quicker than he really is.

Whitney is poised in traffic and well-balanced on his feet. He has exceptionally good hands for passing or shooting. He can lift a backhand shot when he is practically on top of the goalie. He has a deceptive shot because he does not telegraph whether he is going to pass or shoot.

Whitney needs to play with a grinder on his wing because he can't win the battles on the boards.

THE PHYSICAL GAME

Whitney is small, but he plays a wily game for a smaller player. A centre of his ability needs to be protected with a tough winger and defenseman, but Whitney brings so much to the game that a team can make room for him.

THE INTANGIBLES

Whitney was rescued off the NHL's scrap heap by the Panthers and has been one of the team's most reliable forwards over the past two seasons.

PROJECTION

Whitney has the ability to be a consistent 25-goal scorer in the right circumstances, which is the proper expectation for a player of his size and skill.

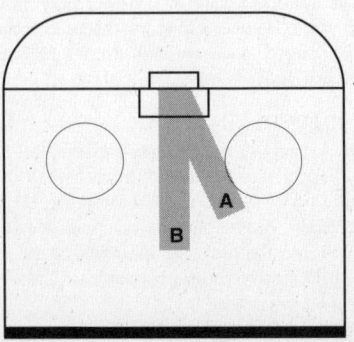

LOS ANGELES KINGS

Players' Statistics 1998-99

POS	NO.	PLAYER	GP	G	A	PTS	+/-	PIM	PP	SH	GW	GT	S	PCT
L	20	LUC ROBITAILLE	82	39	35	74	-1	54	11		7		292	13.4
R	10	DONALD AUDETTE	49	18	18	36	7	51	6		2		152	11.8
D	4	ROB BLAKE	62	12	23	35	-7	128	5	1	2		216	5.6
C	15	JOZEF STUMPEL	64	13	21	34	-18	10	1		1		131	9.9
R	27	GLEN MURRAY	61	16	15	31	-14	36	3	3	3		173	9.2
C	26	RAY FERRARO	65	13	18	31	0	59	4		4		84	15.5
L	9	VLADIMIR TSYPLAKOV	69	11	12	23	-7	32		2	2		111	9.9
C	12	*OLLI JOKINEN	66	9	12	21	-10	44	3	1	1		87	10.3
L	23	CRAIG JOHNSON	69	7	12	19	-12	32	2		2		94	7.4
R	19	RUSS COURTNALL	57	6	13	19	-9	19		1	1		77	7.8
R	55	*PAVEL ROSA	29	4	12	16	0	6					61	6.6
D	3	GARRY GALLEY	60	4	12	16	-9	30	3				77	5.2
D	8	DOUG BODGER	65	3	11	14	1	34					67	4.5
D	6	SEAN O'DONNELL	80	1	13	14	1	186					64	1.6
C	22	IAN LAPERRIERE	72	3	10	13	-5	138			1		62	4.8
C	11	BRANDON CONVERY	15	2	7	9	4	12			1		14	14.3
D	44	DAVE BABYCH	41	2	6	8	-2	22	2				49	4.1
D	43	PHILIPPE BOUCHER	45	2	6	8	-12	32	1				87	2.3
D	14	MATTIAS NORSTROM	78	2	5	7	-10	36		1			61	3.3
R	45	SANDY MOGER	42	3	2	5	-9	26			2		28	10.7
C	24	NATHAN LAFAYETTE	33	2	2	4	0	35		1	1		42	4.8
L	21	*JOSH GREEN	27	1	3	4	-5	8	1				35	2.9
D	48	*MARK VISHEAU	28	1	3	4	-7	107					10	10.0
C	29	SEAN PRONGER	29		4	4	-1	8					14	
L	17	MATT JOHNSON	49	2	1	3	-5	131					14	14.3
C	11	*JASON BLAKE	1	1		1	1						5	20.0
D	54	*JAN NEMECEK	6	1		1	-1	4			1		8	12.5
L	7	STEVE MCKENNA	20	1		1	-3	36					12	8.3
D	33	JAROSLAV MODRY	5		1	1	1						11	
G	32	*MANNY LEGACE	17		1	1	0							
G	1	*JAMIE STORR	28		1	1	0	6						
G	31	*RYAN BACH	3				0							
L	42	DAN BYLSMA	8				-1	2					3	
C	28	JASON PODOLLAN	10				-3	5					9	
G	35	STEPHANE FISET	42				0	2						

GP = games played; G = goals; A = assists; PTS = points; +/- = goals-for minus goals-against while player is on ice; PIM = penalties in minutes; PP = power-play goals; SH = shorthanded goals; GW = game-winning goals; GT = game-tying goals; S = no. of shots; PCT = percentage of goals to shots; * = rookie

DONALD AUDETTE

Yrs. of NHL service: 8
Born: Laval, Que.; Sept. 23, 1969
Position: right wing
Height: 5-8
Weight: 175
Uniform no.: 10
Shoots: right

Career statistics:

GP	G	A	TP	PIM
458	182	143	325	374

1995-96 statistics:

GP	G	A	TP	+/-	PIM	PP	SH	GW	GT	S	PCT
23	12	13	25	0	18	8	0	1	0	92	13.0

1996-97 statistics:

GP	G	A	TP	+/-	PIM	PP	SH	GW	GT	S	PCT
73	28	22	50	-6	48	8	0	5	1	182	15.4

1997-98 statistics:

GP	G	A	TP	+/-	PIM	PP	SH	GW	GT	S	PCT
75	24	20	44	+10	59	10	0	5	1	198	12.1

1998-99 statistics:

GP	G	A	TP	+/-	PIM	PP	SH	GW	GT	S	PCT
49	18	18	36	+7	51	6	0	2	0	152	11.8

LAST SEASON

Acquired from Buffalo for a 1999 second-round draft pick, Dec. 8, 1998. Led team in plus-minus. Second on team in goals, points and power-play goals. Missed 31 games due to contract dispute. Missed one game due to back spasms. Missed one game due to flu.

THE FINESSE GAME

Audette is not very big, yet he makes his living around the net by smartly jumping in and out of the holes.

A bustling forward who barrels to the net at every opportunity, Audette is eager and feisty down low and has good hand skills. He also has keen scoring instincts, along with the quickness to make good things happen. His feet move so fast (with a choppy stride) that he doesn't look graceful, but he can really get moving and he has good balance.

A scorer first, Audette has a great top-shelf shot, which he gets away quickly and accurately. He can also make a play, but he will do this at the start of a rush. Once he is inside the offensive zone and low, he wants the puck. Considering his scoring touch, though, his selfishness can be forgiven.

Audette is at his best on the power play. He is savvy enough not to just stand around and take punishment. He times his jumps into the space between the left post and the bottom of the left circle.

THE PHYSICAL GAME

Opponents hate Audette, which he takes as a great compliment. He runs goalies, yaps and takes dives — then goes out and scores on the power play after the opposition has taken a bad penalty.

Audette will forecheck and scrap for the puck, though he isn't as diligent coming back. He's not very big, but around the net he plays like he's at least a six-footer. He keeps jabbing and working away until he is bowled over by an angry defender.

THE INTANGIBLES

Audette played with fire once he played himself back into shape after missing nearly half the season. His pro-rated totals would have challenged his career best, so he is going to be able to adapt to play in the West. Audette lacks size but not heart. The Kings could use a few more like him.

PROJECTION

Audette's maximum production is around 60 points, which we expect him to attain.

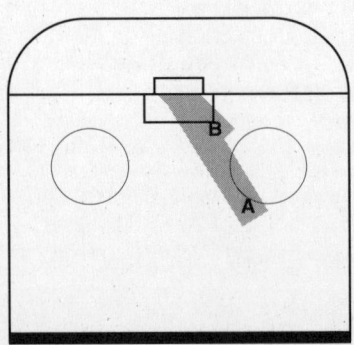

AKI-PETTERI BERG

Yrs. of NHL service: 3
Born: Turku, Finland; July 28, 1977
Position: left defense
Height: 6-3
Weight: 198
Uniform no.: 5
Shoots: left

Career statistics:

GP	G	A	TP	PIM
164	2	21	23	114

1995-96 statistics:

GP	G	A	TP	+/-	PIM	PP	SH	GW	GT	S	PCT
51	0	7	7	-13	29	0	0	0	0	56	0.0

1996-97 statistics:

GP	G	A	TP	+/-	PIM	PP	SH	GW	GT	S	PCT
41	2	6	8	-9	24	2	0	0	0	65	3.1

1997-98 statistics:

GP	G	A	TP	+/-	PIM	PP	SH	GW	GT	S	PCT
72	0	8	8	+3	61	0	0	0	0	58	0.0

1998-99 statistics:
Did not play in NHL

LAST SEASON
Scored 8-7 — 15 in 48 games with TPS Turku (Finland), and led team with 137 PIM.

THE FINESSE GAME
Berg is a pleasing combination of offensive and defensive skills. His skating is topnotch. He has a powerful stride with great mobility and balance. And he gets terrific drive from perfect leg extension and deep knee bends.

He sees the ice well and has excellent passing skills. He can also rush with the puck, but he prefers to make a pass and then join the play. He has more offensive upside and could develop into a solid two-way defenseman.

Berg returned to his native Finland last year after failing to reach agreement on a new contract with the Kings.

THE PHYSICAL GAME
Berg loves to hit. He's big and strong, and has the mobility to lay down some serious open-ice checks. His punishing checks have had some scouts comparing him to Scott Stevens. Berg plays hard and finishes his checks.

THE INTANGIBLES
After being rushed into the NHL at age 18, Berg wisely took a step back. Playing in Finland for the league champions did a lot to restore his confidence. Now all the Kings have to do is convince him to come back.

PROJECTION
If Berg returns, he can rack up some penalty minutes and 15 to 20 points.

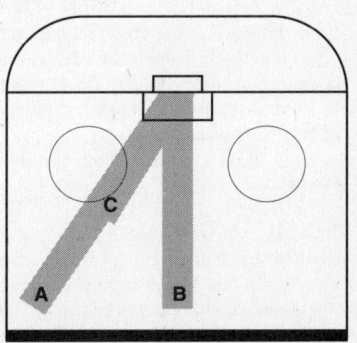

ROB BLAKE

Yrs. of NHL service: 9
Born: Simcoe, Ont.; Dec. 10, 1969
Position: right defense
Height: 6-3
Weight: 215
Uniform no.: 4
Shoots: right

Career statistics:

GP	G	A	TP	PIM
531	103	220	323	870

1995-96 statistics:

GP	G	A	TP	+/-	PIM	PP	SH	GW	GT	S	PCT
6	1	2	3	0	8	0	0	0	0	13	7.7

1996-97 statistics:

GP	G	A	TP	+/-	PIM	PP	SH	GW	GT	S	PCT
62	8	23	31	-28	82	4	0	1	0	169	4.7

1997-98 statistics:

GP	G	A	TP	+/-	PIM	PP	SH	GW	GT	S	PCT
81	23	27	50	-3	94	11	0	4	0	261	8.8

1998-99 statistics:

GP	G	A	TP	+/-	PIM	PP	SH	GW	GT	S	PCT
62	12	23	35	-7	128	5	1	2	0	216	5.6

LAST SEASON

Second on team in assists and shots. Led team defensemen and third on team in points. Third on team in penalty minutes and power-play goals. Missed 15 games due to broken right foot. Missed three games due to suspension for slashing incident. Missed two games due to suspension for cross-checking incident.

THE FINESSE GAME

Lower-body strength is the key to Blake's open-ice hitting, and, of course, his skating. He is a powerful skater, quick and agile, with good balance. He steps up and challenges at the blueline, and has great anticipation. He's also quite bold, forcing turnovers at the blueline with his body positioning and quick stickwork. He is brave but not brash in his decision making.

Blake has finesse skills that make an impact in any zone of the ice. He works the point on the power play, but lacks the vision to be as creative as he could be. He has a good, low shot and rifles it off the pass. He has quality hand skills and is not afraid to skip in deep to try to make something happen low. He is confident about attempting to force the play deep in the offensive zone, and has sharp enough passing skills to use a backhand pass across the goalmouth.

Blake rarely goes a game without getting at least one shot on goal.

THE PHYSICAL GAME

Blake is among the hardest hitters in the league. He has a nasty streak and will bring up his gloves and stick them into the face of an opponent when he thinks the referee isn't watching. He can dominate with his physical play — when he does, he opens up a lot of ice for himself and his teammates. Blake and partner Mattias Norstrom saw the major checking duties against other teams' top lines last season.

THE INTANGIBLES

After an injury-free, Norris Trophy-winning season, Blake suffered a setback last season with a broken foot. He didn't have much help, either, except for Norstrom.

PROJECTION

L.A. expects to break in some new faces on defense this season, which will place an even greater burden on Blake. If healthy, he should score 15 goals and 40 points.

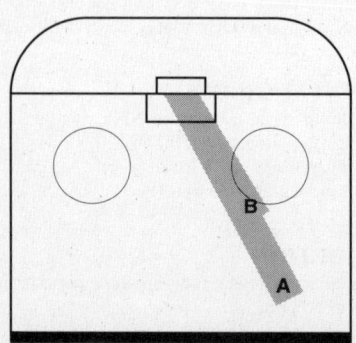

GARRY GALLEY

Yrs. of NHL service: 15
Born: Montreal, Que., Apr. 16, 1963
Position: left defense
Height: 6-0
Weight: 204
Uniform no.: 3
Shoots: left

Career statistics:

GP	G	A	TP	PIM
1023	110	440	550	1107

1995-96 statistics:

GP	G	A	TP	+/-	PIM	PP	SH	GW	GT	S	PCT
78	10	44	54	-2	81	7	1	2	0	175	5.7

1996-97 statistics:

GP	G	A	TP	+/-	PIM	PP	SH	GW	GT	S	PCT
71	4	34	38	+10	102	1	1	1	0	84	4.8

1997-98 statistics:

GP	G	A	TP	+/-	PIM	PP	SH	GW	GT	S	PCT
74	9	28	37	-5	63	7	0	0	0	128	7.0

1998-99 statistics:

GP	G	A	TP	+/-	PIM	PP	SH	GW	GT	S	PCT
60	4	12	16	-9	30	3	0	0	0	77	5.2

LAST SEASON

Appeared in 1,000th NHL game. Missed six games with abdominal strain. Missed 16 games due to coach's decision.

THE FINESSE GAME

Galley is a puck mover. He follows the play and jumps into the attack. He has decent speed to keep up with the play, though he won't be rushing the puck himself. He is mobile and has a good shot that he can get away on the fly. He will pinch aggressively, but he's also quick enough to get back if there's a counterattack.

Galley works well on the power play. His lateral movement allows him to slide away from the point to the middle of the blueline, and he keeps his shots low. He is a smart player and his experience shows. He helps any younger player he is teamed with because of his poise and communication.

Galley uses his finesse ability defensively by playing well positionally, and by using his stick for pokechecks. He has become a fairly reliable two-way defenseman.

THE PHYSICAL GAME

Galley has added a physical element to his game over the past few seasons, but he is not and will never be a big hitter. He will take his man but not always take him out, and more physical forwards take advantage of him. He gets in the way, though, and does not back down. But there are times when he is simply overpowered. He also gets a little chippy now and then, just to keep people guessing.

THE INTANGIBLES

Galley is not likely to be a King this season.

PROJECTION

The days of Galley's best numbers are over, but he can score in the 35- to 40-point range in the right spot.

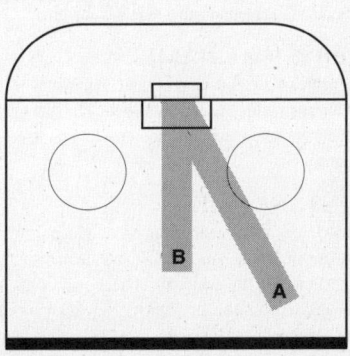

CRAIG JOHNSON

Yrs. of NHL service: 4
Born: St. Paul, Minnesota; Mar. 8, 1972
Position: left wing/centre
Height: 6-2
Weight: 198
Uniform no.: 23
Shoots: left

Career statistics:

GP	G	A	TP	PIM
249	44	50	94	142

1995-96 statistics:

GP	G	A	TP	+/-	PIM	PP	SH	GW	GT	S	PCT
60	13	11	24	-8	4	0	0	0	0	97	13.4

1996-97 statistics:

GP	G	A	TP	+/-	PIM	PP	SH	GW	GT	S	PCT
31	4	3	7	-7	26	1	0	0	0	30	13.3

1997-98 statistics:

GP	G	A	TP	+/-	PIM	PP	SH	GW	GT	S	PCT
74	17	21	38	+9	42	6	0	2	0	125	13.6

1998-99 statistics:

GP	G	A	TP	+/-	PIM	PP	SH	GW	GT	S	PCT
69	7	12	19	-12	32	2	0	2	0	94	7.4

LAST SEASON

Missed four games due to rib contusion. Missed nine games due to coach's decision.

THE FINESSE GAME

Johnson is a quick skater who uses his speed to gain a jump in the neutral zone. He will take a pass in full stride and take the puck to the net. He can also use his speed to create off the forecheck. He doesn't have great hands, so he needs to get rid of the puck quickly to a more talented teammate or get the puck late for a shot.

Although Johnson has played some centre, he is better suited as a left-winger. The Kings frequently use him on the off-wing. He is not a natural scorer and has to work hard for everything he gets. He isn't quite skilled enough to be a top six forward on a better team.

Johnson is fairly alert defensively and brings a level of enthusiasm to the game that is appreciated by coaches. He is a poor man's Paul Ranheim.

THE PHYSICAL GAME

Johnson doesn't have much taste for body work. He prefers to intimidate with his speed. He is a good size, but plays smaller. He needs to gain some strength and assertiveness.

THE INTANGIBLES

Johnson doesn't have a great deal of upside and it's tough sometimes to find a role for him, but he adds speed and energy to a lineup. The benchings indicate how dissatisfied the coaches were with his nightly efforts.

PROJECTION

Johnson's speed will always win him a second chance, but he has to produce in the 40-point range to keep his job as a regular.

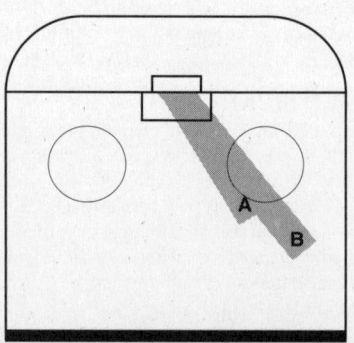

IAN LAPERRIERE

Yrs. of NHL service: 5
Born: Montreal, Que.; Jan. 19, 1974
Position: centre
Height: 6-1
Weight: 195
Uniform no.: 22
Shoots: right

Career statistics:

GP	G	A	TP	PIM
320	36	65	101	611

1995-96 statistics:

GP	G	A	TP	+/-	PIM	PP	SH	GW	GT	S	PCT
71	6	11	17	-11	155	1	0	1	1	70	8.6

1996-97 statistics:

GP	G	A	TP	+/-	PIM	PP	SH	GW	GT	S	PCT
62	8	15	23	-25	102	0	1	2	0	84	9.5

1997-98 statistics:

GP	G	A	TP	+/-	PIM	PP	SH	GW	GT	S	PCT
77	6	15	21	0	131	0	1	1	0	74	8.1

1998-99 statistics:

GP	G	A	TP	+/-	PIM	PP	SH	GW	GT	S	PCT
72	3	10	13	-5	138	0	0	1	0	62	4.8

LAST SEASON

Second on team in penalty minutes with career high. Missed nine games with sprained left knee. Missed one game with left knee inflammation.

THE FINESSE GAME

Despite some scary head injuries in the past, Laperriere is one of the best players in the league at working hard and finishing his checks.

The knock on Laperriere earlier in his career was his skating ability, but he has improved tremendously in that department. Although he'll never be a speed demon, he doesn't look out of place at the NHL level. He always tries to take the extra stride when he is backchecking so he can make a clean check, instead of taking the easy way out and committing a lazy hooking foul. He wins his share of races for the loose puck.

Laperriere grew up watching Guy Carbonneau in Montreal, and he studied well. Laperriere knows how to win a draw between his feet. He uses his stick and his body to make sure the opposing centre doesn't get the puck. He gets his bottom hand way down on the stick and tries to win draws on his backhand. He gets very low to the ice on draws.

Laperriere is ever willing to use the backhand, either for shots or to get the puck deep. He is reliable defensively and shows signs of becoming a two-way centre. He doesn't think the game very well, however, and his offensive reads are brutal.

THE PHYSICAL GAME

Laperriere is an obnoxious player in the Bob Bassen mold. He really battles for the puck. Although smallish, he has absolutely no fear of playing in the "circle" that extends from the lower inside of the face-off circles to behind the net. He will pay any price. He's a momentum changer. He thrives on being the first man in on the forecheck.

Laperriere shows a ton of heart. If the Kings are again well out of the playoff race, he would make an excellent deadline-time acquisition for a Cup hopeful. If they continue to improve and contend, he will be a key chemistry guy.

THE INTANGIBLES

Laperriere adds true grit to the lineup despite his small size, which is his major weakness. His nightly effort puts a lot of bigger guys to shame. He lost any bad habits the hard way by playing for a hard-nosed coach (Mike Keenan) early in his career. He is one of L.A.'s most consistent forwards.

PROJECTION

Laperriere is best suited as a third- or fourth-line centre. His skills are limited, but what he does he does well. His top range appears to be 30 points.

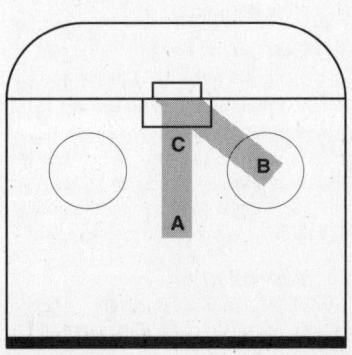

GLEN MURRAY

Yrs. of NHL service: 7
Born: Halifax, N.S.; Nov. 1, 1972
Position: right wing
Height: 6-2
Weight: 220
Uniform no.: 27
Shoots: right

Career statistics:

GP	G	A	TP	PIM
436	104	95	199	281

1995-96 statistics:

GP	G	A	TP	+/-	PIM	PP	SH	GW	GT	S	PCT
69	14	15	29	+4	57	0	0	2	0	100	14.0

1996-97 statistics:

GP	G	A	TP	+/-	PIM	PP	SH	GW	GT	S	PCT
77	16	14	30	-21	32	3	0	1	0	153	10.5

1997-98 statistics:

GP	G	A	TP	+/-	PIM	PP	SH	GW	GT	S	PCT
81	29	31	60	+6	54	7	3	7	0	193	15.0

1998-99 statistics:

GP	G	A	TP	+/-	PIM	PP	SH	GW	GT	S	PCT
61	16	15	31	-14	36	3	3	3	0	173	9.2

LAST SEASON

Led team in shorthanded goals. Third on team in goals, game-winning goals and shots. Missed 19 games with torn knee ligaments. Missed two games with groin injury.

THE FINESSE GAME

Murray is a lumbering skater who needs a good old dump-and-chase game, on a line with a playmaker who can get him the puck and set him up in the slot. He found his man in Jozef Stumpel, but if Stumpel gets teamed with Ziggy Palffy this season, what's to become of Murray? Murray is at his best on the right side, jamming in his forehand shots.

Murray has good size and a good short game. He has a quick release and, like a lot of great goal scorers, he just plain shoots. He doesn't even have to look at the net because he feels where the shot is going, and he protects the puck well with his body. Murray is more consistently using his speed and strength to get in better scoring position.

THE PHYSICAL GAME

On nights when he's playing well, Murray is leaning on people and making his presence felt. He'll bang, but on some nights he doesn't want to pay the price and prefers to rely on his shot. When he sleepwalks, he's useless. When he's ready to rock 'n' roll, he's effective. If he's going to be a topnotch power forward he needs to bring his top game every night.

THE INTANGIBLES

Murray was L.A.'s number one right-winger, but he is going to lose that position (and the ice time) to Palffy.

Murray needed the off-season to recover fully from his knee injury. He wasn't the same player coming back off the injury, and he scored only one goal in his last 24 games.

PROJECTION

If he gets his shifts and doesn't lose any confidence with the arrival of Palffy, Murray is capable of scoring 25 goals.

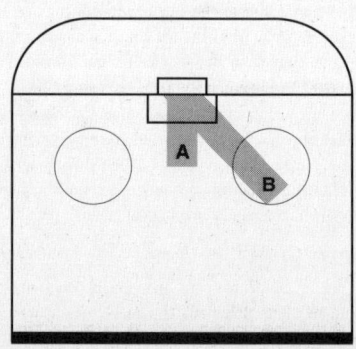

MATTIAS NORSTROM

Yrs. of NHL service: 4
Born: Mora, Sweden; Jan. 2, 1972
Position: left defense
Height: 6-1
Weight: 205
Uniform no.: 14
Shoots: left

Career statistics:

GP	G	A	TP	PIM
285	6	44	50	258

1995-96 statistics:

GP	G	A	TP	+/-	PIM	PP	SH	GW	GT	S	PCT
36	2	2	4	-3	40	0	0	0	0	34	5.9

1996-97 statistics:

GP	G	A	TP	+/-	PIM	PP	SH	GW	GT	S	PCT
80	1	21	22	-4	84	0	0	0	0	106	0.9

1997-98 statistics:

GP	G	A	TP	+/-	PIM	PP	SH	GW	GT	S	PCT
73	1	12	13	+14	90	0	0	0	0	61	1.6

1998-99 statistics:

GP	G	A	TP	+/-	PIM	PP	SH	GW	GT	S	PCT
78	2	5	7	-10	36	0	1	0	0	61	3.3

LAST SEASON
Missed four games due to rib contusion.

THE FINESSE GAME
Norstrom has attained a fairly high level of play on a team that needs him desperately and uses him extensively. He's a good skater, one who is still working on his pivots and turns. He does have straight-ahead speed, to a degree, thanks to a long stride. Along the boards he delivers strong hits, but in open ice he has more misses.

Norstrom's foot skills outdistance his hand skills. He can make a decent pass but mostly he'll keep things simple with the puck — smacking it around the boards if he gets into trouble, rather than trying to make a play.

For so large a player, Norstrom uses a surprisingly short stick that cuts down on his reach defensively and limits some of his offensive options. However, he feels his responsibility is to break down the play, rather than create it. He will pinch down the boards occasionally, but only to drive the puck deeper, not to take the puck and make a play. And he won't jump into the play on offense until he has more confidence with his puck skills.

THE PHYSICAL GAME
Norstrom is hard-nosed; when he hits, you feel it. And he is willing to do what it takes to help his team win. He is solidly built and likes to throw big, loud hits. If he doesn't hit, he's not going to be around long because his talent is not going to carry him, and his hockey sense (especially his defensive reads) needs a lot of improvement. He sacrifices his body by blocking shots.

He knows what he's good at. Norstrom has tremendously powerful legs and is strong on his skates. He has confidence in his power game and has developed a great enthusiasm for physical play.

THE INTANGIBLES
Norstrom is a hard-working athlete who loves to practise, a player acquired more for his character than for his abilities, which are average. He is a defensive-style defenseman who will give his coach what's asked for, but won't try to do things that will put the puck, or the team, in trouble. He was Rob Blake's steady partner last season against other teams' top lines.

PROJECTION
Norstrom will continue to get a big chunk of ice time, but his offensive skills limit him to 15 to 20 points at best.

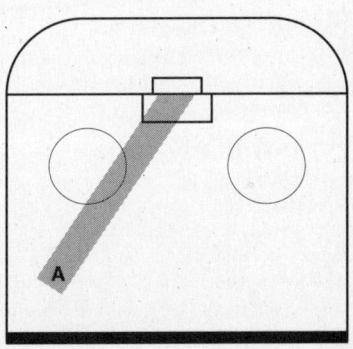

SEAN O'DONNELL

Yrs. of NHL service: 4
Born: Ottawa, Ont.; Oct. 13, 1971
Position: left defense
Height: 6-2
Weight: 225
Uniform no.: 6
Shoots: left

Career statistics:

GP	G	A	TP	PIM
301	10	47	57	685

1995-96 statistics:

GP	G	A	TP	+/-	PIM	PP	SH	GW	GT	S	PCT
71	2	5	7	+3	127	0	0	0	0	65	3.1

1996-97 statistics:

GP	G	A	TP	+/-	PIM	PP	SH	GW	GT	S	PCT
55	5	12	17	-13	144	2	0	0	0	68	7.4

1997-98 statistics:

GP	G	A	TP	+/-	PIM	PP	SH	GW	GT	S	PCT
80	2	15	17	+7	179	0	0	1	0	71	2.8

1998-99 statistics:

GP	G	A	TP	+/-	PIM	PP	SH	GW	GT	S	PCT
80	1	13	14	+1	186	0	0	0	0	64	1.6

PROJECTION

O'Donnell will collect close to 200 penalty minutes if he stays healthy. His point total won't be nearly as impressive. Take him if you've got a goon pool.

LAST SEASON

Led team in penalty minutes. Led team defensemen and tied for second on team in plus-minus. Career high in games played. Missed one game due to suspension. Missed one game due to coach's decision.

THE FINESSE GAME

O'Donnell has worked hard to rise above being a one-dimensional player, but his skating holds him back. He is not very good laterally and that results in his being beaten wide. He tries to line up someone and misses, because he doesn't have the quickness to get there.

O'Donnell has some offensive upside because he is alert and tries so hard, but he is really at his best when he can play a stay-at-home style. He makes a suitable partner for a high-risk defenseman. His hand skills are average at best.

O'Donnell has to improve his defensive reads. He has become a decent shot-blocker.

THE PHYSICAL GAME

O'Donnell is fearless. He is a legitimate tough guy who fights anybody. He hits hard. He uses his stick. He's a nasty customer.

THE INTANGIBLES

O'Donnell has paid his dues in the minors, and there are a lot of rough edges to his game. He has a good distance to go yet, but he could learn to supplement his game and develop along the lines of Paul Laus, who was once considered a pure goon but is now a serviceable, tough defenseman. O'Donnell is a project.

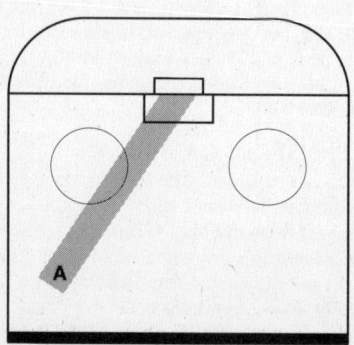

ZIGMUND PALFFY

Yrs. of NHL service: 5
Born: Skalica, Slovakia; May 5, 1972
Position: left wing
Height: 5-10
Weight: 183
Uniform no.: 16
Shoots: left

Career statistics:
GP	G	A	TP	PIM
331	168	163	331	173

1995-96 statistics:
GP	G	A	TP	+/-	PIM	PP	SH	GW	GT	S	PCT
81	43	44	87	-17	56	17	1	6	0	257	16.7

1996-97 statistics:
GP	G	A	TP	+/-	PIM	PP	SH	GW	GT	S	PCT
80	48	42	90	+21	43	6	4	6	1	292	16.4

1997-98 statistics:
GP	G	A	TP	+/-	PIM	PP	SH	GW	GT	S	PCT
82	45	42	87	-2	34	17	2	5	1	277	16.2

1998-99 statistics:
GP	G	A	TP	+/-	PIM	PP	SH	GW	GT	S	PCT
50	22	28	50	-6	34	5	2	1	0	168	13.1

LAST SEASON

Acquired from N.Y. Islanders with Bryan Smolinski and Marcel Cousineau for Olli Jokinen, Josh Green, Mathieu Biron and a 1999 first-round draft pick, June 20, 1999. Led Islanders in goals and points. Tied for Islanders' lead in shorthanded goals. Second on Islanders in assists and shooting percentage. Third on Islanders in shots. Missed 32 games in contract dispute.

THE FINESSE GAME

Palffy has elite, intellectual instincts with the puck and great vision. He knows he can play in the league now and has the confidence to try the moves that only world-class players can execute.

Palffy has deceptive quickness. He is an elusive skater with a quick first step and is very shifty; he can handle the puck while dancing across the ice. He won't burn around people, but when there's an opening he can get to it in a hurry. Sometimes a defender will let up on him for a fraction of a second, and when he does, Palffy has gained a full stride.

Palffy has excellent hands for passing or shooting. Early in his career he would look to make a play before shooting, but he has since become a bona fide sniper. He is an aggressive penalty killer, always looking for the shorthanded break.

THE PHYSICAL GAME

Palffy has a little bit of an edge to him. He's got the magic ingredient that sets the superior smaller players apart from the little guys who can't make the grade. He's not exactly a physical specimen, either. One player said of Palffy, "He's as unathletic a superstar as you'll ever find."

Palffy is decidedly on the small side. He can't afford to get into any battles in tight areas where he'll get crunched. He can jump in and out of holes and pick his spots, and he often plays with great spirit. He never puts himself in a position to get bowled over but he has become less of a perimeter player and is more willing to take the direct route to the net, which has paid off in more quality scoring chances. He's not really a soft player, but he won't go into the corner if he's going to get massacred. Palffy's not against hacking an opponent. He wants the puck.

THE INTANGIBLES

Palffy is a point-a-game player in the regular season. In the playoffs . . . well, he's never been there, and that is the sole knock against him.

PROJECTION

Over a full season, Palffy can score 50 goals, and he should love playing with disher Jozef Stumpel in L.A. The West should suit him.

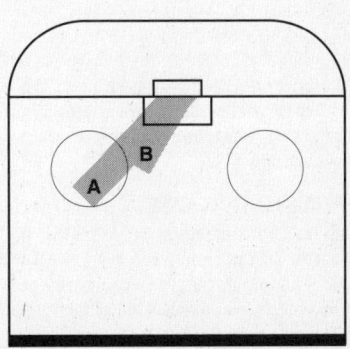

LUC ROBITAILLE

Yrs. of NHL service: 13
Born: Montreal, Que.; Feb. 17, 1966
Position: left wing
Height: 6-1
Weight: 195
Uniform no.: 20
Shoots: left

Career statistics:

GP	G	A	TP	PIM
971	517	559	1076	847

1995-96 statistics:
GP	G	A	TP	+/-	PIM	PP	SH	GW	GT	S	PCT
77	23	46	69	+13	80	11	0	4	2	223	10.3

1996-97 statistics:
GP	G	A	TP	+/-	PIM	PP	SH	GW	GT	S	PCT
69	24	24	48	+16	48	5	0	4	0	200	12.0

1997-98 statistics:
GP	G	A	TP	+/-	PIM	PP	SH	GW	GT	S	PCT
57	16	24	40	+5	66	5	0	7	0	130	12.3

1998-99 statistics:
GP	G	A	TP	+/-	PIM	PP	SH	GW	GT	S	PCT
82	39	35	74	-1	54	11	0	7	0	292	13.4

LAST SEASON

Led team in goals, assists, points, power-play goals, game-winning goals and shots. Most goals since 1993-94. Tied for 10th in NHL in goals. Second on team in shooting percentage. Scored 500th NHL goal. Only King to appear in all 82 games.

THE FINESSE GAME

Robitaille gets the most done when he determines one course of action and follows through on it, because he simply does not have the quickness of hand, foot or mind to do multiple tasks. Slow on his feet to begin with, his problems are magnified by questionable balance. It doesn't seem to take much to knock him off his feet.

Carrying the puck slows Robitaille even more because it requires him to read a defense and identify a passing option. He is far better served by getting the puck, moving the puck and moving his feet to the holes. He benefited from playing with playmaker Jozef Stumpel, an excellent passer, most of last season.

Robitaille needs to be an instinctive player. When he works to an opening in the front of the net and shoots off the pass he can be devastatingly effective, because the shot is accurate and the release too quick for defensemen to block.

THE PHYSICAL GAME

Although he's considered a finesse player, the physical aspect is an under-noticed part of Robitaille's game. He's among the first to avenge any cheap shot against one of his teammates. He isn't a fighter but his sense of team is significant.

Robitaille goes to the grungy parts of the ice; he mucks for the puck. He also pays more of a physical price. He absorbs a fair amount of hits because he isn't quick enough to get out of the way. And, because he does not think or act quickly, he gets whacked while making up his mind. Still, Robitaille has such upper-body strength that a defender will think he has him wrapped up, only to see the puck in the net after Robitaille has somehow gotten his hands free.

THE INTANGIBLES

Robitaille's positive attitude and his luck in staying healthy made him one of the few bright spots on the Kings last season. Whether he is used on a line with newcomer Ziggy Palffy this season, or whether new coach Andy Murray will decide to share the wealth and take Robitaille away from Stumpel to play on another line, could impact on Robitaille's production.

PROJECTION

Robitaille nearly doubled the output we predicted for him last season with an impressive comeback year. He could flirt with 40 again.

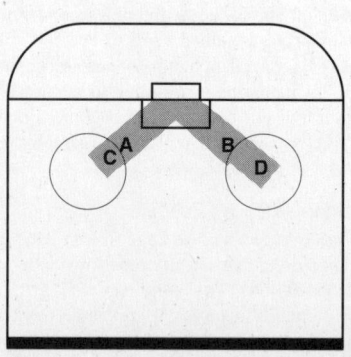

PAVEL ROSA

Yrs. of NHL service: 1
Born: Most, Czech.; June 7, 1977
Position: right wing
Height: 6-0
Weight: 195
Uniform no.: 55
Shoots: right

Career statistics:

GP	G	A	TP	PIM
29	4	12	16	6

1998-99 statistics:

GP	G	A	TP	+/-	PIM	PP	SH	GW	GT	S	PCT
29	4	12	16	0	6	0	0	0	0	61	6.6

LAST SEASON
First NHL season. Appeared in 31 games with Long Beach (IHL), scoring 17-13 — 30. Missed nine games due to coach's decision.

THE FINESSE GAME
Rosa's skating is the biggest drawback to his achieving success at the NHL level. It is more than adequate for the minors — and the juniors, where he was a sniper in the Quebec League — but he will have to work to improve it in order to score in the bigs.

He has very nice hands and a good scoring touch around the net. Once he gets a little bigger he will be more of a factor in the trenches.

Rosa got off to a very slow start last season, but was promoted once he got into a groove. Still, he wasn't able to maintain his scoring touch at the NHL level.

THE PHYSICAL GAME
Rosa is on the weedy side, and needs to get much more muscular to compete with the big boys in the NHL.

THE INTANGIBLES
Rosa suffered from a concussion and an inner-ear disorder in 1997. It has taken him some time to get over the setback they caused, as they essentially robbed him of that entire season (he appeared in only three minor-league games). The Kings promoted him and used him down the stretch, but he produced only two assists in his last eight games, not a strong finish.

PROJECTION
The Kings want to get younger, and by cutting players like Ray Ferraro and Russ Courtnall they're trying to make room for players like Rosa. Rosa's had a taste of the NHL. Now it's time to take a big bite. He's a point-a-game player in the minors, but 40 would be an attainable goal for his first full NHL season.

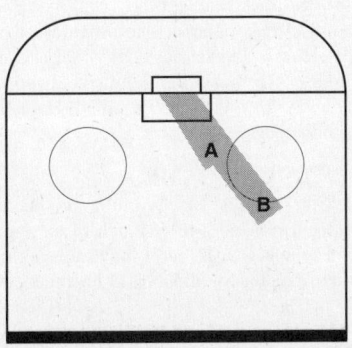

BRYAN SMOLINSKI

Yrs. of NHL service: 6
Born: Toledo, Ohio; Dec. 27, 1971
Position: centre/right wing
Height: 6-1
Weight: 200
Uniform no.: 20
Shoots: right

Career statistics:

GP	G	A	TP	PIM
444	131	158	289	294

1995-96 statistics:

GP	G	A	TP	+/-	PIM	PP	SH	GW	GT	S	PCT
81	24	40	64	+6	69	8	2	1	0	229	10.5

1996-97 statistics:

GP	G	A	TP	+/-	PIM	PP	SH	GW	GT	S	PCT
64	28	28	56	+8	25	9	0	1	1	183	15.3

1997-98 statistics:

GP	G	A	TP	+/-	PIM	PP	SH	GW	GT	S	PCT
81	13	30	43	-16	34	3	0	4	0	203	6.4

1998-99 statistics:

GP	G	A	TP	+/-	PIM	PP	SH	GW	GT	S	PCT
82	16	24	40	-7	49	7	0	3	0	223	7.2

THE INTANGIBLES

Smolinski has a lot going for him physically, but zero emotionally. He is not a player to be counted on at crunch time. Teams get frustrated with him because of his lack of drive and intensity.

PROJECTION

Smolinski will get a lot of ice time in Los Angeles, and maybe the switch to the West will perk up his offense. Don't expect much more than 20 goals, though.

LAST SEASON

Acquired by Los Angeles with Ziggy Palffy and Marcel Cousineau for Olli Jokinen, Josh Green, Mathieu Biron and a 1999 first-round draft pick, June 20, 1999. Led Islanders in shots. Second on Islanders in power-play goals and game-winning goals. Third on Islanders in assists and points. One of three Islanders to appear in all 82 games.

THE FINESSE GAME

Smolinski brings a centre's vision to the wing. He has a quick release and an accurate shot, and, on nights when he brings his "A" game, he works to get himself into quality shooting areas. Confidence is a big factor; Smolinski has a history of being a streaky/slumpy player. When he is in a slump, he turns into Mr. Perimeter.

Smolinski's skating is adequate, but it could improve with some lower-body work. He has good balance and lateral movement but is not very quick. He has a railroad-track skating base.

Smolinski has the smarts to be an asset on both specialty teams, and he has really stepped up as a penalty killer. He has good defensive awareness — his play away from the puck is sound. He is good in tight with the puck.

THE PHYSICAL GAME

Smolinski has a thick, blocky build, and he can be a solid hitter. He doesn't have much of an aggressive nature on a nightly basis, but it shows up sporadically, and on those nights Smolinski is at his most effective.

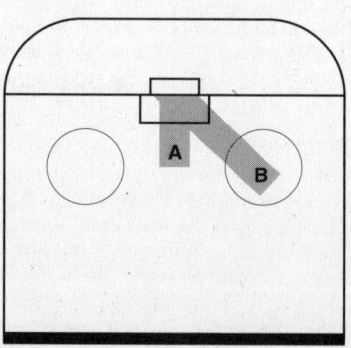

JAMIE STORR

Yrs. of NHL service: 2
Born: Brampton, Ont.; Dec. 28, 1975
Position: goaltender
Height: 6-0
Weight: 170
Uniform no.: 1
Catches: left

Career statistics:

GP	MIN	GA	SO	GAA	A	PIM
60	3235	135	6	2.50	1	6

1995-96 statistics:

GP	MIN	GAA	W	L	T	SO	GA	S	SAPCT	PIM
5	262	2.75	3	1	0	0	12	147	.918	0

1996-97 statistics:

GP	MIN	GAA	W	L	T	SO	GA	S	SAPCT	PIM
5	265	2.49	2	1	1	0	11	147	.925	0

1997-98 statistics:

GP	MIN	GAA	W	L	T	SO	GA	S	SAPCT	PIM
17	920	2.22	9	5	1	2	34	482	.929	0

1998-99 statistics:

GP	MIN	GAA	W	L	T	SO	GA	S	SAPCT	PIM
28	1525	2.40	12	12	2	4	61	724	.916	6

LAST SEASON

Named to NHL All-Rookie Team for second consecutive season. Missed 16 games with groin strain. Missed eight games with sprained ankle.

THE PHYSICAL GAME

Technically, Storr is pretty sound for a young player. He plays his angles well. And he's a stand-up goalie who challenges shooters and forces them to make the first move, rather than scrambling and relying on his reflexes.

Although Storr is somewhat lean, his technique doesn't take much out of him physically, much in the style of a young Kirk McLean. When he has to scramble, he can. He has good reflexes for his size and can be in a position for a second shot, something he will see a lot of with the Kings.

Storr has a quick glove hand. He is adequate with his stick but needs to improve his work out of his net. He is indecisive and mixes up his defensemen.

THE MENTAL GAME

Easily the weakest part of Storr's game is stored in his head. He has trouble with his concentration.

THE INTANGIBLES

The Kings keep trying to give the number one role to Storr. He's still young (24 this season), and this could finally be the year he takes command.

PROJECTION

Storr should be playing behind a slightly improved team this season, and could get 50 starts and 20 wins.

JOZEF STUMPEL

Yrs. of NHL service: 6
Born: Nitra, Slovakia; June 20, 1972
Position: centre/right wing
Height: 6-1
Weight: 208
Uniform no.: 15
Shoots: right

Career statistics:

GP	G	A	TP	PIM
415	88	201	289	117

1995-96 statistics:

GP	G	A	TP	+/-	PIM	PP	SH	GW	GT	S	PCT
76	18	36	54	-8	14	5	0	2	0	158	11.4

1996-97 statistics:

GP	G	A	TP	+/-	PIM	PP	SH	GW	GT	S	PCT
78	21	55	76	-22	14	6	0	1	0	168	12.5

1997-98 statistics:

GP	G	A	TP	+/-	PIM	PP	SH	GW	GT	S	PCT
77	21	58	79	+17	53	4	0	2	1	162	13.0

1998-99 statistics:

GP	G	A	TP	+/-	PIM	PP	SH	GW	GT	S	PCT
64	13	21	34	-18	10	1	0	1	0	131	9.9

LAST SEASON

Third on team in assists. Missed 10 games with hip flexor and abdominal strain. Missed five games with right knee sprain. Missed three games with sprained right ankle.

THE FINESSE GAME

Stumpel keeps getting put in situations where he is expected to be a number one centre, but he is not in that elite class. He was probably the most valuable forward on the Kings last season, which only illustrates their lack of depth. On a deeper team than the Kings, Stumpel's lack of skating speed would drop him down farther on the depth chart.

However, he has good hand skills, which allow him to compensate for his skating up to a point. He also has a deft scoring touch and is a passer with a good short game. He is very patient. Stumpel uses his feet well to keep the puck alive, kick it up onto his stick or keep it in the attacking zone.

Stumpel has keen hockey sense and is still adjusting to a full-time job — and he has responded to the best of his ability to fulfil that role. He does not shoot nearly enough, and if he ends up playing with fellow Slovak Ziggy Palffy this season, he may not shoot at all.

THE PHYSICAL GAME

Stumpel is quite powerfully built, but he doesn't play to his size. He can be intimidated, and teams go after him early. Opponents know how crucial Stumpel is to the Kings' attack, and that Stumpel will take a hit to make a play in the offensive zone. He goes into the corners and bumps and protects the puck with his body, but when the action gets really fierce he backs off. He was really banged up last season, too.

THE INTANGIBLES

Stumpel's assist and point totals could soar with Palffy, though developing a strong second-line centre would accomplish almost as much.

PROJECTION

Stumpel's injuries and L.A.'s lack of depth cut Stumpel's production after a career year. Look for a return to the 70-point mark.

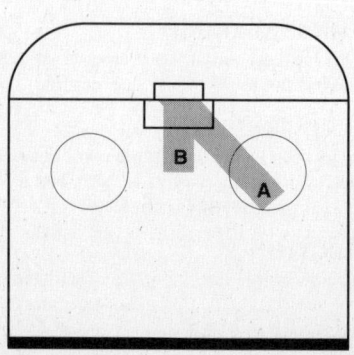

VLADIMIR TSYPLAKOV

Yrs. of NHL service: 4
Born: Moscow, Russia; Apr. 18, 1969
Position: left wing
Height: 6-0
Weight: 185
Uniform no.: 9
Shoots: left

Career statistics:

GP	G	A	TP	PIM
232	50	74	124	66

1995-96 statistics:

GP	G	A	TP	+/-	PIM	PP	SH	GW	GT	S	PCT
23	5	5	10	+1	4	0	0	0	0	40	12.5

1996-97 statistics:

GP	G	A	TP	+/-	PIM	PP	SH	GW	GT	S	PCT
67	16	23	39	+8	12	1	0	2	0	118	13.6

1997-98 statistics:

GP	G	A	TP	+/-	PIM	PP	SH	GW	GT	S	PCT
73	18	34	52	+15	18	2	0	1	0	113	15.9

1998-99 statistics:

GP	G	A	TP	+/-	PIM	PP	SH	GW	GT	S	PCT
69	11	12	23	-7	32	0	2	2	0	111	9.9

PROJECTION

If he wins a job again, Tsyplakov could be a 20-goal scorer, but he will find ice time on the top two lines almost impossible to come by.

LAST SEASON

Second on team in shorthanded goals. Missed 12 games due to left knee sprain. Missed one game due to coach's decision.

THE FINESSE GAME

Tsyplakov is a highly skilled forward who likes to play an up-tempo game. He's a run-and-gun, give-and-go kind of player who'll get the puck and find the open man or jump into the holes for a pass. He has good anticipation and quick acceleration. He has very good hands and a quick release on his shot.

Tsyplakov was drafted as a 26-year-old by the Kings in 1995 to fill a specific need: scoring. He plays on a second power-play unit. He is not as effective on the power play as he should be with his shot because he shies away from the high-percentage areas, where he has to pay a price to stake out his territory. He is a perimeter player, and that minimizes his NHL-calibre skills.

THE PHYSICAL GAME

Tsyplakov dislikes physical contact and is easily intimidated. He has been through several injuries and surgeries in past seasons (shoulder, hernia, knee), which may have had an effect, but he simply just doesn't seem to have the taste for it.

THE INTANGIBLES

Tsyplakov was on the bubble last season, but was saved due to some injuries and the paucity of talent on the Kings. It was his worst season in the NHL. If he repeats it, he'll be gone or watching from the press box.

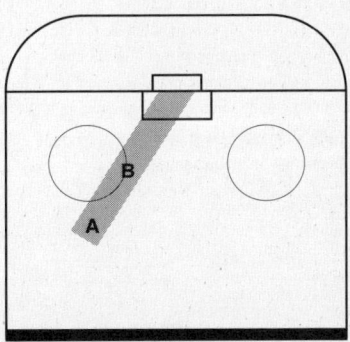

MONTREAL CANADIENS

Players' Statistics 1998-99

POS.	NO.	PLAYER	GP	G	A	PTS	+/-	PIM	PP	SH	GW	GT	S	PCT
C	11	SAKU KOIVU	65	14	30	44	-7	38	4	2			145	9.7
L	26	MARTIN RUCINSKY	73	17	17	34	-25	50	5		1		180	9.4
D	38	VLADIMIR MALAKHOV	62	13	21	34	-7	77	8		3		143	9.1
L	27	SHAYNE CORSON	63	12	20	32	-10	147	7		4		142	8.5
L	17	BENOIT BRUNET	60	14	17	31	-1	31	4	2			115	12.2
R	23	TURNER STEVENSON	69	10	17	27	6	88			2	1	102	9.8
D	5	STEPHANE QUINTAL	82	8	19	27	-23	84	1	1	4		159	5.0
L	49	BRIAN SAVAGE	54	16	10	26	-14	20	5		4	1	124	12.9
C	37	PATRICK POULIN	81	8	17	25	6	21		1	1		87	9.2
C	34	SERGEI ZHOLTOK	70	7	15	22	-12	6	2		3		102	6.9
D	22	ERIC WEINRICH	80	7	15	22	-25	89	4		1	1	119	5.9
R	44	JONAS HOGLUND	74	8	10	18	-5	16	1			1	122	6.6
R	28	DAINIUS ZUBRUS	80	6	10	16	-8	29		1	1		80	7.5
R	21	JASON DAWE	59	6	8	14	0	22	1		1		81	7.4
D	43	PATRICE BRISEBOIS	54	3	9	12	-8	28	1		1		90	3.3
D	55	IGOR ULANOV	76	3	9	12	-3	109					55	5.5
C	24	SCOTT THORNTON	47	7	4	11	-2	87	1		1	1	56	12.5
D	20	SCOTT LACHANCE	76	2	9	11	-21	41	1				59	3.4
D	52	CRAIG RIVET	66	2	8	10	-3	66					39	5.1
D	29	BRETT CLARK	61	2	2	4	-3	16					36	5.6
C	15	ERIC HOUDE	8	1	1	2	-2	2			1		4	25.0
C	46	*MATT HIGGINS	25	1		1	-2						12	8.3
D	48	*MILOSLAV GUREN	12		1	1	-1	4					11	
G	31	JEFF HACKETT	63		1	1	0	12						
L	14	*TERRY RYAN	1			0		5						
R	42	*JONATHAN DELISLE	1			0								
D	53	*SYLVAIN BLOUIN	5			0		19					1	
R	30	JEAN-FRANCOIS JOMPHE	7			0		2					4	
C	45	*ARRON ASHAM	7				-4						5	
L	36	DAVE MORISSETTE	10				1	52					2	
L	35	ANDREI BASHKIROV	10				-3						4	
G	39	FREDERIC CHABOT	11				0	2						
D	56	*ALAIN NASREDDINE	15				-1	52					3	
G	60	*JOSE THEODORE	18				0							
C	6	TRENT MCCLEARY	46				-1	29					18	

GP = games played; G = goals; A = assists; PTS = points; +/- = goals-for minus goals-against while player is on ice; PIM = penalties in minutes; PP = power-play goals; SH = shorthanded goals; GW = game-winning goals; GT = game-tying goals; S = no. of shots; PCT = percentage of goals to shots; * = rookie

PATRICE BRISEBOIS

Yrs. of NHL service: 8
Born: Montreal, Que.; Jan. 27, 1971
Position: right defense
Height: 6-1
Weight: 188
Uniform no.: 43
Shoots: right

Career statistics:

GP	G	A	TP	PIM
445	42	136	178	347

1995-96 statistics:

GP	G	A	TP	+/-	PIM	PP	SH	GW	GT	S	PCT
69	9	27	36	+10	65	3	0	1	0	127	7.1

1996-97 statistics:

GP	G	A	TP	+/-	PIM	PP	SH	GW	GT	S	PCT
49	2	13	15	-7	24	0	0	1	0	72	2.8

1997-98 statistics:

GP	G	A	TP	+/-	PIM	PP	SH	GW	GT	S	PCT
79	10	27	37	+16	67	5	0	1	0	125	8.0

1998-99 statistics:

GP	G	A	TP	+/-	PIM	PP	SH	GW	GT	S	PCT
54	3	9	12	-8	28	1	0	1	0	90	3.3

LAST SEASON

Missed 21 games with separated shoulder. Missed six games with back injury. Missed one game with sprained knee.

THE FINESSE GAME

Brisebois has some nice skills, but he doesn't have the hockey sense to put them in a complete package so he can be an elite level defenseman. He has a decent first step to the puck, plus a good stride with some quickness, though he won't rush end-to-end. He carries the puck with authority but will usually take one or two strides and look for a pass, or else make the safe dump out of the zone. He steps up in the neutral zone to slow an opponent's rush.

Brisebois plays the point well enough to be on the first power-play unit, but he doesn't have the rink vision and lateral movement that marks truly successful point men. He has a good point shot, with a sharp release, and he keeps it low and on target. He doesn't often venture to the circles on offense, but when he does he has the passing skills and the shot to make something happen.

Brisebois has improved his positional play but often starts running around as if he is looking for someone to belt. He winds up hitting no one, while his partner is left outnumbered in the front of the net. He is a good outlet passer and is getting steadier under pressure.

THE PHYSICAL GAME

Brisebois has learned to pay the price physically. Although not a punishing hitter, he is strong and will make his take-outs. He doesn't have much of a mean streak, so he has to dedicate himself to taking the body — which wasn't always easy last season given his back and shoulder injuries.

THE INTANGIBLES

Brisebois has worked hard to develop better defensive presence and has become a legitimate number three defenseman in the league. He takes a lot of heat in Montreal, where even more is expected of him; he might blossom in another environment.

PROJECTION

Brisebois can score in the 40-point range if healthy.

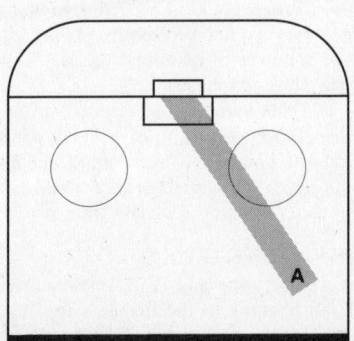

BENOIT BRUNET

Yrs. of NHL service: 7
Born: Pointe-Claire, Que.; Aug. 24, 1968
Position: left wing
Height: 5-11
Weight: 195
Uniform no.: 17
Shoots: left

Career statistics:

GP	G	A	TP	PIM
393	75	121	196	192

1995-96 statistics:

GP	G	A	TP	+/-	PIM	PP	SH	GW	GT	S	PCT
26	7	8	15	-4	17	3	1	4	0	48	14.6

1996-97 statistics:

GP	G	A	TP	+/-	PIM	PP	SH	GW	GT	S	PCT
39	10	13	23	+6	14	2	0	2	1	63	15.9

1997-98 statistics:

GP	G	A	TP	+/-	PIM	PP	SH	GW	GT	S	PCT
68	12	20	32	+11	61	1	2	2	1	87	13.8

1998-99 statistics:

GP	G	A	TP	+/-	PIM	PP	SH	GW	GT	S	PCT
60	14	17	31	-1	31	4	2	0	0	115	12.2

LAST SEASON

Tied for team lead in shorthanded goals. Second on team in shooting percentage. Tied for third on team in goals with career high. Missed 16 games with back injury. Missed four games with strained rib cage muscle. Missed one game with groin injury.

THE FINESSE GAME

Brunet is one of the best unknown defensive forwards in the league. He is virtually anonymous in Montreal because of his quiet, efficient role as a checking winger on the third line. Developing into a top penalty killer, he is strong on his skates and forechecks tenaciously.

When Brunet does choose to do anything offensively, he cuts to the net and uses a confident, strong touch in deep. He is always hustling back on defense, though, and seldom makes any high-risk plays deep in his own zone. He takes few chances and seems to come up with big points. Although he is a checking-line player, Brunet could, if needed, step up to fill in on a first or second line because his skills and intelligence are a powerful combination. He is the best breakaway player on the team.

Brunet's hands aren't great, or he would be able to create more scoring off his forecheck. His goals come from hard work, not pretty finesse plays, and his game is heavily defense oriented. Brunet would be somebody's dream come true at playoff time.

THE PHYSICAL GAME

Brunet isn't very big and is overmatched when he plays against many of the league's top lines. His strength is his positional play. He takes fewer steps than other players to accomplish the same chore. He's not a big hitter, but he will tie up an opponent's stick and play smothering defense. He tends to be injury prone.

THE INTANGIBLES

Brunet took less money in order to stay with the Canadiens in 1998 — he is one of the last of a dying breed, a true-bleu Montrealer who is proud to pull on the famous sweater. He is also a tremendous internal leader. He has a strong work ethic and comes to play every night. He is like a good referee. On his best nights you seldom notice him.

PROJECTION

Brunet is a hard worker who will score 15 to 20 goals in his checking role.

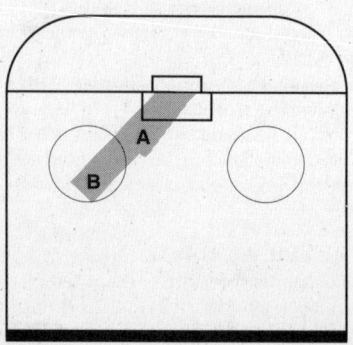

SHAYNE CORSON

Yrs. of NHL service: 13
Born: Barrie, Ont.; Aug. 13, 1966
Position: centre/left wing
Height: 6-1
Weight: 200
Uniform no.: 27
Shoots: left

Career statistics:

GP	G	A	TP	PIM
872	233	348	581	1855

1995-96 statistics:

GP	G	A	TP	+/-	PIM	PP	SH	GW	GT	S	PCT
77	18	28	46	+3	192	13	0	0	2	150	12.0

1996-97 statistics:

GP	G	A	TP	+/-	PIM	PP	SH	GW	GT	S	PCT
58	8	16	24	-9	104	3	0	2	0	115	7.0

1997-98 statistics:

GP	G	A	TP	+/-	PIM	PP	SH	GW	GT	S	PCT
62	21	34	55	+2	108	14	1	1	0	142	14.8

1998-99 statistics:

GP	G	A	TP	+/-	PIM	PP	SH	GW	GT	S	PCT
63	12	20	32	-10	147	7	0	4	0	142	8.5

LAST SEASON

Led team in penalty minutes. Tied for team lead in game-winning goals. Second on team in power-play goals. Third on team in assists. Served six-game suspension. Missed six games with rib injury. Missed four games with neck injury. Missed three games with sprained ankle.

THE FINESSE GAME

Corson makes a lot of things happen by overpowering people around the net. Like Bob Probert in his prime, he has surprising scoring ability for a player who is considered a mucker. People give Corson an extra foot or two because of his muscle, which allows him extra time to pick up loose pucks out of scrums and jam his shots in tight, or lift them over a goalie's stick.

Corson gets a lot of rebound goals if he plays on a line with people who throw the puck to the net, because he will go barrelling in for it. He's free to play that style more on the left wing than at centre, but he also has some nice playmaking abilities when put in the middle. He won't do anything too fancy, but he is intelligent enough to play a basic short game. Corson can win draws outright on his backhand.

Corson is a powerful skater but not very fast or agile. He has good balance for his work along the boards, and has all the attributes of a power forward. He does his dirty work in front of the net for screens and deflections, and has the hands to guide hard point shots. He is wildly inaccurate with any shots that aren't at close range, so on the off nights when he is not winning the duels around the net, he is a nonfactor. From eight to 10 feet around the net, he can't be moved when he puts his mind to it.

THE PHYSICAL GAME

The way Corson is successful is by fighting for his ice in the slot area, which he has to start doing again with consistency. He creates second chance opportunities for himself and his teammates because he is tremendous along the wall. He has grit and plays tough and hard every shift. He is dangerous because of his short fuse. Opponents never know when he will go off; since he's strong and can throw punches, few people want to be around when he does. He inspires fear. He hits to hurt and is so unpredictable he earns himself plenty of room on the ice.

THE INTANGIBLES

Injuries again took a big toll on Corson. Last year was a step back for him, and he has to re-dedicate himself to being the best player he can be.

PROJECTION

At 33, Corson could still have a few productive seasons left, but we doubt 40 goals is in his range. He has become a question mark because of his injuries, yet he is an effective player when healthy.

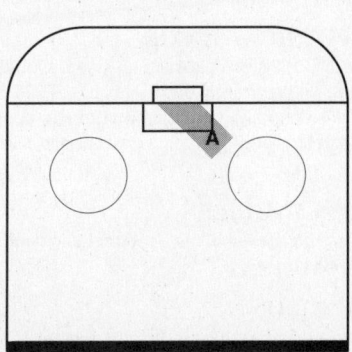

JASON DAWE

Yrs. of NHL service: 6
Born: North York, Ont.; May 29, 1973
Position: left wing
Height: 5-10
Weight: 195
Uniform no.: 21
Shoots: left

Career statistics:

GP	G	A	TP	PIM
362	86	89	175	160

1995-96 statistics:

GP	G	A	TP	+/-	PIM	PP	SH	GW	GT	S	PCT
67	25	25	50	-8	33	8	1	0	2	130	19.2

1996-97 statistics:

GP	G	A	TP	+/-	PIM	PP	SH	GW	GT	S	PCT
81	22	26	48	+14	32	4	1	3	0	136	16.2

1997-98 statistics:

GP	G	A	TP	+/-	PIM	PP	SH	GW	GT	S	PCT
81	20	19	39	+8	42	4	1	3	1	134	14.9

1998-99 statistics:

GP	G	A	TP	+/-	PIM	PP	SH	GW	GT	S	PCT
59	6	8	14	0	22	1	0	1	0	81	7.4

up and needs to score about 40 points to be useful.

LAST SEASON

Acquired on waivers from N.Y. Islanders, Dec. 15, 1998. Missed two games with concussion. Missed 21 games due to coach's decision.

THE FINESSE GAME

Dawe is a skill player with the added element of being an eager forechecker. He is not very big, but he comes in with some speed and picks off passes with his anticipation. He is also intelligent enough to trail into the play if he is being used with faster forwards who are less alert defensively.

Dawe has a quick release on his shot, usually from the top of the left circle in. He has the good sense to read the play and knows when to back off and support the defense as the third man high.

He is a good skater with a fluid stride and good balance. He's shifty and handles the puck well at high tempo (though he isn't much of a one-on-one threat) and in traffic. He is very effective on the power play.

THE PHYSICAL GAME

Dawe's lack of size is always an issue, though he is willing to do the grunt work for his line. He's not big, but he is stocky and strong and will bang people off the puck. He is a diligent backchecker and has an aggressive streak.

THE INTANGIBLES

Dawe was on the bubble in Montreal and could be on the move again.

PROJECTION

Dawe will need to earn his ice time wherever he ends

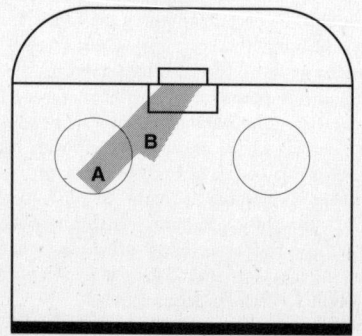

JEFF HACKETT

Yrs. of NHL service: 9
Born: London, Ont.; June 1, 1968
Position: goaltender
Height: 6-1
Weight: 180
Uniform no.: 31
Catches: left

Career statistics:
GP	MIN	GA	SO	GAA	A	PIM
347	19425	974	19	3.01	7	52

1995-96 statistics:
GP	MIN	GAA	W	L	T	SO	GA	S	SAPCT	PIM
35	2000	2.40	18	11	4	4	80	948	.916	8

1996-97 statistics:
GP	MIN	GAA	W	L	T	SO	GA	S	SAPCT	PIM
41	2473	2.16	19	18	4	2	89	1212	.927	6

1997-98 statistics:
GP	MIN	GAA	W	L	T	SO	GA	S	SAPCT	PIM
58	3441	2.20	21	25	11	8	126	1520	.917	8

1998-99 statistics:
GP	MIN	GAA	W	L	T	SO	GA	S	SAPCT	PIM
53	3091	2.27	24	20	9	5	117	1360	.914	6

LAST SEASON
Acquired from Chicago with Eric Weinrich, Alain Nasreddine and a fourth-round draft pick in 1999 for Jocelyn Thibault, Dave Manson and Brad Brown, Nov. 16, 1998. Career high in wins and minutes played. Missed seven games with hip flexor. Missed one game with knee injury.

THE PHYSICAL GAME
Hackett's mechanics are quite good. His positional play is strong. He knows when to challenge a shooter at the top of the crease, and, if anything, has a tendency to be overly aggressive. He plays his angles well and doesn't give the shooter much room.

He is a student of goaltending and is one of the hardest-working players on the team — if anything, he works too hard and has to be urged to conserve his energy, since he's an active goalie and isn't the most robust guy in the world. Hackett actually bulked up a little too much in the off-season last year. During the off-season, he attends camps and works to hone his skills.

Hackett has very quick reflexes for bang-bang plays around the net. His glove is a great asset. He will be conservative and hold the puck for a draw to cool off the action.

Hackett's stickhandling has improved slightly over the years, but still remains the weakest aspect of his game. He is sometimes guilty of trying to do too much. He is much better off letting his defensemen handle the puck and staying out of their way.

THE MENTAL GAME
Hackett thrives on being the number one goalie. He can handle a lot of minutes and isn't fazed when facing a high number of shots. It's been awhile since Hackett played for a contender, though it's hardly his fault. Hackett has the character of a winner.

THE INTANGIBLES
Hackett is very popular with his teammates. If goalies could be captains he would be one for the Canadiens. He is tough, gritty — the kind of goalie his teammates love to play for. He needs to feel needed, and the lucrative three-year contract extension the Canadiens gave him at the end of last season should do the trick.

PROJECTION
Hackett is solid enough to record 25 wins behind what will not be a very good Montreal team.

SAKU KOIVU

Yrs. of NHL service: 4
Born: Turku, Finland; Nov. 23, 1974
Position: centre
Height: 5-9
Weight: 175
Uniform no.: 11
Shoots: left

Career statistics:

GP	G	A	TP	PIM
266	65	137	202	164

1995-96 statistics:

GP	G	A	TP	+/-	PIM	PP	SH	GW	GT	S	PCT
82	20	25	45	-7	40	8	3	2	1	136	14.7

1996-97 statistics:

GP	G	A	TP	+/-	PIM	PP	SH	GW	GT	S	PCT
50	17	39	56	+7	38	5	0	3	0	135	12.6

1997-98 statistics:

GP	G	A	TP	+/-	PIM	PP	SH	GW	GT	S	PCT
69	14	43	57	+8	48	2	2	3	0	145	9.7

1998-99 statistics:

GP	G	A	TP	+/-	PIM	PP	SH	GW	GT	S	PCT
65	14	30	44	-7	38	4	2	0	0	145	9.7

LAST SEASON

Led team in assists for second consecutive season. Led team in points. Tied for team lead in shorthanded goals. Third on team in goals and shots. Missed 12 games with abdominal strain. Missed three games with elbow infection. Missed two games with knee injury.

THE FINESSE GAME

A highly skilled, versatile player, Koivu brings brilliance and excitement to every shift. Considered one of the world's best playmakers, he makes things happen with his speed and intimidates by driving the defense back, then uses the room to create scoring chances.

Koivu has great hands and can handle the puck at a fast pace. He stickhandles through traffic and reads plays well. He is intelligent and involved.

Koivu has a variety of shots. Like many Europeans, he has an effective backhand for shooting or passing. He also has a strong wrist shot and is deadly accurate. The feisty Finn draws a lot of checking attention — teams facing the Canadiens simply load up against him — and he fights his way through most of it, but he is small enough to get worn down.

Koivu made a complete recovery from torn knee ligaments a year ago, with his speed and mobility restored.

THE PHYSICAL GAME

The lone knock on Koivu is his lack of size. He gets involved in a scrappy way, but gets shoved around and occasionally broken. He plays through pain, but the Habs need to keep him from getting so damaged. He won't be intimidated, though, and uses his stick as an equalizer.

THE INTANGIBLES

Koivu simply doesn't have the size to survive the battering as a number one centre in the Eastern Conference, despite his amazing skill level and work ethic. He needs a better supporting cast, or he will be spending more time in sick bay than at the top of the Canadiens' scoring list. Gritty and determined, he is well-respected by his teammates and is a probable future captain of the Canadiens, if the team is daring enough to hand the "C" to a non-Francophone.

Koivu may have suffered both professionally and personally after Mark Recchi was traded to Philadelphia late in the season, but his strong World Championships (in which he suffered a non-displaced fracture in his wrist) may restore some of his good mood.

PROJECTION

If he can stay physically intact, and if Montreal increases its size up front a little bit, there is no reason why Koivu can't be a 25-goal, 60-assist man next season.

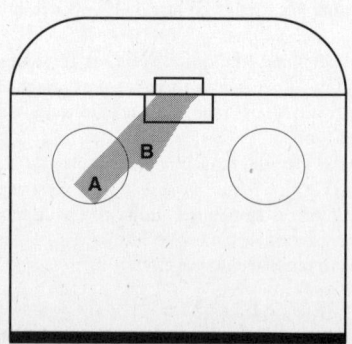

SCOTT LACHANCE

Yrs. of NHL service: 7
Born: Charlottesville, Va.; Oct. 22, 1972
Position: left defense
Height: 6-1
Weight: 196
Uniform no.: 20
Shoots: left

Career statistics:
GP	G	A	TP	PIM
467	27	80	107	326

1995-96 statistics:
GP	G	A	TP	+/-	PIM	PP	SH	GW	GT	S	PCT
55	3	10	13	-19	54	1	0	0	0	81	3.7

1996-97 statistics:
GP	G	A	TP	+/-	PIM	PP	SH	GW	GT	S	PCT
81	3	11	14	-7	47	1	0	0	0	97	3.1

1997-98 statistics:
GP	G	A	TP	+/-	PIM	PP	SH	GW	GT	S	PCT
63	2	11	13	-11	45	1	0	0	0	62	3.2

1998-99 statistics:
GP	G	A	TP	+/-	PIM	PP	SH	GW	GT	S	PCT
76	2	9	11	-21	41	1	0	0	0	59	3.4

LAST SEASON
Acquired from N.Y. Islanders for a third-round draft pick in 1999, Mar. 9, 1999.

THE FINESSE GAME
Lachance is the ultimate tease. He has so many good things going for him that you can't wait for him to put it all together, but at this stage of his career it appears he never will.

He has good hockey sense. He moves the puck well and is poised under pressure. He's one of the few defensemen with the patience to beat a trapping team. He will never have truly impressive offensive numbers, though, because his skating isn't good enough to propel him into the elite class, but he can complement another defenseman who does have good offensive instincts. Lachance is smart enough not to take too many chances. He doesn't have great hands.

Lachance's development has been slowed by injuries. He has to work on his quickness (his feet look a little heavy at times), but he is balanced and strong on his skates.

Defensively, Lachance does some little things well. His positioning is sound and he always keeps his body between his man and the goal.

THE PHYSICAL GAME
After whistles, after his goalie is whacked, in scrums around the net, in pileups in the corner, Lachance's courage wavers. Instead of getting in people's faces or at least into a stare-down, Lachance lowers his eyes and backs away submissively. He never wants a confrontation. During play he'll try hard to eliminate guys, but play is dead the second the whistle blows, and that prevents Lachance from staking out his territory the way the NHL's more dominating defensemen do. He is an efficient defenseman, soft but reliable.

THE INTANGIBLES
Once thought of as a potential number two defenseman, Lachance is a number four on his best nights. His skill level isn't high enough to compensate for his lack of competitiveness.

PROJECTION
Lachance could score a very quiet 20 points a season.

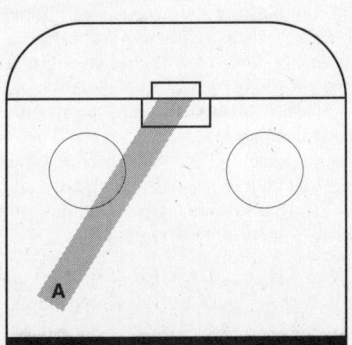

TREVOR LINDEN

Yrs. of NHL service: 11
Born: Medicine Hat, Alta.; Apr. 11, 1970
Position: centre/right wing
Height: 6-4
Weight: 210
Uniform no.: 32
Shoots: right

Career statistics:

GP	G	A	TP	PIM
809	275	357	632	634

1995-96 statistics:

GP	G	A	TP	+/-	PIM	PP	SH	GW	GT	S	PCT
82	33	47	80	+6	42	12	1	2	0	202	16.3

1996-97 statistics:

GP	G	A	TP	+/-	PIM	PP	SH	GW	GT	S	PCT
49	9	31	40	+5	27	2	2	2	0	84	10.7

1997-98 statistics:

GP	G	A	TP	+/-	PIM	PP	SH	GW	GT	S	PCT
67	17	21	38	-14	82	5	2	2	0	133	12.8

1998-99 statistics:

GP	G	A	TP	+/-	PIM	PP	SH	GW	GT	S	PCT
82	18	29	47	-14	32	8	1	1	0	167	10.8

LAST SEASON

Acquired from N.Y. Islanders for a 1999 first-round draft pick, May 29, 1999. Led Islanders in assists and power-play goals. Second on team in points. Third on team in goals. One of three Islanders to appear in all 82 games.

THE FINESSE GAME

Linden is a good player during the regular season who lifts his game a notch in the playoffs or other big games. But in the last few seasons with the Canucks and the Islanders he has had few opportunities to shine, and his stock has fallen.

Linden would be more effective as a winger than a centre. However, because of his size, the Canadiens are likely to keep him in the middle to match up against some of the East's big centres, so he is pretty much stuck. Not a graceful skater, at times Linden looks awkward, and he's not as strong on his skates as a player of his size should be. Despite his heavy feet his agility is satisfactory, but he lacks first-step quickness and doesn't have the all-out speed to pull away from a checker. He has a big turning radius.

Linden has improved his release, but it is not quick. He has a long reach, although unlike, say, Dave Andreychuk's (who is built along similar lines), his short game is not as effective as it should be.

Linden is unselfish and makes quick, safe passing decisions that help his team break smartly up the ice, often creating odd-man rushes. He has improved tremendously in his defensive coverage.

THE PHYSICAL GAME

Linden is big but doesn't always play tough, and so doesn't make good use of his size. He will attack the blueline and draw the attention of both defensemen, but will pull up rather than try to muscle through and earn a holding penalty. There are people he should nullify who still seem able to get away from him. He does not skate through the physical challenges along the boards.

If only he would keep his feet moving, Linden would be so much more commanding. Instead, he can be angled off the play fairly easily because he will not battle for better ice.

When Linden is throwing his weight around, he drives to the net and drags a defender or two with him, opening up a lot of ice for his teammates. He creates havoc in front of the net on the power play, planting himself for screens and deflections. When the puck is at the side boards, he's smart enough to move up higher, between the circles, forcing the penalty killers to make a decision. If the defenseman on that side steps up to cover him, space will open behind the defenseman; if a forward collapses to cover him, a point shot will open up.

THE INTANGIBLES

Linden is very likable and is a team leader.

PROJECTION

Linden will get his 20 to 25 goals and 50 to 60 points on a regular basis. Playing with yet another bad team has to wear on him.

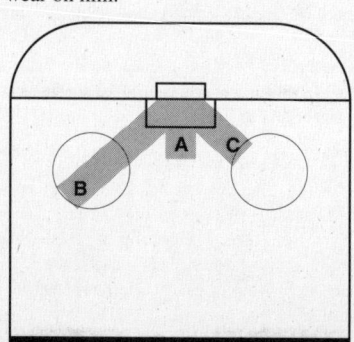

VLADIMIR MALAKHOV

Yrs. of NHL service: 7
Born: Sverdlovsk, Russia; Aug. 30, 1968
Position: right defense
Height: 6-3
Weight: 220
Uniform no.: 38
Shoots: left

Career statistics:

GP	G	A	TP	PIM
442	69	197	266	454

1995-96 statistics:

GP	G	A	TP	+/-	PIM	PP	SH	GW	GT	S	PCT
61	5	23	28	+7	79	2	0	0	0	122	4.1

1996-97 statistics:

GP	G	A	TP	+/-	PIM	PP	SH	GW	GT	S	PCT
65	10	20	30	+3	43	5	0	1	0	177	5.6

1997-98 statistics:

GP	G	A	TP	+/-	PIM	PP	SH	GW	GT	S	PCT
74	13	31	44	+16	70	8	0	2	0	166	7.8

1998-99 statistics:

GP	G	A	TP	+/-	PIM	PP	SH	GW	GT	S	PCT
62	13	21	34	-7	77	8	0	3	0	143	9.1

LAST SEASON

Led team defensemen in scoring for third consecutive season. Led team in power-play goals. Second on team in assists. Tied for second on team in points. Missed 10 games with back spasms. Missed nine games with knee injury.

THE FINESSE GAME

Malakhov has elite pro skills and an amateur attitude. (We don't mean to insult hardworking amateurs, we're just trying to make a point.) He continues to be one of the most enigmatic defensemen in the game.

Malakhov has an absolute bullet of a shot, and may have the hardest shot in the league that no one talks about. He rifles off a one-timer or on the fly, and has outstanding offensive instincts for both shooting and playmaking. He moves the puck and jumps into the play, but lacks vision, lateral movement and confidence.

Malakhov is so talented he never looks like he's trying hard. Most nights he's not. He seems discouraged at times when things aren't going smoothly. If he tries a few plays early in a game that don't work, you might as well put him on the bench for the rest of the night. If he has a few good shifts early, especially offensively, odds are he'll be one of the three stars. He is very gifted defensively as well.

Malakhov can be used on both special teams. He is a mobile skater, with good agility and balance. He has huge strides, which he developed playing bandy — a Russian game similar to hockey that is played on an ice surface the size of a soccer field.

THE PHYSICAL GAME

Malakhov relies on his positioning and anticipation for his defensive plays more than his hitting. He could be a major physical force because of his size and strength, but he has a very low pain threshhold; he really doesn't have the taste for the physical game. He gives up on the play and leaves his defense partner to his own devices.

THE INTANGIBLES

Malakhov should be a Norris Trophy winner — his skills are that world-class. But he has never put the whole package together, and until he does he will remain the number one tease in the NHL. But at least a half-dozen teams will look to make him their problem before the season starts.

PROJECTION

Malakhov will get his 30 to 40 points without being anywhere near the impact player he could and should be.

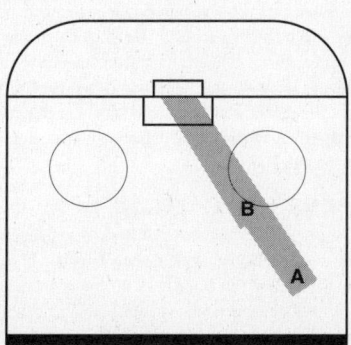

PATRICK POULIN

Yrs. of NHL service: 7
Born: Vanier, Que.; Apr. 23, 1973
Position: left wing
Height: 6-1
Weight: 210
Uniform no.: 37
Shoots: left

Career statistics:

GP	G	A	TP	PIM
472	82	113	195	263

1995-96 statistics:

GP	G	A	TP	+/-	PIM	PP	SH	GW	GT	S	PCT
46	7	9	16	+7	16	1	0	0	1	51	13.7

1996-97 statistics:

GP	G	A	TP	+/-	PIM	PP	SH	GW	GT	S	PCT
73	12	14	26	-16	56	2	3	1	0	124	9.7

1997-98 statistics:

GP	G	A	TP	+/-	PIM	PP	SH	GW	GT	S	PCT
78	6	13	19	-4	27	0	1	1	0	88	6.8

1998-99 statistics:

GP	G	A	TP	+/-	PIM	PP	SH	GW	GT	S	PCT
81	8	17	25	+6	21	0	1	1	0	87	9.2

LAST SEASON

Tied for team lead in plus-minus. Missed one game with sprained knee.

THE FINESSE GAME

Poulin has all the tools — size, strength, speed, shot, hands — to be an elite player, but he never uses all of those qualities on a nightly basis. Once projected as a top-line player, he has been transformed into a third-line checking centre, which may be his future.

Although intelligent and attentive, Poulin is also high-maintenance: he gets down on himself and needs to be shored up mentally. He has to take more of the burden upon himself to motivate his game. It's not an uncommon tendency for a player who starred at the junior level with little effort, as Poulin did, to try to cruise on talent alone his first season or two in the NHL. But Poulin is not in that elite group of athletes who can get away with that kind of game, and he's experienced enough now to know better.

Possessing explosive speed, Poulin can peel off the wing and barrel in with a rifle shot from the circle. He has an excellent shot with a quick release, and his wrist shot is very strong. Although he does not skate well with the puck, he has a fluid stride and a good eye for the openings, plus good hockey instincts and a grasp of positional play.

THE PHYSICAL GAME

Poulin is large in stature but not in on-ice presence. He does not use his body well, doesn't finish his checks and doesn't create the openings a player of his ability should. Floating should be something he does in the pool, not on the ice. He doesn't drive to the net or fight through checks.

THE INTANGIBLES

Poulin will never develop the mental toughness to enhance his skills. But anyone with his skills will keep getting second, third and fourth chances.

PROJECTION

Poulin is a 15-goal scorer in the body of a 40-goal scorer, but he couldn't even attain that modest number again last season.

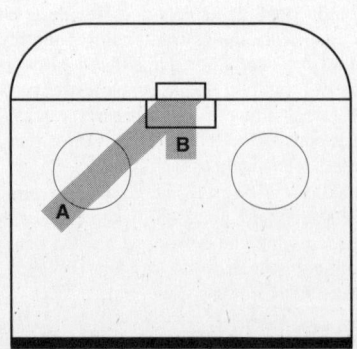

MARTIN RUCINSKY

Yrs. of NHL service: 7
Born: Most, Czech Republic; March 11, 1971
Position: left wing
Height: 6-0
Weight: 198
Uniform no.: 26
Shoots: left

Career statistics:

GP	G	A	TP	PIM
462	126	182	308	389

1995-96 statistics:

GP	G	A	TP	+/-	PIM	PP	SH	GW	GT	S	PCT
78	29	46	75	+18	68	9	2	4	0	181	16.0

1996-97 statistics:

GP	G	A	TP	+/-	PIM	PP	SH	GW	GT	S	PCT
70	28	27	55	+1	62	6	3	3	1	172	16.3

1997-98 statistics:

GP	G	A	TP	+/-	PIM	PP	SH	GW	GT	S	PCT
78	21	32	53	+13	84	5	3	3	0	192	10.9

1998-99 statistics:

GP	G	A	TP	+/-	PIM	PP	SH	GW	GT	S	PCT
73	17	17	34	-25	50	5	0	1	0	180	9.4

LAST SEASON

Led team in goals and shots. Tied for second on team in points. Tied for third on team in power-play goals. Missed three games with shoulder injury.

THE FINESSE GAME

Rucinsky is very quick, with hand skills to match at high tempo. He is most dangerous off the rush, where he can use his speed to intimidate the defense and then use the room they give him to fire his shot.

His flaw is that he is not overly patient. He has nice little moves and can beat people one-on-one. He loves to shoot, though, unlike many European players.

Rucinsky always gives the impression that there is a lot more left in the tank.

THE PHYSICAL GAME

Rucinsky is wiry but isn't a big banger. He will takes hits to protect the puck and make a play, but he does not drive to the net through traffic and seldom initiates. He can be intimidated.

THE INTANGIBLES

Rucinsky may have worn out his welcome even in offense-starved Montreal. He does not compete hard enough every night to make him that valuable a commodity. Rucinsky will also suffer from the loss of pal Vincent Damphousse.

PROJECTION

Rucinsky's inconsistency continues to plague him. He'll score 50 unsatisfying points.

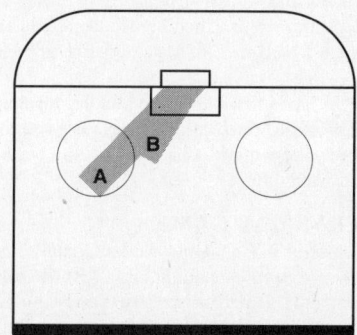

BRIAN SAVAGE

Yrs. of NHL service: 5
Born: Sudbury, Ontario; Feb. 24, 1971
Position: centre/left wing
Height: 6-1
Weight: 190
Uniform no.: 49
Shoots: left

Career statistics:

GP	G	A	TP	PIM
314	103	79	182	150

1995-96 statistics:

GP	G	A	TP	+/-	PIM	PP	SH	GW	GT	S	PCT
75	25	8	33	-8	28	4	0	4	0	150	16.7

1996-97 statistics:

GP	G	A	TP	+/-	PIM	PP	SH	GW	GT	S	PCT
81	23	37	60	-14	39	5	0	2	0	219	10.5

1997-98 statistics:

GP	G	A	TP	+/-	PIM	PP	SH	GW	GT	S	PCT
64	26	17	43	+11	36	8	0	7	2	152	17.1

1998-99 statistics:

GP	G	A	TP	+/-	PIM	PP	SH	GW	GT	S	PCT
54	16	10	26	-14	20	5	0	4	1	124	12.9

LAST SEASON

Tied for team lead in game-winning goals. Led team in shooting percentage. Second on team in goals. Tied for third on team in power-play goals. Missed 11 games with groin/hip injury. Missed 11 games with abdominal strain. Missed one game with groin injury.

THE FINESSE GAME

Savage has tremendous outside speed and a lethal shot. He has the goods to be a 40-goal scorer but has yet to make that leap, though he has improved his playmaking without losing much off his finishing touch. He lacks the creativity and vision for playing centre (he suffers from a bit of tunnel vision), but his experience as a centre helps him as a left wing. He has a quick release and is accurate with his shot. He feasts from the hash marks in and seldom passes up a shot to make a play.

Savage is a streaky scorer and he doesn't bring much to the game when he isn't scoring. He lets the slumps slow him down instead of working harder through the dry spells. Then it becomes a vicious circle where it's hard for him to get ice time to break out of it.

Savage has quick hands for picking up the puck and for working on face-offs. He's a good skater. Defensively, he remains a liability, mostly because of his inconsistent effort.

THE PHYSICAL GAME

Savage doesn't use his body well and can be intimidated when playing a team that does. He is strong on his skates and has decent size. He needs to compete more. Maybe playing with Trevor Linden will do the trick, though he doesn't seem like the answer.

THE INTANGIBLES

Savage has got to stop looking for external forces to juice up his game and find his own motivation. He can produce much more than he has so far in his young career.

PROJECTION

We predicted 25 goals for Savage last year; that still appears to be his limit. His stats will always be heavier on goals than assists.

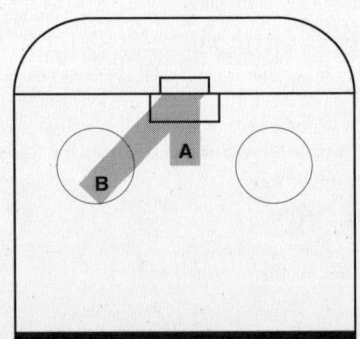

TURNER STEVENSON

Yrs. of NHL service: 5
Born: Prince George, B.C.; May 18, 1972
Position: right wing
Height: 6-3
Weight: 215
Uniform no.: 23
Shoots: right

Career statistics:

GP	G	A	TP	PIM
321	37	53	90	550

1995-96 statistics:

GP	G	A	TP	+/-	PIM	PP	SH	GW	GT	S	PCT
80	9	16	25	-2	167	0	0	2	0	101	8.9

1996-97 statistics:

GP	G	A	TP	+/-	PIM	PP	SH	GW	GT	S	PCT
65	8	13	21	-14	97	1	0	0	0	76	10.5

1997-98 statistics:

GP	G	A	TP	+/-	PIM	PP	SH	GW	GT	S	PCT
63	4	6	10	-8	110	1	0	0	0	43	9.3

1998-99 statistics:

GP	G	A	TP	+/-	PIM	PP	SH	GW	GT	S	PCT
69	10	17	27	+6	88	0	0	2	1	102	9.8

LAST SEASON

Tied for team lead in plus-minus. Third on team in shooting percentage. Career highs in goals, assists and points. Missed 10 games with sprained ankle. Missed one game with back spasms. Served two-game suspension.

THE FINESSE GAME

Effort isn't an issue, but Stevenson lacks the hand speed to combine with his decent skating speed, or he could be more of a contributor. He doesn't shoot enough and has to take the puck to the net with more authority. He is strong along the offensive boards, especially below the goal line. When he gets to a situation, he always makes the opposition player pay the price.

Stevenson's biggest flaw is his lack of foot speed, though he is a fair skater for his size. He has a good, long stride and is balanced and agile.

Stevenson has a variety of shots and uses all of them with power and accuracy, but his release needs improvement. He will follow the puck to the net and not give up on shots. He is also a decent passer and possesses some vision and creativity. He plays a short power game.

THE PHYSICAL GAME

Stevenson isn't tall but he is solidly built and thick through his trunk. He can lay on some serious hits. It's too bad he doesn't have more of a mean streak. He seems to have no idea what kind of physical presence he could add to the team.

THE INTANGIBLES

Stevenson has become a quiet leader on the Canadiens, but doesn't merit enough quality minutes to be more of an impact player. He adds some much-needed grit but can't play with the elite players.

PROJECTION

Stevenson can develop into a two-way winger with 20-goal potential, but "potential" is always a scary word. He has been slow to develop, like many big forwards, but the Canadiens believe he will be worth the wait. They're still waiting.

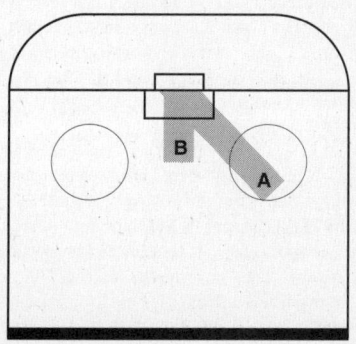

IGOR ULANOV

Yrs. of NHL service: 8
Born: Krasnokamsk, Russia; Oct. 1, 1969
Position: left defense
Height: 6-1
Weight: 205
Uniform no.: 55
Shoots: left

Career statistics:

GP	G	A	TP	PIM
427	14	77	91	815

1995-96 statistics:

GP	G	A	TP	+/-	PIM	PP	SH	GW	GT	S	PCT
64	3	9	12	+11	116	0	0	1	0	37	8.1

1996-97 statistics:

GP	G	A	TP	+/-	PIM	PP	SH	GW	GT	S	PCT
59	1	7	8	+2	108	0	0	1	0	56	1.8

1997-98 statistics:

GP	G	A	TP	+/-	PIM	PP	SH	GW	GT	S	PCT
49	2	8	10	-7	97	1	0	0	0	36	5.6

1998-99 statistics:

GP	G	A	TP	+/-	PIM	PP	SH	GW	GT	S	PCT
76	3	9	12	-3	109	0	0	0	0	55	5.5

LAST SEASON

Led team in penalty minutes. Missed two games due to personal reasons. Missed four games due to coach's decision.

THE FINESSE GAME

Ulanov's skills are magnified by the kind of tough, physical game he is capable of playing. A player who can skate and handle the puck as well as he can, or level you with a hit, is going to command a lot of space. And he knows what to do with that space once he gets it. He loves to join the attack. He has good first-step quickness, with agility and balance.

Ulanov anticipates well. He will break up a rush at his own blueline and start a quick counterattack. He has very good puck skills, but he's not a real offensive defenseman because he does not finish and has only a modest point shot. He starts breakouts with a smart, short pass. He can carry the puck, though he would rather have a teammate lug it.

He made a successful comeback last season from a knee injury. He plays with passion, especially when he is given an assignment against a top-flight player like Eric Lindros or Mats Sundin. The challenge brings out the best in him.

THE PHYSICAL GAME

Ulanov is a punishing open-ice hitter and has a real nasty streak. Some nights he won't hesitate to make a vicious hit right in front of the opponent's bench. But in the same game he'll lose an attacker by failing to make a simple take-out check, leaving his defense partner outnumbered. He raises the temperature of the opposition by raising his stick, too. He competes hard every night. He's not afraid of anybody.

THE INTANGIBLES

Ulanov is too unreliable to be much more than a fifth defenseman, though the Canadiens need this nasty boy and he'll get a lot of chances. He is scary when he plays like a head hunter, but gets too involved in running around instead of playing his game. He will give you all he has got every night, but he will also take dumb penalties and make disastrous reads in the defensive zone, which is why he has worn out his welcome on so many teams (five in six seasons).

PROJECTION

His points will be low (15 to 20); his PIM will be high (around 180).

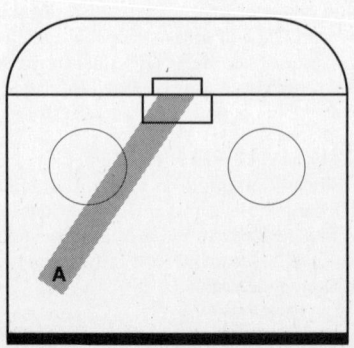

ERIC WEINRICH

Yrs. of NHL service: 9
Born: Roanoke, Va.; Dec. 19, 1966
Position: right defense
Height: 6-1
Weight: 210
Uniform no.: 22
Shoots: left

Career statistics:

GP	G	A	TP	PIM
682	48	200	248	580

1995-96 statistics:

GP	G	A	TP	+/-	PIM	PP	SH	GW	GT	S	PCT
77	5	10	15	+14	65	0	0	0	0	76	6.6

1996-97 statistics:

GP	G	A	TP	+/-	PIM	PP	SH	GW	GT	S	PCT
81	7	25	32	+19	62	1	0	0	1	115	6.1

1997-98 statistics:

GP	G	A	TP	+/-	PIM	PP	SH	GW	GT	S	PCT
82	2	21	23	+10	106	0	0	0	0	85	2.4

1998-99 statistics:

GP	G	A	TP	+/-	PIM	PP	SH	GW	GT	S	PCT
80	7	15	22	-25	89	4	0	1	1	119	5.9

LAST SEASON

Acquired from Chicago with Jeff Hackett, Alain Nasreddine and a fourth-round draft pick in 1999 for Jocelyn Thibault, Dave Manson and Brad Brown, Nov. 16, 1998. Tied career high in goals.

THE FINESSE GAME

Weinrich is a fine, underrated number three or four defenseman who is perfectly spotted in his current role in Montreal. His skating is above average. He accelerates quickly and has good straightaway speed, though he doesn't have great balance for pivots or superior leg drive for power. He has improved his skating but he is not sturdy on his feet. He jumps into the rush but needs to get his shots through from the point.

Weinrich is strong on the puck: shooting and passing hard. He received more quality power-play ice time in Montreal than he did in Chicago. He has a low, accurate shot that he gets away quickly. He will not gamble down low, but will sometimes sneak into the top of the circle for a one-timer. His offensive reads are far keener than his defensive reads.

Weinrich plays better with an offensive-minded partner. He is more useful when he is the support player who can move the puck up and shift into the play.

THE PHYSICAL GAME

A good one-on-one defender, Weinrich has reached an age where he needs to watch his minutes. When he starts averaging over 17 minutes a game, he starts to break down. He is not a soft player (a criticism that dogged him early in his career). He'll fight — it's not in his nature, but he won't get pushed around and will stand up for his teammates. His experience playing with Chris Chelios in Chicago taught him to battle hard, and Weinrich has tried to bring that with him to Montreal.

THE INTANGIBLES

Weinrich has taken on more responsibility and become a better player. He provides some quiet leadership and is an inspiration, but at 33 might not have that much left in the tank.

PROJECTION

Weinrich should score in the 25- to 30-point range.

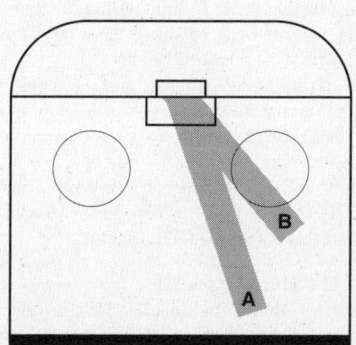

DAINIUS ZUBRUS

Yrs. of NHL service: 3
Born: Elektrani, Lithuania; June 16, 1978
Position: right wing
Height: 6-3
Weight: 215
Uniform no.: 9
Shoots: left

Career statistics:

GP	G	A	TP	PIM
217	22	48	70	93

1996-97 statistics:

GP	G	A	TP	+/-	PIM	PP	SH	GW	GT	S	PCT
68	8	13	21	+3	22	1	0	2	0	71	11.3

1997-98 statistics:

GP	G	A	TP	+/-	PIM	PP	SH	GW	GT	S	PCT
69	8	25	33	+29	42	1	0	5	0	101	7.9

1998-99 statistics:

GP	G	A	TP	+/-	PIM	PP	SH	GW	GT	S	PCT
80	6	10	16	-8	29	0	1	1	0	80	7.5

LAST SEASON

Acquired from Philadelphia with a second-round draft pick in 1999 or 2000 and other conditional picks for Mark Recchi, Mar. 10, 1999. Third on team in plus-minus.

THE FINESSE GAME

Zubrus plays the game in a North-South direction, goal line to goal line, rather than in the East-West fashion favoured by most imports. He's helped in this regard by a long stride that covers lots of ground. His puck control is quite impressive, as though the puck is on a very short rope that is nailed to his stick. His great ability is to control the puck down low and create scoring chances for himself and his teammates.

Splendid acceleration is a key component of Zubrus's game. He is both confident in his skating and competent enough to burst between defensemen to take the most direct path to the net. He also features enough power and balance to control a sweep behind the net, pull in front and roof a backhand shot under the crossbar from close range.

Zubrus uses his edges well and is difficult to knock off the puck. He is quite willing to zoom in off the wing, use his body to shield the puck from a defender and make something happen.

The soft touch in his hands and the quick release of his shot complements the power in Zubrus's legs. He can make a deft pass or a slick move, and can set up a goal or score one with roughly equal skill.

Zubrus still has a way to go to become a complete player. He is very poor in his own zone and in the neutral zone, with and without the puck.

THE PHYSICAL GAME

Zubrus will fight his own battles. He uses his size to advantage, finishes checks with authority and outmuscles as many people as he can muster. He's gritty in the corners and along the boards, and is adept at using his feet to control the puck if his upper body is tied up.

THE INTANGIBLES

Zubrus has played 217 NHL games and is just 21 years old. He is a work in progress.

PROJECTION

Zubrus has his impressive rookie year in Philadelphia to live up to. He needs a big start to his season because the Canadiens' coaching staff has already soured on him.

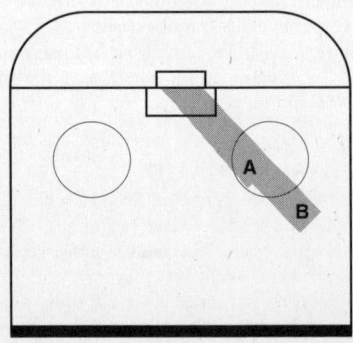

NASHVILLE PREDATORS

Players' Statistics 1998-99

POS.	NO.	PLAYER	GP	G	A	PTS	+/-	PIM	PP	SH	GW	GT	S	PCT
C	7	CLIFF RONNING	79	20	40	60	-3	42	10		4		257	7.8
C	22	GREG JOHNSON	68	16	34	50	-8	24	2	3			120	13.3
R	25	SERGEI KRIVOKRASOV	70	25	23	48	-5	42	10		6	1	208	12.0
C	71	SEBASTIEN BORDELEAU	72	16	24	40	-14	26	1	2	3		168	9.5
R	24	SCOTT WALKER	71	15	25	40	0	103		1	2		96	15.6
R	21	TOM FITZGERALD	80	13	19	32	-18	48			1		180	7.2
R	10	PATRIC KJELLBERG	71	11	20	31	-13	24	2		2		103	10.7
L	19	ANDREW BRUNETTE	77	11	20	31	-10	26	7		1		65	16.9
R	20	JAMIE HEWARD	63	6	12	18	-24	44	4		1		124	4.8
R	43	VITALI YACHMENEV	55	7	10	17	-10	10		1	2		83	8.4
D	15	DRAKE BEREHOWSKY	74	2	15	17	-9	140					79	2.5
L	28	DENNY LAMBERT	76	5	11	16	-3	218	1				66	7.6
D	42	JOEL BOUCHARD	64	4	11	15	-10	60					78	5.1
D	27	JOHN SLANEY	46	2	12	14	-12	14			1		84	2.4
D	6	BOB BOUGHNER	79	3	10	13	-6	137			1		59	5.1
D	44	*KIMMO TIMONEN	50	4	8	12	-4	30	1				75	5.3
D	5	JAN VOPAT	55	5	6	11	0	28					46	10.9
L	16	VILLE PELTONEN	14	5	5	10	1	2	1				31	16.1
C	9	DARREN TURCOTTE	40	4	5	9	-11	16			1		73	5.5
C	12	ROBERT VALICEVIC	19	4	2	6	4	2			2		23	17.4
R	18	*MARK MOWERS	30		6	6	-4	4					24	
L	32	JEFF DANIELS	9	1	3	4	-1	2					8	12.5
C	7	JEFF NELSON	9	2	1	3	-1	2					8	25.0
L	17	*PATRICK COTE	70	1	2	3	-7	242					21	4.8
D	4	JAY MORE	18		2	2	2	18					24	
L	8	DOUG FRIEDMAN	2	1	1	2	0	14					3	
D	40	*KARLIS SKRASTINS	2	1	1	2	0							
G	29	*TOMAS VOKOUN	37		1	1	0	6					1	
D	2	DAN KECZMER	38		1	1	-5	34					24	
C	11	*DAVID LEGWAND	1				0						2	
D	2	ROB ZETTLER	2				-2	2						
C	50	*PETR SYKORA	2				-1						2	
L	47	*MATT HENDERSON	2				-1	2						
R	12	BRAD SMYTH	3				-1	6					5	
G	30	*CHRIS MASON	3				0							
G	35	ERIC FICHAUD	9				0							
G	1	MIKE DUNHAM	44				0	4						

GP = games played; G = goals; A = assists; PTS = points; +/- = goals-for minus goals-against while player is on ice; PIM = penalties in minutes; PP = power-play goals; SH = shorthanded goals; GW = game-winning goals; GT = game-tying goals; S = no. of shots; PCT = percentage of goals to shots; * = rookie

DRAKE BEREHOWSKY

Yrs. of NHL service: 6
Born: Toronto, Ontario; Jan. 3, 1972
Position: right defense
Height: 6-2
Weight: 212
Uniform no.: 15
Shoots: right

Career statistics:

GP	G	A	TP	PIM
269	9	47	56	486

1995-96 statistics:

GP	G	A	TP	+/-	PIM	PP	SH	GW	GT	S	PCT
1	0	0	0	+1	0	0	0	0	0	0	0.0

1996-97 statistics:

Did not play in NHL

1997-98 statistics:

GP	G	A	TP	+/-	PIM	PP	SH	GW	GT	S	PCT
67	1	6	7	+1	169	1	0	1	0	58	1.7

1998-99 statistics:

GP	G	A	TP	+/-	PIM	PP	SH	GW	GT	S	PCT
74	2	15	17	-9	140	0	0	0	0	79	2.5

LAST SEASON

Led team defensemen in scoring. Third on team in penalty minutes. Missed two games with sprained knee.

THE FINESSE GAME

Expansion rescues some players from the NHL's junk drawer, and Berehowsky was salvaged by the Predators. His career was nearly ended by a knee injury, and Berehowsky had to fight his way back into the league by playing in places like San Antonio.

Berehowsky's foot speed is not great, but he has very good hands for a big guy. He plays on the second power-play unit (by necessity, since Nashville doesn't have anyone else) and logs a lot of ice time.

He would probably be a fifth or sixth defenseman on most teams; here he is a top four. He does the best he can even though he is pressed into tough assignments for his skill level.

THE PHYSICAL GAME

Berehowsky is strong and tough and loves to mix it up. He plays with a lot of confidence and fire.

THE INTANGIBLES

Berehowsky drew more attention for his dating (attractive country singers) than his skating. Off the ice he has a good time, but he is serious about the game. He gets to the rink early and prepares himself well. He nearly lost this life, which is why he appreciates it more than many young players. He is a good character player who has persevered.

PROJECTION

Berehowksy may lose ice time as the Predators improve on defense, but as there is no immediate threat of that occurring, he should be in the 20-point scoring range and 150-PIM neighbourhood.

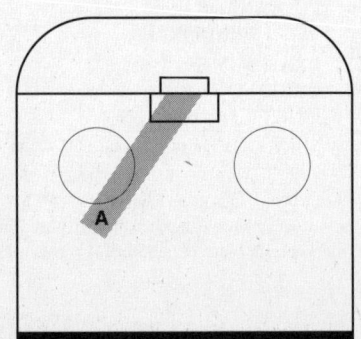

SEBASTIEN BORDELEAU

Yrs. of NHL service: 3
Born: Vancouver, B.C.; Feb. 15, 1975
Position: centre
Height: 5-11
Weight: 188
Uniform no.: 71
Shoots: right

Career statistics:

GP	G	A	TP	PIM
157	24	41	65	64

1995-96 statistics:

GP	G	A	TP	+/-	PIM	PP	SH	GW	GT	S	PCT
4	0	0	0	-1	0	0	0	0	0	0	0.0

1996-97 statistics:

GP	G	A	TP	+/-	PIM	PP	SH	GW	GT	S	PCT
28	2	9	11	-3	2	0	0	0	0	27	7.4

1997-98 statistics:

GP	G	A	TP	+/-	PIM	PP	SH	GW	GT	S	PCT
53	6	8	14	+5	36	2	1	0	1	55	10.9

1998-99 statistics:

GP	G	A	TP	+/-	PIM	PP	SH	GW	GT	S	PCT
72	16	24	40	-14	26	1	2	3	0	168	9.5

LAST SEASON

Tied for third on team in goals. Third on team in game-winning goals. Missed four games with sprained thumb. Missed three games with neck injury.

THE FINESSE GAME

Bordeleau has quickness and mobility. He is quick to the puck and smart around the net. He reads plays well and has good anticipation, though he doesn't have great hands. He has a pretty big shot, which he has gained more confidence in, but he usually looks to make plays first.

Bordeleau has good two-way potential and can work both special teams. He is an excellent penalty killer — a mini Guy Carbonneau. He might also earn some time on the power play in the future, but right now he is a valuable role player. He is among the best in the league in face-offs.

Bordeleau's effort is what sets him apart. He is a very determined player.

THE PHYSICAL GAME

Bordeleau is a small guy, but he is feisty and abrasive and gets in people's way. He will use his body but won't be a big hitter, for obvious reasons.

THE INTANGIBLES

Late in the season, Bordeau suffered a potential career-ending injury when he was cross-checked in the back of the neck by Sean O'Donnell and suffered disk damage. He could be out for four to six months.

PROJECTION

Bordeleau probably won't be ready for the start of the season and we predict it will be another year until he returns to the form he showed last season. He can be a steady 15- to 20-goal scorer at the NHL level.

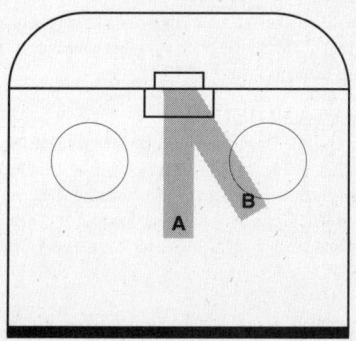

JOEL BOUCHARD

Yrs. of NHL service: 3
Born: Montreal, Que.; Jan. 23, 1974
Position: left defense
Height: 6-0
Weight: 190
Uniform no.: 42
Shoots: left

Career statistics:

GP	G	A	TP	PIM
190	13	23	36	170

1995-96 statistics:

GP	G	A	TP	+/-	PIM	PP	SH	GW	GT	S	PCT
4	0	0	0	0	4	0	0	0	0	0	0.0

1996-97 statistics:

GP	G	A	TP	+/-	PIM	PP	SH	GW	GT	S	PCT
76	4	5	9	-23	49	0	1	0	0	61	6.6

1997-98 statistics:

GP	G	A	TP	+/-	PIM	PP	SH	GW	GT	S	PCT
44	5	7	12	0	57	0	1	1	0	51	9.8

1998-99 statistics:

GP	G	A	TP	+/-	PIM	PP	SH	GW	GT	S	PCT
64	4	11	15	-10	60	0	0	0	0	78	5.1

PROJECTION

Bouchard will get a lot of ice time again this season and can score 20 points.

LAST SEASON

Missed 18 games with ankle injury.

THE FINESSE GAME

Bouchard's greatest asset is his skating. He can log a lot of ice time because he covers a lot of ground fairly effortlessly, and he uses his skating almost exclusively in a defensive posture. He is a very good penalty killer, who can match strides with some of the game's better skaters.

Because his skating is so impressive, more was expected of Bouchard earlier in his career, however, his hockey sense and his hands aren't as good as his skating. He can play the second power-play unit, but only because these are the Predators. He will never rack up impressive point totals.

Bouchard doesn't take it for granted that he's in the league, and he is young enough that he can develop into a better player.

THE PHYSICAL GAME

Bouchard has good size and his skating helps him generate a little more power in his checks, but he is not a big hitter.

THE INTANGIBLES

At some point, Bouchard will be a replaceable player, but at this stage of his career and at this point in Nashville's development, he fits among the team's top defensemen. He is a very good competitor who wants to do well and works hard to improve himself in practice.

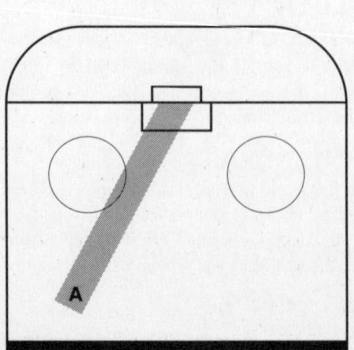

BOB BOUGHNER

Yrs. of NHL service: 4
Born: Windsor, Ont.; Mar. 8, 1971
Position: right defense
Height: 6-0
Weight: 206
Uniform no.: 6
Shoots: right

Career statistics:

GP	G	A	TP	PIM
256	5	21	26	631

1995-96 statistics:

GP	G	A	TP	+/-	PIM	PP	SH	GW	GT	S	PCT
31	0	1	1	+3	104	0	0	0	0	14	0.0

1996-97 statistics:

GP	G	A	TP	+/-	PIM	PP	SH	GW	GT	S	PCT
77	1	7	8	+12	225	0	0	0	0	34	2.9

1997-98 statistics:

GP	G	A	TP	+/-	PIM	PP	SH	GW	GT	S	PCT
69	1	3	4	+5	165	0	0	0	0	26	3.8

1998-99 statistics:

GP	G	A	TP	+/-	PIM	PP	SH	GW	GT	S	PCT
79	3	10	13	-6	137	0	0	1	0	59	5.1

LAST SEASON
Career high in points. Missed three games with flu.

THE FINESSE GAME
Boughner gets the most out of his talent. For the most part he's a defensive defenseman who plays a conservative game, but who competes hard every night and maxes out his modest skills.

Boughner plays every night against other teams' top lines. He wouldn't be a top two defenseman on many other teams, but he has to pay the price in that role for Nashville.

Boughner doesn't have great hands, so he doesn't get involved much in the offense. He doesn't (or shouldn't) try to make the first pass out of the zone. He has to be reminded to keep it simple and just bang the puck off the glass. He killed penalties last season for the first time in his career.

THE PHYSICAL GAME
Boughner is very aggressive and usually the Predators' nightly leader in hits. His teammates appreciate the way he pays the price.

THE INTANGIBLES
Boughner is one of those steady, experienced character guys; the perfect fit for an expansion team.

PROJECTION
Boughner will log his 17 to 18 minutes a night and 12 to 13 points a season.

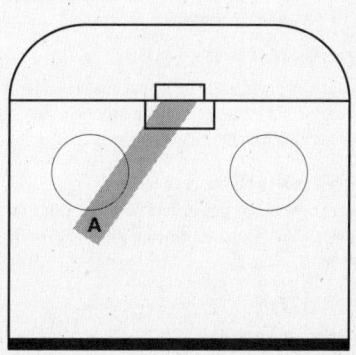

PATRICK COTE

Yrs. of NHL service: 1
Born: Lasalle, Que.; Jan. 24, 1975
Position: left wing
Height: 6-3
Weight: 199
Uniform no.: 17
Shoots: left

Career statistics:
GP	G	A	TP	PIM
78	1	2	3	289

1995-96 statistics:
GP	G	A	TP	+/-	PIM	PP	SH	GW	GT	S	PCT
2	0	0	0	-2	5	0	0	0	0	0	0.0

1996-97 statistics:
GP	G	A	TP	+/-	PIM	PP	SH	GW	GT	S	PCT
0	0	0	0	0	27	0	0	0	0	1	0.0

1997-98 statistics:
GP	G	A	TP	+/-	PIM	PP	SH	GW	GT	S	PCT
3	0	0	0	-1	15	0	0	0	0	3	0.0

1998-99 statistics:
GP	G	A	TP	+/-	PIM	PP	SH	GW	GT	S	PCT
70	1	2	3	-7	242	0	0	0	0	21	4.8

LAST SEASON
First NHL season. Led team and all NHL rookies in penalty minutes. Missed three games with separated shoulder. Missed one game with flu. Missed one game with groin strain.

THE FINESSE GAME
Cote scored his first NHL goal in Tampa late in the season, and it was such a momentous event that he asked assistant coach Paul Gardner if he could leave the bench during the period to call home to his dad.

Cote probably won't have to excuse himself too often in the near future. However, if they install a pay phone in the penalty box, he'll have plenty of time to chat.

Cote never was able to move up the depth chart in Dallas, but he's a hit in Nashville. His hands and his skating have to improve, though, in order for him to stay in the league in the future. Cote went to Europe during the off-season to work on his skills. He needs to be a better hockey player.

THE PHYSICAL GAME
Cote fought everybody. He's good at it and he loves it. He has good size but he could increase his strength since he tackles all the heavyweights.

THE INTANGIBLES
Maybe enforcers are going out of style, but they aren't extinct yet, and Cote is among the best of the next generation.

PROJECTION
A sure pick for your goon pool.

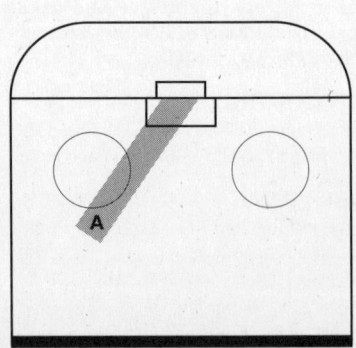

MIKE DUNHAM

Yrs. of NHL service: 3
Born: Johnson City, N.Y.; June 1, 1972
Position: goaltender
Height: 6-3
Weight: 195
Uniform no.: 1
Catches: left

Career statistics:

GP	MIN	GA	SO	GAA	A	PIM
85	4258	199	4	2.80	1	6

1996-97 statistics:

GP	MIN	GAA	W	L	T	SO	GA	S	SAPCT	PIM
26	1013	2.55	8	7	1	2	43	456	.906	2

1997-98 statistics:

GP	MIN	GAA	W	L	T	SO	GA	S	SAPCT	PIM
15	773	2.25	5	5	3	1	29	332	.913	0

1998-99 statistics:

GP	MIN	GAA	W	L	T	SO	GA	S	SAPCT	PIM
44	2472	3.08	16	23	3	1	127	1387	.908	4

PROJECTION

Dunham's injury makes him an iffy prospect but he should net 20 wins.

LAST SEASON

Games played career high. Missed 25 games with recurring groin injuries.

THE PHYSICAL GAME

Dunham is built well for the stand-up style he favours. He injects some butterfly elements, but for the most part makes the best use of his size by staying upright and letting the puck hit him. He has to stay on his feet or his knees since he does not have great reflexes for close-in scrambles.

Dunham played his first season as a number one goalie, and while he was mentally ready, his injuries were a major problem. In addition to the games he missed outright, there were many games he started and could not finish because of his groin injury.

Dunham handles the puck fairly well. He is no Martin Brodeur, but he has obviously learned a great deal from being Brodeur's teammate for two years, and he will be able to help out his defense by moving the puck. He also uses his stick well to break up passes around the crease.

THE MENTAL GAME

Dunham was more relaxed after getting the number one job in Nashville. He was very good in the first two months, before the injury hit him at the end of November.

Dunham has the ability to steal games. He hadn't been a number one goalie in a long time. He shared the starting role with Garth Snow at the University of Maine, and with the U.S. Olympic team he was co-goalie with Corey Schwab (and co-MVP of the 1995 Calder Cup with Albany of the AHL), then backed up Martin Brodeur in New Jersey. He can't be fairly judged until he stays healthy enough to get in a groove. He has a lot of experience for his age.

TOM FITZGERALD

Yrs. of NHL service: 11
Born: Melrose, Mass.; Aug. 28, 1968
Position: right wing/centre
Height: 6-1
Weight: 191
Uniform no.: 21
Shoots: right

Career statistics:

GP	G	A	TP	PIM
649	94	131	215	451

1995-96 statistics:

GP	G	A	TP	+/-	PIM	PP	SH	GW	GT	S	PCT
82	13	21	34	-3	75	1	6	2	0	141	9.2

1996-97 statistics:

GP	G	A	TP	+/-	PIM	PP	SH	GW	GT	S	PCT
71	10	14	24	+7	64	0	2	1	1	135	7.4

1997-98 statistics:

GP	G	A	TP	+/-	PIM	PP	SH	GW	GT	S	PCT
80	12	6	18	-4	79	0	2	1	0	119	10.1

1998-99 statistics:

GP	G	A	TP	+/-	PIM	PP	SH	GW	GT	S	PCT
80	13	19	32	-18	48	0	0	1	0	180	7.2

LAST SEASON

Third on team in shots. Missed one game with stiff neck.

THE FINESSE GAME

Fitzgerald is a good penalty killer but has elevated his game another step above the average third-liner by becoming a reliable crunch-time player.

He is very quick and uses his outside speed to take the puck to the net. He is also less shy about using his shot, perhaps because he is working to get himself into better shooting situations. He doesn't have the quickest release and the goalie can usually adjust in time despite Fitzgerald's speed. He isn't very creative. His chances come off earnest work around the net.

Fitzgerald is versatile and he can play both centre and right wing. He makes a better winger than centre. He is only average on draws. His hands aren't very quick and he seems to be at a disadvantage against bigger centres.

THE PHYSICAL GAME

Fitzgerald is gritty and strong. He has fairly good size and he uses it along the boards and in front of the net. Although he's a pesky checker who gets people teed off, his own discipline keeps him from taking many cheap penalties. He gives his team some bang and pop and finishes his checks. He isn't huge, but he's among the best open-ice hitters in the league.

Fitzgerald is an iron man. He is very durable and handles a lot of ice time. He plays through pain.

THE INTANGIBLES

Fitzgerald got off to a slow start — probably from the unaccustomed pressure of being the highest-paid player on the team ($1.6 million) and the responsibility of being captain of a first-year team. He regained his focus midway through the season and had a fine second half. He helped sell the game on and off the ice, and on *Late Night with David Letterman*.

PROJECTION

Fitzgerald will contribute 15 to 20 goals in a checking role, but lacks the finishing touch to do much more.

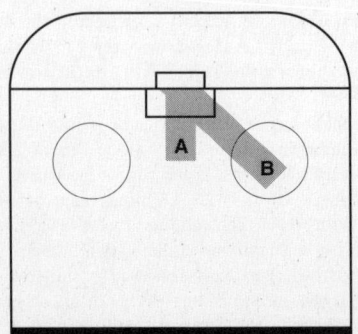

GREG JOHNSON

Yrs. of NHL service: 4
Born: Thunder Bay, Ontario; Mar. 16, 1971
Position: centre
Height: 5-10
Weight: 185
Uniform no.: 22
Shoots: left

Career statistics:

GP	G	A	TP	PIM
351	68	113	181	134

1995-96 statistics:

GP	G	A	TP	+/-	PIM	PP	SH	GW	GT	S	PCT
60	18	22	40	+6	30	5	0	2	0	87	20.7

1996-97 statistics:

GP	G	A	TP	+/-	PIM	PP	SH	GW	GT	S	PCT
32	7	9	16	-13	14	1	0	0	0	52	13.5

1997-98 statistics:

GP	G	A	TP	+/-	PIM	PP	SH	GW	GT	S	PCT
74	12	22	34	-2	40	4	0	3	0	89	13.5

1998-99 statistics:

GP	G	A	TP	+/-	PIM	PP	SH	GW	GT	S	PCT
68	16	34	50	-8	24	2	3	0	0	120	13.3

PROJECTION

Expansion has been very, very good to Johnson, but he is still not likely to max out over the 20-goal mark. His goals to assists ratio will be about 2:1.

LAST SEASON

Led team in shorthanded goals. Second on team in assists, points and shooting percentage. Tied for third on team in goals. Missed five games with stress fracture of ankle. Missed five games with groin strain. Missed four games with concussion.

THE FINESSE GAME

Johnson was one of the biggest pleasant surprises for the Predators last season, fulfilling his role as a number two centre and at times outplaying the number one, Cliff Ronning. After being a spare part early in his career, Johnson took advantage of his chance in Nashville.

A former Hobey Baker candidate, Johnson has explosive speed. He has fine finesse skills, too. He's a smart and creative passer who doesn't shoot enough. When he chooses, he has an accurate wrist shot. Johnson isn't a hard player but he competes well.

It was a good change of scenery for Johnson, who was used on four-on-four and in penalty killing and power-play situations.

THE PHYSICAL GAME

Johnson is small and gets bounced around a lot. Being one of the faster skaters in the league at least allows him to avoid some trouble.

THE INTANGIBLES

Johnson's durability over the course of a full season was a question mark, but he was up to it last year. Now the issue will be whether he takes another step forward this season. He is going into a contract year, which should make him hungrier.

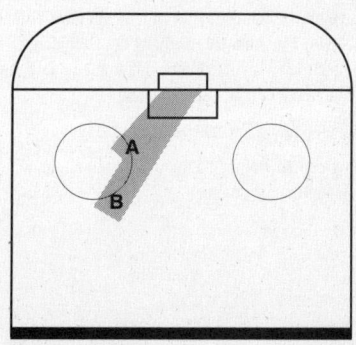

PATRIC KJELLBERG

Yrs. of NHL service: 1
Born: Falun, Sweden; June 17, 1969
Position: left wing
Height: 6-2
Weight: 196
Uniform no.: 10
Shoots: left

Career statistics:

GP	G	A	TP	PIM
78	11	20	31	26

1998-99 statistics:

GP	G	A	TP	+/-	PIM	PP	SH	GW	GT	S	PCT
71	11	20	31	-13	24	2	0	2	0	103	10.7

LAST SEASON
First full NHL season.

THE FINESSE GAME
After a taste of North American hockey with the Montreal system in 1992-93, Kjellberg returned to his native Sweden until the Predators signed him as a free agent prior to last season.

Kjellberg is a big, strong skater, but not a very swift one. His skating is average. He is good along the wall and in the corners. He is a bigger Andreas Dackell.

Kjellberg saw a lot of ice time last season and was very reliable defensively. He's not very flashy. He makes smart plays, though, and you really have to pay attention to notice the little things he does well. He's not a big offensive threat, but he has the finesse skills to play alongside two of the better Predators forwards, Cliff Ronning and Sergei Krivokrasov.

THE PHYSICAL GAME
Kjellberg likes to get involved around the net. He will dig in for rebounds and garbage goals. Most of his goals will come from five to 10 feet out, in the dirty areas. He'll take a beating to get open.

THE INTANGIBLES
Kjellberg had a strong first half but tailed off in the second, probably due to this being his first full season in the NHL. He had to readjust to the length of the NHL schedule. He needs to show more offense and consistency to keep a full-time job.

PROJECTION
Kjellberg could score 15 to 20 goals if he keeps his energy level up all season.

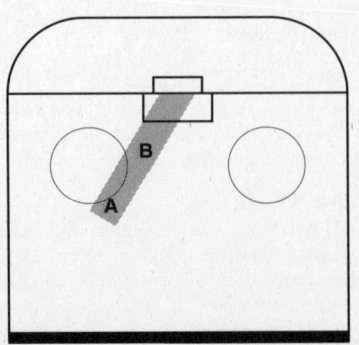

SERGEI KRIVOKRASOV

Yrs. of NHL service: 5
Born: Angarsk, Russia; Apr. 15, 1974
Position: right wing
Height: 5-11
Weight: 185
Uniform no.: 25
Shoots: left

Career statistics:

GP	G	A	TP	PIM
295	67	64	131	188

1995-96 statistics:

GP	G	A	TP	+/-	PIM	PP	SH	GW	GT	S	PCT
46	6	10	16	+10	32	0	0	1	0	52	11.5

1996-97 statistics:

GP	G	A	TP	+/-	PIM	PP	SH	GW	GT	S	PCT
67	13	11	24	-1	42	2	0	3	0	104	12.5

1997-98 statistics:

GP	G	A	TP	+/-	PIM	PP	SH	GW	GT	S	PCT
58	10	13	23	-1	33	1	0	2	0	127	7.9

1998-99 statistics:

GP	G	A	TP	+/-	PIM	PP	SH	GW	GT	S	PCT
70	25	23	48	-5	42	10	0	6	1	208	12.0

LAST SEASON

Led team in goals and game-winning goals. Tied for team lead in power-play goals. Third on team in assists and shooting percentage. Missed 10 games with leg injury. Missed two games with sprained ankle.

THE FINESSE GAME

Krivokrasov is Russian for "exasperating." He is highly skilled but he has never been consistent, even as the first-line right wing for Nashville.

Krivokrasov controls the puck well and reads offensive plays. He will shoot or pass and has good timing in both areas. He draws defenders and opens up ice for a teammate, before dishing off and heading to the net himself for a give-and-go. Sometimes he overhandles the puck, gets too fancy and doesn't shoot when he should. He can score some phenomenal one-on-one goals, but he is tough to play with because he doesn't use his linemates well.

Krivokrasov's skating needs to get a hair quicker. He is strong and will drive to the net. He scores a lot of goals from in tight. He has improved defensively but still has lapses. He can be utterly electrifying, yet he's not a great finisher.

Krivokrasov is a threat on every shift — both ways. Although his defensive play has improved it still has a long way to go.

THE PHYSICAL GAME

On most nights, Krivokrasov is not a physical player and can be intimidated, but other nights he breathes competitive fire and is a force on the ice. He is very strong and stocky.

THE INTANGIBLES

Krivokrasov has major-league talents but never seems to be able to bring his "A" game to the ice every night. He can be a game breaker or a heartbreaker. He gets a little leeway in playing for a new team like the Predators, who are willing to exchange his flaws for 25 goals.

PROJECTION

This is going to be a huge year for Krivokrasov, to see if he can take his game forward another step or if he will tail off. It's likely he'll remain right where he is, in the 25-goal range.

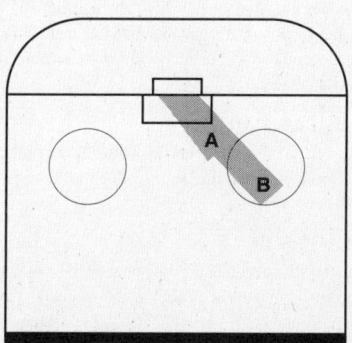

DAVID LEGWAND

Yrs. of NHL service: 0
Born: Detroit, Mich.; Aug. 17, 1980
Position: centre
Height: 6-1 1/2
Weight: 175
Uniform no.: 11
Shoots: left

Career statistics:

GP	G	A	TP	PIM
1	0	0	0	0

1998-99 statistics:

GP	G	A	TP	+/-	PIM	PP	SH	GW	GT	S	PCT
1	0	0	0	0	0	0	0	0	0	2	.0

LAST SEASON
First NHL season. Third in goals (31) and points (80) for Plymouth (OHL).

THE FINESSE GAME
Drafted after Vincent Lecavalier in 1998, Legwand will be linked with Tampa Bay's centre for the first few years of his career, but the parallels just aren't there because they are two very different kinds of players. In fact, move Legwand to left wing and they would probably make very nice linemates.

Legwand is more of a shooter, possibly the best shooter available in the 1998 draft. He handles the puck well in traffic and shoots well in stride. He wants the puck when the game is on the line, because he has that goal scorer's mentality that the team is better off when the puck is on his stick rather than anyone else's. He isn't totally unselfish and is a good passer, but his first option will always be to take the shot.

Legwand is also considered the best skater available from his draft. He's absolutely dynamic. Junior is no longer a challenge, but he is not quite ready for the NHL.

THE PHYSICAL GAME
Legwand has been compared to Mike Modano, but physically and mentally, Legwand is years away from being a Modano type of player (of course, it took Modano six years after his draft to become the kind of player he is now). Legwand is still very boyish in build and needs to get a lot stronger to be able to compete in the NHL.

THE INTANGIBLES
Legwand missed some playing time due to mono, and he was disappointed in being sent back to junior to start the season.

PROJECTION
Legwand will need to take baby steps. He is not ready for the big time yet, although the Predators may give him a shot.

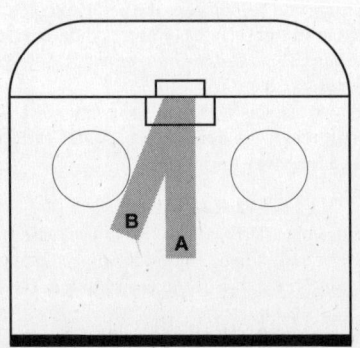

CLIFF RONNING

Yrs. of NHL service: 12
Born: Vancouver, B.C.; Oct. 1, 1965
Position: centre
Height: 5-8
Weight: 170
Uniform no.: 7
Shoots: left

Career statistics:

GP	G	A	TP	PIM
774	216	403	619	333

1995-96 statistics:

GP	G	A	TP	+/-	PIM	PP	SH	GW	GT	S	PCT
79	22	45	67	+16	42	5	0	1	1	187	11.8

1996-97 statistics:

GP	G	A	TP	+/-	PIM	PP	SH	GW	GT	S	PCT
69	19	32	51	-9	26	8	0	2	0	171	11.1

1997-98 statistics:

GP	G	A	TP	+/-	PIM	PP	SH	GW	GT	S	PCT
80	11	44	55	+5	36	3	0	0	1	197	5.6

1998-99 statistics:

GP	G	A	TP	+/-	PIM	PP	SH	GW	GT	S	PCT
79	20	40	60	-3	42	10	0	4	0	257	7.8

LAST SEASON
Led team in assists, points and shots. Tied for team lead in power-play goals. Missed three games due to coach's decision.

THE FINESSE GAME
Ronning's forte is not scoring goals but creating chances for his wingers. He lets bigger linemates attract defenders so that he can dipsy-doodle with the puck. He's quick, shifty and smart . . . he has to be smart, otherwise he'll be flattened along the boards like an advertisement.

Ronning likes to work from behind the net, using the cage as a shield and daring defenders to chase him. Much of his game is a dare. He is a tempting target, and even smaller-sized defensemen fantasize about smashing Ronning to the ice, but he keeps himself out of the trouble spots by dancing in and out of openings and finding free teammates.

A quick thinker and unpredictable, Ronning can curl off the wall into the slot, pass to the corners or the point and jump to the net, or beat a defender wide at the top of the circle and feed a teammate coming into the play late. He's not afraid of going into traffic.

Ronning puts a lot of little dekes into a compact area. He opens up the ice with his bursts of speed and his fakes. Unless the defense can force him along the wall and contain him, he's all over the ice trying to make things happen.

THE PHYSICAL GAME
No one asks jockeys to tackle running backs. Ronning is built for speed and deception. He is smart enough to avoid getting crunched and talented enough to compensate for his lack of strength. He has skills and a huge heart and competes hard every night.

Ronning is so small that usually the best he can do is tug at an opponent like a pesky little brother. He gets involved with his stick, hooking at a puck carrier's arm and worrying at the puck in a player's skates. He keeps the puck in his skates when he protects it, so that a checker will often have to pull Ronning down to get at the puck, which creates a power play.

THE INTANGIBLES
Tough in his own way, Ronning has excelled at a game that everyone told him he was too small to play. He was just what the doctor ordered for an expansion team like Nashville, which had a desperate need for some offense. Ronning came in with the right attitude and saw this move as a big chance for more ice time and responsibility.

PROJECTION
Ronning's forecast in last year's *HSR* was right on the money (60 points, a majority of which were assists). You can stick with those numbers this season as well. He will be Nashville's number one centre again.

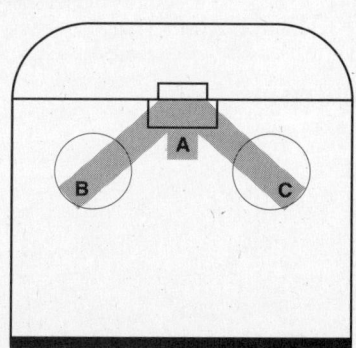

KIMMO TIMONEN

Yrs. of NHL service: 1
Born: Kuopio, Finland; Mar. 18, 1975
Position: left defense
Height: 5-9
Weight: 180
Uniform no.: 44
Shoots: left

Career statistics:

GP	G	A	TP	PIM
50	4	8	12	30

1998-99 statistics:

GP	G	A	TP	+/-	PIM	PP	SH	GW	GT	S	PCT
50	4	8	12	-4	30	1	0	0	0	75	5.3

LAST SEASON

First NHL season. Appeared in 29 games with Milwaukee (IL), scoring 2-13 — 15. Missed one game with facial lacerations.

THE FINESSE GAME

Timonen is the closest thing the Predators have to an offensive defenseman. He has good quickness and adds a lot of skill to the Nashville defense, which doesn't have much in that department. He is not a defensive liability, however, and he has worked to improve the defensive aspects of his game.

Timonen has to produce points because he does not bring enough to the ice in other ways. He is effective on the power-play point. He has competed for Finland in the World Championships, so he has good ability in all offensive areas. He is not elite class, but he moves the puck and sees the ice well.

THE PHYSICAL GAME

Timonen is on the small side and is not very strong. He isn't going to get bigger, so he has to try to get stronger.

THE INTANGIBLES

Timonen will have a job with Nashville and be in a position to get a lot of ice time in key offensive situations, unless his game backslides dramatically. His power play ranked 25th in the league, so getting a role on the top unit shouldn't be a challenge.

PROJECTION

Timonen can score 25 to 30 points.

DARREN TURCOTTE

Yrs. of NHL service: 10
Born: Boston, Mass.; Mar. 2, 1968
Position: centre
Height: 6-0
Weight: 178
Uniform no.: 9
Shoots: left

Career statistics:

GP	G	A	TP	PIM
626	195	215	410	297

1995-96 statistics:

GP	G	A	TP	+/-	PIM	PP	SH	GW	GT	S	PCT
68	22	21	43	+5	30	2	1	4	0	167	13.2

1996-97 statistics:

GP	G	A	TP	+/-	PIM	PP	SH	GW	GT	S	PCT
65	16	21	37	-8	16	3	1	4	0	126	12.7

1997-98 statistics:

GP	G	A	TP	+/-	PIM	PP	SH	GW	GT	S	PCT
62	12	6	18	+6	26	3	0	1	0	75	16.0

1998-99 statistics:

GP	G	A	TP	+/-	PIM	PP	SH	GW	GT	S	PCT
40	4	5	9	-11	16	0	0	1	0	73	5.5

LAST SEASON

Missed 24 games with torn knee ligaments. Missed 15 games with strained knee. Missed two games with back spasms.

THE FINESSE GAME

Balance is the key to Turcotte's contribution to a team; he does a little bit of everything. He is much better on special teams than at even strength, though he is a capable five-on-five player. With the extra open ice — even when his team is shorthanded — he makes things happen. He's a fine skater who appears to hover over the ice. He takes long, fluid strides that cover a lot of territory and creates space with his speed, driving defenders back and daring them to come up to challenge him.

Turcotte kills penalties aggressively. He forces the play and when he gets a turnover he springs down-ice on a break. He makes point men nervous, and teams who use forwards at the point are especially vulnerable to his pressure.

On the power play, Turcotte works down low but can drop back to handle the point if the defenseman comes in deep. He has a fine snap shot, as well as a good wrister and one-timer. He has sharp hand-eye coordination and is skilled on draws. He's a centre who prefers to shoot rather than pass.

THE PHYSICAL GAME

Turcotte will take a hit to make a play but he's not a physical player. He goes into traffic with the puck and has the hand skills to control the puck in a crowd. Still, intimidate him in the first period and you won't see him in the second or third. He wants to be a leader but never seemed to learn how.

THE INTANGIBLES

Turcotte is expected to be ready for the start of the season after knee surgery.

PROJECTION

Turcotte's increasing fragility and declining skills make him a question to score even 30 points.

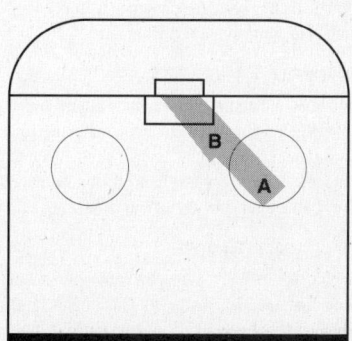

SCOTT WALKER

Yrs. of NHL service: 4
Born: Montreal, Que.; July 19, 1973
Position: right wing
Height: 5-10
Weight: 189
Uniform no.: 24
Shoots: right

Career statistics:
GP	G	A	TP	PIM
268	25	59	84	569

1995-96 statistics:
GP	G	A	TP	+/-	PIM	PP	SH	GW	GT	S	PCT
63	6	7	13	-2	137	0	1	1	0	45	8.9

1996-97 statistics:
GP	G	A	TP	+/-	PIM	PP	SH	GW	GT	S	PCT
64	3	15	18	+2	132	0	0	0	0	55	5.5

1997-98 statistics:
GP	G	A	TP	+/-	PIM	PP	SH	GW	GT	S	PCT
59	3	10	13	-8	164	0	1	1	0	40	7.5

1998-99 statistics:
GP	G	A	TP	+/-	PIM	PP	SH	GW	GT	S	PCT
71	15	25	40	0	103	0	1	2	0	96	15.6

LAST SEASON
Led team in plus-minus and shooting percentage. Third on team in assists. Missed nine games with shoulder injury. Missed two games with ear infection.

THE FINESSE GAME
Walker played defense in junior, but when he started his pro career in Vancouver's system he was switched to right wing, because of his size. He can still be dropped back on defense in an emergency. He is actually versatile enough to play all three forward positions, too. No one's asked him to try goal yet.

Walker has very good speed. He is an excellent penalty killer. He grinds and gets his nose in and doesn't quit on the puck. He played on the checking line but, along with Tom Fitzgerald and Sebastian Bordeleau, was contributing more than his share of points.

He doesn't have great hands, which is why Walker will never be much of an offensive threat, but he works hard for his scoring chances and creates off the forecheck. He gets involved in traffic.

THE PHYSICAL GAME
Walker plays a feisty game. Instead of just stirring things up, he has concentrated on being more of a hockey player, so his penalty minutes have dropped. He still competes every night and has an edge to his game. He can be a pain to play against.

THE INTANGIBLES
Walker is a role player who can add energy and flexibility to a lineup. He has to maintain his consistency and focus to keep his job, as the Predators upgrade their talent.

PROJECTION
Walker made a big leap last season and will have to continue his strong work ethic to repeat his 15 goals.

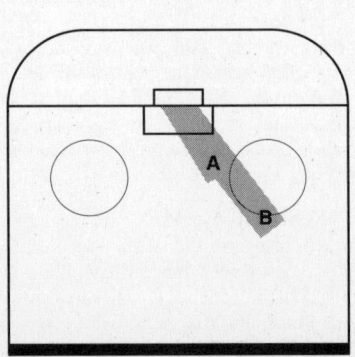

VITALI YACHMENEV

Yrs. of NHL service: 4
Born: Chelyabinsk, USSR; Jan. 8, 1975
Position: R ???
Height: 5-9
Weight: 180
Uniform no.: 43
Shoots: left

Career statistics:

GP	G	A	TP	PIM
204	36	67	103	40

1995-96 statistics:

GP	G	A	TP	+/-	PIM	PP	SH	GW	GT	S	PCT
80	19	34	53	-3	16	6	1	2	0	133	14.3

1996-97 statistics:

GP	G	A	TP	+/-	PIM	PP	SH	GW	GT	S	PCT
65	10	22	32	-9	10	2	0	2	1	97	10.3

1997-98 statistics:

GP	G	A	TP	+/-	PIM	PP	SH	GW	GT	S	PCT
4	0	1	1	+1	4	0	0	0	0	4	0.0

1998-99 statistics:

GP	G	A	TP	+/-	PIM	PP	SH	GW	GT	S	PCT
55	7	10	17	-10	10	0	1	2	0	83	8.4

LAST SEASON

Appeared in 16 games with Milwaukee (IHL), scoring 7-6 — 13. Missed 10 games with shoulder injury.

THE FINESSE GAME

In his rookie year with Los Angeles, Yachmenev played on a line with Wayne Gretzky. It was probably the best and the worst thing to happen to the young player.

Yachmenev's shot is what got him to the NHL. He has a sniper's touch and he has to score, because he doesn't bring much else to the table. He has a tendency to hang onto the puck too long. He has some quickness but no real speed.

He is an intelligent player with good hockey sense who can be used to kill penalties. He is a left-handed shot who plays the right wing; defensively he makes the right play on the wall. He is reliable no matter where he plays.

THE PHYSICAL GAME

Yachmenev isn't very big, but he is strong on his skates and solidly built. He protects the puck well but must show more willingness to fight through traffic.

THE INTANGIBLES

Yachmenev needs to play with linemates who will get him the puck. Unfortunately for him, those players are currently in short supply in Nashville.

PROJECTION

Yachmenev needs to play well enough to earn a spot on the top two lines. He'll never match his Gretzky numbers, but he could score 15 goals.

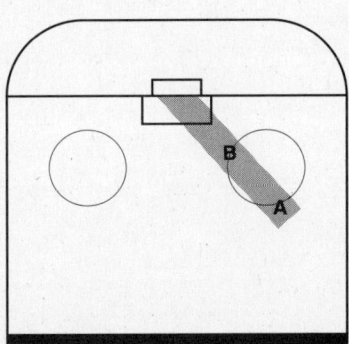

NEW JERSEY DEVILS

Players' Statistics 1998-99

POS	NO.	PLAYER	GP	G	A	PTS	+/-	PIM	PP	SH	GW	GT	S	PCT
C	17	PETR SYKORA	80	29	43	72	16	22	15		7		222	13.1
C	16	BOBBY HOLIK	78	27	37	64	16	119	5		8		253	10.7
L	14	BRIAN ROLSTON	82	24	33	57	11	14	5	5	3		210	11.4
R	25	JASON ARNOTT	74	27	27	54	10	79	8		3	1	200	13.5
L	26	PATRIK ELIAS	74	17	33	50	19	34	3		2		157	10.8
C	9	*BRENDAN MORRISON	76	13	33	46	-4	18	5		2		111	11.7
D	27	SCOTT NIEDERMAYER	72	11	35	46	16	26	1	1	3		161	6.8
R	21	RANDY MCKAY	70	17	20	37	10	143	3		5		136	12.5
D	24	LYLE ODELEIN	70	5	26	31	6	114	1			1	101	5.0
L	23	DAVE ANDREYCHUK	52	15	13	28	1	20	4		3	1	110	13.6
L	20	JAY PANDOLFO	70	14	13	27	3	10	1	1	4		100	14.0
R	8	*VADIM SHARIFIJANOV	53	11	16	27	11	28	1		2		71	15.5
D	4	SCOTT STEVENS	75	5	22	27	29	64			1		111	4.5
C	10	DENIS PEDERSON	76	11	12	23	-10	66	3		1		145	7.6
C	12	SERGEI NEMCHINOV	77	12	8	20	-13	28	2		1		74	16.2
C	18	SERGEI BRYLIN	47	5	10	15	8	28	3		1		51	9.8
L	29	KRZYSZTOF OLIWA	64	5	7	12	4	240			1		59	8.5
D	3	KEN DANEYKO	82	2	9	11	27	63					63	3.2
D	28	KEVIN DEAN	62	1	10	11	4	22	1				51	2.0
C	19	BOB CARPENTER	56	2	8	10	-3	36					69	2.9
D	6	BRAD BOMBARDIR	56	1	7	8	-4	16					47	2.1
D	2	SHELDON SOURAY	70	1	7	8	5	110					101	1.0
G	30	MARTIN BRODEUR	70		4	4	0	4						
L	32	SASHA LAKOVIC	16		3	3	0	59					10	
D	7	KEN SUTTON	5	1		1	1						5	20.0
L	11	*JOHN MADDEN	4		1	1	-2						4	
G	31	CHRIS TERRERI	12		1	1	0							
L	22	SCOTT DANIELS	1					0						

GP = games played; G = goals; A = assists; PTS = points; +/- = goals-for minus goals-against while player is on ice; PIM = penalties in minutes; PP = power-play goals; SH = shorthanded goals; GW = game-winning goals; GT = game-tying goals; S = no. of shots; PCT = percentage of goals to shots; * = rookie

JASON ARNOTT

Yrs. of NHL service: 6
Born: Collingwood, Ont.; Oct. 11, 1974
Position: centre/right wing
Height: 6-3
Weight: 220
Uniform no.: 25
Shoots: right

Career statistics:

GP	G	A	TP	PIM
395	132	176	308	532

1995-96 statistics:

GP	G	A	TP	+/-	PIM	PP	SH	GW	GT	S	PCT
64	28	31	59	-6	87	8	0	5	1	244	11.5

1996-97 statistics:

GP	G	A	TP	+/-	PIM	PP	SH	GW	GT	S	PCT
67	19	38	57	-21	92	10	1	2	1	248	7.7

1997-98 statistics:

GP	G	A	TP	+/-	PIM	PP	SH	GW	GT	S	PCT
70	10	23	33	-24	99	4	0	2	0	199	5.0

1998-99 statistics:

GP	G	A	TP	+/-	PIM	PP	SH	GW	GT	S	PCT
74	27	27	54	+10	79	8	0	3	1	200	13.5

LAST SEASON

Tied for second on team in goals. Second on team in power-play goals. Fourth on team in points. Missed one game with finger injury. Missed one game with thigh injury. Missed two games with flu. Missed one game with foot injury. Missed three games with hip injuries.

THE FINESSE GAME

Petr Sykora must be one hell of a player. Arnott started the season on the fourth line, but once he was put on a line with Sykora his whole future changed.

Part of the difference was due to Arnott's move from right wing to centre, where, quite simply, he's a better player. For a player of his size, Arnott has tremendous skills. As a skater, he has speed, balance, a long stride, plus agility in turning to either side. He has also added muscle to his frame, without losing any edge in his skating. Arnott has one of the hardest shots on the team; last season he used it.

Arnott is a decent passer, although he is better getting the puck late and deep. His timing with passes is fine, as he holds onto the puck until a teammate is in the open. Still, he passes up too many shots. He can play the point on the power play but does not have a quick enough release to be truly effective. Loud shots off the glass are largely useless.

THE PHYSICAL GAME

Arnott can throw his weight around. He is strong and can challenge all but the biggest NHL defensemen — he just doesn't do it frequently enough.

THE INTANGIBLES

Arnott enjoyed the game again last season, probably for the first time since his impressive rookie season in Edmonton.

PROJECTION

Can Arnott do it again? With Sykora at his side for a full season, there is no reason why he can't score 30.

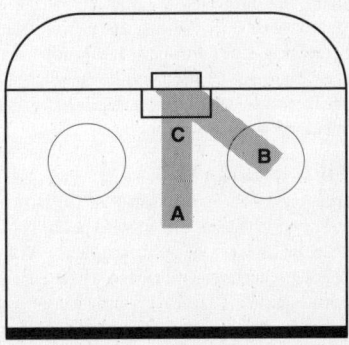

MARTIN BRODEUR

Yrs. of NHL service: 6
Born: Montreal, Que.; May 6, 1972
Position: goaltender
Height: 6-1
Weight: 205
Uniform no.: 30
Catches: left

Career statistics:

GP	MIN	GA	SO	GAA	A	PIM
375	21626	789	36	2.19	14	32

1995-96 statistics:

GP	MIN	GAA	W	L	T	SO	GA	S	SAPCT	PIM
77	4434	2.34	34	30	12	6	173	1954	.911	6

1996-97 statistics:

GP	MIN	GAA	W	L	T	SO	GA	S	SAPCT	PIM
67	3838	1.88	37	14	13	10	120	1633	.927	8

1997-98 statistics:

GP	MIN	GAA	W	L	T	SO	GA	S	SAPCT	PIM
70	4128	1.89	43	17	8	10	130	1569	.917	10

1998-99 statistics:

GP	MIN	GAA	W	L	T	SO	GA	S	SAPCT	PIM
70	4239	2.29	39	21	10	4	162	1728	.906	4

LAST SEASON

Led NHL in wins for second consecutive season. Led NHL in minutes played. Sixth goalie in NHL history to record 30 or more wins for four consecutive seasons. Tied for second among NHL goalies in assists (4).

THE PHYSICAL GAME

Brodeur makes the most of his generous size. He stands upright in the net and squares himself so well to the shooter that he looks enormous. He has become one of the game's best at using his stick around the net. He breaks up passes and will make a quick jab to knock the puck off an opponent's stick.

Opponents want to get Brodeur's feet moving — wraparound plays, rebounds, anything involving his skates exposes his weaknesses. Because of his puck control, Brodeur prevents a lot of scrambles and minimizes his flaws. When he falls into bad streaks, it is usually because of his footwork.

Brodeur has improved his play out of the net, but has to guard against cockiness. He gets carried away with his clearing shots through the middle of the ice, though the majority of the time he handles the puck intelligently and is effective on the penalty kill sending the puck up-ice.

THE MENTAL GAME

Bad games and bad goals don't rattle Brodeur for long. Although he has a tendency to show his frustration on-ice, he also bounces back quickly with strong efforts. He concentrates and doesn't lose his intensity throughout a game. Teammates love playing in front of him because of the confidence he exudes — even through the layers of padding and the mask. When Brodeur is on, his glove saves are snappy and he bounces on his feet with flair.

Although the Devils acquired a veteran backup goalie (Chris Terreri), whom Brodeur likes and trusts, Brodeur was again given too much playing time last season and needs to have his minutes cut.

THE INTANGIBLES

The playoffs raised huge questions about Brodeur's ability to perform under pressure. If he hadn't already won a Cup, there would be doubts about his status as a championship-calibre goalie. But Brodeur has shown that he can do it, although he won't be able to do it again by allowing the kind of stoppable shots that plagued him against Pittsburgh.

PROJECTION

We predicted another 35 wins for Brodeur last season. It's a good habit. No need to break it.

KEN DANEYKO

Yrs. of NHL service: 15
Born: Windsor, Ont.; Apr. 17, 1964
Position: left defense
Height: 6-0
Weight: 210
Uniform no.: 3
Shoots: left

Career statistics:

GP	G	A	TP	PIM
992	34	119	153	2238

1995-96 statistics:

GP	G	A	TP	+/-	PIM	PP	SH	GW	GT	S	PCT
80	2	4	6	-10	115	0	0	0	0	67	3.0

1996-97 statistics:

GP	G	A	TP	+/-	PIM	PP	SH	GW	GT	S	PCT
77	2	7	9	+24	70	0	0	0	1	63	3.2

1997-98 statistics:

GP	G	A	TP	+/-	PIM	PP	SH	GW	GT	S	PCT
37	0	1	1	+3	57	0	0	0	0	18	.0

1998-99 statistics:

GP	G	A	TP	+/-	PIM	PP	SH	GW	GT	S	PCT
82	2	9	11	+27	63	0	0	0	0	63	3.2

LAST SEASON

Second on team in plus-minus. One of two Devils to appear in all 82 games.

THE FINESSE GAME

Break down Daneyko's game — average skater, average passer, below-average shooter — and he looks like someone who would have trouble getting ice time. But the edge is his competitive drive: he will do anything to win a hockey game. Add to that his strength and sound hockey sense, and the result is a powerful defensive defenseman who has been coveted by other teams for many years.

Despite his lack of footwork, Daneyko has evolved into one of his team's top penalty killers. He is a good shot-blocker, though he could still use some improvement. When he goes down and fails to block a shot, he does little more than screen his goalie with his burly body.

A Daneyko rush is a rare thing. He's smart enough to recognize his limitations and he seldom joins the play or gets involved deep in the attacking zone. His offensive involvement is usually limited to a smart, safe breakout pass.

THE PHYSICAL GAME

Daneyko is powerful, with great upper- and lower-body strength. His legs give him drive when he's moving opposing forwards out from around the net. He is a punishing hitter; when he makes a take-out the opponent stays out of the play. He is smart enough not to get beaten by superior skaters and will force an attacker to the perimeter. He has cut down on his bad penalties. Emotions still sometimes get the better of him, but he will usually get his two or five minutes' worth.

Daneyko is a formidable fighter, a player few are willing to tangle with, so he now has to prove himself less frequently. If somebody wants a scrap, though, he's willing and extremely able, and he stands up for his teammates. It helps that players such as Randy McKay and Krzysztof Oliwa are on hand, so that he can spend more time on the ice than in the box.

THE INTANGIBLES

Daneyko is a classic throwback to an era when guys dragged themselves onto the ice and played on fractured ankles. Despite his age, he is in exceptional shape. He truly takes the game of hockey to heart.

PROJECTION

Although he will face a challenge from younger defensemen like Sheldon Souray, Brad Bombardir and Colin White, Daneyko is a survivor and a likely Devils lifer.

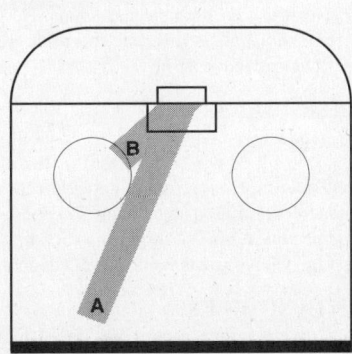

PATRIK ELIAS

Yrs. of NHL service: 2
Born: Trebic, Czech Republic; Apr. 13, 1976
Position: left wing
Height: 6-0
Weight: 195
Uniform no.: 26
Shoots: left

Career statistics:
GP	G	A	TP	PIM
166	37	55	92	64

1995-96 statistics:
GP	G	A	TP	+/-	PIM	PP	SH	GW	GT	S	PCT
1	0	0	0	-1	0	0	0	0	0	2	0.0

1996-97 statistics:
GP	G	A	TP	+/-	PIM	PP	SH	GW	GT	S	PCT
17	2	3	5	-4	28	0	0	0	0	23	8.6

1997-98 statistics:
GP	G	A	TP	+/-	PIM	PP	SH	GW	GT	S	PCT
74	18	19	37	+19	28	5	0	6	1	147	12.2

1998-99 statistics:
GP	G	A	TP	+/-	PIM	PP	SH	GW	GT	S	PCT
74	17	33	50	+19	34	3	0	2	0	157	10.8

LAST SEASON
Second NHL season. Third on team in plus-minus. Missed five games with flu. Missed three games due to coach's decision.

THE FINESSE GAME
Having played centre in the Devils' farm system, Elias brings a centre's creativity and playmaking sensibility to the wing. His primary assets are his skating and a powerful shot, which he can let rip on the fly. The less Elias thinks, the better. Once he starts to feel comfortable in his role he will let the game come to him naturally. He is not quite a power forward, though he is strong enough to muscle his way into traffic areas for scoring chances. He has an excellent release on his wrist shot.

Elias falls into bad slumps where he fails to get shots away on net. This is either a byproduct of his tendency to look for a pass first, or a lapse in his confidence.

Elias can work on both special teams. He is reliable defensively and is a threat to create scoring chances off shorthanded rushes.

THE PHYSICAL GAME
Elias has good upper-body strength for work along the boards and good lower-body strength for skating speed and balance. He is tough to knock off his skates and plays with controlled aggression. He doesn't take many bad penalties, but will bring his stick up or take a swing if he believes he is being taken advantage of.

THE INTANGIBLES
For the second straight season, Elias hit a late-season wall. If this trend continues, consider him a first-half pool player and trade him by the All-Star break to someone unsuspecting.

PROJECTION
Given his ice time and the privilege of playing with Petr Sykora, Elias has to produce 20 to 25 goals or be in danger of losing his prime slot.

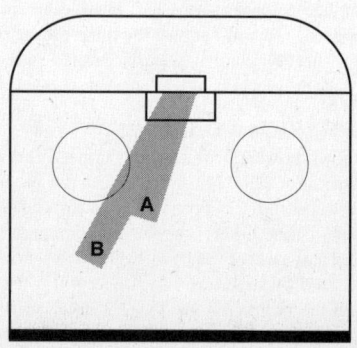

BOBBY HOLIK

Yrs. of NHL service: 9
Born: Jihlava, Czech Republic; Jan. 1, 1971
Position: centre
Height: 6-3
Weight: 220
Uniform no.: 16
Shoots: right

Career statistics:

GP	G	A	TP	PIM
638	177	224	401	654

1995-96 statistics:

GP	G	A	TP	+/-	PIM	PP	SH	GW	GT	S	PCT
63	13	17	30	+9	58	1	0	1	1	157	8.3

1996-97 statistics:

GP	G	A	TP	+/-	PIM	PP	SH	GW	GT	S	PCT
82	23	39	62	+24	54	5	0	6	0	192	12.0

1997-98 statistics:

GP	G	A	TP	+/-	PIM	PP	SH	GW	GT	S	PCT
82	29	36	65	+23	100	8	0	8	1	238	12.2

1998-99 statistics:

GP	G	A	TP	+/-	PIM	PP	SH	GW	GT	S	PCT
78	27	37	64	+16	119	5	0	8	0	253	10.7

LAST SEASON

Led team in shots and game-winning goals. Tied for third in NHL in game-winning goals. Second on team in assists and points. Tied for second on team in goals. Third on team in penalty minutes. Missed two games with suspension for tripping/slewfoot. Missed two games with suspension for slashing.

THE FINESSE GAME

Holik is limited as a creative playmaker, because he lacks vision, but he knows where longtime linemate Randy McKay is headed: to the corners or to the net. Holik plays a fairly straightforward power game. He does not play well when forced to carry the puck. His, and McKay's, best style is dump-and-chase, cycle and create off the forecheck.

Holik has a terrific shot, a bullet drive that he gets away quickly from a rush down the left side. He also has great hands for working in tight, in traffic and off the backhand. On the backhand (at which Europeans are so much more adept than North Americans), Holik uses his bulk to obscure the vision of his defenders, protecting the puck and masking his intentions. He has a fair wrist shot.

He's a powerful skater with good balance, but lacks jump and agility. Once he starts churning, Holik can get up a good head of steam yet can be caught out of position. He is more responsible defensively.

THE PHYSICAL GAME

Holik is just plain big. And mean. He's a serious hitter who can hurt and who applies his bone-jarring body checks at the appropriate times. He takes some bad penalties, and he can be easily frustrated when he feels he is being hooked and held and the opposition isn't penalized.

THE INTANGIBLES

Holik was again quiet at all the wrong times for the Devils — down the stretch and into the playoffs. Two straight seasons of this should have New Jersey seriously rethinking its centre-ice depth.

PROJECTION

Holik was rewarded with a new contract prior to last season and didn't stagger under the burden, but why does that 30-goal mark frighten this fearless athlete so much?

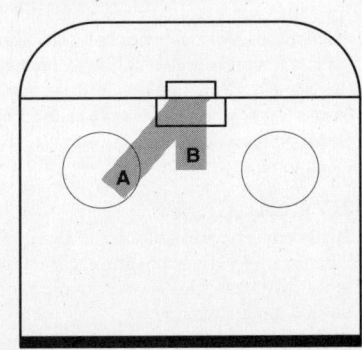

RANDY MCKAY

Yrs. of NHL service: 10
Born: Montreal, Que.; Jan. 25, 1967
Position: right wing
Height: 6-1
Weight: 205
Uniform no.: 21
Shoots: right

Career statistics:

GP	G	A	TP	PIM
644	110	134	244	1457

1995-96 statistics:

GP	G	A	TP	+/-	PIM	PP	SH	GW	GT	S	PCT
76	11	10	21	+7	145	3	0	3	1	97	11.3

1996-97 statistics:

GP	G	A	TP	+/-	PIM	PP	SH	GW	GT	S	PCT
77	9	18	27	+15	109	0	0	2	0	92	9.8

1997-98 statistics:

GP	G	A	TP	+/-	PIM	PP	SH	GW	GT	S	PCT
74	24	24	48	+30	86	8	0	5	0	141	17.0

1998-99 statistics:

GP	G	A	TP	+/-	PIM	PP	SH	GW	GT	S	PCT
70	17	20	37	+10	143	3	0	5	0	136	12.5

LAST SEASON

Second on team in penalty minutes. Missed four games with groin injury. Missed five games with infected elbow/flu. Missed one game with back injury. Missed one game with knee injury. Missed one game due to coach's decision.

THE FINESSE GAME

There is never a lack of effort on McKay's part. His reputation earns him extra ice and extra time, and he makes use of both. He is one of those rare tough guys who has enough skills to make himself a useful player in other areas, including the power play. He has the ability to beat a defender one-on-one by setting his skates wide, dangling the puck, then drawing it through the defenseman's legs and blowing past him for a shot.

McKay is also alert enough to find a linemate with a pass. He doesn't have great hockey vision, but he doesn't keep his eyes glued to the puck, either. Still, most of his points come from driving to the net.

The problem for McKay comes in the assessments of him as an overachieving fourth liner, which is how he made his name, or weighing him as the second-line winger on the team, which is how he is used by the Devils, probably to his detriment. He doesn't have the scoring touch to be a top six forward.

THE PHYSICAL GAME

McKay has become so valuable to the Devils in his new role that he rarely drops his gloves. Even though he is an absolutely ferocious fighter, don't expect to see him duking it out anymore.

That doesn't mean McKay is any less intense. He is astoundingly strong on his skates, tough to knock down and nearly impossible to knock out. His problems arise when he plays too fancy and thinks about being a goal scorer instead of working for his chances.

THE INTANGIBLES

McKay makes everyone around him braver. He will leap to the defense of a teammate, yet he seldom gets involved in histrionics. Coaches never have to worry about McKay being up for a game.

PROJECTION

To be judged a success as a number two winger, McKay needs better numbers — like a 25-goal season. It's possible if he and Bobby Holik find the right left wing.

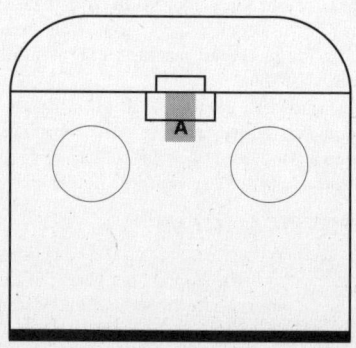

BRENDAN MORRISON

Yrs. of NHL service: 1
Born: North Vancouver, B.C.; Aug. 12, 1975
Position: centre
Height: 5-11
Weight: 180
Uniform no.: 9
Shoots: left

Career statistics:

GP	G	A	TP	PIM
87	18	37	55	18

1997-98 statistics:

GP	G	A	TP	+/-	PIM	PP	SH	GW	GT	S	PCT
11	5	4	9	+3	0	0	0	1	1	19	26.3

1998-99 statistics:

GP	G	A	TP	+/-	PIM	PP	SH	GW	GT	S	PCT
76	13	33	46	-4	18	5	0	2	0	111	11.7

LAST SEASON

First NHL season. Second among NHL rookies in assists and points. Led NHL rookies in power-play points (20). Tied for sixth among NHL rookies in goals. Tied for second among NHL rookies in power-play goals. Missed six games due to coach's decision.

THE FINESSE GAME

Morrison's hockey sense and vision are outstanding. He works especially well with players of a similar mind, like Petr Sykora and Patrik Elias, but he wasn't able to play much with that calibre of player at even strength last season. Much of his offensive production came in his role as a power-play specialist.

Morrison has soft hands for passing and he isn't shy about shooting, using a selection of deceptive and accurate shots. He can work low on the power play or at the point, and he sees all of his options quickly. He doesn't panic and is poised with the puck.

He is a strong skater with balance, quickness, agility and breakaway speed. Morrison made the adjustment to the NHL speed fairly easily.

THE PHYSICAL GAME

Small but wise enough to stay out of trouble, Morrison has wiry strength for playing in the high traffic areas. He loves to create plays from behind the net, and the two extra feet will make it tougher to defend against him. He plays with a little edge to him that demonstrates he will not be intimidated. He is strong on his skates and tough to knock off-balance.

THE INTANGIBLES

Morrison is a potential candidate to become the Devils' number one centre, though he might not be ready for that step yet (given the checking attention he would face). He also needs to work more diligently on his defensive role if he is to face other teams' top centres, but Morrison has a quiet confidence that makes us believe he can do the job.

PROJECTION

Morrison just missed the 50-point target we projected for his rookie season. He racked up fairly impressive numbers given his part-time status. Since he will continue to see first-unit power-play shifts, an upgrade to 55 to 60 points is likely.

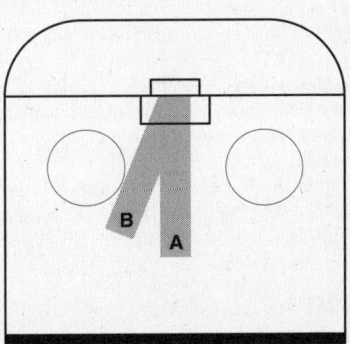

SERGEI NEMCHINOV

Yrs. of NHL service: 15
Born: Moscow, Russia; Jan. 14, 1964
Position: centre
Height: 6-0
Weight: 200
Uniform no.: 12
Shoots: left

Career statistics:
GP	G	A	TP	PIM
575	129	150	279	207

1995-96 statistics:
GP	G	A	TP	+/-	PIM	PP	SH	GW	GT	S	PCT
78	17	15	32	+9	38	0	0	2	0	118	14.4

1996-97 statistics:
GP	G	A	TP	+/-	PIM	PP	SH	GW	GT	S	PCT
69	8	16	24	+9	16	1	0	2	0	97	8.2

1997-98 statistics:
GP	G	A	TP	+/-	PIM	PP	SH	GW	GT	S	PCT
74	10	19	29	+3	24	2	1	1	0	94	10.6

1998-99 statistics:
GP	G	A	TP	+/-	PIM	PP	SH	GW	GT	S	PCT
77	12	8	20	-13	28	2	0	1	0	74	16.2

LAST SEASON
Acquired from N.Y. Islanders for fourth-round draft pick in 1999, Mar. 22, 1999. Led Devils in shooting percentage. Missed six games with hip injuries. Missed two games with knee injuries.

THE FINESSE GAME
If there is a five-on-three against, this is the forward who is sent out for the draw. Nemchinov backchecks well: coming back on his man, throwing him off-stride with a shoulder-check, collecting the puck and then trying to do something with it.

Nemchinov has the hand skills to play with almost any finesse player. He is very fond of the backhand shot but isn't as accurate as he wants to be most of the time. Just as his strength powers his defensive game, it is critical to his offensive game as well, such as it is. He will win a battle for the puck along the boards, with his stick or his skates, muscle it into the scoring zone and create a chance. He is strong enough, also, to get away a shot when his stick is being held or when he is fending off a checker. He lacks only a finishing touch.

Nemchinov carries the puck in a classic fashion, well to the side, which makes him much more difficult to forecheck. He is unpredictable in whether he will shoot or pass, because the puck is always ready for either option and he does not telegraph his moves.

He isn't a dazzling skater, but he is strong and balanced and is a dedicated chopper. His leg strength makes him sneaky-fast.

THE PHYSICAL GAME
Powerfully built, Nemchinov forechecks with zest and drives through the boards and the corners. Linemates have to be alert because he will churn up loose pucks. He is adept at holding an opponent's stick when the two players are tied up in a corner, and his body shields the infraction from the officials. He takes every hit and keeps coming. Nemchinov is as mentally tough as any player in the league. He is enormously strong and never stops competing.

He gets checking assignments against big centres and more than holds his own. He always seems to pin an opponent's stick to the ice at the last second when a pass is arriving in a quality scoring area. He blocks shots, hits, takes hits to make plays and ties up his opposing centre on draws.

THE INTANGIBLES
Don't mistake his stoicism for lack of emotion or intensity. Nemchinov is a quiet leader, and a player of character who is committed to winning. He will probably inherit a lot of the checking responsibility left after the Devils cut Bob Carpenter loose.

PROJECTION
Nemchinov is becoming more and more of a defensive specialist, so 20 goals would be the optimistic top end for him.

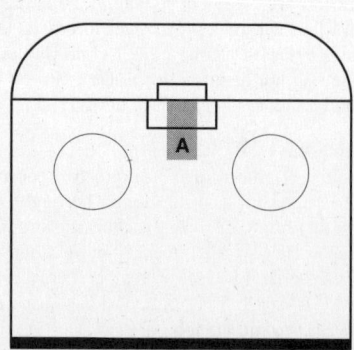

SCOTT NIEDERMAYER

Yrs. of NHL service: 7
Born: Edmonton, Alta.; Aug. 31, 1973
Position: right defense
Height: 6-0
Weight: 200
Uniform no.: 27
Shoots: left

Career statistics:

GP	G	A	TP	PIM
526	63	214	277	272

1995-96 statistics:

GP	G	A	TP	+/-	PIM	PP	SH	GW	GT	S	PCT
79	8	25	33	+5	46	6	0	0	0	179	4.5

1996-97 statistics:

GP	G	A	TP	+/-	PIM	PP	SH	GW	GT	S	PCT
81	5	30	35	-4	64	3	0	3	0	159	3.1

1997-98 statistics:

GP	G	A	TP	+/-	PIM	PP	SH	GW	GT	S	PCT
81	14	43	57	+5	27	11	0	1	0	175	8.0

1998-99 statistics:

GP	G	A	TP	+/-	PIM	PP	SH	GW	GT	S	PCT
72	11	35	46	+16	26	1	1	3	0	161	6.8

LAST SEASON
Led team defensemen in scoring for fourth consecutive season. Third on team in assists. Missed nine games due to contract dispute. Missed one game due to personal reasons.

THE FINESSE GAME
Niedermayer is poised on that border that separates the truly elite offensive defensemen (Brian Leetch, Al MacInnis) from the wannabes, and we're not so sure he is going to make it across.

Niedermayer carries the puck well on the rush. The 26-year-old is an exceptional skater, one of the best-skating defensemen in the NHL. He has it all: speed, balance, agility, mobility, lateral movement and strength. Plus he has unbelievable edge for turns and eluding pursuers. That said, Niedermayer doesn't seem to have the vision that the great ones have, or the snakey lateral movement that makes a point shot so dangerous.

But Niedermayer is a far better defensive player than many of the other top scorers at his position. Even when he makes a commitment mistake in the offensive zone, he can get back so quickly his defense partner is seldom outnumbered.

THE PHYSICAL GAME
An underrated body checker because of the focus on the glitzier parts of his game, Niedermayer has continued to improve his strength and is a willing, if not vicious, hitter. His skating ability helps him tremendously, giving more impetus to his open-ice checks. He makes rubouts along the wall. He would rather be in open ice but he will pay the price in the trenches. He knows the defensive game well.

THE INTANGIBLES
It's laughable every time a Niedermayer trade rumour pops up. Sure, any other NHL team would want him, but he is virtually impossible for the Devils to deal because of his unique blend of talent. There is not a player like him in their system, or in anyone else's.

PROJECTION
Niedermayer continues to mature into an excellent all-around defenseman. With no contract dispute on this year's horizon, he can be expected to post a 55- to 60-point season.

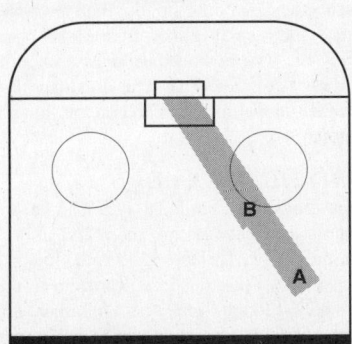

LYLE ODELEIN

Yrs. of NHL service: 9
Born: Quill Lake, Sask.; July 21, 1968
Position: right defense
Height: 5-11
Weight: 210
Uniform no.: 24
Shoots: left

Career statistics:

GP	G	A	TP	PIM
648	32	133	165	1762

1995-96 statistics:

GP	G	A	TP	+/-	PIM	PP	SH	GW	GT	S	PCT
79	3	14	17	+8	230	0	1	0	0	74	4.1

1996-97 statistics:

GP	G	A	TP	+/-	PIM	PP	SH	GW	GT	S	PCT
79	3	13	16	+16	110	1	0	2	0	93	3.2

1997-98 statistics:

GP	G	A	TP	+/-	PIM	PP	SH	GW	GT	S	PCT
79	4	19	23	+11	171	1	0	0	0	76	5.3

1998-99 statistics:

GP	G	A	TP	+/-	PIM	PP	SH	GW	GT	S	PCT
70	5	26	31	+6	114	1	0	0	1	101	5.0

LAST SEASON

Second among team defensemen in scoring. Missed nine games with knee injury. Missed two games with flu. Missed one game due to personal reasons.

THE FINESSE GAME

Defense is Odelein's forte. He is very calm with the puck and able to wait until a player is on top of him, then carry the puck or find an open man. His skating is average at best, but he keeps himself out of trouble by playing a conservative game and not getting caught out of position. An attacker who comes into Odelein's piece of the ice will have to pay the price by getting through him.

Odelein's finesse skills are modest at best, but he has developed sufficient confidence to get involved in the attack if needed. He prefers to limit his contribution to shots from the point.

Odelein deserves credit for having molded himself into more than an overachieving goon. He is a physical presence despite being smaller than most NHL defensemen — and smaller than many NHL forwards. He played his best hockey last season once he was paired with Scott Stevens. The duo usually plays against other teams' top lines and on the first penalty-killing unit.

THE PHYSICAL GAME

Odelein is a banger, a limited player who knows what those limits are, stays within them and plays effectively as a result. He's rugged and doesn't take chances. He takes the man at all times in front of the net and he plays tough. Heavy but not tall, he gives the impression of being a much bigger man. He will fight, but not very well.

Odelein can be taken off his game easily and gets caught up in yapping matches, which does his game no good.

THE INTANGIBLES

Odelein is likely to be the next victim of the Devils' youth movement; it would be a surprise to see him still in a New Jersey uniform in the playoffs.

PROJECTION

Odelein will give you minutes on the ice and in the box. He won't give you points, but that's not what he's here for.

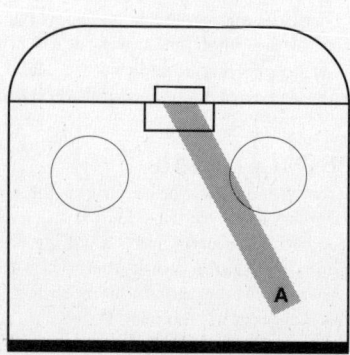

DENIS PEDERSON

Yrs. of NHL service: 3
Born: Prince Albert, Sask.; Sept. 10, 1975
Position: centre/left wing
Height: 6-2
Weight: 190
Uniform no.: 10
Shoots: right

Career statistics:

GP	G	A	TP	PIM
236	41	46	87	225

1995-96 statistics:

GP	G	A	TP	+/-	PIM	PP	SH	GW	GT	S	PCT
10	3	1	4	-1	0	1	0	2	0	6	50.0

1996-97 statistics:

GP	G	A	TP	+/-	PIM	PP	SH	GW	GT	S	PCT
70	12	20	32	+7	62	3	0	3	0	106	11.3

1997-98 statistics:

GP	G	A	TP	+/-	PIM	PP	SH	GW	GT	S	PCT
80	15	13	28	-6	97	7	0	1	1	135	11.1

1998-99 statistics:

GP	G	A	TP	+/-	PIM	PP	SH	GW	GT	S	PCT
76	11	12	23	-10	66	3	0	1	0	145	7.6

LAST SEASON
Missed six games with back injuries.

THE FINESSE GAME
Pederson is so good at doing so many things that the team seldom leaves him alone to excel in one area. He will be asked to centre a rough-and-tumble fourth line, work on a checking line and score as a winger on a top line. He can perform capably in all roles, but needs to find a niche. Maybe with Bob Carpenter finally out of the picture, the Devils will open up a third-line centre's role for Pederson.

Pederson is an intelligent hockey player who has the potential to develop into a solid two-way centre. His skills aren't elite level, but he makes the most of all of his abilities with his hockey sense. He showed some heady flashes of playmaking and is alert around the net for loose pucks. Most of his goals come from hard work around the cage, not pretty rushing plays.

Pederson can work on the power play, where he uses his size down low and crashes the net. He works well in traffic, and has nice hands for picking the puck out of a tangle of skates and sticks. He is a puck magnet because he gives a second and third effort; the puck always seems to end up on his stick. He has a decent array of shots, including a backhand and a wrist shot, the latter being his best weapon.

THE PHYSICAL GAME
Pederson is strong and competes hard for the puck. He has a little bit of a mean streak in him, enough to keep his opponents on their toes, and he will come unglued once in awhile. But for the most part he is a disciplined player and does not take lazy penalties. He protects the puck well with his body.

Pederson is still gaining size and strength. He should have the goods to compete against any team's power forwards on a nightly basis.

THE INTANGIBLES
Pederson is so quiet off the ice, but is a season or two away from making a lot of noise on the ice. This kid was a scorer in junior, so don't pigeonhole him as strictly a defensive player. He is a character guy and a quiet leader, with a sound work ethic.

PROJECTION
What we like about Pederson is that he's not dainty. He will get down and dirty and earn his ice time honestly. He has a lot to learn yet, but a 20- to 25-goal season would not surprise us if he earns a full-time role in training camp.

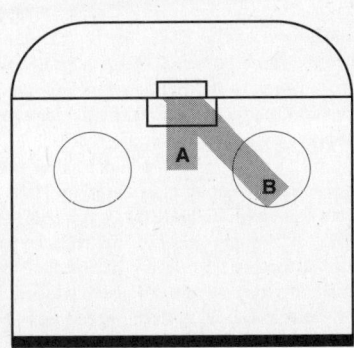

BRIAN ROLSTON

Yrs. of NHL service: 5
Born: Flint, Mich.; Feb. 21, 1973
Position: left wing
Height: 6-2
Weight: 185
Uniform no.: 14
Shoots: left

Career statistics:

GP	G	A	TP	PIM
337	78	96	174	75

1995-96 statistics:

GP	G	A	TP	+/-	PIM	PP	SH	GW	GT	S	PCT
58	13	11	24	+9	8	3	1	4	1	139	9.4

1996-97 statistics:

GP	G	A	TP	+/-	PIM	PP	SH	GW	GT	S	PCT
81	18	27	45	+6	20	2	2	3	0	237	7.6

1997-98 statistics:

GP	G	A	TP	+/-	PIM	PP	SH	GW	GT	S	PCT
76	16	14	30	+7	16	0	2	1	0	185	8.6

1998-99 statistics:

GP	G	A	TP	+/-	PIM	PP	SH	GW	GT	S	PCT
82	24	33	57	+11	14	5	5	3	0	210	11.4

LAST SEASON

Led team in shorthanded goals for second consecutive season. Tied for NHL lead in shorthanded goals. Third on team in shots. One of two Devils to appear in all 82 games. Career highs in goals, assists and points.

THE FINESSE GAME

Rolston will get into goal-scoring grooves in the season, then just as maddeningly will lurch into a slump that lasts weeks. As a shooter, he can be woefully impatient. He has a cannon from the top of the circles in with a quick release. But he tends to hurry his shots, even when he has time to wait, which results in wildly inaccurate shots. He wastes many odd-man-rush opportunities, especially shorthanded ones, by not forcing the goalie to handle the puck and denying the trailing player an opportunity at a rebound. Rolston was third on the team in shots on goal but he probably led them in shots at goal — shots that went off the glass or into the crowd. Watching Rolston waste one scoring opportunity after another is an exercise in rapid-fire frustration.

Rolston's game is speed. He is a fast, powerful skater who drives to the net and loves to shoot. He passes well on his forehand and backhand, and reads breakout plays by leading his man smartly.

Rolston is an aggressive penalty killer who deserves some Selke Trophy consideration. He uses his quick getaway stride to pull away for shorthanded breaks. He takes some pride in this role, and works diligently. Although he doesn't like it, he has been shoehorned into the role of a defensive winger, and he is one of the few Devils with the speed and sense to match strides with a Jaromir Jagr or Pavel Bure.

THE PHYSICAL GAME

Rolston will take a hit to make a play, and has taken the next step to start initiating fights for pucks. He can be intimidated, however, and the Devils are leery of his lack of grit. His better games are against skating clubs rather than Devil clones.

THE INTANGIBLES

Rolston chafed under former coach Jacques Lemaire and was a much happier player under Robbie Ftorek. You saw the results on the ice in Rolston's best season.

PROJECTION

Rolston nearly cracked the 25-goal barrier. He looks like he should score 30, but 20 is more his limit.

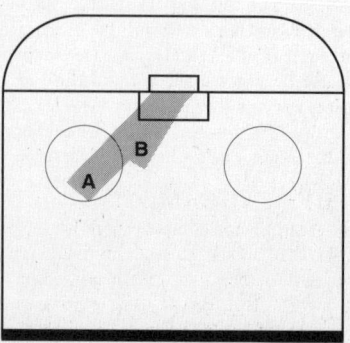

SHELDON SOURAY

Yrs. of NHL service: 2
Born: Elk Point, Alberta; July 7, 1976
Position: right defense
Height: 6-4
Weight: 235
Uniform no.: 2
Shoots: left

Career statistics:

GP	G	A	TP	PIM
130	4	14	18	195

1997-98 statistics:

GP	G	A	TP	+/-	PIM	PP	SH	GW	GT	S	PCT
60	3	7	10	+18	85	0	0	1	0	74	4.0

1998-99 statistics:

GP	G	A	TP	+/-	PIM	PP	SH	GW	GT	S	PCT
70	1	7	8	+5	110	0	0	0	0	101	1.0

LAST SEASON
Second NHL season. Missed 12 games due to coach's decision.

THE FINESSE GAME
Souray has worked hard on his skating but still needs improvement in his turns and his lateral movement. He has good straightaway speed once he gets going. He is very strong on his skates for corner and board work, which he relishes.

Souray plays a conservative style — maybe too conservative, since he looks hesitant at times about his defensive assignments. Being coached by Larry Robinson this year is not going to hurt his development. He has some finesse skills and as he gains more experience and confidence, he could become a point man on the second power-play unit. He has a heavy point shot and isn't shy about teeing it up.

Souray blocks shots and plays a fairly sound positional game, though he will get rattled in his coverage now and then.

THE PHYSICAL GAME
Souray is an imposing physical specimen and an all-around athlete. He is a little too hair-trigger in coming to the aid of his teammates, but that beats the opposite reaction. He is a good fighter and excells in a physical game. He has a major-league mean streak. Souray laid a serious hit on Toronto's Alyn McCauley late last season that unintentionally ended the Leaf player's season with a concussion.

THE INTANGIBLES
Souray shot up the Devils' depth chart, and he can get too comfortable once he feels he has a job won. With a number of excellent young defensemen vying for jobs this season, complacency should not be an issue. Souray is still young and raw, but he was one of the first players other teams were interested in.

PROJECTION
Souray could score 20 points in a full-time role.

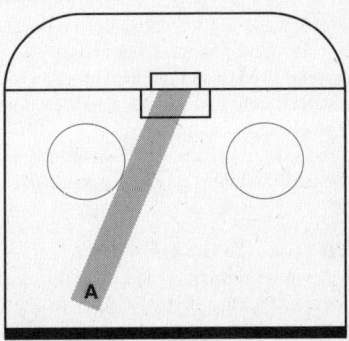

SCOTT STEVENS

Yrs. of NHL service: 17
Born: Kitchener, Ont.; Apr. 1, 1964
Position: left defense
Height: 6-2
Weight: 210
Uniform no.: 4
Shoots: left

Career statistics:

GP	G	A	TP	PIM
1275	171	628	799	2458

1995-96 statistics:

GP	G	A	TP	+/-	PIM	PP	SH	GW	GT	S	PCT
82	5	23	28	+7	100	2	1	1	0	174	2.9

1996-97 statistics:

GP	G	A	TP	+/-	PIM	PP	SH	GW	GT	S	PCT
79	5	19	24	+26	70	0	0	1	0	166	3.0

1997-98 statistics:

GP	G	A	TP	+/-	PIM	PP	SH	GW	GT	S	PCT
80	4	22	26	+19	80	1	0	1	0	94	4.3

1998-99 statistics:

GP	G	A	TP	+/-	PIM	PP	SH	GW	GT	S	PCT
75	5	22	27	+29	64	0	0	1	0	111	4.5

LAST SEASON

Led team in plus-minus. Missed five games with groin injury. Missed one game with flu. Missed one game with back injury.

THE FINESSE GAME

A very good skater, Stevens is secure and strong, capable both forwards and backwards and with good lateral mobility. He has a tendency to overhandle the puck in the defensive zone, though. Instead of quickly banging the puck off the boards to clear the zone, it seems to take Stevens an unusual amount of time to get the puck teed up and it's often kept in by the attacking team. Stevens then digs in twice as hard to win the puck back, but he often creates more work for himself.

Stevens has a tremendous work ethic that more than makes up for some of his shortcomings (and most of those are sins of commission rather than omission). He is a bear on penalty killing because he just won't quit, and he is a fearless shot-blocker. Stevens occasionally gets suckered into chasing the puck carrier behind the net at inopportune moments.

Opponents used to delight in goading a young, immature Stevens into taking bad penalties. The tactic can still be effective.

Stevens's offensive contributions to a game have all but vanished. Did this guy really score 78 points in 1993-94?

THE PHYSICAL GAME

One of the most punishing open-ice hitters in the NHL, Stevens has the skating ability to line up the puck carrier, and the size and strength to explode on impact. He simply shovels most opponents out from in front of the net and crunches them along the boards. He is one of the few NHL defensemen willing and able to tackle Eric Lindros head-on. Most of Stevens's best games occur against the Flyers because he thrives on the challenge. By contrast, some of the league's quicker, sleeker forwards can make him look silly.

THE INTANGIBLES

Stevens is a captain because of his leadership by example, but he is an introspective and sometimes moody individual. He takes great pride in his physical conditioning, but someone (returning assistant coach Larry Robinson?) is going to have to tell this guy to sit down during the regular season and stop playing so many minutes, because the cracks keep showing in the playoffs.

PROJECTION

Perhaps the best defenseman never to win the Norris Trophy, Stevens's skills may be on the wane, but he can still play at the top of his defensive game at crunch time. The point totals are negligible.

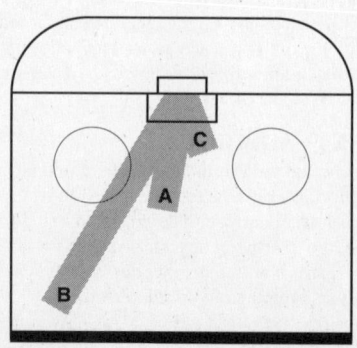

PETR SYKORA

Yrs. of NHL service: 4
Born: Plzen, Czech Republic; Nov. 19, 1976
Position: centre
Height: 5-11
Weight: 185
Uniform no.: 17
Shoots: left

Career statistics:

GP	G	A	TP	PIM
142	35	46	81	58

1995-96 statistics:

GP	G	A	TP	+/-	PIM	PP	SH	GW	GT	S	PCT
63	18	24	42	+7	32	8	0	3	0	128	14.1

1996-97 statistics:

GP	G	A	TP	+/-	PIM	PP	SH	GW	GT	S	PCT
19	1	2	3	-8	4	0	0	0	0	26	3.8

1997-98 statistics:

GP	G	A	TP	+/-	PIM	PP	SH	GW	GT	S	PCT
58	16	20	36	0	22	3	1	4	0	130	12.3

1998-99 statistics:

GP	G	A	TP	+/-	PIM	PP	SH	GW	GT	S	PCT
2	0	0	0	-1	0	0	0	0	0	2	.0

LAST SEASON

Led team in goals, assists, points and power-play goals, all career highs. Second on team in game-winning goals and shots. Tied for fifth in NHL in power-play goals. Missed two games with food poisoning.

THE FINESSE GAME

Sykora has excellent hands in tight, for passing or shooting. He defies the usual European stereotype of the reluctant shooter because he's a goal scorer, but he does tend to pass up a low-percentage shot to work for a better one. His wrist shot is excellent, he also has an adequate snap and slap shot. He is one of the Devils' better power-play specialists.

There are only a few things Sykora doesn't do well technically, but what really sets him apart is his intelligence. Playing against men as a 17-year-old in the IHL in 1994-95 obviously spurred his development, and taught him how to survive as a smaller player in the mean NHL.

Sykora is a fine skater. He has a fluid stride and he accelerates in a few steps. He is quick on a straight-away, with or without the puck, and is also agile in his turns. He picks his way through traffic well, and would rather try to outfox a defender and take the shortest path to the net than drive wide.

Sykora sees the ice well and is a heads-up passer with a great touch. He needs to improve on his face-offs. His defensive play has improved, though he blew a few key assignments at crucial points last season. He can be used to kill penalties because of his ability to read the play and his quickness.

THE PHYSICAL GAME

Sykora won't be intimidated. He'll battle for the puck behind or in front of the net but he is simply not a big or mean player. He is strong for his size and his skating provides him with good balance. His work ethic is strong.

THE INTANGIBLES

Like many young players, Sykora needs to develop consistency. Former Devils coach Jacques Lemaire thought that Sykora and Patrik Elias provided too much of the same quality — as if too much skating, vision and scoring were a bad thing. Sykora brought a centre's sense to the right wing last season, and he made a perfect complement for the less complex play of big centre Jason Arnott.

PROJECTION

Sykora far surpassed the 55 points we anticipated for him last season. He needs someone to help take some of the checking pressure off him as the Devils' number one offensive threat if he is to duplicate his breakthrough season.

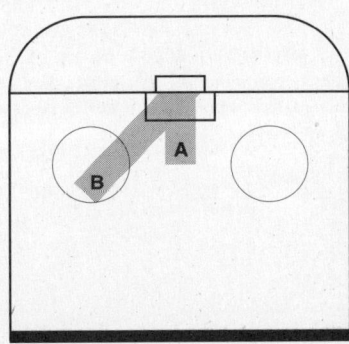

NEW YORK ISLANDERS

Players' Statistics 1998-99

POS.	NO.	PLAYER	GP	G	A	PTS	+/-	PIM	PP	SH	GW	GT	S	PCT
R	16	ZIGMUND PALFFY	50	22	28	50	-6	34	5	2	1		168	13.1
C	32	TREVOR LINDEN	82	18	29	47	-14	32	8	1	1		167	10.8
C	20	BRYAN SMOLINSKI	82	16	24	40	-7	49	7		3		223	7.2
R	25	MARIUSZ CZERKAWSKI	78	21	17	38	-10	14	4		1	2	205	10.2
C	13	CLAUDE LAPOINTE	82	14	23	37	-19	62	2	2	1		134	10.4
R	44	MARK LAWRENCE	60	14	16	30	-8	38	4		2	1	88	15.9
C	11	CRAIG JANNEY	56	5	22	27	-15	14	2			1	45	11.1
D	29	KENNY JONSSON	63	8	18	26	-18	34	6				91	8.8
C	10	MATS LINDGREN	60	10	15	25	6	24	3	1	1		83	12.0
L	12	*MIKE WATT	75	8	17	25	-2	12			4		75	10.7
D	38	BARRY RICHTER	72	6	18	24	-4	34			2		111	5.4
D	4	*ERIC BREWER	63	5	6	11	-14	32	2				63	7.9
D	3	*ZDENO CHARA	59	2	6	8	-8	83		1			56	3.6
D	6	DAVID HARLOCK	70	2	6	8	-16	68					35	5.7
L	24	GINO ODJICK	23	4	3	7	-2	133	1		2		28	14.3
C	11	KEVIN MILLER	33	1	5	6	-5	13					37	2.7
D	2	RICHARD PILON	52		4	4	-8	88					27	
L	14	JOE SACCO	73	3		3	-24	45		1	2		84	3.6
D	36	TED CROWLEY	13	1	2	3	-1	2	1				20	5.0
D	33	ERIC CAIRNS	9		3	3	1	23					2	
C	37	*DMITRI NABOKOV	4		2	2	4	2					4	
R	49	*VLADIMIR ORSAGH	12	1		1	2	6					5	20.0
D	39	DEAN MALKOC	2		1	1	3	7					1	
C	67	MIKE KENNEDY	1				0	2						
D	36	*RAY SCHULTZ	4				-2	7					2	
G	1	*MARCEL COUSINEAU	6				0							
D	55	*VLAD CHEBATURKIN	8				6	12					4	
L	18	MIKE HOUGH	11				-2	2					4	
R	48	*WARREN LUHNING	11				-4	8					11	
G	28	FELIX POTVIN	16				0							
G	30	WADE FLAHERTY	20				0	4						
R	8	STEVE WEBB	45				-10	32					18	

GP = games played; G = goals; A = assists; PTS = points; +/- = goals-for minus goals-against while player is on ice; PIM = penalties in minutes; PP = power-play goals; SH = shorthanded goals; GW = game-winning goals; GT = game-tying goals; S = no. of shots; PCT = percentage of goals to shots; * = rookie

ERIC BREWER

Yrs. of NHL service: 1
Born: Vernon, B.C.; Apr. 17, 1979
Position: left defense
Height: 6-3
Weight: 195
Uniform no.: 4
Shoots: left

Career statistics:

GP	G	A	TP	PIM
63	5	6	11	32

1998-99 statistics:

GP	G	A	TP	+/-	PIM	PP	SH	GW	GT	S	PCT
63	5	6	11	-14	32	2	0	0	0	63	7.9

LAST SEASON
First NHL season. Missed four games with strained Achilles tendon. Missed 15 games due to coach's decision.

THE FINESSE GAME
Brewer grew in confidence during the season. In the last month and a half, he started taking control of some games, using his great skating and puck control to dominate. He's an excellent skater with quick acceleration and lateral movement. He has been compared to a young Scott Niedermayer.

Brewer needs more time and confidence to develop into more of an offensive force. He has a little cockiness to him (which Niedermayer does not have) that shows an innate awareness of his skill level. It will get him in trouble sometimes, but it will also encourage him to try some of the high-risk moves that only elite players make. Brewer can make them.

Brewer can be used in all game situations. In the second half of the season, he concentrated much better throughout the course of the full 60 minutes and was far more effective.

THE PHYSICAL GAME
Brewer is very strong in the defensive zone. He has good size — he will fill out more as he matures — and he likes to hit. He's smart in his own end.

THE INTANGIBLES
He may be playing for a sad-sack team, but Brewer has huge upside. Expect the usual sophomore slump, but he will still be the number two defenseman behind Kenny Jonsson. That's a pretty big step for a 20-year-old.

PROJECTION
Brewer will eventually be a 50-point defenseman, and maybe more, but 25 points would be a good second-year output.

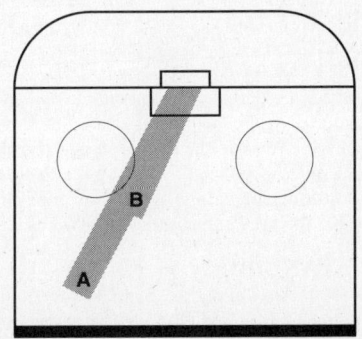

ERIC CAIRNS

Yrs. of NHL service: 3
Born: Oakville, Ont.; June 27, 1974
Position: defense
Height: 6-5
Weight: 225
Uniform no.: 33
Shoots: left

Career statistics:

GP	G	A	TP	PIM
88	0	7	7	262

1996-97 statistics:

GP	G	A	TP	+/-	PIM	PP	SH	GW	GT	S	PCT
40	0	1	1	-7	147	0	0	0	0	17	0.0

1997-98 statistics:

GP	G	A	TP	+/-	PIM	PP	SH	GW	GT	S	PCT
39	0	3	3	-3	92	0	0	0	0	17	.0

1998-99 statistics:

GP	G	A	TP	+/-	PIM	PP	SH	GW	GT	S	PCT
9	0	3	3	+1	23	0	0	0	0	2	.0

LAST SEASON

Appeared in 11 games with Hartford (AHL), scoring 0-2 — 2. Appeared in 24 games with Lowell, scoring 0-0 — 0. Missed two months in contract dispute.

THE FINESSE GAME

It is natural to think a player as big as Cairns would be clumsy, but he has some smarts with the puck and enough skill to skate the puck out of the defensive zone. Occasionally, he can beat a forechecker, but Cairns knows better than to make a habit of that. He doesn't have great foot speed and can get caught flat-footed.

With the puck, Cairns favours backhand moves that allow him to use his body to shield the puck from defenders. He is content to get the puck deep in the zone and let the forwards do the offensive work, but his point shot is accurate when he elects to use it. Out of his own zone, he makes an accurate outlet pass.

Although not a great skater, Cairns turns pretty smoothly and makes up for any shortcomings on speed by using his size and reach. He may look like someone who can be beaten easily to the outside, but he generally does a nice job of angling a puck carrier to less dangerous ice.

THE PHYSICAL GAME

Cairns is a willing fighter and seems to like playing policeman if any opponent starts taking liberties with his teammates. He likes the big hits and mean rubouts, but does a pretty good job of avoiding the cheap hooking and holding penalties big defensemen always seem to get against smaller, quicker forwards.

THE INTANGIBLES

Cairns lost the start of his season to a contract dispute and could be facing another move this off-season. He can't feel like he has made a team. He has to keep working to earn it.

PROJECTION

Cairns will never be a star and he isn't going to score much, but he has made himself a decent NHL prospect. He's still a project — it's going to take lots of extra work before and after practice — but size, strength and reach, sensibly packaged and deployed, are a commodity in the NHL. If he plays his cards right he can have a good career as a dependable stay-at-home, and as a partner for the offensive guy who's going to be up-ice all night.

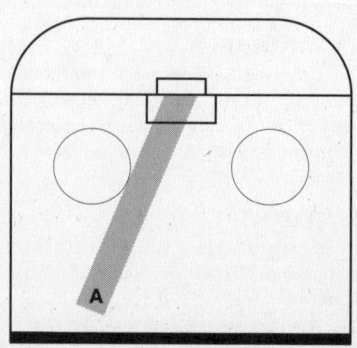

ZDENO CHARA

Yrs. of NHL service: 2
Born: Trencin, Czech Republic; Mar. 18, 1977
Position: right defense
Height: 6-9
Weight: 255
Uniform no.: 3
Shoots: left

Career statistics:

GP	G	A	TP	PIM
84	2	7	9	133

1997-98 statistics:

GP	G	A	TP	+/-	PIM	PP	SH	GW	GT	S	PCT
25	0	1	1	+1	50	0	0	0	0	10	0.0

1998-99 statistics:

GP	G	A	TP	+/-	PIM	PP	SH	GW	GT	S	PCT
59	2	6	8	-8	83	0	1	0	0	56	3.6

LAST SEASON

Second NHL season. Appeared in 23 games with Lowell (AHL), scoring 2-2 — 4. Missed one game due to coach's decision.

THE FINESSE GAME

For a player of his height, Chara is very well-coordinated. He has to get a half-step quicker to be in a better position for his checks, though. If he is out of position at all his hits are sure to be called high sticks and elbows, for the simple reason that he is so much taller than everyone else — their faces just happen to be in the wrong place. By keeping his hands down and his feet moving, Chara can avoid taking those needless penalties. He was much better at this at the end of last season.

Chara moves the puck well but he has a tendency to admire his passes, like a baseball player waiting to break into a slow home run jog around the bases. This leaves him open to hits when he is off-balance.

With his long arms and long stick, Chara can be a bigger, tougher version of Kjell Samuelsson. He needs to improve his puck control and adjust to the NHL pace, but he is well on his way.

THE PHYSICAL GAME

Chara is solid, with a good centre of gravity that is rare to find in a player of his altitude. Players simply bounce off him. He goes through phases when he loses his edge, though. He needs to hit, but when he starts getting those high-sticking calls he has a tendency to back down for awhile. He doesn't mind a good scrap, and he has a long reach. He has handled assignments against other teams' top lines.

THE INTANGIBLES

Chara had a bad start in training camp and began the year in the minors. He is very hard on himself — he is his own worst enemy — but he worked hard in the minors and was one of the Isles' top four defensemen at the end of the season. He has a great reputation as a trier, and as a kid who is coachable and willing to work to improve his game. At six foot nine, Chara is the tallest defenseman in NHL history.

PROJECTION

Chara will do very little offensively but will grow into a stable top four defenseman. His penalty-minute total will be impressive.

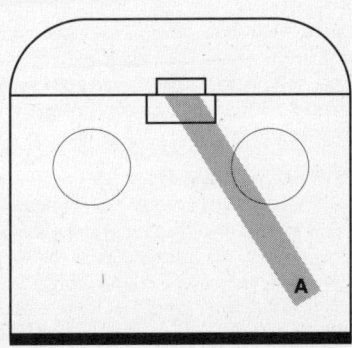

MARIUSZ CZERKAWSKI

Yrs. of NHL service: 5
Born: Radomsko, Poland; Apr. 13, 1972
Position: right wing
Height: 6-0
Weight: 195
Uniform no.: 25
Shoots: left

Career statistics:

GP	G	A	TP	PIM
343	90	89	179	102

1995-96 statistics:

GP	G	A	TP	+/-	PIM	PP	SH	GW	GT	S	PCT
70	17	23	40	-4	18	3	0	1	0	142	12.0

1996-97 statistics:

GP	G	A	TP	+/-	PIM	PP	SH	GW	GT	S	PCT
76	26	21	47	0	16	4	0	3	0	182	14.3

1997-98 statistics:

GP	G	A	TP	+/-	PIM	PP	SH	GW	GT	S	PCT
68	12	13	25	+11	23	2	0	1	0	136	8.8

1998-99 statistics:

GP	G	A	TP	+/-	PIM	PP	SH	GW	GT	S	PCT
78	21	17	38	-10	14	4	0	1	2	205	10.2

LAST SEASON

Second on team in goals and shots. Missed four games due to coach's decision.

THE FINESSE GAME

Although highly skilled, Czerkawski has still not shaken a common fault of gifted European puckhandlers — he will not make the simple play. He often plays as if the objective is to dance through all five opponents on the ice before shooting or passing, leaving his teammates exasperated. He plays on the Islanders' first line because of his skill level but does not give them first-line numbers.

Czerkawski does not get into quality scoring positions in high-traffic areas. He is superb in open ice, with great one-on-one moves and a phenomenal shot. He likes to use all of the ice, and will cut across the middle or to the right side to make the play. He is a shifty skater, not one with great straightaway speed, but he puts the slip on a defender with a lateral move and is off.

His quick wrist shot is Czerkawski's best weapon. With the extra room on the power play he is at his best. He has soft hands for passes and good vision. He needs to play with someone who will get him the puck, since he will not go into the corners for it.

THE PHYSICAL GAME

Czerkawski has to get better at protecting the puck and perform at least a willing game along the boards. He uses his body in the offensive zone, but in a perfunctory manner, and he doesn't like to get involved too much in the defensive zone. He can be intimidated physically. He is quick enough to peel back and help out with backchecking, since he is very smart at anticipating passes, but he will rarely knock anyone off the puck.

THE INTANGIBLES

Czerkawski is the most skilled forward on the Islanders with the departure of Ziggy Palffy. He'll be the go-to guy by default, though he must improve his intensity and his consistency to be a true gamer. Czerkawski showed some nice chemistry after the arrival of Mats Lindgren last season.

PROJECTION

Czerkawski is a chronic underachiever. If he would go to the net harder he would get 35 goals. The Islanders will probably have to settle for 25.

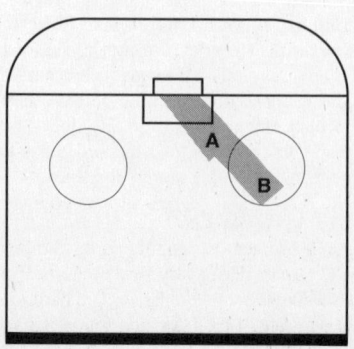

JOSH GREEN

Yrs. of NHL service: 1
Born: Camrose, Alta.; Nov. 16, 1977
Position: left wing
Height: 6-4
Weight: 212
Uniform no.: 21
Shoots: left

Career statistics:

GP	G	A	TP	PIM
27	1	3	4	8

1998-99 statistics:

GP	G	A	TP	+/-	PIM	PP	SH	GW	GT	S	PCT
27	1	3	4	-5	8	1	0	0	0	35	2.9

LAST SEASON

First NHL season. Acquired from Los Angeles with Olli Jokinen, Mathieu Biron and a 1999 first-round draft pick for Ziggy Palffy, Bryan Smolinski and Marcel Cousineau, June 20, 1999. Appeared in 41 games with Springfield (AHL), scoring 15-15 — 30. Missed three games with shoulder injury. Missed five games due to coach's decision.

THE FINESSE GAME

Green could become an Adam Graves-type player. He is a good skater with average hands, but he's very smart with the puck and he knows what to do with it in key areas. His feet are just a little bit slow off the mark, but he has decent speed once he gets moving. He is strong on his skates and he can get a lot better if he works at his skating. He is not a plodder.

Green is a good passer and playmaker. Since his hands aren't great, he will need to dig for his goals around the net, the way Graves does every night. Green is a fairly advanced two-way player for his age (he'll turn 22 during the season).

THE PHYSICAL GAME

Green is a big, strong kid. He underwent reconstructive surgery on his left shoulder during the off-season, and he can't let it affect his willingness to hit. Because his finesse skills are above average, he sometimes falls into the lazy habit of taking the easy way out and not playing the price physically. He can't afford to do that, because he has a bright future as a power forward if he keeps desire and grit in his game.

THE INTANGIBLES

Assuming Green rehabs well off his shoulder injury, he could start on the third line for the Islanders this season, with the potential to move up into the team's top six forwards.

PROJECTION

Power forwards take time to develop. If Green gets 10 to 15 goals this season and is able to earn a full-time role that would be a positive and logical first step.

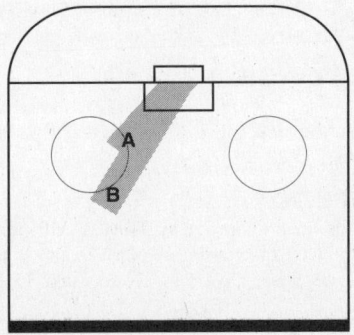

BRAD ISBISTER

Yrs. of NHL service: 2
Born: Edmonton, Alberta; May 7, 1977
Position: right wing
Height: 6-3
Weight: 222
Uniform no.: 16
Shoots: right

Career statistics:

GP	G	A	TP	PIM
98	13	12	25	148

1997-98 statistics:

GP	G	A	TP	+/-	PIM	PP	SH	GW	GT	S	PCT
66	9	8	17	+4	104	1	0	1	0	115	7.8

1998-99 statistics:

GP	G	A	TP	+/-	PIM	PP	SH	GW	GT	S	PCT
32	4	4	8	+1	46	0	0	2	0	48	8.3

LAST SEASON

Second NHL season. Acquired from Phoenix with a third-round draft pick in 1999 for Robert Reichel, a 1999 third-round and fourth-round draft pick, Mar. 20, 1999. Missed 29 games with groin strain/hernia.

THE FINESSE GAME

Isbister is not a very creative sort, but fits in well in a strong forechecking scheme because he plays up and down his left wing. He is a solid skater with straight-away speed and quickness. It remains to be seen how he rehabs from an injury that bears so directly on his skating.

Isbister's hand skills are a shade below average. He is a decent passer when he has a little time, but, unlike more creative players, doesn't quickly see more than one option. His goals will come from driving to the net.

With better hands and a quicker shot, Isbister could be a power forward in the making. He certainly tries to play like one.

THE PHYSICAL GAME

Isbister is strong, able to fend off a defender with one arm and keep going. He protects the puck well. He is an enthusiastic forechecker and likes to be the first man in. He will take or make a hit to make a play happen. He has an aggressive nature and will aggravate a lot of players by making them eat glass.

THE INTANGIBLES

Isbister is still relatively young (22), and will get a chance to crack the top six forwards with the Islanders.

PROJECTION

If he continues his progress, Isbister will get more shifts and we expect a slight improvement — say, 15 goals — because players of his sort take longer to develop.

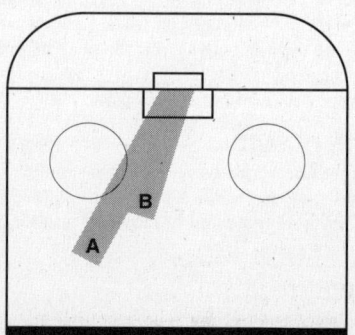

OLLI JOKINEN

Yrs. of NHL service: 1
Born: Kuopio, Finland; Dec. 5, 1978
Position: centre
Height: 6-2
Weight: 198
Uniform no.: 12
Shoots: left

Career statistics:

GP	G	A	TP	PIM
74	9	12	21	50

1998-99 statistics:

GP	G	A	TP	+/-	PIM	PP	SH	GW	GT	S	PCT
66	9	12	21	-10	44	3	1	1	0	87	10.3

LAST SEASON

First NHL season. Acquired from Los Angeles with Mathieu Biron, Josh Green and a first-round draft pick in 1999 for Ziggy Palffy, Bryan Smolinski and Marcel Cousineau, June 20, 1999. Third on Kings in shooting percentage. Appeared in nine games with Springfield (AHL), scoring 3-6 — 9. Missed four games due to coach's decision.

THE FINESSE GAME

Jokinen is an offensive-minded player with terrific hockey sense. He has performed well on the world stage, usually against older players, and he makes things happen with his creativity and up-tempo skills. He has an added dollop of power in his game, which improves his upside.

The Kings played Jokinen at left wing last season, but he is better at centre and will probably play that role with the Islanders. He is a better playmaker than scorer. He has excellent vision and a wonderful sense of timing with his passes. He is probably too unselfish and will need to develop a shot he has confidence in, because he has the ability to.

He has a good head for the game and good vision.

THE PHYSICAL GAME

Jokinen is solidly built and won't be intimidated. He is well used to being a boy playing among men and elevates his game by combining an edge with his high skill level. He has some grit, too. He has a nasty, agitating side and does not play many quiet games.

THE INTANGIBLES

Jokinen would make an ideal number two centre on most teams. The Islanders will probably push him into the number one role, simply because there is no one else available. He is young and needs to mature, especially in his off-ice habits.

PROJECTION

Jokinen is just about guaranteed a top six role, and if he can develop chemistry with a finisher — if the Isles have one — 40 points is a conservative estimate. His totals will be much heavier on assists.

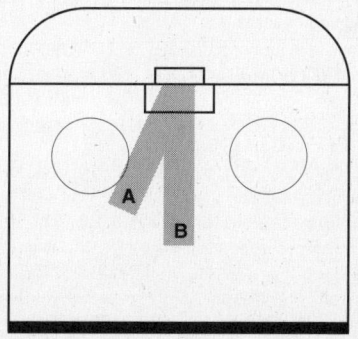

KENNY JONSSON

Yrs. of NHL service: 5
Born: Angelholm, Sweden; Oct. 6, 1974
Position: left defense
Height: 6-3
Weight: 195
Uniform no.: 29
Shoots: left

Career statistics:

GP	G	A	TP	PIM
330	31	95	126	164

1995-96 statistics:

GP	G	A	TP	+/-	PIM	PP	SH	GW	GT	S	PCT
66	4	26	30	+7	32	3	0	1	0	130	3.1

1996-97 statistics:

GP	G	A	TP	+/-	PIM	PP	SH	GW	GT	S	PCT
81	3	18	21	+10	24	1	0	0	0	92	3.3

1997-98 statistics:

GP	G	A	TP	+/-	PIM	PP	SH	GW	GT	S	PCT
81	14	26	40	-2	58	6	0	2	0	108	13.0

1998-99 statistics:

GP	G	A	TP	+/-	PIM	PP	SH	GW	GT	S	PCT
63	8	18	26	-18	34	6	0	0	0	91	8.8

LAST SEASON

Led team defensemen in scoring. Third on team in power-play goals. Missed nine games with sprained knee. Missed eight games with concussion. Missed one game with broken finger.

THE FINESSE GAME

Jonsson is probably one of the top eight defensemen in the league, but no one knows it. He reads the ice and passes the puck very well. He's not overly creative, nor is he a risk taker. He makes a very good first pass out of the zone, but he will also bank it off the boards if that is the safer play. He doesn't shoot for the home run pass on every shift, but he will recognize the headman play when it's there.

Jonsson moves the puck up and plays his position. He always makes sure he has somebody beaten before he makes a pass. He can be used in almost every game situation. He kills penalties, works the point on the power play, plays four-on-four and can be used in the late stages of a period or a game to protect a lead. He's reliable and coachable.

Jonsson is a talented skater, big and mobile, yet he tends to leave himself open after passes and gets nailed.

THE PHYSICAL GAME

Jonsson is smart and plays with an edge. The knock on him earlier in his career was that he was a bit soft and didn't like to play through traffic, but that has changed. He competes hard every night and in the hard areas of the ice. He could stand to improve his off-season conditioning a little, especially considering all the minutes he gets.

THE INTANGIBLES

Jonsson is the Islanders' number one defenseman, and if he weren't playing for such a bad team or in the shadow of the Rangers' Brian Leetch, he would merit Norris Trophy consideration. His confidence in his game has grown.

PROJECTION

Jonsson can score in the 40-point range and provide a solid all-around game and quiet leadership.

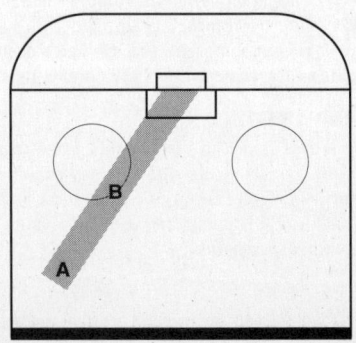

CLAUDE LAPOINTE

Yrs. of NHL service: 8
Born: Lachine, Que.; Oct. 11, 1968
Position: centre
Height: 5-9
Weight: 181
Uniform no.: 13
Shoots: left

Career statistics:

GP	G	A	TP	PIM
521	81	116	197	477

1995-96 statistics:

GP	G	A	TP	+/-	PIM	PP	SH	GW	GT	S	PCT
35	4	5	9	+1	20	0	2	1	0	44	9.1

1996-97 statistics:

GP	G	A	TP	+/-	PIM	PP	SH	GW	GT	S	PCT
73	13	5	18	-11	49	0	3	3	1	80	16.3

1997-98 statistics:

GP	G	A	TP	+/-	PIM	PP	SH	GW	GT	S	PCT
78	10	10	20	-9	47	0	1	3	0	82	12.2

1998-99 statistics:

GP	G	A	TP	+/-	PIM	PP	SH	GW	GT	S	PCT
82	14	23	37	-19	62	2	2	1	0	134	10.4

LAST SEASON

Tied for team lead in shorthanded goals. One of three Islanders to appear in all 82 games.

THE FINESSE GAME

Lapointe is so quick and smart that he gets a breakaway every other game, but he doesn't have the hands to finish off his chances. He is heady and aggressive. As a low draft pick (234th overall in 1988), he has always had to fight for respect. His effort is what's kept him hanging around this long.

Lapointe is one of those useful veteran forwards who will always find a spot in a lineup because of his intelligence, yet he'll always be worried about his job because he doesn't do anything special.

He drives to the front of the net, knowing that that's where good things happen. He has good acceleration and quickness with the puck, plus decent hand skills to make things work down low. He isn't blessed with great vision, but he doesn't take unnecessary chances, either, and can be used in clutch situations.

Lapointe was used as a checking-line winger, where he can make use of his speed, but he might be a third-line centre this season. He is very good penalty killer.

THE PHYSICAL GAME

Lapointe is small but solidly built. He uses his low centre of gravity and good balance to bump people much bigger than he is; he surprises some by knocking them off the puck. He doesn't quit and is dogged in the corners and in front of the net. He is gritty and hardworking.

THE INTANGIBLES

Lapointe is used as a checker, an energy guy, a penalty killer and on face-offs. He doesn't score many goals but the ones he does score tend to be big. He is an excellent team man. Lapointe wore down midway through the season because he was overused, but he bounced back late in the year.

PROJECTION

Lapointe is a useful role-playing centre who can get 15 goals and contribute 15 hard minutes every night.

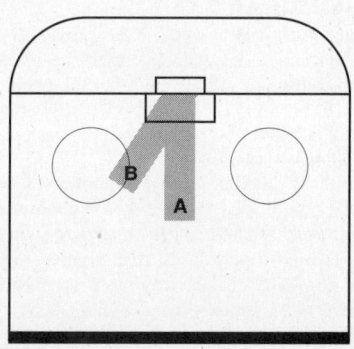

MARK LAWRENCE

Yrs. of NHL service: 1
Born: Burlington, Ont.; Jan. 27, 1972
Position: right wing
Height: 6-4
Weight: 215
Uniform no.: 44
Shoots: right

Career statistics:
GP	G	A	TP	PIM
77	14	17	31	57

1995-96 statistics:
GP	G	A	TP	+/-	PIM	PP	SH	GW	GT	S	PCT
13	0	1	1	0	17	0	0	0	0	13	0.0

1996-97 statistics:
Did not play in NHL

1997-98 statistics:
GP	G	A	TP	+/-	PIM	PP	SH	GW	GT	S	PCT
2	0	0	0	0	2	0	0	0	0	4	0.0

1998-99 statistics:
GP	G	A	TP	+/-	PIM	PP	SH	GW	GT	S	PCT
60	14	16	30	-8	38	4	0	2	1	88	15.9

LAST SEASON
First full NHL season. Led team in shooting percentage. Appeared in 21 games with Lowell (AHL), scoring 10-6 — 16.

THE FINESSE GAME
The knock against Lawrence — and the flaw that prevented him from getting a job as an NHL regular all these years — was that he couldn't keep up with the pace of the major league game. But Lawrence has worked hard to improve his skating, and he has picked up that extra step that now allows him to compete.

Lawrence stands in front of the net on the power play and uses his good hands for tip-ins and rebounds. He drives hard to the net and plays with intensity. He goes through traffic and ties the defender up to give his smaller linemates a chance to get to loose pucks. He has a quick, hard, accurate shot.

Lawrence is good in his own end and protects the puck well.

THE PHYSICAL GAME
Lawrence's game is power. He has good size and he uses it, in front of the net and along the boards. He is a better-conditioned athlete than he has been at any point in his career.

THE INTANGIBLES
After years of kicking around the minors, Lawrence made the best of his (possible) last crack at the NHL last season and it paid off. It's like a light switch went on. He is finally putting all of the pieces together. Power forwards take longer to develop, and Lawrence, at 27, is proof.

PROJECTION
Lawrence has come from out of nowhere to land a job as one of the Isles' top six forwards for this season. Based on his NHL performance last season, a 25-goal output is possible.

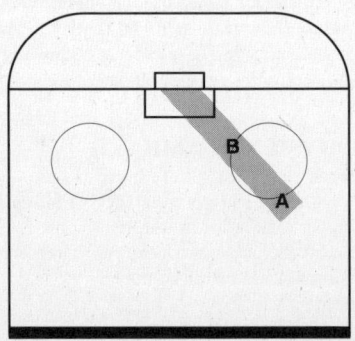

MATS LINDGREN

Yrs. of NHL service: 3
Born: Skelleftea, Sweden; Oct. 1, 1974
Position: left wing
Height: 6-2
Weight: 200
Uniform no.: 10
Shoots: left

Career statistics:

GP	G	A	TP	PIM
211	34	42	76	78

1996-97 statistics:

GP	G	A	TP	+/-	PIM	PP	SH	GW	GT	S	PCT
69	11	14	25	-7	12	2	3	1	0	71	15.5

1997-98 statistics:

GP	G	A	TP	+/-	PIM	PP	SH	GW	GT	S	PCT
82	13	13	26	0	42	1	3	3	0	131	9.9

1998-99 statistics:

GP	G	A	TP	+/-	PIM	PP	SH	GW	GT	S	PCT
60	10	15	25	+6	24	3	1	1	0	83	12.0

PROJECTION

Lindgren has a 25-goal, 50-point season in him. This might be the year he lets it out.

LAST SEASON

Acquired from Edmonton with a 1999 eighth-round draft pick for Tommy Salo, Mar. 20, 1999. Led team in plus-minus. Third on team in shooting percentage. Missed seven games with dislocated shoulder. Missed one game with flu.

THE FINESSE GAME

Lindgren was used primarily as a defensive player with the Oilers, but in coming to the Islanders has been able to unleash the offensive side of his game that he was known for in Sweden. He scored 5-3 — 8 in 12 games with the Islanders. He has a real future as a solid two-way centre.

Lindgren is a fine skater with balance, agility and quickness. He is especially clever in tight, moving the puck at the right moment and knowing when to shoot and when to pass. He has very good puckhandling skills and can do many clever things with the puck.

Lindgren also kills penalties and is a shorthanded threat. He needs to gain more confidence in his shot, though, because it could be a more dangerous weapon. He has a wrister with a lot on it. With his size, hands and vision, he is a poor man's Mats Sundin.

Lindgren has terrific hockey sense, and plays equally well in all zones.

THE PHYSICAL GAME

Lindgren is solidly built and capable of playing a power game. He'll never dominate physically, but he will battle for the puck in high-traffic areas.

THE INTANGIBLES

Lindgren clicked well with Mariusz Czerkawski after his arrival on the Island. They are likely to be the core of the Isles' top line.

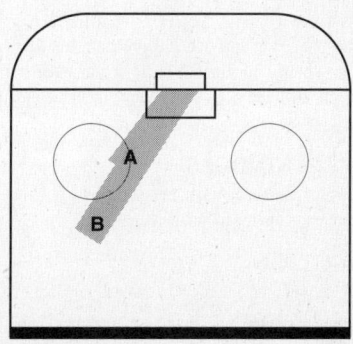

GINO ODJICK

Yrs. of NHL service: 9
Born: Maniwaki, Que.; Sept. 7, 1970
Position: left wing
Height: 6-3
Weight: 210
Uniform no.: 24
Shoots: left

Career statistics:

GP	G	A	TP	PIM
480	50	55	105	2291

1995-96 statistics:

GP	G	A	TP	+/-	PIM	PP	SH	GW	GT	S	PCT
55	3	4	7	-16	181	0	0	0	0	59	5.1

1996-97 statistics:

GP	G	A	TP	+/-	PIM	PP	SH	GW	GT	S	PCT
70	5	8	13	-5	371	1	0	0	0	85	5.9

1997-98 statistics:

GP	G	A	TP	+/-	PIM	PP	SH	GW	GT	S	PCT
48	3	2	5	-2	212	0	0	1	0	52	5.8

1998-99 statistics:

GP	G	A	TP	+/-	PIM	PP	SH	GW	GT	S	PCT
23	4	3	7	-2	133	1	0	2	0	28	14.3

LAST SEASON

Missed 59 games with groin/abdominal strain.

THE FINESSE GAME

Odjick is a goon who knows that goons are facing extinction in the NHL. To preserve his job, he has added important elements to his game.

Odjick's scoring chances come from in tight. He works tirelessly around the net for loose pucks, slamming and jamming. He could use a little more patience, since he gets a lot of room for his first move, but his theory seems to be that three whacks at the puck (which he can get easily) are worth one finesse move (which he might not be able to make anyway).

A determined player, he has fought his way back from a serious abdominal/groin injury. His skating is adequate, and he has surprising hockey sense for a player of his ilk. He knows where to be on the ice.

THE PHYSICAL GAME

Odjick takes cheap penalties. He aggravates, hits late and hits from behind, yet is a legitimate tough guy when the gloves come off. He protects his teammates. He is also strong enough to simply run over people en route to the net. He needs to maintain his conditioning better.

THE INTANGIBLES

Odjick is a question mark because of his injury. The Islanders are hoping to move him.

PROJECTION

As long as fighting isn't outlawed, outlaws will remain hockey players.

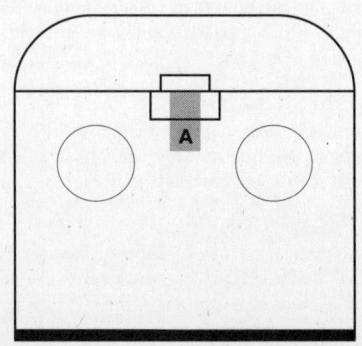

RICHARD PILON

Yrs. of NHL service: 11
Born: Saskatoon, Sask.; Apr. 30, 1968
Position: left defense
Height: 6-0
Weight: 205
Uniform no.: 2
Shoots: left

Career statistics:

GP	G	A	TP	PIM
500	6	51	57	1491

1995-96 statistics:

GP	G	A	TP	+/-	PIM	PP	SH	GW	GT	S	PCT
27	0	3	3	-9	72	0	0	0	0	7	0.0

1996-97 statistics:

GP	G	A	TP	+/-	PIM	PP	SH	GW	GT	S	PCT
52	1	4	5	+4	179	0	0	0	0	17	5.9

1997-98 statistics:

GP	G	A	TP	+/-	PIM	PP	SH	GW	GT	S	PCT
76	0	7	7	+1	291	0	0	0	0	37	0.0

1998-99 statistics:

GP	G	A	TP	+/-	PIM	PP	SH	GW	GT	S	PCT
52	0	4	4	-8	88	0	0	0	0	27	.0

Islanders are likely to deal him.

PROJECTION

Pilon scores a goal once every other year, so he's overdue. A better bet is 250-plus penalty minutes, if he can remain intact.

LAST SEASON

Missed 16 games with back injuries. Missed seven games with sprained knee. Missed two games with sprained wrist.

THE FINESSE GAME

Pilon is power. He takes command of his own end of the ice and is a very steady defensive rearguard. He is not remotely involved in offense. His career scoring totals look like a month's work for Sandis Ozolinsh.

But unlike Ozolinsh, Pilon's main concern is getting the puck out of his own zone safely. He will make a conservative chip off the glass rather than gamble on a pass up the middle. He is a much better passer than he is given credit for, but he won't waste time looking for the high-risk play. He can also skate the puck out of the zone, but he will not venture beyond the redline with it. His offensive input is limited to a so-so shot from the point.

Pilon is not a speedball, but he is above average in mobility and balance. He is a very determined penalty killer and blocks shots willingly.

THE PHYSICAL GAME

Pilon is a fierce, mean hitter. He usually hits high instead of low, and he can topple players. He can also fight, but the impulse is curtailed because of the visor he is forced to wear (an eye injury he received years ago nearly ended his career). He can snap, which makes opponents wary of him.

THE INTANGIBLES

Pilon is a throwback to the six-team era. He plays so hard that injuries are inevitable. He's a rock. The

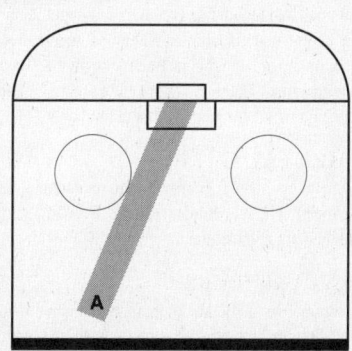

FELIX POTVIN

Yrs. of NHL service: 7
Born: Anjou, Que.; June 23, 1971
Position: goaltender
Height: 6-0
Weight: 190
Uniform no.: 29
Catches: left

Career statistics:

GP	MIN	GA	SO	GAA	A	PIM
380	22067	1063	12	2.89	8	43

1995-96 statistics:

GP	MIN	GAA	W	L	T	SO	GA	S	SAPCT	PIM
69	4009	2.87	30	26	11	2	192	2135	.910	4

1996-97 statistics:

GP	MIN	GAA	W	L	T	SO	GA	S	SAPCT	PIM
74	4271	3.15	27	36	7	0	224	2438	.908	19

1997-98 statistics:

GP	MIN	GAA	W	L	T	SO	GA	S	SAPCT	PIM
67	3864	2.73	26	33	7	5	176	1882	.906	8

1998-99 statistics:

GP	MIN	GAA	W	L	T	SO	GA	S	SAPCT	PIM
11	606	3.66	2	7	1	0	37	345	.893	0

LAST SEASON

Acquired from Toronto with a 1999 sixth-round draft pick for Bryan Berard and a sixth-round draft pick, Jan. 9, 1999. Missed 22 games with groin strain.

THE PHYSICAL GAME

Potvin still has a habit of playing deep in his net. He prefers to keep his skates in the paint at all times, but seems to be honestly trying to play at the top of his crease instead of back on his goal line. It's a constant battle getting Potvin out of his comfort zone.

Excellent on low shots, Potvin's style is similar to that of his idol, Patrick Roy: he likes to butterfly and flirt with leaving a five-hole for shooters. The best place to beat Potvin is high, but shooters see that tempting gap between the pads and go for it, and he snaps the pads shut.

Potvin allows very few bad rebounds. He either controls them into the corners or deadens them in front of him. He is a poor stickhandler. He doesn't use his stick well around the net to break up passes and hates to come out of his net to try to move the puck. Potvin is one goalie who is happy with the extra two feet of ice behind his net, where he can leave the work to his defensemen and not feel guilty.

THE MENTAL GAME

Players love to play for him because of his unruffled temperament. He is a leader in the dressing room and never alibis his mistakes.

THE INTANGIBLES

Potvin cares not only about his own game but about the team. There is nothing wrong with his game that couldn't be cured with better talent in front of him. His groin injury is a question mark, but he was rehabbing well over the summer in preparaion for the season.

PROJECTION

Potvin will upgrade the Islanders' goaltending and could get 25 wins.

BARRY RICHTER

Yrs. of NHL service: 2
Born: Madison, WI; Sept. 11, 1970
Position: left defense
Height: 6-2
Weight: 200
Uniform no.: 38
Shoots: left

Career statistics:

GP	G	A	TP	PIM
126	11	32	43	66

1995-96 statistics:

GP	G	A	TP	+/-	PIM	PP	SH	GW	GT	S	PCT
4	0	1	1	+2	0	0	0	0	0	3	0.0

1996-97 statistics:

GP	G	A	TP	+/-	PIM	PP	SH	GW	GT	S	PCT
50	5	13	18	-7	32	1	0	0	0	79	6.3

1997-98 statistics:
Did not play in NHL

1998-99 statistics:

GP	G	A	TP	+/-	PIM	PP	SH	GW	GT	S	PCT
72	6	18	24	-4	34	0	0	2	0	111	5.4

LAST SEASON
Third on team in plus-minus. Missed three games with shoulder injury.

THE FINESSE GAME
Richter's game is tilted towards his offense, though he has developed into a capable all-around defenseman. He is one of those players who kicked around in the minors and as a part-timer in two organizations (Rangers and Boston) before getting his first full-time job this season.

Richter was used heavily by the Islanders in the first half of the year and when Kenny Jonsson was hurt. He played 28 minutes a game and, not surprisingly, was burned out.

Richter has some nice finesse skills. He is a good skater, with good vision and hands. None of his skills are elite level but he can make a lot of major-league plays. He is an intelligent player. He kills penalties and works the power play.

THE PHYSICAL GAME
Richter is strong although he is not a real force. He competes hard and has a little bit of an edge to his game.

THE INTANGIBLES
The Islanders did not make a qualifying offer to Richter by July 1, which made him a free agent. He could be a nice fifth defenseman on all but the strongest NHL squads.

PROJECTION
Richter can score 25 to 30 points in the right situation.

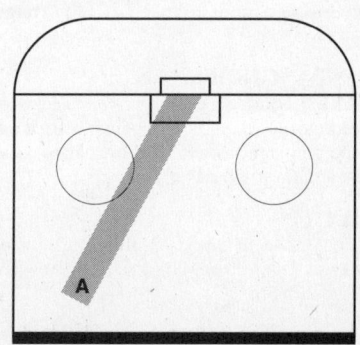

MIKE WATT

Yrs. of NHL service: 1
Born: Seaforth, Ont.; Mar. 31, 1976
Position: left wing
Height: 6-2
Weight: 212
Uniform no.: 12
Shoots: left

Career statistics:

GP	G	A	TP	PIM
89	9	19	28	16

1997-98 statistics:

GP	G	A	TP	+/-	PIM	PP	SH	GW	GT	S	PCT
14	1	2	3	-4	4	0	0	1	0	14	7.1

1998-99 statistics:

GP	G	A	TP	+/-	PIM	PP	SH	GW	GT	S	PCT
75	8	17	25	-2	12	0	0	4	0	75	10.7

LAST SEASON

First NHL season. Tied for team lead in game-winning goals. Second on team in plus-minus. Missed one game with charley horse. Missed five games due to coach's decision.

THE FINESSE GAME

Watt was a go-to guy in college (Michigan State) and for Canada in the World Junior championships. Just two years out of college, he is starting to make his adjustments to playing at the NHL level. He has a knack for the big goal — half of his eight goals last season were game winners, and the Islanders didn't have all that many wins.

Watt has a great shot and decent hands. He needs to shoot more (he averaged only a shot per game last season), and needs more ice time. He has a very good wrist shot. His skating is fine. He is quick into the openings and will use his speed forechecking.

He is a smart two-way player. He knows how to play the game and doesn't get lost in his own end.

THE PHYSICAL GAME

Watt has very good size and uses it along the boards. He isn't an aggressive player, which may cost him some points with coaches who like more of an edge, but John LeClair could be a Lady Byng candidate, and you don't hear the Flyers complaining. Watt could turn out to be a poor man's LeClair: tough and durable.

THE INTANGIBLES

Watt had an impressive training camp last season, but he couldn't score when the real games started and was under the gun right away. He works hard to get his chances, and they will pay off.

PROJECTION

The Islanders seem intent on shipping him out, so Watt may score his 20 goals this season elsewhere, but he *will* score them.

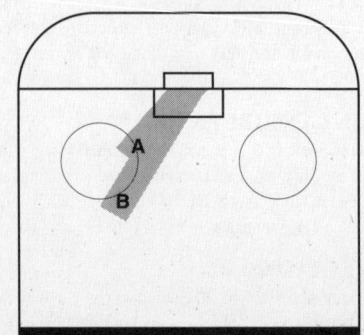

NEW YORK RANGERS

Players' Statistics 1998-99

POS	NO.	PLAYER	GP	G	A	PTS	+/-	PIM	PP	SH	GW	GT	S	PCT
C	99	WAYNE GRETZKY	70	9	53	62	-23	14	3		3	1	132	6.8
R	15	JOHN MACLEAN	82	28	27	55	5	46	11	1	2		231	12.1
D	2	BRIAN LEETCH	82	13	42	55	-7	42	4		1		184	7.1
L	9	ADAM GRAVES	82	38	15	53	-12	47	14	2	7		239	15.9
C	93	PETR NEDVED	56	20	27	47	-6	50	9	1	3		153	13.1
C	33	MARC SAVARD	70	9	36	45	-7	38	4		1		116	7.8
L	17	KEVIN STEVENS	81	23	20	43	-10	64	8		3		136	16.9
R	24	NIKLAS SUNDSTROM	81	13	30	43	-2	20	1	2	3		89	14.6
R	22	MIKE KNUBLE	82	15	20	35	-7	26	3		1		113	13.3
D	25	MATHIEU SCHNEIDER	75	10	24	34	-19	71	5		2		159	6.3
R	20	TODD HARVEY	37	11	17	28	-1	72	6		2	1	58	19.0
C	6	*MANNY MALHOTRA	73	8	8	16	-2	13	1		2		61	13.1
R	26	*MIKE MANELUK	45	6	9	15	5	20	1		1		55	10.9
L	37	BRENT FEDYK	67	4	6	10	-11	30		1			47	8.5
D	23	JEFF BEUKEBOOM	45		9	9	-2	60					8	
C	21	SCOTT FRASER	28	2	4	6	-12	14	1				35	5.7
D	4	CHRIS TAMER	63	1	5	6	-14	124			1		48	2.1
D	34	PETER POPOVIC	68	1	4	5	-12	40					64	1.6
L	28	ERIC LACROIX	64	2	2	4	-12	18			1		38	5.3
D	12	*RICHARD BRENNAN	24	1	3	4	-4	23					36	2.8
D	36	*RUMUN NDUR	39	1	3	4	-1	62					22	4.5
L	10	ESA TIKKANEN	32		3	3	-5	38					25	
D	8	JAN MERTZIG	23		2	2	-5	8					10	
C	18	DEREK ARMSTRONG	3				0						1	
D	14	GEOFF SMITH	4				-5	2						
L	14	JOHAN WITEHALL	4				0						1	
C	28	P.J. STOCK	5				-1	6						
C	14	CHRISTIAN DUBE	6				0							
G	39	*DAN CLOUTIER	22				0	2						
L	19	DARREN LANGDON	44				-3	80					8	
G	35	MIKE RICHTER	68				0							

GP = games played; G = goals; A = assists; PTS = points; +/- = goals-for minus goals-against while player is on ice; PIM = penalties in minutes; PP = power-play goals; SH = shorthanded goals; GW = game-winning goals; GT = game-tying goals; S = no. of shots; PCT = percentage of goals to shots; * = rookie

PAVEL BRENDL

Yrs. of NHL service: 0
Born: Opocno, Czech Rep.; Mar. 23, 1981
Position: right wing
Height: 6-0
Weight: 204
Uniform no.: n.a.
Shoots: right

Career junior statistics:

GP	G	A	TP	PIM
68	73	61	134	40

LAST SEASON

Drafted fourth overall by N.Y. Rangers in 1999 Entry Draft. Led WHL in goals (73) and points (134) in 68 games. Tied for second in WHL in assists (61).

THE FINESSE GAME

When you start throwing the name "Mike Bossy" around when trying to describe an 18-year-old's playing style, you know you are dealing with something special. Brendl could be that kind of player.

Certainly the Rangers thought so, since they traded two players (Niklas Sundstrom and Dan Cloutier) to Tampa Bay in order to be able to move up in the draft and take Brendl. It is said that three things happen when Brendl shoots the puck: he misses the net, he hits the goalie, or he scores. In other words, the goalie is virtually helpless to make a save, so accurate and heavy are Brendl's wrist and slap shots.

The only potential drawback is the question of whether Brendl's skating is NHL calibre. He is strong and balanced on his skates, but until he is tested at the top level his foot speed is suspect. Brendl also isn't the most accomplished defensive player, but then again, neither was Bossy.

THE PHYSICAL GAME

Brendl has excellent size and the desire to take the puck to the net in traffic. He is poised under fire and can shoot or make a play in a throng of defenders; most checkers at the junior level bounced off him.

THE INTANGIBLES

If he makes the jump to the NHL this year, Brendl needs to play. The Rangers signed so many veterans that getting a lot of ice time will be difficult, and he might be better off going back to junior instead of playing six minutes a game. Given the Rangers' investment in him, it's likely he will stay with the big club.

PROJECTION

Brendl looks to be among the most impressive rookies of this year's crop, if he stays with the Rangers.

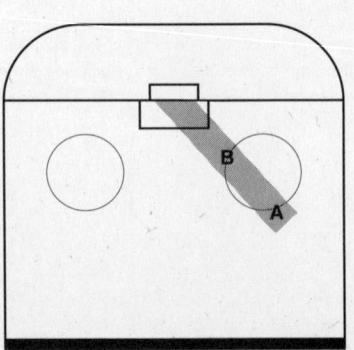

THEOREN FLEURY

Yrs. of NHL service: 11
Born: Oxbow, Sask.; June 29, 1968
Position: right wing/centre
Height: 5-6
Weight: 160
Uniform no.: 14
Shoots: right

Career statistics:

GP	G	A	TP	PIM
806	374	480	854	1490

1995-96 statistics:

GP	G	A	TP	+/-	PIM	PP	SH	GW	GT	S	PCT
80	46	50	96	+17	112	17	5	4	0	353	13.0

1996-97 statistics:

GP	G	A	TP	+/-	PIM	PP	SH	GW	GT	S	PCT
81	29	38	67	-12	104	9	2	3	3	336	8.6

1997-98 statistics:

GP	G	A	TP	+/-	PIM	PP	SH	GW	GT	S	PCT
82	27	51	78	0	197	3	2	4	1	282	9.6

1998-99 statistics:

GP	G	A	TP	+/-	PIM	PP	SH	GW	GT	S	PCT
75	40	53	93	+26	86	8	3	5	2	301	13.3

LAST SEASON

Signed as free agent, July 8, 1999. Acquired by Colorado from Calgary for Rene Corbet, Wade Belak and future considerations, Feb. 28, 1999. Led Avalanche and fifth in NHL in shots. Tied for seventh in NHL in goals. Second on Avalanche in goals and plus-minus. Tied for sixth in NHL and third on Avalanche in assists. Tied for seventh in NHL and third on Avalanche in points. Second on Avalanche in shorthanded goals. Missed seven games with sprained knee.

THE FINESSE GAME

Fleury continues to prove that a small man can excel in a big man's game. Possessing great speed and quickness, he often seems to be dancing over the ice with his blades barely touching the frozen surface. He is always on the move, which is as much a tactic as an instinct for survival. You can't catch what you can't hit. Fleury uses his outside speed to burn slower, bigger defensemen, or he can burst up the middle and split two defenders. He uses all of the ice.

Although Fleury is a better finisher than playmaker, he can handle the puck well enough to play centre. He doesn't cough the puck up very often or make a hasty play. He is very patient.

Fleury always has his legs churning, and he draws penalties by driving to the net. He has a strong wrist shot that he can get away from almost anywhere. He can score even if he is pulled to his knees.

Fleury is an effective penalty killer, blocking shots and getting the puck out along the boards. He is very poised and cool with the puck under attack, holding it until he finds an opening instead of just firing blindly. His defensive play has improved, and he does a good job as a backchecker in holding up opposing forwards so his defensemen have extra time with the puck.

His hand quickness makes him very effective on draws, and he takes offensive-zone draws.

THE PHYSICAL GAME

Fleury can take a hit and not get knocked down because he is so solid and has a low centre of gravity. He uses his stick liberally and will take a lot of penalties sticking up for himself and his teammates. The abuse over a long season tends to wear him down, yet Fleury is remarkably durable.

THE INTANGIBLES

Fleury ended up a Ranger after Colorado paid a heavy rental price, then decided not to re-sign him. The pressure of a four-year, $28-million deal, coupled with his first-ever shift to the East, would terrify most players, but not the confident Fleury.

PROJECTION

Because of the overall lack of depth on the Rangers, expect Fleury's point totals to drop, but not drastically. He will likely score in the 80-point range and will get a ton of ice time.

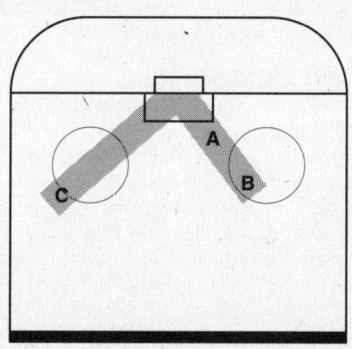

ADAM GRAVES

Yrs. of NHL service: 11
Born: Toronto, Ont.; Apr. 12, 1968
Position: left wing
Height: 6-0
Weight: 205
Uniform no.: 9
Shoots: left

Career statistics:

GP	G	A	TP	PIM
830	270	231	501	1361

1995-96 statistics:

GP	G	A	TP	+/-	PIM	PP	SH	GW	GT	S	PCT
82	22	36	58	+18	100	9	1	2	0	266	8.3

1996-97 statistics:

GP	G	A	TP	+/-	PIM	PP	SH	GW	GT	S	PCT
82	33	28	61	+10	66	10	4	3	5	269	12.3

1997-98 statistics:

GP	G	A	TP	+/-	PIM	PP	SH	GW	GT	S	PCT
72	23	12	35	-30	41	10	0	2	1	226	10.2

1998-99 statistics:

GP	G	A	TP	+/-	PIM	PP	SH	GW	GT	S	PCT
82	38	15	53	-12	47	14	2	7	0	239	15.9

LAST SEASON

Led team in goals, power-play goals, game-winning goals and shots. Tied for team lead in shorthanded goals. Second on team in shooting percentage. One of four Rangers to appear in all 82 games.

THE FINESSE GAME

Graves is a short-game player who scores a whopping percentage of his goals off deflections, rebounds and slam dunks. A shot from the top of the circle is a long-distance effort for him. He favours the wrist shot; his rarely used slap shot barely exists. He is much better when working on instinct because, when he has time to make plays, he will outthink himself.

Although not very fast in open ice and something of an awkward skater, Graves's balance and strength are good and he can get a few quick steps on a rival. He is smart with the puck. He protects it with his body and is strong enough to fend off a checker with one arm and shovel the puck to a linemate with the other.

Graves is a former centre who can step in on draws. He is an intelligent penalty killer.

THE PHYSICAL GAME

A return to good physical health brought Graves back to the form that made him a 50-goal player in 1993-94 (38 goals in the current drought-stricken scoring climate is roughly the equivalent of 50 five years ago). Graves has confidence in his game again, thanks to a successful rehab from a serious back injury. He was able to play a fierce game again, and that makes all the difference in the kind of player Graves can be.

THE INTANGIBLES

Graves is a natural leader who shows up in the grandest fashion on those nights when the rest of his teammates fail to. Those nights when the points aren't coming, Graves never hurts his club and finds other ways to contribute. A frequent winner of "Players' Player" awards, such is the respect he has earned. Off the ice, the absurdly modest Graves is one of the genuine good guys.

PROJECTION

We didn't foresee Graves's return on such a phenomenal scale. It couldn't have happened to a nicer or more determined individual. He can be expected to top 30 goals this season.

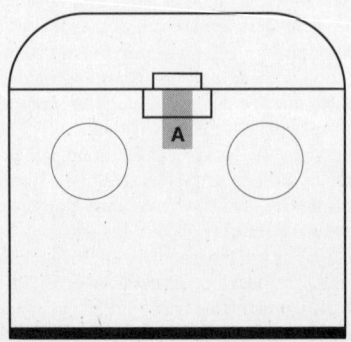

TODD HARVEY

Yrs. of NHL service: 5
Born: Hamilton, Ont.; Feb. 17, 1975
Position: centre/right wing
Height: 6-0
Weight: 195
Uniform no.: 10
Shoots: right

Career statistics:

GP	G	A	TP	PIM
276	49	78	127	521

1995-96 statistics:

GP	G	A	TP	+/-	PIM	PP	SH	GW	GT	S	PCT
69	9	20	29	-13	136	3	0	1	0	101	8.9

1996-97 statistics:

GP	G	A	TP	+/-	PIM	PP	SH	GW	GT	S	PCT
71	9	22	31	+19	142	1	0	2	0	99	9.1

1997-98 statistics:

GP	G	A	TP	+/-	PIM	PP	SH	GW	GT	S	PCT
59	9	10	19	+5	104	0	0	1	0	88	10.2

1998-99 statistics:

GP	G	A	TP	+/-	PIM	PP	SH	GW	GT	S	PCT
37	11	17	28	-1	72	6	0	2	1	58	19.0

LAST SEASON

Second on team in penalty minutes. Missed 27 games with broken thumb. Missed 10 games with sprained left knee. Missed two games with hip injury. Missed three games with bruised thumb. Missed one game with elbow laceration.

THE FINESSE GAME

Harvey's skating is rough. In fact, it's pretty choppy, and as a result he lacks speed. To make up for that, he has good anticipation and awareness. He's clever and his hands are very good. When Harvey gets the puck, he has patience and strength with it. He is not a legitimate first-line player, but he can fit in with skilled players if asked because of his effort.

Harvey's goals are ugly ones. He works the front of the net with grit. He goes to the net and follows up shots with second and third effort. He always has his feet moving and he has good hand-eye coordination. He doesn't have the greatest shot, but he battles to get into the prime scoring areas.

Harvey needs to play big every night to maximize his abilities, but he also has to become smarter in picking his spots. It's not going to do Harvey's career any good to start spending half the season in the trainer's room.

THE PHYSICAL GAME

Harvey's talent level rises when he gets more involved. He's not big enough to be a legitimate NHL heavyweight, but he doesn't back down from challenges. When he's at his best, he gets inside other people's jerseys and heads.

THE INTANGIBLES

Harvey was a big hit in New York because on most nights he was their biggest hitter. Harvey could face a talent squeeze, however, if youngster Pavel Brendl makes the team and if the Rangers are successful in their pursuit of free agent Theo Fleury.

PROJECTION

To get 20 goals, Harvey will have to earn some power-play time, which could happen this season (on the second unit, at least). All Harvey has to do is stay in one piece — not the easiest assignment given his gung-ho style.

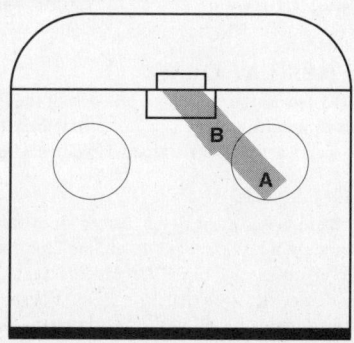

VALERI KAMENSKY

Yrs. of NHL service: 7
Born: Voskresensk, Russia; April 18, 1966
Position: left wing
Height: 6-2
Weight: 198
Uniform no.: 13
Shoots: right

Career statistics:

GP	G	A	TP	PIM
460	166	248	414	303

1995-96 statistics:

GP	G	A	TP	+/-	PIM	PP	SH	GW	GT	S	PCT
81	38	47	85	+14	85	18	1	5	0	220	17.3

1996-97 statistics:

GP	G	A	TP	+/-	PIM	PP	SH	GW	GT	S	PCT
68	28	38	66	+5	38	8	0	4	1	165	17.0

1997-98 statistics:

GP	G	A	TP	+/-	PIM	PP	SH	GW	GT	S	PCT
75	26	40	66	-2	60	8	0	4	0	173	15.0

1998-99 statistics:

GP	G	A	TP	+/-	PIM	PP	SH	GW	GT	S	PCT
65	14	30	44	+1	28	2	0	2	0	123	11.4

LAST SEASON

Signed as free agent, July 6, 1999. Missed two games with broken foot. Missed 15 games with broken forearm.

THE FINESSE GAME

Kamensky is primarily a one-way forward. A gifted skater with speed and quickness, he is as dangerous without the puck as he is with it because of his sense for open ice. He's also as effective in four-on-four situations as he is as an outstanding transition player. His passes are flat and on the money, with just the right velocity. The recipient does not have to slow down but can collect the puck in stride.

Kamensky has quick hands and a good release on his wrist shot. He gets a lot of power-play time and excells at getting open in the left slot; he just rips his one-timer. Given his amount of ice time with the extra man, however, Kamensky should produce more on the power play than he has in recent seasons. He is going to get first-unit power-play time with the Rangers.

THE PHYSICAL GAME

Kamensky is a tough customer, and one of the reasons he is so dinged up every season is that he pays the price to go into high-traffic areas. He takes a beating.

THE INTANGIBLES

Would Kamensky have better career numbers if he had played on a less talented team than Colorado and been given more ice time? Or did the fact that he played alongside someone like Peter Forsberg enhance his career and allow him to land the big free agent deal with the Rangers? That question will be answered this season in New York, where Kamensky will have to shoulder a lot of scoring responsibility.

PROJECTION

Kamensky will find more pressure on him in New York as the number one winger (or at least number one-A, with Adam Graves) and should score 60 points.

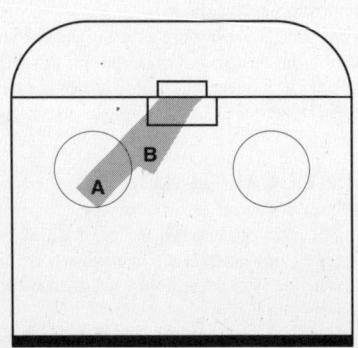

ERIC LACROIX

Yrs. of NHL service: 5
Born: Montreal, Que.; July 15, 1971
Position: left wing
Height: 6-1
Weight: 205
Uniform no.: 28
Shoots: left

Career statistics:

GP	G	A	TP	PIM
347	61	58	119	294

1995-96 statistics:

GP	G	A	TP	+/-	PIM	PP	SH	GW	GT	S	PCT
72	16	16	32	-11	110	3	0	1	0	107	15.0

1996-97 statistics:

GP	G	A	TP	+/-	PIM	PP	SH	GW	GT	S	PCT
81	18	18	36	+16	26	2	0	4	0	141	12.8

1997-98 statistics:

GP	G	A	TP	+/-	PIM	PP	SH	GW	GT	S	PCT
82	16	15	31	0	84	5	0	6	0	126	12.7

1998-99 statistics:

GP	G	A	TP	+/-	PIM	PP	SH	GW	GT	S	PCT
64	2	2	4	-12	18	0	0	1	0	38	5.3

LAST SEASON
Acquired from Los Angeles for Sean Pronger, Feb. 12, 1999. Traded by Colorado to Los Angeles for Roman Vopat and a 1999 sixth-round draft choice Oct. 29, 1998.

THE FINESSE GAME
Lacroix brings zest and inspiration to every shift. There is nothing fancy to his game: he's not the fastest skater and he doesn't have the biggest shot, he just goes to the net and gets his stick down on the ice.

Lacroix is a bigger, more skilled version of Detroit's Kirk Maltby. He can certainly complement some finesse players by working the wall and grinding.

If Lacroix has the proper work ethic, he'll become more than a big banger. Hitters and fighters such as Rick Tocchet turned themselves into productive scorers, first by earning room on the ice then by practising shooting drills to make use of that extra space. Lacroix appears willing to work and is a good skater with balance and speed. He forechecks hard and forces turnovers.

THE PHYSICAL GAME
Lacroix hits to hurt, and some of his checks cross the line. He often makes such thunderous contact he gets penalized, because he leaves his feet and sometimes brings his elbows up. He is grating and fearsome to play against along the boards.

THE INTANGIBLES
Lacroix was rather unfairly driven out of Colorado because of who his father is (Avalanche GM Pierre Lacroix). A fresh start this season is what he needs. The Rangers regard him as a fourth-line winger. If he wants to make anything more of himself, this is the season to step up.

PROJECTION
Lacroix is a tempo-changer who can chip in 10 goals a season.

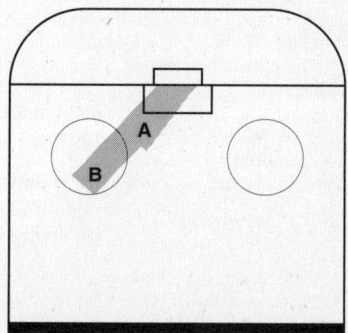

BRIAN LEETCH

Yrs. of NHL service: 11
Born: Corpus Christi, Tex.; Mar. 3, 1968
Position: left defense
Height: 5-11
Weight: 190
Uniform no.: 2
Shoots: left

Career statistics:

GP	G	A	TP	PIM
807	187	578	755	399

1995-96 statistics:

GP	G	A	TP	+/-	PIM	PP	SH	GW	GT	S	PCT
82	15	70	85	+12	30	7	0	3	0	276	5.4

1996-97 statistics:

GP	G	A	TP	+/-	PIM	PP	SH	GW	GT	S	PCT
82	20	58	78	+31	40	9	0	2	0	256	7.8

1997-98 statistics:

GP	G	A	TP	+/-	PIM	PP	SH	GW	GT	S	PCT
76	17	33	50	-36	32	11	0	2	2	230	7.4

1998-99 statistics:

GP	G	A	TP	+/-	PIM	PP	SH	GW	GT	S	PCT
82	13	42	55	-7	42	4	0	1	0	184	7.1

LAST SEASON

Led team defensemen and tied for second on team in points. Tied for fifth among NHL defensemen in scoring. Second on team in assists. Third on team in shots. One of four Rangers to appear in all 82 games.

THE FINESSE GAME

Leetch is a premier passer who sees the ice clearly, identifies the optimum passing option on the move and hits his target with a forehand or backhand pass. He is terrific at picking passes out of the air and keeping attempted clearing passes from getting by him at the point.

Leetch has a fine first step that sends him towards top speed almost instantly. He can be posted at the point, then see an opportunity to jump into the play down low and bolt into action. His anticipation is superb. He seems to be thinking about five seconds ahead of everyone else on the ice. He instantly starts a transition from defense to offense, and always seems to make the correct decision to pass or skate with the puck.

Leetch has a remarkable knack for getting his point shot through traffic and to the net. He even uses his eyes to fake. He is adept at looking and/or moving in one direction, then passing the opposite way.

Leetch smartly jumps into holes to make the most of an odd-man rush, and he is more than quick enough to hop back on defense if the puck goes the other way. He has astounding lateral movement, leaving forwards completely out of room when it looked like there was open ice to get past him. He uses this as a weapon on offense to open up space for his teammates.

Leetch has a range of shots. He'll use a slapper from the point, usually through a screen because it won't overpower any NHL goalie, but he'll also use a wrist shot from the circle. He is gifted with the one-on-one moves that help him wriggle in front for 10-footers on the forehand or backhand, and he has worked on one-timers from close to the net.

THE PHYSICAL GAME

Leetch initiates contact and doesn't hesitate to make plays in the face of being hit. Although not strong enough, or mean spirited-enough, to manhandle people, he still gets physically involved. He competes for the puck and is a first-rate penalty killer.

Leetch cuts off the ice, gives the skater nowhere to go, strips the puck or steals a pass, then starts the transition game. He'll then follow the rush and may finish off the play with a goal. He works best paired with a stay-at-home partner with a mean streak.

THE INTANGIBLES

Leetch re-signed with the Rangers rather than tempt a record-setting auction for his services on the free agent market. While it was a financial risk, it underscores his quiet commitment to the team and his teammates.

PROJECTION

Leetch has finally snapped out of his post-Mark Messier funk and now must grow fully into the role of a leader on a team that is going to go through some growing pains this season. Expect a 55- to 60-point season.

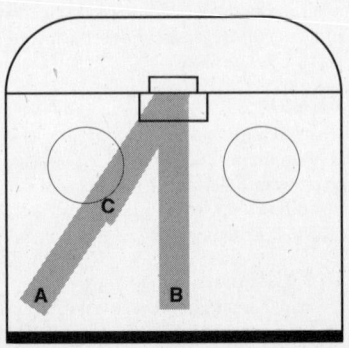

SYLVAIN LEFEBVRE

Yrs. of NHL service: 10
Born: Richmond, Que.; Oct. 14, 1967
Position: right defense
Height: 6-2
Weight: 205
Uniform no.: 2
Shoots: left

Career statistics:

GP	G	A	TP	PIM
716	26	124	150	543

1995-96 statistics:

GP	G	A	TP	+/-	PIM	PP	SH	GW	GT	S	PCT
75	5	11	16	+26	49	2	0	0	0	115	4.3

1996-97 statistics:

GP	G	A	TP	+/-	PIM	PP	SH	GW	GT	S	PCT
71	2	11	13	+12	30	1	0	0	0	77	2.6

1997-98 statistics:

GP	G	A	TP	+/-	PIM	PP	SH	GW	GT	S	PCT
81	0	10	10	+2	48	0	0	0	0	66	.0

1998-99 statistics:

GP	G	A	TP	+/-	PIM	PP	SH	GW	GT	S	PCT
76	2	18	20	+18	48	0	0	0	0	64	3.1

LAST SEASON

Signed as free agent by N.Y. Rangers, July 19, 1999. Missed six games with eye injury.

THE FINESSE GAME

Lefebvre is a good argument for instituting an NHL award for best defensive defensemen (as opposed to the Norris Trophy, which in recent years has gone to offensive defensemen). If there was such a piece of hardware, Lefebvre would have been a finalist through much of his career, if not a winner. He's one of the best at one-on-one coverage. He's always in position and always square with his man. He reads the play well and makes good outlet passes from his own end.

Lefebvre plays his position the way any coach would try to teach it to a youngster. Safe and dependable, he makes the first pass and then forgets about the puck. He couldn't be any less interested in the attack. If he has the puck at the offensive blueline and doesn't have a lane, he just throws it into the corner. His game is defense first, and he is very basic and consistent in his limited role. He does it all playing against the other teams' top lines on a nightly basis.

Lefebvre actually has below-average skills in speed and puckhandling, but by playing within his limits and within the system he is ultrareliable.

THE PHYSICAL GAME

Tough without being a punishing hitter, Lefebvre patrols and controls the front of his net and plays a hard-nosed style. He plays a containment game.

THE INTANGIBLES

Lefebvre is a quiet leader, well respected by teammates and opponents. At 32, he is starting to hit the back end of his career.

PROJECTION

Lefebvre prevents points, he doesn't score them.

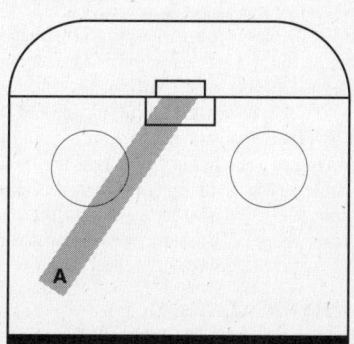

JOHN MACLEAN

Yrs. of NHL service: 15
Born: Oshawa, Ont.; Nov. 20, 1964
Position: right wing
Height: 6-0
Weight: 200
Uniform no.: 15
Shoots: right

Career statistics:

GP	G	A	TP	PIM
1021	371	388	759	1210

1995-96 statistics:

GP	G	A	TP	+/-	PIM	PP	SH	GW	GT	S	PCT
76	20	28	48	+3	91	3	3	3	0	237	8.4

1996-97 statistics:

GP	G	A	TP	+/-	PIM	PP	SH	GW	GT	S	PCT
80	29	25	54	+11	49	5	0	6	0	254	11.4

1997-98 statistics:

GP	G	A	TP	+/-	PIM	PP	SH	GW	GT	S	PCT
77	16	27	43	-6	42	6	0	3	1	213	7.5

1998-99 statistics:

GP	G	A	TP	+/-	PIM	PP	SH	GW	GT	S	PCT
82	28	27	55	+5	46	11	1	2	0	231	12.1

LAST SEASON

Tied for team lead in plus-minus. Second on team in goals, power-play goals and shots. Tied for second on team in points. One of four Rangers to appear in all 82 games.

THE FINESSE GAME

There is no such thing as an impossible angle for MacLean. He will shoot anytime, from anywhere on the ice, and will usually put the puck on net or out into traffic in front of the crease — where there is always a chance the puck will hit someone or something and go skittering into the net. So what if all of his scoring chances are no longer the brilliant highlight shots that characterized his presurgery (1991) career? His pure goal-scoring instincts still make him a threat.

MacLean still thinks of himself as a goal scorer, but he is such a good defensive forward that he can be used in a checking role, and provide offense on the counterattack. He lacks the speed to be an effective shadow against the league's faster forwards, but he is an intelligent player positionally and harasses puck carriers into clumsy passes with his forechecking. He pressures the points when killing penalties. And he has great anticipation for picking passes out of lanes that he fools the opposition into thinking are open.

Slow in open ice but strong along the boards and in the corners, MacLean chugs and churns and draws restraining fouls. He also indulges in a bit of diving. Somehow, he gets to where he has to go, but his wheels are average on a good night.

THE PHYSICAL GAME

MacLean uses a wide-based skating stance and is tough to budge from the front of the net. He will take a lot of abuse to get the job done in traffic, and will not be intimidated. He has cut down on his retaliatory penalties, but won't take much garbage before snapping. Despite his problems with his knee, he is remarkably durable. He is extremely competitive and fights down to the last second of a game.

THE INTANGIBLES

Should the Rangers actually play any of their younger prospects, MacLean is an ideal guy to have around. He's a veteran with a solid NHL reputation, but he also goes out of his way to make kids feel part of a team. They could also learn a thing or two from his work ethic and savvy.

PROJECTION

MacLean's big-number days are over as he has become more of a two-way forward, but he can still kick in 25 goals a season.

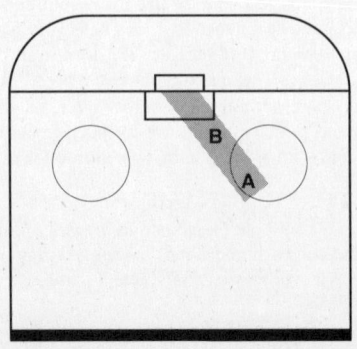

MANNY MALHOTRA

Yrs. of NHL service: 1
Born: Mississauga, Ont.; May 18, 1980
Position: centre
Height: 6-1 1/2
Weight: 210
Uniform no.: 6
Shoots: left

Career statistics:

GP	G	A	TP	PIM
73	8	8	16	13

1998-99 statistics:

GP	G	A	TP	+/-	PIM	PP	SH	GW	GT	S	PCT
73	8	8	16	-2	13	1	0	2	0	61	13.1

LAST SEASON

First NHL season. Drafted seventh overall by N.Y. Rangers, June 27, 1998. Will be entering first NHL season.

THE FINESSE GAME

Malhotra is a versatile player who may turn into a young Rod Brind'Amour, able to check, work on the power play, play centre, play wing, give a team a lead or protect it. He's the perfect player for the Rangers, who have so many holes to fill it's difficult to even start. Malhotra is one way to begin because he brings so many things to a team.

Malhotra is a two-way centre who was used mainly as a checking forward in his last year of junior, and he's probably pegged as the same for the Rangers this season. He will never be a big-time scorer, because his shot is not an awesome weapon, but by working to get in position and dig for short-range chances he will get his share. Malhotra also has a terrific first step and reads offensive plays well. He gets more than his fair share of breakaways.

Malhotra's game is fuelled by his will and determination. Few recent young players have been so highly ranked in terms of character. He understands the game well and is highly coachable.

THE PHYSICAL GAME

Malhotra is big and strong and likes to play a physical game, but he needs to bulk up a bit more to play against the big boys, against whom he looked coltish. He has been described as an ultimate team player and a kid who thrives on hard work and improving himself. He's a low-maintenance player. He will not take a night, or a shift, off.

THE INTANGIBLES

Malhotra was labelled the most NHL-ready of any of the prospects of the 1998 draft, with the lone warning being that there might not be as much upside to his game as there is to players like Vincent Lacavalier or David Legwand. The last 18-year-old draftee we can remember being described in these terms was Mike Ricci, who broke in with the Flyers at 18 and scored 41 points. If that's a safe pick, the Rangers will gladly take it and the consistent 10-year career that goes along with it.

PROJECTION

The Rangers will ask Malhotra to assume a fairly regular third-line role this season. The kid is ready. Consider this: he scored one goal less than Wayne Gretzky last season given about one-fourth the ice time. He is a mature, solid player who can play full-time and maybe score 25 to 30 points in his sophomore year.

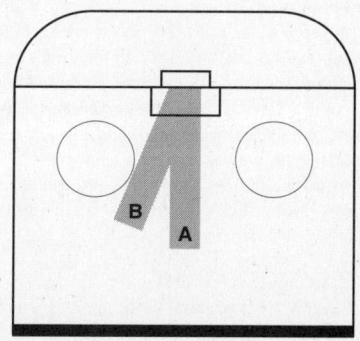

PETR NEDVED

Yrs. of NHL service: 8
Born: Liberec, Czech Republic; Dec. 9, 1971
Position: centre
Height: 6-3
Weight: 195
Uniform no.: 93
Shoots: left

Career statistics:

GP	G	A	TP	PIM
497	178	206	384	370

1995-96 statistics:

GP	G	A	TP	+/-	PIM	PP	SH	GW	GT	S	PCT
80	45	54	99	+37	68	8	1	5	1	204	22.1

1996-97 statistics:

GP	G	A	TP	+/-	PIM	PP	SH	GW	GT	S	PCT
74	33	38	71	-2	66	12	3	4	0	189	17.5

1997-98 statistics:
Did not play in NHL

1998-99 statistics:

GP	G	A	TP	+/-	PIM	PP	SH	GW	GT	S	PCT
56	20	27	47	-6	50	9	1	3	0	153	13.1

LAST SEASON

Acquired from Pittsburgh with Sean Pronger and Chris Tamer for Alexei Kovalev and Harry York, Nov. 25, 1998. Third on team in power-play goals and shooting percentage. Missed 19 games in contract dispute. Missed seven games with rib cage injury.

THE FINESSE GAME

Tall but slightly built, Nedved is good at handling the puck in traffic or in open ice at tempo. He uses his forehand and backhand equally well for a pass or a shot. He sees the ice very well and has a creative mind.

Nedved makes use of the time and space. He may have the best wrist shot in the NHL, with a hair-trigger release and radar-like accuracy. He likes to go high on the glove side, picking the corner. Although he lacks a big slap shot, he has the vision to handle the power play from the point.

Nedved was out of the league for more than a year, but when he stepped in with the Rangers he was able to adapt back quickly to the NHL pace. He is an intelligent player who handles the defensive responsibilities and shows his creative side on the attack.

Good on attacking-zone draws, Nedved knows his way around a face-off. He has good hand quickness and cheats well. On offensive-zone draws, he turns his body so that he's almost facing the boards. That is about it for his defensive contribution, though he can kill penalties because of his quickness and anticipation.

THE PHYSICAL GAME

The knock on Nedved early in his career was his inconsistency and his distaste for the physical aspect of the game. But he has filled out and grown up in every sense of the word. When Wayne Gretzky went down with an injury in February, Nedved blossomed under the mantle of the team's number one centre, which he now is with Gretzky's retirement. Nedved competes hard and isn't deterred when facing some of the league's top forwards, such as Philadelphia's Eric Lindros. In fact, he's starting to thrive on it.

THE INTANGIBLES

Nedved has a new hockey life in New York. If rookie Pavel Brendl is NHL-ready, Nedved could be sitting on a career year.

PROJECTION

It's been a long wait, but Nedved is ready to step into the number one role with the Rangers and we expect a big season. He scored 99 points with Pittsburgh in 1996-97, and could flirt with those numbers again.

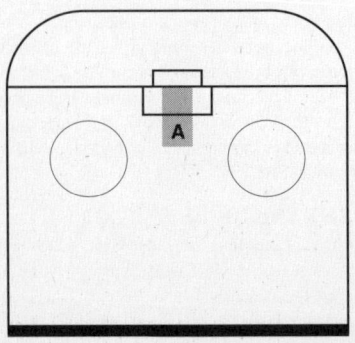

STEPHANE QUINTAL

Yrs. of NHL service: 11
Born: Boucherville, Que.; Oct. 22, 1968
Position: right defense
Height: 6-3
Weight: 225
Uniform no.: 5
Shoots: right

Career statistics:

GP	G	A	TP	PIM
875	46	128	174	944

1995-96 statistics:

GP	G	A	TP	+/-	PIM	PP	SH	GW	GT	S	PCT
68	2	14	16	-4	117	0	1	1	1	104	1.9

1996-97 statistics:

GP	G	A	TP	+/-	PIM	PP	SH	GW	GT	S	PCT
71	7	15	22	+1	100	1	0	0	0	139	5.0

1997-98 statistics:

GP	G	A	TP	+/-	PIM	PP	SH	GW	GT	S	PCT
71	6	10	16	+13	97	0	0	0	0	88	6.8

1998-99 statistics:

GP	G	A	TP	+/-	PIM	PP	SH	GW	GT	S	PCT
82	8	19	27	-23	84	1	1	4	0	159	5.0

LAST SEASON

Tied for team lead in game-winning goals. Only Canadien to appear in all 82 games.

THE FINESSE GAME

Quintal's game is limited by his lumbering skating. He has some nice touches, including a decent point shot, and a good head and hands for passing, but his best moves have to be executed at a virtual standstill. He needs to be paired with a quick skater or his shifts will be spent solely in the defensive zone. Consider this stat: Quintal was -23 on the season, while his regular defense partner, Vladimir Malakhov, was -7. Most of those minuses for Quintal were amassed in the 20 games Malakhov missed.

Fortunately, Quintal is aware of his flaws. He plays a smart positional game and doesn't get involved in low-percentage plays in the offensive zone. He won't step up in the neutral zone to risk an interception but will fall back into a defensive mode. He takes up a lot of ice with his body and stick, and when he doesn't overcommit, he reduces the space available to a puck carrier. Quintal does not like to carry the puck. He tends to get a little panicky under pressure.

Although he can exist as an NHL regular in the five-on-five mode, Quintal is a risky proposition for any specialty-team play.

THE PHYSICAL GAME

Strong on his skates, Quintal thrives on contact and works hard along the boards and in front of the net. He hits hard without taking penalties and is a tough and willing fighter if he has to do it. He has the strength to clear the crease and is good skater for his size.

THE INTANGIBLES

Quintal is ideally a number five or six defenseman, but a dearth of defensive talent in Montreal requires him to play in the top four. A more limited role is in his future as the Canadiens break younger defensemen into the lineup.

PROJECTION

Quintal can score 20 to 25 points and he is a serviceable, second-pairing defenseman only if he is paired with a mobile partner.

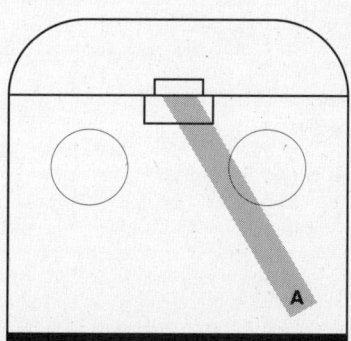

MIKE RICHTER

Yrs. of NHL service: 9
Born: Abingdon, Pa.; Sept. 22, 1966
Position: goaltender
Height: 5-11
Weight: 185
Uniform no.: 35
Catches: left

Career statistics:

GP	MIN	GA	SO	GAA	A	PIM
492	28037	1332	22	2.85	8	26

1995-96 statistics:

GP	MIN	GAA	W	L	T	SO	GA	S	SAPCT	PIM
41	2396	2.68	24	13	3	3	107	1221	.912	4

1996-97 statistics:

GP	MIN	GAA	W	L	T	SO	GA	S	SAPCT	PIM
61	3598	2.68	33	22	6	4	161	1945	.917	4

1997-98 statistics:

GP	MIN	GAA	W	L	T	SO	GA	S	SAPCT	PIM
72	4143	2.66	21	31	15	0	184	1888	.903	2

1998-99 statistics:

GP	MIN	GAA	W	L	T	SO	GA	S	SAPCT	PIM
68	3878	2.63	27	30	8	4	170	1898	.910	0

LAST SEASON

Fifth among NHL goalies in minutes played. GAA was second-best of career.

THE PHYSICAL GAME

The Rangers should consider putting a collar around Richter's neck and an invisible fence around the perimeter of his crease. Richter is a stickhandling nightmare: puck exchanges with his defensemen are often laughable and, at times, life-threatening, because Richter simply cannot decide whether to leave the puck behind the net or try a cute little pass to help the cause. The results are usually calamitous. Either there is a turnover for an easy goal, or some defenseman, trying to find Richter's pass in his feet, gets creamed from behind by a forechecker. He would be far better off just staying in the paint.

Richter uses his stick for poke-checks in one-on-one confrontations, but still doesn't use it enough as a pass-blocking tool. Too often, he concedes the pass across the crease and relies on his lateral movement to make a quick save he wouldn't have to make at all if he merely prevented the puck from reaching the shooter.

Nonetheless, Richter is agile, flexible and athletic, and boasts exceptional post-to-post quickness. Quick reflexes allow him to reach second-chance shots off rebounds or one-timers off odd-man rushes.

Richter rarely gets beat to the low corners. Shooters beat him high on the glove side or on slam-dunks to the weak side after he has overplayed an angle. He gets a whopping percentage of the first shots. While he catches more pucks now, and holds onto them more, he still leaves some big rebounds.

THE MENTAL GAME

Richter may be the most patient one-on-one goalie in the NHL. Confident and fluid, he simply lets himself make whatever save is necessary. If that results in him losing his stick and at least one of his gloves, no problem. When he trusts his instincts and just flows, he is the NHL's best package of concentration, reflexes and puckstopping skill in clutch situations.

He is exceptional at finding the puck through traffic, and able to make solid stops on close-range shots off passes from behind the net. Similarly, when the puck is moving from point to point, Richter stays focussed, stays crouched, sees the puck and stays with it. He tends to lose his concentration on long shots, and gets beaten every now and then by a ridiculous goal.

THE INTANGIBLES

Richter rebounded with a strong season last year, his own numbers vastly improved despite playing behind a team that was not much better. If you have to stop one penalty shot or breakaway, pick Richter as your goalie.

PROJECTION

Richter's numbers improved but he could use a little more time off. The Rangers will need to add a reliable veteran backup to give him some off nights.

MATHIEU SCHNEIDER

Yrs. of NHL service: 10
Born: New York, N.Y.; June 12, 1969
Position: left defense
Height: 5-11
Weight: 192
Uniform no.: 25
Shoots: left

Career statistics:

GP	G	A	TP	PIM
631	105	240	345	582

1995-96 statistics:

GP	G	A	TP	+/-	PIM	PP	SH	GW	GT	S	PCT
78	13	41	54	-20	103	7	0	1	0	191	6.8

1996-97 statistics:

GP	G	A	TP	+/-	PIM	PP	SH	GW	GT	S	PCT
26	5	7	12	+3	20	1	0	1	0	63	7.9

1997-98 statistics:

GP	G	A	TP	+/-	PIM	PP	SH	GW	GT	S	PCT
76	11	26	37	-12	44	4	1	1	0	181	6.1

1998-99 statistics:

GP	G	A	TP	+/-	PIM	PP	SH	GW	GT	S	PCT
75	10	24	34	-19	71	5	0	2	0	159	6.3

LAST SEASON

Acquired from Toronto for Alexander Karpovstev and a 1999 fourth-round draft choice, Oct. 14, 1998. Missed four games with groin strain.

THE FINESSE GAME

Schneider is an excellent skater, plus he's strong. He sees the ice and moves the puck very well coming out of his own end, and is capable of controlling the pace. He has developed into a good two-way defenseman with the offensive skills to get involved in the attack and to work the point on the power play. His major concern is his solid positional play. He makes fewer high-risk plays as he has gained more experience.

Strong, balanced and agile, Schneider lacks breakaway speed but is quick with his first step and changes directions smoothly. He can carry the puck but does not lead many rushes. He gets the puck out of the corner quickly. He makes good defensive decisions.

Schneider has improved his point play, doing more with the puck than just drilling shots. He handles the puck well and looks for the passes down low. Given the green light, he is likely to get involved down low more often. He has the skating ability to recover quickly when he takes a chance.

THE PHYSICAL GAME

Schneider is a poor man's version of Chris Chelios. He plays a lot meaner than most people think. He's extremely strong on his feet. He's great at making the first pass and he's not very flashy, so he doesn't stand out the way a Chelios would.

Schneider's goal is to play a containment game and move the puck quickly and intelligently out of the zone, which he does well. He is often matched against other teams' top scoring lines and always tries to do the job. He is best when paired with a physical defenseman. He has a tendency to hit high and gets penalties because of it.

THE INTANGIBLES

Schneider's major problem has to do with confidence. He's one of those guys you have to tell, all the time, when he's doing well, and then he'll respond. Conversely, criticism from a coach can get Schneider into a funk. He doesn't react well to being ridden hard, even though, like all players, sometimes he needs it. The Rangers didn't exactly make Schneider (Group 2 free agent) feel like a high priority at the end of last season. That and coach John Muckler's apparent dislike for him could have Schneider on the move again.

PROJECTION

Schneider fell shy of the 45 points we predicted for him last season. He is capable of those numbers.

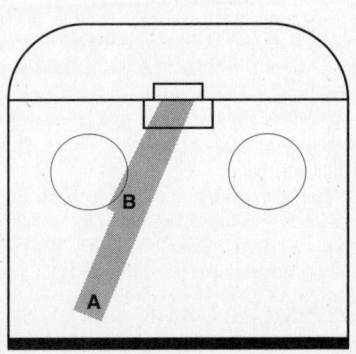

KEVIN STEVENS

Yrs. of NHL service: 11
Born: Brockton, Mass.; Apr. 15, 1965
Position: left wing
Height: 6-3
Weight: 217
Uniform no.: 17
Shoots: left

Career statistics:

GP	G	A	TP	PIM
748	315	366	681	1329

1995-96 statistics:

GP	G	A	TP	+/-	PIM	PP	SH	GW	GT	S	PCT
61	13	23	36	-10	71	6	0	1	0	170	7.6

1996-97 statistics:

GP	G	A	TP	+/-	PIM	PP	SH	GW	GT	S	PCT
69	14	20	34	-27	96	4	0	1	1	175	8.0

1997-98 statistics:

GP	G	A	TP	+/-	PIM	PP	SH	GW	GT	S	PCT
80	14	27	41	-7	130	5	0	3	1	144	9.7

1998-99 statistics:

GP	G	A	TP	+/-	PIM	PP	SH	GW	GT	S	PCT
81	23	20	43	-10	64	8	0	3	0	136	16.9

LAST SEASON
Led team in shooting percentage. Third on team in goals. Missed one game due to coach's decision.

THE FINESSE GAME
Perception is everything, and the perception in New York was that Stevens was a high-priced underachiever. Just because he no longer belongs among the league's elite scorers, however, doesn't mean Stevens is no longer an effective winger.

Stevens has the size and strength to battle for and win position in front of the net. He has lost a lot of confidence in what used to be an astonishingly quick release on his shot. In the past, he didn't think twice about where his shot was going. Now his positioning isn't as good, and he has to concentrate on where he is and where to shoot; the whole process has slowed to a crawl.

Stevens simply drops anchor in the slot on the power play. His huge frame blocks the goalie's view and he has good hand-eye coordination for tips and deflections. Those moves aren't instinctive, but came from hours of practise. He also has a devastating one-timer. He does not have to be overly clever with the puck, since he can overpower goalies with his shot. He's a power-play specialist; his shot is simply no longer that special.

Stevens is an average skater at best, and often seems overanxious to get started on the attacking rush to keep up with his fleeter linemates. His reach and range make him appear faster than he is.

THE PHYSICAL GAME
Stevens looked a little fresher last season, though he was by no means the devastating force he was as a younger player. But when Stevens is on, he initiates his hits and leaves a trail of bodies in his wake. He isn't as consistent with his physical play as he could be, however — probably the result of some horrific injuries he has picked up through his career.

THE INTANGIBLES
Stevens produced his best goal-scoring season since 1993-94, but it just never looks like enough when you consider his past track record. The Rangers will probably move him as part of their rebuilding plans. He is a good team man.

PROJECTION
Stevens can produce 20 to 25 goals in the right spot.

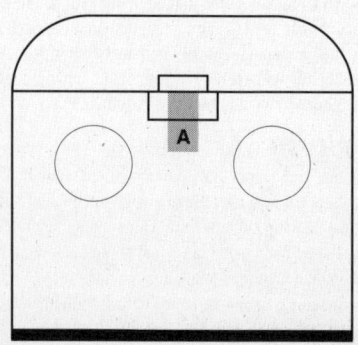

OTTAWA SENATORS

Players' Statistics 1998-99

POS.	NO.	PLAYER	GP	G	A	PTS	+/-	PIM	PP	SH	GW	GT	S	PCT
C	19	ALEXEI YASHIN	82	44	50	94	16	54	19		5	1	337	13.1
L	15	SHAWN MCEACHERN	77	31	25	56	8	46	7		4	1	223	13.9
R	10	ANDREAS DACKELL	77	15	35	50	9	30	6		3		107	14.0
L	20	MAGNUS ARVEDSON	80	21	26	47	33	50		4	6		136	15.4
L	21	ANDREAS JOHANSSON	69	21	16	37	1	34	7		6		144	14.6
R	7	NELSON EMERSON	65	13	24	37	8	51	3		1	2	188	6.9
C	13	VACLAV PROSPAL	79	10	26	36	8	58	2		3		114	8.8
D	33	JASON YORK	79	4	31	35	17	48	2			1	177	2.3
R	11	DANIEL ALFREDSSON	58	11	22	33	8	14	3		5		163	6.7
C	14	RADEK BONK	81	16	16	32	15	48		1	6		110	14.5
R	18	*MARIAN HOSSA	60	15	15	30	18	37	1		2	2	124	12.1
D	6	WADE REDDEN	72	8	21	29	7	54	3		1	1	127	6.3
L	28	TED DONATO	82	11	16	27	-8	41	3				106	10.4
D	29	IGOR KRAVCHUK	79	4	21	25	14	32	3				171	2.3
D	5	*SAMI SALO	61	7	12	19	20	24	2		1		106	6.6
C	22	SHAUN VAN ALLEN	79	6	11	17	3	30		1			47	12.8
C	25	BRUCE GARDINER	59	4	8	12	6	43			1		70	5.7
D	27	JANNE LAUKKANEN	50	1	11	12	18	40					46	2.2
D	3	*PATRICK TRAVERSE	46	1	9	10	12	22					35	2.9
D	2	LANCE PITLICK	50	3	6	9	7	33					34	8.8
C	16	STEVE MARTINS	36	4	3	7	4	10	1		1		27	14.8
R	12	DAVID OLIVER	17	2	5	7	1	4					18	11.1
D	4	CHRIS PHILLIPS	34	3	3	6	-5	32	2				51	5.9
L	9	BILL BERG	44	2	2	4	4	28			1		40	5.0
G	1	DAMIAN RHODES	45	1	1	2	0	4					1	100.0
C	7	VIACHESLAV BUTSAYEV	3		1	1	-1	4					5	
R	26	PHILIP CROWE	8		1	1	1	4					2	
L	37	YVES SARAULT	11		1	1	1	4					7	
D	24	JOHN GRUDEN	13		1	1	0	8					10	
G	31	RON TUGNUTT	43				0							

GP = games played; G = goals; A = assists; PTS = points; +/- = goals-for minus goals-against while player is on ice; PIM = penalties in minutes; PP = power-play goals; SH = shorthanded goals; GW = game-winning goals; GT = game-tying goals; S = no. of shots; PCT = percentage of goals to shots; * = rookie

DANIEL ALFREDSSON

Yrs. of NHL service: 4
Born: Grums, Sweden; Dec. 11, 1972
Position: right wing
Height: 5-11
Weight: 187
Uniform no.: 11
Shoots: right

Career statistics:

GP	G	A	TP	PIM
271	78	132	210	90

1995-96 statistics:

GP	G	A	TP	+/-	PIM	PP	SH	GW	GT	S	PCT
82	26	35	61	-18	28	8	2	3	1	212	12.3

1996-97 statistics:

GP	G	A	TP	+/-	PIM	PP	SH	GW	GT	S	PCT
76	24	47	71	+5	30	11	1	1	2	247	9.7

1997-98 statistics:

GP	G	A	TP	+/-	PIM	PP	SH	GW	GT	S	PCT
55	17	28	45	+7	18	7	0	7	0	149	11.4

1998-99 statistics:

GP	G	A	TP	+/-	PIM	PP	SH	GW	GT	S	PCT
58	11	22	33	+8	14	3	0	5	0	163	6.7

LAST SEASON

Missed five games with abdominal pull. Missed five games with knee injury. Missed four games with facial laceration. Missed one game with flu.

THE FINESSE GAME

Alfredsson has a big-time NHL shot. His release is hair-trigger. He also has a solid work ethic; he didn't make it to the NHL on cruise control. He has to work for his space, and he does. One of the reasons why he is so good on the power play is because of his work in open ice. He has excellent vision and hands.

Alfredsson has not played much with centre Alexei Yashin, which fuels rumours that the two Ottawa stars don't like each other. The fact is that their games don't complement one another. Both players like to play a puck possession game. After the acquisition of Vinny Prospal from Philadelphia, Alfredsson had a linemate who likes to distribute the puck more.

Alfredsson is well schooled in the defensive aspects of the game. He works diligently along the wall.

THE PHYSICAL GAME

Alfredsson has a very thick and powerful lower body to fuel his skating. He is fearless and takes a lot of abuse to get into the high-scoring areas. He will skate up the wall and cut to the middle of the ice. He might get nailed by the off-side defenseman, but on the next rush he will try it again. He won't be scared off, and on the next chance he may get the shot away and in.

Alfredsson learned to handle the rigours of the NHL schedule in his second season. He pays close attention to conditioning and nutrition.

THE INTANGIBLES

You can chalk it up to coincidence for now, but between contract hassles and injuries Alfredsson never gets off to a good start. His frequent absences from the lineup prevent him from establishing a groove.

PROJECTION

Alfredsson won't be a 40-goal scorer, but he should be a reliable 30-goal man every season.

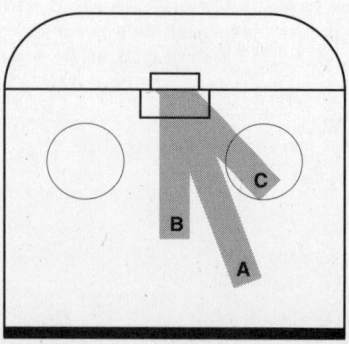

MAGNUS ARVEDSON

Yrs. of NHL service: 2
Born: Karlstad, Sweden; Nov. 25, 1971
Position: left wing
Height: 6-2
Weight: 198
Uniform no.: 20
Shoots: left

Career statistics:

GP	G	A	TP	PIM
141	32	41	73	86

1997-98 statistics:

GP	G	A	TP	+/-	PIM	PP	SH	GW	GT	S	PCT
61	11	15	26	+2	36	0	1	0	1	90	12.2

1998-99 statistics:

GP	G	A	TP	+/-	PIM	PP	SH	GW	GT	S	PCT
80	21	26	47	+33	50	0	4	6	0	136	15.4

LAST SEASON

Selke Trophy finalist. Second NHL season. Led team and tied for fourth in NHL in plus-minus. Led team and tied for fourth in NHL in shorthanded goals. Led team in shooting percentage. Tied for team lead in game-winning goals. Tied for third on team in goals. Missed two games with back spasms.

THE FINESSE GAME

Arvedson has great speed and is strong on the puck. He was not much of a scorer in Sweden but he has a good shot — like many Europeans he doesn't use it enough. He is unselfish and will usually look to set up a teammate.

Arvedson has a lot of potential. He is good and smart enough to play on one of the top two lines. However, he was used as a third-line checking winger and in only his second NHL season excelled at the job to the point where he became a Selke Trophy candidate.

THE PHYSICAL GAME

Arvedson is big and strong and able to handle the rigours of an NHL schedule. He can handle a checking assignment to cover the top players, kill penalties and contribute offensively.

THE INTANGIBLES

Arvedson suffered from a bulging disk in his back that hampered his playoff performance and caused him to miss the final game of the postseason. Surgery was being weighed during the off-season. If he has it, he could get a late start to the season. He could also miss playing time because of a contract hassle. He is an unrestricted free agent who is due for a big raise (he earned U.S.$450,000 last season).

PROJECTION

Arvedson could score 20 goals if he continues to see the ice time he did last year, and if he's healthy.

RADEK BONK

Yrs. of NHL service: 5
Born: Krnov, Czech Republic; Jan. 9, 1976
Position: centre
Height: 6-3
Weight: 215
Uniform no.: 14
Shoots: left

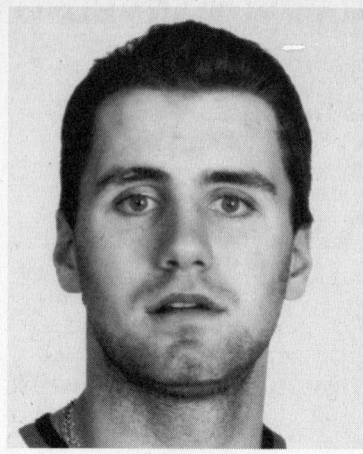

Career statistics:

GP	G	A	TP	PIM
317	47	65	112	142

1995-96 statistics:

GP	G	A	TP	+/-	PIM	PP	SH	GW	GT	S	PCT
76	16	19	35	-5	36	5	0	1	0	161	9.9

1996-97 statistics:

GP	G	A	TP	+/-	PIM	PP	SH	GW	GT	S	PCT
53	5	13	18	-4	14	0	1	0	1	82	6.1

1997-98 statistics:

GP	G	A	TP	+/-	PIM	PP	SH	GW	GT	S	PCT
65	7	9	16	-13	16	1	0	0	0	93	7.5

1998-99 statistics:

GP	G	A	TP	+/-	PIM	PP	SH	GW	GT	S	PCT
81	16	16	32	+15	48	0	1	6	0	110	14.5

LAST SEASON

Tied for team lead in game-winning goals. Games played career high. Goals matches career high. Missed one game with hip flexor.

THE FINESSE GAME

Bonk's skating is a detriment. He's fine when he gets a good head of speed up but he doesn't explode in his first two strides (the way Joe Sakic does, for example). He can't utilize his skills when he can't accelerate away from stick-checks. His skating is the primary reason why he has not been able to be an impact scorer in the NHL as he was in the minors.

Bonk is a puck magnet; the puck always seems to end up on his stick in the slot. He scores the majority of his goals from work in tight, getting his stick free. He has a heavy shot but doesn't have a quick release. He is a smart and creative passer and plays well in advance of his years, with a great deal of poise.

Defensively, Bonk keeps improving. He performed frequently as a third-line centre. He is decent on face-offs and can be used to kill penalties because of his anticipation. He is a poor man's Bobby Holik when he plays with a little edge.

THE PHYSICAL GAME

Although Bonk has good size, he does not show signs of becoming a power forward. He is aggressive only in his pursuit of the puck. He goes into the corners and wins many one-on-one battles because of his strength and hand skills.

THE INTANGIBLES

Only one person in the Ottawa organization — maybe the league — believed in Bonk, and it wasn't Bonk himself. Coach Jacques Martin deserves all the credit for turning Bonk into a serviceable player. He will always be known as a first-round bust, but at least he can make an honest living.

PROJECTION

Bonk's absolute top end is 20 goals. He is not a top six forward.

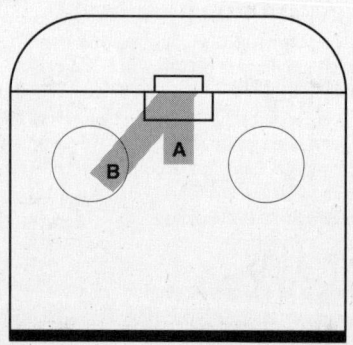

ANDREAS DACKELL

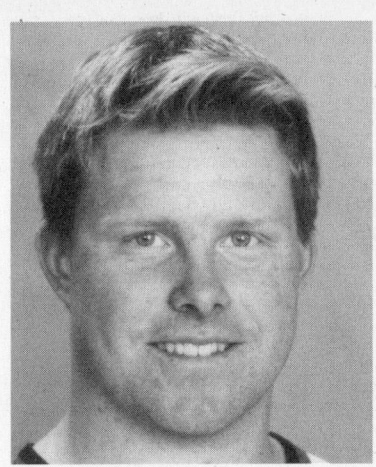

Yrs. of NHL service: 3
Born: Gavle, Sweden; Dec. 29, 1972
Position: right wing
Height: 5-10
Weight: 191
Uniform no.: 10
Shoots: right

Career statistics:

GP	G	A	TP	PIM
238	42	72	114	62

1996-97 statistics:

GP	G	A	TP	+/-	PIM	PP	SH	GW	GT	S	PCT
79	12	19	31	-6	8	2	0	3	0	79	15.2

1997-98 statistics:

GP	G	A	TP	+/-	PIM	PP	SH	GW	GT	S	PCT
82	15	18	33	-11	24	3	2	2	1	130	11.5

1998-99 statistics:

GP	G	A	TP	+/-	PIM	PP	SH	GW	GT	S	PCT
77	15	35	50	+9	30	6	0	3	0	107	14.0

LAST SEASON
Second on team in assists. Third on team in points. Missed four games with concussion. Missed one game with knee injury.

THE FINESSE GAME
Dackell has good hockey sense and is very sound defensively. He does a lot of subtle things well. Tapes of his game could be used to illustrate hustling on backchecks to knock the puck away from an attacker, attacking in the neutral zone without committing yourself, playing strong along the wall and keeping your man out of the play. Dackell is a last-minute man, one of the guys put on the ice in the final minute of a period or game to protect a lead. He kills penalties and protects the puck well.

Dackell has a decent, accurate shot that he could utilize more. He seems to score timely goals. He doesn't have blazing speed but works hard to be where he's supposed to be. He's very smart and hard to knock off the puck.

THE PHYSICAL GAME
Dackell isn't overly big and he's not a banger, however, he'll make his checks and he won't be intimidated. He took a wicked lick into the end boards by Eric Lindros early in the season, but it didn't reduce his enthusiasm when he returned after suffering a concussion and facial lacerations. He could be the toughest 30-PIM-a-year player in the NHL.

THE INTANGIBLES
Much of what Dackell contributes to a team is subtle, but he is a valuable role player on the Senators.

PROJECTION
Dackell can handle a second-line role as a safety-valve winger, but he is better suited as a third-line checking forward who can provide a steady 15 to 20 goals a season.

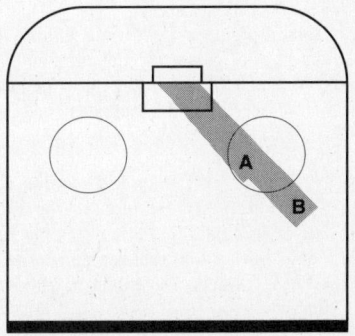

MARIAN HOSSA

Yrs. of NHL service: 1
Born: Stara Lubovna, Slovakia; Jan. 12, 1979
Position: left wing
Height: 6-1
Weight: 185
Uniform no.: 18
Shoots: left

Career statistics:

GP	G	A	TP	PIM
60	15	15	30	37

1997-98 statistics:

GP	G	A	TP	+/-	PIM	PP	SH	GW	GT	S	PCT
7	0	1	1	-1	0	0	0	0	0	10	0.0

1998-99 statistics:

GP	G	A	TP	+/-	PIM	PP	SH	GW	GT	S	PCT
60	15	15	30	+18	37	1	0	2	2	124	12.1

LAST SEASON

First NHL season. Named to NHL All-Rookie Team. Tied for third on team in plus-minus. Missed 22 games recovering from knee surgery.

THE FINESSE GAME

Hossa is a pure goal scorer. He has excellent hands and the kind of instincts that cannot be taught or drilled into a player. He has shown in his brief NHL stint that he will able to bring the brilliance he showed in junior to this level. He could be a great scorer.

Hossa is a swift and mobile skater, who is always dangerous one-on-one. There are some similarities between him and fellow Slovak, Ziggy Palffy. Hossa works hard in the offensive zone but needs to work on his defensive game and his play without the puck. He also needs to be more consistent in his effort.

Hossa works very well down low. He has keen hockey sense and excellent vision.

THE PHYSICAL GAME

Hossa made a remarkable comeback following major reconstructive knee surgery. He seemed to have no lack of confidence in his rebuilt knee. He uses his size well — better in the offensive zone than the rest of the ice.

THE INTANGIBLES

Hossa is something special. He will quickly be elevated to the kind of player the Senators employ as a go-to guy. He had a disappointing playoffs, but so did his much more experienced teammates.

PROJECTION

Hossa played very well for a kid coming into the league off a serious injury. He might hit the wall in the second half of this year as he handles his first full NHL schedule, but he didn't miss a game after returning to the Ottawa lineup December 5, after his successful rehab.

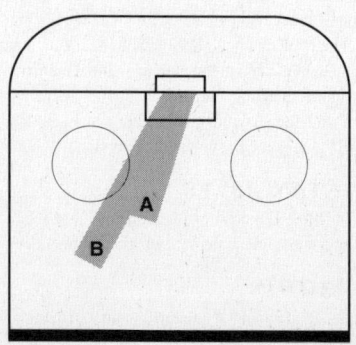

JANNE LAUKKANEN

Yrs. of NHL service: 4
Born: Lahti, Finland; Mar. 19, 1970
Position: left defense
Height: 6-0
Weight: 180
Uniform no.: 27
Shoots: left

Career statistics:

GP	G	A	TP	PIM
220	9	51	60	198

1995-96 statistics:

GP	G	A	TP	+/-	PIM	PP	SH	GW	GT	S	PCT
23	1	2	3	-1	14	1	0	0	0	35	2.9

1996-97 statistics:

GP	G	A	TP	+/-	PIM	PP	SH	GW	GT	S	PCT
76	3	18	21	-14	76	2	0	0	0	109	2.8

1997-98 statistics:

GP	G	A	TP	+/-	PIM	PP	SH	GW	GT	S	PCT
60	4	17	21	-15	64	2	0	2	0	69	5.8

1998-99 statistics:

GP	G	A	TP	+/-	PIM	PP	SH	GW	GT	S	PCT
50	1	11	12	+18	40	0	0	0	0	46	2.2

same energetic player he was a season ago.

PROJECTION

Laukkanen's recovery from his injury bears watching. He can play a top four role and score 25 points if healthy.

LAST SEASON

Tied for third on team in plus-minus. Missed 19 games recovering from abdominal surgery. Missed four games with groin injury. Missed five games with concussion. Missed four games with back injuries.

THE FINESSE GAME

Laukkanen's hockey sense is about average, but his courage, will to win and character are all very much above average. He is one of the defensemen that his coaches want on the ice in the last minutes of the game, because he will rarely lose a battle. He will do anything to win.

Laukkanen's best physical asset is his skating. He has learned to shift gears smoothly. He will never be a big point producer, though, because he doesn't have a great shot. His hands are pretty good for passing, however. He makes an alert first pass out of the zone and can spot a breaking forward for a home run pass. He earns some power-play time because he is poised with the puck.

Laukkanen kills penalties aggressively and intelligently. He was buried for a time in the strong Colorado system, and is a late bloomer.

THE PHYSICAL GAME

Laukkanen is a brave defenseman who will block shots and battle defensively, even though he is much smaller than most NHL heavyweight forwards.

THE INTANGIBLES

Laukkanen suffered his abdominal injury during training camp and underwent surgery at the start of the season. His game never got untracked, and he wasn't the

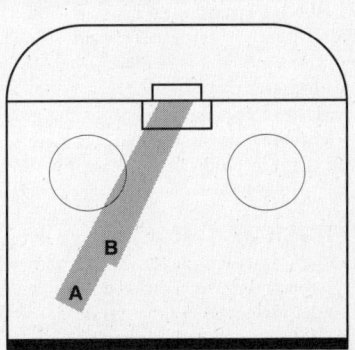

SHAWN MCEACHERN

Yrs. of NHL service: 7
Born: Waltham, Mass.; Feb. 28, 1969
Position: centre/left wing
Height: 5-11
Weight: 195
Uniform no.: 15
Shoots: left

Career statistics:
GP	G	A	TP	PIM
524	151	170	321	242

1995-96 statistics:
GP	G	A	TP	+/-	PIM	PP	SH	GW	GT	S	PCT
82	24	29	53	-5	34	3	2	3	0	238	10.1

1996-97 statistics:
GP	G	A	TP	+/-	PIM	PP	SH	GW	GT	S	PCT
65	11	20	31	-5	18	0	1	2	0	150	7.3

1997-98 statistics:
GP	G	A	TP	+/-	PIM	PP	SH	GW	GT	S	PCT
81	24	24	48	+1	42	8	2	4	2	229	10.5

1998-99 statistics:
GP	G	A	TP	+/-	PIM	PP	SH	GW	GT	S	PCT
77	31	25	56	+8	46	7	0	4	1	223	13.9

LAST SEASON
Second on team in goals, points and shots. Tied for second on team in power-play goals. Missed four games with groin injury. Missed one game with wrist injury.

THE FINESSE GAME
McEachern suffers from serious tunnel vision, which negates some of the advantage his speed brings to the lineup. He skates with his head down, looking at the ice instead of the play around him. He is strong and fast, with straightaway speed, but he tends to expend his energy almost carelessly and has to take short shifts.

McEachern's skating is what keeps him employed on the first line. He can shift speeds and direction smoothly without losing control of the puck. He can play both left wing and centre but is better on the wing because he doesn't use his linemates as well as a centre should. A very accurate shooter with a hard wrister, he has a quick release on his slap shot, which he likes to let go after using his outside speed. He is strong on face-offs and is a smart penalty killer who pressures the puck carrier.

McEachern feasts on the chances that result from both the checking attention on Alexei Yashin and the rebounds that are produced by Yashin's devastating shots.

THE PHYSICAL GAME
Generally an open-ice player, McEachern will also pursue the puck with some diligence in the attacking zone. But he is light, and although he can sometimes build up momentum with his speed for a solid bump, he loses most of the close-in battles for the puck. He's a yapper, and many nights he can distract opponents who want to rip his head off.

THE INTANGIBLES
McEachern is a versatile player who can fill a lot of roles with his speed. He isn't what would be considered a true first-line winger, but he'll fill that role with the Senators until someone takes his job away.

PROJECTION
As long as McEachern continues to earn prime ice time, he can score 30 goals and 60 points.

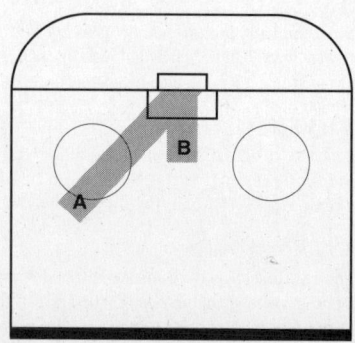

CHRIS PHILLIPS

Yrs. of NHL service: 2
Born: Fort McMurray, Alta.; Mar. 9, 1978
Position: left defense
Height: 6-2
Weight: 200
Uniform no.: 4
Shoots: left

Career statistics:

GP	G	A	TP	PIM
106	8	14	22	70

1997-98 statistics:

GP	G	A	TP	+/-	PIM	PP	SH	GW	GT	S	PCT
72	5	11	16	+2	38	2	0	2	0	107	4.7

1998-99 statistics:

GP	G	A	TP	+/-	PIM	PP	SH	GW	GT	S	PCT
34	3	3	6	-5	32	2	0	0	0	51	5.9

LAST SEASON

Second NHL season. Missed 23 games with ankle surgery. Missed three games with back spasms. Missed one game due to coach's decision.

THE FINESSE GAME

Phillips is a very good skater for his size. He has all of the attributes — decent speed, lateral mobility, balance and agility. He skates well backwards and has a small turning radius. Carrying the puck doesn't slow him down much. He is skilled enough to be used up front, though when the Senators did it last season it was in more of an attempt to wake up Phillips's game.

He will never post Ray Bourque numbers, but Phillips can handle Bourque-like ice time. He has a feel for the offensive part of the game. He joins the attack intelligently and has a hard shot from the point, as well as a good wrist shot when he goes in deep. He is a heads-up passer and sees the ice well.

Lots of kids in the defenseman-heavy 1996 draft were being compared to Scott Stevens, but Phillips may actually be the closest to him in style and leadership. He may even turn out to be better than advertised.

THE PHYSICAL GAME

Phillips is solidly built and there are very few question marks about his honest brand of toughness. He likes to hit, and he's mobile enough to catch a defender and drive with his legs to pack a wallop in his checks. His ankle injury obviously hampered his skating last season.

THE INTANGIBLES

Phillips is leadership material, and his struggles last season grated on him more than they did on the coaching staff. He should be healthy and have a big comeback season.

PROJECTION

Phillips is a solid two-way defenseman whose emphasis will be defense, but he could still provide 40 points a season.

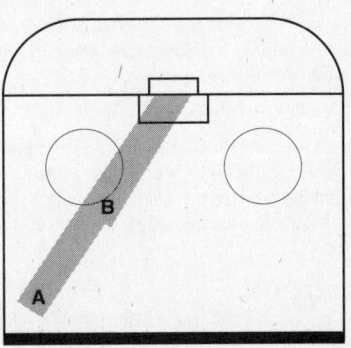

VACLAV PROSPAL

Yrs. of NHL service: 2
Born: Ceske-Budejvice, Czech Republic; Feb. 17, 1975
Position: centre
Height: 6-2
Weight: 185
Uniform no.: 13
Shoots: left

Career statistics:

GP	G	A	TP	PIM
153	21	55	76	83

1996-97 statistics:
GP	G	A	TP	+/-	PIM	PP	SH	GW	GT	S	PCT
18	5	10	15	+3	4	4	0	0	0	35	14.3

1997-98 statistics:
GP	G	A	TP	+/-	PIM	PP	SH	GW	GT	S	PCT
56	6	19	25	-11	21	4	0	0	0	88	6.8

1998-99 statistics:
GP	G	A	TP	+/-	PIM	PP	SH	GW	GT	S	PCT
79	10	26	36	+8	58	2	0	3	0	114	8.8

LAST SEASON

Second NHL season. Led team in penalty minutes. Missed one game with flu. Missed two games due to coach's decision.

THE FINESSE GAME

Prospal has a power-play weapon. It's not an overpowering shot that makes him effective, but his ability to thread the puck through penalty killers to an open man.

Prospal loves to score (his wrist shot and one-timers are accurate) and make plays. He had to learn to play without the puck, and he's succeeded. His defensive game has improved. He thinks the game well and is an unselfish player, which makes him a natural fit with Daniel Alfredsson.

The only rap on Prospal is his skating ability, but it's NHL calibre and his view of the ice and his hockey sense compensate for any lack of pure speed.

THE PHYSICAL GAME

Prospal is tall but lean and needs a little more muscle for one-on-one battles. Right now he gives the impression of being a little smaller than he is, but he's an eager player who will get involved. He didn't do this enough on a nightly basis last season and has to fire up his intensity level more often.

THE INTANGIBLES

The Senators want Prospal to be a number two centre, but he endured a lengthy slump last season (0-for-30 goals) and did not step up when the checking attention of the Buffalo Sabres homed in on Alexei Yashin in the playoffs.

PROJECTION

Prospal needs to show more. He has a job that is his for the taking, but if he feels complacent about it he will have another dud year instead of scoring the 50 points he is capable of.

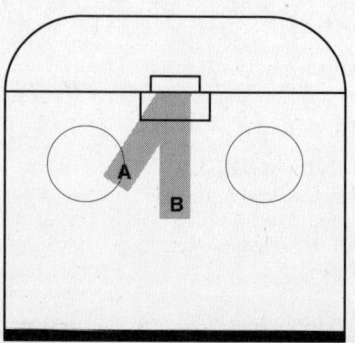

WADE REDDEN

Yrs. of NHL service: 3
Born: Lloydminster, Sask.; June 12, 1977
Position: left defense
Height: 6-2
Weight: 193
Uniform no.: 6
Shoots: left

Career statistics:

GP	G	A	TP	PIM
234	22	59	81	122

1996-97 statistics:

GP	G	A	TP	+/-	PIM	PP	SH	GW	GT	S	PCT
82	6	24	30	+1	41	2	0	1	0	102	5.9

1997-98 statistics:

GP	G	A	TP	+/-	PIM	PP	SH	GW	GT	S	PCT
80	8	14	22	+17	27	3	0	2	0	103	7.8

1998-99 statistics:

GP	G	A	TP	+/-	PIM	PP	SH	GW	GT	S	PCT
72	8	21	29	+7	54	3	0	1	1	127	6.3

LAST SEASON

Tied for second on team in penalty minutes. Missed eight games with shoulder injury. Missed two games with back spasms.

THE FINESSE GAME

Redden has tried to pattern his game after Ray Bourque, and the young defenseman does have a few things in common with the Boston great. Redden is a good skater who can change gears swiftly and smoothly, and his superb rink vision enables him to get involved in his team's attack. He has a high skill level. His shot is hard and accurate and he is a patient and precise passer.

Redden plays older than his years and has a good grasp of the game. As he has been tested at higher and higher levels of competition he has elevated his game. His poise is exceptional.

Redden's work habits and attitude are thoroughly professional. He seems to be a player who is willing to learn in order to improve his game. He is very cool and steady, comprising half of Ottawa's top defense pairing with Jason York.

THE PHYSICAL GAME

Redden is not a big hitter, but he finishes his checks and stands up well. What he lacks in aggressiveness he makes up for with his competitive nature. He can handle a lot of ice time. He plays an economical game without a lot of wasted effort, and he is durable and can skate all night long. He would move up a step if he dished it out instead of just taking it.

THE INTANGIBLES

Redden has a laid-back nature, but he raises his game when something is on the line. An unrestricted free agent, he could miss the start of the season if negotiations don't go smoothly. Redden suffered a fractured ankle in the World Championships.

PROJECTION

Redden plays defense first but he has good offensive upside and can produce 35 to 40 points if he maintains his high level of play through a full year.

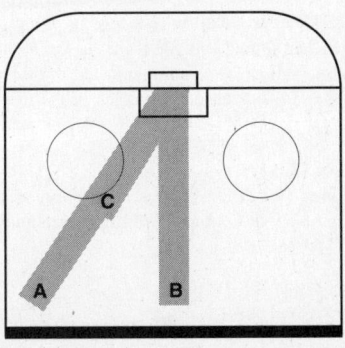

SAMI SALO

Yrs. of NHL service: 1
Born: Turku, Finland; Sept. 2, 1974
Position: right defense
Height: 6-3
Weight: 190
Uniform no.: 5
Shoots: right

Career statistics:

GP	G	A	TP	PIM
61	7	12	19	24

1998-99 statistics:

GP	G	A	TP	+/-	PIM	PP	SH	GW	GT	S	PCT
61	7	12	19	+20	24	2	0	1	0	106	6.6

LAST SEASON

First NHL season. Named to NHL All-Rookie Team. Led team and led all NHL rookies in plus-minus. Missed 11 games with groin injuries. Missed two games with shoulder injury. Missed one game with bruised thigh.

THE FINESSE GAME

Salo is highly skilled. He has very quick feet and good mobility, which, combined with his long reach, make him hard to beat one-on-one. He possesses one of the hardest shots in the NHL, and he likes to get involved offensively. He steps up into the play alertly.

Salo has good hands for passing or receiving the puck. He makes a crisp first pass out of the zone. He has a good head for the game. He was an older rookie last season and was very poised.

Salo has quickly established himself as a top four defenseman on a solid team.

THE PHYSICAL GAME

Salo won't punish anyone. He is more of a positional defenseman who will ride guys out.

THE INTANGIBLES

The Senators aren't paying their European scouts enough. Every season they seem to come up with a surprise gem. Salo, a low pick (239th overall in 1996), was last year's revelation. He took a pay cut and a one-year deal (since extended) just to get a chance to play in the NHL. He had some injuries and wore down a little late in the season, which is probably why he had a poor playoffs.

PROJECTION

If he doesn't take the expected sophomore step backwards, Salo should improve off his rookie numbers to 25 to 30 points.

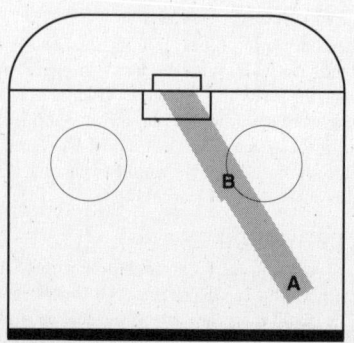

RON TUGNUTT

Yrs. of NHL service: 11
Born: Scarborough, Ont.; Oct. 22, 1967
Position: goaltender
Height: 5-11
Weight: 155
Uniform no.: 31
Catches: left

Career statistics:

GP	MIN	GA	SO	GAA	A	PIM
347	18797	3.32	11	1041	5	6

1995-96 statistics:
Did not play in NHL

1996-97 statistics:

GP	MIN	GAA	W	L	T	SO	GA	S	SAPCT	PIM
37	1991	2.80	17	15	1	3	93	882	.895	0

1997-98 statistics:

GP	MIN	GAA	W	L	T	SO	GA	S	SAPCT	PIM
42	2236	2.25	15	14	8	3	84	882	.905	0

1998-99 statistics:

GP	MIN	GAA	W	L	T	SO	GA	S	SAPCT	PIM
43	2508	1.79	22	10	8	3	75	1005	.925	0

LAST SEASON
Led NHL in goals-against average with career best. Third in NHL in save percentage. Career high in wins. Missed two games with knee injury.

THE PHYSICAL GAME
NHL goalies don't come much smaller than Tugnutt these days. He has to come out to the top of his crease to make himself as big as possible. He is a good skater who is able to follow the play and square himself to the shooter.

Tugnutt is fine with his rebounds, but he also plays behind a team that skates well, and he gets plenty of help clearing loose pucks.

Tugnutt has a good glove hand, though he is not an adept stickhandler. He comes out of his net well to stop hard-arounds and isn't bothered by the extra space behind the net. He communicates well with his defensemen, who like playing for him.

THE MENTAL GAME
Tugnutt did not have a very good playoffs, or a strong World Championships, and there are question marks about his ability to handle the pressure of the big save in the big game. He's going to be 32 when the season starts, so maturity is not an issue.

What is a question mark is Tugnutt's upcoming role as a number one goalie. The Senators moved Damian Rhodes, with whom Tugnutt was virtually platooned, and with no backup on the immediate horizon Tugnutt stands alone.

THE INTANGIBLES
Tugnutt's critics say that his stats are padded because he plays behind a well-disciplined trapping team. He needs to be kept to about 55 starts, meaning the Senators will have to find him some reliable help.

PROJECTION
Tugnutt should net 30 wins in what will be his first full-time role since 1990-91.

ALEXEI YASHIN

Yrs. of NHL service: 6
Born: Sverdlovsk, Russia; Nov. 5, 1973
Position: centre
Height: 6-3
Weight: 215
Uniform no.: 19
Shoots: right

Career statistics:

GP	G	A	TP	PIM
422	178	225	403	203

1995-96 statistics:

GP	G	A	TP	+/-	PIM	PP	SH	GW	GT	S	PCT
46	15	24	39	-15	28	8	0	1	0	143	10.5

1996-97 statistics:

GP	G	A	TP	+/-	PIM	PP	SH	GW	GT	S	PCT
82	35	40	75	-7	44	10	0	5	1	291	12.0

1997-98 statistics:

GP	G	A	TP	+/-	PIM	PP	SH	GW	GT	S	PCT
82	33	39	72	+6	24	5	0	6	0	291	11.3

1998-99 statistics:

GP	G	A	TP	+/-	PIM	PP	SH	GW	GT	S	PCT
82	44	50	94	+16	54	19	0	5	1	337	13.1

LAST SEASON

Led team in goals, points and shots for third consecutive season. Tied for third in NHL in goals. Third in NHL in shots. Sixth in NHL in points. Led team in assists for second consecutive season. Career highs in goals, assists and points. Led team and second in NHL in power-play goals. Tied for second on team in penalty minutes. One of two Senators to appear in all 82 games. Has appeared in 292 consecutive games.

THE FINESSE GAME

Yashin isn't a flashy skater, but he has drawn comparisons to Ron Francis with his quiet effectiveness, and he is spectacular at times. He doesn't go all-out every shift, though, and on those occasions it looks like he's either pacing himself or he's fatigued. Because it looks as if he isn't trying, when things go poorly for him people assume he's loafing. His protracted contract battles of the past have also made the critics quick to attack. Still, Yashin had nearly an MVP season last year, and he was more consistent in his effort on a nightly basis.

Yashin's skills are world class — on par with those of any other player of his generation. He has great hands and size. As he stickhandles in on the rush, he can put the puck through the legs of two or three defenders en route to the net. He has to learn, though, that he can go directly to the net and not wait for the defense to come to him, so that he can dazzle by using their legs as croquet wickets.

Last year, Yashin unleashed his powerful shot with more certainty and regularity; the results said it all. He doesn't have pure breakaway speed but he is powerful and balanced. He doesn't utilize his teammates well. He wants the puck a lot and has to play with unselfish linemates.

THE PHYSICAL GAME

Yashin is big and rangy and he protects the puck well. He has stepped up his desire to play through checks and pay the price in traffic. He is also smart and skilled enough to avoid unnecessary wallops.

THE INTANGIBLES

Taking over as team captain meant a lot to Yashin, who continued to mature in many ways last season. But, guess what? Another contract hassle looms, as Yashin is going into the last year of a deal and wants to get it done before this season is underway. He would benefit if the Senators could develop a second-line centre, since teams will focus checking attention on him and shut him down, as Buffalo did in the playoffs.

PROJECTION

Yashin's all-around game has evolved, and he can be a 100-point scorer, too.

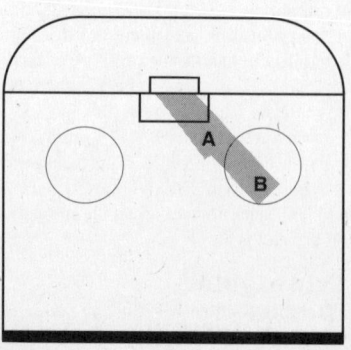

JASON YORK

Yrs. of NHL service: 6
Born: Ottawa, Ont.; May 20, 1970
Position: right defense
Height: 6-2
Weight: 195
Uniform no.: 33
Shoots: right

Career statistics:
GP	G	A	TP	PIM
340	16	94	110	281

1995-96 statistics:
GP	G	A	TP	+/-	PIM	PP	SH	GW	GT	S	PCT
79	3	21	24	-7	88	0	0	0	0	106	2.8

1996-97 statistics:
GP	G	A	TP	+/-	PIM	PP	SH	GW	GT	S	PCT
75	4	17	21	-8	67	1	0	0	0	121	3.3

1997-98 statistics:
GP	G	A	TP	+/-	PIM	PP	SH	GW	GT	S	PCT
73	3	13	16	+8	62	0	0	0	0	109	2.8

1998-99 statistics:
GP	G	A	TP	+/-	PIM	PP	SH	GW	GT	S	PCT
79	4	31	35	+17	48	2	0	0	1	177	2.3

PROJECTION
York moved into the 30-point ranks and maintained a solid defensive base. He can do it again.

LAST SEASON
Tied for third on team in assists. Career highs in assists and points. Missed three games with shoulder injury.

THE FINESSE GAME
York is just entering his defensive prime. He is a smart, all-around defenseman, who concentrated on learning the defensive part of the game first at the NHL level. Now the offensive ability he showed in the minors is coming into play as well.

York's finesse skills are fine. He is a good skater with a very hard point shot, and he can handle the point on the second power-play unit — though he isn't quite good enough to step up to the first five. He's a fine penalty killer. He reads plays well (his offensive reads are far superior to his defensive reads) and has the skating ability to spring some shorthanded chances. He can be used in any game situation.

York was the Senators' best all-around defenseman last season and made a solid pair with Wade Redden.

THE PHYSICAL GAME
York is not very physical. He is not a big checker but employs positional play to angle attackers to the boards, using his stick to sweep-check or poke pucks. Once he gains control of the puck, he moves it quickly with no panicky mistakes. He doesn't have a polished defensive game but he does work hard.

THE INTANGIBLES
York stepped up his game considerably last season. Now all he has to do is stay there.

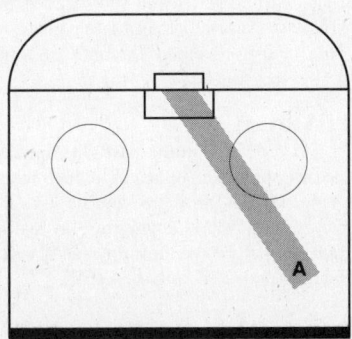

ROB ZAMUNER

Yrs. of NHL service: 7
Born: Oakville, Ont.; Sept. 17, 1969
Position: left wing
Height: 6-2
Weight: 202
Uniform no.: 7
Shoots: left

Career statistics:

GP	G	A	TP	PIM
484	85	118	203	325

1995-96 statistics:

GP	G	A	TP	+/-	PIM	PP	SH	GW	GT	S	PCT
72	15	20	35	+11	62	0	3	4	0	152	9.9

1996-97 statistics:

GP	G	A	TP	+/-	PIM	PP	SH	GW	GT	S	PCT
82	17	33	50	+3	56	0	4	3	0	216	7.9

1997-98 statistics:

GP	G	A	TP	+/-	PIM	PP	SH	GW	GT	S	PCT
77	14	12	26	-31	41	0	3	4	1	126	11.1

1998-99 statistics:

GP	G	A	TP	+/-	PIM	PP	SH	GW	GT	S	PCT
58	8	11	19	-15	24	1	1	2	0	89	9.0

LAST SEASON

Acquired from Tampa Bay as compensation for hiring GM Rick Dudley. Tied for third on team in game-winning goals. Missed 24 games with groin injury.

THE FINESSE GAME

Zamuner is now going to get to prove what he can do on a good team. He doesn't have great speed, but he compensates for it in other ways, including all-out effort. He is a complementary player, a grinder who can also handle the puck and has some good hand skills. Lacking speed, he plays well positionally and takes away the attacker's angles to the net. He doesn't skate as well as many of today's third-line checking wingers, but he is smart enough.

Zamuner was a sniper at the minor-league level but has not been able to make the same impact in the NHL. He has a decent touch for scoring or passing, but it's average at best. He is a shorthanded threat because of his anticipation and work ethic, and he easily turns penalty-killing shifts into shorthanded counterattacks. He has a knack for scoring key goals.

A groin injury prevented Zamuner from being at his most effective last season.

THE PHYSICAL GAME

Zamuner had problems in the past with fitness, until he realized what a big edge he could have with better conditioning. He has good size and he uses it effectively. He is pesky and annoying to play against. On many nights he will be the most physically active forward, adding a real spark with his effort.

THE INTANGIBLES

Few players work as hard every night, every shift, as Zamuner, who was Tampa Bay's captain. Ottawa needs some forwards with a grittier game, and Zamuner should fit the bill.

PROJECTION

Zamuner has become a checking winger and possible Selke Trophy contender who can provide a steady 15 goals a season.

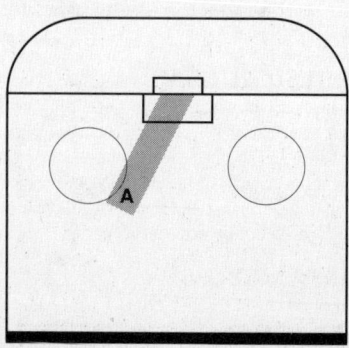

PHILADELPHIA FLYERS

Players' Statistics 1998-99

POS.	NO.	PLAYER	GP	G	A	PTS	+/-	PIM	PP	SH	GW	GT	S	PCT
C	88	ERIC LINDROS	71	40	53	93	35	120	10	1	2	3	242	16.5
L	10	JOHN LECLAIR	76	43	47	90	36	30	16		7	3	246	17.5
C	17	ROD BRIND'AMOUR	82	24	50	74	3	47	10		3	2	191	12.6
R	20	KEITH JONES	78	20	33	53	23	98	3		3		135	14.8
R	11	MARK RECCHI	71	16	37	53	-7	34	3		2		171	9.4
D	37	ERIC DESJARDINS	68	15	36	51	18	38	6		2		190	7.9
D	3	DANIEL MCGILLIS	78	8	37	45	16	61	6		4		164	4.9
R	19	MIKAEL RENBERG	66	15	23	38	5	18	6		2		154	9.7
C	18	DAYMOND LANGKOW	78	14	19	33	-8	39	4	1	2		149	9.4
D	25	STEVE DUCHESNE	71	6	24	30	-6	24	2		2		118	5.1
L	26	VALERI ZELEPUKIN	74	16	9	25	0	48			5		129	12.4
D	6	CHRIS THERIEN	74	3	15	18	16	48	1				115	2.6
R	8	JODY HULL	72	3	11	14	-2	12			1	1	73	4.1
L	21	SANDY MCCARTHY	80	5	8	13	-24	160	1				107	4.7
C	28	MARC BUREAU	71	4	6	10	-2	10					52	7.7
D	5	*DMITRI TERTYSHNY	62	2	8	10	-1	30	1				68	2.9
L	32	CRAIG BERUBE	77	5	4	9	-10	194					52	9.6
D	24	KARL DYKHUIS	78	4	5	9	-23	50	1				88	4.5
L	14	MIKAEL ANDERSSON	47	2	4	6	-7	4					51	3.9
D	22	LUKE RICHARDSON	78		6	6	-3	106					49	
R	9	MARK GREIG	7	1	3	4	1	2					9	11.1
D	2	ADAM BURT	68		4	4	4	60					61	
L	29	ROMAN VOPAT	54		3	3	-7	90					27	
G	27	RON HEXTALL	23		2	2	0	2						
D	43	*ANDY DELMORE	2		1	1	-1						2	
D	32	*RYAN BAST	2		1	1	0						1	
G	34	JOHN VANBIESBROUCK	62		1	1	0	12						
R	54	*BRIAN WESENBERG	1				1	5						
G	49	*JEAN-MARC PELLETIER	1				0							
D	25	CHRIS JOSEPH	2				0	2					1	
L	21	DAN KORDIC	2				-1	2						
L	40	JASON ZENT	2				0						1	
C	14	PETER WHITE	3				0							
C	15	RICHARD PARK	7				-1						5	

GP = games played; G = goals; A = assists; PTS = points; +/- = goals-for minus goals-against while player is on ice; PIM = penalties in minutes; PP = power-play goals; SH = shorthanded goals; GW = game-winning goals; GT = game-tying goals; S = no. of shots; PCT = percentage of goals to shots; * = rookie

ROD BRIND'AMOUR

Yrs. of NHL service: 10
Born: Ottawa, Ont.; Aug. 9, 1970
Position: centre/left wing
Height: 6-1
Weight: 202
Uniform no.: 17
Shoots: left

Career statistics:

GP	G	A	TP	PIM
778	273	430	703	698

1995-96 statistics:

GP	G	A	TP	+/-	PIM	PP	SH	GW	GT	S	PCT
82	26	61	87	+20	110	4	4	5	4	213	12.2

1996-97 statistics:

GP	G	A	TP	+/-	PIM	PP	SH	GW	GT	S	PCT
82	27	32	59	+2	41	8	2	3	2	205	13.2

1997-98 statistics:

GP	G	A	TP	+/-	PIM	PP	SH	GW	GT	S	PCT
82	36	38	74	-2	54	10	2	8	0	205	17.6

1998-99 statistics:

GP	G	A	TP	+/-	PIM	PP	SH	GW	GT	S	PCT
82	24	50	74	+3	47	10	0	3	2	191	12.6

LAST SEASON

Second on team in assists. Tied for second on team in power-play goals. Third on team in goals, points and shots. Only Flyer to appear in all 82 games. Raised consecutive games-played streak to 484, leading all active players.

THE FINESSE GAME

Versatility and dependability are among Brind'Amour's trademarks. He is one of the best two-way centres in the league. He wins face-offs. He checks. He has the strength and speed and stride to handle every defensive aspect of the game, the grit and desire to earn the loose pucks, the temperament and credibility to be on the ice in the last minute of a close game.

Brind'Amour may not beat many players one-on-one in open ice, but he outworks defenders along the boards and uses a quick burst of speed to drive to the net. He's a playmaker in the mucking sense, with scoring chances emerging from his commitment. Brind'Amour is a better player at centre than wing, though he can handle either assignment.

Brind'Amour has a long, powerful stride with a quick first step to leave a defender behind; his hand skills complement the skating assets. He drives well into a shot on the fly, and has a quick-release snap shot and a strong backhand.

When Brind'Amour does not have the puck he works ferociously to get it back. An excellent penalty killer and the centre the Flyers send out if they are two men short, Brind'Amour thinks nothing of blocking shots. His work ethic led him to wear the "C" while Eric Lindros was sidelined.

THE PHYSICAL GAME

A king in the weight room, Brind'Amour uses his size well and is a strong skater. He can muck with the best in the corners and along the boards. He will carry the puck through traffic in front of the net and battle for position for screens and tip-ins. He is among the hardest workers on the team, even in practice, and is always striving to improve his game.

THE INTANGIBLES

Brind'Amour is a coach's treasure because he can be deployed in any situation and will provide trustworthy work. The fact that he provides steady play without glitter or fanfare on a high-visibility team undercuts the recognition he deserves but doesn't always receive. The Flyers, however, may be looking to trade this valuable player.

PROJECTION

Brind'Amour should score in the 30-goal range.

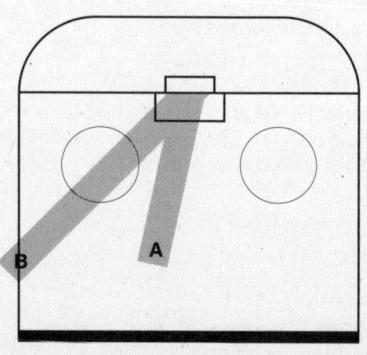

MARC BUREAU

Yrs. of NHL service: 8
Born: Trois-Riviere, Que.; May 19, 1966
Position: centre
Height: 6-1
Weight: 202
Uniform no.: 28
Shoots: right

Career statistics:

GP	G	A	TP	PIM
504	52	78	130	315

1995-96 statistics:

GP	G	A	TP	+/-	PIM	PP	SH	GW	GT	S	PCT
65	3	7	10	-3	46	0	0	1	0	43	7.0

1996-97 statistics:

GP	G	A	TP	+/-	PIM	PP	SH	GW	GT	S	PCT
43	6	9	15	+4	16	1	1	2	0	56	10.7

1997-98 statistics:

GP	G	A	TP	+/-	PIM	PP	SH	GW	GT	S	PCT
74	13	6	19	0	12	0	0	2	0	82	15.9

1998-99 statistics:

GP	G	A	TP	+/-	PIM	PP	SH	GW	GT	S	PCT
71	4	6	10	-2	10	0	0	0	0	52	7.7

PROJECTION

Bureau can score 10 to 15 goals in a third-line checking role.

LAST SEASON

Missed seven games with sprained left wrist. Missed four games due to coach's decision.

THE FINESSE GAME

Bureau plays with concentration and intensity, and is terrier-like in his pursuit of the puck. His tenacity makes penalty killing and shutting down the opposition his best assets. He is also dogged on face-offs and can be used to take key defensive draws. He works consistently on his forechecking and forces turnovers.

Bureau has overcome a skating deficiency. He is a chopper when he moves and his skating is laboured, but he gets to where he has to be with vigour and effort. He has no end-to-end speed to speak of, but in the heated throes of a game he remains highly effective.

He will get to the puck as quickly as he can and is able to do something with it when he arrives. He has decent hands and an average shot, but he thinks defensively.

THE PHYSICAL GAME

Bureau is a blue-collar player and an agitator. He's very feisty and gets opponents ticked off enough to take runs or punches at him. He could be a stronger checker, but he lacks good balance. When he hits people he's usually the one to fall. To his credit, he pops right back up and rejoins the fray.

THE INTANGIBLES

Bureau is used to handling other teams' top lines, but had a tough time getting started in the checking role after Philly spent a bundle to sign him as a free agent from Montreal in 1998.

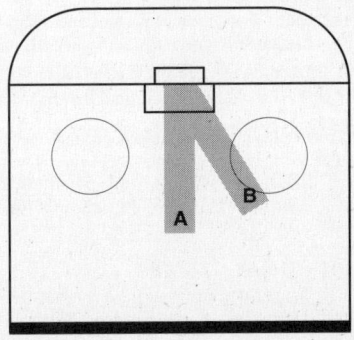

ERIC DESJARDINS

Yrs. of NHL service: 11
Born: Rouyn, Que.; June 14, 1969
Position: right defense
Height: 6-1
Weight: 200
Uniform no.: 37
Shoots: right

Career statistics:

GP	G	A	TP	PIM
746	88	292	380	532

1995-96 statistics:

GP	G	A	TP	+/-	PIM	PP	SH	GW	GT	S	PCT
80	7	40	47	+19	45	5	0	2	0	184	3.8

1996-97 statistics:

GP	G	A	TP	+/-	PIM	PP	SH	GW	GT	S	PCT
82	12	34	46	+25	50	5	1	1	0	183	6.6

1997-98 statistics:

GP	G	A	TP	+/-	PIM	PP	SH	GW	GT	S	PCT
77	6	27	33	+11	36	2	1	0	0	150	4.0

1998-99 statistics:

GP	G	A	TP	+/-	PIM	PP	SH	GW	GT	S	PCT
68	15	36	51	+18	38	6	0	2	0	190	7.9

LAST SEASON

Led team defensemen in points for fifth consecutive season. Tied for eighth among NHL defensemen in points. Led team defensemen in plus-minus. Missed four games with groin injury. Missed seven games with left knee injury. Missed three games with stomach virus.

THE FINESSE GAME

Desjardins has the puckhandling skills and poise to beat the first forechecker, and carry the puck out of the defensive zone. He makes accurate breakout passes and has enough savvy to keep the play simple, gain the redline and dump the puck deep in attacking ice if no other option is available. He makes the smart, safe play all the time.

Stable and capable enough to handle power-play duty, Desjardins is wise enough to realize only the ultra-elite overpower NHL goalies with point shots. Although he has a strong one-timer, his slap shot is not always accurate. He is much more dangerous offensively when he uses his wrist shot, or simply flips deflectable pucks towards the net.

A fine skater with light, agile feet and a small turning radius, Desjardins goes up-ice well with the play, keeping the gap to the forwards small and remaining in good position to revert to defense if there is a turnover. A long reach helps him challenge puck carriers to make plays more quickly, change their minds or shoot from a lower-percentage angle. Desjardins keeps his stick active while killing penalties, sweeping it on the ice to contest passing lanes and intercept pucks.

THE PHYSICAL GAME

Desjardins is a solid combination of mental and physical strength. Particularly while penalty killing in front of the net, he immobilizes the opponent's stick first, then ties up the body — which separates him from the huge percentage of defensemen who are satisfied to do one or the other but not both. He plays a hard game more than a punishing one, but uses his strength in more subtle ways to gain position in front of both goals. On offense, he will venture to the corners from time to time and will beat his check to the front of the net after winning a battle for the puck.

Desjardins is quietly tough. He finished the season and played in the playoffs on a knee that required off-season surgery to repair a torn ACL.

THE INTANGIBLES

A quiet leader on the ice and in the dressing room, Desjardins wants it more than you do, unless you prove different. He patrols the front of his net like a Doberman, but plays a clean, controlled game and rarely takes stupid penalties. He always seems to be where he is most needed, does not panic and does not fight. He is steady and professional and easy to under-appreciate. He also suffers from overwork. The Flyers need to find him some defensive help. Everyone looks good playing with Desjardins, but he can't play every shift.

PROJECTION

Desjardins scores consistently in the 40-point range. He isn't a dominating defenseman, but he gives a lot of steady minutes.

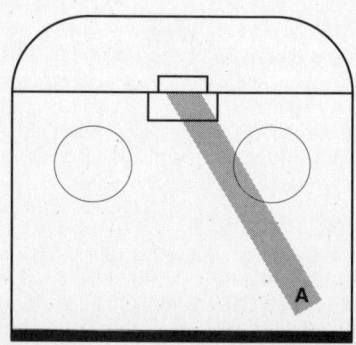

KARL DYKHUIS

Yrs. of NHL service: 6
Born: Sept-Iles, Que.; July 8, 1972
Position: right defense
Height: 6-3
Weight: 205
Uniform no.: 14
Shoots: left

Career statistics:

GP	G	A	TP	PIM
351	21	58	79	337

1995-96 statistics:

GP	G	A	TP	+/-	PIM	PP	SH	GW	GT	S	PCT
82	5	15	20	+12	101	1	0	0	0	104	4.8

1996-97 statistics:

GP	G	A	TP	+/-	PIM	PP	SH	GW	GT	S	PCT
62	4	15	19	+7	35	2	0	1	0	101	4.0

1997-98 statistics:

GP	G	A	TP	+/-	PIM	PP	SH	GW	GT	S	PCT
78	5	9	14	-8	110	0	1	0	0	91	5.5

1998-99 statistics:

GP	G	A	TP	+/-	PIM	PP	SH	GW	GT	S	PCT
78	4	5	9	-23	50	1	0	0	0	88	4.5

LAST SEASON

Acquired from Tampa Bay for Petr Svoboda, Dec. 28, 1999. Missed one game with broken cheekbone.

THE FINESSE GAME

Dykhuis has learned the importance of keeping his feet moving, because it helps him stay up with the play. His game edges towards the offensive side, but he also uses his finesse skills well in his own end.

Dykhuis keeps the passes short, accurate and crisp. He banks the puck off the boards or glass if that's the only option available to clear the zone.

He is a natural for penalty killing and four-on-four play because he has fine mobility and quickness, with a quick shift of gears that allows him to get up the ice in a hurry. Smart, with good hands for passing or drilling shots from the point, Dykhuis also leans towards conservatism; he won't venture down low unless the decision to pinch is a sound one.

THE PHYSICAL GAME

Although tall and rangy, Dykhuis isn't a heavyweight. But he goes out of his way to screen off opposing forecheckers and to buy time for his partner. There are times, on a regular basis, when his physical aspect is almost non-existent. He is strong and makes solid contact on those occasions when he does hit, though. He's also such a good skater that he can break up a play, dig out the loose puck and be off in just a stride or two to start an odd-man rush. He also uses his reach to break up plays.

THE INTANGIBLES

Dykhuis had a strangely inconsistent half-season following his return to the Flyers. He went from a seventh defenseman near the end of the regular season to frequently playing against the top line in the playoffs. He will have to re-establish his form to be a top four defenseman.

PROJECTION

Dykhuis will not score many points (15 to 20), even if he nabs a full-time role.

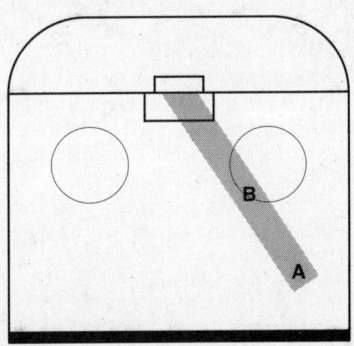

KEITH JONES

Yrs. of NHL service: 7
Born: Brantford, Ont.; Nov. 8, 1968
Position: right wing
Height: 6-2
Weight: 200
Uniform no.: 20
Shoots: left

Career statistics:

GP	G	A	TP	PIM
423	108	128	233	679

1995-96 statistics:

GP	G	A	TP	+/-	PIM	PP	SH	GW	GT	S	PCT
68	18	23	41	+8	103	5	0	2	0	155	11.6

1996-97 statistics:

GP	G	A	TP	+/-	PIM	PP	SH	GW	GT	S	PCT
78	25	23	48	+3	118	14	1	7	0	170	14.7

1997-98 statistics:

GP	G	A	TP	+/-	PIM	PP	SH	GW	GT	S	PCT
23	3	7	10	-4	22	1	0	2	0	31	9.7

1998-99 statistics:

GP	G	A	TP	+/-	PIM	PP	SH	GW	GT	S	PCT
78	20	33	53	+23	98	3	0	3	0	135	14.8

LAST SEASON

Acquired from Colorado for Shjon Podein, Nov. 12, 1998. Third on team in plus-minus and shooting percentage. Missed one game with bruised left knee. Missed two games due to suspension.

THE FINESSE GAME

Jones doesn't have the greatest hands in the world and he'll never be confused with John LeClair, but he has a good shot. Most of his power-play goals came from within 10 feet of the net. He's a spark plug. He likes to make things happen by driving to the front of the net, taking a defenseman with him. His skating is adequate, and he uses quick bursts of speed to power himself to and through the traffic areas.

An eager finisher who plays well at both ends of the ice, Jones keeps the game simple and does his job. He isn't very creative, but his efforts churn up loose pucks for teammates smart enough to trail in his wake. He is the antithesis of a natural scorer, because everything he accomplishes is through effort.

THE PHYSICAL GAME

Jones is energetic and uses his size well. He is tough and willing to pay a physical price, and the Flyers could use a couple of more players like him. He isn't the biggest player on the ice, but there are nights when you come away thinking he is.

Jones finishes every check in every zone. He sometimes runs around a bit but he is becoming more responsible defensively.

THE INTANGIBLES

Jones loves the game and knows what he has to do to stay in the lineup. This is one of the few recent trades made by GM Bob Clarke that weighs heavily in the Flyers' favour.

PROJECTION

No one deserves success more than the hard-working Jones. He hit 20 goals last season despite coming off a serious knee injury — a real testament to his commitment. He should score another 20 to 25.

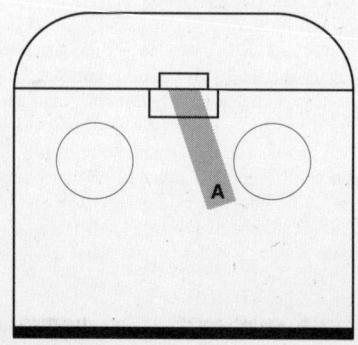

DAYMOND LANGKOW

Yrs. of NHL service: 3
Born: Edmonton, Alberta; Sept. 27, 1976
Position: centre
Height: 5-11
Weight: 175
Uniform no.: 18
Shoots: left

Career statistics:

GP	G	A	TP	PIM
229	37	47	84	136

1995-96 statistics:

GP	G	A	TP	+/-	PIM	PP	SH	GW	GT	S	PCT
4	0	1	1	-1	0	0	0	0	0	4	0.0

1996-97 statistics:

GP	G	A	TP	+/-	PIM	PP	SH	GW	GT	S	PCT
79	15	13	28	-1	35	3	1	1	1	170	8.8

1997-98 statistics:

GP	G	A	TP	+/-	PIM	PP	SH	GW	GT	S	PCT
68	8	14	22	-9	62	2	0	1	0	156	5.1

1998-99 statistics:

GP	G	A	TP	+/-	PIM	PP	SH	GW	GT	S	PCT
78	14	19	33	-8	39	4	1	2	0	149	9.4

LAST SEASON
Acquired from Tampa Bay with Mikael Renberg for Chris Gratton and Mike Sillinger, Dec. 12, 1998. Career highs in assists and points.

THE FINESSE GAME
Langkow is the complete package. The only problem is, it's such a darned small package.

Small men can succeed in the NHL, however, and it appears that Langkow could be one of them, especially on a fairly large Flyers team. He has terrific hockey sense, which is probably his chief asset, to go along with his stickhandling ability and shot. He is a fine passer with good vision and he's patient with the puck. He is not shy about shooting and possesses an effective wrist shot and slap shot.

Langkow has good speed, spies his options quickly and works hard. He knows what's going to happen before it does, which is the mark of an elite playmaker. He will harass opponents on the forecheck and create turnovers. He could become a solid two-way forward. His defensive awareness is above average for a young player.

THE PHYSICAL GAME
Langkow is a spunky, fast, in-your-face kind of player. He has a little sandpaper in his game, which gives him an edge over small forwards who rely only on their finesse skills. He doesn't mind aggravating people, and he'll throw punches at far bigger men. He won't be intimidated, either, and does his scoring in the trenches despite getting hit. He has a high pain threshold.

THE INTANGIBLES
Langkow made a favourable impression at the start of his half-season as a Flyer, but then scored no goals in 22 regular-season and playoff games.

PROJECTION
Langkow needs to be a top six forward but, assuming the Flyers are healthy, there doesn't seem to be a regular job for him. He is capable of 20 goals.

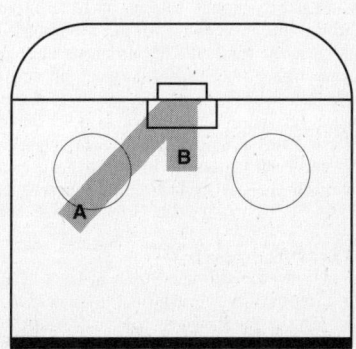

JOHN LECLAIR

Yrs. of NHL service: 8
Born: St. Albans, Vermont; July 5, 1969
Position: left wing
Height: 6-3
Weight: 226
Uniform no.: 10
Shoots: left

Career statistics:

GP	G	A	TP	PIM
583	269	408	538	285

1995-96 statistics:

GP	G	A	TP	+/-	PIM	PP	SH	GW	GT	S	PCT
82	51	46	97	+21	64	19	0	10	2	270	18.9

1996-97 statistics:

GP	G	A	TP	+/-	PIM	PP	SH	GW	GT	S	PCT
82	50	47	97	+44	58	10	0	5	2	324	15.4

1997-98 statistics:

GP	G	A	TP	+/-	PIM	PP	SH	GW	GT	S	PCT
82	51	36	87	+30	32	16	0	9	1	303	16.8

1998-99 statistics:

GP	G	A	TP	+/-	PIM	PP	SH	GW	GT	S	PCT
76	43	47	90	+36	30	16	0	7	3	246	17.5

LAST SEASON

Led team and fifth in NHL in goals. Led team and second in NHL in plus-minus. Led team in power-play goals, game-winning goals, shots and shooting percentage. Second on team and ninth in NHL in points. Third on team in assists. Missed four games with left hip flexor. Missed two games with back spasms.

THE FINESSE GAME

You rarely find a player who shoots as often as LeClair does and who has such a high shooting percentage. Most snipers waste a lot of shots, and high-percentage shooters are most selective. LeClair combines the two by working to get into the highest quality scoring areas and using a terrific shot with a quick release.

A team can defend against LeClair all night long, then lose position on him once, and the puck is in the net. He knows his job is to score goals and he doesn't let up from the opening whistle to the final second of the game.

LeClair is big enough to post up in front and pile drive through the melees for all the rebounds, deflections and garbage goals his teammates can create. He also has enough power in his skating and confidence in his strength to cut in from the wing and drive to the net, but the left wing's attributes as a scorer far outweigh his abilities as a puckhandler. If the puck were a football, you could imagine him putting it under his arm, lowering his head and ramming it across the goal line.

THE PHYSICAL GAME

LeClair may be the strongest man in the NHL and is just about impossible to push off the puck legally. He wants to win the puck, wants the puck in the net and will use every ounce of his strength to try to put it there. He always draws the attention of at least one defender, but accepts his role willingly. Because of a long reach and a big body, LeClair finds a way to place himself between the puck and the defender. Those times when he has a defender under each arm behind the net, he happily will kick the puck to the front.

The frequent disappointment is that LeClair puts so much into winning the puck behind the goal line but doesn't really have the deft touch to make a smooth relay to someone who might be driving to the net. His passing skills are rather dubious and his puck-handling skills are erratic. Teams try to neutralize him by forcing him to carry the puck and make plays.

LeClair can be a mean hitter. And with that size and strength, the combination can be devastating. More often than not, though, he remains a gentle giant. He plays hard, but clean, and really is much easier to control if you play him the same way.

THE INTANGIBLES

LeClair suffered from two things down the stretch and in the playoffs: back spasms, and the absence of Eric Lindros.

PROJECTION

LeClair scores goals on his knees, on his back, whatever. He isn't happy until the puck has been put in the net — either by himself or a teammate. At 30, he is entering prime time, and should net 50.

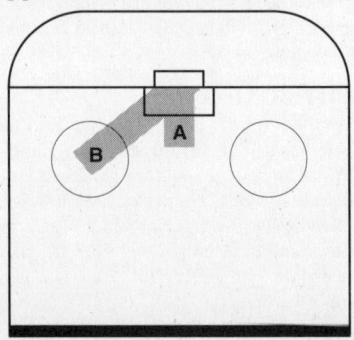

ERIC LINDROS

Yrs. of NHL service: 7
Born: London, Ont.; Feb. 28, 1973
Position: centre
Height: 6-4
Weight: 236
Uniform no.: 88
Shoots: right

Career statistics:

GP	G	A	TP	PIM
431	263	337	600	863

1995-96 statistics:

GP	G	A	TP	+/-	PIM	PP	SH	GW	GT	S	PCT
73	47	68	115	+26	163	15	0	4	0	294	16.0

1996-97 statistics:

GP	G	A	TP	+/-	PIM	PP	SH	GW	GT	S	PCT
52	32	47	79	+31	136	9	0	7	2	198	16.2

1997-98 statistics:

GP	G	A	TP	+/-	PIM	PP	SH	GW	GT	S	PCT
63	30	41	71	+14	134	10	1	4	0	202	14.9

1998-99 statistics:

GP	G	A	TP	+/-	PIM	PP	SH	GW	GT	S	PCT
71	40	53	93	+35	120	10	1	2	3	242	16.5

LAST SEASON

Led team in assists for third consecutive season. Tied for sixth in NHL in assists. Led team in points. Second on team in goals, plus-minus, shots and shooting percentage. Tied for seventh in NHL in goals. Tied for second on team in power-play goals. Third on team in penalty minutes. Missed seven games with collapsed lung. Missed two games with concussion. Missed two games due to suspension.

THE FINESSE GAME

Lindros was on his way to closing out his best regular season, and perhaps writing the first chapter to a better personal playoff history, when a freak injury not only ended his season but very nearly cost him his life. Lindros shrugged off a hit during a game in Nashville, only to collapse in the middle of the night with a damaged lung. Lindros was still recovering from the injury during the off-season.

A healthy Lindros can bore straight ahead, freight-train you with the puck and drive to the net. There are times, though, when opponents so completely prepare themselves for his brute power that they are stunned when he puts the puck through their feet, steps around them and regains it instead of driving through them. As his game matures, Lindros will make better use of this change-up, which beautifully complements his "fastball."

Lindros has the balance and soft hands to control the puck in extremely tight quarters and make those nimble moves at the high speed he reaches quickly. That said, it remains more his nature to muscle the puck to a teammate or to the front of the net, and to let his strength do most of the work because strength remains the watchword of his game.

To offset the torque his arms can generate, the stick Lindros uses has an extremely firm shaft with only a slight curve to the blade. That helps on face-offs, adds velocity to his wrist and snap shots, and makes his backhand shot a very significant weapon both for its speed and its accuracy to the upper corners from close range.

THE PHYSICAL GAME

When you go to hit Lindros, you are going to run into his stick or his elbow eight times out of 10. The remaining times, you are simply going to run into Lindros — which can be just as painful. Those times when you do not run into Lindros, he will make a point of running into you, which makes long evenings against him even longer. And if you thought that stick was a weapon for shooting, imagine how it feels if, by some accident, you get slashed with it.

Nonetheless, a player who plays that way pays a physical toll. Lindros already wears braces on both knees, and suffered his second concussion — a worry since the same injury knocked his younger brother, Brett, out of hockey altogether.

THE INTANGIBLES

Lindros answered the public challenge issued by GM Bob Clarke prior to the start of last season, at least until his lung injury. The Flyers gave him a one-year, $8.5-million contract extension as proof of their faith. You have to wonder, though, about his propensity towards getting injuries, and serious ones, season after season.

PROJECTION

He'll be among the league's scoring leaders if he can stay healthy. He still has a lot to prove in the postseason.

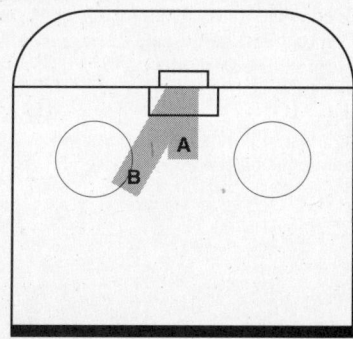

DANIEL MCGILLIS

Yrs. of NHL service: 3
Born: Hawkesbury, Ont.; July 1, 1972
Position: left defense
Height: 6-2
Weight: 220
Uniform no.: 3
Shoots: left

Career statistics:

GP	G	A	TP	PIM
231	25	73	98	222

1996-97 statistics:

GP	G	A	TP	+/-	PIM	PP	SH	GW	GT	S	PCT
73	6	16	22	+2	52	2	1	2	0	139	4.3

1997-98 statistics:

GP	G	A	TP	+/-	PIM	PP	SH	GW	GT	S	PCT
80	11	20	31	-21	109	6	0	3	1	137	8.0

1998-99 statistics:

GP	G	A	TP	+/-	PIM	PP	SH	GW	GT	S	PCT
78	8	37	45	+16	61	6	0	4	0	164	4.9

LAST SEASON

Third on team in game-winning goals. Career highs in assists and points. Missed two games with neck injury. Missed one game with knee injury.

THE FINESSE GAME

McGillis was an offensive defenseman in college. Now that he has graduated to the NHL, he has become a promising two-way defenseman. His scoring skills are not elite class — he'll never be an "offenseman" — but he can provide point production with an edge.

McGillis played with Kevin Lowe in Edmonton and learned to use his finesse skills in a defensive role. He is a smart player: he knows how to read defenses and play angles, and he studies player tendencies.

McGillis is not a quick skater, but he is strong and agile enough for his size.

THE PHYSICAL GAME

McGillis steps up and challenges, and he's a big, big hitter. He's not afraid to go after the stars, either. He is powerfully built and explodes into his hits.

THE INTANGIBLES

McGillis continues to show improvement. He was the Flyers' second-best defenseman last season behind the all-purpose Eric Desjardins.

PROJECTION

McGillis can put points on the point (45 to 50) and will continue to upgrade his defensive play.

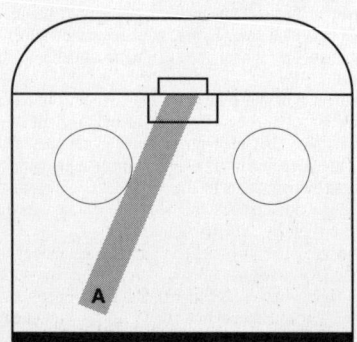

MARK RECCHI

Yrs. of NHL service: 10
Born: Kamloops, B.C.; Feb. 1, 1968
Position: right wing
Height: 5-10
Weight: 180
Uniform no.: 11
Shoots: left

Career statistics:
GP	G	A	TP	PIM
781	333	509	842	569

1995-96 statistics:
GP	G	A	TP	+/-	PIM	PP	SH	GW	GT	S	PCT
82	28	50	78	+20	69	11	2	6	0	191	14.7

1996-97 statistics:
GP	G	A	TP	+/-	PIM	PP	SH	GW	GT	S	PCT
82	34	46	80	-1	58	7	2	3	0	202	16.8

1997-98 statistics:
GP	G	A	TP	+/-	PIM	PP	SH	GW	GT	S	PCT
82	32	42	74	+11	51	9	1	6	0	216	14.8

1998-99 statistics:
GP	G	A	TP	+/-	PIM	PP	SH	GW	GT	S	PCT
71	16	37	53	-7	34	3	0	2	0	171	9.4

LAST SEASON
Acquired from Montreal for Dainus Zubrus and two draft picks, Mar. 10, 1999. Missed four games with pneumonia, ending his "iron man" streak at 570 consecutive games played (eighth longest in NHL history). Missed seven games with concussion and related symptoms.

THE FINESSE GAME
Which is the real Mark Recchi? The durable forward and consistent scorer that played for Montreal? Or the suddenly sidelined winger who produced only one assist in the playoffs? The Flyers gambled on the former, signing him to a five-year, $25-million deal before Recchi became an unrestricted free agent.

Certainly history favours a return to form for Recchi, a little package with a lot of firepower. He is one of the top small players in the game and certainly one of the most productive. He's a feisty and relentless worker in the offensive zone. He busts into open ice, finding the holes almost before they open, and excels at the give-and-go. He's versatile enough to play wing or centre, though he is at his best on the wing.

Recchi has a dangerous shot from the off(right)-wing. Although he is not as dynamic as Maurice Richard, he likes to use the Richard cut-back while rifling a wrist shot back across. It's heavy, it's on net and it requires no backswing. He follows his shot to the net for a rebound and can make a play as well. He has excellent hands, vision and anticipation for any scoring opportunity.

Recchi has worked hard to improve his defensive play. He kills penalties well because he hounds the point men aggressively and knocks the puck out of the zone. Then he heads off on a breakaway or forces the defender to pull him down.

He isn't a pretty skater but he always keeps his feet moving. While other players are coasting, Recchi's blades are in motion, and he draws penalties. He is ready to spring into any play. He resembles a puck magnet because he is always going where the puck is. He protects the puck well, keeping it close to his feet.

THE PHYSICAL GAME
Recchi gets chopped at because he doesn't hang around the perimeter. He accepts the punishment to get the job done. He is a solid player with a low centre of gravity, and he is tough to knock off the puck.

THE INTANGIBLES
Recchi is a solo artist, not a player who makes others around him better, but he can upgrade a team if he is given a decent supporting cast, which he now has in Philadelphia.

PROJECTION
Recchi could return to the 100-point ranks.

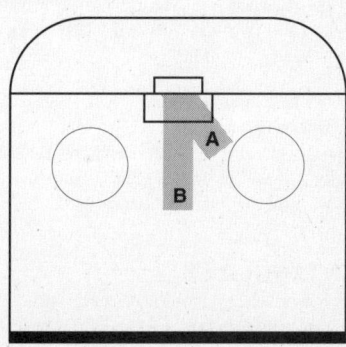

MIKAEL RENBERG

Yrs. of NHL service: 6
Born: Pitea, Sweden; May 5, 1972
Position: right wing
Height: 6-2
Weight: 218
Uniform no.: 19
Shoots: left

Career statistics:

GP	G	A	TP	PIM
392	140	177	295	218

1995-96 statistics:

GP	G	A	TP	+/-	PIM	PP	SH	GW	GT	S	PCT
51	23	20	43	+8	45	9	0	4	0	198	11.6

1996-97 statistics:

GP	G	A	TP	+/-	PIM	PP	SH	GW	GT	S	PCT
77	22	37	59	+36	65	1	0	4	1	249	8.8

1997-98 statistics:

GP	G	A	TP	+/-	PIM	PP	SH	GW	GT	S	PCT
68	16	22	38	-37	34	6	3	0	1	175	9.1

1998-99 statistics:

GP	G	A	TP	+/-	PIM	PP	SH	GW	GT	S	PCT
66	15	23	38	+5	18	6	0	2	0	154	9.7

line. He'll be a number two right wing in Philadelphia after the financial commitment given to Mark Recchi.

PROJECTION

Renberg should be a steady 25-goal scorer, but he hasn't hit that since his first NHL season.

LAST SEASON

Acquired from Tampa Bay with Daymond Langkow for Chris Gratton and Mike Sillinger, Dec. 12, 1999. Lowest goal total of NHL career. Missed nine games with separated shoulder.

THE FINESSE GAME

Renberg has a long, strong stride and excellent balance, but only average speed. Anticipation is the key that gives him a head start on the defense.

He drives to the net, and is strong enough to shrug off a lot of checks, or even shovel a one-handed shot or pass if one arm is tied up. He likes to come in on the off-wing, especially on the power play, and snap a strong shot off his back foot. He sees the ice well and is always looking for a teammate he can hit with a pass. But Renberg finally got it into his head that the more shots you take, the likelier it is you'll score — or that someone else might put in your rebound.

Renberg's best shots are his quick-release wrists or snaps with little backswing. He is defensively aware — a solid two-way forward who can be on the ice in almost any situation.

THE PHYSICAL GAME

Renberg doesn't fight but he is extremely strong, and he has a nasty streak and likes to hit hard. He won't be intimidated. Since he isn't a great skater, his adjustment to the smaller ice surfaces actually helped his game.

THE INTANGIBLES

Renberg has never regained the form he showed in his rookie season as a member of the Legion of Doom

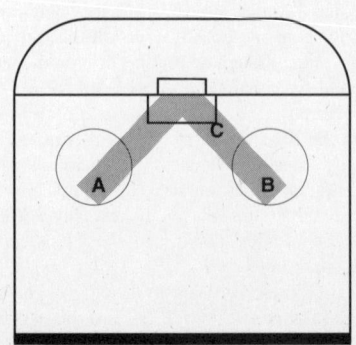

LUKE RICHARDSON

Yrs. of NHL service: 12
Born: Ottawa, Ont.; Mar. 26, 1969
Position: left defense
Height: 6-4
Weight: 210
Uniform no.: 22
Shoots: left

Career statistics:

GP	G	A	TP	PIM
873	26	110	136	1431

1995-96 statistics:

GP	G	A	TP	+/-	PIM	PP	SH	GW	GT	S	PCT
82	2	9	11	-27	108	0	0	0	0	61	3.3

1996-97 statistics:

GP	G	A	TP	+/-	PIM	PP	SH	GW	GT	S	PCT
82	1	11	12	+9	91	0	0	0	0	67	1.5

1997-98 statistics:

GP	G	A	TP	+/-	PIM	PP	SH	GW	GT	S	PCT
81	2	3	5	+7	139	2	0	0	0	57	3.5

1998-99 statistics:

GP	G	A	TP	+/-	PIM	PP	SH	GW	GT	S	PCT
78	0	6	6	-3	106	0	0	0	0	49	.0

LAST SEASON
Missed four games due to coach's decision.

THE FINESSE GAME
Richardson can sometimes play solid defense, but he is more often indecisive. When to step up at the blue, when to back off: you can see the thought process at work in his head, and so can the attacker.

Richardson is a good skater with lateral mobility and balance, but not much speed. To a degree, he overcomes some of his skating flaws by simply taking up as much space as he can with his size. He can't carry the puck and doesn't jump up into the rush well. He seldom uses his point shot, which is merely adequate.

Defensively, Richardson doesn't know when to stay in front of his net and when to challenge in the corners. Despite his 11 years in the league, the necessary improvement hasn't always shown. At least Richardson has become less of a headhunter and doesn't run around looking for the big hit.

THE PHYSICAL GAME
Richardson is the kind of player you hate to play against but love to have on your side. He hits to hurt and is an imposing presence on the ice. He scares people. When he checks he separates the puck carrier from the puck and doesn't let the man get back into play. When he is on the ice his teammates play a bit bigger and braver. He plays hurt.

THE INTANGIBLES
Coach Roger Neilson benched Richardson at the end of the year and for the playoffs, and the defenseman requested a trade. He has three years left on a $12.6-million deal, which means the Flyers will probably have to pay to get someone to take him off their hands.

PROJECTION
Richardson's role is as a physical stay-at-home defender, and his point totals will remain low (10 to 15 points).

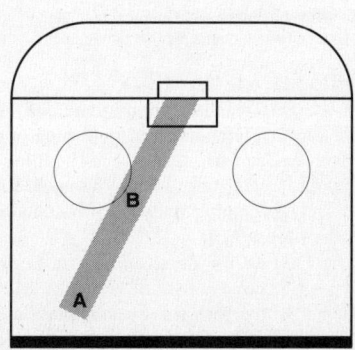

CHRIS THERIEN

Yrs. of NHL service: 5
Born: Ottawa, Ont.; Dec. 14, 1971
Position: left defense
Height: 6-4
Weight: 230
Uniform no.: 6
Shoots: left

Career statistics:

GP	G	A	TP	PIM
353	17	80	97	319

1995-96 statistics:

GP	G	A	TP	+/-	PIM	PP	SH	GW	GT	S	PCT
82	6	17	23	+16	89	3	0	1	0	123	4.9

1996-97 statistics:

GP	G	A	TP	+/-	PIM	PP	SH	GW	GT	S	PCT
71	2	22	24	+26	64	0	0	0	0	107	1.9

1997-98 statistics:

GP	G	A	TP	+/-	PIM	PP	SH	GW	GT	S	PCT
78	3	16	19	+5	80	1	0	1	0	102	2.9

1998-99 statistics:

GP	G	A	TP	+/-	PIM	PP	SH	GW	GT	S	PCT
74	3	15	18	+16	48	1	0	0	0	115	2.6

LAST SEASON

Missed three games with collarbone injury. Missed three games with bruised thigh. Missed one game due to personal reasons.

THE FINESSE GAME

Although not particularly quick, Therien is a fluid skater for his size and has improving offensive instincts. He handles the puck well and looks to move it as his first option, but he can skate it out of the defensive zone and make a crisp pass while in motion. If that option is not available, he keeps it simple and bangs the puck off the boards.

Good balance allows Therien to maximize his size when, rather than use the typical big-man play and slide on the ice, he takes a stride, drops to one knee and keeps his stick flat on the ice — making himself a larger and wider obstacle.

Therien doesn't have much lateral speed, but he is a strong straight-ahead skater who can get up the ice in a hurry. He also has a good enough sense of offense that he can play the point on the power play.

THE PHYSICAL GAME

Therien uses his reach to good advantage. He can dominate physically and started punishing opposing forwards in front of the net in penalty-killing situations. Extremely alert away from the puck, he dedicates himself to gaining body position and making sure his man doesn't get it.

Therien knows big defensemen can be penalty magnets, but he keeps much of his game within the rules. He keeps the elbows down, and plays an effective, clean physical game. When he hits along the boards or battles in the corners, he tends to lower his body position and use his weight to smear an opponent along the boards. (Other big defensemen are too upright in those situations or try to use their arms to pin opponents, which isn't as effective.) Therien makes his heft and bulk work for him.

THE INTANGIBLES

Therien is a top four defenseman in Philadelphia and handles a lot of ice time, but he will never be a dominating rearguard. He needs to play with a mobile defenseman. He is a bit exposed when he doesn't get to play with a partner like Eric Desjardins.

PROJECTION

Therien's offensive instincts do not translate into points, because he usually takes only one or two shots per game. Nonetheless, he plays fairly mistake-free hockey and has channelled his enthusiasm into dogged, effective play, making him a key contributor.

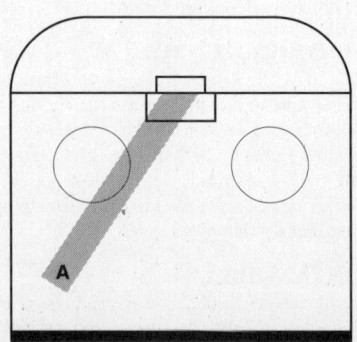

JOHN VANBIESBROUCK

Yrs. of NHL service: 15
Born: Detroit, Mich.; Sept. 4, 1963
Position: goaltender
Height: 5-8
Weight: 176
Uniform no.: 34
Catches: left

Career statistics:

GP	MIN	GA	SO	GAA	A	PIM
779	44595	2259	35	3.04	31	292

1995-96 statistics:

GP	MIN	GAA	W	L	T	SO	GA	S	SAPCT	PIM
57	3178	2.68	26	20	7	2	142	1473	.904	10

1996-97 statistics:

GP	MIN	GAA	W	L	T	SO	GA	S	SAPCT	PIM
57	3347	2.29	27	19	10	2	128	1582	.919	8

1997-98 statistics:

GP	MIN	GAA	W	L	T	SO	GA	S	SAPCT	PIM
60	3451	2.87	18	29	11	4	165	1638	.899	6

1998-99 statistics:

GP	MIN	GAA	W	L	T	SO	GA	S	SAPCT	PIM
62	3712	2.18	27	18	15	6	135	1380	.902	12

LAST SEASON

Tied for fourth in NHL in shutouts. Career highs in games played and minutes played.

THE PHYSICAL GAME

There are few goalies who play a better positional game than Vanbiesbrouck. He doesn't make wild, diving saves, because he doesn't have to. He blends a strong technical game with good reflexes, anticipation and confidence. He isn't very big, so he plays his angles and squares himself to the shooter to take away as much of the net as possible. He makes himself look like a much bigger goalie. He is very aggressive, forcing the shooter to make the first move.

Those facts made his playoff performance baffling, since he allowed some highly questionable — okay, soft — goals that didn't help the offensively challenged Flyers in their first-round loss to Toronto.

Vanbiesbrouck plays a butterfly-style that takes away a lot of low shots and he has a quick glove hand, so most shooters try to go high stick-side on him, but that's a hard corner to pick. He reads wraparound plays well and seldom gets beaten. He gets into occasional trouble when he plays too deep in his net and holds his glove hand too low.

Vanbiesbrouck is a good skater with fine lateral motion. Active with his stick, he uses it to poke-check, guide rebounds, break up passes or whack at any ankles camping out too close to his crease. He won't surrender a centimetre of his ice. He is also confident out of his net with the puck, sometimes overly so. He'll get burned by trying to force passes up the middle.

THE MENTAL GAME

Vanbiesbrouck is highly competitive and keeps himself in superb condition. After his playoff blunders he will start the season under a microscope.

THE INTANGIBLES

Losing in a head-to-head playoff battle with Curtis Joseph (who along with Mike Richter was one of the three hotshot free agent goalies the Flyers had to choose from in the 1998 market) can't have done much for Vanbiesbrouck's stock in Philadelphia.

PROJECTION

Vanbiesbrouck's days as an elite goalie may be over, but at least he won't beat himself too often — in the regular season, anyway. He can easily reach 30 wins.

PHOENIX COYOTES

Players' Statistics 1998-99

POS.	NO.	PLAYER	GP	G	A	PTS	+/-	PIM	PP	SH	GW	GT	S	PCT
C	97	JEREMY ROENICK	78	24	48	72	7	130	4		3		203	11.8
C	16	ROBERT REICHEL	83	26	43	69	-13	54	8	1	4	1	236	11.0
L	7	KEITH TKACHUK	68	36	32	68	22	151	11	2	7	1	258	14.0
R	22	RICK TOCCHET	81	26	30	56	5	147	6	1	5		178	14.6
L	17	GREG ADAMS	75	19	24	43	-1	26	5		3		176	10.8
D	27	TEPPO NUMMINEN	82	10	30	40	3	30	1			2	156	6.4
R	11	DALLAS DRAKE	53	9	22	31	17	65			3		105	8.6
D	20	JYRKI LUMME	60	7	21	28	5	34	1		4		121	5.8
D	10	OLEG TVERDOVSKY	82	7	18	25	11	32	2		2		117	6.0
C	36	JUHA YLONEN	59	6	17	23	18	20	2		1		66	9.1
C	8	*DANIEL BRIERE	64	8	14	22	-3	30	2		2		90	8.9
R	19	SHANE DOAN	79	6	16	22	-5	54					156	3.8
C	21	BOB CORKUM	77	9	10	19	-9	17					146	6.2
C	14	MIKE STAPLETON	76	9	9	18	-6	34		2	2		106	8.5
D	3	KEITH CARNEY	82	2	14	16	15	62		2			62	3.2
D	5	DERON QUINT	60	5	8	13	-10	20	2				94	5.3
D	33	J.J. DAIGNEAULT	70	2	9	11	-12	70	1		1		65	3.1
R	16	BRAD ISBISTER	32	4	4	8	1	46			2		48	8.3
R	15	JIM CUMMINS	55	1	7	8	3	190					26	3.8
L	26	MIKE SULLIVAN	63	2	4	6	-11	24		1	1		66	3.0
C	50	*TREVOR LETOWSKI	14	2	2	4	1	2					8	25.0
R	23	STEPHEN LEACH	31	1	3	4	-7	43					27	3.7
C	47	*TAVIS HANSEN	20	2	1	3	-4	12					14	14.3
C	12	ROB MURRAY	13	1	2	3	2	4					11	9.1
D	24	STAN NECKAR	32		3	3	1	18					16	
D	6	JAMIE HUSCROFT	37		2	2	-4	90					27	
D	4	GERALD DIDUCK	44		2	2	9	72					39	
D	55	*JASON DOIG	9		1	1	2	10						
L	44	ANDREI VASILYEV	1				-2							
G	31	*SCOTT LANGKOW	1					0						
L	49	JOE DZIEDZIC	2				-2							1	
D	48	*SEAN GAGNON	2				-2	7					1	
G	42	*ROBERT ESCHE	3					0						
R	18	BRIAN NOONAN	7				-3							1	
D	39	BRAD TILEY	8				-1							1	
L	29	LOUIE DEBRUSK	15				-2	34					6	
G	28	JIM WAITE	16				0	2						
G	30	MIKHAIL SHTALENKOV	38				0	2						
G	35	NIKOLAI KHABIBULIN	63				0	8						

GP = games played; G = goals; A = assists; PTS = points; +/- = goals-for minus goals-against while player is on ice; PIM = penalties in minutes; PP = power-play goals; SH = shorthanded goals; GW = game-winning goals; GT = game-tying goals; S = no. of shots; PCT = percentage of goals to shots; * = rookie

GREG ADAMS

Yrs. of NHL service: 15
Born: Nelson, B.C.; Aug. 1, 1963
Position: left wing
Height: 6-3
Weight: 195
Uniform no.: 17
Shoots: left

Career statistics:

GP	G	A	TP	PIM
927	325	349	674	302

1995-96 statistics:
GP	G	A	TP	+/-	PIM	PP	SH	GW	GT	S	PCT
66	22	21	43	-21	33	11	1	1	0	140	15.7

1996-97 statistics:
GP	G	A	TP	+/-	PIM	PP	SH	GW	GT	S	PCT
50	21	15	36	+27	2	5	0	4	1	113	18.6

1997-98 statistics:
GP	G	A	TP	+/-	PIM	PP	SH	GW	GT	S	PCT
49	14	18	32	+11	20	7	0	1	0	75	18.7

1998-99 statistics:
GP	G	A	TP	+/-	PIM	PP	SH	GW	GT	S	PCT
75	19	24	43	-1	26	5	0	3	0	176	10.8

LAST SEASON
Missed six games with groin injury. Missed one game with flu. Games played highest since 1991-92.

THE FINESSE GAME
Adams is faster than he looks because he has a long, almost lazy stride, but he covers a lot of ground quickly and with an apparent lack of effort.

He can shoot a hard slap shot on the fly off the wing, but most of his goals come from within five feet of the net. He drives fearlessly to the goal and likes to arrive by the most expedient route possible. If that means crashing through defensemen, then so be it. Adams has good, shifty moves in deep and is an unselfish player. He played a lot of centre early in his career and is nearly as good a playmaker as a finisher. He has excellent hands for re-directions and rebounds — not as good as Joe Nieuwendyk's, but close.

One of Adams's best scoring moves is a high backhand in tight. He always has his head up and is looking for the holes; one of the few knocks on him is that he doesn't shoot enough. He has worked hard at improving his defensive awareness and has become a reliable player. He reads his defensemen's pinches well and is always back to cover up at the point.

THE PHYSICAL GAME
Adams has a light frame and always plays hard, which is why he is so vulnerable to injury. He is nearly always wearing an ice pack or getting medical attention for a nick or bruise, if not a broken bone or nerve damage. Although he enjoyed a fairly healthy season last year, Adams has become increasingly fragile, but keeps coming back. For someone who spends as much time getting whacked in the high-traffic areas, he has a remarkably long fuse. He remains calm and determined, and seldom takes bad retaliatory penalties.

THE INTANGIBLES
The problem with Adams is that he is often hurt, and usually with a serious injury. He can accomplish so much when he is in the lineup, but you can never count on a full season out of him.

PROJECTION
A healthy Adams produced 43 points last year, which means you can expect a point out of every two games from the veteran, whom Phoenix re-signed during the off-season.

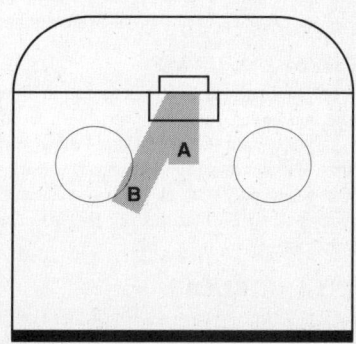

DANIEL BRIERE

Yrs. of NHL service: 1
Born: Gatineau, Quebec; Oct. 6, 1977
Position: centre
Height: 5-9
Weight: 160
Uniform no.: 8
Shoots: left

Career statistics:

GP	G	A	TP	PIM
64	8	14	22	30

1997-98 statistics:

GP	G	A	TP	+/-	PIM	PP	SH	GW	GT	S	PCT
5	1	0	1	+1	2	0	0	0	0	4	25.0

1998-99 statistics:

GP	G	A	TP	+/-	PIM	PP	SH	GW	GT	S	PCT
64	8	14	22	-3	30	2	0	2	0	90	8.9

LAST SEASON

First NHL season. Missed two games with concussion. Appeared in 13 games with Springfield (AHL), scoring 2-6 — 8. Appeared in one game with Las Vegas (IHL), scoring 1-1 — 2. Missed one game due to coach's decision.

THE FINESSE GAME

Briere is an exciting young player whose only drawback is his lack of size. Fortunately for him, the Coyotes have some good-sized wingers to use up front with him, and with a player of Briere's talent, room can be made for a smaller player — but Briere has to earn it.

He has a great release on an accurate shot, but Briere's chief asset is as a playmaker. He will be dynamite on the power play, with the extra space allowing him the extra half-second of time to make a play. He uses his time and space wisely. He has a great passing touch with the puck, plus terrific hockey sense and vision. He knows how to play this game.

Briere is an excellent, shifty skater, which serves him well in the offensive zone since players will be forced to restrain him rather than hit him. If the crackdown on restraining fouls continues into the new season, Briere will be a dynamic force. Defensively, he has to use his skating and his hand skills to survive. He will be outmuscled in any physical matchups.

THE PHYSICAL GAME

Briere's season began with a concussion in an exhibition game and never quite got untracked. He did not play in the NHL with the feisty side he has shown in the minors, which could have been a result of the injury. He needs to play with an edge, like Theo Fleury. Briere was sent to Finland during the off-season to step up his training.

THE INTANGIBLES

Consider this a starting over season for Briere. He finished the season in the minors and was not on the Coyotes' playoff roster. He'll have a new coach, which is also a boon to a fresh start.

PROJECTION

Briere could eventually become a point-a-game player in the NHL. Most of his points will be assists, not goals, and we would wait a season to see how he develops. But it wouldn't be a surprise to see Briere score 45 to 50 points this season.

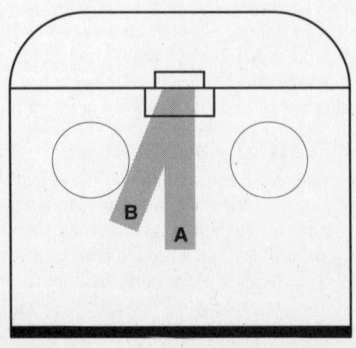

KEITH CARNEY

Yrs. of NHL service: 7
Born: Providence, R.I.; Feb. 3, 1970
Position: left defense
Height: 6-2
Weight: 205
Uniform no.: 3
Shoots: left

Career statistics:

GP	G	A	TP	PIM
424	21	76	97	432

1995-96 statistics:

GP	G	A	TP	+/-	PIM	PP	SH	GW	GT	S	PCT
82	5	14	19	+31	94	1	0	1	0	69	7.2

1996-97 statistics:

GP	G	A	TP	+/-	PIM	PP	SH	GW	GT	S	PCT
81	3	15	18	+26	62	0	0	1	0	77	3.9

1997-98 statistics:

GP	G	A	TP	+/-	PIM	PP	SH	GW	GT	S	PCT
80	3	19	22	-2	91	1	1	0	0	71	4.2

1998-99 statistics:

GP	G	A	TP	+/-	PIM	PP	SH	GW	GT	S	PCT
82	2	14	16	+15	62	0	2	0	0	62	3.2

LAST SEASON
Led team defensemen in plus-minus. Tied for team lead in shorthanded goals. One of four Coyotes to appear in all 82 games.

THE FINESSE GAME
Carney was considered an offensive defenseman when he first tried to break into the league, but he lacked the elite skills to succeed on that style alone. He has turned his finesse skills to his defensive advantage and emphasizes play in his own zone, though he is very capable of contributing some offense.

Carney is quick and agile and he positions himself well defensively. He is a smart power-play point man who works on the second unit on the right side. He is among the NHL's better penalty killers, and he has good hockey sense and great anticipation. He reads the play well, is a fine skater and moves the puck smoothly and quickly out of the zone. He is a very good shot-blocker.

Carney compliments an offensive partner well. He is not strictly stay-at-home, though. He picks his spots wisely.

THE PHYSICAL GAME
Carney is not a hitter but he will get in the way of people; instead of punishing he ties up his man effectively. He is a well-conditioned athlete and an honest worker who is about the last one off the ice in practice.

THE INTANGIBLES
Carney is a capable fifth defenseman, and can even step up to a number four role in the right circumstances, as he does in Phoenix. He has steadily and quietly improved year by year.

PROJECTION
His concentration on defense will limit Carney's point total to around 20 to 25.

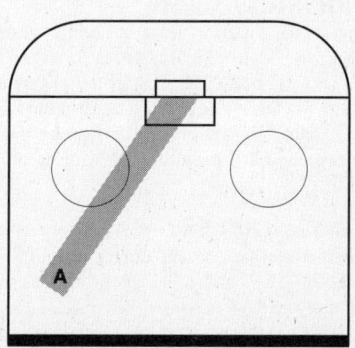

BOB CORKUM

Yrs. of NHL service: 8
Born: Salisbury, Mass.; Dec. 18, 1967
Position: centre/right wing
Height: 6-2
Weight: 210
Uniform no.: 21
Shoots: right

Career statistics:

GP	G	A	TP	PIM
525	82	85	167	223

1995-96 statistics:

GP	G	A	TP	+/-	PIM	PP	SH	GW	GT	S	PCT
76	9	10	19	+3	34	0	0	3	0	126	7.1

1996-97 statistics:

GP	G	A	TP	+/-	PIM	PP	SH	GW	GT	S	PCT
80	9	11	20	-7	40	0	1	3	0	119	7.6

1997-98 statistics:

GP	G	A	TP	+/-	PIM	PP	SH	GW	GT	S	PCT
76	12	9	21	-7	28	0	5	0	0	105	11.4

1998-99 statistics:

GP	G	A	TP	+/-	PIM	PP	SH	GW	GT	S	PCT
77	9	10	19	-9	17	0	0	0	0	146	6.2

PROJECTION
Corkum can get 20 points in a checking role.

LAST SEASON
Missed four games with groin injury. Missed one game with hip injury.

THE FINESSE GAME
Corkum has average skills but makes the most of them with his effort. He has good overall speed, balance and acceleration. He drives to the net for short-range shots and likes to use a strong wrist shot, though he doesn't get it away quickly. He also has a decent backhand. He doesn't score often for a player who could take advantage of a counter-attack against another team's top lines. He's ideally suited as a third-line checking centre.

Corkum likes to use a short, sure pass. He will pass off rather than carry the puck. He anticipates well and hits the open man. He is not terribly clever with the puck, but he makes the bread-and-butter play with confidence.

THE PHYSICAL GAME
Corkum stands tough in front of the net and works hard along the boards. He is a strong forechecker who likes to take the body. He relishes the physical game and makes big hits — anyone hit by Corkum knows it. He works hard and uses his size and strength well. He takes draws and kill penalties. He'll bring energy to each shift.

THE INTANGIBLES
An unrestricted free agent during the off-season, Corkum would be a nice role player for a team looking for crunch-time help.

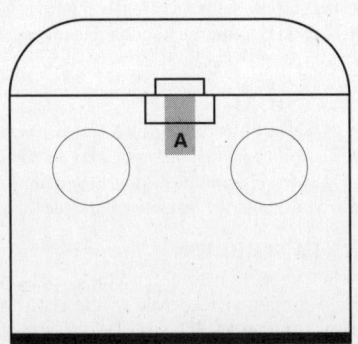

SHANE DOAN

Yrs. of NHL service: 4
Born: Halkirk, Alberta; Oct. 10, 1976
Position: right wing
Height: 6-1
Weight: 215
Uniform no.: 19
Shoots: right

Career statistics:

GP	G	A	TP	PIM
249	22	40	62	239

1995-96 statistics:

GP	G	A	TP	+/-	PIM	PP	SH	GW	GT	S	PCT
74	7	10	17	-9	101	1	0	3	0	106	6.6

1996-97 statistics:

GP	G	A	TP	+/-	PIM	PP	SH	GW	GT	S	PCT
63	4	8	12	-3	49	0	0	0	0	100	4.0

1997-98 statistics:

GP	G	A	TP	+/-	PIM	PP	SH	GW	GT	S	PCT
33	5	6	11	-3	35	0	0	3	0	42	11.9

1998-99 statistics:

GP	G	A	TP	+/-	PIM	PP	SH	GW	GT	S	PCT
79	6	16	22	-5	54	0	0	0	0	156	3.8

LAST SEASON

Missed one game with eye injury. Missed one game with forearm injury. Missed one game due to coach's decision.

THE FINESSE GAME

Doan's game is speed. He is fast and strong, and forechecks aggressively and intelligently along the wall and in the corners. He intimidates with his skating because he gets in on a defenseman fast. Once he gains control of the puck he finds the open man in front of the net. He isn't overly creative, but will thrive on the dump-and-chase play, where he can just skate on his wing and race for the puck.

Doan has an acceptable wrist and slap shot but he doesn't shoot as much as he should. He will become more of a threat if he gains some confidence in his shot. He was a scorer in junior but he's now acting, thinking and scoring like a checker. He turns away from chances or throws the puck into the corner, when he could go in and shoot or make a play.

Doan needs to see power-play time and be put into more offensive situations to revive his game. There's no question he is a fine penalty killer and can handle the checking role, but he's too talented to waste as a one-way player.

THE PHYSICAL GAME

Doan is strong and a very good body checker. He seems to have a mean streak lurking under his exterior. He will lay some hard hits on people. He could play a little more abrasive.

THE INTANGIBLES

Doan came into his own last season as a checking-line winger. Now he needs to study some Jere Lehtinen tapes and see how a defensive forward can be an offensive threat.

PROJECTION

Doan will probably score 10 goals and 30 points, but he has more upside.

DALLAS DRAKE

Yrs. of NHL service: 7
Born: Trail, B.C.; Feb. 4, 1969
Position: centre
Height: 6-0
Weight: 180
Uniform no.: 11
Shoots: left

Career statistics:

GP	G	A	TP	PIM
422	95	161	256	396

1995-96 statistics:

GP	G	A	TP	+/-	PIM	PP	SH	GW	GT	S	PCT
69	19	20	39	-7	36	4	4	2	1	121	15.7

1996-97 statistics:

GP	G	A	TP	+/-	PIM	PP	SH	GW	GT	S	PCT
63	17	19	36	-11	52	5	1	1	0	113	15.0

1997-98 statistics:

GP	G	A	TP	+/-	PIM	PP	SH	GW	GT	S	PCT
60	11	29	40	+17	71	3	0	2	0	112	9.8

1998-99 statistics:

GP	G	A	TP	+/-	PIM	PP	SH	GW	GT	S	PCT
53	9	22	31	+17	65	0	0	3	0	105	8.6

LAST SEASON

Third on team in plus-minus. Missed 20 games due to separated shoulder and related injuries. Missed two games due to concussion. Missed one game with ankle injury. Missed one game with elbow injury. Missed four games due to suspension.

THE FINESSE GAME

Drake sees some playing time with the likes of Jeremy Roenick, by assuming the grinder's role and going into the corners. This is something of a reach for the overachieving Drake, who is better suited to a second-line role, but the chemistry often works because Drake does.

Drake is an aggressive forechecker (the best forechecker on the Coyotes), strong along the boards and in front of the net. He's on the small side, so he doesn't stand in and take a bashing, but he'll jump in and out of traffic to fight for the puck or bounce in on rebounds.

Drake is quick and powerful in his skating. He'll get outmuscled but not outhustled. His scoring chances come in deep.

THE PHYSICAL GAME

Drake gets noticed because he runs right over people. He is limited by his size but he will give a team whatever he's got. He's feisty enough to get the other team's attention, and he works to keep himself in scoring position.

THE INTANGIBLES

Drake is a coach's dream except when he's in the trainer's room. In addition to the injuries listed above, he had to have surgery to repair a broken nose. But he had a terrific playoffs, which should give him a confidence boost going into next season.

PROJECTION

We predicted Drake would score 15 goals (we were shy by six) and miss 15 games due to injury (we were off by 10), and would expect the same this season.

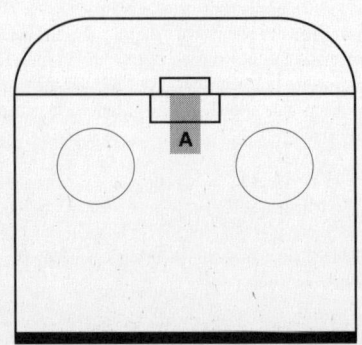

TRAVIS GREEN

Yrs. of NHL service: 7
Born: Castlegar, B.C.; Dec. 20, 1970
Position: centre
Height: 6-1
Weight: 193
Uniform no.: 39
Shoots: right

Career statistics:

GP	G	A	TP	PIM
489	109	173	282	355

1995-96 statistics:

GP	G	A	TP	+/-	PIM	PP	SH	GW	GT	S	PCT
69	24	45	69	-21	42	14	1	2	1	186	12.9

1996-97 statistics:

GP	G	A	TP	+/-	PIM	PP	SH	GW	GT	S	PCT
79	23	41	64	-5	38	10	0	3	0	177	13.0

1997-98 statistics:

GP	G	A	TP	+/-	PIM	PP	SH	GW	GT	S	PCT
76	19	23	42	-29	82	9	0	2	2	141	13.5

1998-99 statistics:

GP	G	A	TP	+/-	PIM	PP	SH	GW	GT	S	PCT
79	13	17	30	-7	81	3	1	2	0	165	7.9

LAST SEASON

Acquired from Anaheim with a first-round draft pick for Oleg Tverdovsky, June 26, 1999. Missed three games with knee injury.

THE FINESSE GAME

Green continues to have trouble finding his niche. Even Anaheim, which was desperate for someone to step up as a second-line centre, frequently dropped Green to the fourth line. He is likely to get another shot as a number two in Phoenix.

Green's abilities are weighted on the defensive side. He is on the ice in the waning seconds of the period or the game to protect a lead. But his skating is flawed. When he stops pushing and stops moving, there's no glide to him, so his skating really falls off. He has decent balance and agility with some quickness, though he lacks straight-ahead speed.

He controls the puck well. He plays more of a finesse game than a power game. An unselfish player, Green passes equally well to either side. He sees the ice well, but he has a very heavy shot. His release needs to be quicker, which is why he'll never be the scorer at the NHL level that he was in the minors.

Green is good on face-offs. He has quick hands and he uses his body to tie up an opponent, enabling his linemates to skate in for the puck.

THE PHYSICAL GAME

Green has good size and he's competitive, but hockey courage doesn't come naturally to him. He talks himself into going into the corners and around the net, knowing that he has to get into the dirty areas to produce. If he wants to be on the ice, he has to pay the price to be there.

THE INTANGIBLES

Green's skating keeps him from ascending to a higher quality of play. We would like to see him compete with a little more fire, but don't anticipate that happening.

PROJECTION

Ideally suited to be a third-line centre, Green will have to push himself to provide some offense as a number two. Phoenix expects he will score 20 to 25 goals. We expect 15 to 20.

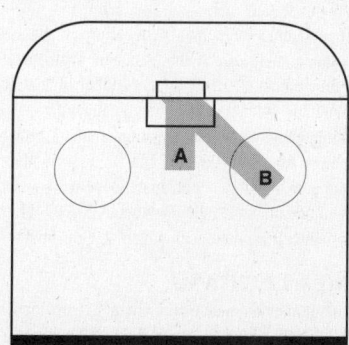

NIKOLAI KHABIBULIN

Yrs. of NHL service: 5
Born: Sverdlovsk, Russia; Jan. 13, 1973
Position: goaltender
Height: 6-1
Weight: 176
Uniform no.: 35
Catches: left

Career statistics:

GP	MIN	GA	SO	GAA	A	PIM
284	16027	735	21	2.75	6	62

1995-96 statistics:

GP	MIN	GAA	W	L	T	SO	GA	S	SAPCT	PIM
53	2914	3.13	26	20	3	2	152	1656	.908	12

1996-97 statistics:

GP	MIN	GAA	W	L	T	SO	GA	S	SAPCT	PIM
72	4091	2.83	30	33	6	7	193	2094	.908	16

1997-98 statistics:

GP	MIN	GAA	W	L	T	SO	GA	S	SAPCT	PIM
70	4026	2.74	30	28	10	4	184	1835	.900	22

1998-99 statistics:

GP	MIN	GAA	W	L	T	SO	GA	S	SAPCT	PIM
63	3657	2.13	32	23	7	8	130	1681	.923	8

LAST SEASON

Third among NHL goalies in shutouts with career high. Tied for fourth among NHL goalies in save percentage with career best. Tied for fifth in NHL in wins with career high. Career best goals-against average. Missed two games with hand injury. Missed one game with groin injury.

THE PHYSICAL GAME

Khabibulin is a butterfly-style goalie who positions himself like a shortstop. He gets down low and always gets his body behind the shot, and he stays on his feet and moves with the shooter. He may perform the best split-save in the league: it's stunningly graceful and athletic, and his legs look about five feet long. He leaves only the tiniest five-hole because he also gets the paddle of his stick down low across the front of the crease. Shooters have to go upstairs on him but he doesn't give away a lot of net high.

Khabibulin is solid in his fundamentals. He plays well out on the top of his crease, which is unusual for Russian goalies, who tend to stay deep in their net. He is aggressive but patient at the same time, and waits for the shooter to commit first. Khabibulin still needs to improve his puckhandling.

Cutting more than 400 minutes from Khabibulin's playing time in 1997-98 was the best thing that could have happened for the goalie (the second best thing was the addition of coach Benoit Allaire). He stayed sharp through the stretch and into the playoffs.

THE MENTAL GAME

Khabibulin was able to maintain a strong attitude despite a lack of offensive support. The lighter work load was a factor.

THE INTANGIBLES

In last year's *HSR*, we said Khabibulin needed to cut his playing time by about 400 minutes, that he was in serious need of some rest and that he needed intensive goalie coaching. Someone must have been paying attention. As a result, Khabibulin enjoyed his best season.

PROJECTION

Khabibulin is back in a positive groove. As long as he is limited to 60 or so starts, he could post 32 or more wins.

JYRKI LUMME

Yrs. of NHL service: 11
Born: Tampere, Finland; July 16, 1966
Position: right defense
Height: 6-1
Weight: 205
Uniform no.: 20
Shoots: left

Career statistics:

GP	G	A	TP	PIM
714	92	281	373	464

1995-96 statistics:

GP	G	A	TP	+/-	PIM	PP	SH	GW	GT	S	PCT
80	17	37	54	-9	50	8	0	2	2	192	8.9

1996-97 statistics:

GP	G	A	TP	+/-	PIM	PP	SH	GW	GT	S	PCT
66	11	24	35	+8	32	5	0	2	0	107	10.3

1997-98 statistics:

GP	G	A	TP	+/-	PIM	PP	SH	GW	GT	S	PCT
74	9	21	30	-25	34	4	0	1	1	117	7.7

1998-99 statistics:

GP	G	A	TP	+/-	PIM	PP	SH	GW	GT	S	PCT
60	7	21	28	+5	34	1	0	4	0	121	5.8

LAST SEASON
Tied for third on team in game-winning goals. Missed 18 games with shoulder injuries. Missed four games with groin injury.

THE FINESSE GAME
Lumme is one of the better-kept secrets in the NHL. He is an accomplished puck carrier who can rush the puck out of danger and make a smart first pass to start the attack. He likes to gamble a bit offensively, but he has the good skating ability to be able to wheel back into a defensive mode.

Lumme's point shot isn't overpowering, but he keeps it low and on net and times it well. He has very good hands and is adept at keeping the puck in. He also uses his lateral mobility to slide along the blueline into the centre to quarterback the power play. He will also glide to the top of the circle for a shot. He can control a game and make everyone play at his pace.

Defensively, Lumme uses his hand skills for sweep- and poke-checks. He will challenge at the blueline to try to knock the puck free. He is tough to beat one-on-one, and always comes out of the corner with the puck. He uses his feet well along the boards to keep the puck alive, and he's a strong penalty killer because of his range and anticipation.

THE PHYSICAL GAME
Lumme is all finesse. He will take a hit to protect the puck or make a play, but he won't throw himself at anybody. Other teams like to key on Lumme, because if he gets hit often and hard enough, he can be taken out of a game early.

THE INTANGIBLES
Although the Finn is not a number one defenseman because his all-around skills aren't good enough, he's just a cut below the NHL's best rearguards. He has improved defensively, but his key value remains his open-ice play and his involvement in the attack.

PROJECTION
Injuries cost Lumme's production last season, especially the shoulder injury, which hampered his shot. He underwent off-season surgery to repair a torn rotator cuff and torn biceps muscle. He also faced the burden of playing the first season after signing a big free-agent deal. The pressure should ease this season, and if he stays healthy, he should score in the 50- to 60-point range.

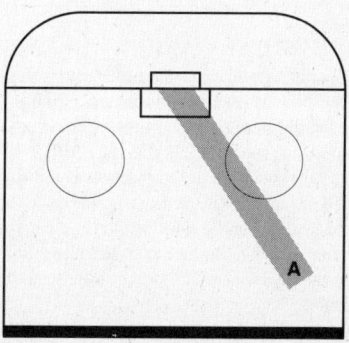

STANISLAV NECKAR

Yrs. of NHL service: 4
Born: Ceske Budejovice, Czech Republic; Dec. 22, 1975
Position: left defense
Height: 6-1
Weight: 196
Uniform no.: 24
Shoots: left

Career statistics:

GP	G	A	TP	PIM
195	6	14	20	124

1994-95 statistics:

GP	G	A	TP	+/-	PIM	PP	SH	GW	GT	S	PCT
48	1	3	4	-20	37	0	0	0	0	34	2.9

1995-96 statistics:

GP	G	A	TP	+/-	PIM	PP	SH	GW	GT	S	PCT
82	3	9	12	-16	54	1	0	0	0	57	5.3

1996-97 statistics:

GP	G	A	TP	+/-	PIM	PP	SH	GW	GT	S	PCT
5	0	0	0	+2	2	0	0	0	0	3	0.0

1997-98 statistics:

GP	G	A	TP	+/-	PIM	PP	SH	GW	GT	S	PCT
60	2	2	4	-14	31	0	0	0	0	43	4.7

LAST SEASON

Acquired from N.Y. Rangers for Jason Doig and a 1999 sixth-round draft pick, Mar. 23, 1999. Acquired by Rangers from Ottawa for Bill Berg and a 1999 second-round draft pick, Nov. 2, 1998. Missed 16 games with broken foot.

THE FINESSE GAME

Neckar understands the position of defenseman but he is fundamentally unsound when it comes time to putting all of the components together. He has to use his body more in addition to learning body position.

Neckar will never put up many points because he doesn't have much offensive sense or very good hands. He has a slow release on his point shot and doesn't do much that's creative, other than put his head down and shoot. He's not a very good puckhandler or passer.

He is a polished skater, especially backwards. He is not often beaten wide. His forte is his defensive play.

THE PHYSICAL GAME

Neckar is not a good open-ice hitter, but is very strong along the boards and in the corners, though he will need to develop confidence in his rebuilt knee (from a 1997 injury) to return to his old self. Although he will fight if provoked he is not very good at it. He needs to get much stronger. His cardiovascular conditioning is fine, and he can handle a lot of ice time (thrives on it, as a matter of fact), but he has to learn to stick and pin his man better. Neckar is a power defenseman, which is valuable.

THE INTANGIBLES

Neckar's confidence has been knocked down a peg and three teams in one season wasn't the way to get it back. The Rangers made it especially tough on him, as he was frequently a healthy scratch. Phoenix thought enough of him to make a side deal with Atlanta to prevent Neckar from going in the Expansion Draft.

PROJECTION

Neckar will have to earn a spot in the top four. His offensive production should be in the single digits.

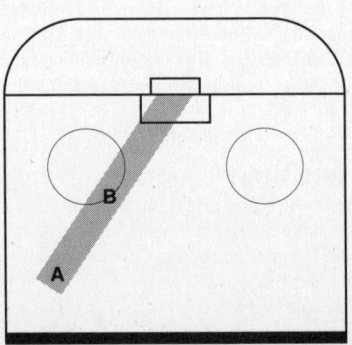

TEPPO NUMMINEN

Yrs. of NHL service: 11
Born: Tampere, Finland; July 3, 1968
Position: left defense
Height: 6-1
Weight: 190
Uniform no.: 27
Shoots: right

Career statistics:

GP	G	A	TP	PIM
793	76	307	383	303

1995-96 statistics:

GP	G	A	TP	+/-	PIM	PP	SH	GW	GT	S	PCT
74	11	43	54	-4	22	6	0	3	0	165	6.7

1996-97 statistics:

GP	G	A	TP	+/-	PIM	PP	SH	GW	GT	S	PCT
82	2	25	27	-3	28	0	0	0	0	135	1.5

1997-98 statistics:

GP	G	A	TP	+/-	PIM	PP	SH	GW	GT	S	PCT
82	11	40	51	+25	30	6	0	2	0	126	8.7

1998-99 statistics:

GP	G	A	TP	+/-	PIM	PP	SH	GW	GT	S	PCT
82	10	30	40	+3	30	1	0	0	2	156	6.4

LAST SEASON

One of four Coyotes to appear in all 82 games (for second consecutive season). Has appeared in 297 consecutive games. Led team defensemen in points for second consecutive season.

THE FINESSE GAME

Numminen's agility and anticipation make him look much faster than he is. A graceful skater with a smooth change of direction, he never telegraphs what he is about to do. His skating makes him valuable on the first penalty-killing unit. He will not get caught out of position and is seldom bested one-on-one.

If he is under pressure, Numminen is not afraid to give up the puck on a dump-and-chase, rather than force a neutral-zone play. He works best with a partner with some offensive savvy. Otherwise, he takes too much of the offensive game on himself, and his plays looks forced. He would rather dish off than rush with the puck, and he is a crisp passer, moving the puck briskly and seldom overhandling it. He is terrific at making the first pass to move the puck out of the zone.

Numminen is not a finisher. He joins the play but doesn't lead it. Most of his offense is generated from point shots or passes in deep. He works the right point on the power play.

Numminen is uncannily adept at keeping the puck in at the point, frustrating opponents who try to clear it out around the boards. He intentionally shoots the puck wide for tip-ins by his surehanded forwards. He is not afraid to pinch, either, and was encouraged by (now ex-) coach Jim Schoenfeld to be more aggressive.

THE PHYSICAL GAME

Numminen plays an acceptable physical game. He can be intimidated and doesn't scare attackers, who will attempt to drive through him to the net. Opponents get a strong forecheck on him to neutralize his smart passing game. He'll employ his body as a last resort, but would rather use his stick and gain the puck. He is even-tempered and not at all nasty.

THE INTANGIBLES

Numminen is underrated. He's not a Norris Trophy type, but no NHL team would hesitate to take him and put him on their top pair.

PROJECTION

Numminen is a complete if not elite defenseman who is capable of scoring 50 points.

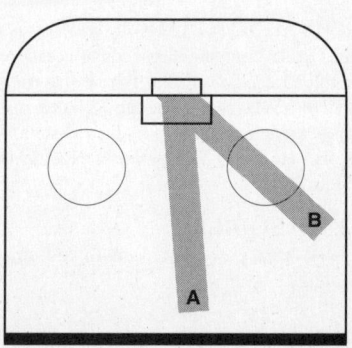

DERON QUINT

Yrs. of NHL service: 4
Born: Durham, NH; March 12, 1976
Position: left defense
Height: 6-1
Weight: 182
Uniform no.: 5
Shoots: left

Career statistics:

GP	G	A	TP	PIM
170	17	39	56	62

1995-96 statistics:

GP	G	A	TP	+/-	PIM	PP	SH	GW	GT	S	PCT
51	5	13	18	-2	22	2	0	0	0	97	5.2

1996-97 statistics:

GP	G	A	TP	+/-	PIM	PP	SH	GW	GT	S	PCT
27	3	11	14	-4	4	1	0	0	0	63	4.8

1997-98 statistics:

GP	G	A	TP	+/-	PIM	PP	SH	GW	GT	S	PCT
32	4	7	11	-6	16	1	0	1	0	61	6.6

1998-99 statistics:

GP	G	A	TP	+/-	PIM	PP	SH	GW	GT	S	PCT
60	5	8	13	-10	20	2	0	0	0	94	5.3

PROJECTION

Quint will be a top point producer in a couple of seasons, but he's still green and 20 points is reasonable for this year. He's still a project.

LAST SEASON

Career high in games played. Missed 16 games with two concussions. Missed three games with separated shoulder. Missed three games due to coach's decision.

THE FINESSE GAME

Quint has some NHL-level skills, starting with his skating. He has very good speed with a change of gears and can shift directions in a fluid motion. He also possesses a fine, accurate slap shot with a quick release. He can rush the puck end-to-end or start a rush with a smart pass and then join the attack.

The problem isn't in Quint's hands or feet, but in his head. He doesn't read the rush well and overcommits to plays. He has to learn to tune into odd-man rushes.

Quint was paired with the veteran J. J. Daigneault, which helped steady him. He would probably thrive if he were paired with a defense-minded partner who would feel comfortable in just telling Quint to go.

THE PHYSICAL GAME

Quint is finesse-oriented and needs to get more physically involved. He doesn't have great size for an NHL defenseman but he is big enough to bump and get in the way of people, though he's inconsistent with his body work. He also has a problem picking the right man to eliminate.

THE INTANGIBLES

Quint was hurt early and late in the season by concussions.

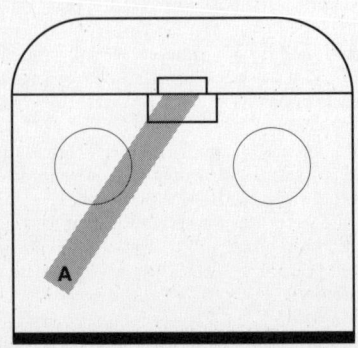

ROBERT REICHEL

Yrs. of NHL service: 9
Born: Litvinov, Czech,; June 25, 1971
Position: centre
Height: 5-10
Weight: 185
Uniform no.: 16
Shoots: left

Career statistics:
GP	G	A	TP	PIM
602	209	298	507	492

1995-96 statistics:
Did not play in NHL

1996-97 statistics:
GP	G	A	TP	+/-	PIM	PP	SH	GW	GT	S	PCT
82	21	41	62	+5	26	6	1	3	0	214	9.8

1997-98 statistics:
GP	G	A	TP	+/-	PIM	PP	SH	GW	GT	S	PCT
82	25	40	65	-11	32	8	0	2	2	201	12.4

1998-99 statistics:
GP	G	A	TP	+/-	PIM	PP	SH	GW	GT	S	PCT
83	26	43	69	-13	54	8	1	4	1	236	11.0

LAST SEASON

Acquired from N.Y. Islanders with a third-round and a fourth-round draft choice in 1999 for Brad Isbister and a third-round draft choice, Mar. 20, 1999. Second on team in assists, points, power-play goals and shots. Tied for second on team in goals. Tied for third on team in game-winning goals. Only player in NHL to appear in 83 games.

THE FINESSE GAME

Reichel's strength in as a playmaker. He thinks "pass" first and needs to play on a line with a pure finisher. He is one of those gifted passers who can make a scoring opportunity materialize when there appears to be no hole; his wingers have to be alert because the puck will find its way to their tape. He has great control of the puck in open ice or in scrums.

Reichel will certainly take the shot when he's got it, but he won't force a pass to someone who is in a worse scoring position than he is. He has an explosive shot with a lot of velocity on it. He pursues loose pucks in front and wheels around to the back of the net to look for an open teammate. He is good in traffic.

At least that's how Reichel plays when things are going well. He's just as likely to go into a slump or a pout, and he doesn't add much to a team when he isn't piling up points.

THE PHYSICAL GAME

Reichel is small but sturdy. He is not a big fan of contact and there are some who question his hockey courage. He's not a player other teams are afraid to play against. He is well-conditioned and can handle a lot of ice time.

THE INTANGIBLES

Reichel was a restricted free agent during the off-season and a protracted contract battle was anticipated. He has taken a season off before to stay in Europe, and it would be no surprise to see him do the again. The Coyotes obtained Travis Green as centre ice insurance, just in case.

PROJECTION

Reichel's commitment to excel in the NHL is a question mark. If he returns in the right frame of mind, he could be an 80-point scorer.

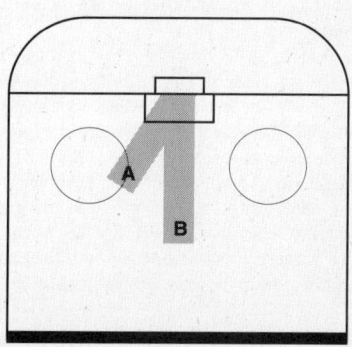

JEREMY ROENICK

Yrs. of NHL service: 10
Born: Boston, Mass.; Jan. 17, 1970
Position: centre
Height: 6-0
Weight: 190
Uniform no.: 97
Shoots: right

Career statistics:

GP	G	A	TP	PIM
753	344	449	793	918

1995-96 statistics:

GP	G	A	TP	+/-	PIM	PP	SH	GW	GT	S	PCT
66	32	35	67	+9	109	12	4	2	2	171	18.7

1996-97 statistics:

GP	G	A	TP	+/-	PIM	PP	SH	GW	GT	S	PCT
72	29	40	69	-7	115	10	3	7	0	228	12.7

1997-98 statistics:

GP	G	A	TP	+/-	PIM	PP	SH	GW	GT	S	PCT
79	24	32	56	+5	103	6	1	3	1	182	13.2

1998-99 statistics:

GP	G	A	TP	+/-	PIM	PP	SH	GW	GT	S	PCT
78	24	48	72	+7	130	4	0	3	0	203	11.8

LAST SEASON

Led team in assists and points. Third on team in shots and shooting percentage. Missed two games with fractured jaw and fractured thumb. Missed two games with concussion.

THE FINESSE GAME

What an enigma Roenick has become. There will be nights when he looks like an uninvolved and somewhat selfish player, yet he shows up to play in a Game 7 in the playoffs with an Imperial Storm Trooper mask to protect a nearly pulverized jaw.

When Roenick is on, he commands a lot of attention on the ice, drawing away defenders to open up ice for his teammates. He has great acceleration and can turn quickly, change directions or burn a defender with outside speed. A defenseman who plays aggressively against him will be left staring at the back of Roenick's jersey as he skips by en route to the net. Roenick has to be forced into the high-traffic areas, where his lack of size and strength are the only things that derail him.

Roenick has great quickness and is tough to handle one-on-one. He won't make the same move or take the same shot twice in a row. He has a variety of shots and can score from almost anywhere on the ice. He can rifle a wrist shot from 30 feet away, or else wait until the goalie is down and lift in a backhand from in tight. He has a drag-and-pull move to his backhand that is highly deceptive, and it also keeps the goalie guessing because he is able to show a backhand but pull it quickly to his forehand once he has frozen the goalie.

THE PHYSICAL GAME

Roenick plays with such a headlong style that injuries are routine. He has had two concussions in the past two seasons that have to be a concern. He has trouble keeping weight on.

Roenick takes aggressive penalties — smashing people into the boards, getting his elbows up — and he never backs down. He plays through pain and is highly competitive.

THE INTANGIBLES

Roenick hasn't been a 50-goal scorer since 1992-93 and no longer belongs among the NHL's goal-scoring elite. It would be interesting to see what happens if the Coyotes get a bona fide number two centre to take some of the checking pressure off him.

PROJECTION

Roenick didn't score many meaningful goals last season (only four on the power play, only three game winners). Not impressive numbers for a guy who used to be considered one of the NHL's best crunch-time players. He's still a pretty safe bet for 75 points.

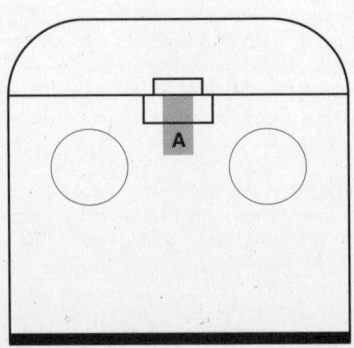

KEITH TKACHUK

Yrs. of NHL service: 7
Born: Melrose, Mass.; Mar. 28, 1972
Position: left wing
Height: 6-2
Weight: 210
Uniform no.: 7
Shoots: left

Career statistics:
GP	G	A	TP	PIM
526	272	237	509	1318

1995-96 statistics:
GP	G	A	TP	+/-	PIM	PP	SH	GW	GT	S	PCT
76	50	48	98	+11	156	20	2	6	0	249	20.1

1996-97 statistics:
GP	G	A	TP	+/-	PIM	PP	SH	GW	GT	S	PCT
81	52	34	86	-1	228	9	2	7	1	296	17.6

1997-98 statistics:
GP	G	A	TP	+/-	PIM	PP	SH	GW	GT	S	PCT
69	40	26	66	+9	147	11	0	8	1	232	17.2

1998-99 statistics:
GP	G	A	TP	+/-	PIM	PP	SH	GW	GT	S	PCT
68	36	32	68	+22	151	11	2	7	1	258	14.0

LAST SEASON
Led team in goals and shots for fourth consecutive season. Scored at least 30 goals for fifth time in career. Led team in power-play goals and game-winning goals for second consecutive season. Led team in plus-minus. Tied for team lead in shorthanded goals. Second on team in penalty minutes and shooting percentage. Third on team in assists and points. Missed two games with groin injury. Missed eight games with broken rib. Missed two games with back injury. Missed two games with knee injury.

THE FINESSE GAME
In front of the net, Tkachuk will bang and crash but he also has soft hands for picking pucks out of skates and flicking strong wrist shots. He can also kick at the puck with his skates without going down. He has a quick release. He looks at the net, not down at the puck on his stick, and finds the openings. He has a great feel for the puck. From the hash marks in, Tkachuk is one of the most dangerous forwards in the NHL. Eliminating the man in the crease rule will increase his effectiveness and his production, because the trenches are where Tkachuk does his best work. He doesn't just stand in the slot, either, but moves in and out.

Tkachuk has improved his one-step quickness and agility. He is powerful and balanced, and often drives through bigger defensemen. Because of his size and strength, he is frequently used to take draws, and it's a rare face-off where the opposing centre doesn't end up getting smacked by Tkachuk.

Tkachuk's numbers last season were really quite amazing when you count up the number of games he missed due to injury (14). He played hurt on quite a few nights, too, even wearing a flak jacket to protect injured ribs. Every time he was out, it took him a few games to regain his rhythm because of the power game he plays.

THE PHYSICAL GAME
Tkachuk is volatile and mean as a scorpion. He takes bad penalties, and since he has a reputation around the league for getting his stick up and retaliating for hits with a quick rabbit-punch to the head, referees keep a close eye on him. He tried to be more disciplined last season, but still took penalties at the wrong times. He can be tough without buying a time-share in the penalty box.

Tkachuk can dictate the physical tempo of a game with his work in the corners and along the boards. He comes in hard with big-time hits on the forecheck.

THE INTANGIBLES
Tkachuk has some growing up to do. He is the heart and soul of this franchise and needs to be more responsible. He is so close to being a complete player.

PROJECTION
A healthy Tkachuk should have a big bounce-back season. He is capable of scoring 50 goals.

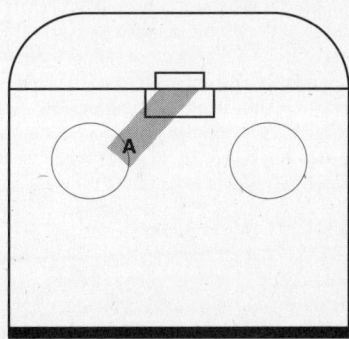

RICK TOCCHET

Yrs. of NHL service: 15
Born: Scarborough, Ont.; Apr. 9, 1964
Position: right wing
Height: 6-0
Weight: 205
Uniform no.: 92
Shoots: right

Career statistics:

GP	G	A	TP	PIM
990	411	666	877	2773

1995-96 statistics:

GP	G	A	TP	+/-	PIM	PP	SH	GW	GT	S	PCT
71	29	31	60	+10	181	10	0	3	1	185	15.7

1996-97 statistics:

GP	G	A	TP	+/-	PIM	PP	SH	GW	GT	S	PCT
53	21	19	40	-3	98	4	0	2	1	157	13.4

1997-98 statistics:

GP	G	A	TP	+/-	PIM	PP	SH	GW	GT	S	PCT
68	26	19	45	+1	157	8	0	6	0	161	16.1

1998-99 statistics:

GP	G	A	TP	+/-	PIM	PP	SH	GW	GT	S	PCT
81	26	30	56	+5	147	6	1	5	0	178	14.6

LAST SEASON

Led team in shooting percentage. Second on team in game-winning goals. Tied for second on team in goals. Third on team in power-play goals and penalty minutes. Missed one game with ankle injury.

THE FINESSE GAME

Tocchet has worked hard to make the most of the finesse skills he possesses, and that makes everything loom larger. His skating is powerful, though he does not have great mobility or breakaway speed. He is explosive in short bursts and is most effective in small areas. He works extremely well down low and in traffic. He drives to the front of the net and into the corners for the puck.

Tocchet's shooting skills are better than his passing skills. He has limited vision of the ice for making a creative play but he is a master at the bang-bang play. He'll smack in rebounds and deflections and set screens as defenders try to knock him down. He does his best work on the goalie's front porch.

Because of his strong, accurate wrist shot, Tocchet gets most of his goals from close range, though he can also fire a one-timer from the tops of the circles. He'll rarely waste a shot from the blueline. He is a good give-and-go player because his quickness allows him to jump into the holes. He beats few people one-on-one because he lacks stickhandling prowess.

THE PHYSICAL GAME

Tocchet gets about 20 shifts a game. That's like going 20 rounds with Joe Frazier, a heavyweight who comes at you again and again with everything he's got. There is no hiding from Tocchet. He is a tough hitter and frequently gets his stick and elbows up. He has long had a history of letting his emotions get the better of him, and although he has matured somewhat, he is acutely aware of his position as one of the few tough, physical forwards on a team of finesse players. Tocchet knows he must play rugged to be effective and he can do that cleanly, but he will also get everyone's attention by bending the rules.

THE INTANGIBLES

Tocchet's work ethic is inspiring. He is always one of the last players off the ice, usually working on puck-handling drills. Before games, he's one of the first to the rink and is riding the bike; after games, he's lifting weights. He started his career as a goon but has remade himself into a solid NHLer. He stayed healthy again last season, and as long as he can stay on his feet he'll be an impact player. Tocchet is a positive role model to have on hand to teach younger players the importance of a work ethic.

PROJECTION

If Tocchet can stay in the lineup, he still has the fire and the goods to be a 30-goal scorer. He'll rack up more than 100 PIM, too. He's 35, but he should still have one top-flight season left in him. The Coyotes think enough of him to commit to a new contract.

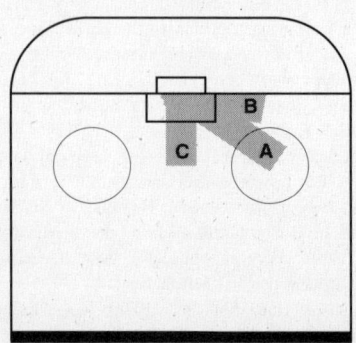

PITTSBURGH PENGUINS

Players' Statistics 1998-99

POS.	NO.	PLAYER	GP	G	A	PTS	+/-	PIM	PP	SH	GW	GT	S	PCT
R	68	JAROMIR JAGR	81	44	83	127	17	66	10	1	7	2	343	12.8
C	82	MARTIN STRAKA	80	35	48	83	12	26	5	4	4	1	177	19.8
L	9	GERMAN TITOV	72	11	45	56	18	34	3	1	3	1	113	9.7
R	27	ALEXEI KOVALEV	77	23	30	53	2	49	6	1	5		191	12.0
C	20	ROBERT LANG	72	21	23	44	-10	24	7		3	3	137	15.3
C	37	KIP MILLER	77	19	23	42	1	22	1		4		125	15.2
C	38	*JAN HRDINA	82	13	29	42	-2	40	3		2		94	13.8
D	4	KEVIN HATCHER	66	11	27	38	11	24	4	2	3		131	8.4
R	44	ROB BROWN	58	13	11	24	-15	16	9		1		78	16.7
D	5	BRAD WERENKA	81	6	18	24	17	93	1		4		77	7.8
D	71	JIRI SLEGR	63	3	20	23	13	86	1				91	3.3
R	36	MATTHEW BARNABY	62	6	16	22	-12	177	1		3		79	7.6
R	95	ALEXEI MOROZOV	67	9	10	19	5	14					75	12.0
R	25	DAN KESA	67	2	8	10	-9	27				1	33	6.1
D	8	BOBBY DOLLAS	70	2	8	10	-3	60					34	5.9
D	24	IAN MORAN	62	4	5	9	1	37		1			65	6.2
D	47	*MAXIM GALANOV	51	4	3	7	-8	14	2			1	44	9.1
D	16	JEFF SEROWIK	26		6	6	-4	16					26	
D	11	DARIUS KASPARAITIS	48	1	4	5	12	70					32	3.1
G	35	TOM BARRASSO	43		3	3	0	20						
L	12	*MARTIN SONNENBERG	44	1	1	2	-2	19					12	8.3
L	18	PATRICK LEBEAU	8	1		1	-2	2					4	25.0
D	49	GREG ANDRUSAK	7		1	1	4	4					2	
D	46	VICTOR IGNATJEV	11		1	1	-3	6					15	
C	18	*RYAN SAVOIA	3				-1							
D	46	*PAVEL SKRBEK	4				2	2					1	
C	17	*BRIAN BONIN	5				-2							2	
D	22	*SVEN BUTENSCHON	17				-7	6					8	
G	30	*J-SEBASTIEN AUBIN	17				0							
D	6	NEIL WILKINSON	24				-2	22					11	
G	1	*PETER SKUDRA	37				0	2						
C	29	TYLER WRIGHT	61				-2	90					16	

GP = games played; G = goals; A = assists; PTS = points; +/- = goals-for minus goals-against while player is on ice; PIM = penalties in minutes; PP = power-play goals; SH = shorthanded goals; GW = game-winning goals; GT = game-tying goals; S = no. of shots; PCT = percentage of goals to shots; * = rookie

MATTHEW BARNABY

Yrs. of NHL service: 6
Born: Ottawa, Ont.; May 4, 1973
Position: right wing
Height: 6-0
Weight: 170
Uniform no.: 36
Shoots: left

Career statistics:
GP	G	A	TP	PIM
335	49	81	130	1282

1995-96 statistics:
GP	G	A	TP	+/-	PIM	PP	SH	GW	GT	S	PCT
73	15	16	31	-2	335	0	0	0	0	131	11.5

1996-97 statistics:
GP	G	A	TP	+/-	PIM	PP	SH	GW	GT	S	PCT
68	19	24	43	+16	249	2	0	1	0	121	15.7

1997-98 statistics:
GP	G	A	TP	+/-	PIM	PP	SH	GW	GT	S	PCT
72	5	20	25	+8	289	0	0	2	0	96	5.2

1998-99 statistics:
GP	G	A	TP	+/-	PIM	PP	SH	GW	GT	S	PCT
62	6	16	22	-12	177	1	0	3	0	79	7.6

PROJECTION
Barnaby's 200 penalty minutes are a sure thing. And so are about 20 points.

LAST SEASON
Acquired from Buffalo for Stu Barnes, Mar. 11, 1999. Third on team in penalty minutes. Missed one game with ankle injury. Missed one game with back spasms. Missed 18 games due to coach's decision.

THE FINESSE GAME
Barnaby's offensive skills are minimal. He gets some room because of his reputation, and that buys him a little time around the net to get a shot away. He is utterly fearless and dives right into the thick of the action going for loose pucks.

But no one hires Barnaby for his scoring touch. His game is marked by his fierce intensity. He hits anyone, but especially loves going after the other team's big names. He is infuriating.

He skates well enough not to look out of place and is strong and balanced on his feet. He will do anything to win. If he could develop a better scoring touch he would start reminding people of Dale Hunter.

THE PHYSICAL GAME
Barnaby brings a lot of energy to the game; considering his size, it's a wonder he survived the season. He has to do some cheap stuff to survive, which makes him an even more irritating opponent. Big guys especially hate him, because it's a no-win when a Bob Probert or Randy McKay takes on the poor underdog Barnaby. But he's so obnoxious they just can't help it.

THE INTANGIBLES
Barnaby took a step back last season to become more of a trash talker and less of a hockey player.

TOM BARRASSO

Yrs. of NHL service: 16
Born: Boston, Mass.; Mar. 31, 1965
Position: goaltender
Height: 6-3
Weight: 211
Uniform no.: 35
Catches: right

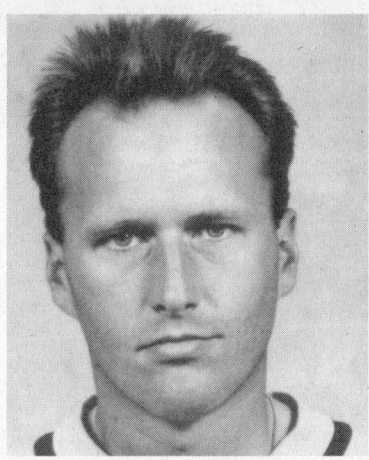

Career statistics:

GP	MIN	GA	SO	GAA	A	PIM
708	40472	2208	34	3.27	48	429

1995-96 statistics:

GP	MIN	GAA	W	L	T	SO	GA	S	SAPCT	PIM
49	2799	3.43	29	16	2	2	160	1626	.902	18

1996-97 statistics:

GP	MIN	GAA	W	L	T	SO	GA	S	SAPCT	PIM
5	270	5.78	0	5	0	0	26	186	.860	0

1997-98 statistics:

GP	MIN	GAA	W	L	T	SO	GA	S	SAPCT	PIM
63	3542	2.07	31	14	13	7	122	1556	.922	14

1998-99 statistics:

GP	MIN	GAA	W	L	T	SO	GA	S	SAPCT	PIM
43	2306	2.55	19	16	3	4	98	993	.901	20

LAST SEASON

Moved into first place on all-time points list for goaltenders (48). Missed 18 games with broken hand. Missed seven games with groin injury. Missed five games with hip injuries. Missed three games with neck injuries.

THE PHYSICAL GAME

One of the most impressive things about Barrasso is that, although he is often on his knees, he is almost never on his side. He might be the best in the league at recovering from going down and will be back on his skates with his glove in position for the next shot.

Barrasso loves to handle the puck; he's like a third defenseman in both his willingness to leave the crease and in his ability to pass. He's a good skater who is able to get to and control a lot of pucks that most goalies wouldn't dare try to reach. Most of the time he uses the boards for his passes, rather than making a risky play up the middle, but every so often he is vulnerable to the interception.

Because of Barrasso's range, teams have to adapt their attack. Hard dump-ins won't work, because he stops them behind the net and zips the puck right back out for an alert counterattack by his teammates. Since he comes out around the post to his right better than his left, teams have to aim soft dumps to his left, making him more hesitant about making the play and giving the forecheckers time to get in on him. His lone weakness appears to be shots low on the glove side.

THE MENTAL GAME

Barrasso is still one of the game's most intense competitors. He has battled through injuries and personal crises through the past few seasons and has lost little of his edge. He will whack guys in the ankle or get his body in the way for a subtle interference play. He played like a man on a mission last season, working extremely hard in practices to stay in shape and keep his edge. He allowed very few soft goals when it mattered most, in the playoffs.

THE INTANGIBLES

Still not the easiest guy to like, you have to give Barrasso credit for coming back time after time from injuries to regain his form.

PROJECTION

Barrasso is just slightly below the league's elite goalies, but more than half the teams in the NHL might upgrade their goaltending if they had him. He should net 20 to 25 wins, since Pittsburgh's younger goalies aren't quite ready to bump him.

BOBBY DOLLAS

Yrs. of NHL service: 9
Born: Montreal, Que.; Jan. 31, 1965
Position: right defense
Height: 6-2
Weight: 212
Uniform no.: 8
Shoots: left

Career statistics:

GP	G	A	TP	PIM
575	38	88	126	421

1995-96 statistics:

GP	G	A	TP	+/-	PIM	PP	SH	GW	GT	S	PCT
82	8	22	30	+9	64	0	1	1	0	117	6.8

1996-97 statistics:

GP	G	A	TP	+/-	PIM	PP	SH	GW	GT	S	PCT
79	4	14	18	+17	55	1	0	1	1	96	4.2

1997-98 statistics:

GP	G	A	TP	+/-	PIM	PP	SH	GW	GT	S	PCT
52	2	6	8	-6	49	0	0	0	0	38	5.3

1998-99 statistics:

GP	G	A	TP	+/-	PIM	PP	SH	GW	GT	S	PCT
70	2	8	10	-3	60	0	0	0	0	34	5.9

PROJECTION

Dollas's contribution isn't measured in points.

LAST SEASON

Missed three games with broken toe. Missed seven games due to coach's decision.

THE FINESSE GAME

Dollas is an excellent skater with speed, mobility and agility, and he's strong on his feet. He doesn't like to get involved too much in the offense, preferring to make a smart, quick pass to start a teammate off. He makes poised plays out of the defensive zone but has become more and more conservative.

Dollas can handle a lot of ice time because he doesn't wear himself out racing up and down the ice. He takes the offensive chance when it's a high-percentage play and is skilled enough to handle point work on the second unit. He has a strong shot from the point, but it takes him awhile to release it and more often than not the shot gets blocked.

Dollas kills penalties well and is one of the game's better shot-blockers.

THE PHYSICAL GAME

Because of his size, Dollas was thrust into the role of an enforcer with three different organizations. But he's not tough, doesn't like to fight and he got an unfair label as a soft player early in his career.

He has tremendous lower-body strength — to bump rather than hammer players around the net. He doesn't scare people but he won't be intimidated.

THE INTANGIBLES

Dollas is a solid citizen, one who is content to play a stay-at-home style and is best suited paired with a more offensive partner.

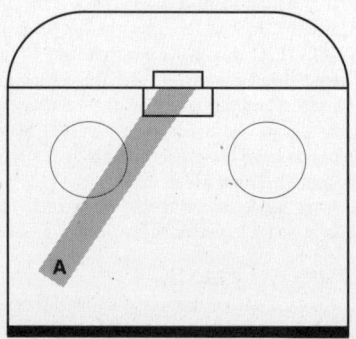

KEVIN HATCHER

Yrs. of NHL service: 14
Born: Detroit, Mich.; Sept. 9, 1966
Position: right defense
Height: 6-4
Weight: 225
Uniform no.: 4
Shoots: right

Career statistics:

GP	G	A	TP	PIM
1026	219	417	636	1318

1995-96 statistics:

GP	G	A	TP	+/-	PIM	PP	SH	GW	GT	S	PCT
74	15	26	41	-24	58	7	0	3	2	237	6.3

1996-97 statistics:

GP	G	A	TP	+/-	PIM	PP	SH	GW	GT	S	PCT
80	15	39	54	+11	103	9	0	1	0	199	7.5

1997-98 statistics:

GP	G	A	TP	+/-	PIM	PP	SH	GW	GT	S	PCT
74	19	29	48	-3	66	13	1	3	1	169	11.2

1998-99 statistics:

GP	G	A	TP	+/-	PIM	PP	SH	GW	GT	S	PCT
66	11	27	38	+11	24	4	2	3	0	131	8.4

LAST SEASON

Led team defensemen in scoring for third consecutive season. Second on team in shorthanded goals. Missed 16 games with broken foot.

THE FINESSE GAME

This is the Hatcher with the offensive nose (it looks like they split the genes). Kevin thinks offense all the time. He anticipates where the puck may be going, so he gets out of position. But when you're as big as he is you shouldn't have to anticipate anything — you should just let it happen. You allow your size to take away everything so that you don't have to force it. Kevin is a little more nimble on his feet, and he has better hands (than Derian) for making plays up the ice and being a little more agile when he has the puck.

Hatcher is not among the elite offensive defensemen for several reasons. He knows he's talented and expects the talent to do the work. He also acts like he's attached to the puck and tends to be a puck chaser.

Hatcher doesn't have a quick take-off; a smart checker will get to him quickly and force a turnover. He can finish in close offensively, but he isn't the smartest puck carrier in the world and is often better off making the short outlet pass or dumping the puck, instead of forcing a play at the blueline. He is smart about jumping into the play, though, and also clever enough to make the best play the situation dictates. He moves to the left point on the power play to open up his forehand for one-timers.

Hatcher has the puck so much during a game that there are times when he'll turn the puck over or carry it dangerously in front of his own net. He makes decisions quickly in all zones. If the heat is on him in his own zone, he's aware of his teammates' positions on the ice and makes the smart outlet pass or bangs the puck off the glass. He is constantly looking to see which attackers might be bearing in on him.

THE PHYSICAL GAME

Who wants a finesse defenseman this big? He's not very brave, and doesn't use his body as well as he should.

THE INTANGIBLES

Hatcher has yet to prove he can be a dominating defenseman and at this stage of the game he doesn't appear to have much more upside. He fits in well with the Penguins, however, because of all their skilled forwards. He just doesn't provide much physical protection for them.

PROJECTION

Hatcher is a 50-point scorer over a full season.

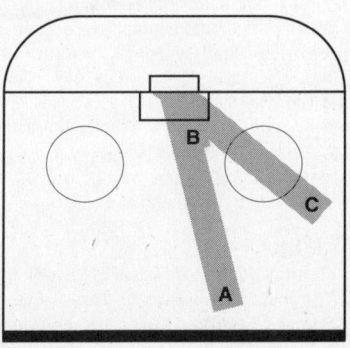

JAN HRDINA

Yrs. of NHL service: 1
Born: Hradec Kralove, Czech.; Feb. 5, 1976
Position: centre
Height: 6-0
Weight: 197
Uniform no.: 38
Shoots: right

Career statistics:

GP	G	A	TP	PIM
82	13	29	42	40

1998-99 statistics:

GP	G	A	TP	+/-	PIM	PP	SH	GW	GT	S	PCT
82	13	29	42	-2	40	3	0	2	0	94	13.8

LAST SEASON

First NHL season. Third among NHL rookies in assists. Fourth among NHL rookies in points. Tied for sixth among NHL rookies in goals. Fifth among NHL rookies in power-play points. Only Penguin to appear in all 82 games.

THE FINESSE GAME

Even taking into account the Jaromir Jagr factor — that anyone playing with the Hart Trophy winner has his status elevated — Hrdina is an impressive specimen.

He is a highly skilled centre whom the Pens have allowed to mature gradually through the minor league ranks. He does everything well. He is a very good skater with the ability to shift gears and directions effortlessly. He doesn't shoot enough — quite typical of European centres — but he has a terrific wrist shot.

Hrdina is a highly intelligent player in all zones. He is very aware defensively for a young player. Offensively, he is a gifted passer with a sure touch and good vision.

THE PHYSICAL GAME

Hrdina is slightly less than average height but he has a wide body. He fights for the puck and is tough to knock off his feet. He is excellent on draws. Not only does he have quick hands, he is able to tie up the opposing centre's stick, and he uses his feet. He cheats a bit on draws, but usually gets away with it.

THE INTANGIBLES

Although he wasn't a Calder Trophy finalist, Hrdina played at least as prominent a role — if not more so — than winner Chris Drury, and he did it on a less powerful team than the Avalanche.

PROJECTION

Hrdina should move forward off his rookie season into the 20-goal, 50-point range. He is quite likely a future 40-goal scorer if he learns to shoot more.

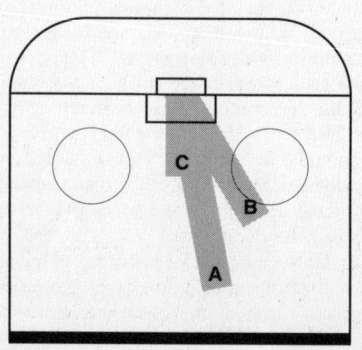

JAROMIR JAGR

Yrs. of NHL service: 9
Born: Kladno, Czech Republic; Feb. 15, 1972
Position: right wing
Height: 6-2
Weight: 216
Uniform no.: 68
Shoots: left

Career statistics:

GP	G	A	TP	PIM
662	345	517	862	501

1995-96 statistics:

GP	G	A	TP	+/-	PIM	PP	SH	GW	GT	S	PCT
82	62	87	149	+31	96	20	1	12	1	403	15.4

1996-97 statistics:

GP	G	A	TP	+/-	PIM	PP	SH	GW	GT	S	PCT
63	47	48	95	+22	40	11	2	6	1	234	20.1

1997-98 statistics:

GP	G	A	TP	+/-	PIM	PP	SH	GW	GT	S	PCT
77	35	67	102	+17	64	7	0	8	2	262	13.4

1998-99 statistics:

GP	G	A	TP	+/-	PIM	PP	SH	GW	GT	S	PCT
81	44	83	127	+17	66	10	1	7	2	343	12.8

LAST SEASON

Won 1999 Hart Trophy. Won third Art Ross Trophy as NHL's leading scorer. Led NHL in assists. Tied for second in NHL in goals. Second on team in plus-minus. Third on team in penalty minutes. Second in NHL in power-play points (44). Led team and second in NHL in shots. Missed one game with groin injury.

THE FINESSE GAME

Jagr's greatness was illustrated by how he elevated other players around him — he made a scoring star out of Kip Miller, for crying out loud — and took his own game to a new level. It's scary to think what Jagr's career numbers would look like if Mario Lemieux had delayed retirement a few more seasons before becoming Jagr's new boss.

Opponents know they have one assignment when they play the Penguins: stop Jagr. Few teams can do it. Jagr's exceptional skating and extraordinary ice time make him tough to shadow, even when checkers sag off his less-imposing linemates to key on him.

Jagr is as close to a perfect skater as there is in the NHL. He keeps his body centred over his skates, giving him a low centre of gravity and making it very tough for anyone to knock him off the puck. He has a deep knee bend, for quickness and power. His strokes are long and sure, and he has control over his body and exceptional lateral mobility. He dazzles with his footwork and handles the puck at high tempo.

Jagr lives and loves to play hockey. His long hair flowing out from beneath his helmet, he's poetry in motion with his beautifully effortless skating style. And, with his Lemieux-like reach, Jagr can dangle the puck while he's gliding and swooping. He fakes the backhand and goes to his forehand in a flash. He is also powerful enough to drag a defender with him to the net and push off a strong one-handed shot. He has a big slap shot and can drive it on the fly or fire it with a one-timer off a pass.

THE PHYSICAL GAME

Considering how often he gets pounded and how much ice time he logs, Jagr's durability over the past six seasons is remarkable. His recurring groin problem resurfaced in the playoffs, but he always seemed to come up with the moves when the team needed him most. Earlier in his career he could be intimidated physically — and he still doesn't like to get hit, but he's not as wimpy as he used to be. He's confident, almost cocky, and tough to catch — impossible to hit in open ice.

THE INTANGIBLES

Jagr continues to criticize his coach, Kevin Constantine (usually to the Czech press), but then turns around and plays his heart out. Forgive him his quirks. Maybe Boss Mario will find him a true number one centre this season, and Jagr can win his fourth scoring title.

PROJECTION

Whew . . . did we underestimate Jagr's ability. Anticipating that the loss of Ron Francis would hurt Jagr's production, we predicted a sharp drop-off. Wrong. Jagr bucked the trend and was one of only three NHL players to break the 100-point mark last season. He should do so again, easily, this season.

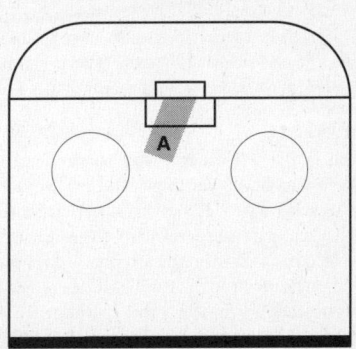

DARIUS KASPARAITIS

Yrs. of NHL service: 7
Born: Elektrenai, Lithuania; Oct. 16, 1972
Position: right defense
Height: 5-10
Weight: 205
Uniform no.: 11
Shoots: left

Career statistics:

GP	G	A	TP	PIM
418	13	68	81	720

1995-96 statistics:

GP	G	A	TP	+/-	PIM	PP	SH	GW	GT	S	PCT
46	1	7	8	-12	93	0	0	0	0	34	2.9

1996-97 statistics:

GP	G	A	TP	+/-	PIM	PP	SH	GW	GT	S	PCT
75	2	21	23	+17	100	0	0	0	0	58	3.4

1997-98 statistics:

GP	G	A	TP	+/-	PIM	PP	SH	GW	GT	S	PCT
81	4	8	12	+3	127	0	2	0	0	71	5.6

1998-99 statistics:

GP	G	A	TP	+/-	PIM	PP	SH	GW	GT	S	PCT
48	1	4	5	+12	70	0	0	0	0	32	3.1

LAST SEASON

Missed eight games with knee injury. Missed two games with groin injury. Missed 21 games with season-ending knee surgery.

THE FINESSE GAME

Kasparaitis is a strong, powerful skater and he can accelerate in all directions. You can run but you can't hide from this defenseman, who accepts all challenges. He is aggressive in the neutral zone, sometimes overly so, stepping up to break up a team's attack when he would be better off backing off.

Kasparaitis has the skills to occasionally get involved in the offense. He will make a sharp outlet pass and then follow up into the play. He also has good offensive instincts, moves the puck well and, if he plays on his off-side, will open up his forehand for the one-timer. He concentrates heavily on the defensive and physical part of his game, and would be blissfully happy going through the season without a point if he could wreak havoc elsewhere.

Kasparaitis has infectious enthusiasm, which is an inspiration to the rest of his team. There is a purpose to whatever he does. He's highly competitive.

THE PHYSICAL GAME

Kasparaitis is well on his way to succeeding Ulf Samuelsson as the player most NHLers would like to see run over by a bus. It's always borderline interference with Kasparaitis, who uses his stick liberally, waiting three or four seconds after a victim has gotten rid of the puck to apply the lumber. Cross-check, butt-end, high stick — through the course of a season Kasparaitis will illustrate all of the stick infractions.

His timing isn't always the best, and he has to think about the good of the team rather than indulging in his own vendettas.

Kasparaitis is legitimately tough. It doesn't matter whose name is on back of the jersey — Tkachuk, Tocchet, McKay, Messier — he will goad the stars and the heavyweights equally. He yaps, too, and is as irritating as a car alarm at 3 a.m.

THE INTANGIBLES

Kasparaitis's grit is badly needed in Pittsburgh, which can tend to be a rather fancy team. He underwent reconstructive surgery in March on a reinjured right knee (which he had played on since the start of the season), and is expected to be ready for October.

PROJECTION

Chalk up another 100 PIM and maybe 20 points, as Kasparaitis will remain one of the Penguins' top three defensemen and get a ton of ice time if he rehabs well.

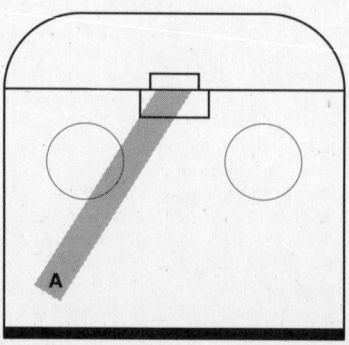

ALEXEI KOVALEV

Yrs. of NHL service: 7
Born: Togliatti, Russia; Feb. 24, 1973
Position: right wing/centre
Height: 6-0
Weight: 205
Uniform no.: 27
Shoots: left

Career statistics:

GP	G	A	TP	PIM
465	139	180	321	496

1995-96 statistics:

GP	G	A	TP	+/-	PIM	PP	SH	GW	GT	S	PCT
81	24	34	58	+5	98	8	1	7	0	206	11.7

1996-97 statistics:

GP	G	A	TP	+/-	PIM	PP	SH	GW	GT	S	PCT
45	13	22	35	+11	42	1	0	0	0	110	11.8

1997-98 statistics:

GP	G	A	TP	+/-	PIM	PP	SH	GW	GT	S	PCT
73	23	30	53	-22	44	8	0	3	1	173	13.3

1998-99 statistics:

GP	G	A	TP	+/-	PIM	PP	SH	GW	GT	S	PCT
77	23	30	53	+2	49	6	1	5	0	191	12.0

LAST SEASON
Acquired from N.Y. Rangers with Harry York for Petr Nedved, Chris Tamer and Sean Pronger, Nov. 25, 1998. Second on team in game-winning goals and shots. Third on team in goals. Fourth on team in points. Missed one game with shoulder injury.

THE FINESSE GAME
Kovalev is skilled enough to make breathtaking plays of exquisite grace, and he is stubborn enough to overhandle the puck and manoeuvre himself completely out of the play without the slightest help from an opponent.

You don't often see hands or feet as quick as Kovalev's on a player of his size. He has the dexterity, puck control, strength, balance and speed to beat the first forechecker coming out of the zone or the first line of defense once he crosses the attacking blueline. He is one of the few players in the NHL agile and balanced enough to duck under a check at the sideboards and maintain possession of the puck. Exceptional hands allow him to make remarkable moves, but his hockey thought process doesn't always finish them off well.

On many occasions, Kovalev's slithery moves don't do enough offensive damage. Sometimes he overhandles, then turns the puck over. Too many times, he fails to get the puck deep. He hates to surrender the puck even when dump-and-chase is the smartest option, and as a result he causes turnovers at the blueline and has to chase any number of opposition breakaways to his team's net.

THE PHYSICAL GAME
The chippier the game, the happier Kovalev is; he'll bring his stick up and wade into the fray. He can be sneaky dirty. He'll run goalies over and try to make it look as if he was pushed into them by a defender. He's so strong and balanced on his skates that when he goes down odds are it's a dive. At the same time, he absorbs all kinds of physical punishment, legal and illegal, and rarely receives the benefit of the doubt from the referees.

Kovalev has very good size and is a willing hitter. He likes to make highlight-reel hits that splatter people. Because he is such a strong skater, he is very hard to knock down unless he's leaning. He makes extensive use of his edges because he combines balance and a long reach to keep the puck well away from his body, and from a defender's. But there are moments when he seems at a 45-degree angle and then he can be nudged over.

THE INTANGIBLES
Kovalev desperately needed to get out of New York, and the move to Pittsburgh's offensive style was just what he required. Despite being happier with the Penguins, however, he still displayed the same inconsistencies (inlcuding an 18-game goalless streak). He is at his best in the playoffs.

PROJECTION
If Kovalev ever plays a consistent game, he is capable of 30 goals and 80 points.

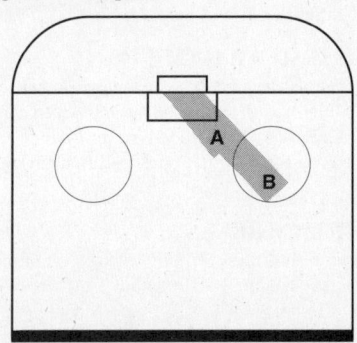

ROBERT LANG

Yrs. of NHL service: 5
Born: Teplice, Czech Republic; Dec. 19, 1970
Position: centre
Height: 6-2
Weight: 216
Uniform no.: 20
Shoots: right

Career statistics:

GP	G	A	TP	PIM
273	49	75	124	66

1995-96 statistics:

GP	G	A	TP	+/-	PIM	PP	SH	GW	GT	S	PCT
68	6	16	22	-15	10	0	2	0	0	71	8.5

1996-97 statistics:
Did not play in NHL

1997-98 statistics:
Did not play in NHL

1998-99 statistics:

GP	G	A	TP	+/-	PIM	PP	SH	GW	GT	S	PCT
72	21	23	44	-10	24	7	0	3	3	137	15.3

PROJECTION
Lang is behind Hrdina and German Titov on the depth chart at centre. He could still get 20 goals, depending on how he is used.

LAST SEASON
Career highs in games played, goals, assists and points. Second on team in shooting percentage. Third on team in power-play goals. Missed 10 games with ankle injury.

THE FINESSE GAME
Lang has so much talent that he is able to turn a game around with several moves, yet he is so inconsistent that there are nights when he is invisible.

He has deceptive quickness and is very solid on his skates. He has great hands, great hockey sense and the ability to make plays on his forehand or backhand. Players on both wings have to be prepared for a pass that could materialize out of thin air or through a thicket of sticks and skates. He has the presence to draw defenders to him to open up ice for his linemates, and he makes good use of them.

Lang is patient with the puck, in fact, he often holds on too long. He will always pass up a shot if he can make a play instead.

Lang is also very aware defensively and is a smart penalty killer because of his anticipation.

THE PHYSICAL GAME
Lang will not take a hit to make a play. He has to show more willingness to hit and be hit in order to earn time on the number one line. He will never trounce anyone, but he has to fight for the puck and fight through his checks.

THE INTANGIBLES
Lang had a shot to become Pittsburgh's number one centre last season, but lost the job to rookie Jan Hrdina.

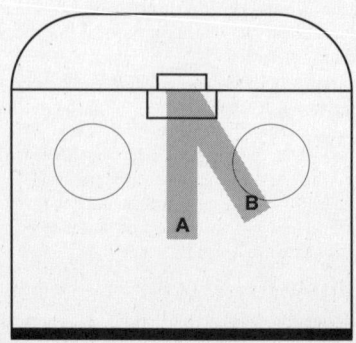

ALEXEI MOROZOV

Yrs. of NHL service: 2
Born: Moscow, Russia; Feb. 16, 1977
Position: right wing
Height: 6-1
Weight: 180
Uniform no.: 95
Shoots: left

Career statistics:
GP	G	A	TP	PIM
143	22	23	45	22

1997-98 statistics:
GP	G	A	TP	+/-	PIM	PP	SH	GW	GT	S	PCT
76	13	13	26	-4	8	2	0	3	0	80	16.3

1998-99 statistics:
GP	G	A	TP	+/-	PIM	PP	SH	GW	GT	S	PCT
67	9	10	19	+5	14	0	0	0	0	75	12.0

LAST SEASON
Second NHL season. Missed 15 games with concussions.

THE FINESSE GAME
Morozov still has some catching up to do in the coordination department. He can be as awkward as a baby giraffe: all legs, and with a lot of skills that look as if they belong with someone else's body. When the pieces do come together, he looks like he will be a swift skater, able to play the uptempo game that is a Penguins hallmark.

Morozov has a very sneaky, deceptive selection of shots and looks like he will be a big-goal scorer — in terms of importance, if not numbers. He tries to be too cute and make the extra play instead of shooting, but once he learns to use his hard and accurate shot to his advantage, he will be extremely effective. He is a good stickhandler and has a good sense of timing with his passes.

Morozov is still learning the game (he is only 22) and will merit more time on the power play once he learns his shot is a bullet that shouldn't be left in the holster.

THE PHYSICAL GAME
Morozov is a little on the stringy side, but he's still growing and will probably fill out into a more solid winger. He'll never be confused with a power forward, though.

THE INTANGIBLES
Morozov suffered a second concussion that affected almost all of the first half of his season and set his development back.

PROJECTION
Morozov can become a solid 20-goal scorer this season, and within the next two or three years could add five to 10 goals to that total.

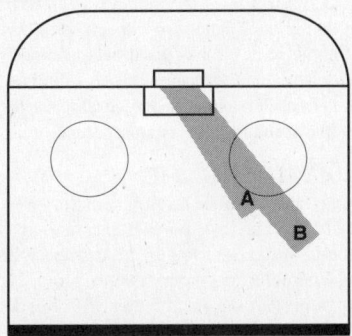

MARTIN STRAKA

Yrs. of NHL service: 7
Born: Plzen, Czech Republic; Sept. 3, 1972
Position: centre
Height: 5-10
Weight: 178
Uniform no.: 82
Shoots: left

Career statistics:

GP	G	A	TP	PIM
450	112	183	295	176

1995-96 statistics:

GP	G	A	TP	+/-	PIM	PP	SH	GW	GT	S	PCT
77	13	30	43	-19	41	6	0	1	0	98	13.3

1996-97 statistics:

GP	G	A	TP	+/-	PIM	PP	SH	GW	GT	S	PCT
55	7	22	29	+9	12	2	0	1	0	94	7.4

1997-98 statistics:

GP	G	A	TP	+/-	PIM	PP	SH	GW	GT	S	PCT
75	19	23	42	-1	28	4	3	4	1	117	16.2

1998-99 statistics:

GP	G	A	TP	+/-	PIM	PP	SH	GW	GT	S	PCT
80	35	48	83	+12	26	5	4	4	1	177	19.8

LAST SEASON

Led team in shorthanded goals and shooting percentage. Tied for fourth in the NHL in shorthanded goals. Second in NHL in shooting percentage. Second on team in goals, assists and points. Third on team in shots. Career high in goals, assists and points. Missed two games with shoulder injuries.

THE FINESSE GAME

Until last season, Straka's game had been a major tease: he would show flashes of brilliance, then go 15 games without being noticed. He has finally achieved a level of consistency that matches his skills.

Straka can do a lot of things. He is a water bug with imagination. He makes clever passes that always land on the tape and give the recipient time to do something with the puck. He's more of a playmaker than a shooter. He will have to learn to go to the net more to make his game less predictable. He draws people to him and creates open ice for his linemates.

Straka doesn't have the outside speed to burn defenders, but creates space for himself with his wheeling in tight spaces. He has good balance and is tough to knock off his feet, even though he's not big.

Not a great defensive player, Straka is effective in five-on-five situations. He is a perpetual threat.

THE PHYSICAL GAME

Straka has shown little inclination for the typical North American style of play. He is small and avoids corners and walls, and has to be teamed with more physical linemates to give him some room. He needs to learn to protect the puck better with his body and buy some time.

THE INTANGIBLES

Straka may have finally found a home on a Pittsburgh team that employs a very European style of attack.

PROJECTION

Straka erased the negatives with a strong regular season and better playoffs. He has arrived as an NHLer, and should be a consistent 35- to 40-goal scorer.

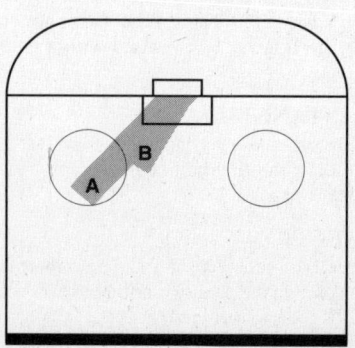

GERMAN TITOV

Yrs. of NHL service: 6
Born: Moscow, Russia; Oct. 16, 1965
Position: centre/left wing
Height: 6-1
Weight: 190
Uniform no.: 13
Shoots: left

Career statistics:

GP	G	A	TP	PIM
417	118	166	284	176

1995-96 statistics:

GP	G	A	TP	+/-	PIM	PP	SH	GW	GT	S	PCT
82	28	39	67	+9	24	13	2	2	2	214	13.1

1996-97 statistics:

GP	G	A	TP	+/-	PIM	PP	SH	GW	GT	S	PCT
79	22	30	52	-12	36	12	0	4	0	192	11.5

1997-98 statistics:

GP	G	A	TP	+/-	PIM	PP	SH	GW	GT	S	PCT
68	18	22	40	-1	38	6	1	2	0	133	13.5

1998-99 statistics:

GP	G	A	TP	+/-	PIM	PP	SH	GW	GT	S	PCT
72	11	45	56	+18	34	3	1	3	1	113	9.7

LAST SEASON

Led team in plus-minus. Third on team in assists with career high. Third on team in points. Missed six games with hamstring injuries. Missed two games with knee injuries. Missed one game with finger injury.

THE FINESSE GAME

Titov constantly drives his coaches and teammates crazy. He works so hard to get himself in a great scoring position and then . . . he doesn't shoot. For the ice time he had last season, Titov's shots should have been 40 tries higher. He uses a short stick and does a lot of one-handed puckhandling. This gives him good control and makes it harder for the defense to knock the puck loose without knocking him down and taking a penalty. It also gives him a quick release on his underutilized wrister.

Titov shows great hockey sense in all zones. He is very creative, but is a streaky scorer. He lacks consistency and doesn't step up on a nightly basis. He can play on the first power-play unit, and is a solid two-way forward.

Titov is an agile skater, if not outstandingly fast. He is very quick coming off the boards and driving to the circle for a shot, and he has a good inside-out move and change of gears. Strong on his skates, he is tough to knock down. He has good hands on the draw. He kills penalties well and blocks shots.

THE PHYSICAL GAME

Titov uses his size well and is very solid. He takes a hit to make a play, blocks shots and sacrifices his body. He protects the puck in an unusual way, by getting his left leg out to kick away the stick of a defender so that he can't be sweep- or poke-checked. It's a move that requires superb balance.

THE INTANGIBLES

Titov excells at the European style of attack the Penguins employ. He was a fish out of water on dump-and-chase teams before his arrival in Pittsburgh.

PROJECTION

Titov should be more productive — in the 20-goal, 65-point range.

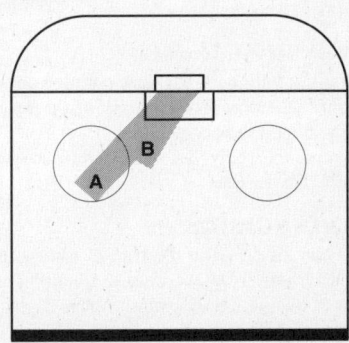

BRAD WERENKA

Yrs. of NHL service: 6
Born: Two Hills, Alberta; Feb. 12, 1969
Position: left defense
Height: 6-1
Weight: 221
Uniform no.: 5
Shoots: left

Career statistics:

GP	G	A	TP	PIM
214	14	47	61	193

1995-96 statistics:

GP	G	A	TP	+/-	PIM	PP	SH	GW	GT	S	PCT
9	0	0	0	-2	8	0	0	0	0	2	0.0

1996-97 statistics:
Did not play in NHL

1997-98 statistics:

GP	G	A	TP	+/-	PIM	PP	SH	GW	GT	S	PCT
71	3	15	18	+15	46	2	0	0	0	50	6.0

1998-99 statistics:

GP	G	A	TP	+/-	PIM	PP	SH	GW	GT	S	PCT
81	6	18	24	+17	93	1	0	4	0	77	7.8

PROJECTION
Werenka is likely to stay in the 20-point range.

LAST SEASON
Career highs in games played, goals, assists and points. Tied for second on team and led team defensemen in plus-minus. Second on team in penalty minutes. Missed one game due to suspension.

THE FINESSE GAME
Werenka makes a stable partner for any player with more offensive inclinations, and often battles against other teams' top lines.

He has a little offensive ability, as he has shown with his numbers in college and the minors. He saw some time as a member of the second power-play unit, but scoring is not his forte. Werenka uses his finesse skills to make the good first pass out of the zone.

Werenka was a good scorer in college (Northern Michigan) and more involved in the attack last season, scoring some big goals, but he is more comfortable with a stay-at-home style.

Werenka kills penalties and blocks shots. He plays a lot like a young Brad Marsh, though he is a better skater.

THE PHYSICAL GAME
Werenka is solidly built but does not play an aggressive game, which is probably one of the reasons it took him so long to become an NHL regular. He displayed more of an edge last season and was rewarded with more playing time.

THE INTANGIBLES
Few players kick around the fringes and the minors for as many seasons as Werenka did before getting a full-time NHL job. He is aware of what a gift this is and is not likely to squander it.

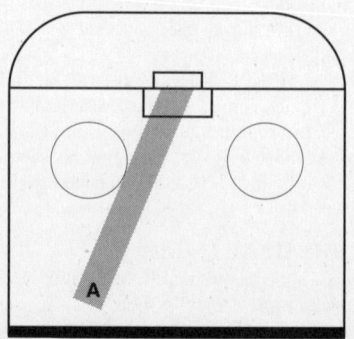

SAN JOSE SHARKS

Players' Statistics 1998-99

POS.	NO.	PLAYER	GP	G	A	PTS	+/-	PIM	PP	SH	GW	GT	S	PCT
L	39	JEFF FRIESEN	78	22	35	57	3	42	10	1	3	1	215	10.2
C	25	VINCENT DAMPHOUSSE	77	19	30	49	-4	50	6	2	3		190	10.0
R	17	JOE MURPHY	76	25	23	48	10	73	7		2	1	176	14.2
C	14	PATRICK MARLEAU	81	21	24	45	10	24	4		4	1	134	15.7
R	11	OWEN NOLAN	78	19	26	45	16	129	6	2	3	1	207	9.2
C	18	MIKE RICCI	82	13	26	39	1	68	2	1	2	1	98	13.3
C	19	MARCO STURM	78	16	22	38	7	52	3	2	3	2	140	11.4
D	2	BILL HOULDER	76	9	23	32	8	40	7		5		115	7.8
R	15	*ALEXANDER KOROLYUK	55	12	18	30	3	26	2			1	96	12.5
R	37	STEPHANE MATTEAU	68	8	15	23	2	73					72	11.1
D	5	JEFF NORTON	72	4	18	22	2	44	2		1		70	5.7
R	22	RONNIE STERN	78	7	9	16	-3	158	1		2		94	7.4
L	26	DAVE LOWRY	61	6	9	15	-5	24	2			1	58	10.3
D	40	MIKE RATHJE	82	5	9	14	15	36	2		1		67	7.5
L	32	MURRAY CRAVEN	43	4	10	14	-3	18		1	1		55	7.3
D	10	MARCUS RAGNARSSON	74		13	13	7	66					87	
L	21	TONY GRANATO	35	6	6	12	4	54	1	1	1	1	65	9.2
D	3	BOB ROUSE	70		11	11	0	44					75	
C	12	RON SUTTER	59	3	6	9	-8	40			1		67	4.5
D	27	BRYAN MARCHMENT	59	2	6	8	-7	101					49	4.1
D	4	ANDREI ZYUZIN	25	3	1	4	5	38	2				44	6.8
L	36	STEPHEN GUOLLA	14	2	2	4	3	6			1		22	9.1
D	42	*ANDY SUTTON	31		3	3	-4	65					24	
C	8	JARROD SKALDE	17	1	1	2	-6	4				1	17	5.9
D	6	*SCOTT HANNAN	5		2	2	0	6					4	
C	9	BERNIE NICHOLLS	10		2	2	-4	4					11	
R	33	BRANTT MYHRES	30	1		1	-2	116					7	14.3
C	13	JAMIE BAKER	1		1	1	1						1	
L	7	SHAWN BURR	18		1	1	-3	29					22	
G	31	STEVE SHIELDS	37		1	1	0	6						
R	25	MIKE CRAIG	1				-1						1	
D	20	GARY SUTER	1				0						1	
G	30	SEAN GAUTHIER	1				0							
D	23	*SHAWN HEINS	5				0	13					4	
G	29	MIKE VERNON	49				0	8						

GP = games played; G = goals; A = assists; PTS = points; +/- = goals-for minus goals-against while player is on ice; PIM = penalties in minutes; PP = power-play goals; SH = shorthanded goals; GW = game-winning goals; GT = game-tying goals; S = no. of shots; PCT = percentage of goals to shots; * = rookie

VINCENT DAMPHOUSSE

Yrs. of NHL service: 13
Born: Montreal, Que.; Dec. 17, 1967
Position: left wing
Height: 6-1
Weight: 200
Uniform no.: 25
Shoots: left

Career statistics:

GP	G	A	TP	PIM
1005	347	582	929	878

1995-96 statistics:

GP	G	A	TP	+/-	PIM	PP	SH	GW	GT	S	PCT
80	38	56	94	+5	158	11	4	3	0	254	15.0

1996-97 statistics:

GP	G	A	TP	+/-	PIM	PP	SH	GW	GT	S	PCT
82	27	54	81	-6	82	7	2	3	2	244	11.1

1997-98 statistics:

GP	G	A	TP	+/-	PIM	PP	SH	GW	GT	S	PCT
76	18	41	59	+14	58	2	1	5	0	164	11.0

1998-99 statistics:

GP	G	A	TP	+/-	PIM	PP	SH	GW	GT	S	PCT
77	19	30	49	-4	50	6	2	3	0	190	10.0

LAST SEASON

Acquired from Montreal for a 2000 second-round draft pick and a 1999 fifth-round draft pick Mar. 23, 1999. Tied for team lead in shorthanded goals. Second on team in assists and points. Third on team in shots. Tied for third on team in game-winning goals. Played in 1,000th NHL game.

THE FINESSE GAME

Cool in tight, Damphousse has a marvellous backhand shot he can roof; he creates opportunites low by shaking and faking checkers with his skating. He likes to set up from behind the net to make plays. Goalies need to be on the alert when Damphousse is on the attack, because he is unafraid to take shots from absurd angles just to get a shot on net and get the goalie and defense scrambling. It's an effective tactic.

Damphousse shows poise with the puck. Although he is primarily a finisher, he will also dish off to a teammate if that is a better option. He's a superb player in four-on-four situations. He has sharp offensive instincts and is good in traffic.

Damphousse won't leave any vapour trails with his skating in open ice, but he is quick around the net, especially with the puck. His foot speed isn't as much of a detriment in San Jose because the Sharks have some skaters who can drive the defense back and give Damphousse more time and space for his shot. He has exceptional balance to hop through sticks and checks. In open ice he uses his weight to shift and change direction, making it appear as if he's going faster than he is — and he can juke without losing the puck while looking for his passing and shooting options.

THE PHYSICAL GAME

Damphousse uses his body to protect the puck, but he is not much of a grinder and loses most of his one-on-one battles. He has to be supported with physical linemates who will get him the puck. He'll expend a great deal of energy in the attacking zone, but little in his own end of the ice, though he is more diligent about this in crunch times.

Damphousse is a well-conditioned athlete who can handle long shifts and lots of ice time. He is not shy about using his stick. He has a pretty high pain threshhold, staying in the lineup despite a concussion. He has missed only 19 games in 12 NHL seasons.

THE INTANGIBLES

Instead of becoming a rent-a-player, Damphousse re-signed with the Sharks after making a good impression in the playoffs.

PROJECTION

Damphousse needs help to get into the 80-point scoring range, which is what his skill level dictates. He scored 13 points in 12 games with the Sharks at the end of the season, an indication he'll adjust nicely to life in the West.

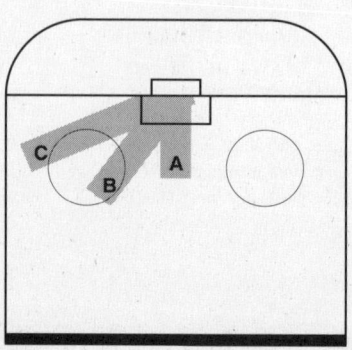

JEFF FRIESEN

Yrs. of NHL service: 5
Born: Meadow Lake, Sask.; Aug. 5, 1976
Position: left wing/centre
Height: 6-0
Weight: 185
Uniform no.: 39
Shoots: left

Career statistics:

GP	G	A	TP	PIM
366	111	142	253	213

1995-96 statistics:

GP	G	A	TP	+/-	PIM	PP	SH	GW	GT	S	PCT
79	15	31	46	-19	42	2	0	0	0	123	12.2

1996-97 statistics:

GP	G	A	TP	+/-	PIM	PP	SH	GW	GT	S	PCT
82	28	34	62	-8	75	6	2	5	2	200	14.0

1997-98 statistics:

GP	G	A	TP	+/-	PIM	PP	SH	GW	GT	S	PCT
79	31	32	63	+8	40	7	6	7	0	186	16.7

1998-99 statistics:

GP	G	A	TP	+/-	PIM	PP	SH	GW	GT	S	PCT
78	22	35	57	+3	42	10	1	3	1	215	10.2

LAST SEASON

Led team in assists for third consecutive season. Career high in assists. Led team in points, power-play goals and shots. Second on team in goals. Tied for third on team in game-winning goals. Missed two games due to contract dispute. Missed two games with shoulder injury. First games missed due to injury in five-year NHL career.

THE FINESSE GAME

Friesen is a fast, strong skater, handles the puck well and has the size to go with those qualities. He is a better finisher than playmaker — he worked well with Vincent Damphousse after the latter's arrival. Damphousse has a lot of patience and can hold onto the puck for a long time, and Friesen can get into holes with his speed for the pass. Friesen has a quick, strong release on his snap or wrist shot and is shifty with a smooth change of speed. Carrying the puck doesn't slow him down.

Friesen never seems to get rattled or forced into making bad plays. In fact, he's the one who forces opponents into panic moves with his pressure. He draws penalties by keeping his feet moving as he drives to the net or digs for the puck along the boards. He is strong on face-offs.

A pure goal scorer in junior, Friesen developed first as a checking-line winger in his rookie year before becoming a complete player. He deserves a lot of credit for making himself into an all-around player.

THE PHYSICAL GAME

Friesen has dedicated himself to his strength and conditioning. He doesn't have much of a mean streak, but he plays tough and honest.

THE INTANGIBLES

Friesen is a potential future captain of the Sharks. Tabbed with a lazy label in his junior days, he has matured into a hard-working player who cares. Just turned 23, he is the leader of the next generation of Sharks.

PROJECTION

Playing with Damphousse over a full year should boost Friesen into the 35-goal range.

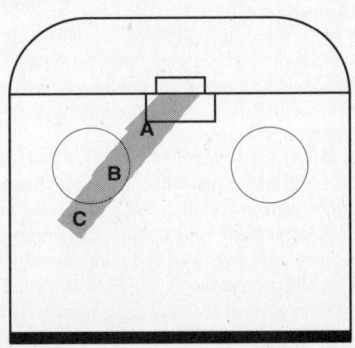

BILL HOULDER

Yrs. of NHL service: 12
Born: Thunder Bay, Ont.; Mar. 11, 1967
Position: left defense
Height: 6-3
Weight: 211
Uniform no.: 2
Shoots: left

Career statistics:

GP	G	A	TP	PIM
530	50	153	203	258

1995-96 statistics:

GP	G	A	TP	+/-	PIM	PP	SH	GW	GT	S	PCT
61	5	23	28	+1	22	3	0	0	1	90	5.6

1996-97 statistics:

GP	G	A	TP	+/-	PIM	PP	SH	GW	GT	S	PCT
79	4	21	25	+16	30	0	0	2	0	116	3.4

1997-98 statistics:

GP	G	A	TP	+/-	PIM	PP	SH	GW	GT	S	PCT
82	7	25	32	+13	48	4	0	2	0	102	6.9

1998-99 statistics:

GP	G	A	TP	+/-	PIM	PP	SH	GW	GT	S	PCT
76	9	23	32	+8	40	7	0	5	0	115	7.8

LAST SEASON

Led team defensemen in scoring for second consecutive season. Led team in game-winning goals. Tied for second on team in power-play goals. Missed five games with knee injury. Missed one game due to coach's decision.

THE FINESSE GAME

Houlder has a big shot, but otherwise his overall skills are average. Although he struggles as a skater, especially with his turns, he has a decent first step to the puck and is strong on his skates.

Houlder is a cerebral player. He makes smart options with his passes and does not like to carry the puck. He prefers to dish off to a teammate or chip the puck out along the wall, rather than try to carry it past a checker.

Houlder inherited some power-play ice time due to the injury to Gary Suter, and responded well. He is not a risktaker. His attack is mostly limited to point shots, though he will get brave once in awhile and gamble to the top of the circle. Most of his goals come from 60 feet out with some traffic in front. He can play on the second unit on the power play and penalty killing, but is best in five-on-five situations.

THE PHYSICAL GAME

Houlder is a gentle giant. There is always the expectation with bigger players that they will make monster hits, but we have the feeling that a lot of them were big as youngsters and were told by their parents not to go around picking on smaller kids. Houlder is definitely among the big guys who don't hit to hurt. If he did get involved he would be a dominating defenseman, but that's not about to happen at this stage of his career.

He will take out his man with quiet efficiency. He has to angle the attacker to the boards because of his lack of agility. He is vulnerable to outside speed when he doesn't close off the lane.

THE INTANGIBLES

Houlder rates as a valuable fifth defenseman.

PROJECTION

Houlder will provide solid defense and 25 to 30 points.

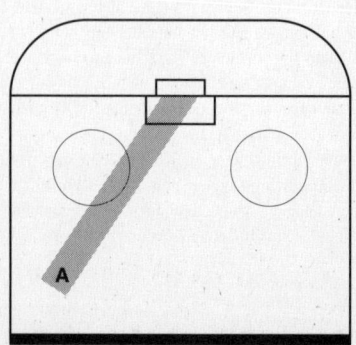

ALEXANDER KOROLYUK

Yrs. of NHL service: 1
Born: Moscow, Russia; Jan. 15, 1976
Position: right wing
Height: 5-9
Weight: 190
Uniform no.: 15
Shoots: left

Career statistics:

GP	G	A	TP	PIM
74	14	21	35	32

1997-98 statistics:

GP	G	A	TP	+/-	PIM	PP	SH	GW	GT	S	PCT
19	2	3	5	-5	6	1	0	0	0	23	8.7

1998-99 statistics:

GP	G	A	TP	+/-	PIM	PP	SH	GW	GT	S	PCT
55	12	18	30	+3	26	2	0	0	1	96	12.5

LAST SEASON

First NHL season. Tied for eighth among NHL rookies in points. Tied for sixth among NHL rookies in assists. Ninth among NHL rookies in goals. Fifth among NHL rookies in shooting percentage. Appeared in 23 games with Kentucky (AHL), scoring 9-13 — 22. Missed one game due to coach's decision.

THE FINESSE GAME

Korolyuk is a gifted player who progressed much more quickly than the Sharks anticipated. His game is puck possession. Although he is small he's not that easy to get a piece of: he's quick and elusive. He draws a lot of penalties, and, in fact, he's a bit of a diver, but he's good enough to draw the call on most occasions.

Korolyuk makes anyone he plays with better because of his creativity. He is short and stocky and a good playmaker. He needs to shoot more because he has a very good, hard shot.

He adapted quickly to the NHL. Strong along the boards, he's an excellent soccer player, capable of keeping the puck alive with his feet.

THE PHYSICAL GAME

The Sharks would like to think that Korolyuk will develop along Doug Gilmour lines. He certainly has an edge to his game, like Gilmour, but it remains to be seen if he will have that "Killer" instinct that has always fuelled Gilmour to play well above his size. Korolyuk has a wide body and is feisty.

THE INTANGIBLES

Korolyuk has the skills and unique style that should allow him to keep a job among the Sharks' top six forwards, as long as he keeps competing as hard as he did last year.

PROJECTION

Korolyuk should graduate into the 45-point range.

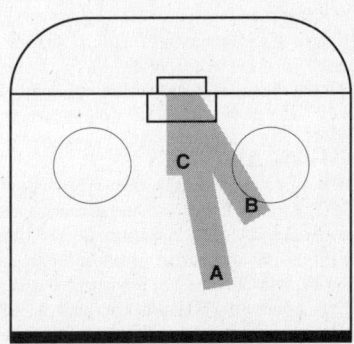

BRYAN MARCHMENT

Yrs. of NHL service: 9
Born: Toronto, Ont.; May 1, 1969
Position: left defense
Height: 6-1
Weight: 205
Uniform no.: 27
Shoots: left

Career statistics:

GP	G	A	TP	PIM
537	27	90	117	1531

1995-96 statistics:

GP	G	A	TP	+/-	PIM	PP	SH	GW	GT	S	PCT
78	3	15	18	-7	202	0	0	0	0	96	3.1

1996-97 statistics:

GP	G	A	TP	+/-	PIM	PP	SH	GW	GT	S	PCT
71	3	13	16	+13	132	1	0	0	0	89	3.4

1997-98 statistics:

GP	G	A	TP	+/-	PIM	PP	SH	GW	GT	S	PCT
61	2	11	13	-3	144	0	0	0	0	56	3.6

1998-99 statistics:

GP	G	A	TP	+/-	PIM	PP	SH	GW	GT	S	PCT
59	2	6	8	-7	101	0	0	0	0	49	4.1

LAST SEASON

Missed 20 games with separated shoulder. Missed one game due to suspension. Missed two games due to coach's decision.

THE FINESSE GAME

Because of Marchment's reputation as a crippling hitter, his skills are often overlooked, but they are impressive for a big man. He loves to play and he loves to get involved from the very first shift. He's never happier than when there's some blood on his jersey, even if it's his own.

During the past few seasons, Marchment has started making better decisions — with and without the puck. He is more aware of when it's appropriate to pinch and when to back off, but he is still overeager. He lacks the skating ability to cover up for some of his mental errors, though he is competent enough to join in on rushes. He has an underrated shot and can drill a one-timer or snap a quick shot on net. He is not much of a passer, since he doesn't sense when to feather or fire a puck to a receiver.

Marchment's mistakes are usually errors of aggression. Where he won't make mistakes is in his down-low coverage. The opposition's transition game is always a little slower when he's on the ice.

THE PHYSICAL GAME

Marchment is a dangerous, low hitter, with controversial hits that damage knees and end careers. One scout describes Marchment as "the ultimate leg breaker." He also hits high, so instead of ending careers with knee injuries, Marchment can end them with concussions. It's a wonder the NHLPA condones this kind of style when the ice has been littered with so many dues-paying Marchment victims.

Marchment can hit clean and tough when he wants to, though, by keeping his shoulder down and his feet on the ice. But even those checks, while honest, are controversial, because Marchment doesn't care who is on the receiving end — a marquee name, a classy veteran or a young stud. He is a throwback to the days of the destructive open-ice hitters. This requires great strength along with good lateral mobility (or else the checker can be left spinning around at centre ice, watching the back of the puck carrier tearing up the ice on a breakaway).

In keeping with the old-fashioned theme, Marchment is a good fighter. He also finishes every check, blocks shots and uses his upper body well. In one-on-one battles, however, he lacks drive from his legs, and he is not a balanced skater.

THE INTANGIBLES

Marchment's dedication to the game during the past few seasons has paid off in better conditioning and more intelligent play. He is as frightening an opponent as there is in the NHL.

PROJECTION

Marchment is a likely PIM leader and just as likely to miss a few games with a suspension somewhere along the way.

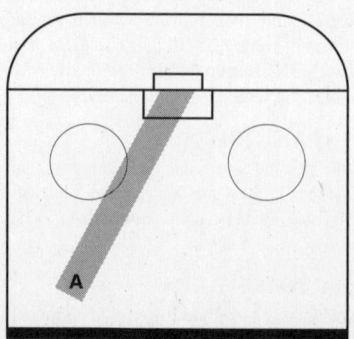

PATRICK MARLEAU

Yrs. of NHL service: 2
Born: Swift Current, Sask.; Sept. 15, 1979
Position: centre
Height: 6-2
Weight: 200
Uniform no.: 14
Shoots: left

Career statistics:
GP	G	A	TP	PIM
155	34	43	77	38

1997-98 statistics:
GP	G	A	TP	+/-	PIM	PP	SH	GW	GT	S	PCT
74	13	19	32	+5	14	1	0	2	0	90	14.4

1998-99 statistics:
GP	G	A	TP	+/-	PIM	PP	SH	GW	GT	S	PCT
81	21	24	45	+10	24	4	0	4	1	134	15.7

LAST SEASON

Second NHL season. Led team in shooting percentage. Second on team in game-winning goals. Tied for third on team in plus-minus. Third on team in goals. Missed one game with injury.

THE FINESSE GAME

Because of Marleau's quickness and intelligence, some scouts have described him as a bigger version of Paul Kariya. Marleau has great first- and second-step acceleration, with an extra gear.

Marleau plays an advanced offensive game; his defensive game is developing. He should become a high-level two-way centre. He pounces on a loose puck and is a scoring threat every time he has it. His offensive reads are outstanding. He anticipates plays and has excellent hands. He is a terrific finisher, as well as a fine playmaker. He has to be encouraged to shoot more. He has a quick release with an accurate touch, and will become a valuable power-play weapon.

The only question mark concerning Marleau is his consistency. He had the occasional lulls in the season, but it remains to be seen whether this was simply the natural learning process for a young player, or a defect in his makeup. It is worth remembering that Marleau barely made the cutoff for the 1997 draft. One more day and he would have been in the 1998 draft.

THE PHYSICAL GAME

Marleau is an imposing athlete, very physically mature for his age. He skates through his checks and when he hits you, you know it. He has a thick build. He does not go looking to run people, but he will battle to get into traffic for the puck. He will take a check to make a play. He has grown gradually in the past few years; lucky to avoid a sudden growth spurt, he has stayed coordinated.

THE INTANGIBLES

Vincent Damphousse's arrival lessened some of the workload on Marleau, and having Damphousse around all season as the number one will alleviate some of the checking pressure on Marleau as well.

PROJECTION

Marleau moved into the 20-goal range last season, as *HSR* predicted, and should continue to progress and raise the bar a little.

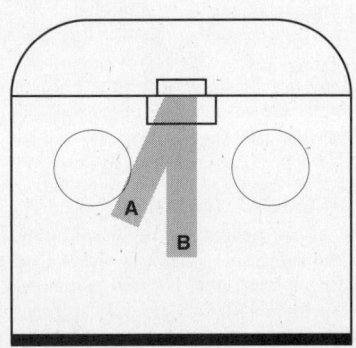

JOE MURPHY

Yrs. of NHL service: 12
Born: London, Ont.; Oct. 16, 1967
Position: right wing
Height: 6-1
Weight: 190
Uniform no.: 17
Shoots: left

Career statistics:

GP	G	A	TP	PIM
710	220	239	459	696

1995-96 statistics:

GP	G	A	TP	+/-	PIM	PP	SH	GW	GT	S	PCT
70	22	29	51	-3	86	8	0	3	0	212	10.4

1996-97 statistics:

GP	G	A	TP	+/-	PIM	PP	SH	GW	GT	S	PCT
75	20	25	45	-1	69	4	1	2	1	151	13.2

1997-98 statistics:

GP	G	A	TP	+/-	PIM	PP	SH	GW	GT	S	PCT
37	9	13	22	+9	36	4	0	0	0	81	11.1

1998-99 statistics:

GP	G	A	TP	+/-	PIM	PP	SH	GW	GT	S	PCT
76	25	23	48	+10	73	7	0	2	1	176	14.2

LAST SEASON

Led team in goals with highest total since 1993-94. Seventh season with 20 or more goals. Tied for second on team in power-play goals. Second on team in shooting percentage. Third on team in points. Tied for third on team in plus-minus. Missed four games with hamstring injury. Missed two games with groin injury.

THE FINESSE GAME

Murphy can be dangerous. He is a goal scorer, and when he's on his game there aren't many better. He has an explosive burst of speed and can take the puck to the net. He has great hands. He is creative off the forecheck and has confidence with the puck. He is sometimes too selfish and single-minded when he has made the decision to shoot, even when a better option to pass suddenly presents itself. He needs a pivot who can get him the puck at the right times.

Murphy has a lot of zip on his slap and wrist shots. He gets both away quickly and through a crowd, and he's been a high-percentage shooter through much of his career.

Murphy has streaks where he is brilliant — and such was the case when he was re-teamed with former Edmonton linemate Vincent Damphousse late in the season — but consistency has always eluded him.

THE PHYSICAL GAME

Murphy makes preemptive hits when going for the puck in the corners — which is a nice way of saying he picks and interferes. He will use his size and strength in front of the net to establish position, and he'll fight along the wall and in the corners. He's not a big banger or crasher, but he does have a nasty streak.

THE INTANGIBLES

Murphy went into the off-season as an unrestricted free agent and talked about getting Mark Recchi money. Good luck, Joe. He has the ability to notch 30 to 35 goals, but he has never done it in 12 NHL seasons. He has a knack for scoring the occasional big goal (he has four overtime winners in the playoffs). He's always a potential game breaker, but the key to Murphy is "potential," and he's never fulfilled his.

PROJECTION

A 25-goal season, with the skill level for 10 more.

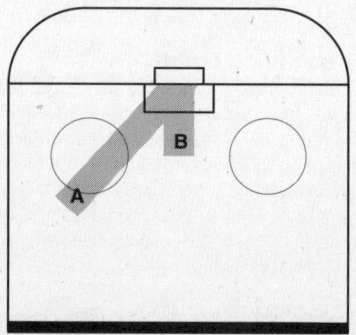

OWEN NOLAN

Yrs. of NHL service: 9
Born: Belfast, N. Ireland; Sept. 22, 1971
Position: right wing
Height: 6-1
Weight: 201
Uniform no.: 11
Shoots: right

Career statistics:

GP	G	A	TP	PIM
559	208	222	440	1100

1995-96 statistics:

GP	G	A	TP	+/-	PIM	PP	SH	GW	GT	S	PCT
81	33	36	69	-33	146	16	1	2	0	207	15.9

1996-97 statistics:

GP	G	A	TP	+/-	PIM	PP	SH	GW	GT	S	PCT
72	31	32	63	-19	155	10	0	3	1	225	13.8

1997-98 statistics:

GP	G	A	TP	+/-	PIM	PP	SH	GW	GT	S	PCT
75	14	27	41	-2	144	3	1	1	0	192	7.3

1998-99 statistics:

GP	G	A	TP	+/-	PIM	PP	SH	GW	GT	S	PCT
78	19	26	45	+16	129	6	2	3	1	207	9.2

LAST SEASON

Led team in plus-minus. Tied for team lead in short-handed goals. Second on team in penalty minutes and shots. Tied for third on team in assists and game-winning goals. Missed two games due to contract dispute. Missed two games with back injury.

THE FINESSE GAME

Nobody knows where Nolan's shot is headed, except Nolan. A pure shooter with good hands, he rips one-timers from the circle with deadly speed and accuracy. His game suffers when he tries to get too fancy and ventures away from a meat-and-potatoes game. When that happens, he holds onto the puck too long and tries to make plays instead of shooting. He has to think like a finisher.

Nolan has an amazing knack for letting the puck go at just the right moment. He has a little move in tight to the goal with a forehand to backhand, and around the net he is about as good as anyone in the game.

Nolan is a strong skater with good balance and fair agility. He is quick straight ahead but won't split the defense when carrying the puck. He's better without the puck, driving into open ice for the pass and quick shot. Defensively, he has improved tremendously.

THE PHYSICAL GAME

Nolan was able to play healthy most of last season, which allowed him to play the physical style he needs to be effective.

THE INTANGIBLES

Nolan's point production was less than expected last season, but coaches were happy with his overall play.

PROJECTION

Nolan could see his goals improve to 25 to 30, with Vincent Damphousse and Gary Suter (if healthy) on hand all season to boost the power play.

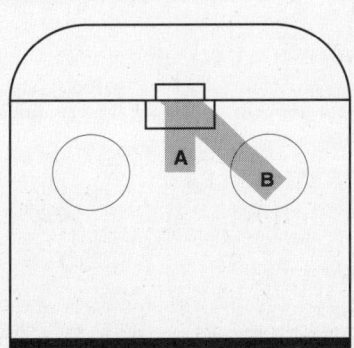

MARCUS RAGNARSSON

Yrs. of NHL service: 4
Born: Ostervala, Sweden; Aug. 13, 1971
Position: left defense
Height: 6-1
Weight: 200
Uniform no.: 10
Shoots: left

Career statistics:

GP	G	A	TP	PIM
293	16	78	94	236

1995-96 statistics:

GP	G	A	TP	+/-	PIM	PP	SH	GW	GT	S	PCT
71	8	31	39	-24	42	4	0	0	0	94	8.5

1996-97 statistics:

GP	G	A	TP	+/-	PIM	PP	SH	GW	GT	S	PCT
69	3	14	17	-18	63	2	0	0	0	57	5.3

1997-98 statistics:

GP	G	A	TP	+/-	PIM	PP	SH	GW	GT	S	PCT
79	5	20	25	-11	65	3	0	2	0	91	5.5

1998-99 statistics:

GP	G	A	TP	+/-	PIM	PP	SH	GW	GT	S	PCT
74	0	13	13	+7	66	0	0	0	0	87	.0

Suter and Vincent Damphousse to the power play.

LAST SEASON

Missed seven games with broken thumb.

THE FINESSE GAME

Ragnarsson has a lot of poise, hand skills and skating ability. He has very quick feet and moves the puck well. He makes a good first pass and also makes some good decisions at the blueline to get the puck through.

He controls a lot of the breakout for San Jose and makes smart choices in the neutral zone. He is given a lot of responsibility on the power play, and while he is not in the elite class of quarterbacks, he has a decent, if not outstanding, point shot and is not afraid to shoot. Ragnarsson will learn more from playing with Gary Suter; the two will probably comprise the first unit on the points.

Defensively, Ragnarsson still has some work to do. He uses his body positionally to take up space, but isn't much of a hitter. He will get the puck out in a hurry when he has time but is vulnerable to a strong forecheck.

THE PHYSICAL GAME

Ragnarsson is built solidly and will play a physical game, though finesse is his forte. He can handle a lot of ice time.

THE INTANGIBLES

Ragnarsson and steady partner Mike Rathje face the opponents' top lines night after night.

PROJECTION

Ragnarsson's offensive game has more upside and he could produce a 40-point season with the additions of

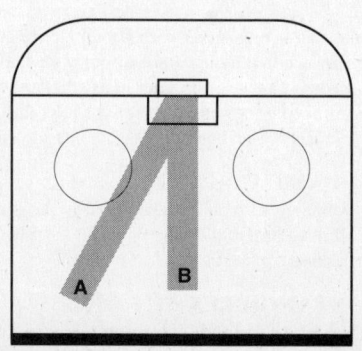

MIKE RATHJE

Yrs. of NHL service: 6
Born: Mannville, Alta.; May 11, 1974
Position: left defense
Height: 6-6
Weight: 220
Uniform no.: 40
Shoots: left

Career statistics:

GP	G	A	TP	PIM
310	11	52	63	218

1995-96 statistics:

GP	G	A	TP	+/-	PIM	PP	SH	GW	GT	S	PCT
27	0	7	7	-16	14	0	0	0	0	26	0.0

1996-97 statistics:

GP	G	A	TP	+/-	PIM	PP	SH	GW	GT	S	PCT
31	0	8	8	-1	21	0	0	0	0	22	0.0

1997-98 statistics:

GP	G	A	TP	+/-	PIM	PP	SH	GW	GT	S	PCT
81	3	12	15	-4	59	1	0	0	0	61	4.9

1998-99 statistics:

GP	G	A	TP	+/-	PIM	PP	SH	GW	GT	S	PCT
82	5	9	14	+15	36	2	0	1	0	67	7.5

LAST SEASON

Second on team and led team defensemen in plus-minus. One of two Sharks to appear in all 82 games.

THE FINESSE GAME

A stay-at-home type, Rathje was probably San Jose's best defenseman all season. He has great quickness for a player of his size. He is a lot like Ken Morrow, the kind of player who is so quiet that you have to watch him every game to appreciate how good he is. He is strong enough to play against the league's power forwards and quick enough to deal with the faster skilled players.

Rathje has the ability to get involved in the attack, but is prized primarily for his defense. He helps get the puck out of the zone quickly. He can either carry the puck out and make a smart headman pass, then follow the play, or make the safe move and chip the puck out along the wall.

Rathje has great poise and worked well paired with the more offensive-minded Marcus Ragnarsson. He combines his lateral mobility with a good low shot, to get the puck on the net without being blocked.

THE PHYSICAL GAME

Rathje has good size and he's adding more muscle. He has learned to play with controlled aggression. He has a little bit of mean in him, and he likes to hit. He has unbelievable strength and good mobility for his size. His penalty minutes look low because he plays hard without taking bad penalties.

THE INTANGIBLES

Rathje is one of the first players rival GMs ask for in a trade. They won't get him. He is the cornerstone of a rapidly improving San Jose defense.

PROJECTION

Rathje is one of the Sharks' top two defensemen. He can get 20 points and play against other teams' top forward lines.

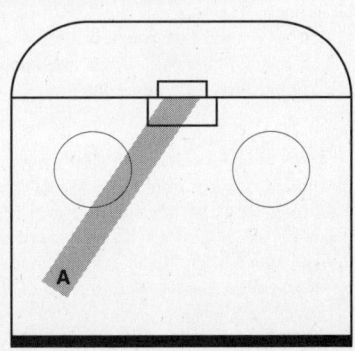

MIKE RICCI

Yrs. of NHL service: 9
Born: Scarborough, Ont.; Oct. 27, 1971
Position: centre
Height: 6-0
Weight: 190
Uniform no.: 18
Shoots: left

Career statistics:

GP	G	A	TP	PIM
626	154	233	387	644

1995-96 statistics:

GP	G	A	TP	+/-	PIM	PP	SH	GW	GT	S	PCT
62	6	21	27	+1	52	3	0	1	0	73	8.2

1996-97 statistics:

GP	G	A	TP	+/-	PIM	PP	SH	GW	GT	S	PCT
63	13	19	32	-3	59	5	0	3	0	74	17.6

1997-98 statistics:

GP	G	A	TP	+/-	PIM	PP	SH	GW	GT	S	PCT
65	9	18	27	-4	32	5	0	2	0	91	9.9

1998-99 statistics:

GP	G	A	TP	+/-	PIM	PP	SH	GW	GT	S	PCT
82	13	26	39	+1	68	2	1	2	1	98	13.3

LAST SEASON

Tied for third on team in assists. One of two Sharks to appear in all 82 games.

THE FINESSE GAME

Ricci is a known quantity. He has terrific hand skills, combined with hockey sense and an outstanding work ethic. He always seems to be in the right place, ready to make the right play. He sees his passing options well and is patient with the puck. He can rifle it as well. He has a good backhand shot from in deep and scores most of his goals from the slot by picking the top corners. His lone drawback is his speed. He's fast enough to not look out of place and he has good balance and agility, but his lack of quickness prevents him from being more of an offensive force.

Very slick on face-offs, Ricci has good hand speed and hand-eye coordination for winning draws outright, or he can pick a bouncing puck out of the air. This serves him well in scrambles in front of the net, or he can deflect midair slap shots. He can play wing in addition to his natural position at centre.

Ricci is a very good penalty killer, with poise and a controlled aggression for forcing the play.

THE PHYSICAL GAME

Ricci is not big, but he is so strong that it's not unusual to see him skate out from behind the net, dragging along or fending off a checker with one arm while he makes a pass or takes a shot with his other arm. He plays a tough game without being overly chippy. He is also very strong in the corners and in front of the net. He plays bigger than he is.

Ricci will play hurt. He pays attention to conditioning and has a great deal of stamina.

THE INTANGIBLES

Ricci will antagonize and draw penalties. He kills penalties and works the power play, and makes timely plays under pressure. Although not as gifted offensively as Ron Francis, he is similar to Francis in that he is a checking centre who can do so much more than just check.

Ricci's quality, character, leadership and dedication to the game and his teammates are impeccable. He is a throwback, and helps provide some grit in a finesse-laden lineup. His teammates love his upbeat off-ice attitude. Ricci has stepped into the gap between the Sharks' kids and the team's older veterans — he is a great addition to team chemistry.

PROJECTION

Ricci can produce 40 points over a full season. He gives the Sharks some options in how to best utilize him.

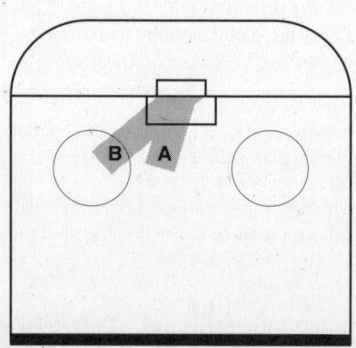

MARCO STURM

Yrs. of NHL service: 2
Born: Dingolfing, Germany; Sept. 8, 1978
Position: centre
Height: 6-0
Weight: 190
Uniform no.: 19
Shoots: left

Career statistics:

GP	G	A	TP	PIM
152	26	42	68	92

1997-98 statistics:

GP	G	A	TP	+/-	PIM	PP	SH	GW	GT	S	PCT
74	10	20	30	-2	40	2	0	3	0	118	8.5

1998-99 statistics:

GP	G	A	TP	+/-	PIM	PP	SH	GW	GT	S	PCT
78	16	22	38	+7	52	3	2	3	2	140	11.4

LAST SEASON

Second NHL season. Tied for third on team in game-winning goals. Missed two games with foot injury. Missed two games due to coach's decision.

THE FINESSE GAME

Sturm may be the best all-around player on the Sharks. He is a versatile skater who can play all three forward positions. There isn't a lot of maintenance to him. He knows where to be without the puck.

He is a fine skater with smooth acceleration. He has elite speed, and finished second in the fastest skater competition at the NHL All-Star Game. He has good hands for stickhandling and shooting (which, like many Europeans, he needs to do more of). He is a natural scorer who should gain confidence in his next few seasons in the league.

Sturm is extremely intelligent and hard working. He is not afraid to block shots. He is going to be the kind of player who scores important goals and makes key plays that determine games. He plays on a third line but has the skill to be a top six, and could give the Sharks what Jere Lehtinen gives the Dallas Stars.

THE PHYSICAL GAME

Sturm is not very big but competes every night. He is chippy and feisty. He plays bigger than he is.

THE INTANGIBLES

Sturm has earned a steady job after only two seasons in the NHL. He is a huge part of the Sharks' foundation of young players.

PROJECTION

Sturm will probably score in the 20-goal range and provide an outstanding all-around game.

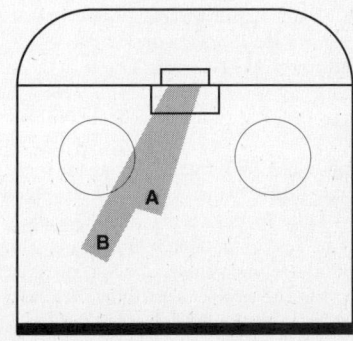

GARY SUTER

Yrs. of NHL service: 14
Born: Madison, Wisc.; June 24, 1964
Position: left defense
Height: 6-0
Weight: 200
Uniform no.: 20
Shoots: left

Career statistics:

GP	G	A	TP	PIM
919	181	563	744	1154

1995-96 statistics:

GP	G	A	TP	+/-	PIM	PP	SH	GW	GT	S	PCT
82	20	47	67	+3	80	12	2	4	0	242	8.3

1996-97 statistics:

GP	G	A	TP	+/-	PIM	PP	SH	GW	GT	S	PCT
82	7	21	28	-4	70	3	0	0	1	225	3.1

1997-98 statistics:

GP	G	A	TP	+/-	PIM	PP	SH	GW	GT	S	PCT
73	14	28	42	+1	74	5	2	0	0	199	7.0

1998-99 statistics:

GP	G	A	TP	+/-	PIM	PP	SH	GW	GT	S	PCT
1	0	0	0	0	0	0	0	0	0	1	.0

LAST SEASON

Missed 81 games with elbow injury.

THE FINESSE GAME

Suter has great natural skills, starting with his skating. He's secure on his skates with a wide stance for balance. He has all of the components that make a great skater: acceleration, flat-out speed, quickness and mobility. He skates well backwards and can't be bested one-on-one except by the slickest skaters. He loves to jump into the attack, and he'll key a rush with a smooth outlet pass or carry the puck and lead the parade.

Suter has a superb shot. It's not scary-hard, but he keeps it low. Not a great playmaker, his creativity comes from his speed and dangerous shot. He can handle some penalty-killing time, though it is not his strong suit.

THE PHYSICAL GAME

Suter may be one of the least-known dirty players in the NHL. Sure, Bryan Marchment gets all the bad press for his knee-to-knee checks, but it was Suter whose hit in the 1991 Canada Cup was the start of Wayne Gretzky's back troubles, and Suter's stick to the head of Paul Kariya threatened that brilliant star's career.

So don't look for his name among the Lady Byng candidates. Like Chelios, Suter is a marathon man who can handle 30 minutes of ice time a game and not wear down. He is exceptionally fit. He can get carried away with the hitting game and will take himself out of position, even when penalty killing. He doesn't like to be hit; he'll bring his stick up at the last second before contact to protect himself. His defensive reads are average to fair.

THE INTANGIBLES

Suter took a lot of money last season and was able to appear in only one game because of his elbow injury. His healthy return would energize the Sharks' power play.

PROJECTION

If he is able to rehab successfully, Suter could power his way back into the 55- to 60-point range.

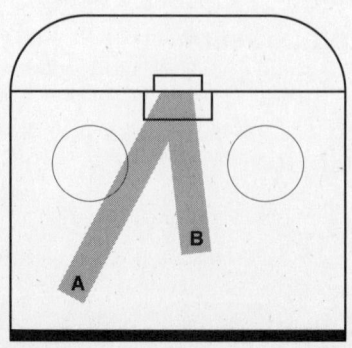

MIKE VERNON

Yrs. of NHL service: 14
Born: Calgary, Alberta; Feb. 24, 1963
Position: goaltender
Height: 5-9
Weight: 165
Uniform no.: 29
Catches: left

Career statistics:

GP	MIN	GA	SO	GAA	A	PIM
673	38587	1932	22	3.00	32	253

1995-96 statistics:

GP	MIN	GAA	W	L	T	SO	GA	S	SAPCT	PIM
32	1855	2.26	21	7	2	3	70	723	.903	2

1996-97 statistics:

GP	MIN	GAA	W	L	T	SO	GA	S	SAPCT	PIM
33	1952	2.43	13	11	8	0	79	782	.899	35

1997-98 statistics:

GP	MIN	GAA	W	L	T	SO	GA	S	SAPCT	PIM
62	3564	2.46	30	22	8	5	146	1401	.895	24

1998-99 statistics:

GP	MIN	GAA	W	L	T	SO	GA	S	SAPCT	PIM
49	2831	2.27	16	22	10	4	107	1200	.911	8

LAST SEASON

Career-best GAA. Missed nine games with groin injury.

THE PHYSICAL GAME

As Vernon gets older he relies more on his angle play than his reflexes, and his technique was never the best part of his game. He has a quick glove hand; he does a good job of setting himself to tempt the shooter to hit the top right corner. However, he is being beaten more on the bread-and-butter save than he was in the past.

Vernon is aggressive, and at the top of his game he is on the top of his crease, trying to make his small body look bigger. He forces the shooter to make a quick decision. He is a good skater from post to post. He handles hard-arounds well, content to stop the puck behind the net and not get involved in any puck-handling, which is a weak point. When he does move the puck, it's usually with a one-handed swing.

Vernon does use his stick well to break up plays around the net. He cuts off low passes, and sweeps his stick at forwards trying to come out from behind the net.

Because he is such an active goalie, Vernon tends to wear down when he gets too much ice time. If the Sharks keep him to around 55 games he'll be just fine.

THE MENTAL GAME

Vernon has won two Stanley Cups with two different teams (Calgary and Detroit), and believes in himself when there are doubters. He is highly competitive.

THE INTANGIBLES

Vernon upgraded San Jose's goaltending immeasurably. His teammates feel that when they go into any game now, they have a chance to win because of their netminder.

PROJECTION

San Jose figures to be an improved team this season, which means Vernon could return to the 30-win level, even if he is slightly past his prime.

ANDREI ZYUZIN

Yrs. of NHL service: 2
Born: Ufa, Russia; Jan. 21, 1978
Position: left defense
Height: 6-1
Weight: 187
Uniform no.: 20
Shoots: left

Career statistics:

GP	G	A	TP	PIM
81	9	8	17	104

1997-98 statistics:

GP	G	A	TP	+/-	PIM	PP	SH	GW	GT	S	PCT
56	6	7	13	+8	66	2	0	2	0	72	8.3

1998-99 statistics:

GP	G	A	TP	+/-	PIM	PP	SH	GW	GT	S	PCT
25	3	1	4	+5	38	2	0	0	0	44	6.8

LAST SEASON

Missed 12 games with team suspension. Missed 19 games due to coach's decision. Appeared in 23 games with Kentucky (AHL), scoring 2-12 — 14.

THE FINESSE GAME

Zyuzin is an offensive-minded defenseman with the kind of speed and anticipation that will prevent him from being too much of a liability on defense — because of his ability to recover and position himself.

Zyuzin could well prove to be the kind of player who can dictate the tempo of a game, or break it wide open with one end-to-end rush, like Brian Leetch. At the moment, he doesn't seem to possess the exceptional lateral movement along the blueline that sets Leetch apart from most of his NHL brethren, but Zyuzin has a big upside.

He doesn't take his offensive chances blindly; Zyuzin knows what the score is. When he takes a chance, it's one that usually results in a play like his overtime goal against Dallas in the playoffs. When he needs to stay back on defense, he will. He will also get burned once in awhile, but he makes smart choices.

The young Russian is a fast skater with quick acceleration and balance. He handles the puck well at a high pace and will pass or shoot: a smart playmaker, but one who will not pass up a golden scoring opportunity. He has a hard point shot and will become a good power-play quarterback.

THE PHYSICAL GAME

Zyuzin is not a physical player. He has adequate size but will need a streak of Chris Chelios-like aggressiveness to make the best use of his ability. He does have a desire to excel, and if it means stepping up his game physically he will probably be able to make that transition. He plays with a lot of energy.

THE INTANGIBLES

Zyuzin went AWOL and was involved in some curious off-ice decisions involving agents, but fortunately his teammates love this kid and he hasn't burned many bridges. He has been compared to Ray Bourque, a do-it-all defenseman, but Zyuzin will need more bulk before he can fulfill those lofty expectations.

PROJECTION

Zyuzin will be given prime power-play ice time and every chance to produce. He could notch 25 to 30 points over a full season.

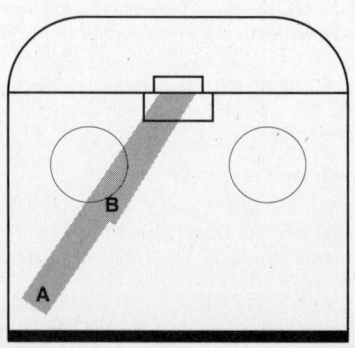

ST. LOUIS BLUES

Players' Statistics 1998-99

POS.	NO.	PLAYER	GP	G	A	PTS	+/-	PIM	PP	SH	GW	GT	S	PCT
R	38	PAVOL DEMITRA	82	37	52	89	13	16	14		10	1	259	14.3
C	77	PIERRE TURGEON	67	31	34	65	4	36	10		5	2	193	16.1
D	2	AL MACINNIS	82	20	42	62	33	70	11	1	2	2	314	6.4
R	48	SCOTT YOUNG	75	24	28	52	8	27	8		4		205	11.7
D	44	CHRIS PRONGER	67	13	33	46	3	113	8				172	7.6
L	33	SCOTT PELLERIN	80	20	21	41	1	42		5	4		138	14.5
C	22	CRAIG CONROY	69	14	25	39	14	38		1	1		134	10.4
C	32	MIKE EASTWOOD	82	9	21	30	6	36					76	11.8
R	27	TERRY YAKE	60	9	18	27	-9	34	3		4		59	15.3
C	25	PASCAL RHEAUME	60	9	18	27	10	24	2				85	10.6
R	10	JIM CAMPBELL	55	4	21	25	-8	41	1				99	4.0
L	34	MICHEL PICARD	45	11	11	22	5	16			2		69	15.9
R	23	BLAIR ATCHEYNUM	65	10	8	18	-8	18	2		2		93	10.8
R	56	*LUBOS BARTECKO	32	5	11	16	4	6			1		37	13.5
C	26	*MICHAL HANDZUS	66	4	12	16	-9	30					78	5.1
D	7	RICARD PERSSON	54	1	12	13	4	94					52	1.9
L	14	GEOFF COURTNALL	24	5	7	12	2	28	1		2		60	8.3
C	15	*MARTY REASONER	22	3	7	10	2	8	1				33	9.1
R	39	KELLY CHASE	45	3	7	10	2	143			1		25	12.0
C	21	*JAMAL MAYERS	34	4	5	9	-3	40					48	8.3
L	18	TONY TWIST	63	2	6	8	0	149					23	8.7
D	6	JAMIE RIVERS	76	2	5	7	-3	47	1				78	2.6
D	36	BRYAN HELMER	40		4	4	5	42					49	
D	37	JEFF FINLEY	32	1	2	3	11	20					16	6.3
D	19	CHRIS MCALPINE	51	1	1	2	-10	50					56	1.8
D	4	MARC BERGEVIN	52	1	1	2	-14	99					40	2.5
D	42	RORY FITZPATRICK	1				-3	2						
L	9	*TYSON NASH	2				-1	5					1	
C	55	*JOCHEN HECHT	3				-2						4	
G	35	JIM CAREY	4				0							
G	1	*BRENT JOHNSON	6				0							
G	30	*RICH PARENT	10				0	2						
D	20	RUDY POESCHEK	16				0	33					8	
D	28	BRAD SHAW	16				0	8					15	
G	29	JAMIE MCLENNAN	33				0							
G	31	GRANT FUHR	39				0	12						

GP = games played; G = goals; A = assists; PTS = points; +/- = goals-for minus goals-against while player is on ice; PIM = penalties in minutes; PP = power-play goals; SH = shorthanded goals; GW = game-winning goals; GT = game-tying goals; S = no. of shots; PCT = percentage of goals to shots; * = rookie

BLAIR ATCHEYNUM

Yrs. of NHL service: 2
Born: Estevan, Saskatchewan; Apr. 20, 1969
Position: right wing
Height: 6-1
Weight: 196
Uniform no.: 23
Shoots: right

Career statistics:

GP	G	A	TP	PIM
130	21	24	45	28

1997-98 statistics:

GP	G	A	TP	+/-	PIM	PP	SH	GW	GT	S	PCT
61	11	15	26	+5	10	0	1	3	0	103	10.7

1998-99 statistics:

GP	G	A	TP	+/-	PIM	PP	SH	GW	GT	S	PCT
65	10	8	18	-8	18	2	0	2	0	93	10.8

LAST SEASON

Acquired from Nashville for a 2000 sixth-round draft pick, Mar. 23, 1999. Missed 15 games with knee injury. Missed two games due to coach's decision.

THE FINESSE GAME

The Blues thought enough of Atcheynum to reacquire him from Nashville in time for the stretch run and the playoffs.

He is a reliable member of the checking line — not flashy — and does a lot of the little things well. He has the intelligence for the NHL game. He is unnoticeable a lot of the time, because he is so low-key, but you will rarely notice him making a crucial mistake, either.

Atcheynum doesn't have great speed but he works hard. He has a good shot and handles the puck well. He also knows where to go on the ice and has some offensive instincts. He scored 42 goals in the minors with Hershey (AHL) in 1996-97, so he has some offensive upside.

THE PHYSICAL GAME

Atcheynum is big, solidly built, but not aggressive. He is a sturdy forechecker.

THE INTANGIBLES

Thoroughly professional, Atcheynum is low-maintenance from a coaching standpoint. He was an unrestricted free agent during the off-season, but he is a particular favourite of the St. Louis coaching staff and was expected to re-sign with the Blues.

PROJECTION

Atcheynum could score 15 goals in a checking role.

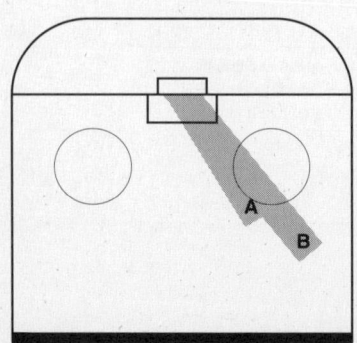

LUBOS BARTECKO

Yrs. of NHL service: 1
Born: Kezmarok, Czech.; July 14, 1976
Position: left wing
Height: 6-1
Weight: 200
Uniform no.: 56
Shoots: left

Career statistics:

GP	G	A	TP	PIM
32	5	11	16	6

1998-99 statistics:

GP	G	A	TP	+/-	PIM	PP	SH	GW	GT	S	PCT
32	5	11	16	+4	6	0	0	1	0	37	13.5

LAST SEASON
First NHL season. Appeared in 47 games with Worcester (AHL), scoring 13-22 — 25. Missed five games due to coach's decision.

THE FINESSE GAME
Bartecko has a stocky build and is quick. Strong on his skates, he has the kinds of skills that stamp him as a pure finisher. Right now, his defensive game is lagging behind his offensive game, but that is hardly unusual for an inexperienced player. He was sometimes a little confused about his job.

He has sure, soft hands and will take the puck to the net for a strong wrist shot. He needs to shoot more often.

Bartecko's biggest problem has been his inconsistency. Every time he was promoted last season, he would play the first half-dozen or so games at a tremendous pace and then tail off.

THE PHYSICAL GAME
Bartecko is solidly built. He won't initiate contact but he won't back down, either.

THE INTANGIBLES
Bartecko has a future as a top six forward. He could make it this season because the Blues would like to get his speed and some youth in their lineup.

PROJECTION
Bartecko could hit 20 goals this season if he lands a full-time job.

CRAIG CONROY

Yrs. of NHL service: 4
Born: Potsdam, N.Y.; Sept. 4, 1971
Position: centre
Height: 6-2
Weight: 198
Uniform no.: 22
Shoots: right

Career statistics:

GP	G	A	TP	PIM
224	35	65	100	129

1995-96 statistics:

GP	G	A	TP	+/-	PIM	PP	SH	GW	GT	S	PCT
7	0	0	0	-4	2	0	0	0	0	1	0.0

1996-97 statistics:

GP	G	A	TP	+/-	PIM	PP	SH	GW	GT	S	PCT
61	6	11	17	0	43	0	0	1	0	74	8.1

1997-98 statistics:

GP	G	A	TP	+/-	PIM	PP	SH	GW	GT	S	PCT
81	14	29	43	+20	46	0	3	1	0	118	11.9

1998-99 statistics:

GP	G	A	TP	+/-	PIM	PP	SH	GW	GT	S	PCT
69	14	25	39	+14	38	0	1	1	0	134	10.4

LAST SEASON
Second on team in plus-minus. Missed 13 games with ankle injuries.

THE FINESSE GAME
Conroy is a determined player who needs a little more confidence in his game to bring out some assets he has yet to display at the NHL level. A numbers man early in his career, he has worked hard at the defensive aspect of the game to become a more well-rounded player.

Conroy kills penalties well, using his speed, size and anticipation. He is a smart player who can make the little hook or hold to slow down an opponent without getting caught. He has quick hands and is good on draws, taking most of the Blues' key defensive-zone face-offs.

Conroy has been a scorer at the college and minor-league levels (he was leading the AHL in scoring when St. Louis obtained him in 1996) and is just starting to come into his own. His hands are much better than the average checking centre's. Although he's been predominantly in a checking role for two seasons, the Blues experiment with him on one of the top two lines from time to time. He can fill in, but he looks like a better fit on the checking line.

He's reliable in all key situations, defending a lead, in the closing minutes of a period and killing penalties at crucial times.

THE PHYSICAL GAME
Conroy isn't mean, but he is tough in a quiet way. He uses his size well and accepts checking roles against elite players without being intimidated. He is relentless on every shift and has a great work ethic.

THE INTANGIBLES
Conroy is a valuable role player for the Blues. He may be asked to pick up the pace offensively. He could even see second-unit power-play time.

PROJECTION
Conroy has considerable upside. Scoring 15 to 20 goals in a checking role is more comfy than being expected to produce 55 points, which he might have come close to if he hadn't been hurt.

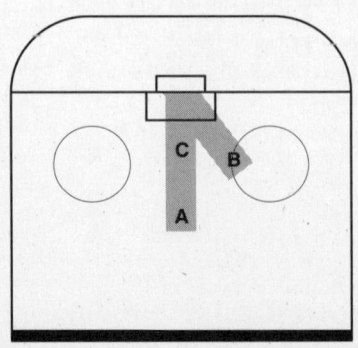

PAVOL DEMITRA

Yrs. of NHL service: 5
Born: Dubnica, Slovakia; Nov. 29, 1974
Position: left wing
Height: 6-0
Weight: 189
Uniform no.: 38
Shoots: left

Career statistics:

GP	G	A	TP	PIM
210	74	96	170	50

1995-96 statistics:

GP	G	A	TP	+/-	PIM	PP	SH	GW	GT	S	PCT
31	7	10	17	-3	6	2	0	1	0	66	10.6

1996-97 statistics:

GP	G	A	TP	+/-	PIM	PP	SH	GW	GT	S	PCT
8	3	0	3	0	2	2	0	1	0	15	20.0

1997-98 statistics:

GP	G	A	TP	+/-	PIM	PP	SH	GW	GT	S	PCT
61	22	30	52	+11	22	4	4	6	1	147	15.0

1998-99 statistics:

GP	G	A	TP	+/-	PIM	PP	SH	GW	GT	S	PCT
82	37	52	89	+13	16	14	0	10	1	259	14.3

LAST SEASON

Led team in goals, assists, points, power-play goals and game-winning goals. Tenth in NHL in points. Tied for 10th in NHL in assists. Tied for eighth in NHL in power-play goals. Second in NHL in game-winning goals. Career highs in goals, assists and points. Third on team in plus-minus. One of three Blues to appear in all 82 games.

THE FINESSE GAME

Brett who? Demitra made the astounding leap forward to not only eclipse Hull (who left as a free agent to Dallas) in nearly every major offensive category, but to ensure that Hull and not the Blues' management would be booed every time the Stars came to town.

Demitra's speed makes things happen. He has great moves one-on-one, and he finds a way to get in the holes. He has good stick skills and loves to shoot. He can really find the top of the net, especially with his one-timer. He is well-versed at picking the top corners and he can do it at speed.

Demitra is a creative and exceptional puckhandler, with a quick, deceptive shot. He's not shy about letting the puck go. He likes to drag the puck into his skates and then shoot it through a defenseman's legs. The move gets the rearguard to move up a little bit, and Demitra gets it by him on net.

Coming in off the right wing, which is his off-side, he will move to the middle on his forehand and throw the puck back against the grain. He needs to work on his puck protection skills. Sometimes he exposes the puck too much and what should be a scoring chance for him gets knocked away. Defensively, he's reliable.

THE PHYSICAL GAME

Demitra is not very big but he has built up his body, adding 10 to 12 pounds of legitimate muscle. He is very competitive and durable. He can take the heat and the ice time.

THE INTANGIBLES

Demitra faced top checking pressure every night — the Blues didn't have much of a second line — and still thrived. He has arrived as an NHL star, though the attention was a bit overwhelming for him at times. He had a strong playoffs. He wants to succeed and appears to be willing to pay the price to stay in the NHL, but expectations will be sky-high now following last season.

PROJECTION

Demitra can be a 40-goal, 90-point guy if the Blues ever develop any depth to take a little attention off him.

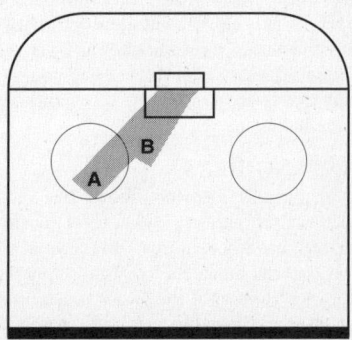

MIKE EASTWOOD

Yrs. of NHL service: 7
Born: Ottawa, Ont.; July 1, 1967
Position: centre
Height: 6-3
Weight: 205
Uniform no.: 32
Shoots: right

Career statistics:

GP	G	A	TP	PIM
404	48	79	127	181

1995-96 statistics:

GP	G	A	TP	+/-	PIM	PP	SH	GW	GT	S	PCT
80	14	14	28	-14	20	2	0	3	1	94	14.9

1996-97 statistics:

GP	G	A	TP	+/-	PIM	PP	SH	GW	GT	S	PCT
60	2	10	12	-1	14	0	0	0	0	44	4.5

1997-98 statistics:

GP	G	A	TP	+/-	PIM	PP	SH	GW	GT	S	PCT
58	6	5	11	-2	22	0	0	1	0	38	15.8

1998-99 statistics:

GP	G	A	TP	+/-	PIM	PP	SH	GW	GT	S	PCT
82	9	21	30	+6	36	0	0	0	0	76	11.8

PROJECTION

Although he did some scoring in college and had one 24-goal season in the American Hockey League, Eastwood's job in the NHL is the denial of opposition offense more than the creation of offense by his team. He is a single-digit goal scorer and will remain as such unless he demands more of himself, more often.

LAST SEASON

One of three Blues to appear in all 82 games. Career highs in assists and points.

THE FINESSE GAME

With a little more spunk, Eastwood could be a strong third-line centre. His problem is a lack of consistency. He is a big player from whom coaches always want more. He has some sparkling games but lacks the confidence and offensive assets — particularly when it comes to the finishing touch — to become an effective everyday player.

Eastwood is sound defensively — alert and aware. He is also deceptively quick as a skater, but doesn't always push himself hard and needs to be urged along by coaches. He kills penalties well and more than holds his own on face-offs.

THE PHYSICAL GAME

Eastwood will never be confused with a body builder. He doesn't have much muscular definition at all and his temperament is equally non-descript. Although he is strong and doesn't get knocked off the puck, he needs to be a presence on the ice and could initiate more contact. He has to work on his conditioning and off-ice strengthening.

THE INTANGIBLES

During the playoffs, Eastwood shows size and spunk, and makes himself play at a higher level than his easygoing nature usually requires. He can make things happen but seems to need a lot of prodding. He handled extra ice time until the Blues reacquired Blair Atcheynum from Nashville late in the season.

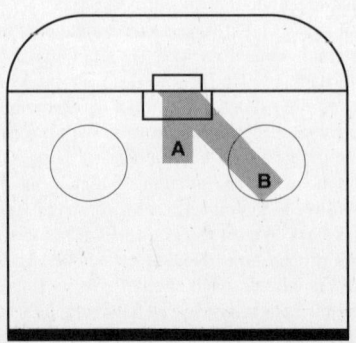

GRANT FUHR

Yrs. of NHL service: 18
Born: Spruce Grove, Alta.; Sept. 28, 1962
Position: goaltender
Height: 5-9
Weight: 190
Uniform no.: 31
Catches: right

Career statistics:

GP	MIN	GA	SO	GAA	A	PIM
845	47740	2679	25	3.37	46	138

1995-96 statistics:

GP	MIN	GAA	W	L	T	SO	GA	S	SAPCT	PIM
79	4365	2.87	30	28	16	3	209	2157	.903	8

1996-97 statistics:

GP	MIN	GAA	W	L	T	SO	GA	S	SAPCT	PIM
73	4261	2.72	33	27	11	3	193	1940	.901	6

1997-98 statistics:

GP	MIN	GAA	W	L	T	SO	GA	S	SAPCT	PIM
58	3274	2.53	29	21	6	3	138	1354	.898	6

1998-99 statistics:

GP	MIN	GAA	W	L	T	SO	GA	S	SAPCT	PIM
39	2193	2.44	16	11	8	2	89	827	.892	12

LAST SEASON
Missed 16 games with knee surgery. Missed 11 games with groin injury. Missed two games with knee injury.

THE PHYSICAL GAME
After a lot of years and a lot of mileage, the strain is finally starting to show on Fuhr's 37-year-old goalie body. Injuries and age have conspired to slow him down a bit, but he can still pull one out of his bag of tricks now and then and let a shooter think he has him beaten, before making the save at the last split-second.

Fuhr is a great skater with outstanding balance. He catches with his right hand, which is disconcerting to some shooters, and his strength is his glove side.

He recovers well for second shots and is so efficient about it that he never seems to be scrambling or panicky. He controls his rebounds well. He isn't overly active with his stick.

THE MENTAL GAME
Fuhr has always possessed a laid-back demeanour, and that calmness gives his defense confidence even when he's under siege. But the cool exterior masks a determined personality. He maintains his concentration well through screens and scrambles, and he doesn't allow many soft goals because his attention doesn't waver.

Fuhr is smart. He reads plays coming at him as well as any top defenseman, and is a master of the read and react.

THE INTANGIBLES
Fuhr's days as a number one goalie are over. He will probably open the season as the starter, unless — or until — Roman Turek proves himself ready to take over.

PROJECTION
Fuhr is the oldest number one goalie in the league, and injuries are getting harder and harder to bounce back from. He has an outside shot at 20 wins.

MICHAL HANDZUS

Yrs. of NHL service: 1
Born: Banska Bystrica, Czech Republic; Mar. 11, 1977
Position: centre
Height: 6-3
Weight: 191
Uniform no.: 26
Shoots: left

Career statistics:

GP	G	A	TP	PIM
66	4	12	16	30

1998-99 statistics:

GP	G	A	TP	+/-	PIM	PP	SH	GW	GT	S	PCT
66	4	12	16	-9	30	0	0	0	0	78	5.1

LAST SEASON
First NHL season. Missed 16 games with shoulder injuries.

THE FINESSE GAME
Handzus has the brains of a much more experienced player. He is so smart that he is the first forward St. Louis will throw onto the ice to kill a penalty when the Blues are two men down. He is very dependable and has a tremendous work ethic.

Now Handzus has to think he can score. He has some offensive skill with a big-league shot. But he concentrated so much on his game defensively that he hasn't developed the offensive part of his game. Handzus is big (six foot five), though still a little weedy. His skating is the only immediate question mark. It is probably adequate for the NHL, but if he works harder to improve he can become an effective player. He has good balance but needs to add a bit of quickness.

Handzus likes to pass a little too much. He need to take the puck to the net and chase down rebounds. He needs a little more greed in his game.

Handzus's skills and hockey sense allow him to play in all game situations. He can develop into a solid all-around centre, with an emphasis on his offensive skills.

THE PHYSICAL GAME
Handzus needs to fill out just a little, but he has gotten much stronger. He can hold off a defender with one arm and still take a shot or make a pass. He doesn't mind the physical game at all. He has the stamina to handle a lot of ice time, and did last season. The Blues had to be careful not to overuse him since he could be employed in so many situations. He is not very aggressive and will have to decide how badly he wants an NHL job, and be willing to pay a higher price.

THE INTANGIBLES
Handzus has the potential to be the number two centre behind Pierre Turgeon. He was used at all three forwards positions last season.

PROJECTION
Handzus didn't post the kind of numbers we hoped he would in his rookie season, but he should improve to 20 to 25 goals this year.

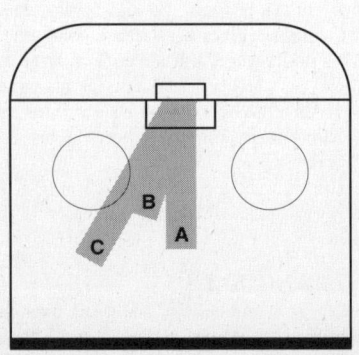

JOCHEN HECHT

Yrs. of NHL service: 0
Born: Mannheim, Germany; June 21, 1977
Position: centre
Height: 6-1
Weight: 180
Uniform no.: 55
Shoots: left

Career statistics:

GP	G	A	TP	PIM
3	0	0	0	0

1998-99 statistics:

GP	G	A	TP	+/-	PIM	PP	SH	GW	GT	S	PCT
3	0	0	0	-2	0	0	0	0	0	4	.0

LAST SEASON
Will be entering first NHL season. Led Worcester (AHL) in goals, assists and points with 21-35 — 56.

THE FINESSE GAME
Hecht is a rangy forward who can handle all three forward positions. He is a good skater with a good passing touch, and is a playmaker more than a scorer. He plays with a straight-up stance that allows him to see everything. He stickhandles in close, and has a great move walking out from the corner or behind the net.

Hecht has deceptive speed. He is a very smart player. He will probably be a better winger since he isn't strong enough on draws to handle playing centre full time. He is tough to read for opposing defensemen because he doesn't do the same thing every time. He is quite unpredictable: he might try to beat a defender one-on-one on one rush and the next time chip the puck in the corner or work a give-and-go. He uses a lot of play selections.

THE PHYSICAL GAME
Physical play doesn't bother Hecht but he doesn't initiate it. He has to get a little stronger and learn to play in the dirty areas of the ice. Hecht physically might not be able to handle a full NHL schedule right off the bat.

THE INTANGIBLES
Hecht joined the Blues late in the season and had a very impressive playoffs. He could probably use more seasoning in the minors, but he will get a good shot at making the Blues.

PROJECTION
Hecht has some nice ingredients to be a quietly effective scorer. His first season could see 15 goals and 30 points with a lot of upside.

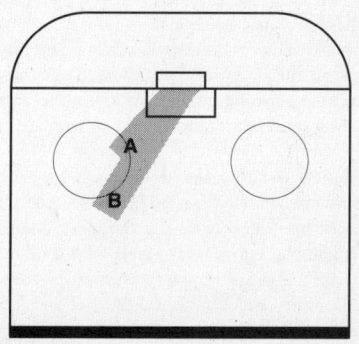

AL MACINNIS

Yrs. of NHL service: 17
Born: Inverness, N.S.; July 11, 1963
Position: right defense
Height: 6-2
Weight: 196
Uniform no.: 2
Shoots: right

Career statistics:

GP	G	A	TP	PIM
1142	290	775	1065	1299

1995-96 statistics:

GP	G	A	TP	+/-	PIM	PP	SH	GW	GT	S	PCT
82	17	44	61	+5	88	9	1	1	1	317	5.4

1996-97 statistics:

GP	G	A	TP	+/-	PIM	PP	SH	GW	GT	S	PCT
72	13	30	43	+2	65	6	1	1	0	296	4.4

1997-98 statistics:

GP	G	A	TP	+/-	PIM	PP	SH	GW	GT	S	PCT
71	19	30	49	+6	80	9	1	2	0	227	8.4

1998-99 statistics:

GP	G	A	TP	+/-	PIM	PP	SH	GW	GT	S	PCT
82	20	42	62	+33	70	11	1	2	2	314	6.4

LAST SEASON

Won 1999 Norris Trophy. Led NHL defensemen in points. Led team and tied for fourth in NHL in plus-minus. Led team and tied for fourth in NHL in shots. Second on team in assists and power-play goals. Third on team in points. One of three Blues to appear in all 82 games.

THE FINESSE GAME

What makes his shot so good is that MacInnis knows the value of a change-up, and he won't always fire with the same velocity. If there is traffic in front, he will take a little off his shot to make it more tippable (and so he doesn't break too many teammates' ankles). One-on-one, of course, MacInnis will fire the laser and can just about knock a goalie into the net. And as much as he likes to shoot, he will also fake a big wind-up, which freezes the defenders, then make a quick slap-pass to an open teammate.

MacInnis knows when to jump into the play and when to back off. He can start a rush with a rink-wide pass, then be quick enough to burst up-ice and be in position for a return pass. Even when he merely rings the puck off the boards, he's a threat, since there is so much on the shot the goaltender has to be careful to stop it. MacInnis has a hard shot even when he's moving backwards.

MacInnis skates well with the puck. He is not very mobile, but he gets up to speed in a few strides and can hit his outside speed to beat a defender one-on-one. He will gamble and is best paired with a defensively alert partner, though he has improved his defensive play and is very smart against a two-on-one.

THE PHYSICAL GAME

MacInnis uses his finesse skills in a defensive posture, always looking for the counterattack. He reads defenses alertly, and positions himself to tie up attackers rather than try to knock them down. In his own way, he is a tough competitor who will pay the price to win. He was the Blues' top defenseman last season, and was always on the ice late to protect a lead.

THE INTANGIBLES

MacInnis is one of the elder statesmen who will stick around while the Blues continue to rebuild with younger talent. The question is if MacInnis, at 36, can continue to handle 30 minutes of ice time a night without breaking down.

PROJECTION

The Norris was well-deserved. MacInnis had a career year and was a leader who logged a lot of ice time. He was the Blues' MVP, since his offensive skills helped players like Pavol Demitra and Pierre Turgeon produce up front. It will be tough for him to duplicate last season, however, and we expect a slight drop-off in production.

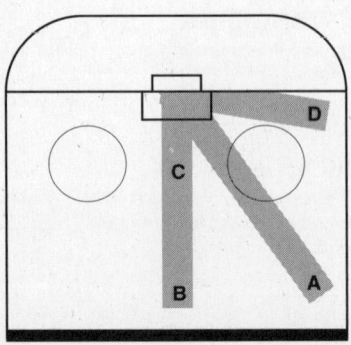

JAMAL MAYERS

Yrs. of NHL service: 1
Born: Toronto, Ont.; Oct. 24, 1974
Position: centre/right wing
Height: 6-0
Weight: 190
Uniform no.: 21
Shoots: right

Career statistics:

GP	G	A	TP	PIM
40	4	6	10	42

1996-97 statistics:

GP	G	A	TP	+/-	PIM	PP	SH	GW	GT	S	PCT
6	0	1	1	-3	2	0	0	0	0	7	0.0

1997-98 statistics:
Did not play in NHL

1998-99 statistics:

GP	G	A	TP	+/-	PIM	PP	SH	GW	GT	S	PCT
34	4	5	9	-3	40	0	0	0	0	48	8.3

LAST SEASON
First NHL season. Appeared in 20 games for Worcester, scoring 9-7 — 16.

THE FINESSE GAME
Mayers has great speed and is very strong on his skates. His legs are sometimes too fast for his brain. He actually had to learn to forecheck, and use his speed in a more intelligent manner instead of just buzzing around without purpose. By the playoffs he was an effective forechecker, using his angles and stick position to force players up the boards. He once broke his wrist so badly it required surgery from a full-tilt rush into the boards, which illustrates how fiercely Mayers charges.

Mayers doesn't have a great scoring touch. Most of his points will come from his effort and his skating. His hands are about average. He has good hockey sense.

THE PHYSICAL GAME
Mayers needs to step up just a bit to become a more agitating player. Once he does, he will become a very hard guy to play against. He finishes all of his checks.

THE INTANGIBLES
The best of Mayers is yet to come. He could win a job on the Blues' checking line, providing energy and speed.

PROJECTION
Mayers could provide 15 goals in a checking role.

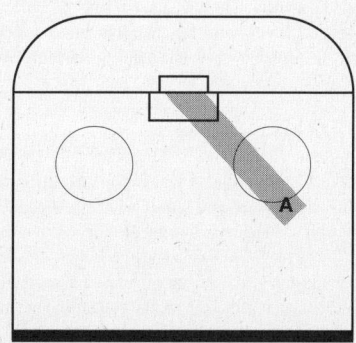

SCOTT PELLERIN

Yrs. of NHL service: 6
Born: Shediac, N.B.; Jan. 9, 1970
Position: right wing
Height: 5-11
Weight: 195
Uniform no.: 33
Shoots: left

Career statistics:

GP	G	A	TP	PIM
266	48	64	112	182

1995-96 statistics:

GP	G	A	TP	+/-	PIM	PP	SH	GW	GT	S	PCT
6	2	1	3	+1	0	0	0	0	0	9	2.2

1996-97 statistics:

GP	G	A	TP	+/-	PIM	PP	SH	GW	GT	S	PCT
54	8	10	18	+12	35	0	2	2	0	76	10.5

1997-98 statistics:

GP	G	A	TP	+/-	PIM	PP	SH	GW	GT	S	PCT
80	8	21	29	+14	62	1	1	0	0	96	8.3

1998-99 statistics:

GP	G	A	TP	+/-	PIM	PP	SH	GW	GT	S	PCT
80	20	21	41	+1	42	0	5	4	0	138	14.5

LAST SEASON

Led team and tied for NHL lead in shorthanded goals. Tied for third on team in game-winning goals. Matched career high in assists. Missed one game with concussion. Missed one game due to coach's decision.

THE FINESSE GAME

Pellerin was a Hobey Baker Award winner as the top U.S. collegiate player with the University of Maine in 1992, and shares the traits most often associated with those so honoured: quickness, intelligence and decent hand skills.

Pellerin works well with Craig Conroy, a player of similar style and temperament, on the Blues' third line, handling most of the first-unit penalty-killing responsibilities. Last season, Pellerin was frequently moved on to one of the top two lines, and did the job there as well as he could.

Pellerin is a heart-and-soul guy who gives you everything he has. Offensively, his biggest asset is his playmaking ability. He was a scorer at the college and minor-league levels and has a fairly good touch with the puck, though his shot isn't quick enough by NHL standards.

THE PHYSICAL GAME

Pellerin is small but stocky, and size is never an issue with him. He plays the same way all the time against opponents both large and small. He's feisty and won't be intimidated. He is a sturdy skater who is hard to knock off his feet. He can handle a lot of ice time. He usually ends up with the most hits in a game for the Blues, and since his line usually plays against the other team's stars, that is a significant stat.

THE INTANGIBLES

Pellerin gives an honest effort every night and was one of the Blues' most consistent forwards again last season.

PROJECTION

Pellerin sees prime checking time against other teams' top lines. He won't score much at this level — 20 goals is really huge — but he has a knack for scoring at the right time.

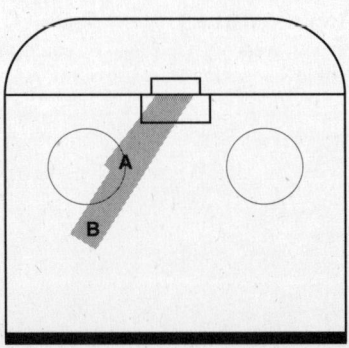

CHRIS PRONGER

Yrs. of NHL service: 6
Born: Dryden, Ont.; Oct. 10, 1974
Position: left defense
Height: 6-5
Weight: 220
Uniform no.: 44
Shoots: left

Career statistics:

GP	G	A	TP	PIM
429	50	137	186	628

1995-96 statistics:

GP	G	A	TP	+/-	PIM	PP	SH	GW	GT	S	PCT
78	7	18	25	-18	110	3	1	1	0	138	5.1

1996-97 statistics:

GP	G	A	TP	+/-	PIM	PP	SH	GW	GT	S	PCT
79	11	25	35	+15	143	4	0	0	0	147	7.5

1997-98 statistics:

GP	G	A	TP	+/-	PIM	PP	SH	GW	GT	S	PCT
81	9	27	36	+47	180	1	0	2	0	145	6.2

1998-99 statistics:

GP	G	A	TP	+/-	PIM	PP	SH	GW	GT	S	PCT
67	13	33	46	+3	113	8	0	0	0	172	7.6

LAST SEASON

Third on team in penalty minutes. Career highs in goals, assists and points. Missed 11 games with ankle injury. Missed four games due to suspension.

THE FINESSE GAME

From the day he was drafted, Pronger has been touted as a young Larry Robinson, and nothing he has done over the past few seasons has shattered that illusion. There are certainly similarities in their physique and style. Pronger is lanky, almost weedy, with a powerful skating stride for angling his man to the boards for a take-out. He blends his physical play with good offensive instincts and skills. His skating is so fluid and his strides so long and efficient that he looks almost lazy, but he is faster than he looks and covers a lot of ground.

Pronger also handles the puck well when skating and is always alert for passing opportunities. His vision shows in his work on the power play. He patrols the point smartly, using a low, tippable shot. Like many tall defensemen, he doesn't get his slap shot away quickly, but he compensates with a snap shot that he uses liberally. He has good enough hands for a big guy and the Blues occasionally use him up front on the power play.

Pronger not only jumps into the rush, he knows when to, which is an art. He'll back off if the opportunity is not there. Playing with Al MacInnis, one of the game's great offensive defensemen, has helped Pronger in this area. He makes unique plays that make him stand out, great breakout passes and clever feeds through the neutral zone. He is also wise enough to dump-and-chase rather than hold onto the puck and force a low-percentage pass. He focusses more on his defensive role, but there is a considerable upside to his offense.

Disciplined away from the puck and alert defensively, Pronger shows good anticipation — going where the puck is headed before it's shot there. He is very confident with the puck in his own end. His defensive reads are excellent for such a young player.

THE PHYSICAL GAME

Pronger finishes every check with enthusiasm and shows something of a nasty streak with his stick. He makes his stand between the blueline and the top of the circle, forcing the forward to react. His long reach helps to make that style effective. He also uses his stick and reach when killing penalties. He averages 25 to 32 minutes a game and doesn't mind it at all. He was a little more headstrong last season and took some bad penalties.

THE INTANGIBLES

Pronger is among the NHL's elite defensemen and will stay there.

PROJECTION

Pronger is a steady defenseman who scores 45 to 50 points a season.

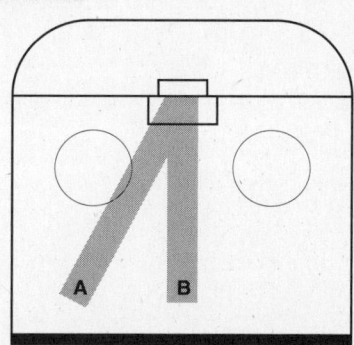

MARTY REASONER

Yrs. of NHL service: 0
Born: Rochester, NY; Feb. 26, 1977
Position: centre
Height: 6-1
Weight: 185
Uniform no.: 15
Shoots: left

Career statistics:

GP	G	A	TP	PIM
22	3	7	10	8

1998-99 statistics:

GP	G	A	TP	+/-	PIM	PP	SH	GW	GT	S	PCT
22	3	7	10	+2	8	1	0	0	0	33	9.1

LAST SEASON
Will be entering first full NHL season. Appeared in 44 games with Worcester (AHL), scoring 17-22-39.

THE FINESSE GAME
Reasoner started off with a bang last season, but when things started going poorly it affected everything — from his feet to his hands to his head.

Reasoner is a playmaker, and most effective when he attacks in straight lines. When he starts to zig-zag, he slows down and loses his speed as a weapon. He has such good hands and vision that he is able to bring the puck in with his deceptive speed and force the defenders to commit.

He has terrific hockey sense.

THE PHYSICAL GAME
Reasoner is average size and hasn't yet shown a knack for the physical part of the game. He can't afford to be a perimeter player. He could afford to work on his upper-body strength and his skating.

THE INTANGIBLES
Reasoner made the Blues at the start of last season after a great training camp, but tailed off and lost ice time. He lost confidence and never rebounded after he was sent down to the minors. It was a difficult season for him mentally. He should be better for the experience.

PROJECTION
Reasoner will get another long look in training camp. Most of his points will be assists.

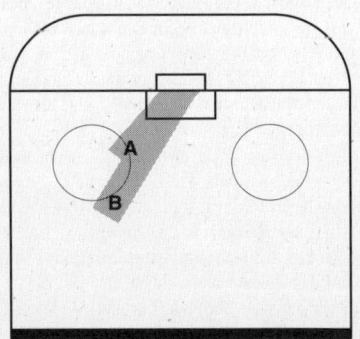

PASCAL RHEAUME

Yrs. of NHL service: 2
Born: Quebec, Que.; June 21, 1973
Position: centre/left wing
Height: 6-1
Weight: 200
Uniform no.: 25
Shoots: left

Career statistics:

GP	G	A	TP	PIM
110	16	27	43	59

1996-97 statistics:

GP	G	A	TP	+/-	PIM	PP	SH	GW	GT	S	PCT
2	1	0	1	+1	0	0	0	0	0	5	20.0

1997-98 statistics:

GP	G	A	TP	+/-	PIM	PP	SH	GW	GT	S	PCT
48	6	9	15	+4	35	1	0	0	0	45	13.3

1998-99 statistics:

GP	G	A	TP	+/-	PIM	PP	SH	GW	GT	S	PCT
60	9	18	27	+10	24	2	0	0	0	85	10.6

LAST SEASON

Career highs in goals, assists and points. Missed 10 games with concussion. Missed 12 games due to coach's decision.

THE FINESSE GAME

Rheaume is built like a power forward but last year he didn't play like one. Buried for years in the strong New Jersey organization, he showed signs of breaking out in his first season with St. Louis but did not continue to progress.

Rheaume is big and has some speed. He doesn't have great hand skills but he has a decent scoring touch. He was a good scorer in the minors.

In the NHL, Rheaume has yet to prove he can be a top six forward. He has a tendency to lay off some of the forecheck and try to be too fancy. He needs a new attitude.

THE PHYSICAL GAME

Rheaume had shoulder surgery prior to last season, which may have affected his play. He struggled because he didn't, or couldn't, play the kind of forceful game he needs to be successful.

THE INTANGIBLES

Rheaume has to decide what kind of player he is going to be. He doesn't have the skill level to be uninvolved and still contribute to his team.

PROJECTION

If the best Rheaume can do is 15 or so goals a season (his pro-rated sum), he will quickly be out of a job.

PIERRE TURGEON

Yrs. of NHL service: 12
Born: Rouyn, Que.; Aug. 28, 1969
Position: centre
Height: 6-1
Weight: 195
Uniform no.: 77
Shoots: left

Career statistics:

GP	G	A	TP	PIM
877	397	600	997	311

1995-96 statistics:

GP	G	A	TP	+/-	PIM	PP	SH	GW	GT	S	PCT
80	38	58	96	+19	44	17	1	6	0	297	12.8

1996-97 statistics:

GP	G	A	TP	+/-	PIM	PP	SH	GW	GT	S	PCT
78	26	59	85	+8	14	5	0	7	1	216	12.0

1997-98 statistics:

GP	G	A	TP	+/-	PIM	PP	SH	GW	GT	S	PCT
60	22	46	68	+13	24	6	0	4	0	140	15.7

1998-99 statistics:

GP	G	A	TP	+/-	PIM	PP	SH	GW	GT	S	PCT
67	31	34	65	+4	36	10	0	5	2	193	16.1

LAST SEASON

Led team in shooting percentage. Second on team in goals, points and game-winning goals. Third on team in assists and power-play goals. Missed 14 games with fractured hand.

THE FINESSE GAME

Turgeon's skills are amazing. He never seems to be looking at the puck yet he is always in perfect control of it. He has a style unlike just about anyone else in the NHL. He's not a fast skater, but he can deke a defender or make a sneaky-Pete surprise pass. He is tough to defend against, because if you aren't aware of where he is on the ice and don't deny him the pass, he can kill a team with several moves.

Turgeon can slow or speed up the tempo of a game. He lacks breakout speed, but because he is slippery and can change speeds so smoothly, he's deceptive. His control with the puck down low is remarkable. He protects the puck well with the body and has good anticipation, reads plays well and is patient with the puck.

Although best known for his playmaking, Turgeon has an excellent shot. He will curl out from behind the net with a wrist shot, shoot off the fly from the right wing (his preferred side of the ice) or stand off to the side of the net on a power play and reach for a redirection of a point shot. He doesn't have a bazooka shot, but he uses quick, accurate wrist and snap shots. He has to create odd-man rushes. This is when he is at his finest.

THE PHYSICAL GAME

Turgeon answered some questions that have dogged him throughout his career when he stepped up big-time in the playoffs and showed he wants to be winner, not just a player with pretty stats. He fought through checks and made the contact he usually avoids.

THE INTANGIBLES

Turgeon didn't miss Brett Hull the way we thought he would. Instead, he meshed beautifully with Pavol Demitra. The Blues were impressed enough to give him a two-year, $10-million contract extension.

PROJECTION

Turgeon is a point-a-game player.

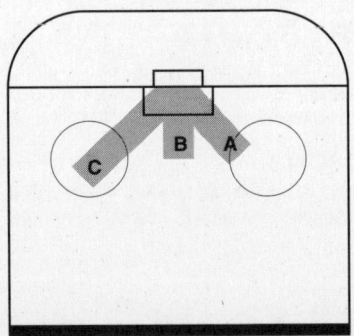

SCOTT YOUNG

Yrs. of NHL service: 10
Born: Clinton, Mass.; Oct. 1, 1967
Position: right wing
Height: 6-0
Weight: 190
Uniform no.: 48
Shoots: right

Career statistics:

GP	G	A	TP	PIM
747	210	287	497	278

1995-96 statistics:

GP	G	A	TP	+/-	PIM	PP	SH	GW	GT	S	PCT
81	21	39	60	+2	50	7	0	5	0	229	9.2

1996-97 statistics:

GP	G	A	TP	+/-	PIM	PP	SH	GW	GT	S	PCT
72	18	19	37	-5	14	7	0	0	0	164	11.0

1997-98 statistics:

GP	G	A	TP	+/-	PIM	PP	SH	GW	GT	S	PCT
73	13	20	33	-13	22	4	2	1	0	187	7.0

1998-99 statistics:

GP	G	A	TP	+/-	PIM	PP	SH	GW	GT	S	PCT
75	24	28	52	+8	27	8	0	4	0	205	11.7

LAST SEASON

Third on team in goals and shots. Tied for third on team in game-winning goals. Missed one game with back injury. Missed four games due to personal reasons. Missed two games due to coach's decision.

THE FINESSE GAME

Young is a hockey machine. He has a very heavy shot that surprises a lot of goalies, and he loves to fire it off the wing. He can also one-time the puck low on the face-off, or he'll battle for pucks and tips in front of the net. He's keen to score and always goes to the net with his stick down, ready for the puck, though he is not a great finisher.

With all of that in mind, his defensive awareness is even more impressive, because Young is basically a checking winger. He reads plays in all zones equally well and has good anticipation. He played defense in college, so he is well-schooled.

Young is a fast skater, which, combined with his reads, makes him a sound forechecker. He will often outrace defensemen to get pucks and avoid icings, and his speed allows him to recover when he gets overzealous in the attacking zone.

THE PHYSICAL GAME

Young's lone drawback is that he is not a physical player. He will do what he has to do in battles along the boards in the defensive zone, but he's more of a defensive force with his quickness and hand skills. He's not a pure grinder, but will bump and get in the way.

THE INTANGIBLES

One of the best free agent signings of 1998, Young gave the Blues strong support on a second line. He finished the season well despite the personal burden of losing his father to cancer. He is a character person as well as an ultrareliable performer. Players with great wheels like Young tend to last a long time, so expect him to display his veteran ability for many more seasons. Just don't expect him to score 50 goals.

PROJECTION

Young will get quality ice time in St. Louis, lots of power-play chances, and 50 points and 20 goals is again likely.

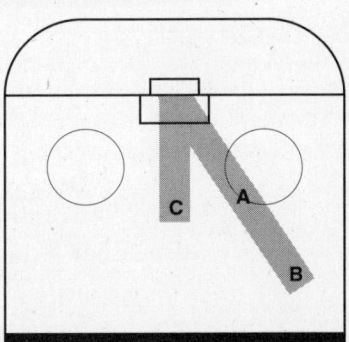

TAMPA BAY LIGHTNING

Players' Statistics 1998-99

POS	NO.	PLAYER	GP	G	A	PTS	+/-	PIM	PP	SH	GW	GT	S	PCT
C	16	DARCY TUCKER	82	21	22	43	-34	176	8	2	3		178	11.8
C	77	CHRIS GRATTON	78	8	26	34	-28	143	1		1	1	181	4.4
R	44	STEPHANE RICHER	64	12	21	33	-10	22	3	2	1		139	8.6
C	8	*VINCENT LECAVALIER	82	13	15	28	-19	23	2		2	1	125	10.4
D	23	PETR SVOBODA	59	5	18	23	1	81	1	1	1		83	6.0
D	13	*PAVEL KUBINA	68	9	12	21	-33	80	3	1	1	1	119	7.6
L	27	COLIN FORBES	80	12	8	20	-5	61		1	4		117	10.3
L	7	ROB ZAMUNER	58	8	11	19	-15	24	1	1	2		89	9.0
D	4	CORY CROSS	67	2	16	18	-25	92					96	2.1
R	21	ALEXANDRE DAIGLE	63	9	8	17	-13	4	4		1	2	82	11.0
D	5	JASSEN CULLIMORE	78	5	12	17	-22	81	1	1	1		73	6.8
C	9	MICHAEL NYLANDER	33	4	10	14	-9	8	1				33	12.1
C	26	MIKE SILLINGER	79	8	5	13	-29	36	2				92	8.7
D	3	*SERGEY GUSEV	36	1	7	8	-3	16			1		46	2.2
D	49	DAVID WILKIE	46	1	7	8	-19	69					35	2.9
C	14	ROBERT PETROVICKY	28	3	4	7	-8	6					32	9.4
D	2	MIKE MCBAIN	37		6	6	-11	14					22	
D	28	KJELL SAMUELSSON	46	1	4	5	-6	38					22	4.5
C	11	STEVE KELLY	34	1	3	4	-15	27			1		15	6.7
G	32	COREY SCHWAB	40		4	4	0	4						
L	27	BRENT PETERSON	20	2	1	3	-2						16	12.5
D	23	MICHAL SYKORA	10	1	2	3	-7				1		24	4.2
D	55	DREW BANNISTER	21	1	2	3	-4	24					29	3.4
C	64	JASON BONSIGNORE	23		3	3	-4	8					12	
D	22	*PAUL MARA	1	1	1	2	-3		1				1	100.0
D	46	ANDREI SKOPINTSEV	19	1	1	2	1	10					17	5.9
D	6	*KAREL BETIK	3		2	2	-3	2					2	
D	3	*SAMI HELENIUS	8	1		1	-5	23		1			4	25.0
C	20	COREY SPRING	8		1	1	0	2					6	
L	15	PAUL YSEBAERT	10		1	1	-5	2					10	
G	93	DAREN PUPPA	13		1	1	0							
G	1	*ZAC BIERK	1				0							
C	43	*XAVIER DELISLE	2				0						1	
C	12	JOHN CULLEN	4				-2	2					3	
G	35	*DEREK WILKINSON	5				0							
D	71	*MARIO LAROCQUE	5				-4	16					3	
G	31	KEVIN HODSON	9				0							

GP = games played; G = goals; A = assists; PTS = points; +/- = goals-for minus goals-against while player is on ice; PIM = penalties in minutes; PP = power-play goals; SH = shorthanded goals; GW = game-winning goals; GT = game-tying goals; S = no. of shots; PCT = percentage of goals to shots; * = rookie

DAN CLOUTIER

Yrs. of NHL service: 1
Born: Mont-Laurier, Que.; Apr. 22, 1976
Position: goaltender
Height: 6-1
Weight: 182
Uniform no.: 39
Catches: left

Career statistics:

GP	MIN	GA	SO	GAA	A	PIM
34	1648	72	0	2.62	0	21

1997-98 statistics:

GP	MIN	GAA	W	L	T	SO	GA	S	SAPCT	PIM
12	551	2.50	4	5	1	0	23	248	.907	19

1998-99 statistics:

GP	MIN	GAA	W	L	T	SO	GA	S	SAPCT	PIM
22	1097	2.68	6	8	3	0	49	570	.914	2

LAST SEASON

Acquired from N.Y. Rangers with Niklas Sundstrom and Rangers' first-round draft pick in 2000 for Tampa Bay's first-round draft pick in 1999. First NHL season.

THE PHYSICAL GAME

Cloutier is an athletic, stand-up goalie — surprising in an era of so many Patrick Roy butterfly clones. He doesn't have the reflexes to excel with a less technical style.

Cloutier follows the play well and squares his body to the shooter. He will learn to play his angles better with more NHL experience, but he has good size to take away a lot of the net from the shooter.

His skills are still a little raw. He doesn't control his rebounds well off his pads and his stickhandling could use work. But he is an eager student who would benefit from a veteran backup goalie and a goalie coach.

THE MENTAL GAME

Cloutier is very combative (he had a memorable goalie fight with Tommy Salo two seasons ago), and he is determined to excel at the NHL level.

THE INTANGIBLES

This will be Cloutier's first stint as a number one, and he's going to do it backing up a team that is dreadful defensively. It's going to be a very long season.

PROJECTION

Cloutier will have to be all-world to get 20 wins with this bunch.

CORY CROSS

Yrs. of NHL service: 5
Born: Lloydminster, Alta.; Jan. 3, 1971
Position: left defense
Height: 6-5
Weight: 212
Uniform no.: 4
Shoots: left

Career statistics:

GP	G	A	TP	PIM
336	12	46	58	377

1995-96 statistics:

GP	G	A	TP	+/-	PIM	PP	SH	GW	GT	S	PCT
75	2	14	16	+4	66	0	0	0	0	57	3.5

1996-97 statistics:

GP	G	A	TP	+/-	PIM	PP	SH	GW	GT	S	PCT
72	4	5	9	+6	95	0	0	2	0	75	5.3

1997-98 statistics:

GP	G	A	TP	+/-	PIM	PP	SH	GW	GT	S	PCT
74	3	6	9	-24	77	0	1	0	0	72	4.2

1998-99 statistics:

GP	G	A	TP	+/-	PIM	PP	SH	GW	GT	S	PCT
67	2	16	18	-25	92	0	0	0	0	96	2.1

LAST SEASON

Third on team in penalty minutes. Career high in assists and points. Missed 12 games with hip pointer. Missed two games with ankly injury.

THE FINESSE GAME

Cross's most impressive asset is his intelligence. He is smart enough to recognize the mistakes he makes and learn from them. He is also highly skilled: a fine skater who can either lug the puck out of his zone or start things with a pass and then jump up into the play. He has a good shot and will make wise pinches to keep the puck in the zone.

Cross was the first player taken in the 1992 supplemental draft and he shot his way up the Lightning depth chart. He may be good enough with the puck to merit more power-play time on the point on the second unit, but he is not a real offensive defenseman. Any power-play time he gets in Tampa usually occurs when the coach runs out of other bodies.

THE PHYSICAL GAME

Cross did not play in a physical environment at the college level, and he's learned that it's okay to hit people hard. He has taken a real shine to NHL play, showing a latent aggressive streak. He is a solid skater with good size and is still discovering how truly big and powerful he is. He gets his stick up at times. He could develop even more upper-body strength.

THE INTANGIBLES

Cross is a top four defenseman largely because he plays on a team that is not well-stocked at the position. He had a very inconsistent year, but injuries may have been a contributing factor.

PROJECTION

Cross provided a little more offense last season, but don't expect more than 20 points out of him.

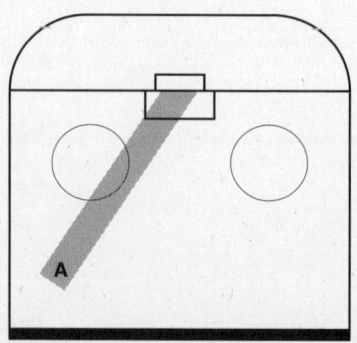

ALEXANDRE DAIGLE

Yrs. of NHL service: 6
Born: Laval, Que.; Feb. 7, 1975
Position: centre
Height: 6-0
Weight: 185
Uniform no.: 21
Shoots: left

Career statistics:

GP	G	A	TP	PIM
401	92	123	215	129

1995-96 statistics:

GP	G	A	TP	+/-	PIM	PP	SH	GW	GT	S	PCT
50	5	12	17	-30	24	1	0	0	0	77	6.5

1996-97 statistics:

GP	G	A	TP	+/-	PIM	PP	SH	GW	GT	S	PCT
82	26	25	51	-33	33	4	0	5	2	203	12.8

1997-98 statistics:

GP	G	A	TP	+/-	PIM	PP	SH	GW	GT	S	PCT
75	16	26	42	-8	14	8	0	5	1	146	11.0

1998-99 statistics:

GP	G	A	TP	+/-	PIM	PP	SH	GW	GT	S	PCT
63	9	8	17	-13	4	4	0	1	2	82	11.0

LAST SEASON

Acquired from Edmonton for Alex Selivanov, Jan. 29, 1999. Missed two games with wrist injury. Missed four games with other injuries. Missed 12 games due to coach's decision.

THE FINESSE GAME

Daigle has NHL speed and acceleration but he doesn't have an NHL body, NHL stick skills or an NHL shot. He was such a brilliant player in certain areas at the junior level that he never had to work at many parts of his game, and he still seems unaware that he can't perform the same tricks in the big leagues.

He has fine, soft hands, but has a tough time controlling the puck in traffic. His skating — his chief asset — is compromised because he gets slower when he's carrying the puck.

Daigle demonstrates a great enthusiasm for the game but is impatient and stubborn. He has problems with teams that play a neutral-zone trap. He has straight-on speed, but when the ice is closed off he looks bewildered because he is not seeking the best options.

A strong forechecker, Daigle is effective as a penalty killer — not because of his defensive awareness but because he wants the puck so desperately.

THE PHYSICAL GAME

Daigle is feisty and will get involved in the offensive zone; he has learned to avoid taking dumb penalties. He could use his body better without getting creamed, but since he's not very big or strong he needs to stay out of the corners.

THE INTANGIBLES

Daigle doesn't seem to have all the pieces to become an impact player in the NHL. He will get ice time in Tampa Bay because of his speed, and by default.

PROJECTION

Expectations remain high for Daigle. He will not fulfil them. He is, at best, a second-line forward whose dream season would be 25 goals.

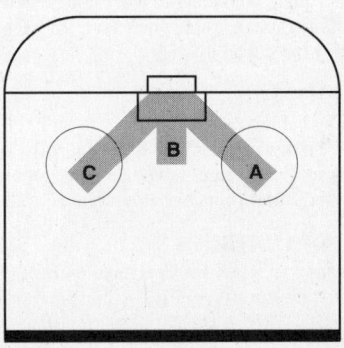

COLIN FORBES

Yrs. of NHL service: 2
Born: New Westminster, B.C.; Feb. 16, 1976
Position: left wing
Height: 6-3
Weight: 205
Uniform no.: 27
Shoots: left

Career statistics:

GP	G	A	TP	PIM
146	25	15	40	120

1996-97 statistics:

GP	G	A	TP	+/-	PIM	PP	SH	GW	GT	S	PCT
3	1	0	1	0	0	0	0	0	0	3	33.3

1997-98 statistics:

GP	G	A	TP	+/-	PIM	PP	SH	GW	GT	S	PCT
63	12	7	19	+2	59	2	0	2	0	93	12.9

1998-99 statistics:

GP	G	A	TP	+/-	PIM	PP	SH	GW	GT	S	PCT
80	12	8	20	-5	61	0	1	4	0	117	10.3

PROJECTION

Don't look for a big bump in Forbes's production. If he can score 20 goals that would be considered positive progress.

LAST SEASON

Acquired from Philadelphia with a conditional draft pick for Sandy McCarthy and Mikael Andersson, Mar. 20, 1999. Second NHL season. Led team in game-winning goals. Second on team in plus-minus. Third on team in shooting percentage. Tied for third on team in goals.

THE FINESSE GAME

Forbes has the build and the physical tools to develop along the lines of a power forward, but he hasn't yet shown the drive that players like John LeClair (his former Flyer teammate) have. Forbes is still young (23) and power forwards take time to develop, but he had better start lighting the fire soon.

There's no guarantee that Forbes will become a LeClair, or a Brendan Shanahan, but he has some nice tools and is off to a pretty good start. He has a good shot and likes to use it. He is a finisher first. His assists will come from linemates driving to the net for rebounds because he wants to fire it.

Forbes saw some power-play time. He could get even more this year. He has a fine one-timer. His skating is adequate but he could use some quickness. He scored four game-winning goals for a team that didn't win many more than that.

THE PHYSICAL GAME

Forbes was able to run people over in junior. He can't do that at this level so he must learn to become stronger and more aggressive. He plays with a lot of energy and enthusiasm, but only when he feels like it.

THE INTANGIBLES

Forbes has a very laid-back personality. He's got to hit the "on" button every night to become an impact player.

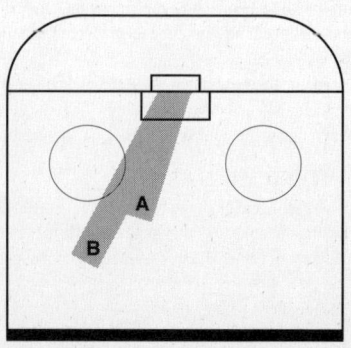

CHRIS GRATTON

Yrs. of NHL service: 6
Born: Brantford, Ont.; July 5, 1975
Position: centre
Height: 6-4
Weight: 218
Uniform no.: 77
Shoots: left

Career statistics:

GP	G	A	TP	PIM
454	97	168	265	820

1995-96 statistics:

GP	G	A	TP	+/-	PIM	PP	SH	GW	GT	S	PCT
82	17	21	38	-13	105	7	0	3	0	183	9.3

1996-97 statistics:

GP	G	A	TP	+/-	PIM	PP	SH	GW	GT	S	PCT
82	30	32	62	-28	201	9	0	4	0	230	13.0

1997-98 statistics:

GP	G	A	TP	+/-	PIM	PP	SH	GW	GT	S	PCT
82	22	40	62	+11	159	5	0	2	0	182	12.1

1998-99 statistics:

GP	G	A	TP	+/-	PIM	PP	SH	GW	GT	S	PCT
78	8	26	34	-28	143	1	0	1	1	181	4.4

LAST SEASON

Acquired from Philadelphia with Mike Sillinger for Mikael Renberg and Daymond Langkow, Dec. 12, 1998. Led team in assists and shots. Second on team in points and penalty minutes. Missed three games due to suspension.

THE FINESSE GAME

Gratton was supposed to be a power centre, and he is happier playing there than when he is on the wing, but he is clearly overmatched in the middle. One of the major reasons is his lack of foot speed, which really hurts him despite a lot of coaching in this area.

Gratton's game is meat and potatoes. He's a grinder and needs to work hard every shift, every night, to make an impact. He has a hard shot, which he needs to use more. He gets his goals from digging around the net and there's some Cam Neely in him, but he lacks the long, strong stride Neely uses in traffic. He has good hand-eye coordination and can pick passes out of midair for a shot.

Gratton is an unselfish playmaker. He's not the prettiest of passers, but he has some poise with the puck and he knows when to pass and when to shoot. He has shown an ability to win face-offs, and works diligently in his own end.

THE PHYSICAL GAME

Gratton is a hard-working sort who doesn't shy from contact, but he has to initiate more. If his skating improves he will be able to establish a more physical presence. He doesn't generate enough speed from leg drive to be much of a checker. He won't be an impact player in the NHL until he does.

THE INTANGIBLES

Gratton was reacquired by Tampa Bay and seems much more relaxed in a Lightning uniform. (He scored seven of his eight goals for Tampa after the trade). He will start the season as a number one centre but is likely to be overtaken by Vincent Lecavalier.

PROJECTION

Gratton scored 30 goals in 1996-97, but it's hard to imagine him repeating that. He is likely to score in the 20-goal range.

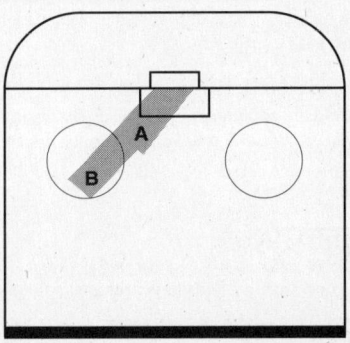

SERGEY GUSEV

Yrs. of NHL service: 1
Born: Nizhny Tagil, Russia; July 31, 1975
Position: left defense
Height: 6-1
Weight: 195
Uniform no.: 3
Shoots: left

Career statistics:

GP	G	A	TP	PIM
36	1	7	8	16

1997-98 statistics:

GP	G	A	TP	+/-	PIM	PP	SH	GW	GT	S	PCT
9	0	0	0	-5	2	0	0	0	0	5	0.0

1998-99 statistics:

GP	G	A	TP	+/-	PIM	PP	SH	GW	GT	S	PCT
36	1	7	8	-3	16	0	0	1	0	46	2.2

LAST SEASON

Acquired from Dallas for Benoit Hogue and a 2001 conditional draft pick, Mar. 21, 1999. First NHL season. Appeared in 12 games with Michigan (IHL), scoring 0-6 — 6. Missed 33 games due to coach's decision.

THE FINESSE GAME

Gusev has a good offensive upside with considerable skills — all NHL quality. He is an excellent skater, with speed, agility and mobility. He handles the puck well and has a good shot. He has fine offensive instincts, but frequently looks to get involved in the attack at the wrong times, something he needs to curb. He can work on the power-play point on the first unit.

Gusev has to improve in his defensive positioning and awareness; he is still learning what it takes to be a well-rounded defenseman. He could develop along Darryl Sydor lines.

Gusev was buried in the deep Dallas system, but will become a top four defenseman and log a lot of ice time with the Lightning. He finished up the season well after the trade, a positive sign.

THE PHYSICAL GAME

Gusev is not a big banger, but he will have to learn to use his body more consistently to get into the lineup. He still needs to grow and gain some confidence. He can play with a little edge.

THE INTANGIBLES

Gusev had the advantage of learning in a strong defensive system. Now he will have to apply his skills to a bad team. His presence upgrades Tampa Bay's defense.

PROJECTION

In his first shot at a full-time role, Gusev had the goods to become a 25-point scorer as a solid two-way defenseman.

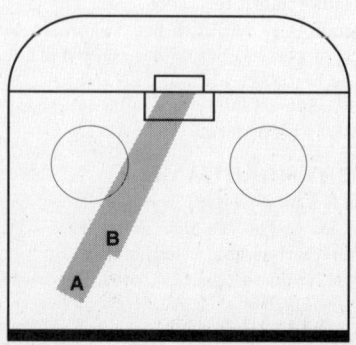

PAVEL KUBINA

Yrs. of NHL service: 1
Born: Vsetin, Czech.; Sept. 10, 1979
Position: right defense
Height: 6-2
Weight: 189
Uniform no.: 13
Shoots: right

Career statistics:

GP	G	A	TP	PIM
78	10	14	24	102

1997-98 statistics:

GP	G	A	TP	+/-	PIM	PP	SH	GW	GT	S	PCT
10	1	2	3	-1	22	0	0	0	0	8	12.5

1998-99 statistics:

GP	G	A	TP	+/-	PIM	PP	SH	GW	GT	S	PCT
68	9	12	21	-33	80	3	1	1	1	119	7.6

LAST SEASON

First NHL season. Tied for second on team in power-play goals. Appeared in six games for Cleveland (IHL), scoring 2-2 — 4. Missed three games with shoulder injury. Missed two games with knee injury. Missed two games with flu.

THE FINESSE GAME

One of the most impressive rookie defensemen in 1998-99, Kubina didn't atract much attention because he played on such an awful team. And he played a lot for said team. He was first among rookies in average ice time (over 22 minutes), logging more action than many veteran defensemen.

Kubina is a good skater for his size. He generates power from his legs for his checks.

His offensive instincts are also good. He passes well and has a decent shot from the point. None of his skills are elite, but coupled with his size they make a solid package.

THE PHYSICAL GAME

Kubina has very good size and he uses it well. He was third in hits among NHL rookies (156). He has a bit of an edge to him.

THE INTANGIBLES

Kubina is going to get a heavy workload again this season. He works well paired with fellow Czech Petr Svoboda, but needs to pay more attention to his conditioning. The Lightning sent him for a brief stint in the minors for being out of shape.

PROJECTION

Kubina has real offensive upside and should lead the Lightning defensemen in scoring with 30 to 35 points.

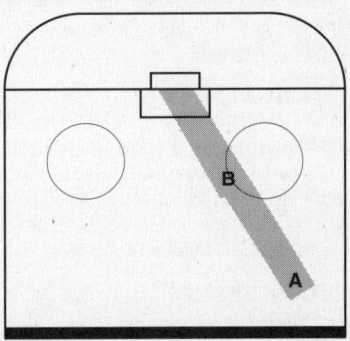

VINCENT LECAVALIER

Yrs. of NHL service: 1
Born: Ile Bizard, Quebec; Apr. 21, 1980
Position: centre
Height: 6-4
Weight: 180
Uniform no.: 8
Shoots: left

Career statistics:

GP	G	A	TP	PIM
82	13	15	28	23

1998-99 statistics:

GP	G	A	TP	+/-	PIM	PP	SH	GW	GT	S	PCT
82	13	15	28	-19	23	2	0	2	1	125	10.4

LAST SEASON

First NHL season. Second on team and eighth among NHL rookies in goals. Fifth among NHL rookies in points. Second on team in shooting percentage. Tied for third on team in game-winning goals. One of two Lightning players to appear in all 82 games.

THE FINESSE GAME

Names like Wayne Gretkzy and Mario Lemieux have been thrown around when people try to dream up comparisons for Lecavalier. Dream on. Although Lecavalier has a bright future, thinking of him in terms of 100-point seasons is way premature.

Things won't happen that quickly for Lecavalier, who was (wisely) brought along carefully by the Lightning in his first season. But he has given scouts few reasons to think he will not become a major point producer at the NHL level. More playmaker than goal scorer, he is a shifty skater who masks his moves. He has good hockey sense and excellent vision, and like the two great centres with whom he has been compared, he will try a wildly creative play that other players wouldn't even dream of.

Lecavalier will need to focus on his defensive play, but he has a good foundation for that already and should be an apt pupil. His speed is major league. He can burst to the outside with the puck and beat a defenseman one-on-one — though he may be surprised by the strength and mobility of NHL defensemen the first few times he tries it.

THE PHYSICAL GAME

Lecavalier is a tall, skinny kid who will have to work the weight room in order to be ready to do battle against the league's heavyweights. He has a nasty streak in him and won't be deterred when he is tested in his first time around the league. He will be just as quick to answer with a whack of the stick.

THE INTANGIBLES

Lecavalier started the season on the fourth line and was a second-line centre by the end of the year. He will evolve into the number one centre, if not this season then next. He could blossom in his sophomore season as did Joe Thornton, who was brought along in a similar fashion by Boston. The main question concerning Lecavalier is whether he will grow into a dominating player like Lemieux, or be an underachieving but gifted centre like Pierre Turgeon?

PROJECTION

Lecavalier's point production was just right for his ice time and the general lack of talent he had surrounding him. Things will probably not improve much in Tampa, though playing with a smart linemate like newcomer Niklas Sundstrom will make Lecavalier a better all-around player. Expect an improvement into the 35-point range.

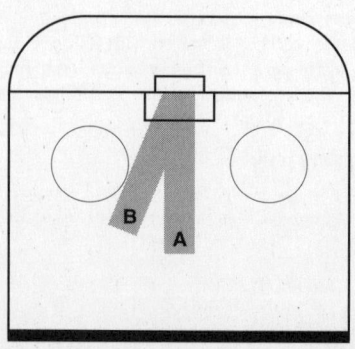

PAUL MARA

Yrs. of NHL service: 0
Born: Ridgewood, NJ; Sept. 7, 1979
Position: D
Height: 6-4
Weight: 202
Uniform no.: 22
Shoots: left

Career statistics:

GP	G	A	TP	PIM
1	1	1	2	0

1998-99 statistics:

GP	G	A	TP	+/-	PIM	PP	SH	GW	GT	S	PCT
1	1	1	2	-3	0	1	0	0	0	1	100.0

LAST SEASON
Will be entering first NHL season. Appeared in 52 games with Plymouth (OHL), scoring 13-41 — 54.

THE FINESSE GAME
Mara is primarily an offensive defenseman. His point shot is a weapon not because of its velocity — he is no Al MacInnis — but because Mara gets it away quickly and keeps it low and on net. He creates the chances for tip-ins and scrambles off his rebounds.

Mara is very mobile for his size. His skating is quite smooth and powerful. He has good vision and is an excellent passer. He is also quick to move the puck out of his zone and will jump up and join the rush.

He is fairly advanced defensively for a young player. He possesses good hockey intelligence.

THE PHYSICAL GAME
Mara makes take-outs, but he is not a punishing hitter. He is tall but lean, and needs to fill out more because he will need more strength to compete in the trenches.

THE INTANGIBLES
Mara could probably use a season in the minors, but if he has a solid camp he could move right into the Lightning lineup.

PROJECTION
Mara has a chance to score 20 points if he lands a job. He will be given every chance to do so.

MICHAEL NYLANDER

Yrs. of NHL service: 5
Born: Stockholm, Sweden; Oct. 3, 1972
Position: centre
Height: 5-11
Weight: 190
Uniform no.: 9
Shoots: left

Career statistics:
GP	G	A	TP	PIM
309	58	136	194	120

1995-96 statistics:
GP	G	A	TP	+/-	PIM	PP	SH	GW	GT	S	PCT
73	17	38	55	0	20	4	0	6	0	163	10.4

1996-97 statistics:
Did not play in NHL

1997-98 statistics:
GP	G	A	TP	+/-	PIM	PP	SH	GW	GT	S	PCT
65	13	23	36	+10	24	0	0	2	0	117	11.1

1998-99 statistics:
GP	G	A	TP	+/-	PIM	PP	SH	GW	GT	S	PCT
33	4	10	14	-9	8	1	0	0	0	33	12.1

LAST SEASON

Acquired from Calgary for Andrei Nazarov, Jan. 19, 1999. Missed 27 games with knee injury. Missed eight games due to personal reasons. Missed five games with concussion.

THE FINESSE GAME

Nylander's production was at odds with his considerable skill. To be fair, he had a tough year physically (injuries) and emotionally (the death of his father). But to be honest, he has never accomplished in the NHL what his skills dictate he should.

Nylander can do things with the puck that are magical. He knows all about time and space. If anything, he is guilty of hanging onto the puck too long and passing up quality shots, as he tries to force a pass to a teammate who is in a worse scoring position than Nylander.

An open-ice player, Nylander is an excellent skater and composed with the puck. He's strictly a one-way forward.

THE PHYSICAL GAME

Nylander is on the small side and plays even smaller. He uses his body to protect the puck but he won't fight hard for possession.

THE INTANGIBLES

Nylander has a chance to play with Vincent Lecavalier and get a lot of ice time if he returns to the NHL, but he was considering playing in Sweden.

PROJECTION

Too quirky a player to predict, Nylander is best avoided by teams and pool players.

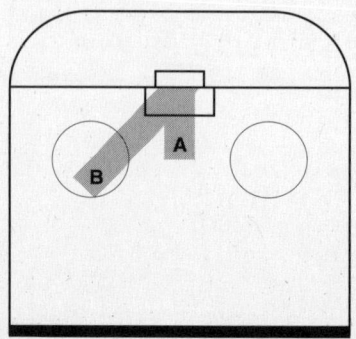

STEPHANE RICHER

Yrs. of NHL service: 14
Born: Ripon, Que.; June 7, 1966
Position: right wing
Height: 6-2
Weight: 215
Uniform no.: 44
Shoots: right

Career statistics:

GP	G	A	TP	PIM
930	392	362	754	582

1995-96 statistics:

GP	G	A	TP	+/-	PIM	PP	SH	GW	GT	S	PCT
73	20	12	32	-8	30	3	4	3	0	192	10.4

1996-97 statistics:

GP	G	A	TP	+/-	PIM	PP	SH	GW	GT	S	PCT
63	22	24	46	0	32	2	0	2	1	126	17.5

1997-98 statistics:

GP	G	A	TP	+/-	PIM	PP	SH	GW	GT	S	PCT
40	14	15	29	-6	41	5	0	2	0	95	14.7

1998-99 statistics:

GP	G	A	TP	+/-	PIM	PP	SH	GW	GT	S	PCT
64	12	21	33	-10	22	3	2	1	0	139	8.5

LAST SEASON

Tied for team lead in shorthanded goals. Tied for second on team in power-play goals. Third on team in assists, points and shots. Tied for third on team in goals with career low. Missed 17 games with ankle injury. Missed one game with shoulder injury.

THE FINESSE GAME

Richer gets great drive from his legs. He has powerful acceleration and true rink-length speed. He can intimidate with his rush, opening up the ice for himself and his linemates. He can also be crafty, slipping in and out of the open ice. He has good vision offensively and keen hockey sense. He possesses a goal scorer's slap shot, a wicked blur that he fires from the tops of the circles. However, he is still bothered by the aftermath of his 1998 surgery to repair an ankle problem.

Unfortunately, Richer is not the dynamic force he once was, despite his size, speed and shot. The mental toughness that once marked him as a game breaker is absent.

He has become a fine penalty killer, but that should enhance his value as a hockey player and not be the sum total of it. Because Richer is so strong on his stick and has a long reach, he can strip an opponent of the puck when his body isn't even close, and the puck carrier is always surprised.

THE PHYSICAL GAME

Richer is much better in open ice than in traffic. Although he has the size, strength and balance for trench warfare, he doesn't always show the inclination, and he can be scared off. He will go to the net with the puck, though, and has a wonderful long reach that allows him to be checked and still whip off a strong shot on net. When he's determined, it is just about impossible to peel him off the puck. He is slow to rile and seldom takes bad penalties.

THE INTANGIBLES

Richer was publicly blasted by former coach Jacques Demers. He claims he wants to be a leader but doesn't act like one. He'll get a second chance, maybe his last, under new coach Steve Ludzik.

PROJECTION

Richer's confidence and ability appear to be at an all-time low. He is a longshot to show 20 goals again.

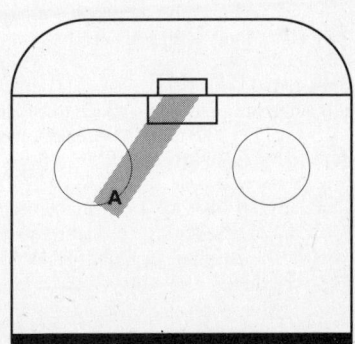

MIKE SILLINGER

Yrs. of NHL service: 7
Born: Regina, Sask.; June 29, 1971
Position: centre
Height: 5-10
Weight: 200
Uniform no.: 26
Shoots: right

Career statistics:
GP	G	A	TP	PIM
450	76	119	195	183

1995-96 statistics:
GP	G	A	TP	+/-	PIM	PP	SH	GW	GT	S	PCT
74	14	24	38	-18	38	7	1	2	0	159	8.8

1996-97 statistics:
GP	G	A	TP	+/-	PIM	PP	SH	GW	GT	S	PCT
78	17	20	37	-3	25	3	3	2	0	112	15.2

1997-98 statistics:
GP	G	A	TP	+/-	PIM	PP	SH	GW	GT	S	PCT
75	21	20	41	-11	50	2	4	1	0	96	21.9

1998-99 statistics:
GP	G	A	TP	+/-	PIM	PP	SH	GW	GT	S	PCT
79	8	5	13	-29	36	0	2	0	0	92	8.7

LAST SEASON
Acquired from Philadelphia with Chris Gratton for Mikael Renberg and Daymond Langkow, Dec. 12, 1998. Tied for team lead in shorthanded goals. Missed one game with sprained left knee. Missed two games due to coach's decision.

THE FINESSE GAME
One of the drawbacks to this veteran's career is his size, but Sillinger is not without his assets. He is a smart player with a knack for positioning himself in the attacking zone. He has a good shot with a quick release.

Sillinger is a good skater with speed and balance. His one-step acceleration is good. He plays well in traffic, using his sturdy form to protect the puck, and he has sharp hand-eye coordination. He is a smart penalty killer and a shorthanded threat, not to mention the best face-off man on the Lightning.

Sillinger kicked around a number of organizations (Detroit, Anaheim, Vancouver, Philadelphia) and has always had a hard time finding his niche.

THE PHYSICAL GAME
Sillinger is small but burly. He is tough to budge from in front of the net because of his low centre of gravity. He is not feisty or aggressive.

THE INTANGIBLES
With Rob Zamuner's departure, Sillinger will be given more of the checking line and penalty-killing duties. He is a grinder, a role player and a leader by example.

PROJECTION
Sillinger can score 15 goals in a largely defensive role.

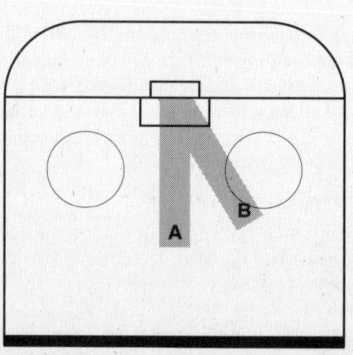

NIKLAS SUNDSTROM

Yrs. of NHL service: 4
Born: Ornskoldsvik, Sweden; June 6, 1975
Position: left wing
Height: 6-0
Weight: 185
Uniform no.: 24
Shoots: left

Career statistics:

GP	G	A	TP	PIM
315	65	98	163	78

1995-96 statistics:

GP	G	A	TP	+/-	PIM	PP	SH	GW	GT	S	PCT
82	9	12	21	+2	14	1	1	2	0	90	10.0

1996-97 statistics:

GP	G	A	TP	+/-	PIM	PP	SH	GW	GT	S	PCT
82	24	28	52	+23	20	5	1	4	0	132	18.2

1997-98 statistics:

GP	G	A	TP	+/-	PIM	PP	SH	GW	GT	S	PCT
70	19	28	47	0	24	4	0	1	0	115	16.5

1998-99 statistics:

GP	G	A	TP	+/-	PIM	PP	SH	GW	GT	S	PCT
81	13	30	43	-2	20	1	2	3	0	89	14.6

LAST SEASON

Acquired from N.Y. Rangers with Dan Cloutier and Rangers' first-round draft pick in 2000 for Tampa Bay's first-round draft pick in 1999. Tied for team lead in shorthanded goals. Career high in assists. Missed one game with flu.

THE FINESSE GAME

Playing as the right wing/safety valve for Wayne Gretzky last season, Sundstrom was one of the few Rangers savvy enough to play successfully off Gretzky and convert the exceptional opportunities Gretzky creates for any teammate. Each player helped provide a vital component for the other. Gretzky helped flesh out Sundstrom's reticent offensive game while Sundstrom covered Gretzky's back whenever possible. Given that the Lightning's prized prospect, Vincent Lecavalier, has been frequently compared to Gretzky in playing style, this seems like a likely duo in Tampa's future.

Keep in mind, however, that Sundstrom is not a true finisher. He will simply make the best of the opportunities he gets.

A deceptively fast skater with good balance and a strong stride, Sundstrom plays a smart game and does a lot of subtle things well.

A puck magnet, he applies his skills to the defensive game. He reads plays very well, is aware defensively and always makes the safe decision. And when he forechecks, especially when killing penalties, he almost always comes up with the puck in a one-on-one battle.

THE PHYSICAL GAME

Sundstrom will not get much bigger and has to get stronger, but he is persistent and consistently physical. One of Sundstrom's talents is lifting an opponent's blade to steal the puck. He absorbs way more punishment than he dishes out, since he doesn't punish anybody, but he's beginning to realize that developing at least a hint of a mean streak is necessary for his survival.

THE INTANGIBLES

Because he doesn't throw big hits or make flashy plays on the ice, and because he almost constantly is smiling off it, Sundstrom gets taken lightly a lot more than he should. He is committed to playing, and playing well. He is also committed to winning, and is enormously respected in the dressing room. He was never a favourite of Ranger coach John Muckler, for some reason, and may flourish with the change of scenery.

PROJECTION

Sundstrom is a passer more than a scorer. Given the right line combination, he could produce 50 points — more than 30 of which would be assists.

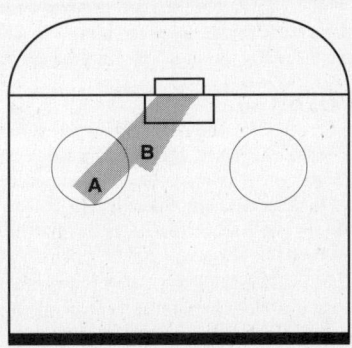

PETR SVOBODA

Yrs. of NHL service: 15
Born: Most, Czech Republic; Feb. 14, 1966
Position: left defense
Height: 6-1
Weight: 190
Uniform no.: 23
Shoots: left

Career statistics:

GP	G	A	TP	PIM
939	55	315	370	1394

1995-96 statistics:

GP	G	A	TP	+/-	PIM	PP	SH	GW	GT	S	PCT
73	1	28	29	+28	105	0	0	0	0	91	1.1

1996-97 statistics:

GP	G	A	TP	+/-	PIM	PP	SH	GW	GT	S	PCT
67	2	12	14	+10	94	1	0	0	0	36	5.6

1997-98 statistics:

GP	G	A	TP	+/-	PIM	PP	SH	GW	GT	S	PCT
56	3	15	18	+19	83	2	0	0	0	44	6.8

1998-99 statistics:

GP	G	A	TP	+/-	PIM	PP	SH	GW	GT	S	PCT
59	5	18	23	+1	81	1	1	1	0	83	6.0

LAST SEASON

Acquired from Philadelphia for Karl Dykhuis, Dec. 28, 1998. Led team defensemen in points. Led team in plus-minus. Missed 10 games with groin injury. Missed two games with knee injury. Missed one game with shoulder injury. Missed 10 games with other injuries.

THE FINESSE GAME

Svoboda has very quick feet and is always in motion. He was never strong on his skates but he has great quickness, balance and agility — and you can't hit what you can't catch. He has a long stride. Not a very solid player, he is lean and wiry. His skating is economical.

Svoboda has excellent instincts. He can carry the puck well and join the rush. He has a quick release on his wrist and snap shots, and also a good one-timer that he uses on the power play. He reads plays well offensively and defensively.

Svoboda is a number four defenseman on his best nights now, but Tampa Bay asked him to be a number one, which is really too much for him to handle.

THE PHYSICAL GAME

Not one for physical play, Svoboda is still a feisty foe who will take the body, then use his stick to rap a player in the choppers or pull his skates out from under him. He ticks off a lot of people. He's taken a couple of pretty big hits in recent years, but he keeps bouncing back.

Svoboda is lean and isn't going to get much done one-on-one in a close battle. He rides an opponent out of the play well when he can use his skating to generate some power.

THE INTANGIBLES

The more teams take the body on him, the lower Svoboda's panic point with the puck seems to get as the game goes along. He has become increasingly fragile. He complements the young defenseman Pavel Kubina well.

PROJECTION

Expect about 60 games and 30 points out of Svoboda.

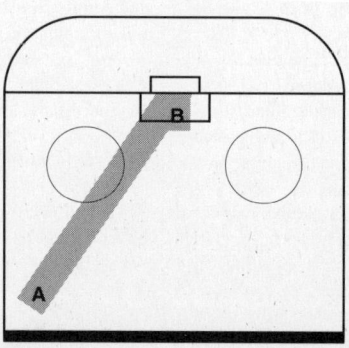

DARCY TUCKER

Yrs. of NHL service: 3
Born: Castor, Alberta; Mar. 15, 1975
Position: centre
Height: 5-11
Weight: 182
Uniform no.: 16
Shoots: left

Career statistics:
GP	G	A	TP	PIM
232	35	48	83	432

1995-96 statistics:
GP	G	A	TP	+/-	PIM	PP	SH	GW	GT	S	PCT
3	0	0	0	-1	0	0	0	0	0	1	0.0

1996-97 statistics:
GP	G	A	TP	+/-	PIM	PP	SH	GW	GT	S	PCT
73	7	13	20	-5	110	1	0	3	1	62	11.3

1997-98 statistics:
GP	G	A	TP	+/-	PIM	PP	SH	GW	GT	S	PCT
74	7	13	20	-14	146	1	1	0	0	63	11.1

1998-99 statistics:
GP	G	A	TP	+/-	PIM	PP	SH	GW	GT	S	PCT
82	21	22	43	-34	176	8	2	3	0	178	11.8

LAST SEASON
Led team in goals, points and penalty minutes, all career highs. Led team in shooting percentage. Tied for team lead in shorthanded goals. Second on team in assists and game-winning goals. One of two Lightning players to appear in all 82 games.

THE FINESSE GAME
Some people are calling Tucker the new Dale Hunter, and that's not a bad comparison. Tucker isn't the street punk that Hunter is, but he brings a level of intensity to his game that supplements — and some might suggest, surpasses — his talent.

Tucker managed to lead Tampa Bay (admittedly one of the NHL's worst teams last season) in nearly every major offensive category. Considering that Tucker is a third-line checking centre, this is a major accomplishment. He was a scorer in junior (137 points in his last year at Kamloops of the WHL) and the minors (93 points with Fredericton of the AHL in 1995-96), and he brings an offensive awareness that enhances his role as a third-line checking centre.

Tucker's major drawback is that he lacks big-league speed. He is a good forechecker who will hound the puck carrier, and he can do something with the puck once it's on his stick.

THE PHYSICAL GAME
Tucker is dogged and enjoys the rough going. His is small but highly annoying to play against. He can distract bigger players who just try to squish him. His efforts are pretty consistent — you don't have to worry about him getting jazzed up to play a big game.

THE INTANGIBLES
Tucker's got spunk. He cares. He's been a winner and he wants to make his team better.

PROJECTION
Tucker surpassed all expectations for his production last season. If he continues to get the ice time he did last year, he could top 40 points again.

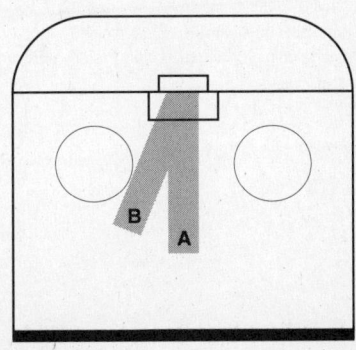

TORONTO MAPLE LEAFS

Players' Statistics 1998-99

POS.	NO.	PLAYER	GP	G	A	PTS	+/-	PIM	PP	SH	GW	GT	S	PCT
C	13	MATS SUNDIN	82	31	52	83	22	58	4		6		209	14.8
L	32	STEVE THOMAS	78	28	45	73	26	33	11		7		209	13.4
L	94	SERGEI BEREZIN	76	37	22	59	16	12	9	1	4		263	14.1
L	7	DEREK KING	81	24	28	52	15	20	8		4		150	16.0
C	22	IGOR KOROLEV	66	13	34	47	11	46	1		2		99	13.1
R	20	MIKE JOHNSON	79	20	24	44	13	35	5	3	2		149	13.4
C	44	YANIC PERREAULT	76	17	25	42	7	42	4	3	3		141	12.1
C	11	STEVE SULLIVAN	63	20	20	40	12	28	4		5		110	18.2
D	34	BRYAN BERARD	69	9	25	34	1	48	4		5	1	135	6.7
L	19	FREDRIK MODIN	67	16	15	31	14	35	1		3	1	108	14.8
R	10	GARRY VALK	77	8	21	29	8	53	1			1	93	8.6
D	3	SYLVAIN COTE	79	5	24	29	22	28			1		119	4.2
D	36	DIMITRI YUSHKEVICH	78	6	22	28	25	88	2	1			95	6.3
D	52	ALEXANDER KARPOVTSEV	58	3	25	28	39	52	1		1		65	4.6
C	18	ALYN MCCAULEY	39	9	15	24	7	2	1		1	1	76	11.8
R	28	TIE DOMI	72	8	14	22	5	198			1		65	12.3
D	15	*TOMAS KABERLE	57	4	18	22	3	12			2		71	5.6
L	8	TODD WARRINER	53	9	10	19	-6	28	1		1		96	9.4
D	55	*DANIIL MARKOV	57	4	8	12	5	47				1	34	11.8
D	38	YANNICK TREMBLAY	35	2	7	9	0	16					37	5.4
G	31	CURTIS JOSEPH	67		5	5	0	6						
L	12	KRIS KING	67	2	2	4	-16	105		1	1		34	5.9
R	39	*LADISLAV KOHN	16	1	3	4	1	4					23	4.3
D	33	CHRIS MCALLISTER	48	1	3	4	-3	102				1	18	5.6
R	16	LONNY BOHONOS	7	3		3	3	4					13	23.1
D	2	DALLAS EAKINS	18		2	2	3	24					11	
C	42	*KEVYN ADAMS	1				0						1	
G	35	JEFF REESE	2				0							
D	4	KEVIN DAHL	3				0	2						
G	30	GLENN HEALY	9				0							

GP = games played; G = goals; A = assists; PTS = points; +/- = goals-for minus goals-against while player is on ice; PIM = penalties in minutes; PP = power-play goals; SH = shorthanded goals; GW = game-winning goals; GT = game-tying goals; S = no. of shots; PCT = percentage of goals to shots; * = rookie

BRYAN BERARD

Yrs. of NHL service: 3
Born: Woonsocket, R.I.; March 5, 1977
Position: left defense
Height: 6-1
Weight: 190
Uniform no.: 34
Shoots: left

Career statistics:

GP	G	A	TP	PIM
226	31	97	128	193

1996-97 statistics:

GP	G	A	TP	+/-	PIM	PP	SH	GW	GT	S	PCT
82	8	40	48	+1	86	3	0	1	0	172	4.7

1997-98 statistics:

GP	G	A	TP	+/-	PIM	PP	SH	GW	GT	S	PCT
75	14	32	46	-32	59	8	1	2	1	192	7.3

1998-99 statistics:

GP	G	A	TP	+/-	PIM	PP	SH	GW	GT	S	PCT
69	9	25	34	+1	48	4	0	5	1	135	6.7

LAST SEASON

Acquired from N.Y. Islanders with a sixth-round draft pick in 1999 for Felix Potvin and a 1999 sixth-round draft pick, Jan. 9, 1999. Led team defensemen in scoring. Tied for third on team in game-winning goals. Missed 13 games with groin injuries. Missed two games with flu.

THE FINESSE GAME

Berard is a little bit of Brian Leetch and a little bit of Chris Chelios, and yet he's his own player. There aren't many defensemen who go all the time like he does.

A terrific skater, Berard has great offensive instincts, a very good shot from the point, and he always manages to get his shot through. He has a lot of confidence in his abilities. On some nights he is dominant, but he hasn't achieved the level of consistency of an elite defenseman. Remember, though, this kid never played in the minors, but stepped right onto a bad team after junior and won the Calder Trophy.

Like Leetch, when Berard is really on he's in perpetual motion. He's the first guy up the ice and the first guy back, and that creates all kinds of excitement and all kinds of pressure on the other team. As long as it's not ultra-risky, that's the way his game should be played. He can win the game one night in the offensive end and maybe lose it another night in his own zone. The most important thing about Berard is that when the game is on the line, he wants the puck. He wants to make the difference.

Berard carries the puck with confidence and does not panic under pressure. His shot is low and accurate; he is also a fine passer. With his combination of skills and intelligence he can control the tempo of a game. He has good vision with the puck and will make the special plays.

THE PHYSICAL GAME

Although not overly physical, Berard has shown a willingness to use his body to slow people down. He is also very good using his stick to poke-check or break up passes, and opponents would be wise not to make cross-ice passes high in the attacking zone or he will easily step up and pick them off. He tends to run around and try to do too much sometimes, but coaches prefer sins of commission to sins of omission. Berard is a competitor and he battles.

THE INTANGIBLES

Berard brings people into the building and then brings them out of their seats. He has shown every indication that he will be among the league's elite offensive defensemen, but needs to add responsible defensive play.

PROJECTION

Berard will get better. He has a lot of learning to do and with patience, maturity and the right coaching will become a 60-point player in a season or two.

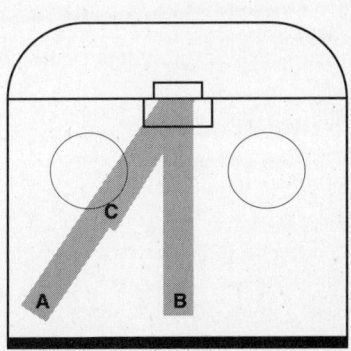

Toronto Maple Leafs

SERGEI BEREZIN

Yrs. of NHL service: 3
Born: Voskresensk, Russia; Nov. 5, 1971
Position: right wing
Height: 5-10
Weight: 197
Uniform no.: 94
Shoots: right

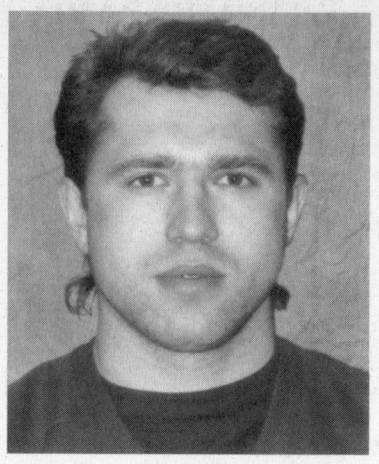

Career statistics:

GP	G	A	TP	PIM
217	79	53	131	24

1996-97 statistics:

GP	G	A	TP	+/-	PIM	PP	SH	GW	GT	S	PCT
73	26	16	41	-3	2	7	0	2	0	177	14.7

1997-98 statistics:

GP	G	A	TP	+/-	PIM	PP	SH	GW	GT	S	PCT
68	16	15	31	-3	10	3	0	3	1	167	9.6

1998-99 statistics:

GP	G	A	TP	+/-	PIM	PP	SH	GW	GT	S	PCT
76	37	22	59	+16	12	9	1	4	0	263	14.1

LAST SEASON

Led team in goals with career high. Led team in shots. Second on team in power-play goals. Third on team in points. Missed four games with hip pointer. Missed two games with bruised foot.

THE FINESSE GAME

Berezin is strictly an offensive player, and a pure goal scorer. Just look at his goals-to-assists ratio. He can be a bit of a puck hog but as long as he's scoring, who cares?

Berezin knows where the net is, and while he is less reluctant to shoot than a lot of Russian players, sometimes he has to see the whites of the goalie's eyes before he will let it go. He shoots one-timers and he knows he's a sniper. He's very creative.

Berezin is a deceptive, quick skater with good balance. He is aware of his defensive shortcomings and needs to continue to improve in that facet of his game.

THE PHYSICAL GAME

Berezin is small but stocky, and he showed more willingness to get into the high-traffic areas instead of hanging around the perimeter. He must work harder to get into the scoring areas and to stay there. He isn't intimidated by physical play, but he also doesn't initiate.

THE INTANGIBLES

Sometimes it just takes awhile for players to "get it." It looks like Berezin's light went on.

PROJECTION

Berezin made a big mental leap last season. If he can sustain that consistency, he is a sure bet for 40 goals.

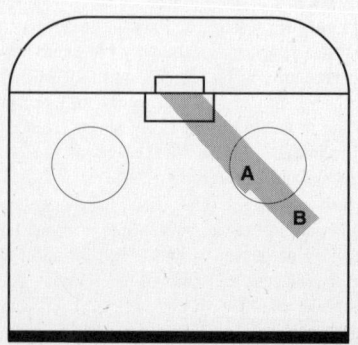

SYLVAIN COTE

Yrs. of NHL service: 14
Born: Quebec City, Que.; Jan. 19, 1966
Position: left defense
Height: 6-0
Weight: 190
Uniform no.: 3
Shoots: right

Career statistics:

GP	G	A	TP	PIM
956	104	264	368	469

1995-96 statistics:

GP	G	A	TP	+/-	PIM	PP	SH	GW	GT	S	PCT
81	5	33	38	+5	40	3	0	2	0	212	2.4

1996-97 statistics:

GP	G	A	TP	+/-	PIM	PP	SH	GW	GT	S	PCT
57	6	18	24	+11	28	2	0	0	0	131	4.6

1997-98 statistics:

GP	G	A	TP	+/-	PIM	PP	SH	GW	GT	S	PCT
71	4	21	25	-3	42	1	0	1	0	103	3.9

1998-99 statistics:

GP	G	A	TP	+/-	PIM	PP	SH	GW	GT	S	PCT
79	5	24	29	+22	28	0	0	1	0	119	4.2

LAST SEASON

Second among team defensemen in points. Missed three games with shoulder injury.

THE FINESSE GAME

Cote is a solid two-way defenseman. He has good puckhandling skills and can make a pass to his forehand or backhand side with confidence. He overhandles the puck at times, especially in his defensive zone, and when he gets into trouble he seems to struggle with his forehand clearances off the left-wing boards.

Cote can do everything in stride. Carrying the puck does not slow him down and he can rush end to end. He is gifted in all of the skating areas: fine agility, good balance, quick stops and starts. He likes to bring the puck up on the power play. He gets a lot on his shot from the point, which causes rebounds, and it's the source of most of his assists.

Cote has decent hockey sense. He can lead a rush or come into the play as a trailer, but he knows enough not to force and to play more conservatively when the situation dictates. His skating covers up for most of his defensive lapses. His instincts lag well behind his skill level. He can be beaten one-on-one but it takes a good player to do it.

THE PHYSICAL GAME

Cote doesn't have great size, but he is a solid hitter who finishes his checks. He isn't mean, however, and will occasionally fall into the trap of playing the puck instead of the man.

THE INTANGIBLES

Cote's skill levels are beginning to erode slightly with age and wear and tear. He could have one more season left as a top four defenseman.

PROJECTION

If Cote can get the ice time, he can score 25 to 30 points.

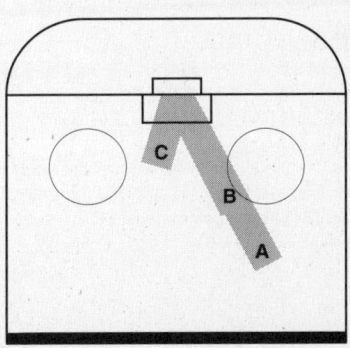

JONAS HOGLUND

Yrs. of NHL service: 3
Born: Hammaro, Sweden; Aug. 29, 1972
Position: left wing
Height: 6-3
Weight: 200
Uniform no.: 44
Shoots: right

Career statistics:

GP	G	A	TP	PIM
220	39	39	78	50

1996-97 statistics:

GP	G	A	TP	+/-	PIM	PP	SH	GW	GT	S	PCT
68	19	16	35	-4	12	3	0	6	1	189	10.1

1997-98 statistics:

GP	G	A	TP	+/-	PIM	PP	SH	GW	GT	S	PCT
78	12	13	25	-7	22	4	0	0	0	186	6.5

1998-99 statistics:

GP	G	A	TP	+/-	PIM	PP	SH	GW	GT	S	PCT
74	8	10	18	-5	16	1	0	0	1	122	6.6

LAST SEASON
Missed eight games due to coach's decision.

THE FINESSE GAME
Hoglund is a natural goal scorer. Every time he gets the puck he has a chance to score. The trick is to encourage him to shoot more, and instill an intense drive. He lacks a goal scorer's mentality but he has a goal scorer's tools. He has a good, hard slap shot and half-wrister.

Hoglund has adapted well to North American hockey in his defensive and positional play. Play along the boards was a new concept to him, but he was unafraid of getting involved.

Hoglund skates well for a big man. He's no speed skater but his skating is NHL calibre.

THE PHYSICAL GAME
Hoglund is a big guy but doesn't play a physical game. He has a long reach, which he uses instead of his body to try to win control of the puck or slow down an opponent. He's getting used to the idea of hitting. Still, he has to get better at it. When he does his whole game perks up.

THE INTANGIBLES
Hoglund needs to feel comfortable to develop confidence, but he also needs a fire lit under him.

PROJECTION
Hoglund has the skills to be an impact scorer but not the drive. He will be out of an NHL job unless he unlocks the toolbox to score at least 20 this season.

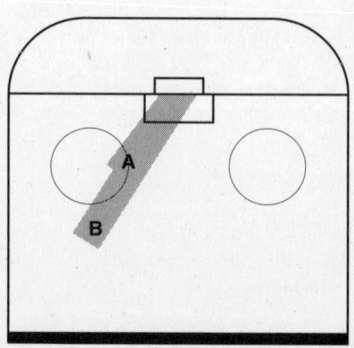

MIKE JOHNSON

Yrs. of NHL service: 2
Born: Scarborough, Ont.; Oct. 3, 1974
Position: right wing
Height: 6-2
Weight: 180
Uniform no.: 20
Shoots: right

Career statistics:

GP	G	A	TP	PIM
174	37	58	95	63

1996-97 statistics:

GP	G	A	TP	+/-	PIM	PP	SH	GW	GT	S	PCT
13	2	2	4	-2	4	0	1	1	0	27	7.4

1997-98 statistics:

GP	G	A	TP	+/-	PIM	PP	SH	GW	GT	S	PCT
82	15	32	47	-4	24	5	0	0	1	143	10.5

1998-99 statistics:

GP	G	A	TP	+/-	PIM	PP	SH	GW	GT	S	PCT
79	20	24	44	+13	35	5	3	2	0	149	13.4

LAST SEASON

Second NHL season. Tied for team lead in short-handed goals. Missed two games due to suspension.

THE FINESSE GAME

Johnson has an amazing, advanced knowledge of how to use the ice offensively and defensively. He protects the puck on the boards. When he's down low in his own end on defensive-zone coverage, he's strong and supports the puck well.

Offensively, Johnson will take the puck to the net. He knows when to move and doesn't just stand around and stay checked. He moves into scoring positions. His puck movement on the power play is exceptional. He has to get a stronger shot, which should come with physical maturity.

Johnson is a terrific skater with the kind of ability that instantly stamps him as a 10-year pro. He can harry puck carriers when killing penalties and has the one-step breakaway quickness to be a shorthanded threat.

THE PHYSICAL GAME

Johnson has to get bigger and stronger. He is tall and reedy, and if he stands too still near the stick rack he'll get packed away for the next road trip.

THE INTANGIBLES

Johnson will do just about anything a coach asks. He needs to develop more consistency, but he is still a young player and that should come.

PROJECTION

Johnson didn't quite make the jump to the 50-point range we anticipated for him last season, but as a top six forward on the Leafs, he is ready this year to score between 50 and 60 points.

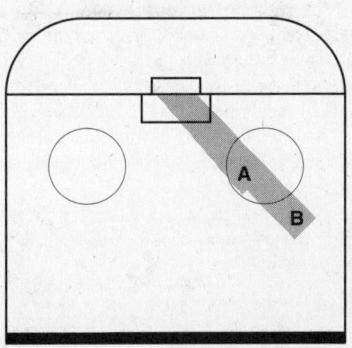

CURTIS JOSEPH

Yrs. of NHL service: 9
Born: Keswick, Ont.; Apr. 29, 1967
Position: goaltender
Height: 5-10
Weight: 182
Uniform no.: 31
Catches: left

Career statistics:

GP	MIN	GA	SO	GAA	A	PIM
524	30156	1473	22	2.93	26	54

1995-96 statistics:

GP	MIN	GAA	W	L	T	SO	GA	S	SAPCT	PIM
34	1936	3.44	15	16	2	0	111	971	.886	4

1996-97 statistics:

GP	MIN	GAA	W	L	T	SO	GA	S	SAPCT	PIM
72	4089	2.93	32	29	9	6	200	2144	.907	20

1997-98 statistics:

GP	MIN	GAA	W	L	T	SO	GA	S	SAPCT	PIM
71	4132	2.63	29	31	9	8	181	1901	.905	4

1998-99 statistics:

GP	MIN	GAA	W	L	T	SO	GA	S	SAPCT	PIM
67	4001	2.56	35	24	7	3	171	1903	.910	6

LAST SEASON

Led NHL goalies in assists (5). Tied for second in NHL in wins. Tied for third in NHL in minutes played.

THE PHYSICAL GAME

Nothing Joseph does is by the book. He always looks unorthodox and off-balance, but he is one of those hybrid goalies whose success can't be argued with. He was the single reason for Toronto's improvement last season.

Joseph positions himself well, angling out to challenge the shooter. He is one of the best goalies against the breakaway in the NHL. He goes to his knees quickly, but bounces back to his skates fast for the rebound. He tends to keep rebounds in front of him. His glove hand is outstanding.

A strong, if bizarre, stickhandler, Joseph has to move his hands on the stick, putting the butt-end into his catching glove and lowering his blocker. His favourite move is a weird backhand whip off the boards. He is a good skater who moves out of his cage confidently to handle the puck. Heck, he outscored teammate Kris King last season.

He needs to improve his lateral movement. He also uses his stick to harass anyone who dares to camp on his doorstep. He's not Billy Smith, but he's aggressive with his whacks.

Joseph gets into technical slumps, which seem to sprout from fatigue and usually result in his staying too deep in his net.

THE MENTAL GAME

Joseph is used to a lot of work, but cutting back his games by a half-dozen or so would result in a fresher goalie for the playoffs. He is never fazed by facing a ton of shots in a night.

THE INTANGIBLES

The problem with Joseph, as it was with Ed Belfour and is with Dominik Hasek, is that you're never a winner until you win the big prize.

PROJECTION

Joseph will hit the 30-win mark again.

ALEXANDER KARPOVTSEV

Yrs. of NHL service: 6
Born: Moscow, Russia; Feb. 25, 1974
Position: left defense
Height: 6-1
Weight: 200
Uniform no.: 52
Shoots: left

Career statistics:

GP	G	A	TP	PIM
336	24	100	114	263

1995-96 statistics:

GP	G	A	TP	+/-	PIM	PP	SH	GW	GT	S	PCT
40	2	16	18	+12	26	1	0	1	0	71	2.8

1996-97 statistics:

GP	G	A	TP	+/-	PIM	PP	SH	GW	GT	S	PCT
77	9	29	28	+1	59	6	1	0	0	84	10.7

1997-98 statistics:

GP	G	A	TP	+/-	PIM	PP	SH	GW	GT	S	PCT
47	3	7	10	-1	38	1	0	1	0	46	6.5

1998-99 statistics:

GP	G	A	TP	+/-	PIM	PP	SH	GW	GT	S	PCT
58	3	25	28	+39	52	1	0	1	0	65	4.6

LAST SEASON

Acquired from N.Y. Rangers with a 1999 fourth-round draft pick for Mathieu Schneider, Oct. 24, 1999. Missed 12 games with fractured thumb. Missed six games with wrist injury. Missed three games with fractured finger. Missed two games with bruised knee. Missed one game due to coach's decision.

THE FINESSE GAME

The strength of Karpovtsev's skating game is best reflected in his terrific lateral movement. He covers acres of ground with a huge stride and a long reach, has excellent balance, turns nicely in both directions and boasts a fair amount of quickness and agility. He has a quick first step to the puck.

Karpovtsev has decent puck-carrying skills and the good sense to move the puck quickly, but displays the defensive defenseman's mindset of getting to the redline and dumping the puck into the corner or making a short outlet pass. Under pressure behind his net he tends to whack the puck around the boards, a play that often gets picked off.

Karpovtsev does, at times, show a good instinct for seeing a better passing option than the obvious in the attacking zone. He has an effective, hard shot from the point, and his accuracy has improved.

THE PHYSICAL GAME

Karpovtsev is extremely strong and is not shy about using his strength in front of the net or in the corners. Battling for loose pucks, he will move a player with a forearm shove, then grab the puck while his opponent is recovering from the jolt. He will also throw himself back-first at a player, immobilize the guy against the boards, then recover quickly and grab the puck.

Karpovtsev plays toughest against the toughest players. He does not hesitate to get involved if things turn nasty, and although he is hardly a polished fighter he is a willing one. He likes the big hit but doesn't mind the smaller ones.

A crease clearer and shot-blocker, Karpovtsev is far more comfortable and poised in front of his net than when he chases to the corners or sideboards. Once he gets away from the slot, with or without the puck, he loses either confidence or focus or both, which can lead to unforced errors or turnovers. Still, he is an effective weapon against a power forward. He can tie up the guy in front, lean on him, and hit and skate with an Eric Lindros.

THE INTANGIBLES

Respect is a very important element to Karpovtsev, who has made his play more than respectable with perseverance. He can kill penalties and work the power play, plus he's comfortable with four-on-four play, but his real value is in the long, tough, bruising nights when he wages war with the Legion of Doom or any of the opposition's top offensive threats. He is a battler who has no problem with the "heavy lifting" assignments. His only drawback is a tendency to get hurt and to not want to play through pain.

PROJECTION

A healthy Karpovtsev can score in the 25-point range and log a lot of ice time.

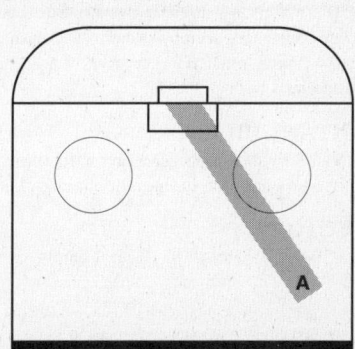

DEREK KING

Yrs. of NHL service: 12
Born: Hamilton, Ont.; Feb. 11, 1967
Position: left wing
Height: 6-0
Weight: 212
Uniform no.: 7
Shoots: left

Career statistics:

GP	G	A	TP	PIM
808	259	344	603	409

1995-96 statistics:

GP	G	A	TP	+/-	PIM	PP	SH	GW	GT	S	PCT
61	12	20	32	-10	23	5	1	0	1	154	7.8

1996-97 statistics:

GP	G	A	TP	+/-	PIM	PP	SH	GW	GT	S	PCT
82	26	33	59	-6	22	6	0	3	0	181	14.4

1997-98 statistics:

GP	G	A	TP	+/-	PIM	PP	SH	GW	GT	S	PCT
77	21	25	46	-7	43	4	0	3	0	166	12.7

1998-99 statistics:

GP	G	A	TP	+/-	PIM	PP	SH	GW	GT	S	PCT
81	24	28	52	+15	20	8	0	4	0	150	16.0

LAST SEASON

Second on team in shooting percentage. Third on team in power-play goals. Missed one game due to coach's decision.

THE FINESSE GAME

There is only one thing King does well, and that is score goals. He is at his best from the face-off dot of the left circle to the front of the net. He has great concentration through traffic and soft, soft hands for cradling passes and then snapping off the shot the instant the puck hits his blade. He has to play with someone who will get him the puck.

At his most effective on the power play, King has good anticipation and reads the offensive plays well. He is not a great skater but has improved his defensive awareness.

THE PHYSICAL GAME

A solid and durable player who takes a pounding in front of the net, King doesn't use his body well in other areas of the ice, which is one of the reasons for his defensive problems. King wore down late in the season and had a poor playoffs.

THE INTANGIBLES

King is bound to start feeling some bubble pressure if the Maple Leafs are able to upgrade their forwards.

PROJECTION

King is a 20-goal skater with 40-goal hands.

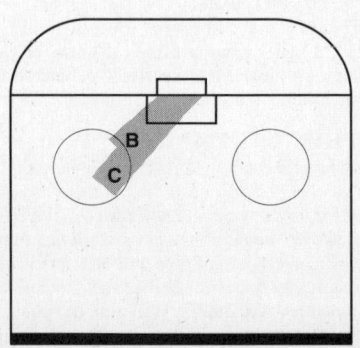

DANIIL MARKOV

Yrs. of NHL service: 2
Born: Moscow, Russia; July 11, 1976
Position: left defense
Height: 6-1
Weight: 196
Uniform no.: 55
Shoots: left

Career statistics:

GP	G	A	TP	PIM
82	6	13	19	75

1997-98 statistics:

GP	G	A	TP	+/-	PIM	PP	SH	GW	GT	S	PCT
25	2	5	7	0	28	1	0	0	0	15	13.3

1998-99 statistics:

GP	G	A	TP	+/-	PIM	PP	SH	GW	GT	S	PCT
57	4	8	12	+5	47	0	0	0	1	34	11.8

LAST SEASON

First NHL season. Missed 11 games with shoulder injury. Missed two games with fractured foot. Missed two games with cracked larynx. Missed two games with lower back spasms. Missed one game with concussion symptoms.

THE FINESSE GAME

Markov is pretty sound positioning-wise, and he is a good skater. Coaches have to constantly keep him in tune with what to do defensively. Markov wants to drift more into an offensive game. He is tempted to make high-risk pinches, and when he gets beat his ice time gets cut. He is just starting to understand that cause-and-effect.

Markov makes a good first pass. Once he gets the puck he is looking to go up-ice for a play, which not all defensemen do, and a stick-to-stick pass gets him out of trouble.

He is still young and learning, but he looked good paired with Dimitri Yushkevich.

THE PHYSICAL GAME

Markov isn't very big but he brings a little edge, and a little chippiness, to his game. He's a bit brash and cocky. He's the Leaf who threw the salute to Jaromir Jagr when Toronto eliminated Pittsburgh in the playoffs.

THE INTANGIBLES

Markov has rapidly developed into a top four defenseman with the Leafs.

PROJECTION

Markov wants to play like an elite "offenseman," but his skills don't put him in that class. If he plays a smarter defensive game he will get a nice chunk of ice time *and* score 20 to 25 points.

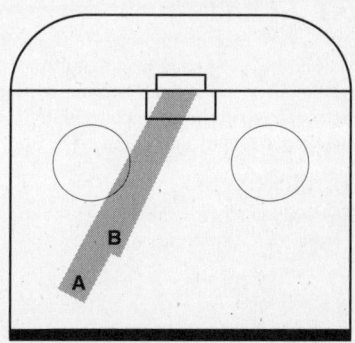

ALYN MCCAULEY

Yrs. of NHL service: 2
Born: Brockville, Ont.; May 29, 1977
Position: centre
Height: 5-11
Weight: 185
Uniform no.: 18
Shoots: left

Career statistics:

GP	G	A	TP	PIM
99	15	25	40	8

1997-98 statistics:

GP	G	A	TP	+/-	PIM	PP	SH	GW	GT	S	PCT
60	6	10	16	-7	6	0	0	1	0	77	7.8

1998-99 statistics:

GP	G	A	TP	+/-	PIM	PP	SH	GW	GT	S	PCT
39	9	15	24	+7	2	1	0	1	1	76	11.8

LAST SEASON

Second NHL season. Missed 22 games with sprained knee. Missed 21 games with concussion.

THE FINESSE GAME

Injuries — serious ones — compromised McCauley's development; until he suffered his knee injury in late December he was showing some very promising signs. He concentrated on defense in his rookie season but last year was promoted to a second-line centre.

McCauley's skating, scoring touch and vision stamp him as one of the most exciting players in the Leafs' system. He is becoming a very good transition player.

He has a good shot and is a topnotch playmaker. He has good hands, good instincts and he sees people well around the net. He's at his best in an up-tempo game because he skates well and can handle the puck at speed. He makes and accepts passes at a quick pace. He has hockey smarts. His hand-eye coordination is terrific.

THE PHYSICAL GAME

McCauley is a small, blocky player without much ferocity. His concussion might affect his willingness to battle along the boards, since that's where he was hurt.

THE INTANGIBLES

McCauley is very hard on himself. He wants to be a top player and has very good work habits, but he has to stop getting down on himself because it affects his game. After recovering from his concussion, he was medically cleared to play during the off-season.

PROJECTION

If McCauley rebounds from his injuries, he could be a 20-goal scorer in a second-line role.

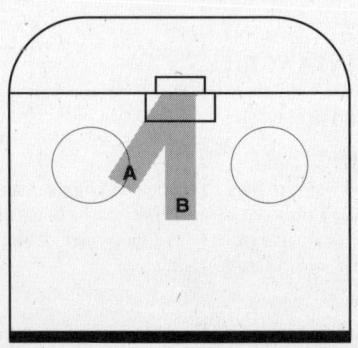

YANIC PERREAULT

Yrs. of NHL service: 5
Born: Sherbrooke, Que.; Apr. 4, 1971
Position: centre
Height: 5-11
Weight: 189
Uniform no.: 44
Shoots: left

Career statistics:

GP	G	A	TP	PIM
313	86	91	177	130

1995-96 statistics:

GP	G	A	TP	+/-	PIM	PP	SH	GW	GT	S	PCT
78	25	24	49	-11	16	8	3	7	0	175	14.3

1996-97 statistics:

GP	G	A	TP	+/-	PIM	PP	SH	GW	GT	S	PCT
41	11	14	25	0	20	1	1	0	0	98	11.2

1997-98 statistics:

GP	G	A	TP	+/-	PIM	PP	SH	GW	GT	S	PCT
79	28	20	48	+6	32	3	2	3	0	206	13.6

1998-99 statistics:

GP	G	A	TP	+/-	PIM	PP	SH	GW	GT	S	PCT
76	17	25	42	+7	42	4	3	3	0	141	12.1

PROJECTION

Perreault works hard and can score 15 to 20 goals as a role player.

LAST SEASON

Acquired from Los Angeles for Jason Podollan and a 1999 third-round draft pick, Mar. 23, 1999. Tied for team lead in shorthanded goals.

THE FINESSE GAME

Perreault's speed is marginal for the NHL level. He tries to compensate with his intelligence, and that alone will keep earning him NHL jobs on third and fourth lines. He is nifty and shifty in tight quarters, but lacks breakaway speed.

Perreault has very good hands and always has his head up, looking for openings. While he doesn't have open-ice speed, he works hard to put on a quick burst in the offensive zone, to gain a half-step on a defender. Once he is open for the shot he waits for the goalie to commit, or he makes a patient pass.

Tricky and solid on his feet, Perreault works the half-boards on the power play. He has an accurate shot with a quick release, and he slithers around to get in the best position for the shot.

THE PHYSICAL GAME

Perreault lacks the size for one-on-one battles in the attacking zone. Defensively, he can't do much except harass a puck carrier with his stick. He is an in-betweener, and if forced to carry the play in any zone his flaws become apparent.

THE INTANGIBLES

It's easy to write off Perreault. It has been done many times over the past few seasons, but he keeps coming into training camp and earning a job.

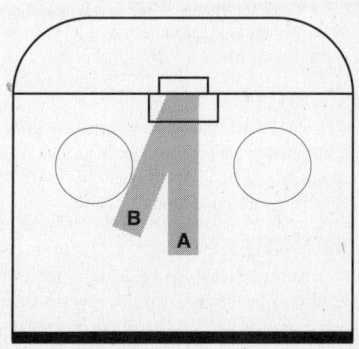

STEVE SULLIVAN

Yrs. of NHL service: 3
Born: Timmins, Ont.; July 6, 1974
Position: centre
Height: 5-9
Weight: 155
Uniform no.: 11
Shoots: right

Career statistics:

GP	G	A	TP	PIM
196	48	67	115	113

1995-96 statistics:

GP	G	A	TP	+/-	PIM	PP	SH	GW	GT	S	PCT
16	5	4	9	+3	8	2	0	1	0	23	21.7

1996-97 statistics:

GP	G	A	TP	+/-	PIM	PP	SH	GW	GT	S	PCT
54	13	25	38	+14	37	3	0	3	1	108	12.0

1997-98 statistics:

GP	G	A	TP	+/-	PIM	PP	SH	GW	GT	S	PCT
63	10	18	28	-8	40	1	0	1	0	112	8.9

1998-99 statistics:

GP	G	A	TP	+/-	PIM	PP	SH	GW	GT	S	PCT
63	20	20	40	+12	28	4	0	5	0	110	18.2

PROJECTION

Sullivan can be a 20-goal scorer with sustained effort, but it will always be a struggle for him to keep an NHL job because of his size.

LAST SEASON

Led team in shooting percentage. Tied for third on team in game-winning goals. Missed one game with back spasms. Missed 18 games due to coach's decision.

THE FINESSE GAME

One advantage to being as small as Sullivan is that you are closer to the puck than a lot of your rivals. Sullivan complicates matters by using a short stick — short even by his standards — to keep the puck in his feet. He draws penalties by protecting the puck so well; foes usually have to foul him to get the puck.

By nature a centre, Sullivan has terrific speed, hands, vision and anticipation. However, he will probably have to make his way in the NHL as a left wing, even though that means sending him into the wars along the boards. Playing wing, he doesn't have to be down low on defensive-zone coverage.

Sullivan is quick and smart enough to get himself out of pending jams, but he does not have elite skills and has to apply himself constantly. He is strictly an offensive threat, almost a specialty player.

THE PHYSICAL GAME

You can't survive in the NHL if you are small and soft. Sullivan has to play with fire. If he gets bounced around he has to get back up, and get his stick up. His effort has to be more consistent.

THE INTANGIBLES

Sullivan's size means his drive has to be more intense than most other players. He doesn't always fire on all cylinders.

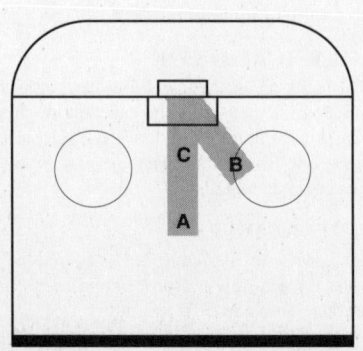

MATS SUNDIN

Yrs. of NHL service: 9
Born: Bromma, Sweden; Feb. 13, 1971
Position: right wing/centre
Height: 6-4
Weight: 215
Uniform no.: 13
Shoots: right

Career statistics:

GP	G	A	TP	PIM
693	296	419	715	545

1995-96 statistics:

GP	G	A	TP	+/-	PIM	PP	SH	GW	GT	S	PCT
76	33	50	83	+8	46	7	6	7	1	301	11.0

1996-97 statistics:

GP	G	A	TP	+/-	PIM	PP	SH	GW	GT	S	PCT
82	41	53	94	+6	59	7	4	8	1	281	14.6

1997-98 statistics:

GP	G	A	TP	+/-	PIM	PP	SH	GW	GT	S	PCT
82	33	41	74	-3	49	9	1	5	1	219	15.1

1998-99 statistics:

GP	G	A	TP	+/-	PIM	PP	SH	GW	GT	S	PCT
82	31	52	83	+22	58	4	0	6	0	209	14.8

LAST SEASON

Led team in assists and points. Second on team in goals with career high. Second on team in game-winning goals. Tied for second on team in shots. Third on team in plus-minus. Only Leaf to appear in all 82 games.

THE FINESSE GAME

Sundin plays centre but he attacks from the off-(left)wing, where he can come off the boards with speed. He protects the puck along the wall and makes it hard for people to reach in without taking him down for a penalty. He gets the puck low in his own end; people can move to him right away, and he has to move the puck. If a checker stays with him Sundin can't get the puck back.

Sundin is a big skater who looks huge, as he uses an ultralong stick that gives him a broad wingspan. For a big man he is an agile skater, and his balance has improved. He has good lower-body strength, supplying drive for battles along the boards. He doesn't stay checked. He's evasive, and once he is on the fly he is hard to stop. He is less effective when carrying the puck. His best play is to get up a head of steam, jump into the holes and take a quick shot.

Sundin can take bad passes in stride, either kicking an errant puck up onto his stick or reaching behind to corral it. He isn't a clever stickhandler. His game is power and speed. He doesn't look fast, but he has ground-eating strides that allow him to cover in two strides what other skaters do in three or four. He is quick, too, and can get untracked in a heartbeat.

Sundin's shot is excellent. He can use a slap shot, one-timer, wrister or backhand. The only liability to his reach is that he will dangle the puck well away from his body and he doesn't always control it, which makes him vulnerable to a poke-check when he is in open ice.

THE PHYSICAL GAME

Sundin is big and strong. He has shown better attention to off-ice work to improve his strength. His conditioning is excellent — he can skate all night. He has even shown a touch of mean, but mostly with his stick.

THE INTANGIBLES

Sundin would probably be better utilized as a winger. But given Toronto's shallow middle and the need for a power guy to play against the rest of the league's power centres, he's stuck in the middle.

PROJECTION

Sundin surpassed the 80 points we predicted for him last year. With a better supporting cast he could squeeze by 90, but, again, 80 is more likely.

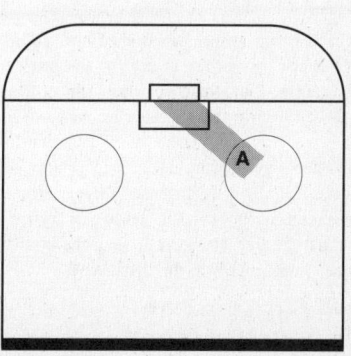

STEVE THOMAS

Yrs. of NHL service: 15
Born: Stockport, England; July 15, 1963
Position: left wing
Height: 5-11
Weight: 185
Uniform no.: 32
Shoots: left

Career statistics:

GP	G	A	TP	PIM
913	352	417	769	1097

1995-96 statistics:

GP	G	A	TP	+/-	PIM	PP	SH	GW	GT	S	PCT
81	26	35	61	-2	98	6	0	6	1	192	13.5

1996-97 statistics:

GP	G	A	TP	+/-	PIM	PP	SH	GW	GT	S	PCT
32	15	19	34	+9	46	1	0	2	0	124	12.1

1997-98 statistics:

GP	G	A	TP	+/-	PIM	PP	SH	GW	GT	S	PCT
55	14	10	24	+4	32	3	0	4	1	111	12.6

1998-99 statistics:

GP	G	A	TP	+/-	PIM	PP	SH	GW	GT	S	PCT
78	28	45	73	+26	33	11	0	7	0	209	13.4

LAST SEASON

Led team in power-play goals and game-winning goals. Second on team in assists, points and plus-minus. Tied for second on team in shots. Third on team in goals, with highest total since 1993-94. Ninth season with 20 or more goals. Missed three games with fractured toe. Missed one game with back spasms.

THE FINESSE GAME

Thomas was born again as a sniper when he signed as a free agent with Toronto in 1998, rejoining the team where he had started his career. The defensive yoke that had been thrown over his neck in New Jersey was discarded, and Thomas played with the joy of a free man.

He has a great shot and loves to fire away. He looks to shoot first instead of pass, sometimes to his detriment, but subtlety is not his forte. Thomas's game is speed and power, and he meshed well with Mats Sundin.

Thomas has a strong wrist shot and a quick one-timer. He likes to win the battle for the puck in deep, feed his centre, then head for the right circle for the return pass. Playing the left side he was not as effective. He has a very short backswing, which allows him to get his shots away quickly.

Thomas is a wildly intense player. His speed is straight ahead, without much deking or trying to put a move on a defender. He works along the boards and in the corners, willing to do the dirty work.

THE PHYSICAL GAME

Thomas is hard-nosed and finishes his checks. He is a very good forechecker because he comes at the puck carrier like a human train. He is not big but he is wide, and tough. He is great along the boards and among the best in the league at keeping the puck alive by using his feet. He is a feisty and fierce competitor and will throw the odd punch. He played through the end of the playoffs despite a bad shoulder separation.

THE INTANGIBLES

Coming home to Toronto gave Thomas a big jolt of adrenaline, but how long will the effects linger? He is 35. We might have seen his last big year.

PROJECTION

Thomas would be hard-pressed to repeat last season's performance, but he is likely to hit 20 again.

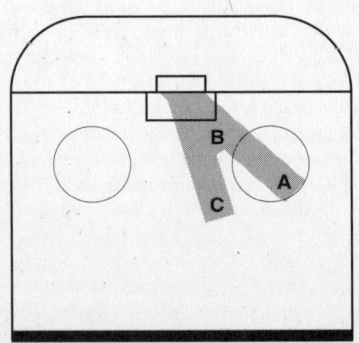

DIMITRI YUSHKEVICH

Yrs. of NHL service: 7
Born: Yaroslavl, USSR; Nov. 19, 1971
Position: right defense
Height: 5-11
Weight: 208
Uniform no.: 36
Shoots: right

Career statistics:

GP	G	A	TP	PIM
490	26	115	141	480

1995-96 statistics:

GP	G	A	TP	+/-	PIM	PP	SH	GW	GT	S	PCT
69	1	10	11	-14	54	1	0	0	0	96	1.0

1996-97 statistics:

GP	G	A	TP	+/-	PIM	PP	SH	GW	GT	S	PCT
74	4	10	14	-24	56	1	1	1	0	99	4.0

1997-98 statistics:

GP	G	A	TP	+/-	PIM	PP	SH	GW	GT	S	PCT
72	0	12	12	-13	78	0	0	0	0	92	0.0

1998-99 statistics:

GP	G	A	TP	+/-	PIM	PP	SH	GW	GT	S	PCT
78	6	22	28	+25	88	2	1	0	0	95	6.3

PROJECTION

Yushkevich appears to have found his groove. He can provide 30 minutes a night and 30 points a season.

LAST SEASON

Highest point total since 1993-94. Missed one game due to personal reasons. Missed three games with groin strain.

THE FINESSE GAME

When Yushkevich pulls everything together mentally and physically, he steps up into a level that isn't elite but is a solid "B" game. His problem in the past was that he did it so infrequently. He has become far more consistent over the past two years.

He is a good skater with a decent shot. It's a real good shot in practice, but in games, he takes too long to unload it. He is strong and well-balanced on his feet. He can move laterally, pivot and put on a short burst of speed, or sustain a rush the length of the rink. Occasionally he can be beaten with outside speed but it takes a pretty good skater to do it.

Yushkevich has improved his defensive reads to where he can be matched against other teams' top lines, and he thrives on the challenge.

THE PHYSICAL GAME

Yushkevich is very fit and, if asked, can play 30 minutes. He'll grind. He'll hit. He plays with a mean streak. He can hit to hurt and be annoying to play against.

THE INTANGIBLES

Yushkevich isn't the easiest player to deal with, but the Leafs have found the right buttons. He feels wanted here and has responded. A restricted free agent, he was looking for a raise in the off-season.

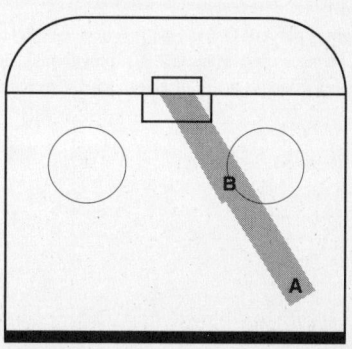

VANCOUVER CANUCKS

Players' Statistics 1998-99

POS	NO.	PLAYER	GP	G	A	PTS	+/-	PIM	PP	SH	GW	GT	S	PCT
L	19	MARKUS NASLUND	80	36	30	66	-13	74	15	2	3	1	205	17.6
C	11	MARK MESSIER	59	13	35	48	-12	33	4	2	2		97	13.4
R	89	ALEXANDER MOGILNY	59	14	31	45	0	58	3	2	1	1	110	12.7
R	17	*BILL MUCKALT	73	16	20	36	-9	98	4	2	1		119	13.4
D	2	MATTIAS OHLUND	74	9	26	35	-19	83	2	1	1		129	7.0
D	6	ADRIAN AUCOIN	82	23	11	34	-14	77	18	2	3	1	174	13.2
C	15	DAVE GAGNER	69	6	22	28	-16	63	2		1	1	100	6.0
D	55	ED JOVANOVSKI	72	5	22	27	-9	126	1		1		109	4.6
C	20	DAVE SCATCHARD	82	13	13	26	-12	140		2	2		130	10.0
D	4	BRYAN MCCABE	69	7	14	21	-11	120	1	2			98	7.1
L	8	DONALD BRASHEAR	82	8	10	18	-25	209	2		1		112	7.1
L	9	BRAD MAY	66	6	11	17	-14	102	1		1		91	6.6
L	44	TODD BERTUZZI	32	8	8	16	-6	44	1		3		72	11.1
C	27	HARRY YORK	56	7	9	16	-3	24	1			1	60	11.7
C	22	PETER ZEZEL	41	6	8	14	5	16	1		2		45	13.3
R	26	TRENT KLATT	75	4	10	14	-3	12					60	6.7
C	14	DARBY HENDRICKSON	62	4	5	9	-19	52	1				70	5.7
L	29	*PETER SCHAEFER	25	4	4	8	-1	8	1		1		24	16.7
D	23	MURRAY BARON	81	2	6	8	-23	115					53	3.8
C	21	*JOSH HOLDEN	30	2	4	6	-10	10	1				44	4.5
D	18	BERT ROBERTSSON	39	2	2	4	-7	13					13	15.4
D	34	JASON STRUDWICK	65		3	3	-19	114					25	
D	5	DANA MURZYN	12		2	2	1	21					7	
C	24	*MATT COOKE	30		2	2	-12	27					22	
R	25	STEVE STAIOS	57		2	2	-12	54					33	
D	3	*BRENT SOPEL	5	1	1	2	-1	4	1				5	20.0
G	30	GARTH SNOW	65		1	1	0	34						
C	7	*ROBB GORDON	4			0		2					1	
G	35	*KEVIN WEEKES	11			0								
C	28	STEVE WASHBURN	12				-1	6					6	
G	31	COREY HIRSCH	20					0						

GP = games played; G = goals; A = assists; PTS = points; +/- = goals-for minus goals-against while player is on ice; PIM = penalties in minutes; PP = power-play goals; SH = shorthanded goals; GW = game-winning goals; GT = game-tying goals; S = no. of shots; PCT = percentage of goals to shots; * = rookie

BRYAN ALLEN

Yrs. of NHL service: 0
Born: Kingston, Ont.; Aug. 21, 1980
Position: left defense
Height: 6-4
Weight: 210
Uniform no.: n.a.
Shoots: left

Career junior statistics:
GP	G	A	TP	PIM
145	15	32	47	279

LAST SEASON
Appeared in 37 games with Oshawa (OHL), scoring 7-15 — 22 with 77 PIM.

THE FINESSE GAME
A first-round (fourth overall) draft pick in 1998, Allen combines size and mobility in the kind of combination that has "blue chip prospect" written all over it. He was considered the most complete young defenseman available in that draft year.

Allen's skating, for his size, is very good. He uses his skating ability mostly in a defensive sense, since he doesn't have a great shot or the creative vision that would elevate the offensive part of his game. He does so many things well in his own zone that the points will hardly be missed. He is a fairly good passer and is able to move the puck smartly out of his end.

Allen loves to compete. He is poised, tough, and will bring his "A" game most nights.

THE PHYSICAL GAME
Allen loves to hit. He has the strength and the mobility to lay the smackdown with big open-ice hits. He works in the corners, along the boards and clears the front of his net. He's got a bit of a mean streak, too.

THE INTANGIBLES
Allen's development was hampered by shoulder and knee injuries that cut seriously into his playing time in junior last season. He is expected to develop along the lines of Derian Hatcher into a tough, stay-at-home style of defenseman. Like Hatcher, he is also a probable future NHL captain.

PROJECTION
Allen is expected to make the jump to the NHL this season, joining a pretty solid defense corps with Mattias Ohlund, Ed Jovanovski and Adrian Aucoin.

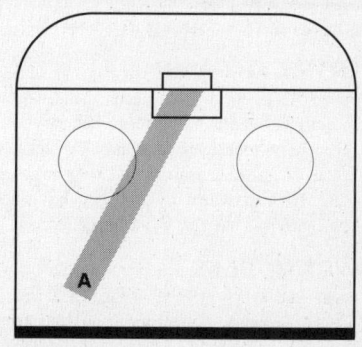

ADRIAN AUCOIN

Yrs. of NHL service: 4
Born: Ottawa, Ont.; July 3, 1973
Position: right defenseman
Height: 6-1
Weight: 194
Uniform no.: 6
Shoots: right

Career statistics:

GP	G	A	TP	PIM
237	36	44	80	195

1995-96 statistics:

GP	G	A	TP	+/-	PIM	PP	SH	GW	GT	S	PCT
49	4	14	18	+8	34	2	0	0	0	85	4.7

1996-97 statistics:

GP	G	A	TP	+/-	PIM	PP	SH	GW	GT	S	PCT
70	5	16	21	0	63	1	0	0	0	116	4.3

1997-98 statistics:

GP	G	A	TP	+/-	PIM	PP	SH	GW	GT	S	PCT
35	3	3	6	-4	21	1	0	1	0	44	6.8

1998-99 statistics:

GP	G	A	TP	+/-	PIM	PP	SH	GW	GT	S	PCT
82	23	11	34	-14	77	18	2	3	1	174	13.2

will both be firsts for him.

PROJECTION

Aucoin exceeded everyone's expectations last season. It's illogical to think he'll surpass, or even match, last season's numbers.

LAST SEASON

Led team and third in NHL in power-play goals. Second on team in goals with career high. Tied for team lead in game-winning goals and shorthanded goals. Second on team in shots. One of three Canucks to appear in all 82 games.

THE FINESSE GAME

Aucoin was a low draft pick (117th overall in 1992), but by playing with the Canadian national team and in the 1994 Olympics he has upgraded his offensive skills and developed into a promising offensive defenseman. Last season was truly a breakthrough year.

Aucoin is a mobile, agile skater who moves well with the puck. He doesn't have breakaway speed, but he jumps alertly into the play. On the power play, he smartly switches off with a forward to cut in deep, and he has good hands for shots in tight. He also has a good point shot. It is not elite, but Aucoin is very intelligent in his shot selection.

Aucoin also kills penalties. Only five of his goals last season came at even strength.

THE PHYSICAL GAME

Aucoin is a strong, good-sized defenseman who often plays smaller. He needs to be more assertive around the net. He has no mean streak to speak of; opponents know he can be pushed around and they take advantage of that. He just wants to play and have nobody notice him, which is usually what happens.

THE INTANGIBLES

Aucoin was due a big raise as a Group 2 free agent during the off-season. The money and the attention

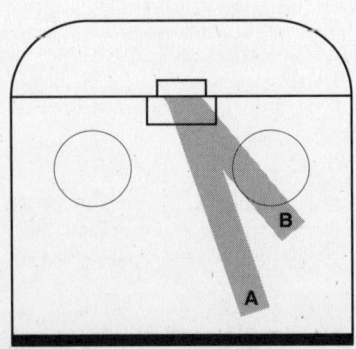

TODD BERTUZZI

Yrs. of NHL service: 4
Born: Sudbury, Ont.; Feb. 2, 1975
Position: left wing
Height: 6-3
Weight: 224
Uniform no.: 44
Shoots: left

Career statistics:

GP	G	A	TP	PIM
243	49	62	111	316

1995-96 statistics:

GP	G	A	TP	+/-	PIM	PP	SH	GW	GT	S	PCT
76	18	21	39	-14	83	4	0	2	0	127	14.2

1996-97 statistics:

GP	G	A	TP	+/-	PIM	PP	SH	GW	GT	S	PCT
64	10	13	23	-3	68	3	0	1	0	79	12.7

1997-98 statistics:

GP	G	A	TP	+/-	PIM	PP	SH	GW	GT	S	PCT
74	13	20	33	-17	121	2	1	2	0	102	12.7

1998-99 statistics:

GP	G	A	TP	+/-	PIM	PP	SH	GW	GT	S	PCT
32	8	8	16	-6	44	1	0	3	0	72	11.1

LAST SEASON

Missed 31 games with broken ribs. Missed 19 games with broken leg and torn knee ligaments.

THE FINESSE GAME

Bertuzzi was injured early and late last season, which made his progress, if any, impossible to assess.

Bertuzzi could become a poor man's John LeClair. He has physically dominating skills, but he doesn't have great vision. He has a tendency to roam all over the ice and doesn't think the game well. What he won't become is a physical, tough, aggressive fighter — a label the Islanders stuck on him when he began his career with that organization. It's not in his makeup.

Bertuzzi is instinctive and has great power to his game. For a big man, he's quick for his size and mobile, and he's got a good, soft pair of hands to complement his skating. With the puck, he can walk over people. He is effective in the slot area, yet he's also creative with the puck and can make some plays. He can find people down low and make things happen on the power play. With the puck, he is powerful and hard to stop, though he needs to improve his game without the puck. When he's not producing, all you notice are the flaws, mentally and defensively.

THE PHYSICAL GAME

Bertuzzi wanders around and doesn't finish his checks with authority. He can beat people, but he won't beat people up. He's a solid physical specimen who shows flashes of aggression and an occasional mean streak, but he really has to be pushed and aggravated to reach a boiling point. He won't run through people or challenge them consistently, and as a result doesn't establish a physical presence. Having Mark Messier as a role model could help Bertuzzi step up some of the physical components of his game, but Messier is mean by nature. Bertuzzi isn't.

THE INTANGIBLES

Still a relatively immature player, Bertuzzi could grow into a leader or he could remain a frustrating enigma. He needs to be handled intelligently, with an arm around his shoulder and a kick to the butt administered at the right times.

PROJECTION

Bertuzzi will get a late start because of rehab from his knee surgery. If he can come back with a 20-goal season, that would be a positive step.

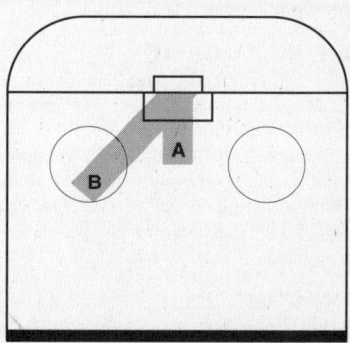

DONALD BRASHEAR

Yrs. of NHL service: 5
Born: Bedford, Ind.; Jan. 7, 1972
Position: left wing
Height: 6-2
Weight: 220
Uniform no.: 8
Shoots: left

Career statistics:

GP	G	A	TP	PIM
329	28	31	59	1146

1995-96 statistics:

GP	G	A	TP	+/-	PIM	PP	SH	GW	GT	S	PCT
67	0	4	4	-10	223	0	0	0	0	25	0.0

1996-97 statistics:

GP	G	A	TP	+/-	PIM	PP	SH	GW	GT	S	PCT
69	8	5	13	-8	245	0	0	2	0	61	13.1

1997-98 statistics:

GP	G	A	TP	+/-	PIM	PP	SH	GW	GT	S	PCT
77	9	9	18	-9	372	0	0	1	1	64	14.1

1998-99 statistics:

GP	G	A	TP	+/-	PIM	PP	SH	GW	GT	S	PCT
82	8	10	18	-25	209	2	0	1	0	112	7.1

LAST SEASON
Led team in penalty minutes. One of three Canucks to appear in all 82 games.

THE FINESSE GAME
No suspensions, no position in the top five PIM leaders in the NHL. Is Brashear getting soft?

Hardly. Brashear is a basher who has developed adequate skills to play a steady role on a grinding-type line. He once scored 38 goals in the AHL, but that is not going to happen in the big leagues. What Brashear will provide in high doses is a high level of energy. He scares opponents when he hones in on a puck carrier, and he finishes every check, often with too much enthusiasm.

Brashear can play on the third and fourth lines, and has to work hard for his scoring chances, most of which come from his churning around the net. He has a hard but predictable shot from the left circle. His puckhandling skills are minimal. His skating is rough and needs more work, but he's fairly fast.

THE PHYSICAL GAME
Brashear is big, tough and mean. He hits to hurt and creates a lot of room for himself. He takes a lot of needless penalties, though, and should learn to hit smarter, because the ref's eyes are always going to be on him and he can't get away with a late or high hit. He's a formidable fighter, and obviously he's had a lot of practice, though there aren't many people willing to test him anymore.

THE INTANGIBLES
Brashear has a great deal of confidence in himself (not for nothing does he have the word "brash" in his name). If he continues to hone his skills, he could be a more valuable member of his team, though he will never develop into a Bob Probert-type scorer.

PROJECTION
If your pool includes penalty minutes, take him. Goal-wise, Brashear will be lucky to break double digits.

ANDREW CASSELS

Yrs. of NHL service: 9
Born: Bramalea, Ont.; July 23, 1969
Position: centre
Height: 6-0
Weight: 192
Uniform no.: 21
Shoots: left

Career statistics:

GP	G	A	TP	PIM
649	134	324	458	292

1995-96 statistics:

GP	G	A	TP	+/-	PIM	PP	SH	GW	GT	S	PCT
81	20	43	63	+8	39	6	0	1	2	135	14.8

1996-97 statistics:

GP	G	A	TP	+/-	PIM	PP	SH	GW	GT	S	PCT
81	22	44	66	-16	46	8	0	2	0	142	15.5

1997-98 statistics:

GP	G	A	TP	+/-	PIM	PP	SH	GW	GT	S	PCT
81	17	27	44	-7	32	6	1	2	1	138	12.3

1998-99 statistics:

GP	G	A	TP	+/-	PIM	PP	SH	GW	GT	S	PCT
70	12	25	37	-12	18	4	1	3	0	97	12.4

LAST SEASON

Signed as free agent, July 13, 1999. Missed 12 games with groin injury.

THE FINESSE GAME

The first word most people associate with Cassels is: smart. He is an intelligent player with terrific hockey instincts, who knows when to recognize passing situations, when to move the puck and who to move it to. He has a good backhand pass in traffic and is almost as good on his backhand as his forehand. He is a creative passer who is aware of his teammates.

Cassels just hates to shoot. He won't do it much, and although he has spent a great deal of time practising it, his release is just not NHL calibre. He has quick hands, though, and can swipe a shot off a bouncing puck in midair. He doesn't always fight through checks to get the kind of shots he should.

A mainstay on both specialty teams, Cassels has improved on draws. He backchecks and blocks shots. He has good speed but lacks one-step quickness. He has improved his puckhandling at a high tempo.

THE PHYSICAL GAME

To complement his brains, Cassels needs brawn. He faces a lot of defensive pressure, although some of that will ease as he is expected to be a number two centre behind Mark Messier in Vancouver. He does not force his way through strong forechecks and traffic around the net. He tends to get run down late in the season or during a tough stretch in the schedule, and when he gets fatigued he is not nearly as effective.

THE INTANGIBLES

Cassels signed a three-year, $7.2-million deal to join the Canucks, which will be pressure in itself.

PROJECTION

Cassels will produce about 40 uneventful points.

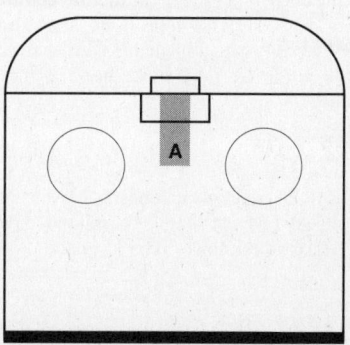

JOSH HOLDEN

Yrs. of NHL service: 1
Born: Calgary, Alta.; Jan. 18, 1978
Position: centre
Height: 6-0
Weight: 190
Uniform no.: 21
Shoots: left

Career statistics:

GP	G	A	TP	PIM
30	2	4	6	10

1998-99 statistics:

GP	G	A	TP	+/-	PIM	PP	SH	GW	GT	S	PCT
30	2	4	6	-10	10	1	0	0	0	44	4.5

LAST SEASON
First NHL season. Appeared in 37 games with Syracuse (AHL), scoring 14-15 — 29.

THE FINESSE GAME
Holden's skating and good hockey sense might be sufficient to help him keep a job in the NHL, but in order to be more of an impact player he has to maintain his intensity.

Holden has been a scorer at the minor-league level and has the potential to be an offensive centre at the NHL level as well. He is a good all-around skater with speed, acceleration and balance. He possesses good puckhandling skills, and is a good passer and playmaker. His shots are hard and accurate.

There were nights last season when Holden didn't put all of his assets together, and he is not talented enough to coast.

THE PHYSICAL GAME
Holden doesn't always play to his size. He is wiry and strong with good stamina. He could use a little more strength and needs to play with an abrasive style on more nights.

THE INTANGIBLES
Holden had a hand injury that hampered him at the end of the season, so much so that he could barely hold his stick. He also had mono about halfway through the year, which made his consistency harder to judge since he may have been worn down physically.

PROJECTION
Holden could be a third- or fourth-line player with the Canucks, or he could play alongside Markus Naslund again, as he did when filling in for injured players last season. His top limit looks to be 15 goals.

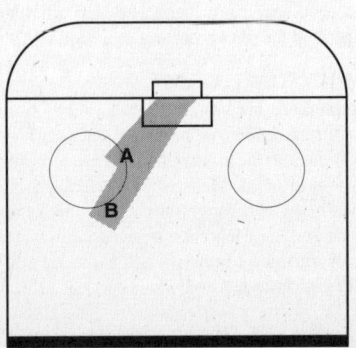

ED JOVANOVSKI

Yrs. of NHL service: 4
Born: Windsor, Ont.; June 26, 1976
Position: left defense
Height: 6-2
Weight: 205
Uniform no.: 55
Shoots: left

Career statistics:
GP	G	A	TP	PIM
284	31	63	94	593

1995-96 statistics:
GP	G	A	TP	+/-	PIM	PP	SH	GW	GT	S	PCT
70	10	11	21	-3	137	2	0	2	0	116	8.6

1996-97 statistics:
GP	G	A	TP	+/-	PIM	PP	SH	GW	GT	S	PCT
61	7	16	23	-1	172	3	0	1	0	80	8.8

1997-98 statistics:
GP	G	A	TP	+/-	PIM	PP	SH	GW	GT	S	PCT
81	9	14	23	-12	158	2	1	3	1	142	6.3

1998-99 statistics:
GP	G	A	TP	+/-	PIM	PP	SH	GW	GT	S	PCT
72	5	22	27	-9	126	1	0	1	0	109	4.6

LAST SEASON
Acquired from Florida with Dave Gagner, Mike Brown, Kevin Weekes and a draft pick for Pavel Bure, Bret Hedican, Brad Ference and a draft pick, Jan. 17, 1999. Third on team in penalty minutes. Tied for third in plus-minus.

THE FINESSE GAME
Jovanovski started playing hockey later than most NHLers, and his skating, which has improved dramatically, may still be improved a notch. He already streaks through the neutral zone like a freight train. He sure isn't pretty, but he's powerful.

Strong on his feet with a dynamic, quick stride, Jovanovski has more quickness than most big men, perhaps because of early soccer training, and he can use his feet to move the puck if his stick is tied up. His powerful hitting is made more wicked by the fact that he gets so much speed and leg drive. He can make plays, too. He gets a little time because his speed forces the opposition to back off, and he has a nice passing touch.

Jovanovski can also score, but he does not possess a great decision-making process yet and still makes some bad pinches. He has an excellent point shot and good vision of the ice for passing. He may develop along Scott Stevens/Ray Bourque lines and become a defenseman who can dominate in all zones. All of his skills are quite raw and are still catching up to his body.

THE PHYSICAL GAME
If he isn't yet the best open-ice hitter in the NHL — and many scouts and GMs affirm that he is — then Jovanovski will be wearing that mantle soon. He hits to hurt. Because of his size and agility, he is able to catch people right where he wants them. They aren't dirty hits, but they are real old-time hockey throwbacks, administered by a modern-sized defenseman.

The problem is that instead of neutralizing the Brendan Shanahans and the Eric Lindroses, Jovanovski is diverted from his game by smaller, peskier players. He is so easy to distract that this must be at the top of every team's game plan against the Canucks. He has to play smarter.

THE INTANGIBLES
Time to concentrate on Jovanovski's most vulnerable area: his head. Jovanovski can't believe he knows it all, because he doesn't. He can't try to do it all, because he can't. In a new setting, Jovanovski must regain his confidence by doing the simple things well, such as chipping the puck off the glass instead of looking for a home run pass, and taking the hit when it's there instead of getting foolishly out of position attempting to make a highlight splat.

PROJECTION
Jovanovski needs to forget about points (OK, not completely; he can still get 30) and the Norris Trophy and regain his rookie form.

TRENT KLATT

Yrs. of NHL service: 7
Born: Robbinsdale, Minn.; Jan. 30, 1971
Position: right wing
Height: 6-1
Weight: 205
Uniform no.: 26
Shoots: right

Career statistics:

GP	G	A	TP	PIM
460	79	124	203	186

1995-96 statistics:

GP	G	A	TP	+/-	PIM	PP	SH	GW	GT	S	PCT
71	7	12	19	+2	44	0	0	2	0	101	6.9

1996-97 statistics:

GP	G	A	TP	+/-	PIM	PP	SH	GW	GT	S	PCT
76	24	21	45	+9	20	5	5	5	0	131	18.3

1997-98 statistics:

GP	G	A	TP	+/-	PIM	PP	SH	GW	GT	S	PCT
82	14	28	42	+2	16	5	0	3	0	143	9.8

1998-99 statistics:

GP	G	A	TP	+/-	PIM	PP	SH	GW	GT	S	PCT
75	4	10	14	-3	12	0	0	0	0	60	6.7

LAST SEASON
Acquired from Philadelphia for a 2000 sixth-round draft pick, Oct. 19, 1998. Missed seven games due to coach's decision.

THE FINESSE GAME
Klatt is something of a choppy skater who doesn't have much use for the fancy stuff. He goes straight ahead — usually until he runs into someone from the other side.

Klatt is a player who can be sent onto the ice for the shift following a goal. In those situations, such players are trusted to continue the momentum if the goal was scored by their team, or reverse the momentum if the goal was scored by the opposition. Deployment at those times is a real compliment; Klatt earns it.

Klatt has a full-bore forechecking style that leads to turnovers. Alas, he doesn't have the hand skills to do much with his chances.

THE PHYSICAL GAME
Klatt looks harmless enough but he is a murderous hitter. He is 210 densely packed pounds, and his body checks can pack the wallop of a warhead. He may like the regular hits but he will go for the monster hit, the one guys feel for a week, every chance he gets. Strong leg drive and a powerful upper body help Klatt make sure the hits just keep on coming.

THE INTANGIBLES
Klatt's body slams can lift the whole bench. Klatt is so good at delivering train-wreck collisions. The more Klatt hits, the more the home fans are in the game. Anything else he provides is a bonus.

PROJECTION
Some checkers remain checkers because there is no pressure to score or do things on the offensive side of the puck; your job is merely to harry your opponent into a turnover or a less dangerous play. It is safe to pencil Klatt in for about 15 goals, and they'll all be honest ones. He is a starter on the NHL's All-Hard-Work Team.

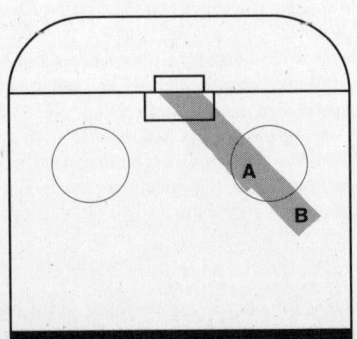

MARK MESSIER

Yrs. of NHL service: 20
Born: Edmonton, Alta.; Jan. 18, 1961
Position: centre
Height: 6-1
Weight: 205
Uniform no.: 11
Shoots: left

Career statistics:

GP	G	A	TP	PIM
1413	610	1050	1660	1687

1995-96 statistics:

GP	G	A	TP	+/-	PIM	PP	SH	GW	GT	S	PCT
74	47	52	99	+29	122	14	1	5	1	241	19.5

1996-97 statistics:

GP	G	A	TP	+/-	PIM	PP	SH	GW	GT	S	PCT
71	36	48	84	+12	88	7	5	9	1	227	15.9

1997-98 statistics:

GP	G	A	TP	+/-	PIM	PP	SH	GW	GT	S	PCT
82	22	38	60	-10	58	8	2	2	0	139	15.8

1998-99 statistics:

GP	G	A	TP	+/-	PIM	PP	SH	GW	GT	S	PCT
59	13	35	48	-12	33	4	2	2	0	97	13.4

LAST SEASON

Led team in assists. Tied for team lead in shorthanded goals. Second on team in points and shooting percentage. Tied for third on team in power-play goals. Missed 18 games with sprained knee. Missed four games with groin injury. Missed one game with concussion.

THE FINESSE GAME

Messier's strength is founded now on his reputation. His skills are eroding; injuries, age and hockey mileage are claiming him as their new victim. But somehow, when the spotlight is on, he rises once again to the occasion. It's the everyday Messier who has become less and less effective.

Messier has always been better at making the utmost use of his teammates, rather than trying one-on-one moves. His hallmark is his bottomless determination to win, which prevents his more skilled but less brave cohorts from faltering. He just drags them right to the front lines with him.

Messier is strong on his skates: he changes directions, pivots, bursts into open ice and, when his game is at its strongest, does it all with or without the puck. He still has tremendous acceleration and a powerful burst of straightaway speed, which is tailor-made for killing penalties and scoring shorthanded goals — even if he cheats into the neutral zone, looking for a breakaway pass, too often.

Messier's shot of choice is a wrister off the back ("wrong") foot from the right-wing circle, which is where he always seems to gravitate. It's a trademark, and it still fools many a goalie. He also makes as much use of the backhand, for passing and shooting, as any other North American player in the league. He will weave to the right-wing circle, fake a pass to the centre, get the goalie to cheat away from the post, then flip a backhand under the crossbar. He shoots from almost anywhere and is unpredictable in his shot selection when the back-foot wrist is not available.

THE PHYSICAL GAME

The Messier mean streak is legendary, even if less frequently evident. He is a master of the preemptive strike, the elbows or stick held teeth-high when a checker is coming towards him. Anyone who goes into the corner with Messier pays the price.

THE INTANGIBLES

There are few better big-game players in NHL history than Messier, but the past is the past, and at 38 he is simply overtaxed by the amount of playing time he sees night after night in Vancouver, where he is frequently the team's best forward.

PROJECTION

Messier will still get a respectable amount of points — he was second on the team in scoring despite missing 23 games — but without much help expected up front he will be hard-pressed to score 60.

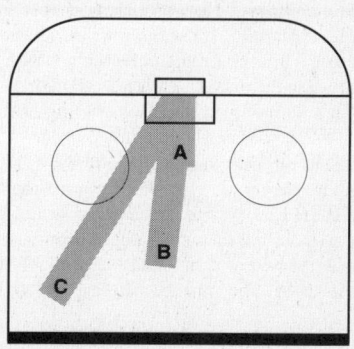

ALEXANDER MOGILNY

Yrs. of NHL service: 10
Born: Khabarovsk, Russia; Feb. 18, 1969
Position: right wing
Height: 5-11
Weight: 187
Uniform no.: 89
Shoots: left

Career statistics:

GP	G	A	TP	PIM
646	329	385	714	331

1995-96 statistics:

GP	G	A	TP	+/-	PIM	PP	SH	GW	GT	S	PCT
79	55	52	107	+14	16	10	5	6	3	292	18.8

1996-97 statistics:

GP	G	A	TP	+/-	PIM	PP	SH	GW	GT	S	PCT
76	31	42	73	+9	18	7	1	4	1	174	17.7

1997-98 statistics:

GP	G	A	TP	+/-	PIM	PP	SH	GW	GT	S	PCT
51	18	27	45	-6	36	5	4	1	1	118	15.3

1998-99 statistics:

GP	G	A	TP	+/-	PIM	PP	SH	GW	GT	S	PCT
59	14	31	45	0	58	3	2	1	1	110	12.7

LAST SEASON

Led team in plus-minus. Tied for team lead in short-handed goals. Second on team in assists. Third on team in points. Missed 19 games with knee injury. Missed four games with abdominal pull.

THE FINESSE GAME

Mogilny's biggest problems continue to be his inconsistency and motivation. He has so many wondrous skills, but most of the time he just doesn't seem interested. What a waste. Even with his injuries there is little excuse for what Mogilny has produced the past few seasons.

Skating is the basis of Mogilny's game. He has a burst of speed from a standstill and hits his top speed in just a few strides. When he streaks down the ice there is a good chance you'll see something new, something you didn't expect. He is unbelievably quick.

Mogilny's anticipation sets him apart from players who are merely fast. He won't skate deeply into his own defensive zone. He waits for a turnover and a chance to get a jump on the defenseman, with a preferred move to the outside. He's not afraid to go inside either, so a defenseman intent on angling him to the boards could just as easily get burned inside.

Mogilny can beat you in so many ways. He has a powerful and accurate wrist shot from the tops of the circles in. He shoots without breaking stride. He can work a give-and-go that is a thing of beauty. He one-times with the best of them. And everything is done at racehorse speed. The game comes easy to Mogilny.

THE PHYSICAL GAME

Mogilny doesn't work as hard as he should, and there always seems to be something left in the tank. There are nights when he is invisible on the ice, and that is unpardonable for a player of his ability and importance.

Mogilny intimidates with his speed but will also add a physical element. He has great upper-body strength and will drive through a defender to the net.

THE INTANGIBLES

Mogilny is not well-liked by his teammates and wants out. But his reputation precedes him; he will be tough to deal. Who would have thought that 1995 trade, which brought him from Buffalo for Mike Peca and Jay McKee, would now be tilted so sharply in the Sabres' favour?

PROJECTION

$4.2 million for 14 goals? He needs to score at least 30 again for anyone to be interested in him.

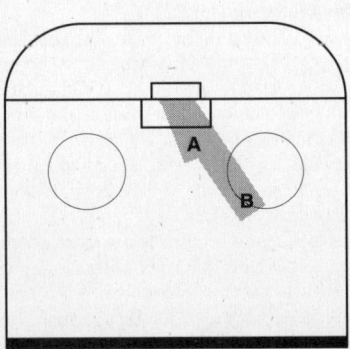

BILL MUCKALT

Yrs. of NHL service: 1
Born: Surrey, B.C.; July 15, 1974
Position: right wing
Height: 6-0
Weight: 190
Uniform no.: 17
Shoots: right

Career statistics:

GP	G	A	TP	PIM
73	16	20	36	98

1998-99 statistics:

GP	G	A	TP	+/-	PIM	PP	SH	GW	GT	S	PCT
73	16	20	36	-9	98	4	2	1	0	119	13.4

LAST SEASON

Third among NHL rookies in goals. Fifth among NHL rookies in assists. Sixth among NHL rookies in points. Tied for team lead in shorthanded goals. Tied for second on team in shooting percentage. Third on team in goals and plus-minus. Tied for third on team in power-play goals. Missed nine games with ankle injury.

THE FINESSE GAME

Muckalt entered the NHL as an older rookie after completing his college career (University of Michigan) — by leading the CCHA in assists and points.

Muckalt has all the skills, and while he could have used a season in the minors to adapt to the pro game, the Canucks needed him right away. His best asset is his hockey sense. He understands the game and has good vision.

He is a late bloomer who shot up the depth chart thanks to his skating (which is NHL calibre), his shot and his passing ability.

THE PHYSICAL GAME

Muckalt is of average size, but he is fairly strong and willing to do the work along the boards.

THE INTANGIBLES

Muckalt was a leading candidate for NHL rookie of the year at midseason but hit the wall, not unusual for a player making the leap from a short college schedule to the NHL. He didn't score a goal in his last 15 games before his season was ended by his ankle injury. He is a restricted free agent and due for a raise.

PROJECTION

Muckalt needs to regain any confidence lost in the second half of the season, which won't be easy to do on this team. He should learn from his rookie year and improve slightly to 40 points.

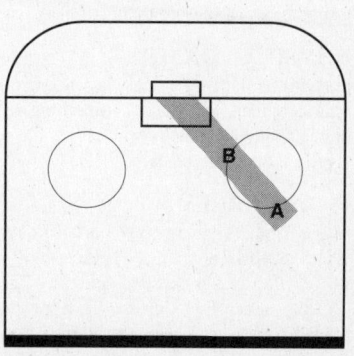

MARKUS NASLUND

Yrs. of NHL service: 6
Born: Bonassund, Sweden; July 30, 1973
Position: left/right wing
Height: 6-0
Weight: 186
Uniform no.: 19
Shoots: left

Career statistics:

GP	G	A	TP	PIM
395	99	112	211	231

1995-96 statistics:

GP	G	A	TP	+/-	PIM	PP	SH	GW	GT	S	PCT
76	22	33	55	+20	42	4	0	5	0	144	15.3

1996-97 statistics:

GP	G	A	TP	+/-	PIM	PP	SH	GW	GT	S	PCT
78	21	20	41	-15	30	4	0	4	0	120	17.5

1997-98 statistics:

GP	G	A	TP	+/-	PIM	PP	SH	GW	GT	S	PCT
76	14	20	34	+5	56	2	1	0	0	106	13.2

1998-99 statistics:

GP	G	A	TP	+/-	PIM	PP	SH	GW	GT	S	PCT
80	36	30	66	-13	74	15	2	3	1	205	17.6

LAST SEASON

Led team in goals and points with career highs. Led team in shots and shooting percentage. Tied for team lead in game-winning goals and shorthanded goals. Second on team in power-play goals. Third on team in assists. Missed two games due to coach's decision.

THE FINESSE GAME

Naslund is a pure sniper. He has excellent snap and wrist shots and can score in just about every way imaginable, including the backhand in tight. He has quick hands and an accurate touch.

He needs to play with people who will get him the puck. He will not play aggressively and dig in the corners for the puck, and he's a little shy in traffic. But he's a jitterbug on the ice and can keep up with the fastest linemates.

Naslund has good hockey sense in the attacking zone, though he does not play well defensively and tends to shy away from the boards. He needs to work on his game to become more than a one-way winger.

THE PHYSICAL GAME

Naslund is erratic in his physical play. Some nights he plays a little bigger, and makes something of a pest out of himself; other nights he's invisible. He needs to be involved on a nightly basis.

THE INTANGIBLES

Naslund and Peter Forsberg were born 10 days apart, but they are a world apart in NHL accomplishment. Naslund, a former first-round draft pick (by Pittsburgh in 1991), has never lived up to the hype that surrounded his first few seasons in the NHL. Although he was the fourth-leading scorer on the Canucks, he ended the season playing on the fourth line.

PROJECTION

Now that Naslund has shown what he can truly accomplish over the course of a season, he must maintain that level of consistency and establish himself as a reliable 30-goal scorer.

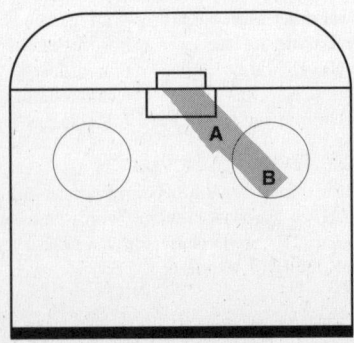

MATTIAS OHLUND

Yrs. of NHL service: 2
Born: Pitea, Sweden; Sept. 9, 1976
Position: defense
Height: 6-3
Weight: 209
Uniform no.: 2
Shoots: left

Career statistics:

GP	G	A	TP	PIM
151	16	49	65	159

1997-98 statistics:

GP	G	A	TP	+/-	PIM	PP	SH	GW	GT	S	PCT
77	7	23	30	+3	76	1	0	0	0	172	4.1

1998-99 statistics:

GP	G	A	TP	+/-	PIM	PP	SH	GW	GT	S	PCT
74	9	26	35	-19	83	2	1	1	0	129	7.0

LAST SEASON
Led team defensemen in points. Missed five games with concussion. Missed three games with shoulder injury.

THE FINESSE GAME
Ohlund has a high skill level and a big body to go with it. He is a lovely, fluid skater with splendid agility for his size. He's very confident with the puck. Because of his skating and his reach, he is difficult to beat one-on-one. He isn't fooled by dekes, either. He plays the crest and maintains his position.

Ohlund is a good power-play player from the right point. He uses an effective, short backswing on his one-timer. He makes a sharp first pass out of the defensive zone, and gets involved in the attack by moving up into the rush (but he won't get caught deep very often).

Ohlund just keeps growing, but unlike many young skaters who experience sudden growth spurts, he has stayed balanced in his skating.

THE PHYSICAL GAME
Ohlund is big and powerful. He is assertive, won't be intimidated and finishes his checks. He clears out the front of the net and works the boards and corners. For a player considered to be a finesse defenseman, Ohlund plays an involved game. He has an iron constitution and can handle 30 minutes of ice time every night.

THE INTANGIBLES
Like many a second-year player, Ohlund hit a mental and physical wall last season. He is one of the best young players in the NHL. He has the mental and physical tools to rebound and improve off his strong rookie season.

PROJECTION
Ohlund could score 40 points if the Canucks improve even slightly over last season.

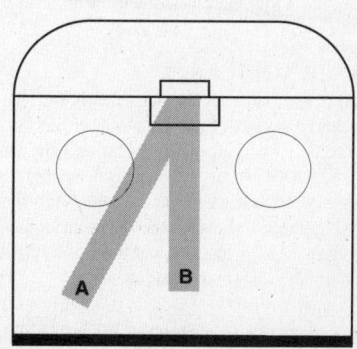

PETER SCHAEFER

Yrs. of NHL service: 0
Born: Yellow Grass, Sask.; July 12, 1977
Position: left wing
Height: 5-11
Weight: 190
Uniform no.: 29
Shoots: left

Career statistics:

GP	G	A	TP	PIM
25	4	4	8	8

1998-99 statistics:

GP	G	A	TP	+/-	PIM	PP	SH	GW	GT	S	PCT
25	4	4	8	-1	8	1	0	1	0	24	16.7

LAST SEASON
Will be entering first NHL season. Missed six games with strained shoulder. Missed three games due to coach's decision. Appeared in 41 games with Syracuse (AHL), scoring 10-19 — 29.

THE FINESSE GAME
Schaefer is pure skill. He is a good skater with a fluid style, and he's hard to knock off his skates. He has quick moves and deceptive speed, especially when busting moves to the outside. He also has excellent one-on-one moves and the potential to become one of Vancouver's top six forwards.

He has very good hands and is smart around the net. He can shoot the puck well with a quick release, and is also a good passer and playmaker. Schaefer forechecks aggressively and has good hockey sense. He is strong on the puck.

Schaefer likes to cheat a little bit in the defensive zone, but he is aware defensively. He just needs to apply himself a bit more.

THE PHYSICAL GAME
Schaefer has fair size and strength. Not a big hitter, he uses his body to angle the opponent out of the play. He could stand to add some upper-body muscle. He doesn't look for trouble but won't back down. He competes most nights and is disciplined with a good work ethic.

THE INTANGIBLES
The worst-case scenario for Schaefer is that he could develop into a speedy checking wing with 20-goal potential and a top-notch penalty killer and shorthanded threat, much like Brian Rolston. But Schaefer could progress beyond that. His first full season in the NHL should give some indication as to which direction he is heading in. One caveat: he had a bit of a run-in with coaches in the Vancouver system.

PROJECTION
Schaefer showed nice flashes in his brief stint with the Canucks last season. A 15-goal full rookie year is likely.

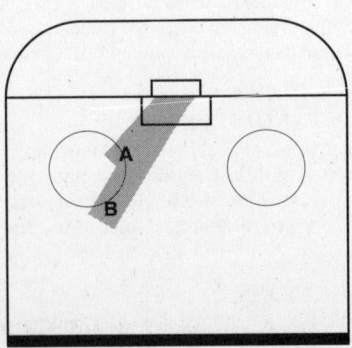

GARTH SNOW

Yrs. of NHL service: 4
Born: Wrentham, Mass.; July 28, 1969
Position: goaltender
Height: 6-3
Weight: 200
Uniform no.: 30
Catches: left

Career statistics:

GP	MIN	GA	SO	GAA	A	PIM
174	9377	441	9	2.82	2	104

1995-96 statistics:

GP	MIN	GAA	W	L	T	SO	GA	S	SAPCT	PIM
26	1437	2.88	12	8	4	0	69	648	.894	18

1996-97 statistics:

GP	MIN	GAA	W	L	T	SO	GA	S	SAPCT	PIM
35	1884	2.52	14	8	8	2	79	816	.902	30

1997-98 statistics:

GP	MIN	GAA	W	L	T	SO	GA	S	SAPCT	PIM
40	2137	2.58	17	14	4	1	92	944	.903	22

1998-99 statistics:

GP	MIN	GAA	W	L	T	SO	GA	S	SAPCT	PIM
65	3501	2.93	20	31	8	6	171	1715	.900	34

LAST SEASON
Led NHL goalies in penalty minutes (34). Tied for fourth in NHL in shutouts.

THE PHYSICAL GAME
Snow is a big, awkward goalie with heavy feet. Few netminders have abused the rules about equipment size (until the recent crackdown) as much as Snow, though it was more for a psychological edge than anything else. We haven't seen those two twin peaks of shoulder pads stopping many pucks. He also sews a padded "cheater" strip on the outside of his shorts. He probably orders early wake-up calls at opponents' hotels. Anything for a perceived advantage.

Snow plays a stand-up style, though not as rigidly as longtime Vancouver goalie Kirk McLean. Snow's relexes aren't razor-sharp and his technique needs a great deal of work. He does not handle the puck well. His size is about all he has going for him.

THE MENTAL GAME
Snow hasn't yet shown that he is able to handle the pressure of being a number one goalie. His moment in the sun came in the 1997 playoffs for the Flyers, but his performances were wholly unmemorable.

THE INTANGIBLES
Snow's position as the number one goalie in Vancouver was being challenged by Kevin Weekes, who was given a lot of Snow's starts late in the season, but has never won an NHL game.

PROJECTION
Snow will have to fight for respect and 20 wins this season. We doubt he'll get either.

JASON STRUDWICK

Yrs. of NHL service: 2
Born: Edmonton, Alberta; July 17, 1975
Position: left defense
Height: 6-3
Weight: 215
Uniform no.: 34
Shoots: left

Career statistics:

GP	G	A	TP	PIM
95	0	5	5	186

1995-96 statistics:

GP	G	A	TP	+/-	PIM	PP	SH	GW	GT	S	PCT
1	0	0	0	0	7	0	0	0	0	0	0.0

1996-97 statistics:
Did not play in NHL

1997-98 statistics:

GP	G	A	TP	+/-	PIM	PP	SH	GW	GT	S	PCT
77	3	4	7	-3	134	0	0	1	0	45	6.7

1998-99 statistics:

GP	G	A	TP	+/-	PIM	PP	SH	GW	GT	S	PCT
65	0	3	3	-19	114	0	0	0	0	25	.0

LAST SEASON
Missed 17 games due to coach's decision.

THE FINESSE GAME
Strudwick is a good skater and strong on his skates, but he lacks the quickness that marks his cousin Scott Niedermayer's game. Strudwick has worked hard to improve his skating but he remains the weakest part of his game.

Strudwick has to concentrate on his positional play to compensate. He plays a fairly conservative game, won't pinch unwisely and won't step up in the neutral zone. He is learning to let the play come to him. He has a long reach and he uses it well.

Strudwick's game is heavily defense-oriented. His puck skills are okay and he is wise to limit himself. He moves the puck adequately. It would help Strudwick to play with a better skater.

THE PHYSICAL GAME
Strudwick plays an energetic and enthusiastic game. He likes to hit and makes good use of his size.

THE INTANGIBLES
Strudwick has struggled adjusting to the pace of the NHL game. If he sticks, it will be because the Canucks like the edge he brings to his game. He will be limited to work on the third defense pair. He is on the bubble and has to play like he knows it.

PROJECTION
Strudwick's point totals will barely approach 10, though his PIM totals could be impressive.

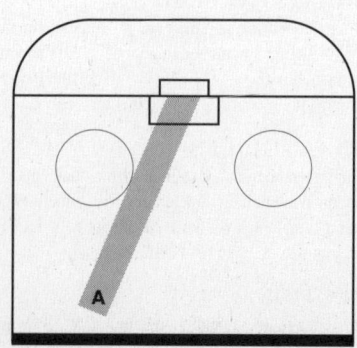

WASHINGTON CAPITALS

Players' Statistics 1998-99

POS.	NO.	PLAYER	GP	G	A	PTS	+/-	PIM	PP	SH	GW	GT	S	PCT
R	12	PETER BONDRA	66	31	24	55	-1	56	6	3	5	1	284	10.9
C	77	ADAM OATES	59	12	42	54	-1	22	3				79	15.2
L	23	BRIAN BELLOWS	76	17	19	36	-12	26	8		3		166	10.2
C	13	ANDREI NIKOLISHIN	73	8	27	35	0	28		1	1		121	6.6
D	55	SERGEI GONCHAR	53	21	10	31	1	57	13	1	3		180	11.7
C	28	JAMES BLACK	75	16	14	30	5	14	1	1	3		135	11.9
D	6	CALLE JOHANSSON	67	8	21	29	10	22	2		2	1	145	5.5
L	22	STEVE KONOWALCHUK	45	12	12	24	0	26	4	1	2		98	12.2
C	8	JAN BULIS	38	7	16	23	3	6	3		3		57	12.3
D	2	KEN KLEE	78	7	13	20	-9	80			1		132	5.3
L	44	RICHARD ZEDNIK	49	9	8	17	-6	50	1		2		115	7.8
D	15	DMITRI MIRONOV	46	2	14	16	-5	80	2				86	2.3
L	34	JAROSLAV SVEJKOVSKY	25	6	8	14	-2	12	4		2		50	12.0
C	20	MICHAL PIVONKA	36	5	6	11	-6	12	2				30	16.7
L	17	CHRIS SIMON	23	3	7	10	-4	48					29	10.3
D	29	JOE REEKIE	73		10	10	11	68					81	
C	48	*BENOIT GRATTON	16	4	3	7	-1	16					24	16.7
D	19	BRENDAN WITT	54	2	5	7	-6	87					51	3.9
L	10	KELLY MILLER	62	2	5	7	-5	29			1		49	4.1
L	36	MIKE EAGLES	52	4	2	6	-5	50					41	9.8
L	21	JEFF TOMS	21	1	5	6	0	2					30	3.3
D	24	MARK TINORDI	48		6	6	-6	108					32	
D	39	ENRICO CICCONE	59	3	1	4	-7	127				1	52	5.8
C	26	*MATTHEW HERR	30	2	2	4	-7	8	1				40	5.0
R	18	TREVOR HALVERSON	17		4	4	-5	28					16	
G	37	OLAF KOLZIG	64		2	2	0	19						
D	41	*PATRICK BOILEAU	4		1	1	-4	2					7	
G	40	MIKE ROSATI	1				0							
C	14	PATRICK AUGUSTA	2				0						4	
G	1	*MARTIN BROCHU	2				0	2						
R	14	PATRICE LEFEBVRE	3				-2	2					2	
D	38	*NOLAN BAUMGARTNER	5				-3						1	
D	4	*ALEXEI TEZIKOV	5				-1						4	
D	3	STEWART MALGUNAS	10				-5	6					2	
D	33	STEVE POAPST	22				-8	8					11	
G	31	RICK TABARACCI	23				0	2						

GP = games played; G = goals; A = assists; PTS = points; +/- = goals-for minus goals-against while player is on ice; PIM = penalties in minutes; PP = power-play goals; SH = shorthanded goals; GW = game-winning goals; GT = game-tying goals; S = no. of shots; PCT = percentage of goals to shots; * = rookie

NOLAN BAUMGARTNER

Yrs. of NHL service: 0
Born: Calgary, Alberta; Mar. 23, 1976
Position: defense
Height: 6-1
Weight: 200
Uniform no.: 38
Shoots: right

Career statistics:

GP	G	A	TP	PIM
10	0	1	1	0

1995-96 statistics:

GP	G	A	TP	+/-	PIM	PP	SH	GW	GT	S	PCT
1	0	0	0	-1	0	0	0	0	0	0	0.0

1996-97 statistics:
Did not play in NHL

1997-98 statistics:

GP	G	A	TP	+/-	PIM	PP	SH	GW	GT	S	PCT
4	0	1	1	0	0	0	0	0	0	4	0.0

1998-99 statistics:

GP	G	A	TP	+/-	PIM	PP	SH	GW	GT	S	PCT
5	0	0	0	-3	0	0	0	0	0	1	.0

LAST SEASON

Will be entering first full NHL season. Appeared in 39 games with Portland (AHL), scoring 5-14 — 19. Missed four games due to coach's decision.

THE FINESSE GAME

Baumgartner is a good skater who is seldom beaten one-on-one. Most of his finesse skills — his skating, his passing — he utilizes in a defensive role. He does not have the elite speed to race up-ice leading rushes, though he can join a rush.

He has good lateral movement, which may make Baumgartner a weapon on the power-play point in the future. He doesn't have a great shot but he can make the kind of passes and low shots that are tippable.

Baumgartner has a good head for the game. He sees the ice well and has a low panic point. He can make a sharp headman pass to set up an odd-man rush. He plays well positionally and doesn't go around looking for big hits. He will become a solid penalty killer with more experience.

THE PHYSICAL GAME

Baumgartner needs to get stronger to survive the everyday battles an NHL defenseman faces. He needs to be able to dominate in front of his net. He works hard on his cardio conditioning but needs to add about 10 pounds of muscle. He is not a very aggressive player, though he can deliver solid body checks.

THE INTANGIBLES

Baumgartner has been a winner (back-to-back Memorial Cups with Kamloops of the WHL) and a leader (captain of gold medalist Team Canada at the 1996 World Junior Championships). He is coachable.

This is a pivotal year for him to make the commitment to being an NHL player.

PROJECTION

It's make or break for Baumgartner, who needs to stick as a fifth or sixth defenseman or get ready to be traded. He won't score much, though his assists (15 to 20 over a full season) will be a respectable contribution.

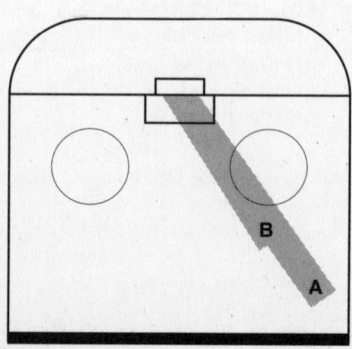

JAMES BLACK

Yrs. of NHL service: 7
Born: Regina, Sask.; Aug. 15, 1969
Position: centre
Height: 6-0
Weight: 202
Uniform no.: 28
Shoots: left

Career statistics:

GP	G	A	TP	PIM
261	49	43	92	74

1995-96 statistics:

GP	G	A	TP	+/-	PIM	PP	SH	GW	GT	S	PCT
13	3	3	6	+1	16	0	0	1	0	23	13.0

1996-97 statistics:

GP	G	A	TP	+/-	PIM	PP	SH	GW	GT	S	PCT
64	12	11	39	+6	20	0	0	3	0	122	9.8

1997-98 statistics:

GP	G	A	TP	+/-	PIM	PP	SH	GW	GT	S	PCT
52	10	5	15	-8	8	2	1	3	1	90	11.1

1998-99 statistics:

GP	G	A	TP	+/-	PIM	PP	SH	GW	GT	S	PCT
75	16	14	30	+5	14	1	1	3	0	135	11.9

PROJECTION
Black can score 15 to 20 goals in a third-line role.

LAST SEASON
Acquired from Chicago for future considerations, Oct. 15, 1998. Career highs in goals, assists and points. Second on team in shooting percentage. Tied for second on team in game-winning goals. Third on team in plus-minus. Appeared in five games with Chicago (IHL), scoring 6-0 — 6. Missed one game due to coach's decision.

THE FINESSE GAME
Black is a reliable, consistent forward who can always be counted on to make the safe play. You can put him on the ice and be pretty sure he is not going to make a play that gets your team scored on again.

Defense always comes first for Black, but he showed a respectable offensive side for the Caps last season as well. He has a big shot but it seldom occurs to him to use it. He doesn't think of himself as a scorer at this level, and it simply doesn't occur to him to try anything creative.

Black is a good skater. He doesn't have any breakaway speed but he capable enough at the NHL level.

THE PHYSICAL GAME
There is no physical element to his game, but Black is good along the boards in terms of always getting the puck in or out.

THE INTANGIBLES
After years of kicking around in the minors and bouncing from one organization to the next, Black may have found a home in Washington.

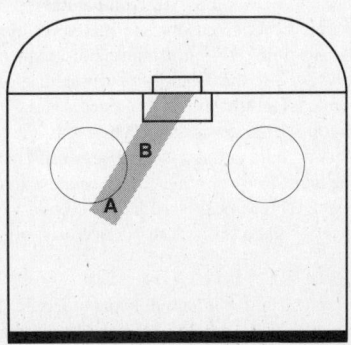

PETER BONDRA

Yrs. of NHL service: 9
Born: Luck, Ukraine; Feb. 7, 1968
Position: right wing
Height: 6-1
Weight: 200
Uniform no.: 12
Shoots: left

Career statistics:

GP	G	A	TP	PIM
610	316	229	545	435

1995-96 statistics:

GP	G	A	TP	+/-	PIM	PP	SH	GW	GT	S	PCT
67	52	28	80	+18	40	11	4	7	3	322	16.1

1996-97 statistics:

GP	G	A	TP	+/-	PIM	PP	SH	GW	GT	S	PCT
77	46	31	77	+7	72	10	4	3	2	314	14.6

1997-98 statistics:

GP	G	A	TP	+/-	PIM	PP	SH	GW	GT	S	PCT
76	52	26	78	+14	44	11	5	13	2	284	18.3

1998-99 statistics:

GP	G	A	TP	+/-	PIM	PP	SH	GW	GT	S	PCT
66	31	24	55	-1	56	6	3	5	1	284	10.9

LAST SEASON

Led team in goals and shorthanded goals, both for fifth consecutive season. Led team in shots, points and game-winning goals. Third on team in assists and power-play goals. Missed 15 games with broken hand. Missed one game with hip injury.

THE FINESSE GAME

Bondra is in the category of players you would pay to watch play. His speed is exceptional and he is intelligent on the ice offensively. He accelerates quickly and smoothly and drives defenders back because they have to play off his speed. If he gets hooked to the ice he doesn't stay down, but jumps back to his skates and gets involved in the play again, often after the defender has forgotten about him. He has excellent balance and quickness.

Bondra skates as fast with the puck as without it, and he wants the puck early. He cuts in on the off-wing and shoots in stride. He has a very good backhand shot and likes to cut out from behind the net and make things happen in tight. He mixes up his shots. He will fire quickly — not many European players have this good a slap shot — or drive in close and deke and wrist a little shot.

Bondra is a dangerous shorthanded threat with 25 shorthanded goals in the past five seasons. He makes opposing teams' power plays jittery because of his anticipation and breakaway speed, and he follows up his shots to the net and is quick to pounce on rebounds.

THE PHYSICAL GAME

Bondra isn't strong, but he will lean on people. He has improved his off-ice conditioning and he handled a lot of ice time last season. He doesn't seem to tire, and is much more determined in fighting through checks.

THE INTANGIBLES

Even taking into account his hand injury, Bondra slid a little last season. It could be a reflection of the overall injury problems on the Caps, or a sign of something more serious.

PROJECTION

Last season was a blip on the radar and Bondra should return to the ranks of the 50-goal scorers.

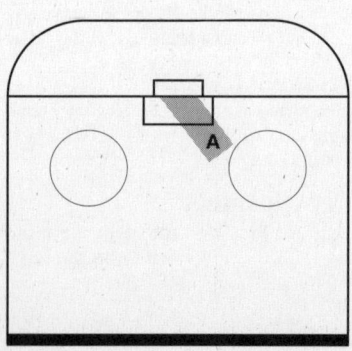

JAN BULIS

Yrs. of NHL service: 2
Born: Paradubice, Czech Republic; Mar. 18, 1978
Position: centre
Height: 6-0
Weight: 194
Uniform no.: 8
Shoots: left

Career statistics:

GP	G	A	TP	PIM
86	12	27	39	24

1997-98 statistics:

GP	G	A	TP	+/-	PIM	PP	SH	GW	GT	S	PCT
48	5	11	16	-5	18	0	0	0	1	37	13.5

1998-99 statistics:

GP	G	A	TP	+/-	PIM	PP	SH	GW	GT	S	PCT
38	7	16	23	+3	6	3	0	3	0	57	12.5

LAST SEASON

Second NHL season. Tied for second on team in game-winning goals. Missed 28 games with ankle injuries. Missed one game due to coach's decision. Appeared in 10 games with Cincinnati (IHL), scoring 2-2 — 4.

THE FINESSE GAME

Bulis has decent size, and the skating and skills that stamp him as a future top forward. He handles the puck well through traffic or in the open at high tempo. He suffered a broken hand midseason, which set back his development slightly.

Bulis is more of a playmaker than a scorer, but he is not a pure passer. He has a quick release on his wrist shot and will take the shot if that is his better option, rather than try to force the pass. He has a good slap shot, too. His shot was clocked at close to 90 m.p.h. when he was in his first year of junior.

Bulis plays a smart positional game and will not need too much tutoring to learn the defensive aspects of the NHL game. He is a well-conditioned athlete and has a lot of stamina to handle the ice time and travel.

THE PHYSICAL GAME

Bulis brings an infectious enthusiasm, whether it's to a game or an everyday practice session. Like Jaromir Jagr, he is one of those players who looks like he is simply having a great time playing hockey, but Bulis is also serious about the sport. He has a work ethic that has earned him the respect of the veterans, and he'll be a quiet leader for his fellow younger players. He isn't aggressive, but he is stocky and strong on his skates. He can compete in a physical game and he likes to hit.

THE INTANGIBLES

Bulis's development was slowed by his serious ankle injury, and he finished the season in the minors. He is the number one centre of the Caps' future. He'll be number two behind Adam Oates this year.

PROJECTION

Bulis should score more than 50 points as he continues to make his way in the NHL. He has a breakthrough season a year or two down the line.

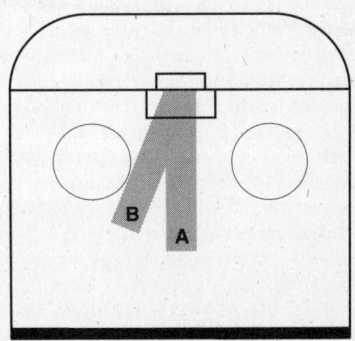

SERGEI GONCHAR

Yrs. of NHL service: 5
Born: Chelyabinsk, Russia; Apr. 13, 1974
Position: left defense
Height: 6-2
Weight: 212
Uniform no.: 55
Shoots: left

Career statistics:

GP	G	A	TP	PIM
291	56	74	130	241

1995-96 statistics:

GP	G	A	TP	+/-	PIM	PP	SH	GW	GT	S	PCT
78	15	26	41	+25	60	4	0	4	0	139	10.8

1996-97 statistics:

GP	G	A	TP	+/-	PIM	PP	SH	GW	GT	S	PCT
57	13	17	30	-11	36	3	0	3	0	129	10.1

1997-98 statistics:

GP	G	A	TP	+/-	PIM	PP	SH	GW	GT	S	PCT
72	5	16	21	+2	66	2	0	0	0	134	3.7

1998-99 statistics:

GP	G	A	TP	+/-	PIM	PP	SH	GW	GT	S	PCT
53	21	10	31	+1	57	13	1	3	0	180	11.7

LAST SEASON

Led team defensemen in points. Led team in power-play goals. Led NHL defensemen in goals. Second on team in goals with career high. Second on team in shots. Third on team in shooting percentage. Missed 10 games with knee injury. Missed eight games with groin injury. Missed seven games with ankle injuries. Missed one game with groin injury. Missed three games due to contract dispute.

THE FINESSE GAME

It's difficult to believe that Gonchar was known as a defensive defenseman when he played in Russia. He sees the ice well and passes well, but he never put up any big offensive numbers before coming into the NHL. Unlike most young defensemen who have to work in their own end to develop an NHL-calibre game, Gonchar made the quick jump to becoming a complete player by adding offense. He becomes a little too involved with the offensive game, however, and frequently lapses into making high-risk passes.

Gonchar jumps up into the play willingly and intelligently. He has a natural feel for the flow of a game, and makes tape-to-tape feeds through people — even under pressure. He sees first-unit power-play time on the point and is maturing into a first-rate quarterback. He plays heads-up. He doesn't have the blazing speed that elite defensemen have when carrying the puck, but he will gain the zone with some speed. He is an excellent passer.

Gonchar's shot is accurate enough but it won't terrorize any goalies. He doesn't push the puck forward and step into it like Al MacInnis. Most of the time he is content with getting it on the net, though he is not reluctant to shoot.

THE PHYSICAL GAME

Gonchar is strong on his skates and has worked hard on his off-ice conditioning. His defense is based more on reads and positional play than on a physical element. He was known as an aggressive player by Russian standards, but he won't run people. He will probably become a little more assertive as he gains confidence, though teams still like to target him early to scare him off his best effort.

THE INTANGIBLES

Gonchar had a huge bounce-back season and if he hadn't missed 26 games would have been among the NHL's scoring leaders on defense.

PROJECTION

We expect a better game fron Gonchar over the course of a full season. He may provide 50 to 55 points backed up by a solid defensive game.

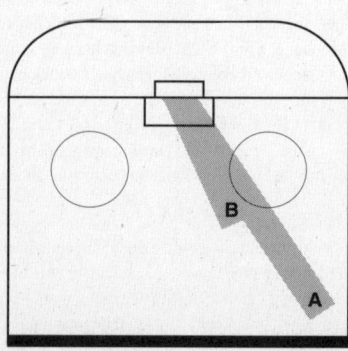

BENOIT GRATTON

Yrs. of NHL service: 0
Born: Montreal, Que.; Dec. 28, 1976
Position: left wing
Height: 5-10
Weight: 163
Uniform no.: 48
Shoots: left

Career statistics:

GP	G	A	TP	PIM
22	4	4	8	22

1997-98 statistics:

GP	G	A	TP	+/-	PIM	PP	SH	GW	GT	S	PCT
6	0	1	1	+1	6	0	0	0	0	5	0.0

1998-99 statistics:

GP	G	A	TP	+/-	PIM	PP	SH	GW	GT	S	PCT
16	4	3	7	-1	16	0	0	0	0	24	16.7

LAST SEASON
Will be entering first NHL season. Appeared in 64 game with Portland (AHL), scoring 18-42 — 60.

THE FINESSE GAME
The new Dale Hunter? That's what the Caps seemed to think. After trading Hunter to Colorado late in the season, they promoted Gratton and watched as he played with the famous Hunter edge.

Like Hunter, Gratton is an agitator with the offensive touches Hunter had early in his career. Gratton has been a good assist man at the minor-league level, and may be able to translate some of that skill in the majors.

Gratton is a smart player, and that is his ticket to the NHL, since he doesn't have NHL legs or size. He is one of those guys who is going to find a way to play.

THE PHYSICAL GAME
The fact that he doesn't have great size does not stop Gratton from getting involved. He is a toy goon.

THE INTANGIBLES
Gratton is a hungry player. His top level is probably as a fourth-line energy player who can make games interesting.

PROJECTION
Gratton could score 20 points in a part-time role.

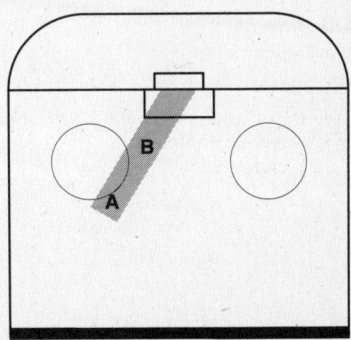

MATTHEW HERR

Yrs. of NHL service: 1
Born: Hackensack, NJ; May 26, 1976
Position: centre
Height: 6-1
Weight: 180
Uniform no.: 26
Shoots: left

Career statistics:

GP	G	A	TP	PIM
30	2	2	4	8

1998-99 statistics:

GP	G	A	TP	+/-	PIM	PP	SH	GW	GT	S	PCT
30	2	2	4	-7	8	1	0	0	0	40	5.0

LAST SEASON
First NHL season. Appeared in 46 games with Portland (AHL), scoring 15-14 — 29.

THE FINESSE GAME
Herr's game is powered by his excellent skating. He shifts direction quickly and easily and is strong on his skates.

A versatile player, Herr can play centre or wing. His hockey sense is only average, and at the moment he is hung up between being a finesse player or a power forward. He will have his greatest success if he chooses to play like the latter. He can take the puck to the net and has a strong wrist shot. He is an opportunist when it comes to scoring, but it doesn't come naturally to him.

At this stage of his development, Herr is a depth player who hasn't carved out his niche.

THE PHYSICAL GAME
Herr is a big kid who has added about 10 pounds of muscle. He likes to hit and needs to do it to play at this level. With his speed and size he can be a frightening forechecker.

THE INTANGIBLES
Herr made the Caps at the start of last season because of injuries and contract hassles. He could use more time in the minors, but the Caps may not have that luxury.

PROJECTION
Herr is still learning the game, and his point production will probably be minimal this season even if he makes the big club.

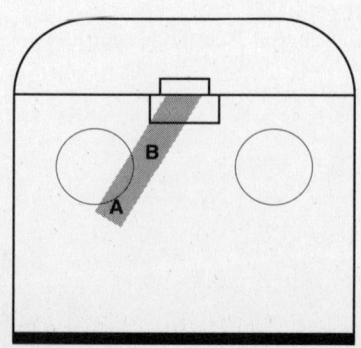

Washington Capitals

CALLE JOHANSSON

Yrs. of NHL service: 12
Born: Goteborg, Sweden; Feb. 14, 1967
Position: left defense
Height: 5-11
Weight: 200
Uniform no.: 6
Shoots: left

Career statistics:
GP	G	A	TP	PIM
850	100	344	444	439

1995-96 statistics:
GP	G	A	TP	+/-	PIM	PP	SH	GW	GT	S	PCT
78	10	25	35	+13	50	4	0	0	0	182	5.5

1996-97 statistics:
GP	G	A	TP	+/-	PIM	PP	SH	GW	GT	S	PCT
65	6	11	17	-2	16	2	0	0	0	133	4.5

1997-98 statistics:
GP	G	A	TP	+/-	PIM	PP	SH	GW	GT	S	PCT
73	15	20	35	-11	30	10	1	1	2	163	9.2

1998-99 statistics:
GP	G	A	TP	+/-	PIM	PP	SH	GW	GT	S	PCT
67	8	21	29	+10	22	2	0	2	1	145	5.5

LAST SEASON
Second on team in plus-minus. Missed 15 games with season-ending knee injury.

THE FINESSE GAME
Johansson has tremendous legs, notably big, strong thighs that generate the power for his shot and his explosive skating. He makes every move look easy. He is agile, mobile and great at moving up the ice with the play. Speed, balance and strength allow him to chase a puck behind the net, pick it up without stopping and make an accurate pass. He is confident, even on the backhand, and likes to have the puck in key spots.

Johansson is also smart offensively. He moves the puck with a good first pass, then has enough speed and instinct to jump up and be ready for a return pass. He keeps the gap tight as the play enters the attacking zone, which opens up more options: he is available to the forwards if they need him for offense, and closer to the puck if it is turned over to the opposition.

Johansson has a low, accurate shot that can be tipped. He is unselfish to a fault, often looking to pass when he should use his shot.

He has good defensive instincts and reads plays well. His skating gives him the confidence (maybe overconfidence) to gamble and challenge the puck carrier. He has a quick stick for poke- and sweep-checks.

THE PHYSICAL GAME
Johansson is not an aggressive player, but he is strong and knows what he has to do with his body in the defensive zone. This part of the game has not come naturally, but he has worked at it. He is not an impact player defensively, though he wins his share of the one-on-one battles because he gets so much power from his legs. He stays in good condition and can (and does) give a team a lot of minutes.

THE INTANGIBLES
Johansson does so many things well that his position among his team's top four defensemen is secure. He is one of the most underrated defensemen in the league.

PROJECTION
Johansson should produce around 35 points.

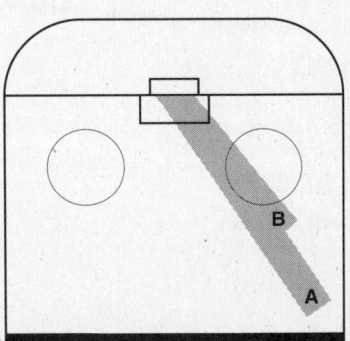

KEN KLEE

Yrs. of NHL service: 4
Born: Indianapolis, IN; Apr. 24, 1971
Position: right wing/defense
Height: 6-1
Weight: 205
Uniform no.: 2
Shoots: right

Career statistics:

GP	G	A	TP	PIM
298	25	27	52	342

1995-96 statistics:

GP	G	A	TP	+/-	PIM	PP	SH	GW	GT	S	PCT
66	8	3	11	-1	60	0	1	2	0	76	10.5

1996-97 statistics:

GP	G	A	TP	+/-	PIM	PP	SH	GW	GT	S	PCT
80	3	8	11	-5	115	0	0	2	0	108	2.8

1997-98 statistics:

GP	G	A	TP	+/-	PIM	PP	SH	GW	GT	S	PCT
51	4	2	6	-3	46	0	0	1	0	44	9.1

1998-99 statistics:

GP	G	A	TP	+/-	PIM	PP	SH	GW	GT	S	PCT
78	7	13	20	-9	80	0	0	1	0	132	5.3

LAST SEASON
Missed four games due to coach's decision.

THE FINESSE GAME
Klee was one of the few players who remained healthy for Washington all season, and it wasn't because he sat on the bench.

Although he is a defenseman by trade, the Caps used Klee as a right wing most of the season. Desperate for help up front, the Caps asked Klee to be a physical presence on the wing, and he responded. He doesn't have great hands to make a lot of things happen, but he is a good skater.

He does nothing fancy. He makes the safe plays, acts as a safety valve for his linemates, and does whatever the coaches ask of him.

THE PHYSICAL GAME
Klee isn't one of the biggest players around but he is solid and he uses his body well, either on the forecheck when he is playing wing or in his own zone when he is on defense.

THE INTANGIBLES
Klee was worth his weight in gold to the Caps last season, because he was able to handle a lot of minutes and keep himself out of the hospital.

PROJECTION
Klee won't score double-digits in goals, but he will provide reliable defense and 15 to 20 points a season.

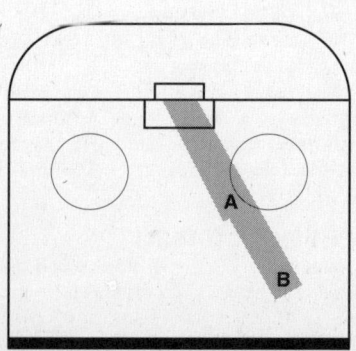

OLAF KOLZIG

Yrs. of NHL service: 4
Born: Johannesburg, South Africa; Apr. 9, 1970
Position: goaltender
Height: 6-3
Weight: 225
Uniform no.: 37
Catches: left

Career statistics:
GP	MIN	GA	SO	GAA	A	PIM
199	11004	474	11	2.58	3	41

1995-96 statistics:
GP	MIN	GAA	W	L	T	SO	GA	S	SAPCT	PIM
18	897	3.08	4	8	2	0	46	406	.887	2

1996-97 statistics:
GP	MIN	GAA	W	L	T	SO	GA	S	SAPCT	PIM
29	1644	2.59	8	15	4	2	71	758	.906	4

1997-98 statistics:
GP	MIN	GAA	W	L	T	SO	GA	S	SAPCT	PIM
64	3788	2.20	33	18	10	5	139	1729	.920	12

1998-99 statistics:
GP	MIN	GAA	W	L	T	SO	GA	S	SAPCT	PIM
64	3586	2.58	26	31	3	4	154	1538	.900	19

LAST SEASON
Surpassed 20 wins for second conescutive season. Matched career high in games played.

THE PHYSICAL GAME
Kolzig is a big goalie with good reflexes and skating ability for a player of his size. Rather than just lumber around and let the puck hit him (think Garth Snow), however, Kolzig is active and positions himself well to block as much of the net as possible from the shooter.

Last season, Kolzig played a little less aggressively than he did in his breakthrough season in 1997-98. He was back on his heels more, and that led to problems. He probably suffered from a lack of confidence because the team in front of him was struggling.

Kolzig needs to improve his stickhandling, though it's not bad. He could use his stick better to break up plays around the net.

THE MENTAL GAME
The biggest problem Kolzig had to lick was in his head. He was a bit of a hothead in his formative years, and last season he was ejected for taking part in a brawl. For the most part, however, he is now competitive but relaxed, more sensible after a bad goal or a bad loss, and able to bounce back quickly.

Kolzig was under a lot of pressure last season because the team wasn't scoring. He started every game knowing he couldn't allow more than one goal or his team might not have a chance to win.

THE INTANGIBLES
Kolzig's fundamentals indicate a probable return to form. The Capitals acquired an ideal veteran backup for him in Craig Billington, and he should help Kolzig in many ways.

PROJECTION
Kolzig's progress and playing behind a healthy team should mean another 30-win season.

STEVE KONOWALCHUK

Yrs. of NHL service: 7
Born: Salt Lake City, Utah; Nov. 11, 1972
Position: left wing
Height: 6-1
Weight: 195
Uniform no.: 22
Shoots: left

Career statistics:

GP	G	A	TP	PIM
418	89	118	232	358

1995-96 statistics:

GP	G	A	TP	+/-	PIM	PP	SH	GW	GT	S	PCT
70	23	22	45	+13	92	7	1	3	0	197	11.7

1996-97 statistics:

GP	G	A	TP	+/-	PIM	PP	SH	GW	GT	S	PCT
78	17	25	42	-3	67	2	1	3	1	155	11.0

1997-98 statistics:

GP	G	A	TP	+/-	PIM	PP	SH	GW	GT	S	PCT
80	10	24	34	+9	80	2	0	2	0	131	7.6

1998-99 statistics:

GP	G	A	TP	+/-	PIM	PP	SH	GW	GT	S	PCT
45	12	12	24	0	26	4	1	2	0	98	12.2

LAST SEASON

Led team in shooting percentage. Missed 22 games with concussion. Missed 15 games with ankle injury. Missed one game due to coach's decision.

THE FINESSE GAME

Konowalchuk is a willing guy who plays any role asked of him. He's a digger who has to work hard for his goals, and an intelligent and earnest player who uses every ounce of energy on every shift.

There is nothing fancy about Konowalchuk's offense. He just lets his shot rip and drives to the net. He doesn't have the moves and hand skills to beat a defender one-on-one, but he doesn't care. He'll go right through him. His release on his shot is improving.

Konowalchuk is reliable and intelligent defensively. On the draw, he ties up the opposing centre if he doesn't win the puck drop outright. He uses his feet along the boards as well as his stick.

THE PHYSICAL GAME

Konowalchuk is very strong. He has some grit in him, too, and will aggravate opponents with his constant effort. He doesn't take bad penalties, but often goads rivals into retaliating. He is very fit and can handle a lot of ice time.

THE INTANGIBLES

Konowalchuk is a heart-and-soul guy. The only thing he did wrong last season was push himself too much when rehabbing his ankle injury, only to reinjure himself.

PROJECTION

Konowalchuk is a quality person to have, on the ice or in the dressing room, and he can score 20 to 25 goals in a second-line role.

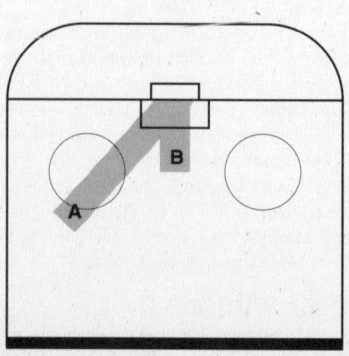

DMITRI MIRONOV

Yrs. of NHL service: 7
Born: Moscow, Russia; Dec. 25, 1965
Position: left defense
Height: 6-3
Weight: 214
Uniform no.: 15
Shoots: right

Career statistics:

GP	G	A	TP	PIM
447	48	182	230	534

1995-96 statistics:

GP	G	A	TP	+/-	PIM	PP	SH	GW	GT	S	PCT
72	3	31	34	+19	88	1	0	1	1	86	3.5

1996-97 statistics:

GP	G	A	TP	+/-	PIM	PP	SH	GW	GT	S	PCT
77	13	39	52	+16	101	3	1	2	0	177	7.3

1997-98 statistics:

GP	G	A	TP	+/-	PIM	PP	SH	GW	GT	S	PCT
77	8	35	43	-7	119	3	0	1	0	170	4.7

1998-99 statistics:

GP	G	A	TP	+/-	PIM	PP	SH	GW	GT	S	PCT
46	2	14	16	-5	80	2	0	0	0	86	2.3

PROJECTION

Mironov's offensive contributions don't always compensate for his defensive shortcomings. He will get a lot of ice time on a thin (even when healthy) defense corps. His top side is 50 points.

LAST SEASON

Missed 32 games with back injury. Missed four games due to coach's decision.

THE FINESSE GAME

Mironov likes to get involved in the attack — probably too much involved. He can do phenomenal things with the puck. He understands the game well and can shoot bullets, but is often reluctant to let fire. He can work the puck up the ice and handle the point on the power play. He sees the ice well and is a good passer.

Mironov can be a bit of a risk factor in his own end. He can be beaten one-on-one and it helps him to play with a defensive defenseman. He has to learn to play as hard in his own zone as he likes to do in the attacking zone.

Mironov was one of the few forays into the free agent market for the Caps in the past two years, and he has likely discouraged the team from trying it again anytime soon.

THE PHYSICAL GAME

Mironov has a long reach and is big, but he plays soft and doesn't use either attribute to his best advantage. He gives up easily on plays in his own end. He likes to step up and challenge in the neutral zone but doesn't take the body well; he often lets the opponent get by him.

THE INTANGIBLES

Mironov has a lot of skill, but a questionable work ethic. He underwent surgery during the off-season to repair his back problem.

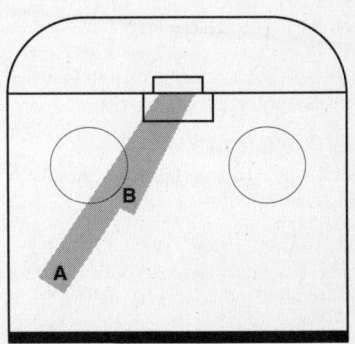

ANDREI NIKOLISHIN

Yrs. of NHL service: 5
Born: Vorkuta, Russia; March 25, 1973
Position: left wing/centre
Height: 5-11
Weight: 180
Uniform no.: 13
Shoots: left

Career statistics:

GP	G	A	TP	PIM
282	45	103	148	118

1995-96 statistics:

GP	G	A	TP	+/-	PIM	PP	SH	GW	GT	S	PCT
61	14	37	51	-2	34	4	1	3	0	83	16.9

1996-97 statistics:

GP	G	A	TP	+/-	PIM	PP	SH	GW	GT	S	PCT
71	9	19	28	+3	32	1	0	0	0	98	9.2

1997-98 statistics:

GP	G	A	TP	+/-	PIM	PP	SH	GW	GT	S	PCT
38	6	10	16	+1	14	1	0	1	0	40	15.0

1998-99 statistics:

GP	G	A	TP	+/-	PIM	PP	SH	GW	GT	S	PCT
73	8	27	35	0	28	0	1	1	0	121	6.6

LAST SEASON

Second on team in assists. Missed nine games due to contract dispute.

THE FINESSE GAME

Nikolishin is a strong skater with a powerful stride, and he makes some of the tightest turns in the league. His great talent is puckhandling, but like many Europeans he tends to hold onto the puck too long and leaves himself open for hits.

He sees the ice well and is a gifted playmaker, but he needs to shoot more so that his game will be less predictable. He needs to play with a finishing winger — like Peter Bondra, with whom he successfully meshed — who can convert his slippery passes.

Nikolishin is defensively aware, he backchecks and blocks shots.

THE PHYSICAL GAME

Nikolishin is extremely strong on his skates and likes to work in the corners for the puck. He is tough to knock off balance and has a low centre of gravity. He has adapted smoothly to the more physical style of play in the NHL, and although he isn't very big he will plow into heavy going for the puck.

THE INTANGIBLES

Nikolishin is popular with his teammates, both for his personality and his work habits.

PROJECTION

Nikolishin is an elite playmaker who should score 60 points — about 45 of those being assists.

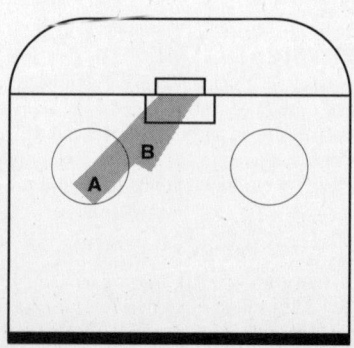

ADAM OATES

Yrs. of NHL service: 14
Born: Weston, Ont.; Aug. 27, 1962
Position: centre
Height: 5-11
Weight: 185
Uniform no.: 77
Shoots: right

Career statistics:
GP	G	A	TP	PIM
967	288	838	1126	321

1995-96 statistics:
GP	G	A	TP	+/-	PIM	PP	SH	GW	GT	S	PCT
70	25	67	92	+16	18	7	1	2	0	183	13.7

1996-97 statistics:
GP	G	A	TP	+/-	PIM	PP	SH	GW	GT	S	PCT
80	22	60	82	-5	14	3	2	5	0	160	13.8

1997-98 statistics:
GP	G	A	TP	+/-	PIM	PP	SH	GW	GT	S	PCT
82	18	58	76	+6	36	3	2	3	0	121	14.9

1998-99 statistics:
GP	G	A	TP	+/-	PIM	PP	SH	GW	GT	S	PCT
59	12	42	54	-1	22	3	0	0	0	79	15.2

LAST SEASON
Led team in assists for third consecutive season. Second on team in points. Missed 23 games with groin injury.

THE FINESSE GAME
Oates remains one of the elite playmakers in the NHL, though age and injuries have begun to erode his effectiveness. He uses a shorter-than-average stick and a minimal curve on his blade, the result being exceptional control of the puck. Although he's a right-handed shooter, his right wings have always been his preferred receivers. He can pass on the backhand but also carries the puck deep; he shields the puck with his body and turns to make the pass to his right wing.

Use of the backhand gives Oates a tremendous edge against all but the rangiest NHL defensemen. He forces defenders to reach in and frequently draws penalties when he is hooked or tripped. If defenders don't harrass him, he then has carte blanche to work his passing magic.

Oates is less reluctant to shoot, though passing is still his first instinct. It doesn't matter how hard you shoot the puck when you have the jeweller's precision of Oates. Taking more shots makes him a less predictable player, since the defense can't back off and anticipate the pass. He is one of the NHL's best playmakers because of his passing ability and his creativity. He is most effective down low where he can open up more ice, especially on the power play. He has outstanding timing and vision.

Yet, Oates isn't stubborn to a fault. He will also play a dump-and-chase game if he is being shadowed closely, throwing the puck smartly into the opposite corner with just the right velocity to allow his wingers to get in on top of the defense.

He is among the top five players in the league on face-offs, which makes him a natural on penalty killing; a successful draw eats up 10 to 15 seconds on the clock, minimum.

THE PHYSICAL GAME
Oates is not a physical player but he doesn't avoid contact. He's smart enough at this stage of his career to avoid the garbage, and he plays in traffic and will take a hit to make the play. He's an intense player with a wiry strength, but he tends to wear down late in the season as his line receives all the checking attention.

THE INTANGIBLES
Oates suffered from his groin injury and from losing linemates right and left. He didn't score a goal after March 13.

PROJECTION
Oates will return to the 80-point level only if he and the Caps can stay healthy.

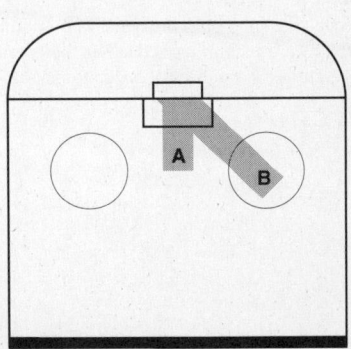

JAROSLAV SVEJKOVSKY

Yrs. of NHL service: 2
Born: Plzen, Czech Republic; Oct. 1, 1976
Position: left wing
Height: 5-11
Weight: 185
Uniform no.: 34
Shoots: right

Career statistics:

GP	G	A	TP	PIM
61	17	12	29	26

1996-97 statistics:

GP	G	A	TP	+/-	PIM	PP	SH	GW	GT	S	PCT
19	7	3	10	-1	4	2	0	1	0	30	23.3

1997-98 statistics:

GP	G	A	TP	+/-	PIM	PP	SH	GW	GT	S	PCT
17	4	1	5	-5	10	2	0	1	0	29	13.8

1998-99 statistics:

GP	G	A	TP	+/-	PIM	PP	SH	GW	GT	S	PCT
25	6	8	14	-2	12	4	0	2	0	50	12.0

LAST SEASON

Missed 37 games with ankle injury. Missed 15 games with concussion. Missed five games due to coach's decision.

THE FINESSE GAME

Svejkovsky is a pure goal scorer. He will work to get himself in high-percentage zones and is astoundingly accurate with his shot. He has great hands for tipping pucks.

He is a good skater without real breakout speed, but he has a nose for the net and he pays the price. He wants the puck and knows what to do with it. He is a threat every time he's near the puck.

Svejkovsky is hardly a defensive specialist, but his overall game is fairly well developed.

THE PHYSICAL GAME

Svejkovsky is not overly aggressive but he will take hits to make plays. He is an average-sized player and needs to get bigger and stronger. He's tenacious and will take a cross-check or a slash to score goals.

THE INTANGIBLES

Svejkovsky is a blue-chip prospect who continues to suffer from hard-luck injuries. He has the potential to be a special player, but he still needs to mature.

PROJECTION

If Svejkovsky earns some decent ice time, he could score 20 to 25 goals.

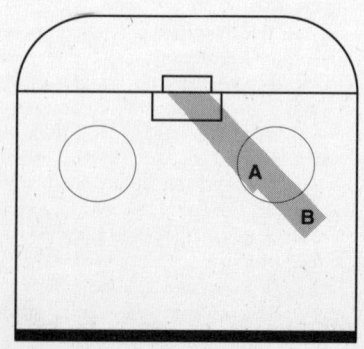

ALEXEI TEZIKOV

Yrs. of NHL service: 0
Born: Togliatti, USSR; June 22, 1978
Position: left defense
Height: 6-1
Weight: 198
Uniform no.: 4
Shoots: left

Career statistics:

GP	G	A	TP	PIM
5	0	0	0	0

1998-99 statistics:

GP	G	A	TP	+/-	PIM	PP	SH	GW	GT	S	PCT
5	0	0	0	-1	0	0	0	0	0	4	.0

LAST SEASON

Acquired from Buffalo with future considerations for Joe Juneau and a third-round draft pick in 1999. Appeared in 25 games with Moncton (QMJHL), scoring 9-21 — 30. Appeared in 31 games with Rochester (AHL), scoring 3-7 — 10. Appeared in five games with Cincinnati (IHL), scoring 0-0 — 0.

THE FINESSE GAME

Tezikov has the skill level of the Caps' current top offensive defenseman, Sergei Gonchar, with a little more edge to his game.

Tezikov cam be compared to another teammate, however, since his game is more like Calle Johansson's. Tezikov is mobile and he can move the puck well. He can't run a power play but he will jump into the play. He will get his points, yet he won't be known primarily for his scoring.

Tezikov is a terrific skater who likes to hit and lines up opponents for rolling hip checks.

THE PHYSICAL GAME

Tezikov dropped the gloves a bit in junior but it's not likely he'll do so at the NHL level. He plays with a bit of a snarl, though, and while he isn't tall, he has a thick body. He could actually stand to lose some weight — he played as high as 225 pounds last season, and would be most effective at 215.

THE INTANGIBLES

The Caps would love to keep Tezikov in the minors for at least another few months, but with their lack of depth on the blueline, he may force his way into the lineup if he has a solid training camp.

PROJECTION

Assuming he only plays a half-season, expect Johansson-like numbers of 15 to 20 points for 40 games.

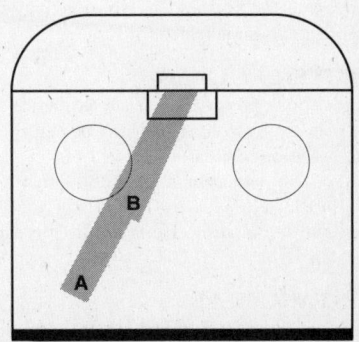

BRENDAN WITT

Yrs. of NHL service: 4
Born: Humboldt, Sask.; Feb. 20, 1975
Position: left defense
Height: 6-1
Weight: 205
Uniform no.: 19
Shoots: left

Career statistics:

GP	G	A	TP	PIM
210	8	17	25	372

1995-96 statistics:

GP	G	A	TP	+/-	PIM	PP	SH	GW	GT	S	PCT
48	2	3	5	-4	85	0	0	1	0	44	4.5

1996-97 statistics:

GP	G	A	TP	+/-	PIM	PP	SH	GW	GT	S	PCT
44	3	2	5	-20	88	0	0	0	0	41	7.3

1997-98 statistics:

GP	G	A	TP	+/-	PIM	PP	SH	GW	GT	S	PCT
64	1	7	8	-11	112	0	0	0	0	68	1.5

1998-99 statistics:

GP	G	A	TP	+/-	PIM	PP	SH	GW	GT	S	PCT
54	2	5	7	-6	87	0	0	0	0	51	3.9

LAST SEASON

Third on team in penalty minutes. Missed 15 games with wrist injury. Missed five games with hip injury. Missed one game with knee injury. Missed five games due to personal reasons. Missed two games due to coach's decision.

THE FINESSE GAME

Witt's skill level is very high and he applies his abilities in his own zone. His skating is capable, though he needs to improve his agility; his turning and passing are also a little raw. Still, he does not overhandle the puck and by making simple plays he keeps himself out of serious trouble. He skates well backwards and has decent lateral mobility.

Witt gets involved somewhat in the attack, but the extent of his contribution is a hard point shot. He won't gamble low and can't run a power play. He won't ever be an offensive force.

Witt was one of the steadier presences on the Caps' blueline last season. He was effective without being flashy. His game is maturing.

THE PHYSICAL GAME

Witt has a strong physical presence on the ice but he needs to get even stronger. He was beaten by some players in one-on-one battles against bigger players, and a defensive defenseman can't allow that to happen. He blocks shots fearlessly and is naturally aggressive and intimidating. He is a little too eager to fight.

THE INTANGIBLES

In addition to injuries, Witt had to deal with the serious illness of his father. Given the dual burdens his season was impressive.

PROJECTION

Witt hasn't reached his best level yet, but he's getting closer. Although he won't score a lot of points he will get a regular turn. He will also rack up some penalty minutes.

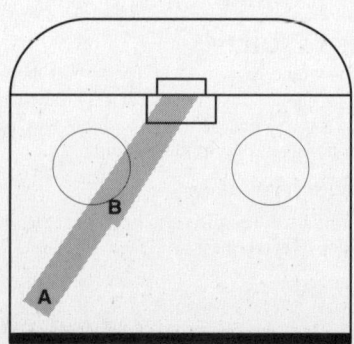

RICHARD ZEDNIK

Yrs. of NHL service: 2
Born: Bystrica, Slovakia; Jan. 6, 1976
Position: right wing
Height: 5-11
Weight: 190
Uniform no.: 44
Shoots: left

Career statistics:
GP	G	A	TP	PIM
126	28	18	46	82

1995-96 statistics:
GP	G	A	TP	+/-	PIM	PP	SH	GW	GT	S	PCT
1	0	0	0	0	0	0	0	0	0	0	0.0

1996-97 statistics:
GP	G	A	TP	+/-	PIM	PP	SH	GW	GT	S	PCT
11	2	1	3	-5	4	1	0	0	0	21	9.5

1997-98 statistics:
GP	G	A	TP	+/-	PIM	PP	SH	GW	GT	S	PCT
65	17	9	26	-2	28	2	0	2	0	148	11.5

1998-99 statistics:
GP	G	A	TP	+/-	PIM	PP	SH	GW	GT	S	PCT
49	9	8	17	-6	50	1	0	2	0	115	7.8

LAST SEASON
Second NHL season. Missed 19 games with groin injury. Missed 10 games with shoulder injury. Missed four games due to suspension for high-sticking incident.

THE FINESSE GAME
Zednik has the skating speed and the hand skills that mark him as a top six forward on a team that is already quite stocked with gifted players. A low draft pick (249th overall in 1994), he has shot up Washington's depth chart.

Zednik is very good down low. He can control the game and go to the net. He has nice hands and he is not shy about shooting. He has a very low crouch and gets a lot on his shot. He could be the Caps' left-wing version of Peter Bondra, he is nearly that dynamic. He also prevents other teams from being able to key on Bondra, because Zednik is almost as dangerous as the 52-goal scorer.

Zednik is especially menacing on the power play and will merit more time there this season.

THE PHYSICAL GAME
Zednik is very strong, even though he is not big. Coming off the wing, he just about carries defenders on his back. Solid and sturdy on his skates, he likes to get involved and isn't rattled by physical play, though he does not initiate contact.

THE INTANGIBLES
Zednik is yet another Capital whose season was disrupted by injuries. He should stake his claim on the top line with Bondra, and be able to do some damage if *he's* not damaged.

PROJECTION
Zednik should score in the range of 20 to 25 goals.

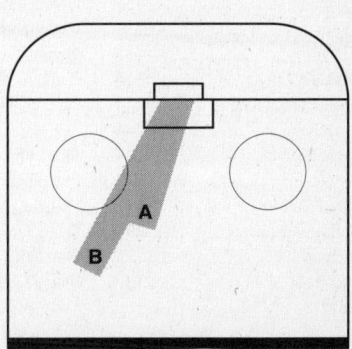

PLAYER INDEX

Adams, Greg 343
Albelin, Tommy 74
Alfredsson, Daniel 312
Allen, Bryan 439
Allison, Jamie 108
Allison, Jason 39
Amonte, Tony 109
Andreychuk, Dave 40
Arnott, Jason 263
Arvedson, Magnus 313
Atcheynum, Blair 390
Aucoin, Adrian 440
Audette, Donald 212
Axelsson, P. J. 41

Barnaby, Matthew 360
Barnes, Stu 56
Barrasso, Tom 361
Bartecko, Lubos 391
Bates, Shawn 42
Battaglia, Bates 92
Baumgartner, Nolan 456
Belfour, Ed 142
Beranek, Josef 177
Berard, Bryan 423
Berehowsky, Drake 246
Berezin, Sergei 424
Berg, Aki-Petteri 213
Bertuzzi, Todd 441
Black, James 457
Blake, Rob 214
Bondra, Peter 458
Bonk, Radek 314
Bordeleau, Sebastien 247
Bouchard, Joel 248
Boughner, Bob 249
Bourque, Ray 43
Brashear, Donald 442
Brendl, Pavel 296
Brewer, Eric 279
Briere, Daniel 344

Brind'Amour, Rod 328
Brisebois, Patrice 229
Brodeur, Martin 264
Brown, Brad 110
Brown, Curtis 57
Brown, Doug 159
Brunet, Benoit 230
Buchberger, Kelly 23
Bulis, Jan 459
Bure, Pavel 195
Bure, Valeri 75
Bureau, Marc 329
Burke, Sean 196

Cairns, Eric 280
Carney, Keith 345
Carter, Anson 44
Cassels, Andrew 443
Chambers, Shawn 143
Chara, Zdeno 281
Chelios, Chris 160
Clark, Wendel 161
Cleary, Daniel 178
Cloutier, Dan 407
Cloutier, Sylvain 24
Conroy, Craig 392
Corbet, Rene 76
Corkum, Bob 346
Corson, Shayne 231
Cote, Patrick 250
Cote, Sylvain 425
Cross, Cory 408
Cullen, Matt 6
Czerkawski, Mariusz 282

Dackell, Andreas 315
Dafoe, Byron 45
Daigle, Alexandre 409
Damphousse, Vincent 374
Daneyko, Ken 265
Dawe, Jason 232

Daze, Eric 111
Deadmarsh, Adam 126
Dean, Kevin 25
DeMitra, Pavol 393
Desjardins, Eric 330
Devereaux, Boyd 179
Doan, Shane 347
Dollas, Bobby 362
Domenichelli, Hnat 77
Donato, Ted 7
Donovan, Shean 127
Drake, Dallas 348
Draper, Kris 162
Drury, Chris 128
Drury, Ted 8
Dubinsky, Steve 78
Dumont, J. P. 112
Dunham, Mike 251
Dvorak, Radek 197
Dykhuis, Karl 331

Eastwood, Mike 394
Elias, Patrik 266
Emerson, Nelson 26
Eriksson, Anders 113

Falloon, Pat 180
Fedorov, Sergei 163
Ference, Brad 198
Fitzgerald, Tom 252
Fleury, Theoren 297
Foote, Adam 129
Forbes, Colin 410
Forsberg, Peter 130
Francis, Ron 93
Friesen, Jeff 375
Fuhr, Grant 395

Galanov, Maxim 27
Galley, Garry 215
Garpenlov, Johan 28

Player Index

Gauthier, Denis...........79
Gelinas, Martin..........94
Gill, Hal....................46
Gilmour, Doug 114
Gonchar, Sergei........460
Gratton, Benoit.........461
Gratton, Chris...........411
Graves, Adam...........298
Green, Josh..............283
Green, Travis............349
Grier, Mike...............181
Grosek, Michal..........58
Guerin, Bill...............182
Gusarov, Alexei........131
Gusev, Sergey..........412

Hackett, Jeff............233
Haller, Kevin............9
Hamrlik, Roman........183
Handzus, Michal.......396
Harlock, David..........29
Harvey, Todd...........299
Hasek, Dominik........59
Hatcher, Derian.......144
Hatcher, Kevin.........363
Hebert, Guy.............10
Hecht, Jochen..........397
Hedican, Bret...........199
Heinze, Steve..........47
Hejduk, Milan...........132
Herr, Matthew.........462
Hill, Sean.................95
Hoglund, Jonas.......426
Hogue, Benoit........145
Holden, Josh..........444
Holik, Bobby...........267
Holmstrom, Tomas..164
Holzinger, Brian......60
Hossa, Marian........316
Houlder, Bill............376
Housley, Phil..........80
Hrdina, Jan.............364
Hull, Brett..............146
Hull, Jody...............30
Hulse, Cale............81

Iginla, Jarome.........82
Irbe, Arturs............96
Isbister, Brad.........284

Jagr, Jaromir..........365
Johansson, Calle....463
Johnson, Craig.......216
Johnson, Greg.......253
Johnson, Mike.......427
Jokinen, Olli...........285
Jones, Keith..........332
Jonsson, Kenny....286

Joseph, Curtis 428
Jovanovski, Ed 445
Juneau, Joe 61

Kamensky, Valeri....300
Kapanen, Sami.......97
Kariya, Paul............11
Karpa, Dave...........98
Karpovtsev, Alexander...429
Kasparaitis, Darius..366
Keane, Mike..........147
Khabibulin, Nikolai..350
Khristich, Dmitri.....48
Kilger, Chad..........184
King, Derek..........430
Kjellberg, Patric....254
Klatt, Trent..........446
Klee, Ken.............464
Klemm, Jon..........133
Koivu, Saku.........234
Kolzig, Olaf..........465
Konowalchuk, Steve...466
Korolyuk, Alexander...377
Kovalenko, Andrei...99
Kovalev, Alexei.....367
Kozlov, Viktor......200
Kozlov, Vyacheslav...165
Krivokrasov, Sergei...255
Krupp, Uwe........166
Kubina, Pavel......413
Kvasha, Oleg......201

Lachance, Scott....235
Lacroix, Eric........301
Laflamme, Christian...185
Lang, Robert.......368
Langenbrunner, Jamie...148
Langkow, Daymond...333
Laperriere, Ian.....217
Lapointe, Claude..287
Lapointe, Martin...167
Laukkanen, Janne..317
Laus, Paul..........202
Lawrence, Mark...288
Lecavalier, Vincent...414
LeClair, John.......334
Leetch, Brian......302
Lefebvre, Sylvain..303
Legwand, David...256
Lehtinen, Jere.....149
Lemieux, Claude..134
Leschyshyn, Curtis..100
Lidstrom, Nicklas..168
Linden, Trevor.....236
Lindgren, Mats....289
Lindros, Eric.......335
Lindsay, Bill........203
Lumme, Jyrki.....351

MacInnis, Al............398
MacLean, John........304
Malakhov, Vladimir...237
Malhotra, Manny.....305
Malik, Marek...........101
Maltby, Kirk............169
Mann, Cameron......49
Manson, Dave........115
Mara, Paul.............415
Marchant, Todd.....186
Marchment, Bryan..378
Marha, Josef.........116
Markov, Daniil.......431
Marleau, Patrick....379
Marshall, Jason.....12
Mayers, Jamal......399
McAmmond, Dean..117
McCabe, Bryan.....118
McCarty, Darren...170
McCauley, Alyn....432
McEachern, Shawn..318
McGillis, Daniel....336
McInnis, Marty.....13
McKay, Randy......268
McKee, Jay..........62
McLaren, Kyle.....50
Mellanby, Scott....204
Messier, Mark......447
Mironov, Boris.....119
Mironov, Dmitri....467
Modano, Mike.....150
Mogilny, Alexander..448
Moreau, Ethan....187
Morozov, Alexei...369
Morris, Derek......83
Morrison, Brendan..269
Muckalt, Bill........449
Murphy, Gord......31
Murphy, Joe........380
Murphy, Larry......171
Murray, Chris......120
Murray, Glen.......218

Naslund, Markus...450
Nazarov, Andrei....84
Neckar, Stanislav..352
Nedved, Petr.......306
Nemchinov, Sergei..270
Niedermayer, Rob..205
Niedermayer, Scott..271
Nielsen, Jeff.........14
Nieuwendyk, Joe...151
Niinimaa, Janne....188
Nikolishin, Andrei...468
Nolan, Owen........381
Norstrom, Mattias..219
Novoseltsev, Ivan..206
Numminen, Teppo..353

Player Index

Nylander, Michael 416

O'Donnell, Sean 220
O'Neill, Jeff 102
Oates, Adam 469
Odelein, Lyle 272
Odjick, Gino 290
Ohlund, Mattias 451
Olausson, Fredrik 15
Olczyk, Ed 121
Osgood, Chris 172
Ozolinsh, Sandis 135

Palffy, Zigmund 221
Parrish, Mark 207
Peca, Michael 63
Pederson, Denis 273
Pellerin, Scott 400
Perreault, Yanic 433
Phillips, Chris 319
Pilon, Richard 291
Plante, Derek 152
Podein, Shjon 136
Poti, Tom 189
Potvin, Felix 292
Poulin, Patrick 238
Primeau, Keith 103
Probert, Bob 122
Pronger, Chris 401
Prospal, Vaclav 320
Pushor, Jamie 153

Quint, Deron 354
Quintal, Stephane 307

Ragnarsson, Marcus 382
Rasmussen, Erik 64
Rathje, Mike 383
Reasoner, Marty 402
Recchi, Mark 337
Redden, Wade 321
Reichel, Robert 355
Renberg, Mikael 338
Rheaume, Pascal 403
Rhodes, Damian 32
Ricci, Mike 384
Richardson, Luke 339
Richer, Stephane 417
Richter, Barry 293
Richter, Mike 308
Roberts, Gary 104
Robitaille, Luc 222
Roenick, Jeremy 356
Rolston, Brian 274
Ronning, Cliff 257
Rosa, Pavel 223
Roy, Patrick 137
Rucchin, Steve 16

Rucinsky, Martin 239

Sakic, Joe 138
Salei, Ruslan 17
Salo, Sami 322
Salo, Tommy 190
Samsonov, Sergei 51
Samuelsson, Ulf 33
Sanderson, Geoff 65
Sandstrom, Tomas 18
Satan, Miroslav 66
Savage, Brian 240
Savard, Marc 85
Schaefer, Peter 452
Schneider, Mathieu 309
Selanne, Teemu 19
Shanahan, Brendan 173
Shantz, Jeff 86
Sheppard, Ray 105
Sillinger, Mike 418
Simpson, Todd 87
Sloan, Blake 154
Smehlik, Richard 67
Smith, Jason 191
Smolinski, Bryan 224
Smyth, Ryan 192
Snow, Garth 453
Souray, Sheldon 275
Spacek, Jaroslav 208
Stefan, Patrik 34
Stevens, Kevin 310
Stevens, Scott 276
Stevenson, Turner 241
Stillman, Cory 88
Storr, Jamie 225
Straka, Martin 370
Strudwick, Jason 454
Stumpel, Jozef 226
Sturm, Marco 385
Sullivan, Steve 434
Sundin, Mats 435
Sundstrom, Niklas 419
Suter, Gary 386
Svehla, Robert 209
Svejkovsky, Jaroslav 470
Svoboda, Petr 420
Sweeney, Don 52
Sydor, Darryl 155
Sykora, Petr 277

Tamer, Chris 35
Tanguay, Alex 139
Tezikov, Alexei 471
Therien, Chris 340
Thibault, Jocelyn 123
Thomas, Steve 436
Thornton, Joe 53
Timonen, Kimmo 258

Tinordi, Mark 36
Titov, German 371
Tkachuk, Keith 357
Tocchet, Rick 358
Trnka, Pavel 20
Tsyplakov, Vladimir 227
Tucker, Darcy 421
Tugnutt, Ron 323
Turcotte, Darren 259
Turgeon, Pierre 404
Tverdovsky, Oleg 21

Ulanov, Igor 242

Vanbiesbrouck, John 341
Varada, Vaclav 68
Verbeek, Pat 156
Vernon, Mike 387

Walker, Scott 260
Ward, Aaron 174
Ward, Dixon 69
Warrener, Rhett 70
Watt, Mike 294
Weight, Doug 193
Weinrich, Eric 243
Werenka, Brad 372
Wesley, Glen 106
Whitney, Ray 210
Wiemer, Jason 89
Wilm, Clarke 90
Wilson, Landon 54
Witt, Brendan 472
Woolley, Jason 71

Yachmenev, Vitali 261
Yake, Terry 37
Yashin, Alexei 324
Yelle, Stephane 140
York, Jason 325
Young, Scott 405
Yushkevich, Dimitri 437
Yzerman, Steve 175

Zamuner, Rob 326
Zednik, Richard 473
Zhamnov, Alexei 124
Zhitnik, Alexei 72
Zubov, Sergei 157
Zubrus, Dainius 244
Zyuzin, Andrei 388